BLACK CONSCIOUSNESS, IDENTITY, AND ACHIEVEMENT

BLACK CONSCIOUSNESS, IDENTITY, AND ACHIEVEMENT

A STUDY OF STUDENTS IN HISTORICALLY BLACK COLLEGES

PATRICIA GURIN

University of Michigan

EDGAR EPPS

University of Chicago

JOHN WILEY & SONS, INC.   New York   London   Sydney   Toronto

Library of Congress Cataloging in Publication Data:

Gurin, Patricia.
  Black consciousness, identity, and achievement.

  Bibliography: p.
  Includes indexes.
  1. College students, Negro—United States.
  2. Negroes—Race identity. I. Epps, Edgar G.,
    1929-   joint author. II. Title

LC2781.G79   378.1'98'1   75-5847
ISBN 0-471-33670-X

Printed in the United States of America.

10 9 8 7 6 5 4 3 2 1

preface

This book is the result of a series of studies conducted in several historically Black colleges from 1964 to 1970. The focus of these studies shifted during the six years that we collected data and during the even longer time that we spent analyzing and writing up the data, just as the perspectives and language of the students shifted over the decade of the 1960s. In 1963 we originally planned to study the impact of the southern student movement on the young Black students who had left their colleges in the early 1960s to work full time in southern communities in "the civil rights movement." These committed activists believed that the "movement" was the beginning of change in the South and the nation. They saw themselves transformed by their own action, awakened to a new sense of group consciousness and pride in being Black. They expected to awaken others and, through the strength of what was then called "the new Negro," to change conditions of life for disenfranchised and poor Blacks in the rural South. We wanted to document the personal and social implications of the involvement and commitment of these young people. However, as we expected, James Forman, Howard Zinn, August Meier, Anne Moody, and others who were more intimately connected to the student movement described and analyzed the personal effects of participation more ably than we could. In addition, the implications of the student movement extended beyond what was happening to its active participants. To understand these broader effects we studied the experiences of students attending the historically Black colleges from which the student movement sprang. Our focus changed from a study of activists to a study of students in an institutional context.

Although full-time activists had already resolved the tension between personal goals and group action, if only temporarily, the Black college students at this time faced a continual conflict between the demands of the college for individual achievement and the demands of the community and the movement for commitment to group goals. When we first worked with students on campuses in 1964, this tension between individualism and collectivism focused on the decision of whether to demonstrate, to risk going to jail, to risk a commitment of time and emotions that might result in academic failure, to risk suspension from college and, in many cases, to risk financial and physical reprisals not only against themselves but also against their parents. A young woman, elected by her student body in 1964 as Miss College, told us of calling her parents to plead for the written permission that the college required if students were to participate in the famous

v

Montgomery demonstrations in the spring of 1965.

First, they talked about what they had seen on the news that day . . . the horses charging into the ranks of the students, students crying and the state police acting like they were cattle being rounded up. They just couldn't let me do it, too. I tried to argue—but Mama, Papa, I have to go, I have to do what I can. Very few have been hurt. I even admitted I knew I would be scared and could understand what they felt; I felt it too but I just had to go. When we weren't getting anywhere down that route, they began talking about how they had sacrificed to send me to college to get a degree and I would be sending that up in smoke by all this civil rights thing. I did feel bad; they have given up almost everything to send me here and they have been so proud of my accomplishments—grades, the honor of representing my college, you know turning into an accomplished student and young lady. And Papa especially feels that you have to be the best in everything—grades, looks, poise, ambition—to get ahead with everything else you face if you're Black. I admitted all that but kept trying to explain that I can't just look after myself; I have to try to make a difference for other people, especially other students who will follow after me and who perhaps haven't had parents who could do what my parents have. But they just kept coming back to their frantic fear that I wouldn't get my degree—I'd be kicked out, I'd get emotional and put my everything into the movement, I'd ruin my grade point average. It was the degree; it just means the whole world to them. I was crying; it was clear they weren't going to send the permission; and I knew down deep even when I was talking to them that I'd find a way to go anyway. And all I could say as I knew there was nothing else any of us could do: But Papa, Mama, what's a degree for? I just kept repeating it—What's a degree for?—and they said they loved me and hung up.

She was not alone. Other students repeatedly talked of their parents' fears that the movement would jeopardize getting a degree, getting ahead, and "making it" as an individual. Students struggled to resolve the dilemma between individual and group commitments, some with compassion for their parents' fears and empathy for the pressures they faced, some with disdain for what they felt had been their parents' generation's lack of courage and indifference to the collective welfare of Blacks.

The tension between individual and collective identity remained, even with the disappearance of large-scale demonstrations. Students turned inward, and the question became not whether you cared enough about others to picket or demonstrate in an attempt to change oppressive institutions but whether you saw yourself as truly part of the

collective whole, whether you understood and accepted group consciousness and the political perspectives of Black Nationalism. As the
language and symbols representing the issue of individual and collective identity changed, so did the context and language of our study;
new questions were introduced in our interviews and questionnaires
as needed, sometimes with the unfortunate effect of making it impossible to document opinion shifts from 1964 to 1970. In the late 1960s,
some issues were cast in language that had not even been used a few
years earlier. For example, when we asked students in 1964 about their
ideal society, we included a statement from Muslim writing, but nothing was included that represented Black Nationalism from a revolutionary collectivist position. Yet by 1968 and 1970 collectivist theory,
especially the writings of Fanon, articulated the dominant critique of
American society for Black students. Sometimes the time-boundedness
of our questions, and therefore of our data, reflects our own limitations in anticipating the shifts in symbols. Very often it reflects the
sheer rapidity of social change that made language and symbolization
change so rapidly—the study spanned the time before Black Power
had been enunciated to the time when it was almost a cliché. No
change is more striking than the shift in what students preferred to be
called between 1968 and 1970. The transition from "Negro" to "Black"
had certainly set in by 1968 when 40 percent of the seniors at one of
the colleges said they wanted to be called Black. By 1970, 89 percent
of the seniors preferred to be called Black. We therefore consistently
use the word Black even when discussing events that occurred in the
early 1960s when Negro was still preferred. We also capitalize Black,
although we leave the word white in lower case. We do so because it
reflected the students' preferences as we collected the last group of
data. It appears still to be preferred, although feelings about this issue
may someday change. This may also apply to some of the other terms
used in this book. We feel, however, that it is appropriate to use the
symbols of the times we have studied.

The last data we collected represent student views in 1970. Much
has changed on college campuses since then. Students now spend less
time debating collectivist theory; they seem more committed to traditional academic pursuits; they are worried about the effects of inflation, and governmental policies to curb it, on their own job prospects;
and few issues ignite student protests. Issues and language have changed
since the late 1960s, but the problem of how to integrate the personal
and collective levels of identity is not dead or dated. Students will go on
facing the tension between individual achievement as a personal base
for identity and collective achievement as a group base for identification and sense of self. We see no way that the basic theme of the book

will disappear short of total assimilation, in which case ethnic and racial status as a meaningful social definition will also disappear. Even if racial assimilation were possible, or if injustice and discrimination were eliminated, we feel that Black Americans will continue to look at the Black experience and sense of "we-ness" with other Blacks as critical to the collective base of personal identity. Pride in the group's history of survival, in its cultural heritage and ties to Africa, and appreciation of the collective strengths of community and family as an antidote to the worst of American individualism will continue to make being Black relevant to identity. Black students, and students from many of our other racial and ethnic minorities, will continue to use their group identifications as important bases of the collective aspect of identity for a long time. Also they will attempt to find ways to integrate their commitments to the group with their longings for individual fulfillment for a long time. The language will shift, but the issue of how to integrate the personal and collective aspects of identity will endure.

Patricia Gurin
Edgar Epps

acknowledgments————————

The field work of the studies reported in this book spanned eight years. Many people from the 10 colleges that participated in the cross-section study from 1964 to 1965 and from the six of these colleges that agreed to participate again in 1970 turned a complicated field operation into rewarding relationships among colleagues. Each college arranged for us to administer the battery of questionnaires to *all* enrolled students in the fall of 1964. This required careful coordination with freshman orientation programs and even more difficult arrangements for upperclass students to answer the questionnaires in campuswide assemblies. Registrars provided test scores and cumulative grade records for all students who were subsequently selected randomly for the analysis sample. At the end of that academic year each college arranged for the freshmen who had been selected for the analysis sample to be reassembled to answer the follow-up questionnaires that provide the measures of freshman change for analyses of college impact. Three colleges worked with us to carry out 200 interviews of students during the second term of that year. Six interviewers lived in dormitories for a month while they interviewed students and observed classes, faculty meetings, campus activities, and generally participated as much as possible in campus life.

The level of collaboration that these data collection activities represent amazes even us as we look back to a period when administrators, faculty, and students were far more optimistic than now about the nation's commitment to developing institutions. By 1970 we could not have undertaken a field operation that involved so much collaboration from the colleges because the benefit of research was far more in question as the availability of financial resources for new programs and educational experimentation became much more problematic. Legitimate suspicion also resulted from the publication of a few uninformed, insensitive, and invidious accounts of the historically Black colleges that nonetheless received unusual attention in educational circles. The six colleges that agreed to participate in our repeat cross-sectional study in 1970 did so despite campus pressures against research. Thus, we aimed for less comprehensive data collection procedures in 1970. We randomly selected 50 men and 50 women in just the freshman and senior classes. That the liaison people at each college managed very successfully to elicit the cooperation of this random sample of students attests to their convictions that research can be useful in educational planning. It was only at one college that some seniors refused to participate, expressly because they questioned our intentions. The liaison people at the other colleges faced suspicion as well, however, and they sensitively and honestly discussed the history of the project, the questionnaires the students were being asked to answer, and the value and limits of research. We simply could not have carried out this series of studies without the collaboration of many people at each of the colleges who handled difficult field situations, admittedly produced by different forces in 1964 and 1970, with extraordinary skill and sensitivity. The list of such persons would be very long had we not promised from the outset to preserve the anonymity of the participating colleges. (Some readers will figure out the identity of particular colleges, although we have tried to make that as difficult as possible. And we know that some people whose experiences should facilitate identifying the colleges accurately have made incorrect guesses.)

We thank first and foremost the administrators, faculty, and students of the colleges who joined with us in this prolonged research endeavor. We have reported research results to the colleges at several points in the eight years of active collaboration. On some campuses this included meeting with student groups, faculty in each major academic division, curriculum committees, student personnel administrators, and executive officers. We do not know if the research has been useful, especially in the sense intended by critics of research who wish to see immediate and direct payoffs. We hope now that this book will make some contributions to an understanding of the struggles of students to integrate their individual and collective goals and also of the efforts of their colleges, operating without adequate resources and in some instances threatened for survival, to help them "put it all together."

Many individuals have provided ideas and approaches to the complex problems of achievement motivation, person-situation interaction, and individual and collective bases of achievement. We are particularly indebted to Daniel Katz, whose work on organization and personality has inspired us as it has many other students of social psychology. We are grateful, however, for far more than his theoretical contributions. He worked closely with us on all aspects of the 1964-1965 cross-section study. He gave endlessly of his time, research experience, and wisdom simply because he wanted to support the work of former students and junior colleagues. He also made many helpful suggestions about previous drafts of this manuscript.

Discussions with many other colleagues have contributed greatly to our approach to the problems we addressed in this book. We especially thank Gerald Gurin, Jack Atkinson, Muriel Beattie, John Bracey, Jr., Kenneth Clark, Carolyn Gaylord, Melinda Willis Green, Tobe Johnson, Lewis Wade Jones, Carl Jorgensen, Irwin Katz, Abigail Krystall, Eric Krystall, Rosina Lao, Hylan Lewis, Grace Mack, Arthur

Mathis, Albert McQueen, Betty Morrison, Theodore Newcomb, Setsu-ko Nishi, Betty Penn, Bert Phillips, Paul Puryear, Daniel Thompson, Marion Thorpe, and Andrew Torrance. We benefited particularly from the thorough and insightful critique that Hylan Lewis and Setsuko Nishi gave to an earlier version of this manuscript. Carolyn Gaylord, our junior colleague who is about to complete her Ph.D. in psychology at the University of Michigan, carried out and wrote up the analyses of the 1970 material on student opinions about Black Nationalism (see Chapter 8). She has also commented on the manuscript in detail; her judgment of our presentation of sensitive concerns of Black students has given us much appreciated guidance. Betty Penn made the 1964-1965 field work possible. Having graduated from one of the participating colleges only the year before the field work started, she managed to coordinate all the questionnaire administrations, handle the intensive interview study at three of the colleges, and keep in close touch with key people at the colleges throughout that academic year. She also supervised the coding process, assuring that the open-ended responses were not misinterpreted by a coding staff of Northerners who were not familiar with the South in general or with the Black college milieu in particular. Finally, the process of reporting results to the colleges could not have been done without Betty Penn's involvement and simultaneous capacity for criticism and commitment.

Various people have typed and proofread the numerous drafts of this manuscript. Most of the work has been done by Arlene Sanderson with competence and good cheer. We are indebted to Elizabeth O'Neill, Douglas Truax, and Rhea Kish for editorial assistance.

We are grateful to several funding agencies for the support of the various studies reported in this book: The Office of Education Cooperative Research Branch for support of the 1964-1965 cross-section study of 10 colleges; the Horace H. Rackham Graduate School, University of Michigan, for support of the study of activism at College H in the spring of 1965; the Office of Education Vocational Educational Branch for support of an evaluation of our research reporting procedures in 1966; the National Science Foundation for support of the 1968 follow-up study of seniors at College H; and the National Institute of Mental Health (The Center for Metropolitan Studies) for support of the 1970 cross-section study of six colleges and of the analysis needed to integrate this series of studies for publication.

We also wish to thank the following publishers for permission to use excerpts in this book: Bantam Books; Beacon Press; Carnegie Foundation for the Advancement of Teaching; Grove Press; Journal of the American Academy of Arts and Sciences; Journal of Social Issues; Macgibbon and Dee; MacMillan; McGraw-Hill; William Morris Agency; Prentice-Hall; Trans-action Press; and the University of Chicago Press.

contents

Overview

Black students are making demands on colleges and universities throughout the country. They are demanding academic excellence in order to perform well in traditional areas of achievement, qualify for admission to graduate schools, and secure jobs of their choice. They also are demanding that both the curriculum and other experiences in college be relevant to their identities as Black students. This ferment is expressed in various ways: formation of Black student organizations; appeals for Afro-American studies programs; expression of Black pride through such symbols as African dress and hair styles, Afro-American music and literature; insistence that colleges and universities become more involved in their surrounding communities; and demands for participation in the decision making at their schools.

These student demands have triggered confrontation protests on many campuses—at first on the campuses of the historically Black colleges and then on white campuses as their Black student populations increased during the second half of the sixties. Sometimes these protests have emphasized only academic excellence; more frequently they have stressed that academics should be both excellent and relevant. Special Black studies courses became the focus of this attempt to integrate intellectual and identity issues. The way some colleges have resisted these demands or relegated special studies that stress identity to secondary academic status ignores a unique opportunity to use the students' desires to understand their relationship to the world as a motivation to pursue more traditional, intellectual achievement. Most Black students who push for special Black courses do not intend to study those courses only, or even to major in them. They want to examine Western thought and history within the broader context of non-Western, especially African, philosophical traditions; they want to analyze the conventional assumptions of social science and the humanities but from a Black perspective; they want not only to apply typical

1

research methods to problems facing the Black community but to change those methods when their own Black experiences reveal methodological inadequacies. While some students may depend on these special Black courses as a shield against personal challenge, most use them as intellectual opportunities in which their unique concerns as Black students can be integrated into the conventional curriculum. Indeed this national push among Black students for an education relevant to their identities as Blacks is yet another instance of a much broader-based student demand for relevancy. Higher education, whether in predominantly white or predominantly Black institutions, is being challenged to create an environment where both traditional intellectual achievement and social relevancy can be fostered and mutually reinforced. Although this book is not a prescription for achieving such an environment, it aims at revealing and clarifying the concerns and dilemmas of Black students during this uneasy period when many questions are being raised about the relevancy of education.

We report here the results of a series of studies conducted in several historically Black colleges from 1964 to 1970, using this controversy between relevant identity goals and the traditional academic goals of higher education as the framework for the book. Both goals—to make certain that students gain the skills necessary to act effectively in the world and that they develop the sense of identity and humanity that provide the reason to act—are compatible elements of what we think of as the educated person. Still the fact that many educators feel that these goals define dichotomous and mutually contradictory directions highlights the need to examine the relationship between them as seen by the student generation crucially affected by this debate.

How do Black students manage to integrate their collective commitments as Blacks with their goals for individual achievement and personal fulfillment? Normative pressures in college generally push toward individual development, expression, and advancement; commitments to social change and group responsibilities may be approved, but they are hardly advocated as a central norm. Black students, like other students, respond to the general cultural stress on individuality and personal fulfillment. But because of their Blackness they must also cope with competing, powerful motives and pressures for selflessness rather than personal gain, for cooperation rather than competition, for collective rather than individual commitments. How do they put it all together? When can individual goals and collective commitments coexist or, even more positively, reinforce each other? When do these goals polarize? What in the students' college experiences and personal strengths promotes a life plan that allows the personal as well as the collective expression of achievement? What situations foster the integration of these goals? These questions form the central thrust of this book.

Our second purpose in writing the book is to present data gathered from questionnaires and interviews with several thousand Black students that either counter common expectations or fill the void of information about Black students. Contrary to popular belief, for example, our data show that growing up without a father in the home did not depress academic performance, future aspirations, or effectiveness in planning or working to achieve personal goals. We will show that family structure was simply never significant in our analyses of student performance, motivation, and aspirations. This was true even though approximately a quarter of the students came to college from families where the father had not been present, a figure that matches the national estimates for urban areas in the north where father absence is highest. Likewise, our studies provide no evidence for the widely held stereotype of the Black woman who is more dominant and ambitious than the Black man. Women consistently chose educational and occupational goals that reflected lower levels of aspiration; they did so in every college, as freshmen and as seniors, in 1964 and 1970. When we describe the social roots of activism among Black students, the study results serve not only to explode myths but to fill gaps in what is known about Black students. Nearly all studies of the political activism of college students have been conducted at just a few major predominantly white institutions. Even though Black students were more active than white students throughout the decade of the sixties, practically nothing in the vast literature on student activism pertains to them.

IDENTITY AND ACHIEVEMENT

We chose to use the concept of identity in the title of this book and as an integrating concept despite its almost clichéd status in popular writing on adolescence. However overused and inevitably imprecise, identity remains one of the concepts that best bridges the personal and social realms. The discussion of identity demands recognition of the mutual relationship of the individual and the group. When Erikson[1] first discussed the concept of ego identity in psychoanalytic theory, he stressed that personal identity refers to the maintenance of inner solidarity with a group's ideal and identity, a persistent sameness with oneself (self-sameness), and persistent sharing of some kind of essen-

1. Erik H. Erikson, "Identity and the Life Cycle," *Psychological Issues*, Monograph 1 (New York: International Universities Press, 1959).

tial character with others. People learn to be most themselves where they mean most to others. Whatever their theoretical persuasion—psychoanalytic, symbolic interactionist, or existential—psychologists who write of identity or self retain this idea of a mutual relationship between the individual's core and an essential aspect of a group's inner coherence. Individuals form personal identity from social interactions in which they learn what others think and expect of them, from assuming the role and perspective of significant others, especially toward themselves. But identity formation is not simply a responsive process. The person tests, selects, and integrates from the many self-representations provided by these social interactions. This means that all individuals will have elements of identity that reflect unique integrations of social experiences as well as elements that are common to other members of the group with which they identify. While each individual will rightfully think of the self as unique, no one forms a comfortable identity independently of social influences. The sense of identity has to involve both the uniquely personal and the collective elements that result from social interaction and group identifications.

Because the identity concept bridges the social and psychological levels, it applies especially well to questions faced by young people of minority status. The fact of minority status sharpens the universal necessity of group belongingness for the development of a sense of identity. Young people belonging to the racial and ethnic majority may be only dimly aware of the collective aspects of personal identity, although they, too, have developed a sense of continuity through social interactions embedded in particular groups. Young people from an ethnic or racial minority group are much more conscious of the group elements of identity because others define them as Black, Chicano, Chinese, or Jewish. Since the ethnic or racial group provides an obvious base for the minority person's collective elements of identity, minority status can be an enormous advantage in the formation of identity. In addition to being an obvious focus for identification, the ethnic or racial minority group also provides special possibilities for developing the sense of history and connectedness to the past and the future that seem so crucial for personal identity. All ethnic and racial groups provide a collective history and a set of traditions that remind the person identified with them of a tie with the past as well as a projection into the future, if only because future generations will also share that history. Not all social groups provide as clear a temporal dimension for personal continuity. The racial or ethnic minority group also provides a healthy basis for spatial continuity—a sense of sameness across different social situations—since racial and ethnic categories are used as meaningful social descriptions by most people in this society. We are a nation of many ethnic and racial groups; we are not a melting pot. Sex, ethnic, and racial status figure prominently in social perception. To enter a new situation with a firm and positive sense of one's sexual, ethnic, and racial identity validates shared meanings of "who we are" and serves as a solid foundation for social interaction as we move on to more differentiated conceptions of our individuality.

Why, then, has ethnic or racial group membership not been advanced as a critical asset in identity formation? Why has so much of our psychological literature focused on the negative implications of minority status? The answer is simple enough. Racial and ethnic identifications have been viewed positively only for groups that the majority has evaluated positively. Since being Black has been devalued by the majority group, racial identification among Black youngsters has been viewed by psychologists as acceptance of oneself in a devalued group. Identification as Black began to be viewed by social scientists as a positive base of personal identity when the history of Black Americans was correctly reinterpreted as a positive struggle and effective survival against systematic exploitation and oppression. Since previous social science literature had reflected the dominant view of historians of the psychological damage done to Blacks through slavery and reconstruction, social scientists were not likely to advance the notion that racial identification could be a source of strength for the identity formation of Black Americans. It was not until the reappraisal of history put the adaptive strengths of Black people in proper perspective that the positive identifications Black youngsters had with parents, Black community figures, and Black symbols began to be recognized for what they were.

This volume shows how the students themselves began to use the fact of being Black as the basis for the collective elements of identity as they reappraised the history of Black people in America. It also shows how students used the civil rights movement to discard victim analyses and to authenticate a perspective that simultaneously stressed the oppression of Blacks and pride in the group's strength and ability to endure. Black Nationalist writing further solidified for them this twofold consciousness of collective oppression and pride in the group. While race pride has always been present among Blacks in America, the civil rights movement and the dissemination of Black pride symbols and nationalist writing later in the sixties effectively countered the negative view of Blacks created by the white majority.

We believe that race identification will continue to serve as a collective base of personal identity, partly because we are not sanguine about the society's capacity to assimilate racial minorities and partly because the shared history and sense of "peoplehood" will gratify important needs even if social inequities were not to force their prominence in identity formation.

What does achievement have to do with identity? Traditional psychological literature on achievement motivation and performance casts achievement in highly individualistic terms. The need for achievement stems from the individual's pleasure in competing with a personal standard of excellence. Actual achievement connotes individual performance at a high standard of excellence. Typical indicators of achievement in psychological research include good performance at academic-type tasks, earning good grades, persisting at difficult tasks, setting educational and occupational goals that realistically test one's mettle, striving to meet those goals, managing to enter and advance in an occupation that represents mobility over one's parents, or maintenance of the parent's high level of achievement where mobility is hardly possible. When we talk about achievement, we generally refer to performance in school or in academiclike settings that lead, we typically believe, to performance in the job world that will bring status and financial rewards. Achievement in this individualistic sense relates to identity in a highly industrialized society such as ours because occupational placement and the work role are so critical to definitions of who we are. Erikson,[2] for example, contends that adolescents must form a commitment to an occupation or work role that allows expression of talent and a sense of industry. This, along with making commitments to heterosexual intimacy, to secondary groups that represent personal ideology and values, and to a time perspective that spans the past and the future, is critical in order to resolve the adolescent identity crisis. Adolescents cannot miss the social pressure for personal achievement in the form of work commitments, since the educational system has institutionalized, with parental support, societal demands for decisions. High school students must decide whether to continue their education and in what setting—decisions that generally hinge upon eventual occupational placement. Recruitment publicity for the armed services stresses occupational training and the opportunity to "find a career that fits you." College students must select an academic major; few miss the connection between that choice and career decisions. All the way along teachers and parents explicitly tie school achievement, personal competence and talent, and achievement motivation to occupational aspirations and placement. The eventual work role ideally provides the niche for the expression of individual achievement and, thus, a major aspect of personal identity. These pressures for

2. *Ibid.*

occupational commitments are not without cost, but young people must face them, successfully or not. The first section of this book examines how students attending historically Black colleges addressed these pressures for future educational and occupational commitments as the individual achievement dimensions of personal identity.

We also view achievement as having a collective meaning in that the individual's contribution to group achievement is a collective medium for forming personal identity. The idea of group achievement as an aggregate of individuals' achievements in pursuit of their own goals easily follows from achievement theory. McClelland,[3] for example, has characterized groups and societies by an aggregate level of achievement that can become culturally normative and exert achievement pressures in socialization of the young. This idea of aggregate achievement also represents one theory of social change. Assuming that opportunities were truly equal and that universal, nondiscriminatory standards were applied to all people, the individual achievements and personal mobility of group members would provide the mechanism for aggregate social change in the status of the group. The idea of group achievement as something more than the aggregate of individual achievements flows less obviously from achievement theory. We will argue, however, that the efforts of members working together to exact legal, economic, and social change also represent collective achievement. The students who were committed to collective action as a social change strategy and expressed their commitments to group activities were striving to achieve, but they were working for group products and accomplishments rather than individual goals. Their motivation carried all the usual connotations of achievement motivation. It prompted hard and persistent effort as well as setting group goals that were both difficult and realistic. When successful in desegregating a public facility, registering impressive numbers of the previously disenfranchised to vote, forcing a policy of affirmative employment, or manning a demonstration that received national attention, the students evinced the kind of pleasure usually associated with achievement. They were elated with a job well done; they were proud of the process of working together as well as with their accomplishments in creating change. Sometimes, when campaigns did not succeed, the process itself was the prime source of gratification, just as it must be in individual achievement settings when individual efforts are not rewarded.

The achievement that results from individuals working in concert provides a tie to identity through what Erikson meant by commitment

3. David C. McClelland, *The Achieving Society* (Princeton, New Jersey: Van Nostrand, 1961).

to groups that represent personal values and ideology. Collective achievements promote the collective aspect of identity. To identify with a group whose achievements you admire and, furthermore, to enhance those achievements by your own actions cements the mutual relationship between the individual and the group, the personal and collective elements of identity. The collective commitments that originally motivated the students' social action were further reinforced by the group process, the sense of "we-ness" and "being-together" with others.

The second section of the book explores the sources of motivation for group action, viewed as collective achievement, that in turn solidified an extended sense of self, the collective aspect of identity. Finally, the third section examines how students handled this collective base of identity as they simultaneously dealt with the pressures for individual achievement that are so critical to personal identity in American society.

GENERAL PLAN OF THE BOOK

This is a book about students—their individual and collective achievements and the influences that acted upon them. We do not pretend to make a detailed analysis of the history of institutional features of historically Black colleges. Several volumes about Black colleges as institutions have been recently published. Nor do we enter the debate about the future of these colleges except as our data on students speak to that issue. Our own position is clear. Many Black students will still prefer to attend colleges where the campus ambience supports their personal development without the level of conflict and isolation experienced on many predominantly white campuses. Such a supportive environment is likely to be predominantly Black; it need not be exclusively Black; it cannot be restrictedly Black. Whatever the eventual racial mixture of the student bodies of these historically Black colleges, it is of utmost importance that they maintain the goal of promoting the racial identity of Black students.

While our major concern is with students, not institutions, we nonetheless believe that our data must be set in an historical context of the place of Black colleges in American higher education. Chapter 2 examines the historical role of Black colleges and trends in enrollment of Black students in higher education.

The remainder of the book is divided into three parts. Part 1 (Chapters 3 to 7) examines the *individual achievement* goals of the students. There we discuss students' academic achievement, their grades, their performance on achievement tasks administered in the study, and whether or not they stayed in college. We also look at their educational and occupational goals and the level of aspiration they represent. Part 2 (Chapters 8 to 12) explores their *collective achievements* as expressed through social action. It describes the students' action commitments at three points in time—at the end of the mass demonstration period highlighted by the famous march led by Martin Luther King from Selma to Montgomery, Alabama in which large numbers of the students in our study participated; again two years later when on-campus student power confrontations had begun to replace conventional off-campus civil rights activities; and then in 1970 when newly emerging Afro-groups were delineating psychological questions of racial identification as raison d'être for student activists. Part 3 (Chapters 13 to 15) takes up the *relationship between individual and collective achievements.* There we look at four groups of seniors whose motivations, ideologies, and college experiences show four ways of handling the pressures for personal and collective commitments. Two groups, which we call Traditional Achievers and Committed Achievers, shared the intention of pursuing major professions and higher degrees in graduate and professional schools; they differed in whether they had been committed during their college years to collective achievement as well. The Traditional Achievers' strong personal goals existed at the expense of collective commitments. They reported as seniors that they had never participated in any form of social action. The equally high personal goals of the Committed Achievers coexisted with strong, stable commitments to collective action. A third group, the Activists, like the Committed Achievers, had been politically involved throughout college but approached graduation with lower personal goals. They either considered the B.A. a terminal degree or talked about advanced education as a more remote goal. If they expected to go eventually to graduate or professional school, they talked about training for lower status professions. As a remote goal graduate education was thought of as a master's degree. Students in this group had not necessarily rejected personal goals, as the activist committed to revolution would have done, but they had not integrated their collective commitments with the same high level of personal aspiration, despite having entered college with much the same goals, that characterized the Committed Achievers. The fourth group, the Unengaged, had neither been involved in collective action nor did they end college with personal goals that reflected unusual individual achievement. What was it that distinguished these groups of seniors?

In each of these three parts we discuss three sets of influences. First, we explore sources of personal motivation for individual and collective achievement. Our analysis of internal pressures for individual achievement is put in the context of the extensive psychological literature on achievement motivation. We examine the significance of achievement motives and values. Motivation also depends on expectations of success, some reflecting confidence in oneself, others reflecting assessments of the environment's response to one's effort. These expectancies of success have proved to be crucial factors in the motivational dynamics of the students we have studied. The self-confidence the students felt about their basic abilities and the likelihood that their talents and efforts would be rewarded greatly influenced how hard they tried, what they tried for, and how effective they were. In our discussion of individual achievement motivation we emphasize several of these expectancy concepts, among them the popular concept of internal and external control, to show how they dominated other aspects of achievement motivation and why they took on heightened significance for students who have had to take seriously the issue of reality payoffs. By contrast, motivation for collective achievement depended on the students' collective consciousness and growing Black Nationalism, not on their individual achievement motivation. Our discussion of collective achievement highlights how victim-deficit interpretations of the status of Blacks in America gave way to awareness of system obstacles, to cynicism about traditional models of creating change, and to commitment to collectivism and the basic ideas of nationalism as the civil rights movement wound down and student political action turned inward to campus targets. Despite these shifts in language and the increasing attention to collectivism over the decade, at a given point in time it was always the students whose ideologies were most collectivist who tried hardest to effect change, first through the civil rights movement and later through student power activities.

Next, we look at the influence of the students' precollege family and demographic backgrounds on their individual goals and aspirations, their collective commitments and, finally, their integration or separation of individual and collective goals. Here we analyze the role of rural-urban background, family income level, family structure, the mother's and father's education, and the importance of religion to the family. We show that family social class mattered less in aspirations and individual achievement than is sometimes believed to be true; none of the family status measures correlated significantly with college grades or performance on standard tests or with measures of achievement motives and values. Only the students' aspirations, and especially their expectancies of achieving their individual goals, reflected precollege home and environmental influences. Generally, the aspects of the student's precollege environment that most pertained to aspirations and expectations of success suggest that social impact operated through the opportunities and the resources of the environment. Family income and rural-urban background, both social variables that reflect differential opportunities and resources, related more consistently than either the educational attainments of parents or the family structure to student aspirations and expectancies. Opportunity likewise appears to be governing the demographic influences on student political action since rural-urban background, not family social status, best distinguished activists from nonactivists. This is one of the ways our results concerning Black student activists appear to differ from their white counterparts who are generally painted as the products of the most privileged, educated, and affluent homes in America. Opportunities to participate and relative freedom from reprisals, both greater in the urban than the rural South, had more to do with the civil rights activism of Black students than having a background of privilege.

Finally, in each section we examine the influence of the environment on student development and change. What kinds of environments resulted in heightened aspiration, increased concern with collectivism and political action, and especially the capacity to integrate collective and personal goals? In keeping with the book's focus on students, we primarily use measures of student experiences and campus climates to present a picture of the 10 colleges and their influences on students. By different kinds of environments we refer to the academic-intellectual atmosphere of the student culture, the diversity of extracurricular activities, the heterogeneity of subcultural groupings, the role of student activism on the campus, the amount of student-faculty contact outside the classroom, the openness of the administration to student influence, and the cosmopolitanism and social status of the student body. We also discuss more traditional indicators of institutional quality: academic selectivity, accreditation ratings, institutional resources. However, they are secondary because they have been over-emphasized in recent writing on Black colleges, while the significance of student life and culture has been neglected.

THE COLLEGES

The 10 colleges we asked to participate in the research in the fall of 1964 were chosen to represent different types of predominantly Black colleges and universities. The historically Black colleges differ in numerous ways (see Chapter 2). We used two important features of their diversity—type of sponsorship and position in an academic status hierarchy—to select an equal number of public and private institutions that were judged by the Southern Association of Schools and Colleges as falling within two categories, those with the highest academic status and those whose status was somewhat lower but who still met basic accreditation requirements. We also wanted to include colleges that differed in their responses to student involvement in the southern civil rights movement so as to study the meaning of activism where constraint operated and where it did not. Administrative constraint was judged according to whether there was public evidence that it existed, as by firing of faculty, expelling of students, or openly instructing students that their status as students would be jeopardized by participation. Lack of constraint did not necessarily indicate that civil rights activism was encouraged. Of only one college could it be said that the administration felt activism should be encouraged; but there were other colleges where it was tolerated, and where students and faculty who chose to participate faced no particular consequences.

By selecting four public and four private colleges that were also judged to be high or low on these other two dimensions, eight types of institutions were included in the study. Two others were also asked to participate for special reasons, one because it is an unusually prestigious college and the other because of its history of providing high quality technical as well as liberal arts education. The 10 colleges thus break down as follows:

	Evidence of Constraint	No Evidence of Constraint
	Public Institutions	
Highest academic status	One College Student population = 4088	One College Student population = 3086
Accredited but somewhat lower status	One College Student population = 2290	One College Student population = 1854
	Private Institutions	
Highest academic status	One College Student population = 1008	Three Colleges Student population = A— 498 B—1026 C—3039
Accredited but somewhat lower status	One College Student population = 1137	One College Student population = 653

This purposive selection resulted in a sample of students that represented very well the characteristics of students attending other historically Black colleges as well. Most of the students in our sample,
like most of the general population of students at Black colleges, were
the first generation in their families to attend college. Seventy-eight
percent of the fathers in our 1964-1965 sample, 73 percent in the
1969-1970 sample, and 80 percent of the fathers in an American Council of Education sample of historically Black colleges had not attended
college. The parents of most of the students worked in semiskilled and
unskilled jobs. Only a quarter of the fathers in our sample and less
than a third in a larger sample of Black colleges were white collar
workers. Nearly a third of the students came from families with incomes that fell below the poverty line; over half came from families
earning less than $6000 per year. These figures match almost exactly
the estimates on other Black colleges provided by the American
Council of Education.[4] Like most students attending Black colleges in
the South, virtually all the students in our sample grew up in southern
states. Most were attending colleges in their own home states. In all of
these ways our sample of colleges provided a sample of students that
represented Black colleges more generally. Thus, while 10 colleges are
only a fraction of all historically Black colleges, those we chose were
serving students from the same backgrounds as those who were attending other Black colleges between 1964 and 1970.

Restricting this study just to historically Black colleges does mean
we should not generalize to all Black students attending colleges and
universities. We will point out in Chapter 2 that Black colleges enrolled
just over half of all Black students in 1964. They enrolled between 25
and 30 percent in 1972. Since Chapter 2 also details that Black students
who entered predominantly white institutions during the period of our
study grew up in somewhat more comfortable circumstances, the
information we will present about students may not apply as well to
students in predominantly white institutions as they do to students in
Black colleges other than the 10 we studied. On the other hand, some
predominantly white colleges serve Black students from much the
same types of backgrounds as those students who entered the particular Black colleges we studied. We were fortunate in being able to compare the demographic and family backgrounds of the students in our
10 colleges with Black students in three northern, predominantly white
colleges. Each of the three served students whose profile was matched

4. Alan E. Bayer and Robert F. Boruch, "Black and White Freshmen Entering Four-Year
   Colleges," *Educational Record* 50 (1969), p. 378, and A. J. Jaffe, Walter Adams, and
   Sandra G. Meyers, *Negro Higher Education in the 1960's* (New York: Frederick A.
   Praeger, 1968).

by at least one of the sample colleges even though the average income, education, and occupational status of the parents of northern Black students attending the predominantly white colleges was significantly greater than the average of students we were studying. Gross comparisons of southern and northern, predominantly white and predominantly Black, rural and urban, private and public can miss the fact that some southern, historically Black colleges attract students whose backgrounds are remarkably similar to Black students attending some predominantly white institutions, certainly in the South but even in the North. Thus, while we caution against generalizing our data too broadly, they can legitimately apply to some Black students in some predominantly white institutions as well.

DESCRIPTION OF THE STUDIES

The results we will present are based on both cross-sectional and longitudinal studies that were carried out at four points in time between the fall of 1964 and the spring of 1970.

The first cross-sectional study involved administering a battery of questionnaires to students attending 10 colleges in the fall of 1964. All 10 colleges were located in deep South states; four were publically, six privately supported. To assure random selection of students, the colleges agreed to let our research team administer the questionnaires to all students during the registration period for the fall term; we then randomly selected 50 questionnaires from men and 50 from women at each class level to code for the analysis sample. This provided a total of 400 students per college at all but three colleges where 50 students were not enrolled in all sex-class groupings.

A longitudinal follow-up of the entering freshmen at these 10 colleges was conducted in the spring of 1965. Questionnaires were repeated to assess change during the freshman year so as to measure the impact of the college. New questions on the meaning of the freshman experience were also asked at that time. This "change sample" figures prominently in the results discussed in Chapter 6 on the influence of the college on student aspirations and motivation. At that time we attempted to question again the 100 freshmen at each college who had been randomly selected into the analysis sample the previous fall. With a 92 percent success rate, the "change sample" totaled approximately 1000 students.

In-depth interviews were conducted at three of the 10 colleges between January and March, 1965. All were private colleges chosen because of their diversity in student groups and subcultures. Of the students interviewed at each college 150 were selected by peer nomination as students who represented different types on the campus: political activists, casual types who spent a lot of time around the student union, intellectuals or scholarly students, and creative non-conformists who were active in the arts on the campus. Fifty additional students at each campus were then randomly chosen to provide control. These interviews figure prominently in Chapter 8 where we describe how students felt in 1965 about a variety of racial issues and also provide the quotations from students that are found throughout the book.

A second cross-sectional study was carried out in the spring of 1970. Six of the 10 original colleges—three public, three private—agreed to participate in the repeat study by administering questionnaires to 50 men and 50 women at the freshman and senior levels, making a total of approximately 200 students per college. Liaison people at the colleges administered these questionnaires. When we compare student opinions, aspiration levels, motivational characteristics, or activism rates in 1964 with 1970, we use only the six colleges that participated both times. This is to assure that any differences found do not derive from comparing a different set of colleges. The tables indicate the number of colleges and students that comprise the base for the appropriate statistics.

Chart A describes the samples for the 1964 10 college and the 1970 six college cross-sectional studies.

A longitudinal study of one freshman class was also conducted at College H. In addition to the entrance questionnaires collected in the fall of 1964 and the readministration of questionnaires at the end of the freshman year, both questionnaires and interviews were collected at the end of the senior year in the spring of 1968. This intensive one-college study provides data for two special analyses in this book. The first, a study of the correlates and consequences of dropping out of college described in Chapter 4, compares the 123 of the original 200 freshmen who were still in residence during the senior year with the 77 who had left before then. We also use the longitudinal data from students at this college to discuss the impact of participation in social action in Chapters 10, 11, and 14. Between the beginning and end of the freshman year large numbers of the students at this college participated in demonstrations near their campus and in a local civil rights group affiliated with the Student Nonviolent Coordinating Committee (SNCC). We selected three groups of freshmen: activists who participated in all of the events and the campus leadership group; moderately active students who had participated in only one event; nonactivists who had not taken part in any civil rights activities during their freshman year. Comparing the entrance and end-of-the-year

CHART A. Description of Samples for the Ten College Study, 1964-1965 and the Six-College Study, 1970

| Colleges | 1964-1965 Sample | | | | | | | | 1970 Sample | | | |
| | Freshmen | | Sophomores | | Juniors | | Seniors | | Freshman | | Seniors | |
	Men	Women	Men	Women	Men	Women	Men	Women	Men	Women	Men	Women
Public institutions												
Mississippi (A)	50	50	50	50	50	50	50	50 (400)	50	50	50	50 (200)
Florida (B)	50	50	50	50	50	50	50	50 (400)	50	50	36	61 (197)
North Carolina (C)	50	50	50	50	50	50	50	50 (400)	53	63	52	65 (223)
South Carolina (D)	50	50	50	50	50	50	50	50 (400)				
Private institutions												
Mississippi (E)	50	50	33	36	41	41	34	32 (317)				
South Carolina (F)	50	50	50	50	50	50	50	50 (400)				
Louisiana (G)	50	50	41	50	44	50	46	50 (381)				
Alabama (H)	50	50	50	50	50	50	50	50 (400)	50	56	45	49 (200)
Alabama (I)	40	50	30	50	36	50	37	50 (343)	31	63	36	31 (161)
Georgia (J)	50	—	50	—	50	—	48	— (198)	75	—	61	— (136)
	(490)	(450)	(454)	(436)	(471)	(441)	(465)	(432)	(309)	(282)	(280)	(256)

Total: Men 1880
Women 1759
Freshmen 940
Sophomores 890
Junior 912
Seniors 897

Grand total: 3639

Total: Men 589
Women 538
Freshmen 591
Seniors 536

Grand total: 1127

CHART B. Description of Samples Involved in the Intensive Studies of Students in College H

Dropout Study of the Class of 1968

Freshmen Who Dropped Out between 1965 and 1968		Freshmen Still In Residence In 1968	
Men	Women	Men	Women
38	39	62	61

Total: Men 100
Women 100
200

Study of Freshmen in 1964-1965 Before and After Civil Rights Events Occurred During Their Freshmen Year

Inactives		Moderately Active		Activists	
Men	Women	Men	Women	Men	Women
42	61	51	50	52	56

Total: Men 155
Women 168
323

Longitudinal Follow-Up of the Freshmen Who Varied in Civil Rights Participation in 1964-1965 as Seniors in 1968

Stable Inactives		Activist Dropouts		Activated Activists		Stable Activists	
Men	Women	Men	Women	Men	Women	Men	Women
28	41	33	50	2	5	40	40

Total: Men 103
Women 136
239

questionnaires of these three groups of freshmen made it possible to assess both predispositions and the effects of civil rights activism. The follow-up interviews and questionnaires administered during their senior year in 1968 also provide data for our discussion of the effects of activism. These senior data were collected immediately after this college reopened following a three-month protest about a series of campus issues that had galvanized concerns about student power. Again, we took advantage of a natural experiment that was created by having "before" questionnaires from the freshman year and "after" questionnaires in the senior year to assess the impact of participating in an intervening political action. In addition, we could analyze the meaning of remaining politically active throughout college by comparing three groups of seniors in 1968: the stable activists who had been active in the civil rights events in their freshman year and reported still being involved in the issues that led to protest on the campus in 1968; the activist dropouts who had been active as freshmen but were no longer involved as seniors; and the stable nonactivists who had not participated as freshmen or at any time later in their college years. The senior activists who had become activated during their college years were too few in number to be included in these analyses. These three samples from College H are described in Chart B.

Large quantities of data were collected in these studies. Since we did not want to include a string of separate tables, we decided to insert some tables in the text itself and to refer the reader to additional tables in the Appendix for fuller detail. The Appendix tables primarily cover the multivariate analyses where we looked at many predictor variables in relationships to many sets of dependent variables. The tables presented in the text primarily describe student or college characteristics on key variables. We also use descriptive statistics in the narrative to illustrate general points we are making. We hope that the reader who prefers to do so can follow the data and arguments without reference to tables and that the reader who is more interested in methodology will make use of both the Appendix tables and those in the text itself.

chapter 2

Black Colleges and American Higher Education

Throughout most of the history of the United States, higher education for Blacks has typically meant segregated education. Black colleges and universities originated and developed in a social system that condoned slavery until 1865 and replaced slavery with a color-caste system after emancipation. Before the Civil War, slaveholders vigorously opposed education for Blacks in the South. In the North, even in the absence of slavery, whites were also extremely reluctant to provide education for Blacks. Both northern and southern whites sometimes used violence or threats of violence to prevent Blacks and their supporters from establishing schools. Few northern institutions were willing to enroll Blacks in their regular programs. This reluctance was based in part on widespread acceptance of the belief that Blacks were inherently incapable of benefiting from higher education, and in part on practical considerations of economics and politics related to a social system in which there was no place for college-educated Blacks.

In spite of these obstacles, Blacks have made determined efforts to obtain college and university training since early in the nineteenth century. A small number of Blacks managed to enroll at white colleges in the North before the Civil War, and an even smaller number obtained degrees from American institutions during the first half of the nineteenth century. It is estimated that about 28 Blacks graduated from American colleges before the Civil War.

With some assistance from whites, a small number of institutions that were intended specifically to provide higher education for Blacks were established or attempted before the Civil War. The colleges were designed primarily to prepare teachers and preachers to serve the needs of free Blacks in America and to do missionary work in Africa. Several of these antebellum institutions are still operating as colleges or universities today. Minor Academy in Washington, D. C. (1851), Avery College (1852), and Ashum Institute (1854) in Pennsylvania, and Wil-

19

berforce University in Ohio are examples of institutions developed for the purpose of providing higher education for "quasi-free Negroes" in the North.[1] These early institutions and the 47 private colleges and universities founded between 1865 and 1900 produced most of the educators and professionals who served the Black community in the first half-century following emancipation.

After the Civil War, Northern philanthropic and religious organizations and the Freedman's Bureau established thousands of elementary and secondary schools and a large number of normal schools and colleges to provide education for the newly freed ex-slaves of the South. Many of these early colleges are still educating the descendants of the original ex-slaves. Among the colleges and universities founded during the period from 1865 to 1870 are Howard University, St. Augustine's College, Atlanta University, Fisk University, and Johnson C. Smith University (formerly Biddle Memorial Institute).[2] The schools opened by northern philanthropic organizations and the Freedman's Bureau were not intended to be exclusively for Afro-Americans. The charters of the schools established before 1870 provided for the education of youth regardless of race, creed, or sex.[3] Some of these institutions have never excluded white students. The institutions that became segregated did so as a result of white public opinion and legal proscription.

From 1870 to 1900, many new private institutions were established, including some that later became public.[4] For example, the Methodist Episcopal Church founded the Centenary Biblical Institute in Baltimore in 1866, which later became Morgan College and is today Morgan State University.[5] The most famous of the private institutions established during this period is Tuskegee Institute, founded in 1881 by Booker T. Washington. Tuskegee Institute was one of the few institu-

---

1. John Hope Franklin, *From Slavery to Freedom* (New York: Vintage Books Edition, 1969), p. 231.
2. *Ibid.,* p. 308.
3. Lewis Wade Jones, "Vantage Points for Viewing the Negro College" (Unpublished Paper, Tuskegee Institute, Alabama, 1968), p. 20.
4. Public support for education in the South was extended to Afro-Americans during the Reconstruction Period. In those states with a large Black electorate Blacks played an important role in the establishment of a system of free public education for all children. In five of these states, Arkansas, Louisiana, Mississippi, Florida, and South Carolina, Black men were elected to the office of State Superintendent of Education. See Horace Mann Bond, *The Education of the Negro in the American Social Order* (New York: Octagon Books, 1970) (Originally published by Prentice-Hall, 1934), pp. 49-50.
5. Virgil A. Clift, "Educating the American Negro," in John P. Davis, Editor, *The American Negro Reference Book* (Englewood Cliffs, New Jersey: Prentice-Hall, 1966), p. 367.

tions with a policy of hiring Afro-American teachers only. There were few Afro-Americans on college faculties in the nineteenth century, even those founded to educate ex-slaves.[6] It was much later that the pattern of Black faculties for Black colleges was established. Some of the early mission schools continued to employ predominantly white faculties and to appoint whites as president until the 1950s.

Like Tuskegee Institute, several of the schools established after 1870 resulted from the efforts of Blacks who were graduates of antebellum institutions. Afro-American churches also established several institutions.

The historic importance of the Black institutions during the nineteenth century can hardly be exaggerated. While the Black private colleges and universities were turning out more than 1000 college graduates, it is estimated that northern white institutions graduated less than 200 Blacks. Seven additional Black private colleges and universities were founded after 1900. New institutions continued to be established well into the twentieth century.[7] Thus the period of constructing colleges for Blacks encompassed more than 100 years.[8]

Public support for institutions designed to provide education for Blacks also experienced its most rapid period of growth during the decades following the Civil War. Seventeen of the 34 historically Black

6. Horace Mann Bond, *Black American Scholars: A Study of Their Beginnings* (Detroit, Michigan: Balamp, 1972), p. 98.
7. Of the 54 private colleges and universities listed in F. A. Bowles' and F. DeCosta's *Between Two Worlds: A Profile of Negro Higher Education* (New York: McGraw-Hill, 1971), 42 were established before the Civil War, 16 were founded immediately after the war (1865-1869), 14 began operations during the 1870s, 11 were established in the 1880s, and 4 others were founded during the 1890s. Seven institutions began operations during the twentieth century; four during the first decade, one in 1912, one in 1925, and the last in 1958. The public colleges and universities "for Negroes" also have a long history, one institution began before the Civil War, others were established immediately after the war. Some institutions began as private schools and became public institutions later in their histories. Of the currently existing public colleges and universities that began as institutions for Blacks, four were established in 1866 and 1867, seven were founded during the seventies, five during the eighties, 10 during the nineties, and seven during the twentieth century, with the latest being established in 1950.
8. We seem to be embarking on a new period of "separate-but-equal" higher education in some areas through the establishment of community colleges in locations that are dominated by the presence of a single racial group. Thus, in Chicago, for example, some city colleges are more than 90 percent Black while others are more than 90 percent white. A state university located in Chicago has experienced a student population shift from about 90 percent white to approximately 60 percent nonwhite since 1965. On the other hand, several historically Black universities in border states have changed from 100 percent Black to predominantly white in recent years.

public colleges now in existence were founded before 1890. The Morrill Act of 1890 (the Second Morrill Act) provided funds for the establishment of separate land-grant colleges for Blacks. In the decade that followed the passage of this act, a Black land-grant college was established or designated in each of the 17 southern and border states. Most of these institutions did not become degree-granting colleges until later. Four Black public colleges were founded between 1899 and 1910, and two were founded after World War II. While most of the public colleges enrolled very few college level students during their early years, by 1940 more than half of the students attending Black colleges were enrolled in public institutions. By 1967, the public Black colleges and universities enrolled 90,583 students. Of the hundreds of institutions for Blacks established through a combination of philanthropy and government support for segregated public institutions, 105 two- and four-year colleges and universities enrolling more than 150,000 students are still in operation today.[9]

During the first half of the twentieth century, Black colleges continued to provide higher education for the majority of Blacks who attended college. This was partially because most Blacks of college age resided in the South where segregation barriers made it impossible for them to attend white colleges. At the same time, admissions barriers at northern colleges limited the number of spaces available to Black students. As a result, both northern and southern Black students found it advantageous to attend Black colleges. Eighty percent of all baccalaureate degrees awarded to Blacks by 1968 were earned at Black colleges and universities.[10] The same pattern exists at the professional level; the handful of professional schools founded for Blacks have produced the majority of Black professionals. Only at the graduate level have the major non-Black institutions produced the majority of Black degreeholders. Few Black colleges and universities had graduate programs until rather late in this century. In the public colleges and universities, these programs were initiated as a direct response to Black attempts to eliminate segregation in graduate and professional education. "Separate but equal" graduate and professional schools were established after World War II in an attempt to keep Blacks from

9. Alan E. Bayer estimated that there were nearly one half-million Black college students in 1971. Of these, he estimated that 35 percent were enrolled in Black four-year colleges and universities, another six percent were enrolled in predominantly Black two-year colleges and the remainder were enrolled in traditionally white colleges. See A. E. Bayer, "The New Student in Black Colleges," *School Review, 81* (May, 1973), p. 415.

10. Elias Blake, Jr., "Future Leadership Roles for Predominantly Black Colleges and Universities in American Higher Education," *Daedalus, 100* (Summer, 1971), p. 746.

attending white universities in the southern and border states. In 1967, 18 of the 34 Black public institutions and eight of the 54 Black private institutions offered graduate or professional degrees.

As recently as 1964, Black colleges and universities continued to enroll more than one-half of all Black students attending colleges and universities in the United States, and more than three-fourths of the Black students attending colleges in the South. Since 1965, increased civil rights pressure from Blacks and federal efforts to enforce compliance with civil rights legislation have led to rapid increases in Black enrollment in white colleges. During the period from 1964 to 1968 total college enrollment for Blacks increased from about 234,000 to 434,000, while enrollment at Black colleges increased from 120,000 to 156,000. This represents a 144 percent increase for non-Black colleges, a 30 percent increase for Black colleges during this period, and a total increase of 85 percent in Black student enrollment. A recent census report presented figures that indicate that the number of Black students in college increased an additional 25 percent in 1969 for a total increase of 110 percent between 1964 and 1969.[11] Census reports indicate that 522,000 Black students were enrolled in American colleges in the fall of 1970,[12] and that 680,000 were enrolled in the fall of 1971.[13] It is estimated that between 25 and 30 percent of all Black students currently attend Black colleges.

The data on Black college student enrollment must be viewed with some caution because the 1964 data and the data for later years are not comparable. After 1966, census reports include students in non-credit courses while this was not true of earlier reports. What proportion of the increase in Black college enrollment is because of changes in reporting practices and what proportion is because of actual changes in attendance patterns is difficult to estimate. It is also difficult to determine the extent to which the reported increase in enrollment will actually result in increased attainment of college degrees because most of the Black students are still in the early years of college. In October 1970, 70 percent of the 482,000 Blacks attending four-year colleges were enrolled in the first two years of college. More recent data are not yet available, but it is probable that much of the increase that has taken place in the past few years has involved students in programs that will not lead to degrees. While Black students constitute about 8 percent of the enrollment in both two-year colleges and four-year

11. Cited in: The Carnegie Commission on Higher Education, *From Isolation to Mainstream: Problems of the Colleges Founded for Negroes* (New York: McGraw-Hill, 1971), pp. 11, 14.
12. United States Bureau of the Census, Series P-23, No. 38, July, 1971.
13. United States Bureau of the Census, Series P-20, No. 234, March, 1972.

colleges, the four-year college statistics include the 88 Black public and private colleges. The two-year colleges also include some colleges that are predominantly Black, but most of these were not founded specifically for Blacks. In any case, the proportion of Black students in the later years of college is higher at Black colleges than is indicated by considering only the total enrollment statistics.

The importance of this issue should not be underestimated. *Graduation* from college is much more important for later economic success than attendance without graduation. The person with "some college" is little better off than the high school graduate. An increase in Black enrollment in two-year colleges will not significantly improve Blacks' occupational and income status unless substantial numbers then transfer to four-year institutions. Nor will an increase in Black enrollment in four-year predominantly white institutions represent an educational gain unless the retention rate equals that of the historically Black colleges. One of the most important questions about the recent increase in Black enrollment in white colleges is how many will graduate. The answer will be very important in assessing the impact of recent trends in enrollment.

Recommendations by the Carnegie Commission on Higher Education to achieve educational equality call for increasing Black student enrollment in higher education to 1,100,000 by 1980 and to 2,000,000 by the beginning of the next century.[14] The Commission suggests that Black colleges could increase their enrollments to about 300,000 by the end of the century, if not by 1980. If these projections are reasonably accurate, it is clear that while white institutions will play an increasingly greater role in the provision of higher education for Blacks, the Black colleges and universities are expected to continue to educate a smaller, but still significant proportion of Black students. Their contribution is especially important for the improvement of educational opportunities for Black students in the South where historical conditions have limited Black opportunities at all levels of the educational system.

CONTRIBUTIONS OF BLACK COLLEGES

In assessing the contribution of the "mission schools" to the development of a system of education for Afro-Americans, Horace Mann Bond stated that:

14. Carnegie Commission on Higher Education, *From Isolation to Mainstream: Problems of the Colleges Founded for Negroes* (New York: McGraw-Hill, 1971), p. 19.

The schools were frequently called "colleges" and "universities" when their enrollments were concentrated on the elementary and secondary school level . . .

. . . For every "college" student actually graduated, these schools gave a thorough elementary and secondary education to scores of students who in their turn passed on, through family and friends, their knowledge of the fundamentals and their acquired habits and discipline. Their children and grandchildren did not have to "start from scratch," or even behind it, in an illiterate home and a wretched school or in no school at all.

Based on the academic successes of first, second and even third generation descendants of the students of the early mission schools, available evidence suggests that these schools provided some of the most effective educational institutions the world has ever known. The Negro scholars of today are, for the most part, the children and grandchildren of persons who received their education in these institutions.[15]

Although their development as college-level institutions occurred at a later point in time, the public institutions have also made important contributions to the overall educational development of Blacks. The Carnegie Commission on Higher Education reported that "the specific accomplishments of colleges and universities founded for Negroes are remarkable." Among the accomplishments cited were the following:

Among their 385,000 alumni are substantial numbers of the country's Black governmental officials, army officers, professors, doctors, lawyers, and members of other professions.

They have prepared most of the teachers employed for the education of many generations of Negro children in the South. One-third of all principals and one-half of all teachers in public schools in Mississippi are graduates of one Negro college—Jackson State.

Some of them have extensive experience in providing higher education for students who come to them under-prepared by reason by inadequate prior schooling.

15. Horace Mann Bond, "The Negro Scholar and Professional in America," in John P. Davis, Editor, *The American Negro Reference Book* (Englewood Cliffs, New Jersey: Prentice-Hall, 1966), p. 560.

They have recruited and educated students from low-income families. The average family income of 37.6 of entering Black students and 17.1 percent of other entering students in Negro colleges in the fall of 1960 was less than $4,000 a year.[16]

The Black college contributed to the cultural, economic, and political development of the Black community.[17] In addition to providing leadership, these institutions brought opera, classical music, drama, and lectures by well-known personalities to communities that had little contact with the outside world. Often the Black colleges provided the only opportunity for whites as well as Blacks to participate in Northern cultural events. The Black college was also a major source of employment for the Black community. Even today, Tuskegee Institute has the second largest payroll in Macon County, Alabama. These colleges and universities employed nearly all of the Black scholars working in academic institutions until after 1960.

Mack Jones, a political scientist at Atlanta University, contends that the most significant role played by the Black college was the creation of a substantial Black middle-class community.

Whatever may have been the objective competence of the graduates of Black colleges when tested against median performances of white college graduates, the alumni of Black colleges became the new Black bourgeoisie . . .

. . . Most of the members of the Black bourgeoisie are the graduates of Black colleges. As teachers in the elementary and secondary schools of the South and of northern segregated systems, these graduates provided not only literacy for their students, but also a vision of the possibility of life-styles other than those provided by contact with white employers . . .

From this Black middle class, created by the Black college, came the core of the leadership that changed the status of Blacks in the United States.[18]

It is, of course, well known that Dr. Martin Luther King and the majority of the leaders of the civil rights movement attended Black colleges as undergraduates as did many of the current political leaders in the South. St. Clair Drake believes that these institutions will continue to

---

16. *From Isolation to Mainstream, op. cit.,* pp. 14-15.
17. Mack H. Jones, "The Responsibility of the Black College to the Black Community: Then and Now," *Daedalus,* 100(3) (Summer, 1971), pp. 745-771.
18. *Ibid.,* p. 723.

provide a type of "socially conscious, well-informed political leader" as Blacks take advantage of recently acquired political opportunities in the rural and urban South.[19]

DIVERSITY AMONG BLACK COLLEGES

The historically Black colleges that are still in operation present a broad range of educational opportunities. The colleges differ considerably in size of enrollment, ranging from about 9000 to less than 100 students. Some offer a wide range of graduate programs; others offer graduate study only in the field of education; and some offer no graduate programs at all. There is one school of veterinary medicine, two medical schools, several schools of nursing, and a few schools of pharmacy and law but, for the most part, the historically Black colleges and universities are primarily undergraduate institutions. Most of the private institutions are church related, although many of the original "mission" schools are now independent and include some of the best endowed and most academically productive of the Black colleges.

Within the Black college world, there has been a fairly well established academic status hierarchy. Among the most prestigious and most selective institutions were the early mission schools designed to educate what W.E.B. DuBois called the "Talented Tenth of Black Youth." From their earliest days, these institutions catered to the "better classes" within the Black population, which usually meant the children of Free Negroes or the more advantaged of the slave community, the house slaves. This tradition, which tended to favor mulattoes and other light-skinned youngsters, continued as successive generations sent their children to their alma maters and passed on similar values. It has only been since World War II that skin color ceased to figure in admissions policies at some of the more selective institutions. As Bond has shown, however, it was the graduates of these institutions who were most likely to become scholars and professionals.[20] Their relatively favored socioeconomic status made it possible for them to attend the best elementary and secondary schools and colleges available to Blacks.

Some private institutions and nearly all of the public institutions developed less elitist programs and attracted larger proportions of students from less advantaged circumstances than the early mission schools. Most of these institutions followed the Hampton-Tuskegee

---

19. St. Clair Drake, "The Black University in the American Social Order," *Daedalus,* *100*(3) (Summer, 1971), p. 877.
20. "The Negro Scholar and Professional in America," *op. cit.*

approach to education in their early years by focusing on agricultural, mechanical, and normal (teacher training) curricula rather than the traditional liberal arts programs of the major private institutions. While all of these institutions had added liberal arts curricula by the 1950s, and all had become full-fledged collegiate institutions by this time, many continued to reflect their vocational-technical-teacher training origins. Even today, as we will show, some institutions attract students who are primarily interested in preparing for an immediate career in a traditional occupation and send relatively few students on to graduate or professional schools.

SOCIAL CHARACTERISTICS OF STUDENTS AT BLACK COLLEGES

Black colleges have traditionally enrolled more women than men, and while this pattern seems to be changing, as recently as 1971 the entering freshman class still contained almost 55 percent females. Among Black students attending white colleges, the discrepancy between the sexes was smaller—51.4 percent females; 48.6 percent males.[21] This imbalance does not hold at the postbaccalaureate level, however. Males predominate among Blacks holding academic doctorates and among physicians, dentists, and lawyers in spite of the high rate of college attendance among Black females. When compared to a national sample of non-Black college students, Black college students as a group tend to be more upwardly mobile. This is because less than one-fourth of the parents of all Black entering freshmen in 1968 had attended college.[22] Almost 60 percent of Black students in Black colleges and about 45 percent of Black students in white colleges had fathers who had not graduated from high school. One-half of the mothers of Black students in Black colleges and 38 percent of mothers of Black students in white colleges had not graduated from high school. Thus, the average Black college student tends to be in the process of increasing social status to the middle class. Occupationally, the parents of Black college students tend to be semiskilled or unskilled workers. Less than one-third of the fathers of students at Black colleges were white collar workers in 1968.

According to a recent survey in 1968 Black students attending Black colleges were more likely to come from low income families than were Black students at white colleges. In 1971 these two groups of Black students differed very little with respect to family income.[23]

21. Bayer, op cit., p. 418.
22. A. E. Bayer and R. F. Boruch, "The Black Student in American Colleges," ACE Research Reports, 4(2) (1969).
23. Bayer, op cit., p. 419.

The differences in the results of the two surveys may be attributable to differences in the samples of colleges surveyed, or they may reflect a change in recruiting patterns of white colleges and an increased tendency for Black students from higher income families to select Black institutions. A significant difference in the circumstances of Black students at Black colleges and those at white colleges was found in patterns of financial support for education. Only one-third of the Black students in Black colleges but one-half of those in white colleges held scholarships or grants that covered most of their college expenses. Thus, it appears that the distribution of financial aid is inequitable and favors the more affluent white institutions.[24]

Considering the financial sacrifices involved, it is not surprising that the majority of Black students attend colleges close to home. We estimate that 90 percent of students attending Black colleges in the South are southerners, the majority residing in the same state as the college attended. Private institutions tend to draw students from a broader geographic area than public institutions and to have smaller proportions of low income students. Given the local nature of the student populations of most institutions, it is unlikely that the number of applications to these colleges will drop sharply within this decade. The available evidence indicates that enrollments are increasing at Black schools as well as at predominantly white schools, although they are increasing more rapidly at the latter. The availability of financial assistance may well determine the extent to which Black colleges and universities will be able to continue as viable institutions. Since Black students tend to be predominantly the offspring of low-income families, they will choose schools that require the least financial sacrifice. If resources continue to be distributed inequitably, it will strike a harsh blow at the Black institutions.

The publicly supported Black colleges are now faced with desegregation as an additional problem (although some of their administrators do not consider it a problem). Several of the border state colleges that were totally Black in 1954 are now more than 50 percent white. It is likely that state governing bodies, under pressure from federal agencies, will increasingly force these schools to become biracial or to merge with nearby predominantly white institutions. The practice of establishing new predominantly white institutions or branches of major state universities in a city that already contains a well-established Black facility has caused much concern in the Black community.

There is a danger that traditionally Black colleges that have served for generations as a repository for Black culture and heritage may be

24. *Ibid.*, p. 424.

integrated out of existence. These schools have long provided training for the leaders of the Black community, and they are valued by the communities they serve and by their alumni. They have proud traditions and continue to provide invaluable educational and social services to their students and the communities in which they are located. They also provide concrete examples of Black achievement in areas where opportunities have been severely limited. The effort to eliminate these institutions is another example of the insensitivity of policymakers which is fostered by the racism that permeates American society. Political pressure from Blacks has caused some states to reconsider their proposals for Black institutions, but there is still considerable uncertainty concerning the future of Black public colleges and universities.

The junior college is not an adequate replacement to Blacks for the four-year colleges. First, students who attend junior colleges are less likely to graduate from college than students who attend four-year colleges. Available information indicates that two-year colleges "have been successful in getting low-income youth into college, but have not increased their chances of getting a degree nearly as much."[25] Second, the four-year residential college provides a more complete socialization experience than the commuter two-year college. An important part of the college experience is the gradual identification of oneself as a "professional-in-training." This kind of transformation can occur most smoothly in a four-year institution where the student does not have to undergo the difficulties of transfering from a two-year program to a four-year one.

To summarize the discussion in this chapter, Black colleges and universities despite limited resources have performed a necessary service to the Black community and to the country. Without them, the educational and occupational gaps between Blacks and whites in this country would be much greater than they are now. In addition to their educational function, these institutions have served as "cultural islands" in often hostile communities, providing opportunities for self-expression, leadership development, and the development of race pride. Moreover, these institutions provided the major source of activist students and much of the adult leadership of the civil rights movement.

Vivian Henderson, president of Clark College in Atlanta, Georgia,

---

25. John K. Folger, Helen S. Astin, and Alan E. Bayer, Editors, *Human Resources and Higher Education: Staff Report of the Commission on Human Resources and Advanced Education* (New York: Russell Sage Foundation, 1970).

has expressed doubts whether some Black institutions will survive. Many are poor, some are located in isolated rural areas, and all are having difficulty attracting top quality Black faculty members because of stiff competition from white institutions. As a result it is extremely difficult for some institutions to maintain their student enrollments and faculty quality at levels that will allow them to continue as viable institutions. Henderson believes, however, that Black colleges must be preserved to provide higher education for many Blacks. "In the South," he says, "I'm not convinced that what we call white higher education is going to take Blacks in any significant numbers. Set aside the junior college enrollment of Blacks, and the rest is not very significant. So in the South it's still very important to provide alternatives, and Black colleges do that."[26]

It seems clear to us that these colleges do indeed play a unique role in American higher education. They provide educational opportunities for a segment of the Black population that would otherwise continue to be neglected. They serve as symbols of Black achievement and protectors of a proud heritage. They also provide opportunities for young people to develop leadership ability and political sophistication as they prepare themselves for careers. These functions cannot be duplicated in predominantly white institutions whose traditions have been and continue to be altogether different from those of the traditionally Black colleges and universities.

26. Quoted in *The Chronicle of Higher Education*, May 30, 1972.

part 1

Individual Achievement: Aspirations, Performance, and Achievement Motivation

This part of the book takes up the conventional meaning of achievement as an individual phenomenon. It focuses on *achievement behavior and resultant achievement motivation*. What do we mean by these terms? We have used as measures of achievement behavior how the students performed in college, whether they stayed in college, and how they performed on tasks typically used in achievement motivation research. Resultant achievement motivation is gauged according to what levels of aspiration their occupational and educational goals represented. These indicators provide the dependent variables in our motivational framework. Why some students achieved better grades than others and why some expressed higher, as well as more challenging, aspirations are the major questions to be explained. First, we describe the students' aspirations and performance (Chapter 3); then, we analyze why students differed motivationally (Chapters 4 to 6).

Why do we call performance and aspirations resultant states? What are they the result of? Our motivational framework looks at three components of achievement motivation as the explanatory variables. The students' aspirations and academic performance reflected, conceptually at least: (1) their needs for achievement and anxieties about failure—their *achievement motives*, (2) the value they placed on hard work and success—their *achievement values*, and (3) their estimates of the probability that their efforts would lead to their goals—their *expectancies of success*.

This perspective on achievement means that students who reflected only minimal achievement motivation in the goals they expressed or in what they seemed to desire or in their classroom behavior may have done so from a variety of motivational reasons. Some could have been directed by the motive to avoid failure that theoretically pushes people away from realistic challenge or causes them to withdraw from achievement settings if at all possible. Some may not have valued high grades or the success and challenge that often go with high status and demanding occupations. Others may have expressed equally low motivation, desire, or performance not because they lacked appropriate motives and values but because they doubted that they could be successful. They may have held lower levels of aspiration than other students because their expectancies of success were lower. This conception of motivation stresses how little we know if all we know is that some students appear more motivated or seem to desire more challenge or strive for higher levels of aspiration. To simply show, for example, that women and men differed in the level of aspiration their occupational goals represented does not tell us why they differed. We need to know what it was about their motivational characteristics— their motives, values, and expectancies—that explained sex differences in aspirations.

We emphasize this distinction between resultant motivation and the components of achievement motivation because goals and performance cannot be used simplistically to infer the need for achievement or the values students place on achievement. We learned in talking about the results of the study that many people in higher education equate motives with motivation; they assume that students lack the appropriate motives or values if they seem listless in class, perform poorly on exams, drop out of college, or aspire to jobs that provide very little challenge. Sometimes poor performance or apparent lack of desire does result from anti-achievement values or insufficient motives for achievement; many times it results from depressed expectancies. Educators will find it hard to "motivate" students if they do not make these conceptual distinctions.

We also press the distinctions among motives, values, and expectancies as the personal characteristics that comprise achievement motivation because the concept of expectancy ties the student's motivations so closely to the immediate situation and the world of reality. Many people assume that motivation resides in the individual, as the personal strengths and failings the individual brings to the situation. Thus we were told during the course of our study, "Of course academic achievement is a matter of motivation. Students differ when they come to college; some just aren't as motivated as others." Or there was the view of a. frustrated educator who had tried to develop new programs and found, "The students don't respond—there is not much we can do about the question of motivation: they either want academic challenge or they don't." Or there were social activists, wary lest a study of motivation would conclude by blaming individuals rather than environmental and institutional forces, who attacked the study as a product of typical psychological reductionism: "The trouble with psychologists is that they always assume the problem lies with the people. They never see the social aspects of the problem. It's not a matter of motivation. It's a problem of opportunities and social restrictions. We ought to work on that, not motivation." Some aspects of achievement motivation do imply a stable personality characteristic that predisposes a person to act in a predetermined way. The expectancy concept, however, connotes a much closer tie to current opportunities and objective probabilities of success. People's expectancies necessarily involve their relationships to the social world since probability estimates depend on their judgments both of themselves and the realities of their situations. Thus, concern with motivational problems does not have to imply denial of reality issues; on the contrary, the reality constraints and payoffs that individuals face are an integral aspect of their motivational dynamics. The expectancy concept links the person and the situation.

The very tie of expectancies to objective opportunities also means that expectancies can be altered by changing the situation, especially its possibilities for success and failure, and thereby increase student motivation by providing greater opportunities and payoffs for achievement. We as educators can influence student motivation more easily through expectancy factors than through some other aspects of motivation because expectancies are so sensitive to the social situation. We need not be so discouraged about apparent lack of motivation if we view student performance, persistence, and aspirations as critically influenced by expectancies that in turn are sensitive to immediate social influences. Higher education can have a motivational impact on students by offering them situations through which they can explore where and how they can be successful and simultaneously express their motives and values. We further believe that this expectancy orientation toward motivation carries special import for colleges that serve students whose previous experiences may have realistically depressed expectancies and confidence about payoffs in society.

The four chapters in Part 1 are structured according to this general model of individual achievement. Chapter 3 describes the variation in students on the dependent variables—their individual achievement goals and the level of aspiration or resultant motivation they represent

Generally, this student population aspired to educational and occupational goals that indicated unusually high achievement motivation. We also show, however, that this was more true of the men than of the women students. Chapter 4 presents motivational analyses of why students' levels of aspiration varied and why some received lower grades and others dropped out despite having entered college with high school performance histories and freshman test results similar to many students who succeeded in college. These motivational analyses follow the framework of this part of the book in distinguishing the respective functions of achievement motives, values, and expectancies of success. Generally, the results show the heightened significance of academic and generalized success expectancies, although motives and values best explained aspirations and performance in one college where the environment made the need for achievement and anxiety about failure especially pertinent. Chapter 4 also presents results that challenge common views about the role of internal control in achievement motivation and behavior. Consonant with our distinction between expectancies and values, we also show that measures of internal control that genuinely reflected a personal expectancy of control operated, as usually expected, to facilitate individual achievement. By contrast, measures of internal control that represented adherence to cultural work-ethic values, an internal ideology about control, generally proved irrelevant for individual achievement and even depressed the aspirations and performance of students whose personal expectancies were unusually low.

Chapters 5 and 6 discuss two sets of influences on the dependent variables (aspirations and performance) and on these three components of motivation (motives, values, and expectancies). Chapter 5 takes up the influences of precollege demographic and family variables. Generally, the results contradict the common expectation that home factors heavily influence student performance and motivation. In most respects the students who entered college from poverty backgrounds were motivationally indistinguishable from those who came from more affluent and privileged backgrounds. It was only their aspirations, not their performance, and only their expectancies of success, not their values or achievement motives, that reflected any impact of the precollege environment, and then only at the time of entering college. By senior year even these precollege influences had almost totally disappeared. Moreover, those aspects of the students' home and environment that most influenced aspirations and expectancies—their family incomes and rural-urban background—argue for a view of social impact that stresses environmental resources and opportunities more than social-class related family socialization patterns. Chapter 6 presents similar analyses but treats the college environment, rather than the precollege environment, as the possible source of influence on aspirations and performance, as well as on the three components of achievement motivation. We will show that individual achievement varied greatly by institution, largely but not totally because freshmen entering some colleges already reflected higher levels of achievement motivation than those entering some other colleges. Although the total number of colleges included in the study limited the variety of analyses of institutional effect, Chapter 6 does show that students' future aspirations were positively affected in colleges where many students reported contact with faculty outside of the classroom, where academic values were especially pronounced, and where extracurricular opportunities were diverse, particularly activities outside the traditional collegiate-social ones. Furthermore, the college environment conditioned the dynamics by which aspiration was enhanced: case examples of three types of institutional impact attest to the complexity of environmental-motivational interaction.

chapter 3

Aspirations

COMMITMENT TO THE PROFESSIONS

Black college students have always sought careers in the professions; responding realistically to closed doors in business and industry, they have recognized that the professions represented their major avenue of escape from laboring and service jobs.[1] They have particularly sought the teaching and social service professions, in which they could simultaneously serve the needs of the Black community and be guaranteed a large clientele within a segregated society. This professional orientation has continued. Eighty to 90 percent of the students both in 1964 and in 1970 said they wanted to enter a profession. Men most often chose public school teaching, medicine, law, and engineering; women most often chose teaching, social work, and nursing.

Black students' preferences for certain professions make them stand out even from other college students. Using the six professions that were most popular in our 1964 sample and comparing the data on the career goals of our students with other 1964 data on students in the nation at large, we found that the Black students consistently showed an edge: public school teaching—31.3 percent Black, 24.9 percent national; social work— 7.9 percent Black, 2.4 percent national; physician—5.7 percent Black, 2.6 percent national; engineer— 4.3 percent Black, 4.7 percent national; lawyer—4.1 percent Black, 3.8 percent national; nurse—3.5 percent Black, 1.7 percent national.[2]

1. K. W. Back and I. H. Simpson, "The Dilemma of the Negro Professional," *Journal of Social Issues XX* (1964), pp. 60-70. J. A. Davis, *Great Aspirations* (Chicago: Aldine, 1964). Frank Bowles and Frank A. DeCosta, *Between Two Worlds* (Berkeley: The Carnegie Foundation for the Advancement of Teaching, 1971). Joseph H. Fichter, *Neglected Talents: Background and Prospects of Negro College Graduates* (Chicago: National Opinion Research Center, 1966) Report No. 112.
2. National figures: Alexander W. Astin and Robert J. Panos, *The Educational and Vocational Development of College Students* (Washington: American Council on Education, 1969), p. 87. Hereafter cited as *Development of College Students*

When twice as many Black male seniors (35 percent) as men in the class of 1965 (16 percent) in the nation at large hoped to enter professional schools for postbaccalaureate training, their heightened commitment to the professions was obvious.[3]

The reasons students in our survey gave for coming to college similarly reflected their strong commitment to vocational and professional development. We asked them to rate 10 possible goals to be reached in college. Those with the clearest vocational meaning—"the opportunity to get training for a better job than I could get otherwise" and "the chance to think through what occupation and career I want and to develop some of the necessary skills for it"—received top priority in both 1964 and 1970. The two goals ranked next also showed a concern for professional development and for defining the sense of identity associated with the future work role: "the chance to develop a deep, perhaps professional grasp of a specific field of study" and "finding myself—developing what kind of person I really want to be."

These preferences in jobs and goals continued to be stated with remarkable steadfastness over the six-year research period. By 1970, however, they had changed in important ways: students then listed a wider variety of jobs; many fewer men mentioned teaching; and freshman men were especially beginning to choose business careers more frequently. These shifts showed up even when we used the gross classifications of the census code. When we coded students' future job aspirations to yield many more distinctions in the professional category, we found even stronger evidence of increased diversity (Appendix Table 3.1). It took 32 more job titles to code job choices in 1970 than in 1964.[4]

Furthermore, jobs mentioned in 1970 indicated an increased concern for social relevance and a stronger commitment to work in the Black community. Twice as many students aspired for what the census calls "public advisor" jobs (e.g., religious, social, and welfare workers; recreation and group workers; personnel and labor relations workers; clergymen; home management advisors; community organization consultants). Twice as many male freshmen planned to major in social science, and there was a corresponding drop in science and math majors. More men students planned to enter graduate programs in social science and business and to attend law school while fewer looked toward medical school in 1970 (Appendix Table 3.2).

---

3. *Ibid.,* p. 33.
4. Since the coding staff included two people who worked on the data in both 1964 and in 1970, this reflects genuine differences in students' choices and not an artifact of the coding process.

TABLE 1.   Census Classification of the Job Aspirations of Men and Women, 1964 and 1970

	1964[a]		1970[b]	
	Men	Women	Men	Women
Physicians	8%	2%	4%	1%
Other medical and paramedical	4	11	4	9
Accountants, auditors	3	1	6	3
Teachers: primary and secondary	22	43	13	41
Teachers: college; social scientists librarians; college administrators	7	8	2	2
Architects, chemists, engineers, physical and biological scientists	12	1	11	4
Skilled technicians	7	6	7	3
Public advisors (clergymen, social workers, personnel and labor relations, etc.)	6	13	18	25
Lawyers and judges	6	*	14	*
Other professional	14	9	5	3
Self-employed businessmen	1	*	1	*
Nonself-employed managers	5	*	9	2
Clerical and kindred workers	*	6	2	6
Sales workers	*	—	1	*
Craftsmen, foremen, kindred workers	2	—	1	—
Farmers	1	—	—	—
Other	2	*	2	1
	100%	100%	100%	100%

*Less than one-half of one percent.

[a]These percents are based on the 1964 data from 535 seniors, 285 men and 250 women, attending the six colleges that participated in the cross-sectional studies in both 1964 and 1970.

[b]These percents are based on 536 seniors, 280 men and 256 women, who participated in the 1970 cross-sectional study of six Black colleges.

The shifts toward law, social science, and business, especially among the men, indirectly support the point that more students wanted to serve the Black community. Direct evidence came from how they described their future jobs: "community organization in the Black community," or "working with Black youth as a counselor or psychologist where I can influence their goals as Blacks," or "social work in agencies serving the Black community," instead of simply "social work." The aspirants to law described "jobs in legal aid clinics," "criminal law that will help bring justice to the Black community" and "civil rights work." The business students talked about "developing Black businesses" or "wanting business training to help develop the ghetto." Most of the students in this group of social science, law, public advisor, and business aspirants also said they expected to work in an "all Black" or "mostly Black" setting, whereas a majority of the other students assumed they would work in an integrated situation. Since they did not evaluate race obstacles and opportunities differently from other students, their much higher expectancy of working in the Black community indicated a preference and complemented how they talked about service and responsibility in describing their future jobs.

LEVEL OF ASPIRATION

Educational Aspirations

Such commitment to the professions attests to a high level of aspiration and motivation. The students' goals and their persistence in trying to reach them despite grave financial obstacles spoke even more clearly of strong motivation. Students in Black colleges are unusually persistent in pursuing their educational goals. Estimating dropout rates from social class background and college test scores, Astin shows that the actual dropout rate in historically Black colleges is below the predicted rate while the actual dropout rate of white students in white colleges is slightly above that predicted.[5] Data compiled by the Carnegie Commission on Higher Education also demonstrate that for three decades now the historically Black colleges have awarded more undergraduate degrees than their proportion of total enrollments would have suggested.[6] It is no small feat for students in Black colleges to place above the national average of students completing bachelor's degrees despite their smaller personal financial resources and a much smaller resource base in the schools they attend.

Like college students in the nation at large, the majority of students in our samples said they hoped to go on to graduate or professional schools. A national sample showed that three-fourths of graduating

5. Alexander W. Astin, "Racial Considerations in Admissions," in David C. Nichols and Olive Mills, Editors, *The Campus and the Racial Crisis* (Washington: American Council on Education, 1970), Table 11, p. 130.
6. During the 1940s historically Black colleges awarded 3.1 percent of all first degrees while they enrolled only 2.7 percent of the nation's students; during the 1950s the comparable figures were 3.2 percent of all degrees and 2.5 percent of all students; during the early sixties the Black college edge was reduced but Black colleges were still awarding more first degrees (3.0 percent in 1961-1962 and 2.8 percent in 1963-1964) than their proportion of total enrollments would have suggested (2.9 percent in 1961-1962 and 2.7 percent in 1963-1964). Frank Bowles and Frank A. DeCosta, *Between Two Worlds* (Berkeley: The Carnegie Foundation for the Advancement of Teaching, 1971), p. 199. Hereafter cited as *Between Two Worlds*.

seniors in 1964 expressed an interest in pursuing postgraduate training.[7] Another survey of students in the class of 1965, a national sample of 246 accredited four-year institutions, found that 70 percent hoped to take a postbaccalaureate degree.[8] Eighty-five percent of the students attending the colleges we studied in 1964, and 90 percent in 1970 wanted to continue their education in graduate or professional school.

However strong their desire for higher education, only between 8 and 20 percent were certain they would be able to continue beyond the baccalaureate. For the rest, the path was obstructed by overpowering financial obstacles. Only 17 percent of the students reported their families' incomes as being $10,000 or more per year, and close to a third reported incomes below $3600 (a figure only slightly above the national criterion of poverty in 1964); their families' incomes mirrored almost exactly the range given by the students in a much larger sample of Black colleges in an American Council of Education report.[9] In fact, the proportion of Black students whose family income was below the poverty line—both in this study and in Black colleges generally—was five times larger than the percentage of white students in white colleges who came from poverty conditions.[10] The data on family income collected from students in 1970 demonstrated only a slight improvement because of a 7 percent shift out of the $4000–$5999 income grouping into the next grouping $6000–$9999. The

7. J. A. Davis, *Great Aspirations* (Chicago: Aldine, 1964).
8. Astin and Panos, *Development of College Students*, p. 32.
9. Alan E. Bayer and Robert F. Boruch, *The Black Student in American Colleges* (Washington: Office of Research, American Council on Education, 1969), Table 4, pp. 377-388.
10. Data from our 1964 and 1970 samples of men can be compared with data provided by Bayer and Boruch from an American Council of Education study conducted in 1967. These data show the following income distributions for male students (and since neither the ACE nor we found significant sex differences, these distributions validly reflect overall differences between Black students in Black colleges from white students in white colleges):

| | | Black Students in Black Colleges | | |
Estimated Family Income	White Students in White College[a]	ACE 1967 Data[a]	Our 1964 Data	Our 1970 Data
Less than $4000	4.2%	37.2%	31.5%	33.9%
$4000–5,999	8.9	25.1	26.4	15.4
$6000–9999	33.5	23.4	24.9	34.0
$10,000 +	53.4	14.3	17.0	16.7
	100%	100%	100%	100%

[a]Table 4, Alan E. Bayer and Robert F. Boruch, "Black and White Freshman Entering Four-Year College," *Educational Record* 50 (1969), p. 378.

percentage who reported incomes of less than $3600 remained nearly the same. Furthermore, 31 percent of the students in our sample said they were helping to support the education of younger brothers and sisters (Table 2).

TABLE 2.   **Aspiration for and Expectancy of Being Able to Pursue Postbacclaureate Education among Seniors in 1964 and 1970**

	1964 Seniors[a]		1970 Seniors[b]	
	Men	Women	Men	Women
Aspiration for graduate or professional school				
Intend to go sometime	89	81	92	88
Do not want to go	11	19	8	12
	100%	100%	100%	100%
Expectancy or level of certainty of going among seniors who wanted to continue				
Completely certain	13	8	20	11
Pretty certain	47	53	47	56
Some possibility will not go	30	25	24	24
Pretty strong possibility will not go	10	14	9	9
	100%	100%	100%	100%

[a]These percents are based on the 1964 data from 535 seniors, 285 men and 250 women, attending the six colleges that participated in the cross-sectional studies in both 1964 and 1970.

[b]These percents are based on 536 seniors, 280 men and 256 women, who participated in the 1970 cross-sectional study of six Black colleges.

How do students in Black colleges manage to graduate in the numbers they do? They do it by working, as 70 percent of our sample did, and by obtaining loans, which 53 percent stated were critical to financing their education. A study of graduating seniors in 1964 found that 62 percent of the graduates of Black colleges, as compared to 36 percent of a national sample of white students, owed money for college expenses at the time they graduated.[11] As previous studies[12]

11. Joseph H. Fichter, *Neglected Talents: Background and Prospects of Negro College Graduates* (Chicago: National Opinion Research Center, 1966), Report No. 112. Hereafter cited as *Neglected Talents.*
12. J. A. Davis, *Great Aspirations* (Chicago, Aldine, 1964). G. L. Gropper and R. Fitzpatrick, *Who Goes to Graduate School?* (Pittsburgh: American Institute for Research, 1959). James D. Stanfiel, "Education and Income of Parents at Predominantly Black Colleges," *Journal of Negro Education XLI*, No. 2 (Spring, 1972), 170-176. Joseph H. Fichter, *Neglected Talents: Background and Prospects of Negro Graduates* (Chicago: National Opinion Research Center, 1966) Report No. 112.

have detailed, many potential candidates are deterred from entering graduate school because previous indebtedness must be added to the cost of several additional years of schooling. Close to half of the graduating seniors in Black colleges, but only 17 percent of a national sample of white students, cited finances as a major reason for not attending graduate school. Or conversely, only 20 percent of the Black, but 52 percent of the white seniors felt that financial issues had nothing to do with their decision about postgraduate training.[13]

Figures derived from our data confirm these estimates: even in 1970, when family income had improved slightly, 63 percent of the seniors talked about financial obstacles, and close to half of them believed they could not garner the resources for graduate school. Moreover, a third of the seniors we interviewed in 1968 felt that the usual graduate fellowship offering $2000 to $2500 for living expenses would not meet their obligations even if they could defer repaying their undergraduate loans until they had finished graduate school.

These financial constraints meant that very many Blacks could not realize their hopes of enrolling in graduate or professional school and that the current disparities between Black and white students would be little changed. A Ford Foundation report states the problem and prospects:

> *According to the recent survey of the Ph.D. degrees awarded from 1964 through 1968, to which 63 American graduate schools of arts and sciences responded, only 294, or 0.8 percent of the 37,456 degrees awarded were received by Black Americans. If this is representative of the number of Ph.D.'s granted by higher education throughout the country, the annual number of new Black Ph.D's would have to be multiplied by 15 in order to reach 11.5 percent, the estimated ratio of Black Americans in the general population.[14]*

The most optimistic estimate this Ford Foundation report could make, barring a substantial increase in financial support for Black doctoral studies, was an increase in Blacks' graduate enrollments that would bring the proportion of Black Ph.D.'s to between 1 and 2 percent of all American Ph.D.'s.[15] We have no reason to expect a substantial growth in support for Black doctoral studies. In fact, it is increasingly popular to argue that students should hypothecate some of their future earnings to pay for the training that makes these higher earnings possible. If such arguments reverse federal policy and make

---

13. Fichter, *Neglected Talents,* pp. 85-86.
14. James W. Bryant, *A Survey of Black American Doctorates* (New York: The Ford Foundation, n.d.), p. 7.
15. *Ibid.,* p. 11.

loans, rather than fellowships, the major source of federal support for graduate training, Black students will face still another inequality just when graduate schools are beginning to mount programs to increase minority enrollment. With lower family incomes and greater indebtedness Black students cannot as easily turn to loans as an investment against future earnings. Black students want advanced training. Facing the hardships they do, Blacks have achieved an extraordinary feat by graduating from college in the numbers they do. But the strength of their motivation for education is not the problem; finding the financial resources is.

Occupational Aspirations

In addition to examining career goals as categorical choices, we can also look at the occupation's prestige in terms of the level of aspiration it represents. A student evinces a high aspiration by choosing a job that is generally considered to be prestigious. In fact, prestige is the meaning traditionally implied when the term "level of aspiration" is applied to career choice. We have extended the term to other meanings as well. For example, jobs that challenge ability and talent surely imply high aspiration although they may not always accord the greatest social status. Jobs that have been virtually closed to Blacks likewise represent another type of high aspiration. To be sure, the professional orientation of the students automatically casts their choices as reasonably prestigious, demanding, and nontraditional for Blacks. Still, even the professions vary somewhat along these dimensions. Take professions normally closed to Blacks. Although the proportion of Blacks in almost every profession falls far below parity with whites, it was previously somewhat easier for Blacks to enter the social service and teaching fields than other professions. In 1960 Blacks made up approximately 10 percent of all social workers and elementary school teachers, 5 percent of all secondary school teachers but less than 1 percent of all engineers, accountants, business executives or managers in large firms, sales representatives, architects, writers, and producers or executives in newspaper, TV, and other communication media. They comprised between 1 and 2 percent of many other occupations. Even in the service professions requiring similar educational attainments there were strong contrasts. Social work employed 10 percent Blacks but psychological counseling employed only 1.4 percent. Moreover, although woefully few Blacks were engaged in the highest prestige professions, the fact that 2 percent of all doctors and 2.5 percent of all dentists but only 1 percent of all lawyers and psychiatrists were Black reaffirms this meaningful difference in nontraditionality. Aside from the prestigious helping professions, the fact that 1.2 percent of all reasearch scientists in the medical sciences were Black makes research a more unusual choice than medicine, although the training for each field requires the same bent for science. The point is clear: many professional roles have been virtually closed to Black college graduates.

In order to examine these different bases of aspiration, we asked an additional random sample of students from the participating colleges to judge the more than 150 occupations that were taken from the choices students had named in the original sample. The students were instructed to judge each occupation as to:

Prestige. By rating from excellent to poor the job's general standing in society.[16]

Ability demands. By evaluating what percent of their college class, ranging from only the top 1 percent to almost everyone, would have the requisite ability for the job.[17]

Social difficulty. By judging the relative chances a Black and a white applicant, equally trained, would have getting the job in the same city in the same sector of the country.

The average ratings determined from the random sample then became the measure by which the prestige, ability demands, and social difficulty of the jobs named by the original sample could be scored. Whether student ratings properly judged these qualities, they certainly indicated what their fellow students believed to be true about different jobs; and these beliefs probably represented the context within which students made their choices. We did not depend on student evaluations, however, to measure whether the job fell within a sector of the labor market previously closed to Blacks, but, instead, used census data showing the proportion of Blacks that were in the occupation by 1960 to score each student's choice for *nontraditionality*.

A fourth of the students aspired to jobs that their peers felt had "excellent standing." Even the lowest aspirations were not very low; only 10 percent of the students listed jobs rated as "fair," and none of their choices fell in the "poor" category. A third also mentioned jobs that fell in the top two levels of ability and social difficulty. Their peers

16. The instructions used to measure occupational prestige are from the classic study of occupations, conducted by the National Opinion Research Center, Albert J. Reiss, *Occupations and Social Status* (Glencoe, Illinois; The Free Press, 1961).
17. The instructions used to measure ability demands come from a study by Mahone of achievement motivation determinants of realistic goal setting. See Charles H. Mahone, "Fear of Failure and Unrealistic Vocational Aspirations," *Journal of Abnormal and Social Psychology*, LX (1960), pp. 253-261.

felt that only the top 10 percent of their classmates had the ability for these jobs and that the jobs would be three times as hard for a Black to get as for a white. However, the students' choices showed a wide range in ability demands and social difficulty. Nearly one-fourth chose jobs their peers felt at least three-fourths of the students in their classes would be qualified to fill and would be able to obtain as easily as a white applicant. The nontraditionality of their choices is highlighted by the fact that no student planned to enter a field in which more than 13 percent of the jobholders were Black by 1960 and that a quarter of the students aspired for jobs where the Black average was only 2 percent or less. The gross underrepresentation of Blacks in professional jobs dictated that the goals held by Black graduates would be nontraditional.

Did the average level of aspiration reflected by the students' job choices increase between 1964 and 1970, a period sometimes viewed as one of optimism before the fall? It did not (Table 5). The level of student aspirations remained remarkably stable throughout this period; students mentioned jobs of almost exactly the same levels of prestige, ability demands, social difficulty, and nontraditionality. It was a high aspirant population in 1964; it still was in 1970.

ASPIRATIONS: MEN AND WOMEN

Contrary to stereotyped notions about the dominance of Black women, the picture of high aspiration fit the men students much better than the women. The goals of women students reflected lower levels on almost every measure of aspiration. Although their desire to go to graduate or professional school nearly matched the aspirations of the men, only 5 percent of the women, compared to 35 percent of the men, intended to pursue professional degrees. In contrast, 64 percent of the women, compared to 35 percent of the men, expected to terminate graduate work at the master's degree. Although a fairly equal group of men (19 percent) and women (12 percent) expressed doctoral aspirations, women felt much less certain of pursuing the doctorate immediately after college. The feelings of a senior woman who did intend to enter graduate school the following fall characterized the doubts held even by this unconventional group of women who were aiming for a doctor's degree:

> I say I plan to stay in school until I finish the doctorate. But there are a lot of ifs about that. So much depends on whether I meet the right guy and what he thinks about it. I can conceive of it all work-

ing out with a certain kind of man. But I also know I'd give it up if that were really important to a guy I loved. And it is not just marriage either. My younger brother needs help. I'm very sure I'd start with a master's degree if the school allowed that. But most schools I have applied to give only the Ph.D. or nothing. That really makes me nervous, like I'm embarking on something that got bigger than I expected.

Men also expressed doubts, of course, but theirs rested almost exclusively on financial problems. They rarely tied their doubts to anticipated attitudes of a hypothetical mate or to the graduate school rules that required them to go for the doctorate rather than for a less time-consuming graduate program.

These data suggest that Black women, compared to Black men, will go on showing lower rates of graduate school enrollment. It is not well known that 80 percent of the doctorates held by Blacks had been earned by men.[18] Even in the social sciences, women accounted for only about one-fourth of the Black Ph.D.'s[19] These data clearly indicate that although Black women slightly outnumber men at lower educational levels, men predominate in the higher degree programs. These findings corroborate our data on aspirations—Black men have higher educational aspirations than Black women. Although it may be that the disparity will decrease as women respond to broader opportunities, data collected on social science graduate students in 1970 showed that Black men still far outnumbered Black women. Sixty-three percent of the Black social science graduate students were men.[20]

The size of these sex differences in graduate school aspirations and enrollments matched the difference for men and women in the nation at large. A study of 246 accredited four-year colleges found that three times as many men as women in their senior year planned to pursue doctorate or professional degrees.[21] Figures collected from our sample at the same time that these national statistics were gathered also showed three times as many men as women expressing aspirations for higher degrees. In contrast, women in the college population at large and in the Black colleges we studied were one and a half to two times as likely as men to look to master's degrees as terminal educational

18. Bryant, *Black American Doctorates*, Table, p. 4. Also, Kent G. Mommsen, "Professionalism and the Racial Context of Career Patterns Among Black American Doctorates: A Note on the 'Brain Drain' Hypothesis," (Unpublished article, 1972).
19. Edgar G. Epps and Glenn R. Howze, *Survey of Black Social Scientists* (Tuskegee: Tuskegee Institute, 1971), Table 2, p. 16.
20. *Ibid.*, Table 22, p. 117.
21. Astin and Panos, *Development of College Students*, p. 33.

TABLE 3. Summary of Sex Differences in Educational Aspirations from Studies of Seniors in Historically Black Colleges, Southern White Colleges, and a National Sample of Colleges, 1964

| | Seniors, Our Sample of 10 Black Colleges[a] | | Seniors, National Sample 246 Four-Year Institutions[b] | | Seniors, NORC Sample of[c]: | | | |
| | | | | | Black Colleges | | Southern White Colleges | |
Portion Who:	Men	Women	Men	Women	Men	Women	Men	Women
Want to go to graduate or professional school sometime	89%	81%	74%	67%	No data		No data	
Intend to pursue the—								
Master's degree	35%	64%	38%	55%	No data		No data	
Ph.D. or Ed.D.	19	12	18	8				
Professional degree	35	5	16	2				
Other	—	—	2	2				
Considered going immediately after graduation	No data		No data		73%	54%	74%	57%
Intend to go immediately	No data		No data		41%	24%	46%	22%
Already decided on a specific school	No data		No data		27%	14%	39%	17%

[a]These percents are based on the 897 seniors, 465 men and 432 women, who participated in the 1964 cross-sectional study of 10 Black colleges.

[b]These percents are reported in Table 14, A. W. Astin and R. J. Panos, *The Educational and Vocational Development of College Students,* (Washington: American Council on Education, 1969), p. 33.

[c]These percents, based on a sample of graduating seniors from 52 colleges collected by the National Opinion Research Center, are presented in Table 9:9 in Joseph H. Fichter, *Neglected Talents: Background and Prospects of Negro College Graduates* (Chicago: National Opinion Research Center, 1966), Report No. 112.

goals. Figures on graduate degrees awarded also confirm similar sex disparities among Black and white young people. The sex breakdown of doctorates earned in the United States between 1955 and 1965 showed that only 10 to 11 percent were earned by women.[22] The male edge in the nation at large was nine to one; among Blacks it was eight to two. More men than women aspired to the highest degrees; and there was an even larger gap between the men and women (Black and white) who actually received their degrees (Table 3).

Work preferences even more strikingly reflected conventional sex-role concerns, as is evinced by which jobs men and women judged attractive and by their future job choices. Although men and women held identical opinions on which occupations carried the greatest prestige and demanded the most ability, they differed greatly in judging which jobs would be the most personally desirable. The students who judged occupations were asked: "How satisfied would you be with this kind of work as an adult, say ten years after college?" The five-point rating scale varied from "extremely desirable, I'd be very satisfied with it" to "very undesirable, I'd be very dissatisfied with it." Judging 150 occupations, men and women agreed on only four of the 25 they rated most desirable. Even then, men and women ranked these four (doctor, school administrator, IBM computer programmer, and IBM machine operator) differently. Doctor ranked second for men but 18th for women; at the opposite extreme, IBM machine operator tied for second among women but fell to 20th among men.

The list of the 25 occupations most desirable to men and the 25 most desirable to women almost stereotypically connoted masculinity and femininity. Socialization for different work roles for men and women has succeeded well when college men and women differ as greatly in what they find attractive as the following lists indicate. The important point is not just that men and women end up pursuing different occupational lines, but that they find different jobs attractive and personally desirable. If we want women to be free to choose within the full range of jobs and academic majors, colleges must counteract rather than reinforce previous sex-role socialization (Table 4).

The implications of sex-linked attitudes toward a job's attractiveness went beyond the demands the job might make. The men and women students who participated in the occupational evaluation study agreed that the jobs men said were desirable also accorded greater prestige; the average prestige rating of the 25 occupations most attrac-

22. Helen Astin, *The Woman Doctorate* (Hartford, Conn.: The Russell Sage Foundation, 1969), p. 5.

TABLE 4. Ranking by Men and Women of the 25 Jobs Highest in Desirability to Men and the 25 Highest to Women

Top 25 for Men

	Rank Position in Desirability	
	Men	Women
Architect or designer	1	55
Doctor in private practice	2	17.5
Staff surgeon at a large hospital	4.5	42
Industrial research scientist	4.5	83.5
Lawyer in private practice	4.5	31.5
Lawyer in civil rights work	4.5	42
School administrator	9	1
Statistician or chief statistician in a government agency	9	42
Engineer	9	69
Marketing or advertising executive		
IBM computer programmer		

Top 25 for Women

	Rank Position in Desirability	
	Men	Women
School administrator	9	1
IBM machine operator	21.5	2.5
Fashion designer	96	2.5
Interior decorator	59	5.5
Administrator in a social welfare agency	29.5	5.5
Child psychologist or child development expert	88	5.5
Special education teacher	88	5.5
Social worker	44	8.5
IBM computer programmer	9	8.5
Counselor or psychological therapist	29.5	12.5

Occupation			Occupation		
Pharmacist	14.5	31.5	Working with youth groups	50	12.5
Foreign service or diplomatic corps	14.5	55	Professional civil rights work	29.5	12.5
Scientific consultant in the space agency	14.5	83.5	Nursery school teacher	68	12.5
Technician (aeronautical, automotive, or similar kind)	14.5	55	Elementary school teacher	68	12.5
College professor of engineering	14.5	83.5	Legal or medical secretary	124	12.5
College professor of physics, chemistry or other science	14.5	69	Airline stewardess	148	17.5
Veterinarian	21.5	55	Typist	131	17.5
College professor of law	21.5	69	Doctor in private practice	2	17.5
Mathematician	21.5	2.5	Social scientist	29.5	17.5
IBM machine operator	21.5	42	Physical or occupational therapist	38	23
Elected public official	21.5	5.5	Stenographer or secretary	130	23
Office manager of a large concern	21.5	5.5	Key punch operator	59	23
Business administrator or executive	21.5	31.5	Home economist	142	23
Psychiatrist	21.5	31.5	Assistant in a science laboratory	74	23
			Librarian	80.5	23
			Nurse	147	23

tive to men was 3.2 on a five-point scale, as compared to 2.6 for the top 25 for women. The jobs also demanded greater ability; the average ability rating of the top 25 for men was 4.5 on a seven-point scale, compared to 3.2 for women. These data clearly show that feminine jobs provide less status and that they less often challenge personal ability and talent. About this men and women agreed.

Given this pattern of evaluation, men's and women's future job choices ought to show large sex differences in level of aspiration, and so they did. Women's job choices carried significantly lower prestige and ability demands, even though all but 15 percent of the women expected to work after marriage (thus, approximating men's expected participation in the labor force). Their choices also fell within the more traditional areas of achievement for Blacks. The differences in level of aspiration cannot be explained entirely by the fact that nearly twice as many women as men expected to become teachers at the secondary or primary levels. Moreover, the pattern of lower aspirations among women was as marked in 1970 as in 1964 and it was true in every college in the study.

There were also striking sex differences in the correlates of choosing an occupation that is highly attractive to one's own sex group. An

TABLE 5. **Level of Occupational Aspiration of Senior Men and Women, 1964 and 1970**

	1964[a]		1970[b]	
Average level of aspiration	Men	Women	Men	Women
Prestige	2.93	2.70	2.95	2.56
(Range 1–5; 5 = high)	$t =$ 7.79, (.001)		$t =$ 8.21, (.001)	
Desirability	2.42	2.45	2.43	2.39
(Range 1–5; 5 = high)	$t =$ .27, (NS)		$t =$ 2.45, (.01)	
Ability demands	3.62	2.85	3.65	2.92
(Range 1–7; 7 = high)	$t =$ 12.33, (.001)		$t =$ 14.28, (.001)	
Nontraditionality	3.14	5.16	3.17	6.12
(Average % Blacks in occupation)	$t =$ 11.73, (.001)		$t =$ 14.2, (.001)	

[a]These average aspiration scores are based on the 1964 data from 535 seniors, 285 men and 250 women, attending the six colleges that participated in the cross-sectional studies in both 1964 and 1970.

[b]These averages are based on 536 seniors, 280 men and 256 women, who participated in the 1970 cross-sectional study of six Black colleges.

occupation rated by the men as very attractive was likely to be a job that demanded exceptional ability (the correlation between attractiveness and ability was +.64), connoted considerable social difficulty (the correlation between attractiveness and social difficulty was +.58), and fell in nontraditional fields where Blacks generally have been excluded (the correlation between attractiveness and nontraditionality was +.61). An occupation attractive to women was likely to be a job that did not demand great ability (the correlation between attractiveness and ability was −.31), was socially easy rather than difficult (the correlation between attractiveness and social difficulty was −.12), and was more traditional than nontraditional for Blacks (the correlation between attractiveness and nontraditionality was −.16). (See Appendix Table 3.3.) If occupational choices thought desirable by peers of the same sex define the appropriate sex role, the implication is that women expressing high job aspirations—choosing a nontraditional occupation or one demanding a great deal of ability—are making an inappropriate choice. High job aspirations inevitably produce conflicts for women who care about social definitions of femininity. In contrast, men who aspire to a difficult or nontraditional occupation are thought to have made a desirable role choice.

The constraining effects of sex-role consideration also showed in the way men and women made decisions about their future jobs. Women included significantly fewer jobs when asked to check from a long list of jobs all the occupations they had ever seriously considered. Furthermore, the occupations that women considered reflected a narrower range of prestige, ability, and nontraditionality. It is no wonder women ended up choosing lower level jobs since they less often explored job possibilities that would demand or challenge their abilities or would provide them with more status. It is understandable (consistent) that they were surer about their occupational choices and decided on them earlier in life. In summary, women approached the choice process with considerably less openness than did the men.

The whole pattern of sex differences in aspirations closely resembles data from national studies of college students and from studies specifically of white students. We have already noted that the size of the male edge in graduate school aspirations and enrollments was approximately the same for white and Black students. Sex differences in the job aspirations of Black students likewise paralleled those of students in the nation at large. Let us look at five occupations defined as masculine by the preponderance of men in them (businessman, lawyer, doctor, physical scientist, engineer) and two occupations defined as feminine by their preponderance of women (teaching in elementary or secondary schools and social work.)[23] The male edge for the masculine occupations among Black students closely paralleled those of white students (Table 6). The female edge for the feminine occupations was not as great, however, among Black as among white students.[24]

When less than 1 percent of either the Black or white women graduates in that study planned to go into law and engineering, 1 percent into medicine, 3 to 4 percent into the physical sciences, and 5 to 6 percent into business, we must conclude it is rare for women, be they Black or white to aspire for masculine fields. This is further shown by applying the criteria used to define occupational role innovation in a study of white college women to the women attending the Black colleges we studied. Women were classified as Role Innovators if they aspired to occupations in which less than 30 percent were women—in other words, to occupations where women were underrepresented relative to their proportion in the experienced, college-educated, civilian labor force. Women were classified as Moderates if they aspired to occupations with 30 to 50 percent women in them, and as Traditionals if they planned to enter occupations with more than 50 percent women. Using those definitions, we see that 19 percent of the white female seniors at a major four-year university were Role Innovators, another 19 percent were Moderates, and 60 percent were Traditionals.[25] Applying the same criteria to the choices listed by senior women in our sample, Black women were every bit as conventional: 17 percent were Role Innovators, another 14 percent were Moderates, and 68 percent were Traditionals.

Studies of white students show also that women make their occupational decisions earlier than men, enter college with lower aspira-

23. These five occupations can also be defined as the most masculine by the size of the weight that sex carried in predicting their choice among the students studied by Astin and Panos in their sample of 246 four-year institutions. Astin and Panos, *Development of College Students*, Table 49, pp. 99-101. Social work and teaching, plus nursing and secretarial work, represent the most feminine fields in the sense that over 70 percent of American working women are in them. Not only do most women go into these fields, but most of the people in these fields—between 70 and 100 percent—are women. Women are particularly underrepresented in those professions in which prestige and financial rewards are greatest. Sandra Schwartz Tangri, "Determinants of Occupational Role Innovation Among College Women," *Journal of Social Issues* 28(2) (1972), p. 178.

24. These comparisons derive from statistics found in Tables 7:4 and 7:5, p. 170, of Fichter, *Neglected Talents*.

25. Sandra Schwartz Tangri, "Determinants of Occupational Role Innovation Among College Women," *Journal of Social Issues* 28(2) (1972), p. 178.

TABLE 6. Comparison of the Proportion of Men and Women Seniors Attending Our 1964-1965[a] Sample of Black Colleges Who Chose Five "Masculine" and Three "Feminine" Occupations with Statistics Provided by a National Survey of Southern Black, Southern White, and Other Graduating Seniors in 1964[b]

	Seniors, Our Sample[a] of 10 Black Colleges		Southern Black Graduating Seniors		Southern White Graduating Seniors		All Other Graduating Seniors	
	Men	Women	Men	Women	Men	Women	Men	Women
Masculine occupations								
Business	10%	2%	12%	6%	28%	6%	28%	5%
Lawyer	7%	1%	4%	<1%	8%	1%	9%	1%
Doctor	9%	1%	6%	1%	6%	1%	5%	1%
Physical scientist	6%	<1%	9%	3%	9%	4%	8%	2%
Engineer	7%	<1%	8%	<1%	16%	<1%	13%	<1%
Feminine occupations								
Elementary and secondary school teacher	22%	42%	31%	55%	9%	56%	15%	59%
Other education fields	ND	ND	27%	23%	8%	25%	13%	28%
Nurse (our data)	1%	7%	—	—	—	—	—	—
Other health fields (NORC data)	—	—	6%	7%	3%	6%	3%	9%
Social worker	4%	12%	5%	10%	1%	5%	1%	4%

[a]These percentages are based on the 897 seniors, 465 men and 432 women, who participated in the 1964 cross-sectional study of 10 Black colleges. The percentages do not add to 100% because all occupational choices of the seniors are not included here.

[b]These percentages, based on data from a sample of graduating seniors from 52 colleges and universities collected by the National Opinion Research Center, are presented in Tables 7:4 and 7:5 in Fichter, *Neglected Talents*.

tions and, when they shift during college, they change to a lower rather than a higher level of aspiration.[26]

Astin and Panos have concluded that the sex of the student, more than any other personal characteristic, entered into the prediction of the careers and the academic majors among the seniors they studied in a national sample of universities and colleges.[27] In fact, one of the most reliable facts about change among college students is the accentuation of sex differences in orientations about career and marriage, in preferences of academic majors and occupational fields, and in number of years or desired education. Sex differences increase during college because men do not change in a "feminine" direction while women do.[28]

We continually see similar sex disparities among Black and white students. But Blacks and whites of the same sex, even among the college population, do not always share the same life experiences or hold the same attitudes and perspectives. Indeed, the insightful study by Ladner of growing up Black and female[29] and the documentary accounts of Black women since the early 1800s recently presented by Lerner argue convincingly that many of the experiences and perspectives of Black women are unique.[30] Black women may express less conflict about working outside the home and perhaps experience less fear of being successful in roles other than mothering. Reactions of Black women to the women's liberation movement highlight these differences. Committed foremost to Black liberation, many Black women further contend that the goals of women's liberation have either been achieved by or forced upon the Black woman, who hardly feels deprived of being a breadwinner in the family.

26. Jerry Lee Lamesnez Miller, "Occupational Choice: The Construction and Testing of a Paradigm of Occupational Choice for the College Graduate," doctoral dissertation, Florida State University, 1959.
27. Astin and Panos, *Development of College Students*, pp. 103-104.
28. S. S. Angrist, "The Study of Sex Roles," *Journal of Social Issues 25*(1) (1969), pp. 215-232; J. L. Holland, "Exploration of a Theory of Vocational Choice and Achievement. A Four-Year Prediction Study," *Psychological Reports 12* (1963), pp. 547-594; Nichols, R. C. and Astin, A. W., *Progress of the Merit Scholars: An Eight-Year Followup*. NMSC Research Reports 1 (Evanston, IL.: National Merit Scholarship Corporation, 1965); S. S. Tangri, "Role Innovation in Occupational Choice Among College Women," unpublished doctoral dissertation, The University of Michigan, 1969; and W. L. Wallace, *Student Culture: Social Structure and Continuity in a Liberal Arts College* (Chicago: Aldine, 1966).
29. Joyce A. Ladner, *Tomorrow's Tomorrow: The Black Woman* (Garden City, New York: Doubleday, Anchor Books, 1972).
30. Gerda Lerner, *Black Women in White America: A Documentary History* (New York: Pantheon Books, 1972).

Data on the work intentions of the women in our sample actually differed very little, however, from white women attending a major university in the Midwest. When asked, "Do you expect to work after you get married before you have children", 90 percent of the white and 93 percent of the Black women seniors said yes. Working after the arrival of children distinguished them somewhat more. Half of the Black and 42 percent of the white women said they did intend to work after having children; 29 percent of the Black and 28 percent of the white women were uncertain; 21 percent of Black but 30 percent of the white women definitely planned not to work after having children.[31] Of course, their intentions tell little about feelings of conflict, and we did not measure the fear of success that has recently received so much attention in the motivation of women. Nonetheless, the Black and white students were more alike than not in their intentions of working and certainly in the kinds of jobs to which they aspired. We argue on the basis of these data only that sex-role demands, certain socialization practices (especially in the schools), and patterns of sex discrimination in the society at large critically determine role-appropriate educational and occupational choices, be the women Black or white.

In highlighting the conventional work-role aspirations of these Black women, as well as the similarity in their career orientations to those of white women in college, we do not intend to imply that sex-role conventionality is a permanent socialization effect. Most women have been raised to prefer "feminine" jobs when they decide to work at all. They come to college with lower and sex-appropriate job aspirations. They change their aspirations less while in college. When they do shift their work goals, they typically lower their sights by choosing an even more conventional job. Although all of this is typical, it is not unavoidable. Indeed, we will show in Chapter 6 that women who attended colleges with unusual opportunities for faculty-student interaction and an exceptional press in the student culture for academic commitments increased rather than decreased their level of occupational aspirations, specifically their aspirations for unconventional jobs for women. Social experiences that convince women they *can* enter challenging, unconventional careers serve to counteract the more common experiences that reinforce previous socialization practices and effects. Data on a national sample of working men and women make the same point. When men and women hold jobs that provide challenge, they equally often value the challenge. When their current

31. These data on white women come from a study directed by Gerald Gurin, at the Institute for Social Research, The University of Michigan, Ann Arbor, Michigan.

jobs are unchallenging, women value work challenge less than men.[32] Earlier socialization of work preferences continues if the current experience does not provide opportunity to express, if not discover, the forms of gratification that result as "natural" preferences for men. Data from the same national study of working conditions of men and women make the same argument about men and women's desires to be promoted. In response to the question of when they would like to take on a job at a higher level, more women than men said they never wanted to be promoted. Women also expressed lower expectations of being given a chance to take on a job at a higher level. However, once the expectations of whether promotion was likely to occur was controlled, the sex difference in desire for promotion disappeared. When women believe they can be promoted, they want to be promoted as much as men.[33]

Moreover, the data we have summarized on the ambitions of Black men and women in college challenge the widely held stereotype of the Black women who is more dominant and ambitious than the Black man. The stereotype depends in part on the belief that, relative to the men, Black women have enjoyed an advantage in the urban labor market. Facts support exactly the opposite picture. Jackson presents evidence of female inequality among Blacks for several aspects of labor force participation.[34] She shows from census data since 1910 that Black men have always outnumbered Black women in the employed labor market, that Black women once in the market have always shown higher unemployment rates, that Black women have not competed for the same jobs as Black men, but much like white women, have found employment in traditionally female jobs, and that Black women have earned less than Black men with the same levels of education. Black women are always at the bottom of the income pyramid: they earn less than white women, who make less than men, white or Black. Nor does anything in our results about job aspirations suggest female dominance. The lower job aspirations of women existed in every college, as freshmen and as seniors, in 1964 and 1970. We know of no data to suggest that Black women face a work advantage relative to Black men, or that they show greater ambition or dominance.

32. Conversations with Teresa Levitan and Robert Quinn relative to work in progress on working conditions of a national sample of American workers, Survey Research Center, University of Michigan, 1973.
33. J. Crowley, T. Levitan and R. Quinn, "The Seven Deadly Half-Truths About Women," *Psychology Today* (March, 1973), pp. 94-96.
34. Jacquelyne J. Jackson, "But Where Are the Men?" *The Black Scholar*, (December, 1971), pp. 30-41.

Harwood and Hodge, referring to the belief that Black women are economically advantaged, conclude:

This stereotype is so familiar, and so widely-accepted, that it is hard to believe it could be false. Yet false is what available evidence shows it to be. Today, even in the poorest urban neighborhoods Negro men enjoy a clear economic superiority over Negro women, as the findings of the United States Bureau of Labor Statistics 1968-69 demonstrated. Moreover, and more surprising, all the evidence we have for past periods offers no significant support for the assumption that Negro women ever were advantaged in the search for jobs.[35]

PERCEPTIONS OF THE OPPORTUNITY STRUCTURE

Student ratings of the social difficulty of jobs related to two questions about job opportunity. First, there was the issue of whether a job's social difficulty depended on its institutional setting. Could, for example, the students distinguish the barriers that obstruct the practice of law in major corporations from those in government service or in private practice? Second, how did the students view the labor markets in the North and the South? Traditionally, Black graduates have looked to the North as the land of opportunity. Even in 1964, half of the students who had made definite plans said they intended to leave the South to find jobs elsewhere. Was there further evidence that they felt the opportunity for the same job would be greater in the North than in the South? Since half the students who judged social difficulty were asked about the relative chances for equally qualified Black and white applicants in a large city in the North and half were asked the same question for the same job but in a large city in the South, these data tell us how southern students evaluated the two labor markets for 150 occupations.

The results provided a mixed picture. The students were acutely realistic about the institutional meaning of social difficulty but far less so in judging its geographical meaning. They knew that certain kinds of institutions and work settings were notoriously discriminatory, at least in certain job functions. The issue for them was not so much that becoming a doctor or setting up a private medical practice presented problems but rather that practicing on a hospital staff or becoming a staff surgeon in a large hospital was extraordinarily difficult for Black doctors. Likewise, the students rated going into private law practice as much easier than obtaining a position in a large law firm. The

35. Edwin Harwood and Claire C. Hodge, "Jobs and the Negro Family: A Reappraisal," *The Public Interest* 23 (Spring, 1971), pp. 125-126.

students also felt the job of bank teller, although not requiring much ability, was far harder than becoming a cashier or a bookkeeper where the business site was not specified. They also indicated that becoming a sales representative for a large firm was five times as hard as getting a job in personnel in a similar company: personnel jobs were not easy to break into, but much easier than jobs in sales. Studies of discriminatory policies in industry substantiate these perceptions.[36] They indicate that sales and other divisions that represent the company to the outside world typically discriminate more than divisions that primarily fill internal functions. A second generalization from the industrial studies —that jobs that lay directly in the line of authority in production prompted more discrimination than special staff jobs outside the production line—also was supported by how our students perceived opportunities and restrictions. Showing their knowledge of this kind of distinction, they said that getting a job as an industrial scientist or as a personnel executive was easier than competing with a white applicant to become a top industrial executive or business manager for a large firm.

Student evaluations of the relative opportunities of the North and South proved to be somewhat less realistic. First, they indicated that the old standard image of the North as the land of opportunity still was believable to students in the mid-sixties. One hundred and twenty-nine of the 150 occupations were judged as easier to obtain in the North; the remaining 21 were viewed as equally accessible in the two regions. Not one of the 150 occupations, including 12 different public school jobs, was viewed as easier to obtain in the South. To rate teaching and school supervisory jobs as less difficult to obtain in the North could only come from a distorted view of the two labor markets, since prior to desegregation most Black teachers found their teaching and administrative jobs in the South. In another way, the students seemed more unaware of differences in the northern and southern situations than they should have been. Beyond viewing the northern labor market as consistently more benign, they did not distinguish the relatively fewer opportunities of certain jobs in the North from the greater opportunities in the South. For example, in 1964 when these data were collected it was easier in two senses to obtain a teaching job in the South than in the North—easier in an absolute sense, and easier relative to other jobs in the South. The students misjudged both facets. They not only felt that all the teaching jobs in elementary and second-

36. Robert P. Quinn, Joyce M. Tabor, Laura K. Gordon, *The Decision to Discriminate: A Study of Executive Selection* (Ann Arbor: Survey Research Center, Institute for Social Research, The University of Michigan, 1968).

ary schools included in the 150 occupations were easier to obtain in the North, they also saw teaching as having the same rank position in the set of 150 in both regions in the country. Teaching was not the only area that showed a lack of differentiation between the northern and southern job worlds, although the actual facts about the distribution of Black teachers, North and South, made the students' misperceptions especially striking. Indeed, all but three of the 150 occupations carried the same rank position in the North and in the South, that is, the occupations were viewed as having the same level of difficulty, relative to others on the list, in both regions of the country. In both ways—viewing the North as providing greater opportunity in an absolute sense, and failing to differentiate the relative difficulty of these 150 jobs in the two regions—the students showed the consequences of their almost exclusively southern origins.

Since we did not repeat the study of evaluation of occupations in 1970, we do not know if these misperceptions from informational gaps continued. The students may have become much more realistic about the North, although we doubt it since even in 1970 few had traveled extensively, let alone worked for any time, outside the South. The students had had little direct test of the northern employment markets in either 1964 or 1970. They had to depend on what they read, on counseling and placement office information, and on the hearsay of friends and relatives. Up-to-date job information is never easy to obtain, especially in times of change. Old opinions serve particularly badly when labor demands are shifting quickly, as they have for teaching jobs in the past five years. When the market deteriorates, as it has for college graduates since 1969, information about opportunities in expanding categories becomes all the more critical. The students need current data on southern job opportunities since the overwhelming majority would prefer to work and live in the South. Given their mental set about opportunity in the North (at least in 1964) and the shifting economic picture, they cannot make decisions based on preference without fuller knowledge of regional opportunities in a detailed breakdown of job categories. That is hard for them to acquire since what they need most—timely, detailed descriptions of job markets—are not readily available. Here is a critical counseling need, one that does not imply changing the students or undoing hypothesized damage of previous discrimination.

HIGHER EDUCATION AND CAREER PREPARATION

The data presented in this chapter have documented ways in which the students' aspirations both reflected and transcended the constraints that Blacks have faced in our society. Their commitment to remaining in school and to getting their degrees, their high aspirations for post-baccalaureate education and professional careers, their readiness to work and borrow to further their education all show that Black students have maintained a high level of motivation and aspiration despite a history of limitations and discrimination. This underscores the critical role that the Black colleges have played in supporting and helping Black people realize these aspirations.

On the other hand, some of the results show the effects of discrimination. In their views of the opportunity structure Black students saw certain professions and occupational settings and roles (e.g., engineering, banking, executive management roles) as relatively closed to them, and their aspirations tended to exclude such careers. While there was some suggestion that this was not as true in 1970 as in 1964, even at the later date there was evidence that the Black students were making career choices within a more restricted set of possibilities than was true of the typical white college student. Note that these constraints apply to Black women as well as to men students. Despite the popular stereotype about the dominance of Black women, the data showed very clearly that, in addition to race discrimination, the occupational aspirations of Black women reflected also the severe limitations of their sex role. In most cases they aspired for traditionally "feminine" occupations, which even they saw as less prestigious and challenging than the careers chosen by the men.

These data inevitably raise policy questions for higher education. Should academic departments and counseling services work actively to change students' rather narrow concepts of work roles appropriate for men and for women? How much should curricular revision and development depend on economic facts and future labor market projections? Indeed, how explicit do we want to make the already well-established connection between institutions of higher education, including even the most exclusively liberal arts colleges, and career preparation? Should certain institutions increasingly specialize in skill training as others focus on liberal arts and the presumably less applied areas of research? Even if it were advisable to achieve certain purposes of higher education, what would that do to our colleges' and universities' responsibilities to address themselves to critical social problems of our times? And in what manner should the historically Black colleges continue to contribute to the American education scene?

Expressing opinions held widely among Black educators, Bowles and DeCosta do not question the appropriateness of higher education redressing job inequality and providing skills for the Black community:

"*. . . It seems evident that, among the many crises facing Negro society, the professional deficit must rank as of high, of possibly highest, importance. If this can be accepted, then we move automatically to the question of how it can be overcome.*

Of the many possible ways of searching for and stating an answer to this, the simplest, and perhaps the best, is to recall what has already been stated—that the Negro professional class is about half the size that it should be. To achieve parity with the white professional labor force by 1990, there should be an immediate doubling of Black enrollments in professional schools. And thereafter, since the size of the professional work force is increasing steadily at the rate of about 5 percent per year, there should be a comparable Black enrollment increase in professional schools each year."[37]

While this task clearly must be shared by both Black and white institutions, Black colleges offer unique opportunities for tying professional training to the needs of the Black community. Training Black professionals has been, in fact, the historical mission—and a successful one—of Black colleges. Although all too often unappreciated in the debate over the future significance of Black colleges, the vast majority of the nearly 300,000 Black professionals noted in the 1960 census were educated in Black colleges. In 1970 three-fourths of the Blacks who held doctorates had attended Black colleges.[38]

Many Black educators argue that the commitments of the Black colleges must continue to lie in professional training if they are to continue to realize their unique contribution. A dean at one of the participating colleges expressed the issue for many educators when he commented about the increasing pressure on Black colleges to provide skill training for business and technical careers:

Having been out of the mainstream, Black colleges have too often taken a responsive stance and let others decide what we should be about. And we may do it again by responding too enthusiastically or defensively to this new flock of recruiters who, at long last, are eager for our students in business and industry. I'm not at all sure we should change our focus from professional training to trying to train the new breed of Black managers. In fact, I'm not even sure we should deemphasize teacher training. We have done a good job of training teachers in the past when that was about the only choice we had. Maybe we should go on specializing in teacher training and

37. Bowles and DeCosta, *Between Two Worlds,* p. 208.
38. K. G. Mommsen, "Professionalism and the Racial Context of Career Patterns Among Black American Doctorates: A Note on the 'Brain Drain' Hypothesis" (Unpublished article, 1972).

preprofessional programs that we know will make a difference to future generations of Black youth in a direct way. More Black engineers and Black managers will eventually matter, but not in any immediate or direct sense. Also, as far as I can tell, the general growth in the economy is going to count on these service professions anyway. And I know for sure that they are what we need in strengthening the Black community.

We agree that Black colleges must not now deemphasize professional training or turn away from service responsibilities in favor of specialized technical or business education. Projections of economic growth, revaluation of national purpose, and especially our critical need for domestic social change all militate against it. Rising Black consciousness, moreover, will likely keep service the primary goal for students. On the other hand, we do not want students to be locked into the professions without the sense of real choice, whether that comes from the history of exclusion, limitation in curricular offerings, inadequate resources for curriculum development, inadequate exposure to new job opportunities, parental pressures for safe and secure paths in which Blacks historically have achieved, or a restrictedly narrow viewpoint about meeting the needs of the Black community. Labor market projections are at best inadequate. The needs of the Black community provide enough diversification for students to choose many different directions and still contribute to its strength. Thus, within the context of continuing the emphasis on professional commitment and service, all colleges, Black or white, where Black students go to school should aim to help them exercise genuine choice about their lives.

They should:
- Help them recognize the choices they *could* make.
- Heighten their awareness of opportunities they have, while, at the same time, support their efforts to change the obstacles large numbers of Black Americans face.
- Encourage students to make decisions positively on the basis of their commitments as Blacks and their own personal talents rather than on negative considerations of constraints of exclusion or fear of failure.
- Provide the skills and knowledge by which students can face these choices with self-confidence.

With these goals higher education would have an impact on the nature of society, although admittedly it would be slower and more conservative than some of the most outspoken of our student critics would like. In doing so, the occupational commitment of the students clearly becomes a strength instead of an educational liability as it is often presented in invidious comparisons between intellectually oriented students in elite colleges and vocationally or mobility oriented students in open-door schools. That such large numbers of these students are committed both to their development as future professionals and to using their skills to benefit other Black Americans eases considerably the problem of making education relevant. Some people in higher education may not want to move in this direction. For those who do, the task is clear. The students want skills, and they want to use them in making a difference to the Black community.

chapter 4

The Motivational Dynamics of Aspirations and Performance

The previous chapter described the students' individual achievement goals: their choices of occupations and the level of aspiration they represented, their future educational goals, and the unusually high achievement motivation these goals reflected for a student population that faced financial hardships far beyond those typical of college students in the nation at large. This chapter presents motivational analyses of aspirations and performance, using the framework of distinguishing among three components of motivation—achievement motives, achievement values, and expectancies of success.

We address four sets of questions:

1. How did these three components of motivation operate in explaining aspirations and performance? We stress especially the importance of distinguishing between cultural values and personal expectancies of success.

2. Did personal expectancies predominate over motives and values as we had anticipated they would? Were expectancies generally more important or only for certain students? Did the significance of expectancies, relative to motives and values, depend on the sex of the student or on particular college environments? Did expectancies stand out in clarifying all, or only some, individual achievement outcomes? Although we emphasize the heightened import of expectancies, we also stress the complexity of motivation, especially the necessity of considering the role of the college environment in conditioning the dynamics of motivation.

3. How did the students' social awareness and sensitivity to reality constraints and opportunities influence their aspirations and performance? Within the context of previous research on internal and external control we stress the positive motivational implications for minority students of a special kind of externality, one that attributes the responsibility for race inequities to the social system rather than to individual members of the minority group.

4. Did the students' aspirations and achievement motivation change over the decade of the sixties, a period sometimes described as one of rising expectations? Did the students in the colleges that participated both in the 1964 and 1970 studies express either higher aspirations or more certain expectancies in 1970?

THREE COMPONENTS OF MOTIVATION: EXPECTANCIES, VALUES, AND MOTIVES

Personal Expectancies and Cultural Values

The significance of distinguishing between values and expectancies as different aspects of motivation is best illustrated in the meaning of internal and external control to the students we have studied. Internal control refers to individuals' expectancies that their own actions, rather than forces outside themselves over which they have no control, will determine the rewards they receive in life.[1] The Internal-External Control Scale that Rotter and his associates[2] designed to measure this concept includes two types of items that they did not distinguish: items that refer explicitly to the person's own life situation and items that tap beliefs about what leads to success or failure for other people. These two types of items relate to the distinction we have drawn between values and expectancies. Individuals' feelings that they can exercise control *in their own lives* reflect their personal expectancies about life chances and opportunities. In contrast, their views about what determines payoffs in the culture at large measure their commitments to traditional Protestant ethic cultural values, but do not necessarily reflect their own expectancies.

THE STUDENTS' CONCEPTIONS OF PERSONAL CONTROL AND CULTURAL VALUES

The students themselves separated these two types of items as they answered the questions on the Internal-External Control Scale. Two distinct factors emerged when we did a factor analysis of the responses of the students who participated in the study in 1964.[3] One included

1. Julian B. Rotter, "Generalized Expectancies for Internal Versus External Control of Reinforcement," *Psychological Monographs* 80(1) whole No. 609, 1966.
2. *Ibid.*
3. The factor structure is presented in tabular form in Patricia Gurin, Gerald Gurin, Rosina C. Lao, and Muriel Beattie, "Internal-External Control in the Motivational Dynamics of Negro Youth," *Journal of Social Issues* XXV(3) (1969), pp. 29-53. Men and women's factor structures were remarkably similar. Veldman coefficients all ranged between .82 and .98.

five items, all phrased in the first person. Students who consistently chose the internal statement on these five items showed a strong conviction that they could control what happened in their own lives. They believed in their own competence. We have called this a sense of *personal control*. In contrast, only one of the 13 items that fell on the second distinct factor used the first person. Referring instead to people generally, the items on the second factor seemed to measure the students' cultural ideologies about success. They probed the students' beliefs about the role of internal and external forces in determining success and failure in the culture at large. Choosing the internal statement on these items meant rejecting the belief that success follows from luck, the right breaks, or knowing the right people in favor of the traditional Protestant ethic explanation of success. Such students consistently held that hard work, effort, skill, and ability determine success in life. We have called this a measure of *control ideology*. The difference between the personal and cultural measures shows up clearly in contrasting the lists of items that fell on the two factors:

Sense of Personal Control

Internal Alternatives	*External Alternatives*
Trusting to fate has never turned out as well for me as making a decision to take a definite course of action.	I have often found that what is going to happen will happen.
What happens to me is my own doing.	Sometimes I feel that I don't have enough control over the direction my life is taking.
When I make plans, I am almost certain that I can make them work.	It is not always wise to plan too far ahead because many things turn out to be a matter of good or bad fortune anyhow.
In my case, getting what I want has little or nothing to do with luck.	Many times we might just as well decide what to do by flipping a coin.
It is impossible for me to believe that chance or luck play an important role in my life.	Many times I feel that I have little influence over the things that happen to me.

Control Ideology

Internal Alternatives	External Alternatives
Becoming a success is a matter of hard work; luck has little or nothing to do with it.	Getting a good job depends mainly on being in the right place at the right time.
People will get ahead in life if they have the goods and do a good job; knowing the right people has nothing to do with it.	Knowing the right people is important in deciding whether a person will get ahead.
Some people just don't use the breaks that come their way. If they don't do well, it's their own fault.	People who don't do well in life often work hard, but the breaks just don't come their way.
Leadership positions tend to go to capable people who deserve being chosen.	It's hard to know why some people get leadership positions and others don't; ability doesn't seem to be the important factor.
Capable people who fail to become leaders have not taken advantage of their opportunities.	Without the right breaks one cannot be an effective leader.
In the case of the well-prepared student, there is rarely if ever such a thing as an unfair test.	Many times exam questions tend to be so unrelated to course work that studying is really useless.
People who can't get others to like them don't understand how to get along with others.	No matter how hard you try some people just don't like you.
Who gets to be boss depends on who has the skill and ability; luck has little or nothing to do with it.	Who gets to be boss often depends on who was lucky to be in the right place first.
How many friends you have depends upon how nice a person you are.	It is hard to know whether or not a person really likes you.
Getting people to do the right thing depends upon ability; luck has little or nothing to do with it.	Without the right breaks, one cannot be an effective leader.
There is really no such thing as "luck."	Most people don't realize the extent to which their lives are controlled by accidental happenings.

Control Ideology (Continued)

Internal Alternatives	External Alternatives
People are lonely because they don't try to be friendly.	There's not much use in trying too hard to please people, if they like you, they like you.
There is a direct connection between how hard I study and the grades I get.	Sometimes I can't understand how teachers arrive at the grades they give.

This separation of the personal from the cultural levels has been replicated on additional Black samples.[4] It emerged again in factor analysis of the responses of the students who participated in the 1968 senior followup at one of the colleges and again in the 1970 cross-sectional study of students in six of the original 10 colleges. More important, the same distinction has emerged in studies of noncollege populations as well. It resulted from factor analyzing the responses of Black inner-city youth who were trainees in a manpower training program.[5] It also appeared in a study of Black high school students in

4. Most factor analytic studies of the Internal-External Control items that have been carried out on white samples show only one general factor rather than two factors that separate the personal from the cultural levels. See the summary by Rotter: "Generalized Expectancies for Internal Versus External Control of Reinforcement," *Psychological Monographs* 80(1) whole No. 609, 1966. However, Mirels (H. L. Mirels, "Dimensions of Internal Versus External Control," *Journal of Consulting and Clinical Psychology* 34 (1970), pp. 226-228.) reports finding two factors in a later study of students at Ohio State University who had also served as subjects in Rotter's original work. One covers influences over personally relevant outcomes; it includes three first-person items and three cultural items that refer explicitly on the external side to chance or luck. Most of the items loading high on the second factor focus on the respondent's acceptance or rejection of the idea that a citizen can exert some control over politics and world affairs. The items refer to people in general and seem to measure attributions of political efficacy. Thus far little research has been reported on differential associations with these two factors, but the separation itself argues that our distinctions apply not *only* to minority group members whose experience may sharpen the capacity to distinguish between cultural values about success and what actually works when social forces inhibit individual mobility. The study by Mirels shows that white students also distinguish personal and political dimensions. We expect politically liberal or radical white students would reflect even greater awareness than a general sample of white students of the difference between personal efficacy and control of social conditions such as poverty, racism, and war. In Chapter 10 we discuss the implications of interpreting the I-E Control Scale as a measure of personal powerlessness when evidence shows a conservative bias in the measure itself.
5. Gerald Gurin, *Inner-City Negro Youth in a Job Training Project; A Study of Factors Related to Attrition and Job Success* (Ann Arbor: Institute for Social Research, University of Michigan, 1968).

Detroit and Atlanta and in data provided by a sample of their mothers as well. Jorgensen, who carried out the analyses of the high school students and their mothers, concluded:

Generally the results are an impressive replication of previous conceptions of IE in Black samples. Now, several Afro-American samples, the Gurin et al. sample of Black southern college students, the sample of northern and southern urban Black high school students, and the sample of Black mothers living in a northern or southern urban center, have produced the same basic belief structure for IE. Additionally, the high school sample and the mothers' sample include persons with a wide range of social and economic status . . . The sense of personal control is separate from ideological beliefs. That is, a respondent's beliefs about his ability to control the direction and outcome of his personal life are distinguished from has beliefs about the ability of "people" as a general category to control the outcomes and directions of their lives.[6]

DIFFERENTIAL IMPORT OF PERSONAL CONTROL AND CONTROL IDEOLOGY

Is the separation of the cultural and personal levels of control just an esoteric distinction or does it really matter in understanding the motivational dynamics of the students we have studied? We believe that it is critically important and that the failure to separate them often results in invidious comparisons between Black and white youngsters. Several previous studies point to the greater externality of Black youth as another example of personal deficits that inhibit their achievement and rise in status, relative to whites.[7] Actually, the pattern of responses

6. Carl Christian Jorgensen, *The Socialization and Meaning of Sense of Internal Versus External Control Among Black High School Students* (The University of Michigan: Unpublished Ph.D. Dissertation, 1971), p. 92. Jorgensen's data show that the personal control factor emerged clearly for both the southern and northern high school girls and mothers of both boys and girls. It did not emerge for high school boys in general but only among those with high vocabulary test scores. He argues, therefore, that verbal sophistication seems to be important in determining when this distinction between the personal and cultural levels is made and that high school girls produced a separate personal control factor because of their greater sophistication, relative to boys of the same age.

7. Esther S. Battle and J. B. Rotter, "Children's Feelings of Personal Control as Related to Social Class and Ethnic Group" *Journal of Personality 31* (1963), pp. 482-490; Adrian Zytkoskee, Bonnie R. Strickland, and James Watson, "Delay of Gratification and Internal Versus External Control Among Adolescents of Low Socioeconomic Status," *Developmental Psychology 4(1)* (1971), pp. 93-98; H. M. Lefcourt and G. W. Ladwig, "The American Negro: A Problem in Expectancies," *Journal of Personality and Social Psychology 1* (1965), pp. 377-380; and Ralph L. Shaw and Norman P. Uhl, "Control of Reinforcement and Academic Achievement," *The Journal of Educational Research, 64(5)* (1971), pp. 226-228.

of Black and white youngsters to the individual items of the Internal-External Control scale show that Black youths endorse general Protestant ethic values just as strongly as their white peers while they express less certainty that they can control what happens in their own lives.[8] The experience of different racial groups in America seems to matter more in how they perceive their opportunities and possibilities for success than in how committed they are to the values that are instrumental to achievement.

The personal and ideological meanings of internal control have also carried different motivational implications in the work we have done

8. This shows up in numerous studies. For example, in the study of Equal Educational Opportunity, Black college students were equally, if not more, internal than white students in responding to statements that seem to measure what we have called control ideology: for example, "If people are not successful it is their own fault." In contrast, race differences did appear in questions that used the personal referent. Black students were less internal than their white peers in answering questions about their own life experiences, for instance, in responding to the statement, "Everytime I try to get ahead something or somebody stops me." See Table 4:12.1 in J. S. Coleman et al., Equality of Educational Opportunity (Washington, D.C.: U. S. Government Printing Office, 1966). Likewise, when we compare the endorsement rates of items in the Internal-External Control Scale by the white students whom Rotter used in standardizing his scale and by the Black students who participated in our study in 1964, we find the same results: while the Black and white percentages on the cultural value items were almost identical, fewer Black than white students endorsed the internal statement on the personal control items. This same racial pattern is also reported by Wittes in his study of high schools in 10 urban areas, north and south. Using our measures of personal control and control ideology, Wittes reports equal adherence to cultural values about internal control but shows that white students expressed stronger feelings of personal control. See S. Wittes, School Power Structure and Belief in Internal-External Control: A Study of Secondary Schools in Conflict (The University of Michigan: Unpublished Ph.D. Dissertation, 1969). Moreover, the same pattern characterized the findings of a national sample of white and Black adults participating in job retraining programs. White and Black trainees agreed in responding to questions tapping general Protestant ethic beliefs (including some items adapted from the Rotter Scale); however, there were clear race differences in responses to questions on the sense of efficacy and control over one's life, the white trainees indicating a greater sense of personal control. See Gerald Gurin, A National Attitude Study of Trainees in MDTA Institutional Programs (Ann Arbor: Institute for Social Research, University of Michigan, 1970). Together, these results show that it is important to make the distinction we have stressed if we are interested in understanding the motivational effects of societal status of very limited opportunities. These barriers and limitations seem to have much more effect on an individual's personal expectancies than on his generalized beliefs and values.

with college students.[9] Repeatedly the sense of personal control has proved to be motivationally significant (Appendix Tables 4.1 A and B). Students with a higher sense of personal control achieved higher grades and performed better on standard tests of academic skill, even when we controlled for their achievement test scores as entering freshmen. Their aspirations also reflected stronger motivation. Both in 1964 and 1970 the students with the greatest sense of personal control more often expressed intentions of going on to graduate school and aspired to jobs that demanded high ability, accorded high prestige, and fell in nontraditional sectors of the labor market.

In contrast to these findings for personal control, our measure of control ideology showed no such relationships to performance and aspirations. In fact, the results suggest that an internal control ideology not only did not positively motivate the students but, under certain circumstances, negatively influenced them. Negative implications occurred when strong adherence to Protestant ethic values was expressed by students who doubted their own sense of personal control (i.e., those students who fell in the lower half of scores on our measure of personal control). We found this in numerous ways. The men who felt least able to control what happened in their own lives but, nevertheless, believed that internal virtues paid off for other people, aspired to occupations that reflected significantly less prestige, ability demands, and nontraditionality. These interactions between personal control,

9. Studies of students at the high school level and in community colleges provide mixed results on this point. Some indicate either equivalent motivational import of personal control and control ideology or even greater significance of the cultural values for achievement. (Jorgensen, *The Socialization and Meaning of Sense of Internal Vs. External Control Among Black High School Students;* Eleanor R. Hall, *Motivation and Achievement in Negro and White Students*) (Final Report, U. S. Department of Health, Education and Welfare, 1971); and David C. Mitchell, "Urban Community College Students' Beliefs in Internal-External Control," (Case Western Reserve University: Unpublished Ph.D. Dissertation, 1970). Jorgensen presents some data that suggests a reason why personal control may be more important motivationally at the college level but not always in groups at lower grade levels or in certain kinds of higher education institutions. While cultural values correlated with grades in high school and performance on standard tests better than personal control for the general samples Jorgensen studied, the pattern we found among college students prevailed for the most verbally skilled of the high school students as well. That is, personal control related positively to achievement while control ideology bore either negative or no relationships to achievement among the subgroup of high schools who were most verbally skilled. This was also the only group of high school boys for whom personal control was distinguished from cultural values in the way they thought about control. Thus, Jorgensen argues that verbal sophistication and social experience are necessary both to conceive of the difference between one's own life and forces in the culture at large and to be influenced motivationally primarily by the personal rather than cultural meanings of control.

CHART A. **Summary of Relationships of Two Types of Internal Control Measures (Personal Control and Control Ideology) and Achievement Outcomes**

Internal Sense of Personal Control:

Positively Related To	Unrelated To	Negatively Related To
Cumulative grades (both sexes)		
Correct performance on anagrams task (men only)		
Low number of errors on anagrams task (women only)		
Prestige of occupational aspiration (both sexes)	Nothing	Nothing
Ability demands of occupational aspiration (both sexes)		
Nontraditionality of occupational aspiration (men only)		
Graduate or professional school aspirations (both sexes)		

Internal Control Ideology:

Positively Related To	Unrelated To	Negatively Related To
Nothing	Occupational aspirations (prestige, ability demands, and nontraditionality for all women and men with *high* sense of personal control)	Occupational aspirations (prestige, ability demands, and nontraditionality for men with *low* sense of personal control)
	Graduate or professional school aspirations (both sexes with *high* sense of personal control)	Graduate or professional school aspirations (both sexes with *low* sense of personal control)
	Cumulative grades (both sexes with *high* sense of personal control)	Cumulative grades (both sexes with *low* sense of personal control)
	Anagrams performance both sexes with *high* sense of personal control)	Anagrams performance both sexes with *low* sense of personal control)

cultural values about internal control, and aspirations were significant for men in both 1964 and in 1970. (Appendix Table 4.1A). The same pattern also characterized the graduate school aspirations of both the men and women in 1970 (Appendix Tables 4.1 A and B). The students in the low personal expectancy group who believed that other people could control events in their lives were especially unlikely to aspire for graduate education. The performance data we collected in 1964 also showed the negative effect of believing in an internal ideology for students with a low sense of personal control (Appendix Tables 4.1 A and B). While performance already was lower when students felt little personal control, it was even lower when they believed that Protestant ethic values were critical for success in the culture at large. In this group below the median in personal control an internal ideology was associated with significantly lower grades in college as well as poorer performance on the anagrams task we administered in the study. The belief that success in the general culture depends on internal virtues, combined with doubts as to one's own strengths, seemed to result in a self-blame that especially depressed both aspiration and performance. By far the least effective among both the men and women were the students who showed this combination of external personal control and internal ideology about control.[10] See Chart A.

ACADEMIC SELF-CONFIDENCE:
ANOTHER PERSONAL EXPECTANCY

These results on the personal and cultural meanings of control repeatedly attest to the significance of the students' personal expectancies of success and failure. Another indicator of personal expectation, the student's academic self-confidence, further confirmed this. Sometimes called self-concept of ability,[11] or level of expectancy,[12] this measure instructed the student to assess his probability of academic success. Specifically it asked, "How do you expect your academic performance this coming year will compare with others in your class?" Choices ranged from "I'll do better than 90 percent" to only "better than 10 percent." We think of both the sense of personal control and academic self-confidence as competency-based expectancies. They reflect the aspect of expectancy that comes from feeling confident about one's own ability. Obviously, they are just a portion of what goes into a student's overall expectancy of being successful since the student can feel very confident about his own competence but still express a low expectancy of reaching a desired goal because discrimi-

10. None of these aspiration-performance results were confounded by so-called ability differences since the students' ranks on college entrance tests were controlled in all of these analyses.

11. W. Brookover, A. Peterson, and S. Thomas, *Self-Concept of Ability and School Achievement: Final Report of Cooperative Research Project 845,* (East Lansing, Michigan: Michigan State University, 1967).

12. W. Mischel and E. Staub, "Effects of Expectancy of Working and Waiting for Larger Rewards," *Journal of Personality and Social Psychology 3* (1965), pp. 625-633.

nation or other social obstacles are likely to interfere. The critical tie between level of expectancy and perception of opportunity, or assessment of the probable environmental response to one's effort, will be explored at the end of this chapter. Here we are examining only the competency-based personal expectancies.

Academic self-confidence was associated with better performance and higher levels of aspiration in much the same way as the more general sense of personal control proved to be. Men and women in both 1964 and 1970 who expressed academic self-confidence above the median, like those who felt most able to control more general outcomes in their own lives, received better grades in college. They also made fewer errors and achieved higher performance scores on our anagrams task, chose future careers that promised greater prestige and challenge, and more often aspired to graduate or professional training.[13] In addition, the most academically self-confident men intended to enter the most nontraditional jobs after completing their training. The multiple analyses of variance that used both of these competency-based expectancies to explain motivation and performance showed that their effects were additive (Appendix Tables 4.2 A and B). The students who were most sure of their general personal control and most self-confident specifically about academic success repeatedly stood out for better performance and heightened aspirations. Those who lacked both a strong sense of personal control and academic self-confidence performed particularly poorly and showed the most depressed aspirations.[14]

13. As would be expected from the ability theme running through these competency-based expectancies, they are positively, although weakly, related to the student's entrance test scores. Even the highest correlations, which occur between academic self-confidence and entrance scores, were only .15. Nonetheless, we controlled for entrance test scores in relating these expectancy measures to college grades, anagrams performance, and aspirations.

14. At this point a comment should be made on some of the causal implications in our argument. Obviously it is hard to tell in these kinds of correlations, even with control for achievement test scores, whether confidence produces achievement or achievement produces confidence. This is particularly true with the correlation between the competence measures and the anagrams performance, since the two tests were administered simultaneously. The causal direction in the relationship with college grades is somewhat clearer since there was at least a temporal difference, with both entrance scores and self-confidence measured at the beginning of the college year, while the GPA reflected grade achievements at the end of the year. We also know that this correlation between self-confidence and subsequent grades holds even when we control both entrance scores and high school rank. Still, it is easier to unravel some of the causal complexities in longitudinal studies; we have done that in looking at the impact of academic success experiences where we were able to follow the same students through their college years. We will return to this issue in Chapter 6 on institutional impact on aspirations.

Is there any evidence that the most self-confident and efficacious students were overaspiring in their job choices—that a general optimism rather than realistic appraisal of themselves underlay their aspirations? Although there is no easy solution to the problem of determining whether an occupational aspiration represents a realistic goal rather than overaspiration or underaspiration for the individual, we followed some standard procedures in achievement motivation research to examine this question for the men who participated in the 1964 study.[15] Following a procedure developed by Mahone[16] and described in Chapter 3, we used the judgments the students themselves made as to the level of ability required for success in various occupations. The occupational realism score, corresponding to the goal discrepancy score traditionally used in experimental studies of level of aspiration, was the discrepancy between the ability required for the student's occupational choice (the percentage of persons judged by peers to have the ability for it) and the percentile of the class that the student's cumulative grade point average represented. A student who aspired to an occupation whose ability requirements were no more than 10 percent higher or 10 percent lower than his own performance was viewed as making a realistic choice. When the discrepancy was more than plus 10, he was overaspiring; when it was more than minus 10, he was underaspiring. There is nothing infallible about these classifications. They simply provided a way to distinguish three groups of men students, those whose choices were relatively underaspirant, another whose choices were relatively realistic, and a group whose choices were relatively overaspirant.[17]

15. These analyses of realism of choice were restricted to men because prior research results have been clearest for men. We also restricted them to men who entered college with tests scores that put them above the median for their class since the issue of setting a realistic goal has been examined most thoroughly for college men with reasonably high achievement.

16. J. L. Morris, "The Relation Between Perceived Probability of Success in Chosen Occupations and Achievement-Related Motivation," (University of California, Berkeley: Ph.D. Thesis, 1964) and C. H. Mahone, "Fear of Failure and Unrealistic Vocational Aspirations," *Journal of Abnormal and Social Psychology* 60 (1960), pp. 253-261.

17. Several examples can be given to illustrate the meaning of this score. If a student's cumulative grades put him in the 50th percentile in his class and he aspired to be an industrial scientist, a job for which the average estimate was that 19 percent would have the requisite ability, the goal discrepancy score would be a high positive, plus 31. That is, the student's aspiration was 31 percentiles higher in ability demands than his performance in college indicates his potential for the job would be. This would be coded as an unrealistically high level of aspiration. On the other hand, if a student scoring at the level of the top 20 percent of his class in grade performance aspired for the same occupation, the goal discrepancy

The men whose occupational choices realistically matched their college performance showed the strongest sense of personal control and were most assured of their academic strengths. Their personal control and academic self-confidence scores were higher than both the under-aspiring and overaspiring men (Appendix Table 4.3). They seemed to prefer goals that represented an intermediate risk, those that would challenge their talents. This association between these two competency-based expectancies, on the one hand, and realism of aspiration, on the other, counters suspicions that might be held about the psychological makeup of students who were unusually self-confident and efficacious. The men who felt comfortable about their own competence were not choosing unrealistic goals. Instead, their confidence seemed to be grounded in self-awareness of their skills and personal strengths that led to goals that would test their mettle.

SUMMARY

We have seen several reasons why it is important to distinguish between values and expectancies. First, the students themselves made this distinction in their views about what determines success in the culture at large and in their own lives. Second, the students' expectancies and feelings of confidence repeatedly related to their performance and aspirations, while their commitments to traditional achievement ideology and values were much less important. To briefly review the results: both aspects of competency-based expectancies, feelings of personal control and academic self-confidence, were consistently related to heightened occupational and educational aspirations, to better performance in college and on experimental achievement tasks, and to realistic aspirations. In contrast to this consistent pattern of positive results with the expectancy measures, the commitment to Protestant ethic values was generally irrelevant for these conventional indicators of individual achievement. There were no direct relationships between the control ideology score and the students' occupational and educational aspirations, the realism of their occupational choices, or their performance scores. It was only among students who questioned their own personal efficacy that believing in the virtues of hard work, effort, and other individual strengths operated at all and for them commit-

---

would be plus .01, suggesting a much more realistic aspiration. An illustration of an unrealistic underaspiration would be a student standing at the top 5 percent of his class who aspired to be a bookkeeper. Since students judged that the percentage having the required ability to be a bookkeeper was, on the average, approximately 40 percent, the index of goal discrepancy would be a high negative, .35. In other words, this student's aspiration would be 35 percentiles lower in ability demands than his performance indicates his potential for the job would be.

ment to the traditional Protestant work ethic inhibited rather than enhanced aspiration and performance. The group whose aspirations were lowest and performance poorest were those who believed strongly that internal virtues paid off for other people but doubted their own capacities to control what happened in their own lives. They must have blamed their achievement problems largely on themselves since they believed anyone can make it by virtue of internal strengths. This suggests the negative motivational state that follows from the attribution of failure to an unchangeable lack of ability.[18]

The Role of Motives

Motives function as generalized activators of behavior. The phrase, *driven* by the need for power (or approval or ambition), captures the role that motives theoretically play in motivating behavior. They are not easily distinguished, either conceptually or operationally, from values. To the extent that values imply something about the importance or attractiveness of a specific goal, such as the value placed on a college degree, motives differ by being much more general in nature. But we often use the term values to denote the basic, generalized beliefs about what is important in life. When we do, values and motives seem to converge in their meanings. In fact, some situational theorists of motivation exclude any notion of a generalized disposition to act; instead, they depend entirely on the more limited meaning of value that accrues to a specific goal which, together with expectations about reaching the goal, prompts a person to act.

We are sympathetic to models of motivation that preserve the possible significance of a generalized disposition, whether it is called a motive or a basic value. Following conflict theories of motivation, which distinguish motives that push a person toward a goal from motives that pull him away from it, we tried to measure both approach and avoidance motives. We limited ourselves to those motives or values that should relate to educational and occupational aspirations and to performance in achievement situations.

POSITIVE MOTIVES

The approach motive that has guided most of the research on level of aspiration and achievement is the "need for achievement," defined

18. For a superb review of the significance of attributions about success and failure for achievement motivation see Bernard Weiner, Irene Frieze, Andy Kukla, Linda Reed, Stanley Rest, and Robert M. Rosenbaum, "Perceiving the Causes of Success and Failure" in Edward E. Jones et al., editors, *Attribution: Perceiving the Causes of Behavior* (Morristown, New Jersey: General Learning Corporation, 1973).

in the McClelland-Atkinson[19] tradition as the disposition to strive for success in competition with some standard of excellence. Prior research carried out on very limited samples—typically white, male college students who were readily available as research subjects—has demonstrated relationships between the need for achievement and persistence at difficult tasks, preference for intermediate risks and realistic occupational challenges, aspiration for prestigious jobs, actual job achievement, intergenerational occupational mobility, and performance in college and on experimental achievement tasks.[20] While there are many just criticisms of this tradition of research, it has produced strong support for the concept that the need for achievement is a meaningful aspect of achievement motivation.

The most commonly used measure of the need for achievement, the Thematic Apperception Test (TAT), would have required asking the students to write stories in response to pictures or to verbal cues. Since several thousand students participated in this study, the TAT was simply not a feasible measuring device. We tried to approximate its meaning by using the criteria traditionally followed in coding the TAT stores for achievement need to code student responses to two questionnaire items about their life goals: "As you think of your future life, what is your picture of the way you would like life to work out for you?" and "when you think of the kind of person you would like to be as an adult, who is the one person you know you would most want to be like—what is it about that person you admire?"

An *achievement orientation* was scored when the student's answers to these questions reflected concern with: (1) a standard of good performance on some standard of excellence, (2) work challenge or a test of one's ability to do a difficult job, (3) putting maximum effort or energy into work, or (4) the process of striving or persistently trying to reach goals set for oneself. The achievement orientation scores represented the proportion of all codable responses to these questions that fit these achievement criteria. The scores ranged from a third of the students giving no achievement themes to a tenth for whom 50 percent of their responses were coded as achievement related; the median score was approximately 20 percent of all themes devoted to achievement.

19. John W. Atkinson, *An Introduction to Motivation* (Princeton, New Jersey: Van Nostrand, 1964) and David C. McClelland, *The Achieving Society* (Princeton, New Jersey: Van Nostrand, 1961).
20. For presentation of these studies see John W. Atkinson and N. T. Feather, *Theory of Achievement Motivation* (New York: John Wiley and Sons, 1966) and John W. Atkinson and Joel O. Raynor, *Motivation and Achievement* (Washington, D.C.: V. W. Winston, in press).

A *success orientation* was scored when the student's answers showed concern with: (1) obtaining a prestigious, respected job; (2) prominence in one's career; (3) recognition for any outstanding achievement; or (4) general success that was not restricted to work, including gaining the respect of the community or being generally well-known. Over all students expressed fewer success than achievement themes; half of them gave none at all, and the upper quartile had only 30 percent of their responses devoted to these success concerns.

How did the achievement and success orientations bear on the students' aspirations and performance? Neither was very important, although the need for achievement measured this way did distinguish some aspects of student motivation, especially among women. The success orientation proved generally insignificant. Its irrelevance may have resulted partly from restricted variance; too few students mentioned these success concerns for them to have explained individual differences in aspiration and performance. The achievement orientation was useful, however, in differentiating level of occupational aspiration among both men and women (Appendix Tables 4.4 A and B). Men and women whose concern with achievement in their descriptions of admired people and of the good life represented at least 30 percent of everything they talked about also chose future occupations that accorded significantly higher prestige and provided for greater challenge and demand of personal ability. Women whose achievement orientations were unusually pronounced also aspired, in greater numbers, for advanced education beyond the baccalaureate. They further achieved significantly higher grades in college. Thus, for women the achievement orientation generally meant something motivationally. Even for men it helped explain the most conventional indicators of occupational aspiration, the job's prestige and ability demands.

NEGATIVE MOTIVES

The avoidance motive that has received the most attention in achievement motivation research, the fear of failure, is defined as a disposition to avoid failure in achievement situations. Frequently measured by the Mandler-Sarason Test Anxiety Questionnaire,[21] which asks the student to report how anxious he feels in test situations, the fear of failure has been shown to inhibit effective performance and to encourage avoidance of intermediate risks both in achievement tasks and in setting unrealistic occupational goals.[22] To aspire for an occupation that is well

21. G. Mandler and S. B. Sarason, "A Study of Anxiety and Learning," *Journal of Abnormal and Social Psychology 47* (1952), pp. 166-173.
22. Atkinson and Feather, *op. cit.*

above or below one's ability is a very good way to avoid the intermediate risk that provides a real test of self and arouses anxiety in
people with a high fear of failure.

We used the Test Anxiety Questionnaire[23] as one measure of avoidance motives. The other measure derived from analyzing the responses
to the same questions about the good life and admired people that
provided measures of the approach motives as well, in this case to
capture concern with security. We felt that *desire for security* would
contribute to avoidance motivation, as least among students who came
to college out of real economic hardships and might seek to avoid risks
in order to assure a more secure future. Criteria for scoring desire for
security were evidence of concern about: (1) basic fear of want; (2)
adequate income; (3) job security; (4) stable family relationships or
(5) a pleasant comfortable life.

These measures of avoidance motives clarified the motivational
dynamics of the men students far more than the women. The security
concerns of the women proved totally irrelevant to their aspirations
and performance (Appendix Table 4.4B). Their anxieties about failure,
and they had them every bit as much as the men did, inhibited only
their occupational strivings. The most anxious women chose future
careers that provided less prestige and demanded less ability, while
women who expressed very little anxiety about failure showed higher
levels of aspiration in their job choices. Some women students were
much more fearful about failing in achievement situations and were
more preoccupied than others about security, but these motive differences just mattered very little for how they behaved. This has also
been true in studies of white women. The motive that has proved important in studies of women (largely white women in certain elite
colleges) has been the fear of succeeding in achievement situations
because of the threat to femininity and social success.[24] Fear of success
might have proved important to the behavior and aspirations of the
women attending these Black colleges but research on women's moti-

---

23. Being a self-report inventory, the Test Anxiety Questionnaire invites problems of
defensiveness. Since the intent of the questions was obvious to the student, it was
easy to defend oneself against exposing anxiety and vulnerability; and, in fact
we found that highly defensive students did score lower on the Test Anxiety Questionnaire (correlations of $-.26$ for men and $-.21$ for women between the TAQ
and the Defensiveness Scale we used). We eliminated the 10 percent of the
students with the highest scores on the defensiveness scale in the analyses using
fear of failure.

24. Matina Horner, "Toward an Understanding of Achievement-Related Conflicts in
Women," *Journal of Social Issues* 28 (2) (1972), pp. 157-175.

vation was only beginning to tap this area[25] when we started our studies and, therefore, we did not attempt to examine its implications for Black women.

In contrast, these avoidance motives, especially the fear of failure, did consistently relate to the men's aspirations and performance (Appendix Table 4.4A). Men with high fear of failure scores performed considerably less well on the anagrams task (correlations of $-.34$ with correct performance and $+.21$ with errors in the 10 college study, and $-.44$ with correct performance and $+.39$ with errors in a special study of freshmen attending an experimental program at one of the colleges). They also achieved lower grades (correlation of $-.31$). Both avoidance motives likewise distinguished level of the men's occupational and educational aspirations. Men who expressed high anxiety about failure and devoted as much as half of their discussion of the good life and what they admired about important models in their lives to security issues chose future careers that accorded less prestige, demanded less ability, and did not represent unusual types of employment for college-educated Blacks. They also aspired to graduate and professional school less frequently than men who were less fearful of failure and less concerned about security. Realism of the job choice also reflected the impact of avoidance motives, although in this case it was only fear of failure that operated. Realistic choices, especially compared to those that represented underaspiration, were most frequently made by the least anxious men.

THE RELATIVE IMPORTANCE OF EXPECTANCIES AND ACHIEVEMENT MOTIVES

We have seen throughout these results on the role of motives that their function depended greatly on the sex of the student. The extent of their concern with achievement in discussing the good life and describing people they particularly admired generally influenced the motivation of the women but related only to the prestige and ability demands of the men's job choices and not to their educational aspirations or college performance. Conversely, fear of failure proved consistently significant in the dynamics of the men but inhibited only the level of the women's job aspirations. The personal expectancy measures, on the other hand, generally worked for both men and

25. Some research suggests that the fear of success is lower among Black than among white women, although not enough research has been done to warrant a comfortable conclusion about that. See Peter J. Weston and Martha T. Mednick, "Race, Social Class and the Motive to Avoid Success in Women," *Journal of Cross-Cultural Psychology 1* (3) (September, 1970), pp. 284-291.

women. In this sense motives were not as important as expectancies. The motive measures were less important in another sense as well. In multivariate analyses, using both the expectancy and motive scores to predict aspiration and performance, the motives never carried as high beta weights as did the expectancy assessments. Thus, just as measures that assessed personal expectations of success were more relevant than those that assessed commitments to cultural values, they likewise clarified the students' motivation somewhat more than the measures of motives we included in this study.[26] Charts B and C summarize the results of analyses using these traditional indicators of achievement motivation.

College Dropout: The Complementary Influence of Motives and Expectancies

While expectancy measures were more important than motive measures in most of the motivational results, analyses of college dropouts showed motives with comparable import, at least for men. Dropout data were collected only in 1964 and only at one of the 10 colleges, a fact that disallows generalizing too broadly. At that college the men, but not the women, who dropped out after their freshman year differed motivationally from those who returned for their sophomore year (Appendix Table 4.5).

Questionnaires were administered at the end of the spring term of their freshman year. Among the men the following differences were found between dropouts and those who returned to college the next year: more dropouts said that college had been a very big and new experience for them (23 percent compared to 6 percent); more dropouts reported that college had been difficult and stressful (66 percent compared to 40 percent); more dropouts felt there were things they

---

26. Recent reinterpretations of motivation theory proposed by attribution theorists presents a somewhat different but related perspective on the distinction between motives and expectancies that we have presented in this chapter. Attribution theory has reinterpreted the experimental findings on achievement motivation to stress the cognitive aspects of motivation. Specifically, attribution theory suggests that motivational differences imply different conceptions of causation of behavioral outcomes, and that these different conceptions are critical mediators between antecedent stimulus-organism transactions and ensuing achievement behavior. For example, they postulate that people with high achievement motives get heightened reward and pride in accomplishment because they more often attribute success to internal factors—their own effort and ability. In their view the achievement motives are primarily a cognitive rather than affective disposition. While this approach of the attribution theorists is different from ours, which has stressed the greater explanatory power of expectancies over motives, both approaches are similar in their view that cognitions are the critical aspects of motivation.

CHART B. **Summary of Significant Relationships between Achievement Motivation and the Aspirations of Men and Women**

Components of Achievement Motivation	Educational and Occupational Aspirations				
	Planning to Go to Graduate or Professional School	Prestige of the Occupational Choice	Ability Demands of the Occupational Choice	Nontraditionality of the Occupational Choice	Realism of the Occupational Choice[b]
Values					
Control ideology	No relationships except in 1970 and then only among students with low personal control where Internals *lower*	No relationships except for men with low personal control where Internals *lower*	No relationships except for men with low personal control where Internals *lower*	No relationships except for men with low personal control where Internals *lower*	Realistic more External than either Over-or-Under aspirants
Positive achievement motives:[a]					
Achievement orientation	Women only	Both sexes	Both sexes	No Relationships	No Relationships
Success orientation	No relationships	No Relationships	No Relationships	Men only	No Relationships

Negative achievement motives:[a]

Fear of failure	Men only	Men only	Both sexes	Both sexes	Men only	Underaspirants more fearful
Desire for security	Men only	Men only	Men only	Men only	No Relationships	No Relationships

Competency-based expectancies:

Sense of personal control	Both sexes	Both sexes	Both sexes	Both sexes	Men only	Realistic higher
Academic self-confidence	Both sexes	Both sexes	Both sexes	Both sexes	Both sexes	Realistic higher

[a]These motive measures were collected only in 1964.
[b]Realism of occupational choice was analyzed only in 1964 and only for men with above median test scores.

CHART C. Summary of Significant Relationships Between Achievement Motivation and the Performance of Men and Women

Components of Achievement Motivation	Performance Measures[b]		
	Correct Performance on the Sixth Trial of Anagrams	Total Number of Errors on Six Anagrams Trials	Cumulative Grade Point Average
Values:			
Control ideology	No relationships except in low personal control group where Internals *poorer performance*	No relationships except in low personal control group where Internals *more errors*	No relationships except in low personal control group where Internals *lower*
Positive achievement motives[a]:			
Achievement orientation	No relationships	No relationships	Women only
Success orientation	No relationships	No relationships	No relationships
Negative achievement motives[a]:			
Fear of failure	Men only	Men only	Men only
Desire for security	No relationships	No relationships	No relationships
Competency-based expectancies:			
Sense of personal control	Men only	Women only	Both sexes
Academic self-confidence	Both sexes	Both sexes	Both sexes

[a]These motives measures were collected only in 1964.
[b]Performance measures were collected only in 1964.

had hoped would be true about college that had not turned out that way (40 percent compared to 19 percent); and fewer dropouts summed up their whole freshman year experience as a success (39 percent compared to 66 percent).

The dropouts were accurate in these appraisals. They had not performed as well despite having entered college with only slightly (nonsignificantly) lower test scores than the freshman men who did not leave after the first year. Twenty-nine percent of the dropouts, compared to only 13 percent of the other freshman men, completed the first year with cumulative grades in the bottom fifth of the class. Conversely, only 6 percent of those who left, compared to 34 percent of those who returned the next year, had achieved grades in the upper fifth of the class. What was it about their motivational makeup that helped explain these subjective feelings of failure as well as their objectively poorer performance that must have led, at least partially, to the decision to leave school? Mostly it was the sense of personal control, academic self-confidence, and anxiety about failure that mattered. Two patterns of problems emerged, one among men who had entered this college with above median test scores, the other among those with lower entrance scores.

The results for men who scored below the median on entrance achievement tests showed that anxiety was greater and confidence was lower among the men who *stayed* in college than among those who dropped out (Appendix Table 4.5). Staying in college when others with comparable entrance scores dropped out did not stem from unusual, if unrealistic, confidence about themselves. Instead, their test anxiety scores at time of entrance had been significantly higher, and both their personal control and academic self-confidence scores significantly lower than those of the dropouts. Indeed, the men who subsequently stayed in college despite lower performance scores showed the least self-confidence and greatest anxiety of any group of male entrants. While their fears and anxieties were perhaps not unwarranted, so long as they remained in college they needed help either to make the college experience less anxious or to find other personal goals and the routes by which to achieve them. We are not suggesting that anxiety and depressed confidence kept them in college. But whatever held them there, it brought the cost of unusual anxiety and confidence problems. The dropouts, by contrast, handled their records of poorer performance and unhappy experiences with college by leaving. Not having entered college the previous fall as anxious or unconfident may have made their leaving easier.

The pattern among men whose entrance test scores had been higher was the exact opposite and altogether more consonant with achievement motivation theory. It was the dropouts who entered college with greater anxiety about failure (Appendix Table 4.5). They also expressed less personal efficacy and lower self-confidence about their academic potential than did their counterparts with comparably high test scores who stayed in school. This picture of the dropout as highly anxious and questioning of his ability and confidence conforms to the traditional experimental findings on the relationship between achievement motivation and persistence of behavior, particularly as they have been reinterpreted in recent attribution theory. The experimental literature has clearly documented that people low in resultant motivation (i.e., people whose anxiety and motivation to avoid failure are higher than their positive achievement motivation) persist less in experimental tasks. Attribution theorists have shown that such people are also those who attribute their failure to lack of ability. Furthermore, they suggest that it is these attributions that help explain their lower persistence. Since lack of ability is something they cannot do anything about, they get discouraged in the face of failure and give up instead of persisting at the task. Extrapolating from these results and interpretations, we suggest that our own example of low persistence—dropping out of college—reflects a syndrome that combines self-doubts of one's ability with a belief that ability is critical in the determination of success and failure. This combination leads both to low competency-based expectancies and high anxiety and motivation to avoid failure.

While theoretically expected, this pattern should be amenable to counseling help. After all, the problems of the dropouts in this group were clearly psychological: they should not have been so anxious, so lacking in self-confidence, or performing so badly. Some of them might not have dropped out had their first year countered their expectations or had they been helped to gain a more realistic and healthy picture of their academic potential. In a sense counseling services or behavioral therapy were peculiarly appropriate for this group. They needed ways of resolving or controlling their anxieties so as to handle failure without attributing it to lack of ability and to respond to success by attributing it to their own strengths and personal control, thereby minimizing arousal of further anxiety and raising both academic self-confidence and performance. While proponents of different psychotherapeutic strategies would not agree on how to do this, most would be optimistic of the outcome with this group of men.

The College Environment: Conditioning the Role of Motives and Expectancies

Some results on the influence of the college environment help also in clarifying the function of motives and expectancies. In Chapter 6 we take up the impact of the college on performance and motivation in greater depth. At this point we note only that certain college environments heightened the significance of motives and values. This was clearly true at one college. We carried out separate multivariate analyses of the motive and expectancy determinants of occupational aspirations for each of the 10 colleges. While most showed the pattern we have already described—the relatively greater significance of expectancies—this was not true at one college. There, expectancies were somewhat less important; motives, particularly avoidance motives, assumed much greater significance. Fear of failure and desire for security turned out to be the best predictors of the men's job aspirations at that college (Appendix Table 4.6).

When we discussed with students and faculty at this college how this pattern of results departed from the general findings of the study, they commented on environmental pressures that seemed relevant to the increased significance of achievement motives there. This college is located in a large city where the Black population has strong cultural traditions in which social status is ascribed largely by ancestry and family position. This, added to the fact that many more daughters than sons of high status families stay home to attend this college, created special pressures on nonresident men students. Through their involvement with the commuting women students, the nonresident men became absorbed in the community's social life, sometimes to the exclusion of much activity on campus. The result could be early marriage and settling down in the local social system. One professor, reflecting on these influences, mused that every year the college lost more talented men to the local social structure than they managed to send on to graduate school. "Women who grew up here are not so willing to sacrifice to go along to graduate school, either to study themselves or support their husbands, because there is a very attractive world right here. And mama pushes all the while for them to be sensible. So they are. The man compromises, settles for the security and status his wife's family provides instead of for the kind of status that comes from personal achievement. That is not a bad decision if they do stay here since family connections matter more than what you do. Many an outsider who comes to an important job here never quite makes it socially. So you have to be strong and value achievement very much if you don't get caught up here." Despite the spider and the fly quality of these remarks, the point he made was reiterated by many others. In this particular environment the motivational strengths needed to hold onto higher levels of occupational achievement depended on an unusual commitment to the values of status-by-achievement rather than to the values of status-by-ascription, and on limiting one's concerns about future insecurity or failure. While expectancies also influenced the men's aspirations, they mattered less here than at colleges where these social pressures did not prevail; expectancies were clearly less important than were the strengths to resist the social pressures.

In pointing out the unique pattern in this one college, we do not mean to belittle the decision to live and work in this community or the reasons underlying the decision. From a traditional mobility and achievement viewpoint such a decision may reflect waste of talent, at least if local opportunities to express the talent are limited; even so, such students may have been making choices for less pressured and more broadly fulfilled lives. We cite the results of this one college as a way of emphasizing that the dynamics of motivation depend heavily on environmental pressures and supports. We will see this again in three colleges with still different motivational climates in the next chapter. Here we simply want to mute conclusions that might otherwise appear too simplistic and "neat." While it was true that expectancies and feelings of competency generally assumed greater significance than most measures we had of achievement values and motives, that was not always the case.

SYSTEM BLAME: A SPECIAL KIND OF EXTERNALITY

Usual conceptions of achievement are limited in two critical ways for understanding the achievement of groups who face either class or race discrimination. The traditional meaning of achievement, limited as it is to *individual* accomplishment or sense of excellence, applies best to the attempts to cope with discrimination through traditional modes of personal success and mobility. By being better prepared than the best prepared white competitor, many a Black youth has set out to prove it and "make it on the white man's terms." That many have, at great social odds, stresses the import of unusual personal motivational strength. But there are also those who define their personal goals in terms of the collective progress of the group, whose success is reflected in *collective achievement* rather than in individual mobility. What motivational strengths are needed to see one's fate inextricably bound with the fate of the group and to judge success by having some part in achieving the freedom of others? Achievement-motivation theory helps little in explaining commitments to collective achievement. The determinants of collective commitments and group action will be the focus of the second half of the book.

The second limitation of the traditional achievement literature is apparent even when our concern is with individual achievement. The theory of achievement motivation is limited by assuming a benign environment in which success in life follows from individual competence and achievement. It assumes equal opportunities and the application of universal standards, both of which race discrimination counteracts. Although the theory's concept of expectancy can tie personal motivation to objective social realities, that is rarely done. Not enough consideration has been given to the implications of life situations that cause serious limitations to personal mobility and individual achievement. Even the attribution theorists who feel that people's views about the causes of success and failure figure prominently in their motivation generally pay little attention to socially structured determinants of success. They study people's perceptions of the difficulty of the task or the role of fate, not their perceptions of labor market conditions or discrimination. While the failure to build social structural and economic considerations explicitly into the theory is no more characteristic of the achievement literature than of other psychological theory, it does have serious consequences, particularly when applied to socially oppressed groups.

We see this clearly in the work on internal and external control where the internal orientation has usually been interpreted as realistic and healthy, and the external orientation—typically meaning a primitive belief in fate or chance—as unrealistic and damaging to effective behavior. In fact, internal control has often been equated with "fate control" in the recent popularization of Rotter's original concept. If the world were benign and opportunities were truly equal, this depiction of external control might be justified, as it probably is when applied to people in favored, advantaged social positions. But the poor, the discriminated minorities, and women in this society face many external obstacles that have nothing to do with fate, indeed, that operate in the opposite way—systematically and predictably. Furthermore, while it may be unhealthy for Black youngsters to believe in chance or fate, their understanding of how the social system conditions individual success and failure can be a strong motivational asset. Since race discrimination does exist, awareness of it attests to a sense of reality. Realistic assessment of the impact of social constraints can not only help people cope with these constraints, but it can protect them from the damage to personal identity that comes from blaming members of their own group for the inequities they face. People subordinated in a social system who react with invidious self-depreciation rather than against the system have already accepted a rationale for the existing system that serves to perpetuate their subordinate position.[27] Not to include some of these positive implications of

27. F. Fanon, *Black Skin, White Masks* (New York: Grove Press, 1967) and R. K. Merton, *Social Theory and Social Structure* (New York: Free Press, 1964).

an external orientation, when it results from assessing the influence of systematic social constraints rather than the exigencies of an unpredictable fate, severely limits the broader applicability of the internal-external control concept.

Accordingly, we emphasized this distinction in the meaning of external control by adding to the typical internal and external control items a set of questions that asked students to explain the status of Blacks in American society. Did they follow an internal explanation by blaming the social position of Blacks on their personal inadequacies, or did they show themselves to be more externally oriented, and at the same time sociologically more sophisticated, by stressing the importance of racial and social discrimination?

While we expected that this measure of individual versus system blame would figure prominently in the students' growing Black consciousness and pride (and we shall see in Chapter 8 that it did), we anticipated that it would also be relevant for some of the more traditional, individual expressions of achievement. The findings suggest that system blame did have such relevance and it did so in ways that supported our assumption that attributing the responsibility for racial inequities to inadequacies of the social system instead of to its victims indicates a healthy realism and social sophistication.

While blame of the social system was not related to traditional measures of job aspiration—to the job's prestige level or its ability demands—it was related to innovative pioneering job choices. Men who more often blamed the system for race inequities also more often aspired to jobs that heretofore were closed to Blacks. (Appendix Table 4.7A). This was true both in 1964 and in 1970. Their greater focus on systematic social forces implied a greater awareness of opportunities as well as constraints. After all, new job areas do not open by chance; these more socially attuned students knew it. We will see in later chapters that the system blamers were also much more committed to collective action and group achievements.

This reality interpretation of the meaning of system blame was further buttressed by results on the realism of job choices. Men who chose occupations that realistically challenged their talents were especially likely to blame social obstacles rather than the personal deficiencies of Black people for race inequities. In contrast, blame of the individual instead of the system was associated with patterns of underaspiration (Appendix Table 4.3). Blaming the system was also associated with more effective performance, at least among those students who felt a strong sense of personal efficacy themselves (Appendix Tables 4.7 A and B). Students who felt that they could control what happened in their own lives but focused on discrimination in accounting for race differentials in income and job status achieved higher grades in college than students who, equally efficacious, adhered to individualistic theories of causality in explaining the status of Blacks in our society. They also made fewer errors and completed more anagrams correctly on the achievement task we administered.

Does this mean that system blame was always healthy, always indicative of effectiveness? As critical as we are of the general tendency to view internality as consistently positive—what we feel has become the myth of the internal hero—there is also no point in idealizing system blame. It can be used stereotypically and therefore inappropriately as a ready explanation for all situations that involve race and it can be used to defend against personal failures. This was suggested by other findings. For example, system blame had opposite performance implications for students with high and low personal control. In contrast to the positive meaning it held for students who felt personally efficacious, men and women with low personal control who blamed the system for race inequities achieved lower grades as well as made more errors and generally performed less well on the anagrams task (Appendix Tables 4.7 A and B). Blaming the system may well have served defensive functions for these students who felt little sense of power over their own lives. Possible misinterpretations or ideological excesses should not blind us, however, to the more consistent and persuasive data about the positive motivational implications that can follow from a healthy focus on system obstacles.

The credibility of these results on system blame and the response to them depend on one's own life experiences and political perspectives. They are readily accepted, indeed viewed as so obvious as to warrant little comment, by people whose own Black perspective calls for rejecting victim-deficit theories in social science. But this is not the only response. Many faculty at the participating colleges shared thoughtful reservations about the motivational meaning of blaming the system. Some few simply did not feel that discrimination matters since they denied that it had affected their own lives. There was also considerable feeling, admittedly less in 1970 than when we began the research, that race should not matter, that the professor's role is to stress the human, not racial, aspect of the student's future. Focusing on ideals of a common humanity, some faculty felt there was altogether too much, not too little, race consciousness among students. Others questioned whether they should deal with what came to be viewed as Black studies material unless they taught in the social sciences where, if anywhere, they argued such issues belonged. Others, even in the hard sciences, felt that the wider ramifications of social conditioning and

TABLE 1. Comparison of Personal Control Responses 1964, 1968, 1970

	1964[a]		1968[b]		1970[c]	
	Men	Women	Men	Women	Men	Women
Individual Items:						
1. a. I have often found that what is going to happen will happen. (External)	40%	49%	24%	42%	36%	47%
b. Trusting to fate has never turned out as well for me as making a decision to take a definite course of action. (Internal)	60%	51%	76%	58%	64%	53%
	100%	100%	100%	100%	100%	100%
2. a. What happens to me is my own doing. (Internal)	62%	55%	58%	53%	52%	48%
b. Sometimes I feel that I don't have enough control over the direction my life is taking. (External)	38%	45%	42%	47%	48%	52%
	100%	100%	100%	100%	100%	100%
3. a. When I make plans, I am almost certain that I can make them work. (Internal)	48%	37%	64%	48%	52%	36%
b. It is not always wise to plan too far ahead because many things turn out to be a matter of good or bad fortune anyhow. (External)	52%	63%	36%	52%	48%	64%
	100%	100%	100%	100%	100%	100%
4. a. In my case, getting what I want has little or nothing to do with luck. (Internal)	77%	83%	74%	76%	78%	84%
b. Many times we might just as well decide what to do by flipping a coin. (External)	23%	17%	26%	24%	22%	16%
	100%	100%	100%	100%	100%	100%

5. a. Many times I feel that I have little influence over the things that happen to me. (External)
    b. It is impossible for me to believe that chance or luck play an important role in my life. (Internal)

47%	49%	40%	52%	52%	57%
53%	51%	60%	48%	48%	43%
100%	100%	100%	100%	100%	100%

Index Based on These Five Items:

All five internal alternatives chosen	17%	13%	23%	18%	15%	8%
Four out of five internal chosen	23%	19%	29%	16%	21%	18%
Three out of five internal	25%	30%	20%	21%	26%	25%
Three out of five external	21%	22%	16%	26%	24%	28%
Four out of five external	11%	14%	8%	13%	10%	17%
All five external alternatives chosen	3%	2%	4%	6%	4%	4%
	100%	100%	100%	100%	100%	100%

[a]These percents are based on the 2141 students (1141 men and 1000 women) attending the six colleges in 1964 that participated in both the 1964 and 1970 cross-sectional studies.

[b]These percents are based on the 239 seniors (103 men and 136 women) who participated in the longitudinal followup at College H.

[c]These percents are based on the 1127 students (589 men and 538 women) attending the six colleges that participated in the cross-sectional study in 1970.

discrimination were integral to their teaching and relationships with students. While not always reflecting the commitments that the more political students might have hoped for, such faculty believed it was their job to focus on the social and economic conditions in ways that would then enhance students' capacities to manipulate the environment to their advantage and to change it for the sake of others.

The question of how this is accomplished remains. Many professors were worried that discussing discrimination would create hopelessness rather than effectiveness in students. They recalled incidents, either in their own lives or in the lives of students they had known, in which teachers and other well-meaning adults treated discrimination as if it were an impossible barrier to overcome and advised students to go into fields much beneath their capabilities. Knowing that this kind of counseling has been offered all too often, they tried to counter it with the opposite emphases. As one professor put it: "I have always considered it my job to inspire students to strive for their goals, to tell them and to show them by models here at the college that discrimination does not stand in the way of a person with high ideals. I haven't felt I could do much about discrimination but I could give them a good education, inspire them to work hard and never to give up their goals because they are Black."

While it is easy to discard these fears as naive or as defensive avoidance of Blackness, as some critics do, real issues are at stake. If not, students would not have felt the conflicts they did. Cynicism, escape, or commitment to revolution—in the face of racism in America—are all viable alternatives to trying to integrate personal goals with social reform. We need not deny the difficulties of increasing students' awareness of the way things are while simultaneously enhancing their commitments to do something about it.

STABILITY OF MOTIVATION

The decade of the sixties brought many changes to the historically Black colleges. For most of this period there was a feeling of growing optimism on the campuses. Through the early civil rights movement and the Civil Rights Act of 1964 there was some alleviation of discrimination's assaults on dignity that had turned most Black campuses into closed, protected enclaves in a hostile environment. Black students and faculty in most parts of the South began coming and going more freely. Accordingly, college rules also were relaxed, although probably as much in response to the growing student demands for institutional change at mid-decade as to the earlier civil rights activism. Job recruiters came in numbers unheard of before the sixties. Financial hope came through the renewed interest of private foundations and federal assistance to developing institutions. Most colleges experienced enrollment expansion, largely attributed to greater student financial assistance. Despite the loss of some prospective students to previously segregated, predominantly white southern colleges and, less often, to northern institutions, a feeling of movement, excitement, and well-being characterized most campuses.

The cause for optimism had dimmed somewhat by 1970 as the general economic situation worsened and brought bleak consequences for support of higher education and job opportunities for graduates. But these economic effects would have their greatest impact on the students that followed the class of 1970. We did not expect the students studied in 1970 to feel that all the social advances for Black colleges had been dissipated, and we had reason to believe that the aspects of student motivation most subject to environmental influence—their aspirations and expectancies in particular—might show an increase beyond their 1964 levels. They did not: the students' job and graduate school aspirations remained almost exactly as they had been in 1964 (Chapter 3, Tables 2 and 5). This was true at every one of the six colleges that participated both in the original and followup study. The expectancy picture likewise showed great stability. Students in 1970 expressed almost the same level of certainty about achieving their goals as had the students in 1964 (Chapter 3, Table 2). There were no shifts in the competency aspects of expectancy either: students were no more and no less self-confident about their abilities. Table 1 also shows that their sense of personal control was no different in 1964 and 1970.

Why should student motivation remain so stable during what has been described as a period of rising expectations? We suspect it is just too simplistic to assume that the social and political climate of the sixties would produce aspirational or motivational shifts in the college population as a whole. Take the issue of personal efficacy. Some writers speculated earlier that the sense of efficacy of Black students would rise as they saw they could influence the world around them through social protest. This seems much too general to us. Feelings of efficacy probably waxed and waned as events supported or thwarted the students' efforts to bring about change. With hindsight most people would agree that the results of the decade of protest were not so clearly successful as to have led a whole generation of students to change their concepts of their power to control either social events or the outcomes of their own lives. By 1970 they were much more ready to engage in social protest than students had been 10 years earlier. That is not to say they expected their commitment to collective action to create immediate or broad changes or that their own feelings of personal confidence or efficacy had changed greatly.

chapter 5

Precollege Family Background and Students' Aspirations, Motivation, and Performance

The role that social background plays in educational performance and attainment stimulates enormous controversy, largely focused on the conflict between egalitarianism and meritocracy. Take the question of who goes to college. One of the best studies of what happens to students after high school—a longitudinal study of approximately 9000 randomly selected Wisconsin high school students who were successfully followed for seven years after graduation[1]—shows enormous differences in the educational opportunities of the various socioeconomic groups. Sewell concludes from that study that differences are great regardless of what socioeconomic indices are used and regardless of how restrictedly or broadly opportunity for higher education is defined—whether it is taken to mean college entry, college graduation, professional or graduate study, or simply the continuation in any kind of formal education beyond high school.[2] The sample was divided into socioeconomic status (SES) quartiles. The students in the upper quarter were found to have almost two and one-half times as great a chance as students in the bottom quarter of continuing in some kind of posthigh school education. The upper SES students had an almost 4 to 1 advantage in access to college, a 6 to 1 advantage in college graduation, and a 9 to 1 advantage in graduate or professional education. We cannot be sure that the same socioeconomic differentials in educational opportunity prevail for Black youngsters since data from longitudinal studies with large numbers of Black high school students are not available. Generally, relationships between family socioeconomic characteristics and the offspring's status attainments are much

1. W. H. Sewell and V. P. Shah, "Socioeconomic Status, Intelligence, and the Attainment of Higher Education," *Sociology of Education 40* (1967), pp.1-23.
2. William H. Sewell, "Inequality of Opportunity for Higher Education," *American Sociological Review 36* (October, 1971), pp. 793-809.

weaker among Black than among white Americans.[3] The structure of opportunities and the facts of discrimination make it less possible for the Black family to pass on to the next generation the advantages that have accrued to substantial status achievement. There is one exception to this: the intergenerational correlation of the second generation's educational attainment with the head of the family's education is very nearly as large in the Black population as in the white.[4] Thus, social background may influence educational opportunity and attainment almost as much for Black as for white youth.

Despite these facts, we are woefully ignorant about the way social background affects young people. That it does is incontestable: how and why it does is altogether more controversial. The people who believe that mobility is guaranteed by an open, meritocratic system generally admit that social background influences college entrance but legitimately so through the well-known relationship between family background and performance on standardized tests. (Indeed, the best data available show that performance on standard tests is a powerful determinant of both who goes to college[5] and how elite a college it is,[6] which also carries implications for annual and lifetime earnings.[7])

3. Many writers have noted that the regression slopes of family background predictors to respondent's status are lower among the Black than among the white population. Duncan makes the point clearly. Blacks who do have favorable social origins cannot, as readily as whites, convert this advantage into higher occupational status and wages. The major exception is that Black families with better than average education levels do, in general, succeed in "passing on" a comparable level of educational attainment to their children. Again, however, Black children are less able than white children to make their educational attainment pay off for occupational achievement and commensurate monetary returns to education. Duncan attributes a large share of this problem to current discrimination. Path analysis results for explaining the Black-white income differential, for example, estimated that of the total $3790 difference, $830 represented occupational discrimination and $1430 income discrimination. Only $520 was estimated as the effect of less education among Blacks. Otis Dudley Duncan, "Inheritance of Poverty or Inheritance of Race?" in Daniel P. Moynihan, Editor, On Understanding Poverty (New York: Basic Books, 1968), pp. 85-110.

4. Ibid., p. 96.

5. Sewell and Shah, "Socioeconomic Status."

6. J. Karabel and A. W. Astin, "Social Class, Academic Ability, and College 'Quality,' " unpublished manuscript.

7. Studies that show the income advantage to a college education typically pertain to white students. Among them are Gary S. Becker, Human Capital (New York: Columbia University Press, 1946); Mary Jean Bowman, "Economics of Education" in Orwig, Editor, Financing Higher Educational Alternatives for The Federal Government (Iowa City: American College Testing Program, 1971); J. T. Innes, P. B. Jacobson, and R. J. Pellegrin, The Economic Returns to Higher Education: A Survey of Findings (Eugene: The Center for Advanced Study of Educational Administration,

According to this point of view, opportunity for education would be equally available to young people from all social backgrounds providing they were equally qualified and test scores are taken as reasonably valid indicators of qualification. Moreover, our differentiated system of higher education, ranging from the most elite four-year institutions to two-year community and private colleges (some with extraordinarily low resources) assures everyone of opportunity for some form of higher education. The correlation between social background and where the child ends up in this differentiated system of education is said not to imply social or racial discrimination but, instead, the failure of the child to compete favorably on performance measures which is then generally attributed to family influences. According to the "social inheritance" argument, young people from less privileged economic backgrounds or from racial or ethnic communities perform less well in school and on standardized tests and complete fewer years of schooling because their parents either do not place as great a value on these forms of achievement or, if they do, are less able to socialize their children to achieve these ends effectively.

Other people are less impressed with the "social inheritance" argument and look to current inequities between lower and upper-status youth. They note that access to education, especially to the highest quality education, and to employment opportunities is by no means equal across socioeconomic groups. They admit that some of the socioeconomic effect on educational attainment is mediated by test-score performance. Sewell estimates, for example, that of the 18 percent of the total variance in posthigh school education explained by socioeconomic background, some 20 to 30 percent is mediated by the child's test scores.[8] Still, even controlling for the effect of performance, young people from less privileged backgrounds face much lower probabilities of success because of the way opportunities are distributed by class and by race. For example, considering only the young

University of Oregon, 1965); J. N. Morgan and M. H. David, "Education and Income," *Quarterly Journal of Economics* (August, 1963), pp. 423-437; Theodore W. Schultz, *The Economic Value of Education* (New York: Columbia University Press, 1963); and B. A. Weisbrod and P. Karpoff, "Monetary Returns to College Education, Student Ability, and College Quality," *Review of Economics and Statistics* (November, 1968), pp. 491-497. There is no question but that a college degree does not pay off with a comparable increase in earnings for Black graduates. This is clearly demonstrated by P. M. Siegel, "On the Cost of Being a Negro," *Sociological Inquiry XXXV*, (April, 1965) and O. D. Duncan, "Inheritance of Poverty." Let us be clear, however, that Black college graduates do earn more than nongraduate Blacks; they simply do not earn as much more as the same educational edge provides whites.

8. William H. Sewell, "Inequality of Opportunity," pp. 798-799.

people in the top 3 percent of the Scholastic Aptitude Test performance distribution, high SES students are about five times as likely to attend an elite college.[9]

These two interpretations of why young people from different social backgrounds experience such different educational paths and of why the stratification system remains so stable despite our apparent commitment to equality of opportunity represent different, highly controversial theories in social science. The differences in their assumptions bear heavily on educational policies, especially on efforts to broaden the class and racial-ethnic spectrum from which students are recruited to four-year institutions of higher education.[10] Since a third of the students in our sample grew up in homes with incomes below the poverty line and 64 percent in homes below the Bureau of Labor Standards minimum standard of living, the data we present about the performance, aspirations, and motivation of these low-income students apply directly to this controversy about the role of social background in educational attainment. They especially pertain to the issue of increasing the enrollment of Black youngsters into higher education since any admission expansion in the Black population would necessarily involve recruiting students from similarly low income backgrounds.

This chapter presents data concerning six sets of questions that relate to this controversy.

1. What were the demographic and family backgrounds of the students attending these 10 historically Black colleges? Did their demographic and family characteristics match the backgrounds of students enrolled in other historically Black colleges reasonably well? Did their backgrounds differ greatly from the national population of

9. J. Karabel and A. W. Astin, "Social Class, Academic Ability and College 'Quality,'" p. 18.

10. Many people assume that the booming college enrollments of the sixties must have resulted in a wider range of backgrounds represented in the nation's colleges and universities. Sewell, ("Inequality of Opportunity,") comments that this is in part true but estimates that 34 percent of the increased college experience in the decade was because of the growth in the size of the age cohort, another 30 percent because of the increased rate of high school graduation and 36 percent because of the increase in the rate of college entry. While it is difficult to establish how much of this increase in the rate of college entry was provided by high school graduates from lower SES groups, Sewell estimates that the proportion of students of manual and service origins enrolled in college increased by 7 percent during the decade, while the proportion of white-collar students increased by less than 2 percent. While this is a notable increase, it does not mean that most of the expansion in enrollment resulted from increased opportunity for categories of students previously out of the higher education circuit.

college students? Did their families' socioeconomic characteristics approximate the average of the national, or at least the southern, non-white population?

2. How did the students' precollege backgrounds influence their performance, aspirations, and motivation? The results on demographic relationships are organized according to our model of motivation. We explore first whether demographic and family background influenced performance and aspirations. Did students from low income families perform more poorly in college? Did they aspire to less education and to lower occupational goals? Next we examine how the precollege environment related to the components of motivation that comprise the dynamics of performance and aspirations. Did the students from low income families enter college with different achievement motives: did they bring greater fear of failure, less need for achievement, less propensity for hard work? Did their goals for college reflect different values from those held by students from more comfortable families? Did they differ primarily in their expectancies of success—which, as seen in Chapter 4, were unusually important in explaining why some students aspired for more education and for more challenging and nontraditional jobs and why some students achieved higher grades and performed better on achievement tasks?

3. What aspects of the students' precollege backgrounds proved most important in explaining these aspects of motivation and resultant performance and aspirations? Did environmental resources and opportunities (as represented by family income and rural-urban residency) carry heavier weight than social class socialization patterns (as represented by parents' education and family structure variables)? Distinguishing the opportunity aspects of the students' precollege environments from home characteristics that imply family socialization patterns should help clarify the way social background impinges on educational attainment. If family structure or the parents' own educational attainments pressed most heavily on the students' aspirations and performance, especially by influencing achievement motives and values, the results would support the social inheritance interpretation of social impact. If family income and rural-urban residency were more influential in explaining aspirations and performance, especially through the students' expectancies of success that presumably reflect their reality situations, the results would buttress instead an opportunity analysis of social impact.

4. Was the impact of precollege environment consistent for all dimensions of occupational aspiration? Here we examine the special implications of choosing a job in sectors of the labor market not previously available for high achievement among college-educated Blacks.

5. What role did family structure play in motivation and aspirations? Since our data show essentially no impact of family structure, they add to the body of data that challenge the idea that growing up in a father-absent family necessarily depresses school achievement and motivation.

6. To what extent did these Black colleges show the usual relationships between college status and student background status? Did the students from low income families end up in a somewhat different circuit of colleges, just as national data show is true in higher education generally?

DEMOGRAPHIC AND FAMILY CHARACTERISTICS OF THE 1964 AND 1970 STUDENT SAMPLES

Two background variables concern the parents' education. The students were asked to check, among alternatives ranging from less than sixth grade up to graduate work beyond the master's degree, the extent of their parents' education. They were also asked to describe any other education or training each parent had obtained that was not covered in the alternatives listed. This additional information was used to clarify responses to the structured alternatives. Six levels of education were used for *mother's education* and *father's education*: eighth grade or less, some high school, completion of high school, some college, college degree, and at least some postbaccalaureate work. Students were also asked about each parent's *occupational* status and to describe the kind of work and job setting for each parent who was employed. These questions were coded using major census categories. We also asked students to check a monthly income figure that they believed represented the total *family income*. If both parents were working, this total figure was to represent the income contributed by both. Four income levels were used in the analyses reported in this chapter: families earning less than $3600; those earning between $3600 and $5999; those earning between $6000 and $9999; and those earning above $10,000. Since we were concerned about the validity of using student reports of family income, we also used 1960 census materials to estimate family income for each student according to what we knew about where the family lived, the parents' occupations, and their work history during the year preceding the study. As expected, the census-based estimate was somewhat more conservative than the student estimates of family income. But this difference primarily reflected a constant tendency on the part of all students to report slightly higher incomes than the census estimate would have suggested. The two were highly correlated and each related in a similar way to other demographic data such as parents' education and the number of people contributing to family income. Either income estimate resulted in the same students being grouped in ordered income categories, although the median income in each of the ordinal groups was consistently higher using the student rather than the census estimates. *Rural-urban residency* referred to the place where the student had lived during the school years. Seven categories were coded: farm; village of 2499 or less; town of 2500 to 9999; small city of 10,000 to 49,999; medium city of 50,000 to 199,999; metropolitan city of 200,000 or over; and suburb of a metropolitan city close to and almost part of the city. *Family structure* characteristics referred to the persons with whom the student had lived during the majority of the school years. Three types of families were included: two-parent nuclear families, mother-only headed families, and multiple adult, extended families.

Comparisons with national and southern nonwhite data show that students attending these 10 colleges grew up in families with somewhat atypical socioeconomic characteristics. In terms of occupational distribution, the 1964 data showed that 25 percent of the students' fathers were employed in white collar jobs, as against 15 percent of all nonwhite men and 10 percent of southern nonwhite men. The employed mothers in this student population likewise stood out from other nonwhite employed women: 39 percent of the students' mothers held white collar jobs but only 24 percent of all employed nonwhite women, and 19 percent of all southern nonwhite working women, did so. The fathers and mothers of this student population had also acquired more education: 43 percent of the students' fathers had completed high school compared to 37 percent of all nonwhite men and 19 percent of all southern nonwhite men. Similarly 53 percent of the students' mothers held high school diplomas compared to 28 percent of all nonwhite women and 20 percent of southern nonwhite women. The $5200 median family income reported by the students was also higher than either the $2888 median for southern nonwhite families or the $3724 median for nonwhite families in the country at large in 1964. The students' family structures, by contrast, resembled very closely figures for nonwhite families in the south. Three-quarters of the students in our 1964 sample grew up in families in which both parents were present. Census data from 1965 showed that 78 percent of all nonwhite families in the south were two-parent families.[11] (See Tables 1 and 2.)

While atypical of Black families in the nation at large and even from the South where 90 percent of our sample grew up, the backgrounds

11. *Population Characteristics, Negro Population: March 1965,* Series P-20, N. 155, U.S. Department of Commerce, Bureau of the Census, September, 1966, p. 23.

TABLE 1. Comparisons of the Occupations of the Employed Parents in the 1964[a] Sample with Those of all Employed Nonwhite Males and Females in the National Population in the South, 1965[b]

	Employed Fathers in This Population	All Employed Nonwhite Males	Employed Nonwhite Males in the South	Employed Mothers in This Population	All Employed Nonwhite Females	Employed Nonwhite Females in the South
Professional, technical, and kindred workers	12%	5%	4%	29%	9%	11%
Managers, officials, and proprietors	8	3	2	3	2	1
Clerical, sales, and kindred workers	5	7	4	7	13	7
Craftsmen and foremen	15	11	8	3	1	1
Operatives and kindred workers	21	28	26	7	15	8
Laborers (except farm)	14	22	27	2	1	1
Service workers and military	13	16	15	47	57	68
Farmers: managers, owners, and laborers	12	8	14	2	2	3
	100%	100%	100%	100%	100%	100%

[a]These percents are based on the 3639 students attending the 10 colleges that participated in the 1964 cross-sectional study.
[b]Source for the national and southern occupational figures for nonwhites: Population Characteristics, Negro Population: March 1965, Series P-20, No. 155, U. S. Department of Commerce, Bureau of the Census, September, 1966, p. 27.

TABLE 2. Comparison of the Educational Attainments and Family Incomes of the Parents of the 1964[a] Sample with that of all Nonwhite Males and Females (25 Years and Older) and Nonwhites in the South, 1965[b]

Amount of Education	Fathers in This Population	All Nonwhite Males	Nonwhite Males in the South	Mothers in This Population	All Nonwhite Females	Nonwhite Females in the South
Grade school or less	36%	53%	62%	23%	48%	60%
Some high school	21	20	19	24	24	20
High school graduation	21	17	12	25	19	12
Some college	7	5	3	8	5	3
College degree or more	15	5	4	20	4	5
	100%	100%	100%	100%	100%	100%

[a]These percents are based on the 3639 students attending the 10 colleges that participated in the 1964 cross-sectional study.

[b]Source for the national and southern education figures for nonwhites: Population Characteristics, Negro Population: March 1965, Series P-20, No. 145, December, 1965, p. 3.

Family Income

Median family income of this population: $5200 (according to student estimates)

$3000 (according to our census-based estimate)

Median income of all nonwhite families in the United States in 1964: $3724

Median income of all nonwhite families in the south in 1964: $2888

Source for national and southern nonwhite figures: Population Characteristics, Negro Population: March 1965, Series P-20, No. 145, U. S. Department of Commerce, Bureau of the Census, December 1965, p. 4.

TABLE 3. Demographic Characteristics of the 1964 and 1974 Cross-Sectional Samples of Entering Freshmen, Compared to Students Entering a National Sample of Universities, a Sub-sample of Southern Universities and a Sub-sample of Predominantly Black Universities and Colleges

| | Our Sample of Black Universities and Colleges | | | | National Sample of Universities | | Sub-sample of Predominantly: | | | |
| | 1964[a] | | 1970[b] | | 1970[c] | | Southern Universities 1970[d] | | Black Universities 1970[e] | |
	Men	Women	Men	Women	Men	Women	Men	Women	Men	Women
Family income										
Less than $3600	29%	34%	29%	43%	5%	7%	7%	10%	27%	31%
$3600 to $5999	29	19	22	25	7	8	10	11	22	24
$5999 to $9999	24	24	25	21	25	23	25	24	28	24
$10,000 and above	18	23	24	11	63	62	58	55	23	21
	100%	100%	100%	100%	100%	100%	100%	100%	100%	100%
Mother's education										
Grammar school or less	21%	22%	12%	12%	7%	7%	9%	10%	12%	13%
Some high school	21	25	24	35	15	14	17	19	33	32
Completed high school	26	22	28	26	44	40	39	36	32	29
Some college	10	10	16	11	17	20	18	18	11	11
Completed college	17	15	11	10	14	16	14	14	9	10
Advanced or professional degree	5	6	9	6	3	3	3	3	3	5
	100%	100%	100%	100%	100%	100%	100%	100%	100%	100%

Father's education

Grammar school or less	31%	32%	27%	32%	11%	11%	14%	15%	25%	25%
Some high school	23	24	21	26	16	15	18	16	33	31
Completed high school	20	26	21	19	30	27	27	26	23	23
Some college	6	7	12	10	17	18	16	18	9	9
Completed college	13	6	7	6	17	19	17	17	7	7
Advanced or professional degree	7	5	12	7	9	10	8	8	3	5
	100%	100%	100%	100%	100%	100%	100%	100%	100%	100%

[a]These percents are based on 540 freshmen in 1964 who entered the six colleges that participated in the cross-sectional studies in both 1964 and 1970.

[b]These percents are based on the 591 freshmen who entered the six colleges who participated in the cross-sectional study of 1970.

[c]American Council on Education, "National Norms for Entering College Freshmen, Fall, 1970." *Research Reports.* Vol. 5, No. 6. Data based on 275 institutions. Income data, pp. 22 and 30; mother's and father's education data, pp. 21 and 29. We have rounded the original percents that were carried to the nearest tenth of a percent to compare to our data.

[d]*Ibid.* Data based on 64 southern universities. Income data, p. 46; father's and mother's education data, p. 45.

[e]*Ibid.* Data based on 15 predominantly Black universities and colleges. Income data, p. 54; father's and mother's education, p. 53.

of the students in our sample did represent very closely those of students attending other historically Black colleges. Almost exactly the same figures on family income result from comparing our 1964 data with information provided by the American Council on Education for students entering Black colleges in 1967[12] and with data reported by Jaffe for a much larger sample of historically Black colleges.[13] More recent comparisons also show remarkably similar figures. Comparing our 1970 data with the American Council of Education 1970 data again indicates that our sample was highly representative of students in other Black colleges (Table 3). This means that our results on the implications of social and demographic background for achievement should also generalize to students in other Black colleges.

By contrast, our sample of students entered college from backgrounds that were *not* typical of students in the nation's college population at large. The one-third who entered Black colleges from poverty backgrounds, for example, was five times larger than the proportion of students in a national sample of colleges and universities from such low income backgrounds. The 17 percent of our sample whose families earned $10,000 or more was nearly one-fourth the proportion of such families in the college population nationally (Table 3). We have already noted in Chapter 3 that this economic disparity put unusual financial burdens on students in Black colleges for handling the costs of a college education and certainly for continuing education beyond the baccalaureate level. (See also Table 4.)

This chapter focuses especially on the motivational differences and similarities between the third of the students whose family incomes put them below the poverty line and the small group of students from more comfortable families who earned more than $10,000. If these two groups of students presented similar motivational profiles, the results would augur well for recruiting the many more Black students from low income families who would have to be reached if admissions were to be broadened sufficiently to reduce occupational inequities. We cannot know, of course, if these students who already were enrolled in college would actually have resembled students from low income backgrounds who had not yet made it to college. We do know that this group of very low income students had experienced the

12. Alan E. Bayer and Robert F. Boruch, "Black and White Freshman Entering Four-Year Colleges," *Educational Record 50* (1969), p. 378.
13. A. J. Jaffe, Walter Adams, Sandra G. Meyers, *Negro Higher Education in the 1960's* (New York: Frederick A. Praeger, 1968).

TABLE 4.   **Other Demographic Characteristics of the 1964 and 1970 Cross-Sectional Samples of Entering Freshmen**

	1964[a]		1970[b]	
	Men	Women	Men	Women
Region of country where student lived most of life				
Deep South states	91%	95%	84%	95%
Border states	1	1	1	1
Northeastern states	1	—	2	—
Northcentral states	3	2	6	2
Western states, Hawaii, Alaska	4	2	5	1
Foreign countries	—	—	2	1
	100%	100%	100%	100%
Rural-urban characteristics of place where student lived most of life				
On a farm	14%	23%	11%	17%
Village (2500 population or less)	12	13	5	3
Town (2500–9999)	12	12	16	22
Small city (10,000–49,999)	20	21	19	17
Medium city (50,000–199,999)	9	13	19	17
Metropolitan city (200,000+)	14	9	23	17
Suburb of metropolitan city	19	9	7	7
	100%	100%	100%	100%
Structures of the families in which the student grew up				
Two-parent families	76%	74%	78%	77%
Mother alone	15	16	10	14
Other types of structures	9	10	12	9
	100%	100%	100%	100%

[a]These percents are based on 540 freshmen in 1964 who entered the six colleges that participated in the cross-sectional studies in both 1964 and 1970.

[b]These percents are based on the 591 freshmen who entered the six colleges who participated in the cross-sectional study of 1970.

economic insecurity fairly typical of poverty in our country.[14] Nearly half of the low income group, but only 15 percent of the most comfortable students with at least $10,000 family income, grew up in homes where the economic head was a woman. Even where the man was the economic head, unemployment was five times greater than in

14. Oscar Ornati, "Poverty in America," in L. A. Ferman, J. L. Kornbluh, and A. Haber, Editors, *Poverty in America* (Ann Arbor, Michigan: The University of Michigan Press, 1965), pp. 24-39.

the most affluent group. Finally, the job status and educational attainments of the parents of this low income group matched almost exactly the nonwhite national average for families below the poverty line. Thus, while students attending Black colleges generally grew up in families with somewhat higher socioeconomic status than is characteristic of the national or southern nonwhite population, a large group of them, far larger than is generally true of college students, came from very low income families. Moreover, other demographic features of these families resembled the much larger group of the nation's Black families with as little as $3600 annual income who would have to be included if admission to higher education were to be meaningfully expanded.

THE DIFFERENCES THAT MAKE A DIFFERENCE

Demographic Relationships With Performance and Aspirations

How did these socioeconomic and demographic variables relate to student performance?[15] There was no significant correlation between these variables, either separately or combined, and any of our measures of performance (Appendix Table 5.1). This was true whether performance was measured by entrance test scores, grades in college, or scores on an anagrams task, a test frequently used in achievement motivation research and administered as part of this study. Whether students came from rural or urban settings, from low or high income families where parents had low or high educational attainments, or from two-parent or other kinds of families simply did not relate to how well they performed. This was equally true of men and of women, and it held for every one of the 10 colleges. While this lack of relationship counters usual expectations about socioeconomic background and performance, we should bear in mind that those usual expectations have been derived primarily from data gathered from high school students. Because a college population already is more homogeneous, the correlation should be reduced simply by virtue of the more restricted range of students. Indeed, data collected from students entering 251 colleges and universities in 1966 showed a correlation of

15. The performance-demography relationships were examined only in the cross-sectional study in 1964 since we did not ask the colleges that participated in the 1970 follow-up study to provide records of students' grades and test scores. Obtaining such records on the sample of 3639 students in 1964 was extraordinarily difficult and represented a serious burden to already understaffed registrars in the 10 colleges.

.29 between socioeconomic background and test scores, a lower relationship than typically reported in national studies of students in high school.[16]

On the other hand, demographic background did influence students' aspirations. The relationships were small; they never exceeded beta weights of .30[17] and were generally less than .20. They were of comparable size in both 1964 and 1970 and appeared primarily among freshmen at the time of college entrance (Appendix Table 5.2). In fact, the nontraditionality of the chosen job was the only dimension of occupational aspiration that class and demographic background still differentiated at the senior year; in both 1964 and 1970 the size of the demographic correlates of nontraditionality remained as large among male seniors as among male freshmen. Otherwise, even the small aspiration difference between freshmen attributable to family social status or place of residence disappeared by the senior year. To some extent the college experience acted as a leveler of social class and demographic influences.

What effect did the demographic variables have when they were the most potent—during the freshmen year? Although freshmen from all backgrounds generally expected to enter the professions, those from

16. Karabel and Astin, "Social Class," p. 23.
17. In many analyses in this book we are interested in examining the effects of a number of variables on a given dependent variable, such as occupational aspirations. One technique particularly well suited to our purpose is the Multiple Classification Analysis. It is a multivariate technique that can deal with predictors that are only nominal in form; it can handle missing data on the predictor variables, simply by treating absence of data as another predictive category; it can handle a wide range of interrelationships among predictors and between predictors and the dependent variable. MCA requires that the dependent variables be either interval scales or dicotomies, and it assumes that the effects of predictor variables are combined additively. The eta provided by MCA is the correlation ratio that, when squared, indicates the proportion of the variance explainable by a predictor operating alone (i.e., without adjustment for correlation with other predictors). The beta coefficients provide a measure of the relationship of each predictor to the dependent variable, after adjusting for the effects of all other predictors. They are analogous to the standardized regression coefficient.

To illustrate what we accomplish using this technique, consider the effect of father absence on whether the father exercised influence over the child's decision to go to college. As expected, fathers who did not live in the home were reported by their children as less influential on the college decision. Since we know that father-absent families also have lower family incomes and, furthermore, that the father's influence in the college decision is affected by total family income, we want to know whether father absence is important after adjusting for the effects of family income. The MCA provides an estimate of the father absence effect by indicating what its effect would be *if* family income among father-absent families were exactly the same as it is for the total sample.

families with higher incomes, higher level of educational attainment, and from more urban backgrounds more often chose from the top professions that accorded the highest prestige and denoted to their peers the greatest test of ability.

Let us look first at men—for whom demography figured both somewhat more prominently and simply than it did for women. Sixty-two percent of the freshmen men who grew up in families who earned more than $10,000, but only 30 percent of those from homes below the poverty line, chose jobs in 1964 with above median prestige scores. Differences related to the parents' educational attainments were larger still. Three-quarters of the freshmen whose fathers held professional or advanced academic degrees, 70 percent of those with college degrees, but only 29 percent of those whose fathers had completed less than high school chose jobs in the upper half of the prestige dimension. While these differences between extreme groups were sizable, the majority of the students whose family characteristics fell somewhere between the extremes held quite homogeneous aspirations, enough so that the income and educational effects in the sample at large were demonstrated by only small beta weights. Social status influences on the ability dimension of job aspiration looked much the same as those on the prestige dimension. Again, the students' choices were noticeably different at the extremes of family income and educational profiles, despite only small relationships in the sample as a whole. One and a half times as many freshman men from the most comfortable homes as from those below poverty, and two and a half times as many from families where the fathers had achieved at least a college degree as those whose fathers had left school before high school, aspired to jobs that were judged to demand more than median ability. Again the students between these extremes entered school with homogeneous job aspirations. The rural-urban characteristics of the places where the students had grown up served primarily to distinguish freshmen from cities of 50,000 or larger from all other entering men students. Twenty percent more men from the large cities than from small cities or the rural South chose jobs with above median prestige and ability ratings.

Among women the role of precollege demographic influences was somewhat less straightforward. While women from poverty backgrounds and whose parents had not completed high school also chose jobs that accorded the least prestige and demanded the least ability, the highest aspirations were expressed by freshman women from families with only moderate, rather than the highest, incomes and where the father had either finished high school or had gone to college but had not completed the baccalaureate degree. To illustrate using the

1964 data: 55 percent of the freshman women from families earning
between $6000 and $10,000 and 68 percent of those whose fathers had
attended but not finished college aspired to jobs with above median
ability ratings. In contrast, just 40 percent of the women from families
whose incomes were above $10,000 and 45 percent of those where
the father held either a college or advanced degree chose comparably
demanding jobs. Only a third of the freshman women from families
below the poverty line and whose fathers had completed less than high
school aspired to jobs of higher than median ability. The same pattern
was demonstrated by the 1970 data as well (Figures 1 and 2). Thus,
aspiration was diminished among both men and women from the least
affluent and least educated families, but the professionally educated,
higher income families did not stimulate the highest aspirations among
women as they did among men. Instead it was the family with moderate
income and some college experience that brought up the women who
entered college choosing jobs that were viewed as demanding especially high personal competence. Remembering that jobs demanding
great ability were also judged by women students as less desirable and
appropriate for their sex, we learn that women who entered college
with unconventional job aspirations most often grew up in families

FIGURE 1. **Ability Demands of the Occupations Chosen By
Freshman Women from Families Varying in Total Family
Income, 1964 and 1970**

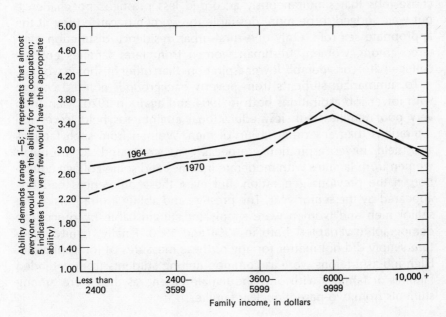

FIGURE 2. **Ability Demands of the Occupations Chosen by Freshman Women from Families Varying in Amount of Education Attained by the Father, 1964 and 1970**

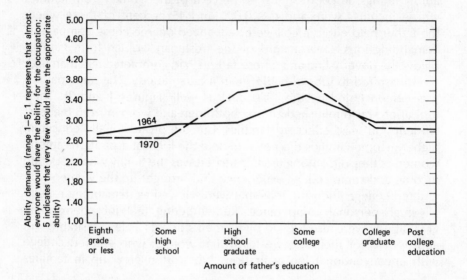

characterized by moderate incomes and educational attainment. Women from families that were the most affluent and highly educated chose jobs that simultaneously accorded less prestige and challenge but were judged to be more desirable for women because they fit the appropriate sex role. Only one rural-urban residence distinction mattered among women; freshman women from farm families entered college with considerably lower aspirations than other freshman women.

To summarize: students from poverty backgrounds entered college with lower job aspirations both in 1964 and again in 1970. Men from very poor families with low educational attainments held lower job aspirations than any other group of men. Women from such families also held lower aspirations, especially as compared to freshman women from families with moderate incomes and some college education in the previous generation. But even these differences had disappeared by the senior year. The prestige and ability aspirations of the senior men and women were simply indistinguishable by precollege demographic variables, both in 1964 and 1970. Finally, family structure simply did not matter for any of these measures of job aspiration. High job aspirations were as common among students from extended families or families with only the female parent, as they were among students from two-parent nuclear families.

**Demographic Relationships Wtih
Motives, Values, and Expectancies**

The measures of motives that we adopted from the achievement motivation literature as well as those we developed for this study (Chapter 4) were consistently unrelated to family and demographic variables. While the strength of the students' fear of failure, desire for security, achievement orientation, and success motives varied and the individual differences, in turn, somewhat influenced students' aspirations, these differences had nothing to do with social background. Students from very low income families entered college with just as much need for achievement and with no greater anxiety about failure than students from much more comfortable backgrounds. Likewise, rural and urban students, those whose parents had attained only grammar school education and those whose parents had graduated from college, were remarkably similar in their achievement motives (Appendix Table 5.3).

Did the students' values differ, especially those values concerning achievement and success that some people argue are less important in people in poverty? The results repeatedly show that students from poverty backgrounds shared the same broad values expressed by the most well-to-do students. For example, rural-urban residency, family income, and parental educational attainments were unrelated to the students' adherence to work-ethic values and to their rankings of the six statements that make up Spranger's[18] measures of theoretical, pragmatic, social, political, religious, and aesthetic values (Table 5.4). Generally, students of all economic backgrounds agreed that hard work was an important virtue. The response to the Spranger value statements was equally heterogeneous among all demographic subgroups; an equal number of students placed each of the six values at the top of their hierarchy of values. Moreover, students from different social backgrounds expressed almost exactly the same ideas about the value of a college education. Pragmatic and vocational values, reflected in viewing college as a way to a better job or as a chance to think through occupational plans, were no stronger in the poverty group; intellectual values, reflected in viewing college as an opportunity to explore new ideas and be stimulated by learning, were no greater in the most comfortable students (Appendix Table 5.5). Likewise, academic commitment was not tied to precollege social background. The importance that students attached to graduating from

18. E. Spranger, *Types of Men*. Translated from the fifth German edition of *Lebensformen* by P. J. Pigors (Halle: Max Niemeyer Verlof, 1928. American Agent: Stechert-Hafner, New York).

college, indicated by their unwillingness to drop out to take a really good job, or to get married, and the importance of going on to graduate or professional school depended in no way on their social backgrounds.

The students' perspectives of the future and their ability to plan toward future goals, two attributes often assumed to be less characteristic of working class, low income groups, were likewise almost completely independent of social background influences. Students from families with low incomes did not differ from the most comfortable students on an index of how purposeful they had been in planning to get to college. Indeed, only two behaviors on this index showed differences even among the most extreme income groups and these two contradicted usual expectations. Students from poverty backgrounds exhibited greater, not lesser, ability to plan (as reflected in applying for scholarships) and to earn money specifically for college. Comparison of the lowest income group with the most well-to-do on the seven behaviors on this index showed the following: applied for scholarships—58 percent from low income families versus 33 percent from families earning over $10,000; earned money specifically for college—62 versus 43 percent; wrote away for college catalogs—51 versus 49 percent; talked to people who had attended various colleges —52 versus 51 percent; sought help from high school counselors— 33 versus 31 percent; took exams for scholarships or college entrance —46 versus 43 percent; took special summer courses—12 versus 13 percent.

Let us turn now to the students' expectancies of success. Even if the more comfortable and the poorer students equally valued graduating from college, going on to professional or graduate school, and entering prestigious, challenging careers, the resultant aspirations of the poorer students might be lower if economic realities made them question the financial feasibility of reaching those goals. The data show that students' expectancies of success were significantly related to family income and rural-urban residency, despite the marked commonality in the values and motives of students from all social backgrounds. For example, although social background did not influence the importance attached to higher education or the desire to go to graduate school, students from affluent and urban families expressed considerably greater certainty that they would be able to realize that goal (Appendix Table 5.6). Thirty-two percent of the students whose family incomes exceeded $10,000 but only 2 percent of those from poverty backgrounds were completely certain of being able to go on for higher degrees. At the other extreme, nearly 40 percent of the lowest income group but only 8 percent of the most comfortable were almost completely certain they would not go on to graduate or professional school. These family income differences in graduate school expectancies existed despite the lack of demographic influences on academic values, motives, self-confidence about ability, and general commitment to education. The same pattern characterizes job expectancies. Despite feeling equally self-confident about ability to do the jobs they had chosen, students from rural areas and from low income families assessed their chances of actually getting those jobs at a much lower level of probability. For example, while a fourth of both the most and least affluent students were completely sure of their ability for their chosen jobs, only 12 percent of the students from poverty backgrounds but 43 percent of the most comfortable students were completely certain of being able to get into the work they had chosen. Students from cities over 50,000 population were three times as likely as those who grew up on farms or in the rural South to assess their chances of getting their chosen jobs as completely certain.

Summary

Chart A summarizes these demographic-family background relationships with both resultant performance and aspirations and with three components of motivation—motives, values, and expectancies of success. This chart illustrates several points:

1. Social background simply did not influence college performance or performance on typical achievement motivation tasks.

2. At the freshman level men from very poor families and from families with low educational attainments held lower job aspirations than any other group of men. Women from such families also held lower aspirations, especially as compared to freshman women from families with moderate incomes and some college education in the previous generation.

3. Social background was not significantly related to either achievement motives or values.

4. The opportunity aspects of the students' precollege environments, especially the level of their family incomes and the rural setting of their homes, did influence expectancies of success. Although students from such backgrounds attached the same importance as other students to getting an advanced degree, they were considerably less certain that they would be able to realize that goal. Similarly, students from rural areas and low income families assessed their chances of actually getting the jobs they desired at a much lower level of probability despite feeling equally self-confident about their abilities to perform at those jobs.

CHART A. **Summary of Demographic Relationships to Student Performance, Aspirations, Motives, Values, and Expectancies**

	Rural-Urban Characteristics of Place Student Grew Up	Family Income	Father's Education	Mother's Education	Family Structure
Occupational aspirations:					
Prestige of the choice	Both sexes	Linear for men Curvilinear for women	Linear for men Curvilinear for women	Linear for men Curvilinear for women	No relationship
Ability demands	Both sexes	Linear for men Curvilinear for women	Linear for men Curvilinear for women	Linear for men Curvilinear for women	No relationship
Nontraditionality	Both sexes	Curvilinear for men and women	Curvilinear for men and women	Curvilinear for men and women	No relationship
Performance:					
Cumulative college grades	No relationship	No relationship	No relationship	No relationship	No relationship
Entrance scores	No relationship	No relationship	No relationship	No relationship	No relationship
Anagrams performance	No relationship	No relationship	No relationship	No relationship	No relationship

Motives:						
Fear of failure	No relationship	No relationship	No relationship	No relationship	No relationship	No relationship
Security orientation	No relationship	No relationship	No relationship	No relationship	No relationship	No relationship
Success orientation	No relationship	No relationship	No relationship	No relationship	No relationship	No relationship
Achievement orientation	No relationship	No relationship	No relationship	No relationship	No relationship	No relationship
Values:						
Work ethic values	No relationship	No relationship	No relationship	No relationship	No relationship	No relationship
Spranger values	No relationship	No relationship	No relationship	No relationship	No relationship	No relationship
Goals for college	No relationship	No relationship	No relationship	No relationship	No relationship	No relationship
Importance attached to completing college	No relationship	No relationship	No relationship	No relationship	No relationship	No relationship
Importance attached to going to graduate or professional school	No relationship	No relationship	No relationship	No relationship	No relationship	No relationship
Expectancies:						
Certainty of being able to complete college	Both sexes	Both sexes	No relationship	No relationship	No relationship	No relationship
Certainty of being able to go to advanced education	Both sexes	Both sexes	No relationship	No relationship	No relationship	No relationship

SOCIAL INHERITANCE AND SITUATIONAL INEQUITIES

The results just summarized on expectancies of success speak directly to the controversy about the social inheritance and the opportunity-situational analysis of social impact. Not only did social background influence expectancies more than it influenced motives and values, but also the influential aspects of the background seemed to be closely tied to opportunity. In the multivariate analyses of expectancies, family income and rural-urban residency were far more influential than either parental education or family structure. (The beta weights attached to family income and rural-urban residency in explaining students' educational expectancies fell between .25 and .40 in both 1964 and 1970 while those attached to parental education and family structure never exceeded .10.) The objective chances of making their graduate schools aspirations or occupational goals a reality were much slimmer for students from farms and villages and from very poor families than for students who came to college from the urban environments and more affluent families where resources were more abundant. When students were asked why they felt uncertain about achieving their goals, talk about the constraints put upon them by reality always distinguished the poor from the nonpoor and the most rural students from all others. Ninety-five percent of the students from poverty backgrounds who expressed doubts about achieving their goals talked about financial or other reality problems. The specifics varied: "I don't want to continue to be a financial drain on my parents"; "I have to repay an uncle who has helped me with my education so far"; "My family needs me to help support them"; "My father died and I have to send money home"; "I have to help support my sister who started college last year"; "I already have a sizable debt for my college education and don't see how I can go on until I make a dent in that"; "With all the financial obligations I have, I cannot begin to make ends meet even if I get a fellowship." The message was clear. In Chapter 3 we noted that these financial concerns were expressed generally by students as they faced the question of advanced education; indeed, nearly 40 percent from even the most comfortable backgrounds, who were not very comfortable relative to the national average of students, likewise talked about financial problems. But financial worries were ubiquitous among the students from poverty.

This general pattern appeared in the results both of the 1964 and 1970 studies: a strong commonality among students of diverse backgrounds in values, achievement motives, ideal goals, commitments to education, test performance and grades earned in college, but dissimilarity in aspirations and even greater divergency in expectancies of reaching those goals. Although these results do not provide exhaustive answers, their replicability across time and their consistency across many measures validate the general point. Social background did influence student motivation; this influence sprung more from environmental resources and opportunities than from the poor family's inability to socialize appropriate achievement motives and values in their children. The differences that counted, primarily those in the expectancy area, were more associated with current reality situations than with the consequences of early class-linked socialization patterns. To recapitulate the major points: (1) social background influenced expectancies, which reflect at the psychological level the objective possibilities and constraints of the environment, more than it influenced motives and values that presumably arise out of early family socialization; (2) the influential aspects of the precollege background that pertained especially to student expectancies were family income and rural-urban residency, each of which points to objective differences in opportunities between the poor and the more well-to-do, the urban and the rural students.

Does this mean that social background provided no psychological consequences for the educational experience? Previous social experience implied psychological effects in the sense that freshmen from farms and the rural South and from the lowest income families entered college with reduced aspirations and expectancies of reaching their goals. Those are genuine differences in the social-psychological characteristics of entering students. Yet they are differences that should disappear as such students are exposed to greater opportunities in the college environment, especially where colleges actively work to provide new opportunities. Expectancies, reflecting as they do the objective probabilities of the world, should be easier to change than motives and values, at least if they represent the residues of early family socialization. And, indeed, the data we have presented indicate that the aspiration and expectancy differences freshmen brought to college no longer prevailed during the senior year. Since this is not explained by a significant relationship between family social status and student attrition, we can only conclude that colleges can and did mute the impact of precollege social background. The only socioeconomically tied expectancy that remained among seniors was the lower expectation of going on to graduate or professional school among students from the poorest families. It is not hard to argue that this expectancy difference, too, would disappear if the reality differences disappeared as well.

We are aware that these results counter numerous expectations about the importance of social, especially family, background. Many of the usual expectations derive from studies of white youngsters and have been applied without sufficient caution to Black life. We also believe, that their impact on white youngsters, even at the high school level, has been exaggerated. Research on the connection between family socioeconomic status and parents' aspirations for their children[19] and children's aspirations for themselves[20] stands up rather well. Several of these studies are based on national, representative samples; moveover, sufficient work with Black youngsters has been done to demonstrate similar effects. Even here, however, it does not follow from previous research that the socioeconomic determinants of aspirations continue to operate as strongly among college as among high school youth. In contrast, the question of how much socioeconomic background conditions the achievement values and motives of young people, even at the high school level, can be answered less certainly. Some research carries dubious value because it is based on small or exceptionally unrepresentative samples[21] or because the measures have not managed to isolate expectancy factors from values. Just as the projective need for achievement measures can be seriously confounded by situational cues and the expectancies they arouse, many questions presumably measuring values are contaminated by situational expectancies. Turner's classic work with high school students

19. R. L. Bell, "Lower Class Negro Mothers and Their Children," *Social Forces XLIII* (1965), pp. 493-501. James Morgan and Martin David, "Race Economic Attitudes and Behavior," *Proceedings*, Social Statistics Section, American Statistical Association (1962), pp. 2-9. B. C. Rosen, "Race, Ethnicity, and Achievement," *American Sociological Review XXIV* (1959), pp. 47-60.

20. J. G. Bachman, "The Impact of Family Background and Intelligence on Tenth Grade Boys," *Youth in Transition,* Volume II (Ann Arbor: Institute for Social Research, 1970). W. S. Bennett and N. P. Gist, "Class, Family and Student Aspirations," *Social Forces 53* (1964), pp. 167-173. E. G. Epps, *Family and Achievement: A Study of the Relation of Family Background to Achievement Orientation and Performance Among Urban Negro High School Students* (Washington, D.C.: U. S. Department of Health, Education and Welfare, 1969). J. A. Kahl, "Educational and Occupational Aspirations of 'Common Man' Boys," *Harvard Education Review XXIII* (1953), pp. 186-203. William H. Sewell, "Inequality of Opportunity for Higher Education," *American Sociological Review 36* (October, 1971), pp. 793-809. W. H. Sewell, A. O. Haller, and M. A. Straus, "Social Status and Educational and Occupational Aspiration," *American Sociological Review XXII* (1957), pp. 67-73. W. H. Sewell and V. P. Shah, "Parents' Education and Children's Educational Aspirations and Achievements," *American Sociological Review 33* (1968), pp. 191-209. Alan B. Wilson, "Residential Segregation of Social Classes and Aspirations of High School Boys," *American Sociological Review 24* (1959), pp. 836-845.

21. B. C. Rosen, "Race, Ethnicity, and Achievement."

makes this very clear.[22] He posed alternative behaviors, for example, going to college or getting a good-paying job right after high school, to high school students. When asked which behavior they admired the most, working class and upper status youth generally shared the same thoughts. When asked which of the two they planned to do themselves, working class and upper status youth differed greatly and in the expected ways.

Why is this important? Values should imply a "categorical ought," a rightness, something admired. Studies that ask young people about their preferences, their goals, or their intentions and assume that such questions indicate something about values fail to separate the confounding influence of expectancies. Thus, we are not at all sure that social background promotes major motive and value differences even at the high school level, let alone among the nation's college population. In some respects we suspect that our results diverge more from research misconceptions than from hard data regarding the socioeconomic determinants of these separate aspects of motivation and performance.

TRADITIONAL AND UNCONVENTIONAL CHOICES

In one crucial way this picture of the demographic correlates of aspiration and motivation oversimplifies the influences that the social status of the parent exerted on students' goals. If the level of job aspiration is assessed in terms of the nontraditionality of the choice, then the goals of the most privileged students did not reflect the highest aspirations. We have already noted this in discussing the social origins of women students who aspired to jobs that were unconventional for women and that were judged by their peers to require high personal competence on the one hand and on the other not to be especially desirable or appropriate for women (Figues 1 and 2). The same holds true for men students if their unconventional choice fell outside the fields in which Blacks have traditionally achieved the highest status. Generally those jobs fall in sectors of the labor market that have been virtually closed to Blacks.

Using the percentage of Blacks in a given occupation in 1960 to indicate its nontraditionality, the data show that men whose family incomes were moderately high (between $6000 and $10,000) but not the highest (over $10,000) and whose parents had attended college but had not achieved college degrees chose careers most nontraditional for Blacks. This curvilinear effect of education and income

22. Ralph Turner, *The Social Context of Ambition*, (San Francisco: Chandler, 1964).

FIGURE 3.   **Nontraditionality of the Occupations Chosen by Freshman Men from Families Varying in Total Family Income, 1964 and 1970**

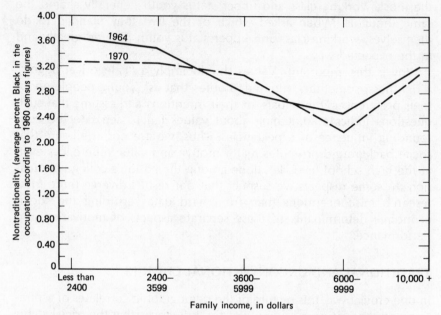

FIGURE 4.   **Nontraditionality of the Occupations Chosen by Freshman Men from Families Varying in Amount of Education Attained by the Father, 1964 and 1970**

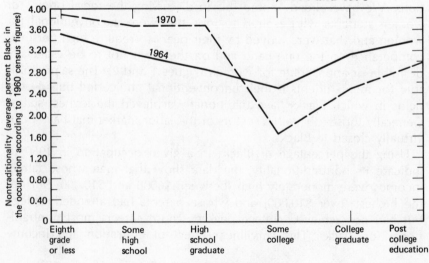

appeared in 1964 and again even more sharply in 1970 (Figures 3 and 4). It was also the one demographic effect that prevailed at the senior level despite the general tendency for the college experience to vitiate the effects of precollege background on aspirations.

This does not imply that men from highly educated, high income families made the most traditional choices. Since men from high status, affluent backgrounds aspired for highly prestigious jobs, and since nontraditionality and prestige scores were positively correlated (+.54), their choices obviously could not fall in the most traditional sector of the professions. In fact, their jobs' nontraditionality scores typically fell between those of the men entering college from the least educated, lowest income families and those of the most nontraditional group from families with moderate incomes and some college experience in the previous generation.

While it would be inaccurate to characterize the choices of men from the highest status backgrounds as traditional, their choices nonetheless reflected relatively greater prestige than nontraditionality. How do we see this? It helps to consider only those men whose career choices fell in the upper 40 percent on the prestige dimension. Despite the positive correlation between prestige and nontraditionality, some of these jobs were more nontraditional, some less nontraditional. We formed three groups of men whose choices were prestigious: one whose choices reflected a higher position on the prestige than on the nontraditionality dimension; a second whose choices reflected a lower position on the prestige than on the nontraditionality dimension; and a third whose choices were equally prestigious and nontraditional, that is, jobs that fell in the upper 20 percent on both dimensions or in the next 20 percent on both dimensions. Clear-cut differences in social background emerged in comparing these groups of men. The men who entered college from families with the highest incomes and highest levels of educational attainment fell disproportionately in the group choosing jobs whose prestige exceeded their nontraditionality position. The men from families with only moderate incomes and with a record of only some college experience disproportionately chose jobs whose nontraditionality either exceeded or equaled their prestige position. These differences were striking: 43 percent of the highest status men but only 11 percent of those with more moderate status chose jobs that reflected greater prestige than nontraditionality; none of the highest status men but 33 percent of those with more moderate status chose jobs that reflected greater nontraditionality than prestige; and 23 percent of the highest status and 33 percent of those with somewhat lower status chose jobs with equal positions on both dimensions.

Why did the sons of the most privileged families elect the more traditionally prestigious professions? We can infer from two sets of data that parental influence was critical. First, income and education both influenced the role students reported their parents to have played in their decisions about college and future jobs. Approximately 20 to 25 percent more of the students from the most comfortable, most highly educated group than those from the lowest income group attributed a "very" or "crucially" important role to the father in affecting their decisions to go to college and in making up their minds about their occupational choices. Second, the men students who reported strong parental influence on their occupational decisions chose jobs that reflected higher ability demands and prestige but lower nontraditionality. In contrast, the men who said that their fathers had not been too important in their career choices intended to enter jobs with higher nontraditionality but lower prestige and ability scores. Therefore, the class-linked influence of parents seemed to mediate, at least in part, the effect of family status on job aspirations. Higher status parents were seen as having more influence; sons who felt their parents had been crucially important chose jobs with higher prestige but lower nontraditionality. On the basis of these findings, a disproportionate number of the highest status men chose jobs with relatively greater prestige than nontraditionality. The fact that the family status difference in the nontraditionality of the high prestige choices disappeared when parental influence was controlled further substantiated the indirect effect of social status through parental influence. While other aspects of precollege environment may also impinge on choices of the most well-to-do men students, these data clearly indicate that their parents contributed at least one significant influence.

For high-status parents to prefer the elite professions, in which at least some Blacks have already made their mark, to the new and more uncertain job opportunities is understandable on many counts. Their sons have the most to lose by risking status for uncertain achievements. Given the parents' own experiences in facing closed doors to achieve their status, they may have viewed with some skepticism the new, presumably nondiscriminatory policies and the flurry of college recruitment of the midsixties. Again and again the faculty emphasized this point when discussing these demographic correlates of nontraditionality. Many faculty in the participating schools identified with high-status parents and were not sure how happy they would be if their scientifically talented sons were to go into industrial research instead of college teaching or medicine or if their politically ambitious sons were to choose the foreign service or careers in the Labor Department or were to aspire to the national political arena without preparing for future uncertainties by also qualifying as lawyers or college professors in these fields. Moreover, in addition to their skepticism, their reluctance to extend risks, and their desire to fortify themselves against the future, they endlessly reiterated that the Black community needs the service of Black professionals. Parents who themselves have worked within the Black community, although perhaps not in ways advocated by those most socially committed or critical of the present student generation, believe that some of the so-called new opportunities drain outstanding talent away from the Black community, especially when they demand geographical isolation from Black life. Finding work commitments that satisfy the self, contribute to Black life and peoplehood, and provide future economic security cause real and genuine conflicts. They are the guts of the identity issue for Black students. That high-status parents, who dealt with similar issues— perhaps cast differently at an earlier time—may prefer the more traditional paths for their sons should not be considered as another invidious characterization of the Black bourgeoisie.

At the same time, the nontraditionality exception to the usual direction of class and status effects on aspiration can have a salutary impact on discussions of social class. Although well supported by research that uses prestige of job choice as the main indicator of aspiration, the enhancing effect of high-status families on their children's aspirations has too often been generalized inappropriately to include all dimensions of aspiration. In reality, young people from the working class and ethnic minorities have always "made it" by being one step ahead of the current labor market and by being sensitive to new opportunities and marginal roles when slots in the mainstream proved inaccessible. Class literature would truly be more balanced if previous research had considered this dimension of aspiration.

THE ROLE OF FAMILY STRUCTURE

Family structure characteristics were included consistently in the analyses of aspiration and motivation that we have reported in this chapter. Whether the student grew up in a nuclear, two-parent family or in one of two father-absent families—the single adult, mother-headed family or the multiple-adult, extended family—simply never figured prominently in aspiration. Family structure had no effect, with or without control for other family and demographic variables, on:

College grades
College entrance test scores
Performance on achievement tasks
Job aspirations of men students

Expectancies of achieving career goals
Graduate/professional school goals and expectancies
Commitments to education
Self-confidence about ability
Achievement motives and values
Work-ethic values
General life values

Family structure significantly influenced only women's job aspirations, where its positive effect was the opposite of usual expectations. Women who grew up in mother-only or extended families aspired to high ability jobs in unconventional fields more often than women from nuclear, two-parent families. Apart from this one positive effect, the absence of the father and the family structure never influenced student motivation and aspiration. In fact, it never explained even so much as one-tenth of one percent of the variance in students' aspirations, motivation, and performance.

Even the question of how much parents influenced their children's educational and career goals was as much a function of family income as of intactness in the home. Obviously, an absent father will not likely match the influence of a father who lives with the child. But the father's role in the college decision was as closely related to family income as to family structure; his importance in the career decision was more closely tied to family income than to family structure. Thus, even in two-parent families only 20 percent of the poverty students, but 55 percent of the most affluent group, mentioned that their fathers (either alone or in combination with their mothers) had the greatest influence on their decisions to go to college. If we look at families where the father was not present, we find a striking corollary: even when the father was not present in the home, a more adequate family income made it possible for him to be influential in the college decision. Only 4 percent of the father-absent students from poverty backgrounds mentioned their fathers, whereas 27 percent of the most affluent mentioned him despite his absence from the home. The absent father who earned a comfortable income and contributed to the support of his family, which was true for almost all father-absent families in the highest income group, continued to influence his children's major decisions.

Why does the widespread but stereotyped opinions about deficits of the single-parent Black family continue despite substantial data to the contrary reported here and elsewhere? The Labor Department report on *The Black Family*,[23] commonly referred to as the Moynihan Report,

---

23. Daniel P. Moynihan, *The Negro Family: The Case for National Action* (Washington, D. C.: U. S. Department of Labor, Office of Planning and Research, 1965).

and characteristic of many social analyses of Black life, popularized the thesis that "the Black family is deteriorating"; it stated, furthermore, that its higher rates of father-absence presumably reduce the Black family's ability to socialize achievement values and behaviors in its young; and, finally, it theorized that these socialization deficits preponderantly account for race differentials in the educational, occupational, and income status of each succeeding generation. Many criticisms of The Black Family have now been published. Most clearly refuted is the misleading impression that the typical Black family is headed by a female, single parent, since the statistics of the report itself made clear that even where father absence was greatest, in the urban North, 77 percent of Black families were comprised of two parents and children. The proportion of intact families rose to 90 percent among the rural farm Black population. Other criticisms have centered on statistical inadequacies in its trend analyses of race differences among the various indicators of family pathology. Beyond that, no data in that report—and very little in the literature on achievement—support the causal negative function attributed to father absence.[24] Generally when father absence is reported as significant in either achievement motivation or behavior, the effect turns out to be spurious; it disappears when other aspects of family background are controlled. It is imperative that social scientists attempt to separate family and demographic influences at a time when one of our racial myths calls for tying race inequities to "the deteriorating structure of the Black family."

The data we have reported add to an increasing body of findings showing that family structure rarely, if ever, explains any unique variance in achievement. For example, Coleman and others carried out one of the most thorough studies of the effects of father absence on school achievement in the literature.[25] While that study has been criticized widely for the conclusions it drew about the relative importance of school and home effects, its analyses of different components of family background cannot be faulted. It did try to isolate

---

24. See especially the following critiques: Andrew Billingsley, Black Families in White America (Englewood Cliffs, New Jersey: Prentice-Hall, 1968); Andrew Billingsley, "Black Families and White Social Science," Journal of Social Issues 26 (March, 1970), pp. 127-142; Elizabeth Herzog, About the Poor: Some Facts and Fictions (Washington, D.C.: U.S. Department of Health, Education and Welfare, 1967); Elizabeth Herzog, "Social Stereotypes and Social Research," Journal of Social Issues 26 (March, 1970), pp. 109-125; Robert Staples, The Black Family (Belmont, California: Wadsworth, 1971), Hill, Robert, Strengths of Black Families (New York: Emerson Hall, 1971).

25. J. S. Coleman et al., Equality of Educational Opportunity (Washington, D.C.: U. S. Government Printing Office, 1966).

the unique variance that could be attributed to father absence from among a set of family variables. It produced the following results: (1) no unique effect of father absence on performance on standard achievement tests could be shown for either Black or white children at either the elementary or high school level; (2) for Black children at the elementary level, the strongest family background effect on school achievement derived from the economic status of the family; at the senior high level, the strongest effects stemmed from the parents' level of education and length of time the family had resided in an urban environment; (3) parents' level of education produced the strongest effect for white children at both the elementary and high school levels. Father absence did not explain a significant portion of the variance in test performance for either group at either level of schooling. In our own work with high school students we also have seen how little father absence counts in the verbal performance of Black students.[26] In fact, what little effect there was of father absence served to heighten students' recognition of their limited opportunities. But it did not emerge materially in any other aspect of student motivation or performance in studies we have conducted with high school students.

Another important study bears directly on the presumed connection between father absence and achievement difficulties of the next generation. This study, conducted by Duncan,[27] utilized a regression analysis of predictors of level of education for various age cohorts in the United States. The variables used as possible predictors were derived from characteristics of the respondents' parents at the time the children were growing up. The father's presence or absence in the home during their school years was considered along with the parents' education, income, occupational status, and geographical residency. Father absence was not a significant predictor of the next generation's educational attainments for any age group of the Black population. There was simply no evidence in this thorough analysis of census materials that father absence in one generation was associated with the level of educational attainment in the next generation.

The evidence of the effects of father absence on other developments in children fares little better when reviewed carefully. Despite widespread beliefs that the broken home causes juvenile delinquency, the best data available provide only limited support. Of 18 studies

26. Edgar G. Epps, *Family and Achievement: A Study of the Relation of Family Background to Achievement Orientation and Performance Among Urban Negro High School Students*. (Ann Arbor, Michigan: Institute for Social Research, 1969)
27. Otis Dudley Duncan, "Discrimination Against Negroes," *Annals of the American Academy of Political and Social Science, 371* (May, 1967), pp. 85-103.

recently reviewed, only seven found clear support and even in these studies the minor differences in delinquency between father-absent and father-present boys were dwarfed by far more important factors, especially depressed income and community influence.[28] Another review of the role of the father in child development highlights some consistency in research showing that boys growing up without fathers in the home are more feminine and dependent, at the same time they sometimes show compensatory aggressiveness.[29] Even this conclusion should be treated cautiously, because most of the relevant studies involved small numbers of white nursery school children whose fathers had been absent fighting in World War II or equally small numbers of Norwegian children whose fathers were recurrently absent for the approved occupational reason of going to sea. Applying these studies to Black youngsters as though they prove that father absence causes masculine identification problems and eventual inability to perform adequately as an adult male leaps far beyond the data.

Why, then, are father absence and presumed socialization deficits of the single-parent Black family so often advanced as the causes of the continued race inequities Black people face? Billingsley suggests that the answer lies in the broader treatment of Black families in social science scholarship.[30] Father absence is the center of focus because Black family life is so badly misunderstood. And that, in turn, derives from the tendency to ignore Black families altogether, to focus almost exclusively on the lowest income group when Black families are considered at all, to ignore the majority of Black families even among this lowest income group who show stable family structures, and to focus on victims instead of the social and economic forces that define the environment in which Black families live.

EDUCATIONAL OPPORTUNITIES OF THE POOR

The results we have presented show a large group of low income students who, by virtue of their academic commitment, performance, self-confidence, and achievement values, were as prepared for college as the most affluent students. They differed from their more affluent peers primarily by expressing somewhat lower job aspirations and lower expectations of achieving their job and postcollege educational ambitions. Unless the low income students differ radically from other

28. Elizabeth Herzog "Social Stereotypes and Social Research," *Journal of Social Issues 26* (1970), pp. 109-125.
29. J. Nash, "The Father in Contemporary Culture and Current Psychological Literature," *Child Development 36* (1965), pp. 261-297.
30. Andrew Billingsley, *Black Families in White America.*

young people not attending college who share much the same objective life conditions, expanding college admissions to include many more students from such backgrounds augurs well. That will be necessary if Blacks are to reach occupational parity with whites anytime in this century.

Despite their apparent motivational readiness for college, the lowest income students have not had equal educational opportunities if only because their financial resources are seriously limited. Only 25 percent of the lowest income students, but 54 percent of the highest income group, reported that their parents were contributing "all or nearly all" of their tuition and living expenses at college. If this inequity were compensated for by scholarships, low income students would not have unique problems. Compensatory supports, however, did not include enough scholarship aid; the proportion of the lowest income group who reported receiving scholarship assistance was almost exactly the same as that of the highest income group. But students from poverty backgrounds were markedly distinguished by more frequent dependence on loans. Three times as many of them reported having all of their college costs covered by some kind of loan. Moreover, virtually all the students from the low income group, as compared with 40 percent of the most affluent group, not only worked, but worked an average of twice as many hours. While college jobs can complement academic work and add to personal character, we need not romanticize their value nor assume they are twice as valuable for the poor as for the more comfortable students. Having to work as many hours as they did and ending college with so much indebtedness clearly put low income students at a disadvantage in financing graduate school.

Low income students not only command unequal resources, but they also end up in a different higher education circuit from their more affluent peers. Despite their apparent equal readiness for college, the lowest income students disproportionately entered institutions of lower academic standing. Only 24 percent of them, in contrast to 60 percent of all other income groups, enrolled in schools ranking in the highest quality categories as judged by the Southern Association of Schools and Colleges. Family income also related to the academic quality of schools students had ever considered and actually applied to. We asked students to list the schools they had ever thought about attending and the ones to which they actually applied. Several important facts emerged. First, students from families with incomes of $10,000 or more were twice as likely as students from poverty backgrounds to have considered out-of-state colleges, colleges outside the South, and predominantly white schools as well as historically Black colleges. Second, students from different income groups chose different kinds of historically Black colleges. A rough measure of academic rank allowed us to code four levels of quality in the schools mentioned—one group of unaccredited schools and three levels of accredited schools. Merely 8 percent of the students from poverty backgrounds, in contrast to approximately 30 percent of all other income groups, considered only the schools in the highest academic category; yet nearly 28 percent of the poverty students, but only 5 percent of the most comfortable students, had considered at least one school in the lowest of the accredited group.

The relationship between family economic resources and the quality of the college children attend exists generally in higher education and by no means pertains solely to predominantly Black colleges. Data collected from students entering 251 colleges and universities in 1966 showed that socioeconomic resources figured prominently in who enrolled in the most elite colleges. Measuring college quality in two ways —selectivity of the student body and affluence—eight categories of institutions were formed. Though few students even in the highest socioeconomic quintile entered schools in the top two categories, high SES students were about eight times as likely as low SES students to attend very high quality colleges. Looking at it another way, over two-thirds of the students at the most affluent institutions were from the top two SES quintiles; almost half were from the highest quintile.[31]

If the quality of the college bore no implications for students' futures, the effect of family economic resources on rank of college the child attends would carry little import. Various studies, however, have demonstrated not only that college quality is linked to the system of social stratification but also that it makes a difference where one attends college, even controlling for student inputs.[32] Even when test score performance is controlled, adults who graduated from the most elite colleges earn more than graduates of colleges of lower quality.[33] Graduates of high ranking colleges are also more likely to enter prestigious professions and to receive the choice positions in the business world.[34] Studies on entrance to graduate school suggest that attending an elite college not only increases the student's chances of graduate school but also makes attendance at a prestigious graduate institution more

31. Karabel and Astin, "Social Class."
32. *Ibid.*
33. Ernest Havemann and Patricia Salter West, *They Went to College* (New York: Harcourt, Brace, 1952). Dael Wolfe, *The Uses of Talent* (Princeton, New Jersey: Princeton University Press, 1971).
34. Laure H. Sharp, *Education and Employment* (Baltimore: John Hopkins University Press, 1970).

likely.[35] While none of these studies directly tests the implications of college rank for the graduates of predominantly Black colleges, there is every reason to believe that status differentiations among Black colleges likewise carry strong import for students' postgraduation lives. In fact, two of the colleges we studied have been much more successful than the other eight in sending their graduates on to graduate or professional colleges and both of these colleges were judged by the Southern Association of Schools and Colleges in the top rank of colleges. Being poor, then, results in less chance for the highest quality of undergraduate education and less likelihood of getting advanced training beyond the baccalaureate degree as well.

Our research did not sufficiently explore the processes by which students selected their colleges for us to be sure why the lowest income students ended up in a different educational circuit. In part it can be explained on purely financial grounds. Although many high quality public colleges exist, the Southern Association's top group of historically Black colleges includes a disproportionately high number of private schools. Given their financial base, these private schools already have been overburdened by large student aid budgets—generally in the form of loans rather than direct scholarship aid—which nonetheless constitute a large share of their total budgets. These schools have not been insensitive to the needs of low income students nor undesirous of recruiting more; but with their sizable dependence upon student tuition, they need a large student body and, especially, they need more students who can afford to pay an even higher tuition than is currently charged. Tuition in the private historically Black colleges is already more per year than in the public schools. Thus, it is no wonder that the lowest income students do not share an equal chance to attend the most elite private institutions. Other factors also contribute to the total picture. While most of the lowest income group entered public schools where tuition was lower, 39 percent were enrolled in private schools and the private schools they attended fell disproportionately in the lower ranked categories. Moreover, when we look at the private schools that low income students mentioned having considered, we see the same kinds of choices. Although financial reasons primarily determined final decisions, they do not explain why this group of students disproportionately considered the lower ranking private schools even when tuition costs were reasonably equivalent to the higher ranking colleges. To the extent that these choices primarily reflected economic factors, financial support

---

35. Joe L. Spaeth, "The Allocation of College Graduates to Graduate and Professional Schools," *Sociology of Education 41* (Fall, 1968), pp. 342-343.

would reduce current inequalities. But if they reflected the recruitment policies and practices of the colleges, the counseling of high school personnel, or the indirect norms of the high school about what colleges are appropriate for whom, financial subsidies to students or to schools would not by themselves alter the picture.

With Black colleges now enrolling only a third of all Black students who attend college, that representing a decrease from a half in 1964, educators in Black colleges understandably worry about losing students from atypically high social status backgrounds to other types of institutions. With a larger age cohort and some increase in the proportion going to college, however, enrollment figures in Black colleges did not drop at the end of the sixties. Admission expansion to students not now attending college would not only protect current rates but provide for growth as well. This need not mean a loss in those student qualities important for high quality education even if the students were increasingly from homes with fewer economic resources. It is to this point that our data are most relevant. Colleges could provide opportunities and develop the talents of low income students who have the kind of academic strengths characteristic of those students from poverty backgrounds already attending Black colleges. They are basically motivated and their aspirations are low enough and flexible enough to be changed; they do not present personality deficits so often assumed to result from cultural restriction and deprivation. Rather, they need the kind of help colleges are uniquely prepared to provide. They need experiences that reinforce their self-confidence; they need information, exposure, and models who represent the viability of realizing high educational and occupational achievement. We do not mean that admitting more such low income, rural youth will produce a level of urbaneness and social sophistication that many of the highest status students currently bring to the most elite Black colleges. But we wish to stress, from the data we have presented, the strong probability that they will bring academic commitments and motivational strengths that should make their potential for change and development the kind of challenge that higher education should symbolize.

chapter 6

College and Its Impact on Motivation and Aspirations

This chapter takes up the impact of college on students' achievement as expressed through their personal, occupational, and educational goals and through their college performance. Did the 10 institutions differ in their average levels of student aspiration, motivation, and performance? Did the differences simply reflect selectivity in recruitment, or did they imply something about the influence of the colleges on their students? Which of the institutions managed to heighten aspiration and motivation, and why? Did the "enhancement" institutions affect students through identical motivational dynamics or did several patterns produce positive effects?

INSTITUTIONAL PATTERNS OF STUDENT ASPIRATIONS, PERFORMANCE, AND MOTIVATION

Aspirations

Students' demographic backgrounds were generally unimportant in explaining individual differences in their college performance and in their achievement values and motives and, therefore, would not be expected to carry much weight in explaining why the colleges might differ in these aspects of student motivation and achievement. But they could partially account for college differences in the students' aspirations and expectancies of achieving their goals. Therefore, we consistently partialled out the effects of precollege background (rural-urban residency and father's education) and the sizable effect of sex on aspiration *before* we examined the average level of aspiration in the 10 colleges. This meant that the colleges that exhibited high levels of student aspiration did so even after adjusting for the fact that, compared to other colleges, they might have recruited more students from reasonably comfortable, urban, and professional families, or that they

143

enrolled a disproportionate number of men who, on the average, held higher levels of aspiration.[1]

Even after controlling for the student input characteristics that we knew influenced aspiration, the average student aspiration levels differed greatly in the 10 colleges we studied in 1964 and the six we studied in 1970. Although the colleges did differ more in 1970 than earlier with respect to their students' graduate school aspirations, in most other ways the size of these college differences was about the same in 1964 and 1970 (Appendix Table 6.1). Moreover, ranking the colleges by their students' average aspiration levels resulted in exactly the same order in 1964 and in 1970.

TABLE 1.   **Rank Order of the Colleges by Their Students' Level of Educational and Occupational Aspirations**[a]

| | Graduate or Professional Aspirations | | Prestige of the Choice | | Occupational Aspirations | | | |
| | | | | | Ability Demands of the Choice | | Nontraditionality of the Choice | |
	1964	1970	1964	1970	1964	1970	1964	1970
College	I	I	J	J	J	J	J	J
College	J	J	I	I	I	I	H	H
College	B	B	H	H	H	H	I	I
College	H	H·	B	B	B	B	B	No data
College	C	C	E	No data	C	C	D	B
College	E	No data	G	No data	E	No data	C	C
College	G	No data	D	No data	D	No data	E	No data
College	D	No data	C	C	G	No data	G	No data
College	F	No data	F	No data	F	No data	F	No data
College	A	A	A	A	A	A	A	A

[a]These rank orders were based on average scores for each college after adjusting for differences in the proportion of women enrolled, the students' rural-urban backgrounds, and fathers' educational attainments. The order of just the six colleges that participated both in 1964 and 1970 was perfectly correlated for all dimensions of aspirations.

1. Statistically adjusting for the fact that these 10 colleges served students from different social backgrounds did not completely eliminate selection effects. It would have been preferable to match colleges on these student input characteristics to see whether student aspirations and motivation still differed despite matched student populations, and whether they were influenced more in one institution than another that served the same kinds of students. The statistical control we exercised made it possible, at least, to answer the hypothetical question of whether the colleges would have differed in their students' aspirations and motivations *if* they had enrolled students with the same average background characteristics.

To illustrate the size of the aspiration differences, it may be helpful to show how the top quarter of the total sample of students was distributed across the colleges. Using an average of the 1964 and 1970 figures, we find the following contrast between the college with the highest average aspiration levels and the one with the lowest:

	College with Highest Level of Student Aspirations	College with Lowest Level of Student Aspirations
Proportion in the upper quarter of the total sample on occupational aspirations:		
Prestige of the choice	50%	11%
Ability demands of the choice	49%	15%
Nontraditionality of the choice	40%	10%
Proportion who where certain they would go to graduate professional school	33%	5%

Two colleges particularly stood out from all others in the number of their students who expressed either doctoral or professional degree aspirations. In 1970 nearly half of the students at these two institutions, compared to less than a quarter of the students at most of the others, planned to pursue the highest degrees. Of course, student aspirations in some of the colleges were very similar; these comparisons of the most extreme colleges simply emphasize the wide range these colleges represented. It was considerable both in 1964 and 1970.

Documentation of these institutional variations should reduce the tendency to view all historically Black colleges as homogeneous institutions. While people who know Black colleges are fully aware of both their common and unique patterns of historical development as well as their current heterogeneity, the wider public often is not. These data on student aspirations complement other recent work, particularly by Bowles[2] and by Jaffe,[3] that demonstrates the diversity within the Black colleges and the commonality between them and predominantly white schools of the same size in the same states. These much needed facts in no way rob the Black colleges of their potential to build on their common histories or to continue to serve unique functions in higher education. In some circles it is feared that stressing the variation within the Black world will foster divisiveness or, at least,

2. Frank Bowles and Frank A. DeCosta, *Between Two Worlds* (Berkeley: the Carnegie Foundation for the Advancement of Teaching, 1971).
3. A. J. Jaffe, Walter Adams and Sandra G. Meyers, *Negro Higher Education in the the 1960's* (New York: Frederick A. Praeger, 1968).

will play into the white world's desire to minimize Black identity and sense of peoplehood at a time when they form the basis for political strength. Indeed, the mutual cooperation of Black colleges has been one of their strengths. Cooperation does not demand identical programs but, rather, their speaking in one voice about policies and developments that affect them all while each college functions in its own way for its own particular student body.

Why did these colleges differ in their students' levels of aspirations? Did they attract students who already held different goals when they entered college? Did certain of them influence their students' aspirations more than others? Despite widespread beliefs about the importance of institutional "quality," Astin and others make very clear that most of the institutional variation in student aspirations and achievement in American colleges results from selection rather than from institutional effect. Studying 246 accredited four-year colleges and universities, Astin and Panos conclude that:

> From half to three-quarters of the observed variance in the five educational criteria (completing four years of college, obtaining a Bachelor's degree, planning graduate study, planning a Ph.D., and planning a professional degree) was attributable to differential student inputs, and only about half of the remaining variance was attributable to institutional variables. Thus, with respect to the problem of interaction between the individual and his environment, these findings suggest the large observed differences among institutions in educational outcomes are more a function of differences in their entering students than of differences in measurable characteristics of their environment.[4]

We ruled out some of the possible effects of selection by originally adjusting for the fact that these colleges served students from different social backgrounds. However, controlling for demographic differences among entering students does not mean that freshmen in the 10 colleges would necessarily show comparable aspirations at time of entrance. And they did not. It only means that colleges differed in their students' average level of aspiration even considering that they attracted students from varied backgrounds.

Selectivity clearly lay behind part of the institutional variation in aspirations. The men students who entered these colleges already ran the gamut of levels of job aspiration, and while their graduate school aspirations did not differ at time of entrance in 1964, they did by 1970.

---

4. Alexander W. Astin and Robert J. Panos, *The Educational and Vocational Development of College Students* (Washington, D.C.: American Council on Education, 1969), p. 63.

Freshman women differed college by college, although less than did the male entrants. These initial differences between entering freshman classes, significant in 1964, were even more marked in 1970 (Appendix Table 6.2).

Selectivity was not the entire explanation. The 1964 study included a follow-up of freshmen at the end of their first year in college. Even after adjusting for selectivity differences among the 10 colleges, freshman aspiration levels still differed significantly at the end of the year. This evidence of institutional effect applied to all dimensions of job choice and aspiration for post baccalaureate education among the men; it occurred only in degree of job difficulty represented by the occupational choice and in graduate school aspirations for women. (Appendix Tables 6.2 and 6.3).

Generally, the nature of this effect was to accentuate[5] the initial differences among the colleges. The college with the highest aspiration levels among its entering freshmen showed even higher levels at the end of the year; the colleges with lower initial scores generally ended up with even lower levels. Still, accentuation did not describe the complete picture since one of the colleges with an initially low score showed such a large increase by the end of the year that it took first place in ranking the colleges after adjusting for entrance differences. We will return to these patterns of effect at the end of this chapter to show the dynamics of three different types: an *accentuation* pattern, a college whose freshmen entered with unusually high aspirations and finished the first year with even higher scores; a *maintenance* pattern, a college whose freshmen entered with high initial scores but whose aspiration scores at the end of the year showed the reduction generally expected of extreme scores in analyses of change; and a *redirection* pattern, a college whose freshmen entered with only moderate scores but completed the year with much higher scores than would be expected simply from regression effects, so much higher that their adjusted scores moved them to the top of the rank order of colleges.

---

5. Feldman and Newcomb have referred to this type of impact as the "accentuation of initial differences." The differences in institutional environments that initially attract students with different characteristics serve to reinforce and accentuate these differences. We see this in these results from examining the raw change scores that typically countered the regression toward the mean that is ordinarily expected in analyzing change. The colleges with initially high student aspiration scores showed even higher, those with initially lower scores showed even lower, at the end of the freshman year. See K. Feldman and Theodore M. Newcomb, *The Impact of College on Students* (San Francisco: Jossey-Bass, 1969).

College Performance

Student performance data were collected only in 1964. Even then they can be used to show only the differences rather than the effects of the 10 colleges. Without change scores on achievement tests, we had no indicator of the improvement in performance that would reflect the educational impact of the college. Moreover, since we did not administer a standard achievement test in the 10 colleges at the end of the freshman year, it was impossible to carry out some of the common analyses of institutional impact on achievement.[6]

We did gather information about student grade-point averages (Appendix Table 6.4). While not indicating much about institutional impact, school variation in college grades does tell us something about the reward and performance climates on the 10 campuses. With approximately C+ at the highest and C− at the lowest school, the average grade level differed greatly among the 10 colleges. In fact the relationship between the grades students received and the school they attended turned out to be the largest of all the institutional correlates we examined. College differences in grade-point averages were as sizable among seniors as among freshmen and were unaltered by controlling for college differences in their sex ratios and their students' demographic backgrounds (Appendix Table 6.1).

Admittedly, these differences could reflect institutional differences in other student characteristics that were more closely related than precollege demographic factors were to college grades. For instance, we know that certain colleges attracted more students whose high school performance put them in the upper 20 percent of their graduating classes. Freshman performance on the SAT also differed significantly among the five colleges that administered that entrance test in 1964. Thus, what looks like different reward climates could simply mean that these colleges attracted students with different performance histories and that superior high school students simply continued their performance into college. This turns out not to be the whole case. Although the control for high school rank reduced the size of college differences in grades, large differences still persisted. (The beta coeffi-

---

6. Many analyses of impact use entrance characteristics of students, including their entrance test scores, in a multivariate analysis that also includes institutional characteristics to predict some outcome measure of achievement, such as Graduate Record Examination scores. Others derive a prediction equation for such outcome achievement scores solely from student characteristics at time of entrance and demonstrate institutional effect according to how much higher or lower the actual achievement outcome scores are than those that were predicted by their students' entrance characteristics. In both cases the dependent variable is a measure of achievement administered at the end of the senior year or at least after attendance in the college for some time.

cient for institutions in predicting grade-point averages was reduced from .52 to .44 when high school rank was controlled.) Furthermore, looking just at the five colleges where SAT's were administered to entering freshmen, we found even greater institutional differences in grades after adjusting for initial test score differences. (The beta coefficient for institution in predicting cumulative grades for these five colleges was raised from .39 to .48 when SAT scores were controlled.) This happened primarily because of two colleges that we will discuss more fully at the end of this chapter. At one freshmen entered with unusually high average SAT scores but nonetheless received the lowest average grades. Therefore, the average grades there were reduced from the low of 1.31 (on a four-point grading system) to an even lower average of 1.11 after adjusting for its students' entrance scores. Students at this college argued that the faculty too often used grades to show them that they would not measure up to standards that the students felt represented the faculty's own exaggerated conceptions of national norms or achievement in white colleges. The faculty often felt that the students' achievements did not live up to their capabilities. Both views could be supported by the fact that the students at this college did not perform badly on the anagrams task that we administered in 1964; they placed fifth in the group of nine colleges. Something was happening at this college that produced poorer grades than the students should have received. We will speculate about this again when we explore the motivation climate of this campus at the end of this chapter. The other college showed the opposite picture. Although the students' SAT scores at time of entrance were the second lowest of the five colleges that administered them, the cumulative grades there were the highest of all. Adjusting for SAT scores, therefore, brought the average grades from a high of 2.49 to an even higher adjusted average of 2.65. Moreover, average performance on the anagrams task was also the highest there. Students were performing unusually well at this college despite their considerably lower entrance scores. We will argue at the end of this chapter that a high expectancy environment in which the faculty believed that all students could learn and perform at high standards accounted in large measure for the higher grade achievements there. At this point we highlight these two examples to show that college differences in grades did not reflect simply their different potential to attract students with superior test scores.

Achievement-Related Motivation

The 10 colleges differed very little in the motives or value aspects of their students' achievement motivation (Appendix Table 6.1). They did not differ at the freshman or at the senior year in their students' average test anxiety scores nor in their scores on our measures of achievement or success motives. It was only on the measure of concern with security that the students attending the 10 colleges differed significantly; students in two colleges showed unusually high concern while students in one expressed unusually low concern with security issues when they talked about their future goals. Also, there was no evidence from examining freshman change that any college affected its students' achievement motives more than others (Appendix Table 6.3).

Commitment to Protestant ethic values did vary somewhat from college to college, although the differences were not large in either 1964 or 1970 (Appendix Table 6.1). There were really three groups of colleges: a group of three where students expressed comparatively strong beliefs in the importance of ability, hard work, perseverance, and other internal virtues in determining success in life; another group of four with intermediate scores on the internal Control Ideology scale; and a final group of three where students much more frequently rejected traditional work ethic beliefs about what determines success in the culture at large. The general effect of college was to alter a rigid adherence to an Horatio Alger ideology and to bring about a more balanced explanation of success and failure. This showed up in two ways: seniors were consistently more external than freshmen on the Control Ideology scale, and freshmen in all schools completed their first year more external than they began it. This college impact was greater at some of the colleges than at others; even after adjusting for initial differences, freshmen in the 10 colleges continued to differ significantly at the end of the freshman year (Appendix Table 6.3). Furthermore, it was clear, as it was with job and educational aspirations, that the differential impact of the colleges generally resulted from accentuation effects. While students shifted toward greater externality at all colleges, the shift was greatest at colleges whose freshmen entered with the greatest skepticism about the Protestant ethic.

Institutional variation in the expectancy aspect of motivation generally followed the picture we have already presented of student aspirations. In both 1964 and 1970 the colleges differed significantly in their students' sense of personal control and in their academic self-confidence (Appendix Table 6.1). These college differences persisted after adjusting for student input characteristics; they existed at both the freshman and senior year. They were attributable to selectivity at least to some extent for men and almost totally for women. Certain colleges attracted the more self-confident students. Again it was the men students who were measurably affected by the colleges they attended, and there was no evidence of institutional effect on women

(Appendix Table 6.3). The impact of college on men mirrors what we have already seen in its effect on aspiration. With one exception, the colleges whose freshman men entered with unusually high self-confidence showed even higher feelings of competency and efficacy at the end of the freshman year; the colleges whose men entered with greater doubts about their academic potential and their capacity to control what happened in their lives ended with even lower scores after the first year in college.

Summary of College Differences and Effects

Several generalizations can be made with reasonable confidence from these analyses of college differences.

1. Even after adjusting for college differences in sex ratios and demographic characteristics of their students, the colleges still differed in the average level of their students' job and educational aspirations, college grades, commitment to Protestant ethic values, preoccupation with security concerns in thinking about their futures, and academic self-confidence and sense of personal efficacy. In contrast, the colleges did not differ in their students' test anxiety or in any of the positive, achievement-related motives that we measured.

2. Differences among the colleges were largest regarding college grades, followed by occupational aspirations; they differed somewhat less with respect to their students' graduate school intentions and competency self-assessments.

3. The size of these differences among the colleges remained reasonably constant from 1964 to 1970. It was only with respect to graduate school aspirations that the colleges differed more in 1970 than in 1964. Moreover, the ranking of the colleges was virtually unchanged. Those colleges that were ranked high in 1964 were still at the top in 1970; the lower ones were still lower.

4. Selectivity effects beyond the colleges' differences in sex ratios and students' social backgrounds accounted for many of the differences in student aspiration and motivation. Freshmen at certain colleges entered college with higher aspirations, greater self-confidence, and more balanced judgments about what determines success and failure, even after adjusting for obvious demographic influences on these student characteristics.

5. Still, there was evidence of some institutional effect as well, particularly on men students. Generally this effect was to accentuate initial differences among the colleges. These accentuation effects characterized what happened regarding all dimensions of the male freshmen's aspirations and competency judgments as well as women's choice of jobs that demanded high ability.

6. Repeatedly we have seen that the particular college a man attended meant more than it did for a woman. Institutional differences were greater among men than among women. Even more important, college clearly affected men more than women. This sex difference in the meaning of college on aspiration and achievement has been found in numerous other studies of college impact and in no way represents a difference unique to historically Black colleges.[7]

FEATURES OF THE COLLEGE BEARING MOTIVATIONAL RELEVANCE FOR STUDENTS

Thus far we have seen that certain colleges attracted students who held unusually high aspirations and, moreover, that some colleges were better able than others to influence their students' aspirations. In this section we turn to why some institutions seemed to have greater impact on their students—what features and qualities of the college made for greater influence. Although we can never capture all the qualities that provided the more positive motivational climates, we can examine several institutional features that varied across the 10 colleges and thus could have affected student motivation. We have tried to go beyond the unique environment of each college by grouping them according to a number of critical qualities: type of sponsorship, academic status, histories of handling student and faculty activism, financial resources, emphasis on teacher training relative to liberal arts, sex ratio of the student body, faculty contact with students, and numerous other characteristics of their environments as perceived by the students themselves.[8]

College Environments

Our purposive selection of colleges according to academic status, public-private sponsorship, and response to student activism also resulted in numerous other differences among the 10 colleges. The additional dimensions that we used in exploring the connection between institutional characteristics and student motivation fell into two

7. Astin and Panos, *Educational and Vocational Development of College Students.* J. A. Davis, *Great Aspirations* (Chicago: Aldine, 1964).

8. The unit of analysis throughout this chapter is students, not institutions, since 10 colleges are too few for institutional comparisons. This means that we classified the 10 by several different institutional characteristics, such as whether they were publically or privately sponsored, and then compared all students attending one type of institution with all students attending the other type(s). Generally, we classified the 10 colleges into no more than three categories of institutions.

categories: features provided by the colleges to the students and features provided by what the students and campus culture were like.

How did the colleges differ in what they presented to students? Student-body size differed greatly among the 10, largely as a function of public or private sponsorship. With one exception all of the public institutions were larger than those that were privately sponsored. Their curricular emphases also varied greatly. In the college that most emphasized liberal arts, 93 percent of the students were enrolled in that curriculum, as compared to 29 percent in the college where the liberal arts were least emphasized. Teacher training varied from a high of one-third of the students enrolled in schools or departments of education to a low of no students majoring in education (although some took enough courses to qualify for a teaching certificate).

While the historic tendency for more women than men to enter Black colleges continues, particularly colleges in the Deep South, the 10 colleges also varied considerably in the sex ratios of their student bodies. In 1964, the sex ratios varied from one college where women represented 68 percent of the student body to one in which they were only 32 percent. By 1970 these extremes were reduced by a growing proportion of men, a phenomenon generally attributed to increased admissions and the larger financial resources available in the sixties. Still, the six colleges differed in 1970, with only two showing sex parity in their student bodies.

We were particularly interested in what going to a college where women predominated might mean to the women's willingness to choose unconventional jobs. If women felt their femininity threatened by pursuing goals few women select, they might opt for the more conventional roles in colleges where competition for dating and marriage was increased by the scarcity of men. On the other hand, a grim social situation could produce heightened desire among women for unusual, challenging careers simply because they eschewed marriage as being problematic and not to be depended upon as an exclusive, or even major, source of gratification in life. Our data indicate this rarely happened. Even in colleges where they far outnumbered men, women just as frequently put marriage as their primary goal. It was true, nonetheless, that significantly fewer women in such colleges listed being a housewife as their only commitment; they more often discussed their futures as involving both marriage and work outside the family.

Three other environmental features related directly to student life on the campuses. One pertained to student personnel services. While we did not pretend to evaluate their quality, the facilities for personal, academic, and occupational counseling, as well as for placement, were more numerous on some campuses than others. Amount of faculty-student interaction also varied greatly across the 10 colleges, with the high represented by a college where 90 percent of the students reported nonclass contacts with at least one faculty person; a third mentioned such contacts with three or more faculty members. In the college at the opposite extreme only 40 percent of the students mentioned any contact at all with the faculty outside of the classroom.

The diversity of student activities was much greater on some campuses than on others. We measured diversity by coding how many different interest areas (e.g., music, art, drama, literary, political, social action, service, religious, social or fraternal clubs involving like-sex memberships, heterosexual social activities, sports, campus loyalty, or booster groups, departmental or academically oriented groups, lecture or cultural events committees) were represented by the activities available on the campus. We depended upon yearbooks and interviews with informed campus leaders, who were asked to mention all the groupings they could think of that might not be listed in their yearbook. The final measure of diversity was weighted so as to give higher scores to colleges that not only had more interest groups but that met two additional criteria: (1) the number of activities in areas other than "collegiate-social or sports" began to approximate the available options in those areas, and (2) there existed within these lesser collegiate social activities not only the formal groups listed in the campus yearbook but also some informal groups created out of student interest. For instance, two colleges that placed equal emphasis on sports and social groups received different scores if the number of music and literary groups was much greater at one than at the other, or if one campus had numerous informal jazz groups, a newly developing literary magazine, or a news sheet that the students themselves were writing. This obviously resulted in a measure of more than simple diversity; rather, it marked the amount of diversity and the degree of self-initiated activity that characterized the noncollegiate aspects of life on the campus. This meaning of the measure is reflected in the fact that using it to rank the schools was negatively related to ranking them according to the average importance that the students felt sports ($-.89$) and parties and social life ($-.65$) had on the campus. Scored this way, the diversity of extracurricular activities ranged from a score of 55 at the college with the largest number of different activity options to 22 at the college with the fewest.

Turning to characteristics of the students and the student culture, we distinguished between inputs of the students' precollege backgrounds and the experiences and attitudes they reported about campus atmosphere. We have repeatedly emphasized that these 10 colleges served students who came from very different social backgrounds. Measuring the social statuses of the student body by an average of how many students grew up in families where the parents had gone to college, held professional jobs, and earned incomes of $10,000 or more per year, the colleges varied from a high of 58 percent that met these criteria to a low of 19 percent. Measuring cosmopolitanism by averaging the proportion of students from cities of at least 50,000 population and the proportion of out-of-state students attending the college, cosmopolitanism varied from one college with 59 percent urban, out-of-state students to one with only 4 percent. We have also previously stressed that the 10 colleges varied in academic selectivity. In 1964 the most select student body included 41 percent from the upper fifth of their high school graduating classes, while the comparable figure was 9 percent in the least selective college.

Variation in student cultures depends on many subtle qualities of student relationships and what is admired and rewarded in day-to-day life. Obviously we do injustice to those subtleties with questionnaire responses, although they do tell us something about life on the campus. For example, the colleges differed markedly in their students' stance toward what were later known as student power issues. In 1964 we asked two sets of questions that were germane to governance and power issues. One asked students how much they approved or disapproved of rather common campus regulations, such as rules about women's hours, parental permission to leave campus, administrative control over conducting civil rights demonstrations on and off campus, and clearance of speakers that student organizations could invite to the campus. The other set asked who were the legitimate decision makers on these kinds of regulations—the administration alone, students and administration working together, or the students alone. On the campus where there was the most criticism of traditional governance, in 1964 nearly 70 percent of the students disapproved of all of the parietal regulations and felt that they either alone, or working with administrators, should make decisions about rules that affected their lives. Where students were most accepting of administrative authority, this figure dropped to less than 20 percent of the students. Student attitudes shifted on all campuses after 1964. (See Chapter 8 for data on the total population shifts regarding college regulations from 1964 to 1970.) Generally students became much more critical of campus regulations and traditional administrative authority. The shifts were most impressive among freshmen: freshmen in 1970 came to college more critical of regulations than the seniors had been in 1964 and were almost as critical as the seniors were in 1970. Colleges clearly faced a different breed of students who entered college already questioning whether the administration should take a paternalistic stance. The students were also less receptive in 1970 than in 1964 to the idea that the college administration should be the sole voice in making decisions about their lives. Whereas students were fairly evenly split in 1964 between favoring traditional governance and advocating a consensual authority structure in which both the administration and students shared power, the modal view about governance in 1970 stressed student participation. Even in 1970 students were not pressing their sole authority to decide anything except how they could spend their time off campus. Thus, although the shifts since 1964 were striking, participation rather than unilateral student power was what students wanted in 1970. Impressive as these shifts are, they occurred at all colleges and in no way changed the 1964 ordering of the 10 colleges. The colleges where students were most critical of traditional governance in 1964 still stood out as the most critical in 1970. The college where these feelings were rare in 1964 likewise still showed the greatest (although diminishing) acceptance of traditional administrative authority in 1970.

Student activism also varied greatly on the 10 campuses. Since activism and Black Nationalism form the central theme of the next section of the book, just a brief description of college differences will suffice here. In 1964-1965 activism primarily meant civil rights participation; campus-power protest was yet to erupt and Afro-American groups had only begun to emerge. The big shift since then was to the much greater diversification in types of activism and in the issues that served to focus student concern. But with the demonstration epoch of protest not yet over in 1964, students in some schools were much more involved than in others. At the most active college 86 percent of the students had taken part in some protest while only 13 percent had participated at the least active campus. This disparity obviously reflected variation in the degree of constraint placed on the student body by the administration. Where there were strong sanctions, there was little participation. The reverse was not true, however. Even in the six colleges where there was little constraint, students were more active at some than at others.

Three other closely interrelated measures indicate something about the social integration of the 10 campuses. Two of these represent how "hooked-in" students were to organized groups on the campus. Breadth of extracurricular involvement, measured by averaging the proportion of students who participated in some extracurricular activity other than fraternities and sororities and also the proportion who had had some leadership experience in these groups, ranged from 57 percent at the most involved campus to 33 percent at the least involved.

Participation rates in campus elections varied from a high of 84 percent to a low of 31 percent.

The third measure will not indicate very much about social integration to those uninformed about the significance of Greek organizations on Black college campuses. In contrast to the decreasing importance and generally conservative and insulating functions that they serve for white students, Greek organizations on Black campuses have attracted students, and continue to attract them, who perform well in college, who become highly involved in campus organizations and politics, and even play significant roles in campus protest and social change. This does not mean the members feel no conflict between status maintenance and social change commitments. They often do. But the conflict is minimized because Black Greek national organizations have long histories of commitment, however moderate, to race responsibility and progress. That tradition provides a context for expressing social concerns among the Greeks on Black campuses. Of course, the conventional kinds of campus leaders have come from Greek organizations at white colleges too; in fact that was where the power lay in preceding decades, as it still does at some small white schools. But on Black campuses Greek leadership frequently has stood, and clearly did in 1964-1965, for commitment to protest and change more than for preservation of status. Observers often miss this aspect of fraternal life on the Black campus since the image of Greek organizations often depends on public presentations of their traditions and rituals. Since student-body size severely limits how many students can join the fraternities and the sororities that have national status, student attitudes about Greek organizations are a more accurate indicator than membership of their place on the campus. We averaged the proportion of students who strongly approved of fraternities and sororities and also the proportion of nonmembers who would have liked to join. At one extreme was a college whose student body was 85 percent pro-Greek affiliation; at the other end, was a campus at which only 40 percent of the students favored fraternities or sororities.

The last measure of the environment that we used in these analyses of impact on student motivation can be thought of as the academic stress in the student culture. At colleges where the academic stress was strongest, large numbers of students said they chose the college because of its academic reputation and because it was a hard school that would really challenge them; also many students showed intrinsic sources of academic motivation—they preferred classes where attendance was not required, where the professor would leave it up to the students to keep up with their work instead of checking to see that assignments were being carried out properly and on time, where stu-

TABLE 2.   **Summary of the Range Represented by the 10 Colleges
That Participated in 1964 on Several Institutional Features**

	Highest College	Lowest College
Size of the student body	4088	498
Curricular emphases:		
Proportion enrolled in the liberal arts	93%	29%
Proportion enrolled in teacher training departments	33%	0%
Sex Ratio: Proportion of women enrolled	68%	32%
Proportion of students who reported nonclass contacts with at least one faculty member	90%	40%
Diversity of extracurricular activities:		
Number of activity options weighted for emphasis on collegiate-social types	55	22
Social status of students: Proportion who grew up in families where parents had gone to college, held professional jobs, and earned incomes of $10,000 or more	58%	19%
Cosmopolitanism of students' backgrounds:		
Average of the proportion from cities of at least 50,000 and proportion from out-of-state	59%	4%
Selectivity: Proportion of students from upper fifth of high school class	41%	9%
Rejection of traditional governance:		
Proportion of students who disapproved of all parietal regulations measured	70%	20%
Proportion of the students who had taken part in some *civil rights activity*	86%	13%
Breadth of participation in campus life:		
Average of the proportion who participated in some activity (other than greek organizations) and proportion who had had some leadership experience	57%	33%
Proportion of students who had voted in previous campus election	84%	31%
Average of proportion of students who strongly approved of greek organizations and proportion who would have liked to join	85%	40%
Academic stress of student culture:		
Proportion of students who stressed academic values in what was important about the college	68%	33%

dents were encouraged to do independent reading instead of the professor giving definite, required assignments, and where the professor discussed a lot of interesting ideas that might not be covered on exams. Averaging these three highly interrelated measures of the students' academic commitments, the colleges varied from one where 68 percent expressed these orientations to one where only 33 percent did.

These institutional features and the various aspects of the student cultures were clearly not independent of each other. While it would facilitate understanding what really affects student motivation if such institutional characteristics were not highly interrelated, that is not the way the world is organized. Colleges with high academic status tended to be chosen for their reputation. Colleges where many students took part in campus groups also had high student participation rates in campus elections.

To examine how these institutional characteristics were patterned, we ranked each of the colleges, relative to others, on each of these 17 dimensions of their environments. One major cluster was what might be thought of as a status-academic cluster. It was comprised of six highly (at least .75) interrelated features: the social status and cosmopolitanism of the student body, the college's academic selectivity, the diversity of the extracurricular activities offered on the campus, the academic stress in the student culture, and the amount of faculty-student interaction reported by students. A second set included size of the student body, number of personnel services, and curricular emphasis. Student services were more numerous and curriculum more diversified in the larger institutions. Size also affected organizational features of student life. Participation in extracurricular activities included a broader spectrum of the students in the smaller schools; student government elections also drew a larger proportion of the students in the smaller colleges. On the other hand, diversity of extracurricular groups was unrelated to student-body size. Another small cluster represented the governance climate of the campus: colleges where large proportions of students approved of shared power between the administration and the students also showed high participation rates in student elections and broad involvement in extracurricular activities. In addition, these three student attitude and participation measures were strongly related to amount of student-faculty interaction, although they were only weakly related to other aspects of the status-academic set in which faculty-student interaction was embedded. Moreover, this governance set was only weakly related to the level of civil rights activism on the campus. In fact, the only institutional feature that was clearly connected to level of campus activism in 1964 was curricular emphasis. Colleges with strong liberal arts emphasis were also likely to show the highest rates of student involvement in civil rights. Interestingly enough, curricular emphasis meant little else, at least with respect to these dimensions of college environment. Finally, the two institutional features that were most independent of all others were the sex ratio of the student body and the level of student approval of Greek organizations.

Relevance of these Features for Institutional Effect

Because of the small number of schools participating in the study, we were not able to partial out the effects of other institutional characteristics when trying to isolate the meaning of a given feature of the college. We simply would have run out of colleges. Thus, we were stuck with the fact that many characteristics of the college also represented others. Therefore, we tried to analyze the implications for freshman change in aspiration of each institutional feature separately and then to discuss the cluster of features that both hung together and similarly influenced student aspirations. We were restricted in this to the 1964 data since that was the only time when freshman students were studied at both the beginning and end of the year, thereby providing a measure of institutional impact.

EFFECT ON WOMEN.

College affected women students primarily in whether they chose jobs perceived by fellow students as demanding great ability and in whether they planned to pursue either a Ph.D. or advanced professional degree at the graduate level (Table 6.2). Both were rare choices for women; they reflected a willingness to pursue unconventional goals that other women students viewed as undesirable and generally unfeminine. Thus, where there was evidence of college impact, it served to challenge sex-role constraints on women's choices. Attending certain kinds of colleges also positively influenced women's sense of personal control.

What institutional features seemed to facilitate these unconventional choices and personal control among women? The academic characteristics of the institution mattered most. Even after controlling for selectivity, freshman women who attended colleges with high academic status, high faculty-student interaction, diverse curricular options, and a strong academic stress in the student culture finished the freshman year with even higher aspirations for demanding and difficult jobs (Appendix Tables 6.5A, and 6.6A). Two of these characteristics, the academic stress of the student culture and faculty-student interaction, also fostered stronger commitments among women to pursue higher degrees at the graduate level. In fact, these were the only two college characteristics that affected women's graduate school plans. Women who attended colleges where students held strong academic values and where faculty-student contact outside of class was reasonably widespread completed their freshman year more committed to advanced education (Appendix Table 6.6A). Faculty-student interaction also fostered personal efficacy among women. Where many students reported getting to know faculty outside of class and where extracurricular offerings were especially diverse women showed an increase in their sense of personal control (Table 6.8A).

One institutional characteristic that was not part of the academic cluster, the level of rejection of traditional governance on the campus, also affected women's aspirations. Women completed their freshman year with stronger aspirations for jobs that would challenge their abilities and with higher personal efficacy at those colleges where students favored a shared power model of governance (Appendix Tables 6.6A and 6.8A). While we cannot be sure that these results reflect the fact that such schools also showed atypically high faculty-student interaction, we suspect that was the case. Governance climate did not relate to other characteristics of the academic cluster, but was clearly related to faculty-student interaction (.65). The impact of governance climate on women's job aspirations and sense of efficacy probably did result, therefore, because faculty and students interacted more frequently on campuses where students were especially critical of traditional governance.

None of the other institutional features we examined affected the aspirations or achievement motivation of the women. The remaining differences resulted mostly from selectivity rather than from institutional impact. For example, women who entered private colleges, those whose student populations were especially cosmopolitan and from unusually high status backgrounds, and those with an emphasis on the liberal arts expressed higher job aspirations and sense of efficacy. Those differences disappeared when their scores at the end of the freshman year were adjusted for selectivity effects (Appendix Tables 6.5A and 6.7).

Several other institutional characteristics were not even important as selection influences. Women expressed much the same aspirations and achievement motivation in colleges that varied in such institutional features as the sex ratio of the college, student body size, number of student personnel services, level of civil rights activism, breadth of student participation in extracurricular affairs, participation rates in student government elections, and level of pro-Greek attitudes. We find especially interesting that women's aspirations were not unduly restricted by attending a college where women outnumbered men. The sex ratio of the college simply had no meaning for women's aspirations or motivation. Women had much the same occupational and educational aspirations regardless of whether they entered a college where men outnumbered women, women outnumbered men, or where both sexes were fairly equal in number. At the end of the freshman year their aspirations were also unaffected by the distribution of men and women at their colleges.

EFFECT ON MEN

The impact of college was greater on men than on women. More of the institutional features we have examined carried effect implications for men and more aspects of the men's aspirations and motivations were affected by them.

Generally, freshman men ended the year having lowered their occupational aspirations, although that was more true in some institutions than in others (Appendix Table 6.2). For example, men who attended public colleges of somewhat lower academic status or colleges where many students came from families with lower social status and grew up in rural areas in the same state where the college was located completed their freshman year having reduced their level of occupational aspiration more than men in private colleges with high academic status that served more predominantly cosmopolitan and high status students (Appendix Table 6.5B). The more elite colleges did not actually heighten aspirations but their freshman men, who entered with higher job aspirations in the first place, had reduced them less at the end of the year. Moreover, the men in such colleges actually became more committed to graduate school while men in public and less elite colleges expressed less certainty about pursuing postbacclaureate training after they had been in college for a year. In this one sense, therefore, the cluster of social and academic status variables accentuated the initial aspiration differences that the freshman men brought with them to college.

Another cluster of institutional characteristics accentuated not only educational aspiration differences but also the job aspirations that male entrants to the different colleges had expressed in the fall of the freshman year. This cluster includes the academic stress of the student culture, the diversity of extracurricular activities, faculty-student interaction, and level of student rejection of traditional governance (Appendix Table 6.6B). At the end of the freshman year men attending colleges where the most students held strong academic values questioned traditional governance, got to know faculty outside of class, and had available to them a wide array of student activities were even more likely than at time of entrance to aspire to difficult, nontraditional jobs and to Ph.D. or professional degrees at the graduate level. Conversely, men attending colleges where academic values were the least widespread in the student culture and where students reported the least contact with faculty and most accepted traditional governance were even less likely to express these job and educational aspirations. The differences that had existed between freshman men at time of entrance had been accentuated in colleges varying in these ways. Faculty-student interaction and diversity of student activities on the campus also influenced men students' sense of personal efficacy and their ideologies about determinants of success and failure (Appendix Table 6.8B). In general, men's sense of efficacy was uninfluenced by a year in college. In colleges where faculty-student interaction was reasonably widespread and where activities were especially diverse, efficacy did increase during the freshman year. And, while students generally became more cynical about the Protestant work ethic, showing more external scores on the Control Ideology scale at the end than at the beginning of the freshman year, this was especially true where men students got to know faculty well and had spent their freshman year on campuses that were rich in extracurricular activities.

Certain aspects of the men's aspirations and motivation were unaffected by the college they attended. For example, their achievement motives did not differ as a function of the type of college they entered nor were they measurably influenced by any of these institutional characteristics. Their academic self-confidence differed at time of entrance: men who entered colleges serving especially cosmopolitan student populations with high academic status were more self-confident academically. However, their level of confidence was not affected by the experience at such colleges since college differences at the end of the freshman year disappeared after these selectivity effects were controlled. The only two institutional variables that actually influenced the men's academic self-confidence, outside of the capacity of the college to attract more self-confident students, were the sex ratio of the college and the academic stress of the student culture. While most freshman men were less self-confident at the end than at the beginning of the freshman year, this was especially the case in colleges where men far outnumbered women (Appendix Table 6.7B) and where the academic stress was especially strong (Appendix Table 6.8B). This negative effect of a strong academic stress culture on the campus must be viewed in the context of its positive effects on the men's aspirations and sense of efficacy. Going to college that many students chose because of its academic reputation and challenge, and where students were more motivated by intrinsic than by extrinsic rewards, promoted the men's commitments to advanced education and to demanding occupational choices. It also reduced their self-confidence more than was usual in other colleges. We suspect this was only a temporary effect, since their general sense of efficacy was simultaneously heightened in such colleges. Once they learned they could compete effectively in colleges where academic values were strongest, the stress itself could become a positive aspect of its motivational climate, even for academic confidence just as it already was for aspirations and the more generalized feelings of efficacy and control in life.

The social integration of the campus was also important for some aspects of the men's achievement motivation, although it had no implications for women. Men who entered colleges where most students were active in some kind of campus organization and where campus elections involved virtually all the students ended their freshman year with heightened feelings of efficacy, even though they had not differed from men entering other kinds of colleges the previous fall (Appendix Table 6.8B). This was one way in which the organizational climate of the campus positively affected students; understandably the effect was not on aspirations or strictly academic expectancies but on the more generalized feelings of mastery and personal control that should result from going to school where students were especially active in campus political and organizational life.

Finally, there were a few institutional characteristics that did not serve as either selection factors or aspects of college impact, even for men. Student body size, number of student personnel services, student attitudes about fraternal organizations, and level of civil rights activism did not distinguish which colleges stood out in any aspect of their men students' aspirations or achievement motivation.

Summary of Motivationally Relevant Features of the College Environment

Chart A summarizes the selection and impact implications of these features of the college environment. Only the features that operated either as selection or impact for at least one sex group are included in the chart. It highlights the fact that more of these institutional characteristics affected the men than the women, as well as affected more aspects of the men's than the women's aspirations and motivations.

Despite the generally greater effect of college on men than on women, a few features of the colleges enhanced the aspirations of both sexes. Amount of faculty-student interaction and the academic stress in the student culture turned out to be the most generally significant institutional features we examined. Going to college where many

CHART A. **Summary of Selection and Impact of Characteristics of the Colleges on Men and Women: Freshman Students**

College Characteristics	Selectivity Effects	Impact
Public-private sponsorship	Private colleges: Higher prestige and ability demands of job choices for both men and women; higher personal control for women; more external work ethic ideology for men.	No effect for women; significant adjusted post scores on prestige and ability demands for men's job choices.
Social status of the student body	More elite student bodies: Higher prestige, ability demands of job choices, and sense of personal control for both men and women; greater nontraditionality of job choices and more external work ethic ideology for men.	No effects for women; significant adjusted post scores on prestige, ability demands, and nontraditionality of job choices, graduate school aspirations, external work ethic ideology for men.
Cosmopolitanism of student body	More cosmopolitan student bodies: Higher prestige, ability demands of job choices and sense of personal control for both men and women; greater nontraditionality of job choices and higher academic self-confidence for men.	No effects for women; significant adjusted post scores on prestige, ability demands, and nontraditionality of job choices, graduate school aspirations, external work ethic ideology for men.
Liberal arts emphasis in curriculum	Strongest emphasis on liberal arts: Higher prestige and ability demands of job choices and sense of personal control for both men and women; greater nontraditionality of job choices for men.	No effects for women; significant adjusted post scores on prestige, ability demands, and nontraditionality of job choices, graduate school aspirations, external work ethic ideology for men.

(Continued on Next Page)

CHART A. **Summary of Selection and Impact of Characteristics of the Colleges on Men and Women: Freshman Students**

College Characteristics	Selectivity Effects	Impact
Academic status as judged by accrediting association	Highest status colleges: Higher prestige and ability demands of job choices and sense of personal control for both men and women; greater nontraditionality of job choices and external work ethic ideology for men.	Significant adjusted post scores on prestige and ability demands of women's job choices; prestige, ability demands, and nontraditionality of job choices, graduate school aspirations, and academic self-confidence for men.
Academic stress in the student culture	Strongest academic stress colleges: Higher prestige and ability demands of job choices of both men and women; greater nontraditionality of job choices, sense of personal control and external work ethic ideology for men.	Significant adjusted post scores on graduate school aspirations, and ability demands of job choices for women; prestige ability demands, and nontraditionality of job choices, graduate school aspirations, academic self-confidence for men (lower confidence where stress strongest).
Diversity of extracurricular activities	Most diverse: Higher prestige and ability demands of job choices and sense of personal control for both men and women; higher nontraditionality of job choices for men.	Significant adjusted post scores on ability demands of job choices and sense of personal control for women; prestige ability demands, and nontraditionality of job choices, graduate school aspirations, sense of personal control, and external work ethic ideology for men.

Faculty-student interaction	Greatest interaction: Higher prestige and ability demands of job choices for both men and women; higher sense of personal control, nontraditionality of job choices, and external work ethic ideology for men.	Significant adjusted post scores on ability demands of job choices, graduate school aspirations, and sense of personal control for women; prestige, ability demands, and nontraditionality of job choices, graduate school aspirations, sense of personal control, and external work ethic ideology for men.
Rejection of traditional college governance	Rejection strongest: Higher prestige, ability demands of job choices, sense of personal control, external work ethic ideology for both men and women.	Significant adjusted post scores for ability demands of job choices and sense of personal control for women; prestige, ability demands, and nontraditionality of job choices, graduate school aspirations for men.
Breadth of student extracurricular participation	No selectivity effects for either men or women.	No effects for women; significant adjusted post scores on sense of personal control for men.
Participation rates in student elections	No selectivity effects for either men or women.	No effects for women; significant adjusted post scores on sense of personal control for men.
Sex ratio of the college	No selectivity effects for either men or women.	No effects for women; adjusted post scores on academic self-confidence for men (lower where men outnumbered women).

students reported contact with faculty outside of the classroom and where academic values were especially widespread fostered many positive developments for both men and women. Even after adjusting for the fact that such colleges attracted high aspirants in the first place, men and women on such campuses completed their freshman year more committed to graduate education, especially to pursuing the Ph.D. or professional degrees; they aspired to more demanding jobs, especially those that were unconventional either in the sense of falling outside traditional sectors of Black employment or deviating from sex-role stereotypes for women; they also felt more efficacious about being able to control their own lives.

Other aspects of the academic cluster of institutional variables were almost as generally important. Diversity of extracurricular offerings on the campus influenced both the men's and women's sense of personal control and their occupational choices. Colleges with unusually diverse activities enhanced students' level of job aspiration specifically for the most demanding and unconventional occupations, and heightened the men's but not the women's graduate school aspirations.

We have already seen that these three institutional features tended to go together—colleges high in one were likely to be high in others. We cannot tell, therefore, whether each has causal significance beyond the general atmosphere in a college that was characterized by high faculty-student interaction, diverse activity options, and heavy emphasis placed on academic values. We could, however, draw some conclusions regarding the importance of faculty contact. In addition to examining what happened to the men's and women's aspirations in colleges that varied in the proportion of students who reported contact with several faculty members, it was also possible to look at the direct relationship between the amount of contact each student reported and aspirations at the end of the freshman year. There was a direct causal relationship. Students who reported the most contact with faculty had significantly higher aspirations, even after controlling for initial aspiration differences between students who subsequently established many rather than few faculty contacts. *With the men these effects of faculty contact operated on both the ability demands and nontraditionality of their job choices as well as on their graduate school plans; with women the effect pertained to both the ability demands of their job choices and to graduate aspirations.* Thus, involvement with faculty outside of the classroom had a positive effect on the least conventional of aspirations. If colleges want to foster these kinds of less conventional aspirations, positive consequences should follow from anything that is done to encourage faculty-student interaction, to increase the diversity of activities that students can participate in, and to support and reward the academic-intellectual values in the student culture.

Institutional status that resulted from the college's capacity to attract students from out-of-state and urban environments and from professional, highly educated, high income families was far less important as an impact feature. With women these institutional features mostly served as selection influences. Women who entered such high status colleges already came with higher aspirations, but their aspirations at the end of the freshman year were not markedly different from women in other colleges after the initial selection effects had been controlled. With men these status variables were influential but primarily served as a buffer against the general tendency of men in all colleges to lower their aspirations during the freshman year. Men who entered public colleges and those serving less cosmopolitan and high status students were especially likely to reduce their educational and occupational aspirations. On the other hand, the aspirations of men who entered the more elite colleges were not enhanced by the experience there, at least not in the same sense that aspirations were enhanced by going to colleges where the academic press, faculty-student interaction, and campus organizational life were especially rich.

Since one of the major purposes of this book is to explore the possibilities of combining commitments to social change with individual achievement goals, it is noteworthy that the level of civil rights activism on the campus neither positively nor negatively influenced any aspect of either the men's or women's aspirations or achievement motivation. Of course, this does not mean that the aspirations and motivation of individual students who were active in civil rights were not positively influenced by their activism. We will explore the impact of activism on the individual achievement goals of individual students in Chapters 10 and 11. The institutional analyses did show that campuses where activism was especially widespread were neither more or less likely to encourage an aggregate shift in students' achievement goals. The activism atmosphere was simply independent of the achievement atmosphere on the campus.

PATTERNS—A LOOK AT THREE COLLEGES

Up to now we have been interested in general patterns of institutional effect. Generally, we have found that the 10 colleges showed different levels of student aspiration and motivation either because they selected students who already differed when they entered college, because certain colleges were able to buffer their students against the general tendency of lowering aspirations during the freshman year while other colleges were not, or because the college experience actually accentuated the initial differences the entering freshman brought to these 10 colleges. But these general patterns do not describe the whole picture. For example, the adjusted aspiration scores at the end of the freshman year at two colleges whose freshmen entered with equally high aspirations indicated that one had accentuated its students' already high aspirations while the' other had not. What explained this difference? A third college, whose students entered with scores that put it sixth in the group of 10, managed to redirect aspirations during the freshman year to the point that it took first place at the end of the first year after adjusting for entrance differences. What went on at these three colleges that might carry implications for others?

The intensive research techniques that we used in 1964-1965 suggest answers to this question. Informal interviews and observations of classes were carried out at all colleges to add depth to the quantitative results on freshman change obtained from the questionnaire data. In addition, two of these three colleges were part of a more systematic and extensive interview project. Six Black, recent college graduates lived in the dormitories and tried to participate as broadly as possible in both the formal and informal campus groups for a month at each of these colleges. They also conducted about 200 interviews with students who were selected to represent various campus subcultures. Although the three interview colleges had been chosen without knowing what the subsequent data analyses would show concerning their effects on aspiration and motivation, one turned out to be the college with the clearest accentuation effects and a second proved to be the college with the most obvious redirection effects.

The Accentuation Pattern

This private college with an enrollment of less than 500 and located in a rural setting drew both rural and urban students. It has traditionally sent large numbers of students on to graduate school. Its graduates stand out for their achievements. Despite extraordinarily limited resources, the school has developed the reputation for education of the highest quality. From our analyses of freshman change we see that it attracts students with high aspirations. Even so, its freshmen finished the first year with even higher scores on all dimensions of occupational aspirations, and with even a greater number planning with reasonable certainty to enter graduate school. Among the aspirants to graduate school, many more than at all other schools but one said they planned to study for professional degrees or the doctorate. This counters the usual expectations that a school with initially high averages should show somewhat lower scores just because of the statistical regression effects. Thus, after adjusting for college differences at the time their freshmen entered, this college stood out even more at the end of the freshman year than at the beginning. Its students also performed unusually well on the achievement task we included in our questionnaire sessions. Even controlling for their verbal Scholastic Aptitude Test scores, they showed the top performance on the anagrams and averaged far fewer errors. Likewise, student grade-point averages were higher although their entrance scores were very ordinary (in fact, the second lowest among the five colleges that administered the SAT in 1964).

What was it about this college that produced this pattern? It was a liberal arts college with limited resources and low per-pupil expenditures for educational and general purposes. This resulted in low faculty salaries and practically no formal counseling or other student personnel services. It attracted both out-of-state and in-state students who, by no means, showed social status characteristics as high as the student bodies at four other schools. Instead it was the social heterogeneity of the students that was so striking here. This college included a group of urban, affluent students, some of whose parents and grandparents had graduated from the same college; but it also included many students from the working classes of a nearby, major metropolitan center and from the rural areas of the state. Many of them came as their family's first generation to attend college. Women outnumbered men but not so much as at two other colleges. While the college administration had never put sanctions on students or faculty who had participated in the civil rights movement of the early sixties, a court injunction on protest at this college had effectively eliminated student participation. Furthermore, the school's geographical isolation, combined with the transportation problems that resulted from not having cars and by difficult bus connections, worked to reduce student involvement in political activities elsewhere in the state. In fact, civil rights participation was the third lowest of the 10 schools. But the campus itself, an enclave in a town that seemed not to have changed in 100 years, provided diverse extracurricular options—second in the group of 10 despite its limited resources and small student body. Almost all students participated in some activity and campus elections drew campuswide support. While many students disapproved of college regulations, of which there were many reflecting the college's history of familial concern and parietal stance toward students, the modal student opinion about governance favored community decision making, in which students, faculty, and administrators shared responsibility. Student-power advocates were few in number, although they were vocal enough. Our interviewers reported that many students, particularly the more sophisticated urbanites, were discontented with the college's general protective atmosphere. But, generally, student unrest was latent and, when expressed, was channeled through a student culture where consensus instead of conflict was the norm. With the highest scores of any college on our measure of academic stress in the student culture, this was a college where serious, scholarly endeavors were admired, although not to the exclusion of playing cards, hanging around the student union, and exhibiting the more casual style of a relaxed, socially minded campus. It tied with two other colleges in being the most pro-Greek in its attitudes.

When students were asked to identify with student subcultural types, more students at this college than at any other simultaneously chose (1) being really serious students who care about studying and achieving good grades or being intellectuals and (2) identifying with the student union crowd and casual students who have a relaxed attitude toward college. More students here viewed themselves as creative and somewhat nonconformist literary types, writers, poets, and musicians who spend a lot of time playing or listening to jazz or other types of music. In contrast, very few students identified as being just "ordinary students," a label that was much more popular at other colleges. In short, many signs indicated an involved, alive student culture where the social atmosphere in no way threatened commitment to scholarly work. Students and faculty also saw more of each other, and more students reported the influence of teachers as a significant force in their college years.

The fact was that the faculty, particularly those who had taught at the college for many years, played key roles in the college's influence on motivation. Their philosophy of education, the college's general familial quality, and the generally supportive student culture converged to make what might be called a "high expectancy environment" in which students came to believe that most of them *could* achieve. It was simply up to them. How do we see this? While many students, notably the out-of-state or urban sons and daughters of college graduates, tended to feel that grades were issued arbitrarily, even they were aware of a larger purpose behind the use of grades. Student progress and development earned the highest reward. From a faculty point of view, this showed primary concern with the intellectual development of the student. Sitting in on freshman faculty meetings, we were struck repeatedly with an incredible concern for each individual student and his or her progress. Why wasn't this student living up to potential? How was the college failing? What could they do to turn things around? Similarly, there was great pleasure taken, though admittedly less time consumed, with students who were making the strides expected of them and those who were blossoming in ways that test scores might not have predicted. While competitive techniques were used by some teachers, the dominant philosophy stressed individual growth and the conviction that there is room at the top for everyone, presuming they all want to be there. Personal achievement at the cost of someone else's failure had no place. In fact, this college, and this one alone, did not grade on the curve. It was not simply that the average grades were higher here but also that the shape of the grade distribution was different. As many students earned A's as C's at this college, which was unheard of at other colleges. These expectancies of the faculty and the expectancy atmosphere on the campus paid off for many students. Although students entered this college with high expectancies to begin with, their academic self-confidence and their sense of personal efficacy grew even higher during their freshman year. A heightening of competency feelings did not occur at all the colleges that attracted students with as initially high self-confidence.

Most students seemed to accept both the challenge and the promise of this developmental philosophy. But not all. The concern that many on the faculty evinced for the students' social and cultural development struck some students as excessive paternalism. One critic put it this way.

> The one-big happy-family point of view that prevails among the older faculty and the administration in general is just an unrealistic outlook. And it works against students who come from good high schools and other advantages that make it easy to coast along with B's. Since you're not living up to your promise and the success motif around here, you do not get a B. You get a C or maybe a D just to show you to shape up. That wouldn't be so bad but the paternalism pervades everything else too—like ridiculous curfew and courses that seem geared to acculturate us to white, northern, middle-class concerns. I admit lots of students think it's great to discuss music and painting as it's described in the New York Times. But I resent being penalized because I'm bored. I've read newspapers before, have at least a passing acquaintance with museums and art galleries, and I don't think much of either. I don't mind the course per se. It's the point of view that sees us as needing constant guidance and encouragement. I'd take a lot less encouragement and stake my chances on just how well I do on exams. Going to class, showing you're interested, and above all else responding—that's what you have to do to make the grade here.

He was right that the students' prior experiences conditioned how they perceived the philosophy and reacted to the general concern about them. While the sizable proportion who came from more cosmopolitan environments neither found the early courses liberating nor accepted the personalism of the faculty's interest in them or the protective social rules, the much larger group of students from more rural parts of the South did. An interviewer reflected this difference in students' reactions:

> *Many students seem to welcome the one-big-happy-family point of view because they need the constant encouragement, the friendly pat on the back, the interest shown in other ways, such as trips to see plays. The communal concern present in lower class Black families and small towns is replaced in a student's mind by this school's familial style and he feels more comfortable, more secure. College life is hard and different but he's not alone. Somebody cares. Communal concern, of course, also carries with it a pressure to succeed. But it is like a parent who believes that all his children can make it since they are after all—his children.*

We suspect that the accentuation of aspiration occurred because the environment, onerous as it may have been for some students, worked well for so many. Partialing out precollege social status and other demographic effects on individual aspiration scores would not affect the role we are suggesting they played in students' reactions to the college experience. Moreover, the more affluent, sophisticated students did not reduce their sights; very few of them did poorly although they, not being as happy about the campus atmosphere, criticized more. While the college may not have heightened their aspirations, motivation, or performance, they held their own. The general stand for academic excellence as a goal that every student could and would be helped to achieve did heighten both the self-confidence and the aspirations of many others; that was what seemed to lie behind the accentuation effects.

The charges of overprotection and outmoded social attitudes made by some student critics in the midsixties underestimated this college's potential for change and its administration's willingness to be influenced by student needs, even their needs for greater freedom and leeway, as they care to be expressed by increasing numbers of students, rural and urban. By 1970 the students in this college almost unanimously disapproved of the custodial rules that generally had been acceptable in 1964. In the context of shared power, they had influenced a change in those rules. As students more and more wanted courses that built on their Afro-American heritage instead of stressing Western civilization, a freshman program that included a strong Black studies component was instituted. In fact, in 1970, more students reported taking Black studies courses at this college than at any other. Moreover, as we will see later, this college's traditional emphasis in no way prevented a general growth of Black consciousness on the campus. In 1970, the students generally showed the strongest commitments to Black Nationalism while at the same time, they continued to exhibit high levels of individual achievement and aspiration. We knew much less about the ambience of the campus in 1970 than we had in 1964, but it seems altogether possible that its cooperative, communal perspective —that one need not rise at a cost to someone else—was particularly congenial to the changed Black mood.

The Maintenance Pattern

Known as an elite Black college, this liberal arts college attracted students from high-status families all over the South. It was also the only college with as many as 10 percent of its students coming from other regions of the country. Fulfilling family traditions, many students represented third, even fourth, generations to attend this college. Located in a major metropolitan center and serving a predominantly urban student body, it provided a cosmopolitan environment with diverse activities both on and off the campus. Throughout the decade of the sixties, students from this college had become leaders in the southern civil rights movement. Still, the number of involved students tended to be smaller than its reputation as an activist campus might imply. In fact, its participation rate in 1964 was fourth lowest among the 10 colleges. Moreover, while the students expressed strong commitments to Black Nationalism in 1970, the proportion of students active in civil rights groups still kept it among the least involved colleges. This discrepancy between belief and action also characterized the student-power scene here. Although more students here than at other colleges advocated student responsibility for determining college regulations, the proportion of students who had been active in either protest or governance committees was very low relative to other colleges. In fact, the breadth of student participation in extracurricular activities was altogether low compared to other colleges, and particularly low when compared to those that had as many different groups and opportunities on the campus. In numerous ways we see a picture of a rich environment offering many opportunities to sophisticated, socially aware students, who, nonetheless, seemed less active than students at other campuses. Loners whose commitments did not seem to be captured by the life on the campus were more obvious here than elsewhere.

The motivational milieu reflected a similar phenomenon. Freshmen entered with very high aspirations. At the end of the year there had been little change. Controlling for its selection advantage, the adjusted aspirations scores pulled it from first or second to third or fourth position among the 10 colleges at the end of the freshman year. Moreover, something happened to reduce the sense of efficacy and academic self-confidence during the freshman year—in striking contrast to the accentuation college where both aspirations and expectancies increased. Performance on the anagrams test likewise was lower than at the accentuation college despite similar test scores. Other data suggest that this may have reflected a lack of engagement as much as anything else. While it was by no means the predominant behavior, many more students here than at other colleges played it cool by trying not to do well on the anagrams tasks. This showed up in several ways. Too many of them who admitted they could finish all 10 anagrams said they were trying to complete only six or seven when they were asked to state a performance goal. More students also showed atypical shifts in their aspirations after succeeding on previous trials. Instead of increasing their goals after meeting the level they previously aspired to, they reduced their goal levels. They knew what it was all about. They were not going to play the game. If they had rejected only this game, which after all was not very important to them, we would make little of it. Some of the most interesting and thoughtful students strongly questioned the value of research and sometimes refused to participate or sabotaged the effort. But this pattern of opting out of the task was more pronounced among students who apparently did much the same thing in their courses. The particular students who showed this pattern turned out to have earned lower grades than the average here, despite higher test scores. As justified as their feelings about our silly task or their courses may have been, their unwillingness to get engaged was a motivational pattern that occurred more often here, and it paralleled the unengaged stance some students took toward college life in general.

This college differed from the accentuation college in other ways that also may relate to its motivational milieu. On the average, grades were lower, although students of the two colleges entered with very similar test scores. Grades also followed a typical bell-shaped curve so that competition for A's was keen indeed. Students mentioned competition frequently when they talked about sources of stress during the freshman year. Generally, though, they approved of the competition. This college's history as a selective, demanding academic environment was confirmed for them by the fact that high grades were so hard to come by. Its graduates have always stood out for unusual achievements. Still, the effect of the college seemed to result from recruiting students who would achieve no matter what happened in college. Students felt special by being there; the image of the school really mattered. But aspirations and expectancies suffered somewhat from the philosophy of the rare achievement. A peculiar message came across. Students showed they would achieve by simply getting into this college. Their future achievements were taken for granted as a function of having attended this college but while they were in college, they did not expect to perform unusually well and their sense of competency actually dropped. The communal milieu fostered at the accentuation college, at which some of their own cosmopolitan students chafed, undoubtedly would not have worked for the vast majority of students at this high-status college. They simply would not have tolerated such supervision and communal concerns at the cost of their rights of privacy and autonomy. What worked in one setting would, in all likelihood, have been disastrous in the other. Many students and faculty wanted to see activism and engagement rise, yet they recognized that it had to be done differently here.

The Redirection Pattern

This small private college located in a small town near the state capital drew students primarily from within the state, many of whom were the first in their families to attend college. More students at this college came from reasonably comfortable families, at least compared to other Black colleges in the same state. Compared to other colleges participating in the study, its students represented average social status. A predominantly liberal arts college, its students traditionally looked forward to a variety of jobs, whereas students attending other Black colleges in this state almost exclusively anticipated going into elementary or secondary school teaching. Compared to students in the other institutions the freshmen who came to this college entered with somewhat low job and postcollege educational aspirations, but at the end of the freshman year their aspirations had risen. After adjusting for initial differences among the schools, the freshmen at this school expressed the highest aspirations of all when ability demands were used to describe job aspirations and on graduate school intentions. While these enhancement effects were greater among men than among women, the pattern existed for women as well.

The performance picture at this college was very different from what happened with aspirations. The average grades here were the lowest among the 10 colleges. Despite high test scores (the highest among the five schools that administered SAT's in 1964), the students did not seem to achieve at a very high level. This fact kindled the feeling of some critics on the campus as well as on the board of the college that strict academic matters assumed too little importance at this college. This is a matter of point of view concerning the meaning of an education; certainly there were many positive and healthy things going on at this campus. The heightening of aspirations was one of them.

When we looked at change in motivation, a very different picture emerged from what we saw at either the accentuation or the maintenance college. While there was very little shift in the students' expectancies or feelings of competency, this college did seem to affect certain motives and values. At the end of the freshman year, students less often expressed security concerns and more often mentioned concern about success and status when they talked about their life goals. These achievement motives also related more closely to job and educational aspirations here than at other colleges. The students who most often aspired for graduate school and for demanding jobs were much less concerned about security and much more concerned about doing something unusual that is recognized as significant.

The heightening both of aspirations and of motives that facilitate the pursuit of goals exceeding those with which they entered college possibly emanated from the school's important role in exposing students to new opportunities and possibilities. This college held a special meaning in the intellectual life of the state and for the state's Black community. It had been the only environment in the state where cross-race contacts had been possible. It became known as an intellectual center, a place where concerts, plays, lectures, and festivals with either interracial casts or audiences could be presented at a time when other places in the state continued to be segregated. At the height of the civil rights movement, it also had been the state center for activism. A forum for political and intellectual discussion that attracted students and faculty from both Black and white colleges in the state was in its third year of existence in 1964. Just as the college was open to activism, political debate, and visits from many and varied guests, it also welcomed new educational experiences for students. It was one of two colleges cooperating with the southern student movement in developing a work-study program, in which students continued to take courses at the college while working in voter registration and other community-organization work in the field. Exchange programs with other schools and coop work experiences had been offered to students here for many years.

The effectiveness of the college seemed to follow from its unique meaning as an environment where the new, the different, and the unconventional were entertained amidst the much more prevailing traditional influences in the state. Although some students had tired of the parade of visitors to this open environment, still the dominant quality on campus was liveliness. Students were critical, far ahead of students in other schools in questioning the internal authority of the college and the college's relationship to white society. They were also much more critical and suspicious of the intents of this research. Interviewing students here was no easy matter, since they were already concerned in 1964 with a possible misuse of research data for purposes of political oppression.

Of course, some people viewed this college as a civil rights outpost rather than a college, and they were eager to turn it around toward concern for "real education." While it was very different from either of the other two colleges we have described, the students were proffered an atmosphere that some of its strongest critics greatly underestimated. By enhancing its student's aspirations, it opened opportunities for achievement that simply did not exist for students attending other Black colleges in the state.

chapter 7

Individual Achievement: Summing Up

Persistent in finishing college, desirous of advanced education beyond the baccalaureate, ready to work and borrow to further their education, and committed to professional careers, the students attending these Black colleges manifested strong motivation for individual achievement. Their personal goals varied, of course, but it was variation at generally high levels of motivation and aspiration.

Much of the variation reflected clear, consistent sex differences. The goals of the women reflected lower levels on almost every measure of aspiration. Although their desire to go to graduate school nearly matched the aspirations of the men, many fewer women intended to pursue professional degrees and many more expected to terminate graduate work at the master's level. The jobs women chose indicated considerably lower aspiration: they accorded less prestige, demanded less ability, and fell more often in sectors of the labor market where Blacks have traditionally found employment. The constraining effects of sex-role considerations also showed in the way men and women made decisions about their future jobs. Women mentioned fewer jobs when asked to list all the occupations they had ever considered and the jobs they had considered showed a narrower range of prestige, ability, and nontraditionality.

This pattern of sex differences in aspiration closely resembles data from national studies of college students. Three times as many men as women, both in the college population at large and in the Black colleges we studied, plan to pursue doctoral or professional degrees. Figures on graduate degrees awarded show that the male edge for doctorates earned is nine to one in the nation at large, eight to two among Blacks. The size of the male edge in aspiration for traditionally masculine fields—law, medicine, engineering, and physical sciences—and the female edge for traditionally feminine fields—social work and teaching at the elementary or secondary levels—is also almost exactly the same among Black and white graduating seniors. The frequency of role innovation, defined by choosing an occupation where women are underrepresented relative to their proportion in the experienced, college-educated labor force, is identical for Black and white women, according to our data and those from a study of white women at a major four-year university. That study also showed approximately the same proportion of white women who intended to work after having children as we found was true of the women attending these Black colleges. The fact that these colleges influenced the future goals of the men more than the women again parallels national data. More dimensions of the men's aspirations were influenced by the college experience, and more aspects of college had an effect on the men. By the senior year men and women differed even more than they had as freshmen. The accentuation of sex differences during the college years in orientations about career and marriage, in preferences of academic majors and occupational fields, and in number of years of desired education is one of the most reliable facts about change in college. Finally, the motivational analyses that showed that the role of anxiety was greater among men than among women and that more aspects of the men's aspirations and performance were tied to typical measures of achievement motivation conform to conclusions about sex differences drawn from studies on the achievement motivation of white college students.

We do not conclude that Black and white women, or Black and white men, even among the college population, experience life the same way or hold the same attitudes about themselves and their worlds. Black women's reactions to the women's liberation movement attest to their own unique perspectives. We do argue that sex-role demands and patterns of sex discrimination in the society at large critically determine role-appropriate educational and occupational choices, be the women Black or white. Sex-role constraints, operating for Black women in college just as they have for white women, serve as one of the critical influences in explaining individual differences in student aspiration and motivation. If we want women to be free to choose within the full range of jobs and academic majors, colleges must counteract rather than reinforce previous sex-role socialization. Certainly these data should challenge, as other recent research has done, the widely held stereotype of the Black woman as more ambitious than the Black man. Nothing here supports a picture of female dominance.

Achievement motivation serves as another source of influence on aspirations and performance. We focused our discussion of motivation on distinctions between motives, values, and expectancies. The students themselves distinguished values from personal expectancies in their views about what determines success in their own lives and in the culture at large. They separated cultural beliefs about the role internal control plays in the success of other people from their own feelings of personal control. Moreover, their own expectancies and sense of control carried motivational significance while adherence to cultural values did not influence aspirations and performance, at least not for students in general. It was only among students who questioned their own personal efficacy that an internal cultural ideology operated at all: for them commitment to conventional work ethic values inhibited rather than enhanced aspirations and performance. By contrast, two competency-based expectancies, the student's sense of personal control and academic self-confidence, were significant for students generally. Repeatedly these personal expectancies related to graduate school aspirations, to level of job aspirations, to college performance, and to performance on an anagrams task we administered. Students who were the most self-confident academically and who attributed their success to their own internal control performed better and held higher aspirations. Analyses of the realism of the occupational choices of men students further indicated that the most self-confident and efficacious students were not overaspiring in their job choices. Instead, their confidence seemed to be grounded in self-awareness of their skills and personal strengths. One indication of the primary importance of expectancies is that they influenced students generally, while the implications of achievement values depended on the student's own level of efficacy and the significance of achievement motives depended on the sex of the student. When expectancies and motives were used in multivariate analyses to explain variation in aspiration and performance, expectancies proved the more important of the two. We also pointed out instances, however, where this general conclusion was not warranted. For example, expectancies and achievement motives, especially the fear of failure, played reasonably equivalent roles in explaining why men at one college dropped out of school. At another college motives predominated over expectancies in explaining the men's job aspirations.

Expectancies that depended on assessing the nature of society, rather than on individual competency, also influenced personal motivation. While internally based expectancies, where success in one's own life was attributed to one's own effort or ability, generally promoted positive motivation, externally based expectancies did so when they concerned the student's beliefs about the role of social and economic forces in determining race inequities in our society. Men who were especially aware of racial discrimination and blamed it for status differentials between Blacks and whites also more often aspired to jobs heretofore closed to Blacks. These external, system-blaming students were unusually attuned to how social and economic realities produce both constraints and opportunities. This reality interpretation of the meaning of system blame was buttressed by the fact that men who chose occupations that realistically challenged their talents particularly stood out for their system-blame ideology. Blaming the system was also associated with more effective performance, at least among students who felt personally efficacious themselves. These results clearly show that an external orientation can promote rather than inhibit healthy motivation when it depends on assessing systematic social forces that realistically do structure the achievements of minorities. We will see in the next section of the book that externally based expectancies were even more important in explaining collective achievement.

The significance of expectancies ties our discussion of motivation to the role of precollege environmental influences on the students' aspirations and performance. Our analyses showed that financial constraints and opportunity factors were the important aspects of the precollege background, and especially for the students' aspirations and expectancies. All the students faced financial problems beyond the experience of college students generally. Their family incomes were much lower: fully a third, a figure five times larger than for college students nationally, came from families whose incomes put them below the poverty line. Close to a third were also helping support the education of younger brothers and sisters. The vast majority were working to help defray educational costs. National data show that nearly twice as many Black as white college graduates owed money for college expenses and that three times as many cited finances as a major reason for not attending graduate school. The impact of these general financial realities nonetheless showed up especially for those who were objectively the worst off, the students from poverty backgrounds. Their educational and occupational aspirations were lower; their expectations about getting to graduate school and into jobs of their choice were reduced, as were those of students who grew up on farms and in villages in the rural South. But these were the only ways they differed from the more comfortable students and from those whose urban environments had provided greater opportunities before coming to college. The low income students matched other students in their performance in college, their entrance test scores, their achievement values, their achievement motives, their capacities for long-term planning, and their reasons for going to college. They differed in just those aspects of motivation, their perceptions of opportunity and expectations of success, that especially reflected the differential opportunities of the poor and nonpoor and further influenced their aspirations.

These results on demographic influences speak directly to the controversy about social inheritance and the opportunity-situational analysis of social impact. We saw no evidence that achievement-related values—those pertaining to ambition, hard work, success, materialism, or immediate and long-term gratification—reflected the students' social backgrounds. But social background did influence expectations of success, which further influenced aspirations. Moreover, the aspects of the background that especially influenced expectancies and aspirations were closely tied to opportunity and resources. Family income and rural-urban residence were far more influential than either parental education or family structure. Family structure never significantly related to student aspiration or motivation. Students from farms and villages and from very poor families did not command the same resources as those who came to college from urban environments and more affluent families. They could not as easily make their graduate school aspirations a reality or achieve their desired occupational goals. We have also seen that the objective opportunities of the poor students for entering the most elite Black institutions in no way matched the opportunities of the most affluent students. Family income clearly influenced what kind of college a student considered and eventually entered, just as it does generally in the nation's stratified system of higher education.

How did the 10 colleges show their impact on student aspirations and performance beyond the fact that the college experience vitiated the influence of precollege social background? Institutional variation in student motivation was great: even after adjusting for college differences in sex ratios and the demographic characteristics of students, the colleges still differed in the average level of their students' job and educational aspirations; in student grade-point averages; in the students' ideologies about internal and external determinants of success; in the students' expectancies, both their general sense of personal control and more specific academic self-confidence. They did not differ in their students' achievement motives. Selectivity effects, even considering that some colleges recruited more men and more students from higher income and urban backgrounds, accounted for many of the differences in student aspiration and motivation. Freshmen at certain colleges entered with higher aspirations, greater self-confidence, and more balanced judgments about what determines success and failure, even after adjusting for the sex and demographic influences we showed were important in aspirations and expectancies.

There was also an institutional effect, particularly on men students, which generally accentuated initial differences among the colleges. Colleges that selected freshmen with unusually high aspiration reinforced such attitudes, while colleges that selected freshmen whose aspirations were initially lower apparently did little to heighten them, at least as a general rule. At the end of the freshman year the students in the 10 colleges differed even more than they had at the beginning of the year.

Despite the generally greater effect of college on men than on women, some features of the colleges enhanced the aspirations of both sexes. Amount of faculty-student interaction and the academic stress of the student culture turned out to be the most generally significant institutional features we examined. Going to college where many students reported contact with faculty outside of the classroom and where academic values were especially prevalent among students seemed to foster many positive developments for both men and women. Even after adjusting for the fact that such colleges attracted high aspirants in the first place, men and women on such campuses completed their freshman year more committed to graduate education, especially to pursuing the Ph.D. or professional degrees; they aspired to more demanding jobs, especially those that were unconventional either in the sense of falling outside traditional sectors of Black employment or deviating from sex-role stereotypes for women; they also felt more efficacious about being able to control their own lives.

Diversity of extracurricular offerings, an institutional feature that was highly intercorrelated with amount of student-faculty interaction and an intellectual press in the student culture, was almost as important. The presence of diverse extracurricular activities influenced both the men's and women's occupational choices. Colleges with unusually diverse activities enhanced students' level of job aspiration specifically for the most demanding and unconventional occupations. Moreover, the men's but not the women's graduate school aspirations and sense of personal efficacy were also heightened in such colleges.

Institutional status that resulted from the college's capacity to attract students from out of state and urban environments and from professional, highly educated, high income families was far less important as an impact feature. With women these institutional features mostly served as selection influences: women who entered such high status colleges came with higher aspirations, but their aspirations at the end of the freshman year were not markedly different from women in other colleges after the initial selection effects had been controlled. With men these status features of the college did have an effect— primarily to buffer against the general tendency of men in all colleges to lower their aspirations during the freshman year. Men who entered public colleges and those serving less cosmopolitan and high status students were especially likely to reduce their educational and occupational aspirations. On the other hand, the aspirations of men who entered the more elite colleges were not enhanced by the experience there, at least not in the same sense that aspirations were heightened by going to colleges where the academic stress of the student culture, faculty-student interaction, and campus organizational life were especially rich.

Students should be encouraged to explore new possibilities for their lives. This does not mean pushing women into masculine fields or pushing Black students, men or women, into nontraditional sectors of the economy. It does mean pushing for real choice, helping students make decisions with full awareness of race and sex-role constraints so that they can choose to pursue unusual achievements if they so desire. If colleges want to foster the exploration of these less conventional aspirations, our results on institutional impact suggest that positive consequences should follow from anything that is done to encourage faculty-student interaction, to increase the diversity of activities that students can participate in, and to support and reward the academic-intellectual values in the student culture. In addition, the case examples of two colleges—the one that accentuated its students' already initially high aspirations and expectancies and the one that enhanced level of aspiration beyond what would have been expected —indicate that these generally significant institutional characteristics assumed somewhat different meaning on the two campuses. The influence of the faculty, while important on both campuses, was especially critical in the heightened expectancy environment of the accentuation college where the faculty believed that absolutely every student could achieve and insisted that they do so. The influence of diverse activity options, while important on both campuses, assumed unusual significance in the open, lively, exciting environment of the college that showed redirection effects. Civil rights activities, work-study opportunities, political and intellectual debates, and the college's special history as an intellectual and cultural center in the state exposed students to new opportunities far beyond what more conventional colleges could offer.

Throughout this section of the book we have noted remarkable stability in student aspirations and motivation. Whenever we repeated the analyses of data collected from students in 1964 on data gathered in 1970, we found almost exactly the same levels of educational and occupational aspirations, the same levels of expectations about reaching their goals, the same levels of self-confidence about their abilities, and almost identical assessments of personal control. The only shifts of consequence showed up in the students' actual occupational choices. Students in 1970 considered and actually chose from a broader range of occupations, and they more often planned to enter professions and business roles that they thought would benefit the Black community. They somewhat less often selected jobs in the physical sciences. Even these shifts did not alter the average level of aspiration that their job choices indicated. Students' values, especially their commitments to a traditional Protestant ethic ideology, also shifted. In 1970 students much less consistently insisted that people get ahead because they work hard or in other ways possess the virtues of the Protestant ethic. Instead they were considerably more balanced by seeing both internal and external forces as operating in people's lives. In the next section we will interpret these ideological shifts as another aspect of the students' increasing collective consciousness that predisposed them in the late sixties to the growth of Black Nationalism.

Stability showed up not only in their levels of aspiration and motivation but also in the analyses we carried out of the influences on aspiration and performance. Generally, the same influences operated in both 1964 and 1970. The general pattern of demographic results appeared in both cross-sectional studies: a strong commonality in values, achievement motives, ideal goals, commitments to education, and test performance and college grades, among students from divergent backgrounds who differed in their levels of aspiration and even more in their expectancies of reaching those goals. These expectancies then influenced aspirations and performance in much the same way at both points in time. Institutional differences also held steadfastly. The size of the differences in average levels of student aspiration and motivation among the six colleges that participated in both 1964 and 1970 remained constant. It was only with respect to graduate school aspirations that the colleges differed more in 1970 than in 1964. Moreover, the ranking of the colleges was virtually unchanged. Those colleges that showed the highest levels of student aspiration and motivation were still at the top in 1970; the lower ones were still lower.

Throughout our studies, we did not see any evidence of rising individual aspirations and expectations. In this respect, the period of the mid to late sixties was a period of stability. In the next section of the book we will see, however, that the ferment of the sixties did affect the students' collective commitments—the way they thought about social, economic, and political issues; their group identifications and collective consciousness; and their sense of responsibility for the collective fate of the group.

part 2

Collective Achievement: Group Action and Collective Commitments

This part of the book examines achievement as a collective phenomenon. It focuses on the collective commitments and action of the students through which they tried to exact legal, economic, and social changes that would benefit Black people. The activists were striving to achieve, but they were working for group products and accomplishments rather than for individual goals. Their motivation carried all the usual connotations of achievement motivation: it prompted hard and persistent effort as well as setting group goals that were both difficult and realistic. When successful in creating change, they evinced the kind of pleasure usually related to achievement. They were elated with a job well done; they were proud of the process of working together. These collective action experiences, first in civil rights activities and later in campus-based activities to alter their own colleges, provide the dependent variables for this part of the book just as individual achievement and aspirations defined the dependent variables for the first part. First, we describe the students' collective commitments and action experiences (Chapter 8); then we analyze why some students were much more active and more collective in their orientations (Chapters 9 to 11). We will present information on the same three sets of influences that we examined regarding individual achievement. Just as we looked at achievement motivation as the social-psychological base of conventional individual achievement, we look at the role of ideology as the social-psychological motivation

189

for collective achievement. Just as we looked at precollege demographic and college influences on individual achievement, we present
data in this part of the book on the demographic and social roots of
activism and collective commitments, as well as the influence of the
college experience on these indicators of collective achievement. The
structure of Part 2 parallels Part 1; we merely shift interest from
explaining individual achievement to collective achievement.

Chapter 8 describes shifts in both the targets of action and ideologies of the students from 1964 at the height of the demonstration
period of the civil rights movement to 1970 when Black Nationalism
had become much more prominent politically. We report material
from questionnaires that were administered in the cross-sectional
studies in both 1964 and 1970 as well as information from intensive
interviews we conducted at three colleges during the spring of 1965
and at the one college where we reinterviewed seniors in 1968 who
had participated as freshmen in the earlier study in 1964. Chapter 9
examines the social roots of collective achievement and ideology. The
data address whether the social bases of participation in collective
action changed as the targets and issues changed. The social profiles
of these Black student activists will be set in the context of previous
work done on student activism, most of it on white students even
though we will show that white students were never as politically
active in the sixties as were students attending Black colleges. Chapter
10 turns to the social-psychological motivation for collective achievement. We will show that the tie between a collectivist ideology and
collective achievement remained intact even as the targets of action,
form of action, and content of the ideology shifted over the decade.
The data we present raise questions about the relative importance of
personal efficacy and ideology as motivators of collective action and
about the meaning of "powerlessness" as an aspect of alienation.
Much of the discussion of urban revolts and college student protest
has been cast, erroneously we believe, as the expressive acts of the
alienated. The students we studied were not "powerless"; instead they
expressed an activist ideology that reflected their awareness of social
determination and the necessity of collective rather than individual
action. Chapter 11 looks to the college experience as a source of influence on collective achievement. It presents information about institutional variation in both ideology and activism rates. Then, effect of
the college on collective achievement is approached in three ways.
First, we will show that campus climate conditioned whether students
expressed their ideologies by becoming involved in action. Second,
we move within the college to show what aspects of the college experience were related to collective achievement and whether a distinctive

subculture *was* associated with activism on all campuses or only on those where participation itself was reasonably widespread. Finally, we examine whether the collective action experience served as one of the sources of college impact on students.

chapter 8

Trends in Activism and Ideology: The Emergence of Nationalism

THE DEMONSTRATION EPOCH

We began this research in 1964, four years after the first sit-in occurred on the first of February, 1960, in Greensboro, North Carolina. Much had happened in those intervening years. During the month following that first famous lunch counter sit-in, similar activities had spread to 15 cities and five southern states. Within the following year, over 50,000 people had participated in one kind of demonstration or another in 100 cities and over 3600 demonstrators had spent time in jail.[1] By 1961 the Student Nonviolent Coordinating Committee was one year old; in that spring and summer the Freedom Rides electrified the nation and toughened the cadre of young people who, joined by others, became the full-time, dedicated field staff of the Southern Student Movement, loosely coordinated by SNCC. Their numbers increased by the fall of 1964 to 150 young people, mostly ex-college students, mostly Black, mostly southern, who had left their colleges and ordinary pursuits to commit themselves indefinitely to changing the fabric of the South.

The critical events between 1961 and 1964 are now history. Voter registration drives that in the fall of 1961 centered around McComb, Mississippi, soon spread throughout Mississippi to southwest Georgia and eventually to all the Deep South states and culminated in the 1964 Mississippi Summer Project and the Mississippi Freedom Democratic Party's abortive attempt to challenge the seating of the state's delegates at the Democratic National Convention in Atlantic City. *The southern movement, symbolized by the names of rural towns and cities—Greenwood, Mississippi; Hattiesburg, Mississippi; Albany, Georgia; Selma, Alabama; Cambridge, Maryland; Danville, Virginia; Pine Bluff, Arkansas, and others—was distinguished by heroic responses to brutal*

1. Howard Zinn, *SNCC: The New Abolitionists* (Boston: Beacon Press, 1964), p. 16.

violence—bombings that killed four little girls attending Sunday School in Birmingham, cattle prods, police dogs, and fire hoses. The nation watched it all on their televisions.

The students who participated in the study in the fall of 1964 had watched it all too. The college freshmen had been freshmen in high school when the sit-ins first began. Coming of age and simultaneously coming to terms with adult decisions were occurring in a new milieu for Black youngsters in the South. Some, 7 percent of our sample, had already participated actively; they had worked summers in the movement, had gone to jail, and had continued to work in campaigns in their home towns or near their colleges while they held on, somehow, to their lives as high school or college students. Another 23 percent had participated in several different activities, still another 16 percent had taken part in at least one event. The majority (54 percent) had thus far not participated at all. But they knew about these events.

They also had had opportunities to assess the impact of four years of action, a mixed picture of success and failure. By the end of 1961 several hundred lunch counters had been desegregated in scores of cities, mostly in border states. Desegregating public accommodations in the Deep South was to take longer. The public accommodations sections of the Civil Rights Act that had been passed in July, 1964, represented to the students that autumn a victory that had emerged from the sit-in phase of the student movement. After the first bitter agonies of impenetrable resistance in McComb, there had been victories in voter registration drives too. When the Mississippi Freedom Ballot campaign of 1963 was over, 80,000 Blacks—four times the number officially registered in the state—had marked ballots for Aaron Henry and Edwin King for Governor and Lt. Governor. That had shown that Mississippi Blacks, in huge numbers, would vote if given the chance to register. In fact, the effect of the Voting Rights Act of 1965 would nowhere be more striking than in Mississippi where registration rose from the prelegislation level of 6.7 percent to 59.8 percent of the Black voting-age population by three years after the passage of the Act.[2] This was a period when Blacks of many different social change persuasions maintained faith in the impact of Black voters on the electoral process. Black political parties and Black caucuses within the traditional parties had begun to look viable.

But the students had also experienced or knew about frustrations, disappointments, setbacks, and downright failures. The compromise worked out in the 1964 Democratic National Convention in Atlantic

2. "Voting Rights," *Civil Rights Digest* 4(4) (December, 1971), p. 32.

City in response to the Mississippi Freedom Democratic Party's challenge to traditional white control convinced many activists that there was no hope for change by working through established party politics. Notes of futility and cynicism were sounded amidst the chorus of greater optimism and of growing sense of power by the fall of 1964. In that year the last great demonstrations of the decade were to take place, the march on Selma in February, 1965, and the march from Selma to Montgomery the following month. A new period was developing, during which concerted efforts would turn from public accommodations to the knottier problems of economic power and of use of the vote to achieve meaningful political change once registration began to pay off. Black Power was hardly yet a slogan but it was soon to be.

Our study began at a turning point. What did students feel? How did they view the events of the previous four years? What directions and strategies did they advocate? What responsibilities did they sense belonged to their generation of Black students? Indeed, what did it mean to be Black in Black colleges after this period of ferment that had been stimulated so largely by the action of their fellow students?

These questions have received little attention in systematic research. We generally have to look to the short stories, novels, poetry, and drama written by Black authors for the feelings of Black young people about being Black in America. While not approaching the sensitivity of Black literature, quantitative research can add a sometimes neglected focus on how generally certain attitudes and feelings are expressed as students talk about themselves and their worlds, especially if our methods allow them to do just that—to talk in their own words. In exploring these questions we relied heavily on information from intensive interviewing, where students could talk freely about their feelings, ideas, and analyses of the way our society works.

Interview Themes, Spring of 1965

Two hundred interviews were conducted at each of three colleges during the spring of 1965. The interviewers, Black college graduates who were only one or two years older than the students themselves, lived at each of the campuses for a month, observing classes and campus life as well as interviewing individual students. The interviews were coded in two ways: one to preserve the students' comments to particular questions; the other to summarize over the whole interview the students' concerns about four major themes—integration and separatism, racial identity and pride, causes of racial inequities, and strategies for social change.

INTEGRATION-SEPARATION

Almost all the students in 1965 voluntarily talked about integration as either a goal or a strategy at some point in the interview; three-quarters of them discussed it more than once; a third brought it up several times. In fact, the prointegration theme was the most frequently mentioned of the themes we coded across the total interview (Table 1).

We asked students to choose among four statements describing the kind of society in which they would like to live and rear their children. One-half chose a statement that describes the kind of society we know now but with full integration; these students felt that "the present American system and the life it promises would be a good one if it provided for the full integration of all races in that system; except for the racial issue I have no basic criticism of American society." Another 40 percent preferred a statement that stressed integration but along with it a "complete moral rebirth where basic human values become central to the society." Only 10 percent felt that integration was not sufficient and selected the statement stressing the need for "a radical change in the whole economic base of the American system—a revolution that goes much beyond race, challenging all the economic injustice of this society." None of them preferred a separate Black state, as described in this way: "Society must be free—to be free, the races must be separated because the white man will never give justice, equality, and freedom to other peoples; only with a separate state can there be real freedom." Almost all the students went further and said they disagreed most with that statement.

To be sure, none of these statements captured what the students later were to consider the most important themes of Black Nationalism. It is of topical interest that we had pretested several statements that would have better represented the growing nationalism of the late sixties but dropped them when none of the students responded favorably in 1965. By 1970, of course, the controversy over integration versus separation rarely contained the issue of a separate state. Nevertheless, most of the students in 1965 viewed an integrated society as a desirable goal and considered desegregation-and-integration as significant strategy targets. Furthermore, when students talked about the racial setting of the situation in which they would eventually like to work, the kind of neighborhood where they would prefer to live, and the type of school they would like their children to attend, they generally described a racially mixed situation. At least three-quarters of them preferred racially mixed neighborhoods and schools; an even larger proportion preferred racially mixed work environments. That picture shifted greatly between 1965 and 1970. A third of the students in 1970

TABLE 1. Number of Times Students Voluntarily Mentioned Four Major Themes In Responding To Unstructured Interview Questions in 1965[a]

Proportion of Students Who Mentioned Each Theme	Integration as Either a Goal or Strategy	Themes					
		Racial Identity		Analyses of Racial Inequities		Social Change Strategies	
		Racial Pride	Negative Identification	Economic-Social Explanations	Individualistic Explanations	Collective Action	Individual Mobility
Never	2%	0%	82%	3%	8%	46%	15%
Once	23	40	4	31	30	34	35
Twice	42	32	5	46	32	12	36
Three or more times	33	28	9	20	30	8	14
	100%	100%	100%	100%	100%	100%	100%

[a]These percents are based on 600 students who were interviewed, 200 at each of three colleges, in the spring of 1965

preferred predominantly Black work settings, half preferred predominantly Black neighborhoods, and 40 percent said they wanted to send their children to predominantly Black schools.

Racial Pride

We began a series of questions about racial pride with the general question: "People have a lot of different ideas about what it means to be Black in this society. I wonder if you could tell me a little about what it means to you?" Less than a fifth of the students denied that there was any special identity issue for them. Some of this small group simply asserted: "It doesn't mean anything; I'm a darker skin color, that's all." Others rejected a special Black identity out of a more universal commitment: "It means I'm human, like people everywhere," "It means I'm part of the *human* race—I'm the child in India, the old man in Sweden, the father in Africa, as well as the young man who also happens to be Black." A few others in this group expressed primary identification with being an American: "I'm just like any other American with the same rights and possibilities," "I'm like any other guy next door; it is no more special to be Black than it is to be Polish or to be young or to be a man. You are what you are." Then there were a few students who talked exclusively about the uniqueness of the human individual: "It means I'm a particular person, admittedly with life experiences in common with other Blacks, but I'm unique—I feel what I feel, I'm aware of the things around me in my own personal way, I'm alive, and I'm me."

Most students, however, talked about something special that grows from a shared Black experience. Half of them focused, at least initially, on the realities of restrictions, discrimination, and other negative life conditions. They mentioned: "denial of my rights," "being a second-class citizen," "facing segregation, whether dejure or defacto," "job and housing discrimination," "income disadvantage even when you have appropriate education," "restrictions on freedom of movement and access to public accommodations," "assault on dignity—whites treat you like dirt," "denial of basic respect," "facing derogatory statements and social humiliations," and "the necessity of hard work, fighting, a constant struggle." None of these responses showed interiorization of the oppressor's view of Blacks; they simply expressed irritation, frustration, and anger about injustice, discrimination, and lack of freedom that are realities for Black Americans. Moreover, a preponderant number of the students in this group who focused first on restrictions and discrimination went on to talk about the pride they felt in being part of a group that has the ability to overcome these obstacles and a history of survival in the face of overwhelming hardship. They talked about strength of character: "I don't know any other group that has seen so much injustice and keeps right on fighting and moving," "It means being a part of a group that has enormous determination and courage—nobody can miss that and I wouldn't trade places with anyone," "It means being part of a proud group of people—you don't come through three hundred years of history like we have without a sense of awe for your own strength, resiliency, and perseverance." Others mentioned specific historical events, landmarks of progress and accomplishment, and figures who have stood for determination, courage, and revolution, especially DuBois, Frederick Douglass, and Malcolm X.

Pride in survival and in the group's determination and accomplishments predominated the students' discussion of their feelings of racial pride. While only 13 percent of the students talked about group pride when they were first asked about what it means to be Black, most of those who originally focused on restrictions and discrimination then switched to the other side of the coin, pride in the group's response to these restrictions. Furthermore, group pride was even stronger when the students responded to our next probe: "A number of people have written recently about it being very special and exciting to be Black at this particular point in time and I wonder how you feel about that notion?" This question invited pride responses, although not necessarily these particular themes of pride. Yet two-thirds of the students did talk about the group's ability to overcome obstacles and their pride in the gains and accomplishments that have resulted from the struggle. "We're on the move, there's no stopping, yes, it's exciting to be part of a revolution," "I've a special sense of the unity of Blacks in this struggle, what we're able to do when we join together to overcome for all—I guess a lot of whites never experience a sense of being part of something bigger than self," "Yes, it's exciting to look around you and see all these Blacks, even tenant farmers and people who have a real reason to fear repression, stand up for their rights—I always knew we were courageous people but it means something special to have the world stand back and take note," "It's exciting to be writing a new epoch of history, I believe historians will look back on this period and finally write down what we Blacks have always known—we're proud, we're aggressive, and we can turn this system around." These were not the only types of pride responses. Students also talked about pride in their African heritage, pride in their involvement in a larger Afro-Asian block, pride in cultural artifacts and life-style, pride in being Black, a priceless pearl. Some students also mentioned the personal consequences of involvement, an acute sense of being alive and aware of oneself with a special sense of commitment. Some mentioned heightened sensitivity: "Your antennae are sharpened, you see things that others don't," "You gain a special perceptivity and insight out of the Black experience, you're aware of more things, you go about this world with a special sense of alertness—I suspect other people often miss a great deal about what's going on around them." A few students also talked about the positive strengths that come from the challenge to one's personal identity, noting that: "You get to know yourself better, you have to face up to what you really believe, what is really you and what is simply some form of pressure, whether it's pressure to think white or think Black; other people maybe don't have to separate what they are as people from social pressures that try to define them in stereotyped ways."

Were there no students who responded to these. questions with self-hate? Where is the evidence of damage to self-esteem that some treatments of Black personality have implied is almost ubiquitous. We coded throughout the interview for evidence of identification with the aggressor, acceptance of stereotypes about immorality or laziness of the Black masses, a sense of burden of having to prove oneself against these stereotypes, and disassociation from Black people. Only 14 percent of the students showed as many as two of these themes; nine percent showed them all. The students in this group indeed had problems. Without minimizing the pain, suffering, or psychopathology of this small group, it is important to stress how few students reflected the serious damage that some writers assume is the almost universal heritage of the Black experience. (See Table 1 for the relative stress on pride and negative identification in the overall content of the interviews.)

Clinicians perhaps will doubt the level of personal exposure that our interviews evoked. Surely more students would have shown that they harbored self-doubt or self-hate had we used more appropriate clinical instruments and techniques to probe their feelings about themselves. We make no pretense that one interview, even as unstructured and open as this one, can draw out the complexities and vulnerabilities of the human psyche. On the other hand, overdependence on clinical methods and on patient populations has resulted in portraits of Black personality that exaggerate damage and psychopathology. As sensitive, moving, and popular as some of these clinical accounts have been, they have also served to reinforce prejudice and stereotypes by focusing on a limited set of issues in the psychology of being Black. The threat to self-esteem and personal authenticity is real enough. The critical question centers on the balance between endurance and hopelessness, resiliency and resignation, damage and strength. Much of our literature has overblown the negative and thereby minimized both the role of the oppressor and the adaptive strengths of Blacks themselves.

ANALYSES OF RACIAL INEQUITIES

Several questions in the interview asked students to talk about their everyday theories about injustice. How did they explain income, educational, and occupational differentials between Blacks and whites? What did they feel most needed to be done to change these disparities? How did they differ, if at all, from their parents' views about the basic causes of racial inequality?

Repeatedly we saw complexity as students were beginning to rethink what they believed about these questions. They were by no means so critical of conventional individualism as students would become as revolutionary-collectivist theory came to provide the intellectual base for Black Nationalism later in the decade. But they thought of themselves as less conventional than their parents. The third of the students who felt their analyses of race in America differed from their parents' viewpoints focused on their parents' individualistic thinking. They generally described their parents as believing too wholeheartedly in the American dream—that success will eventually reward individual effort; the Black man only has to work a little harder. Feeling that their parents too often underestimated social and economic forces, many of them concluded that their parents implicitly rested the burden for injustice on inadequacies of Blacks themselves; if anyone can make it, then the failure to do so must stem from personal deficits. These students were questioning their parents' traditional victim analyses much as Bayard Rustin described such a generational shift in discussing the urban uprisings in 1967:

> The miserable yield to their fate as divinely ordained or as their own fault, and, indeed, many Negroes at earlier generations felt that way. Today young Negroes aren't having any. They don't have the feeling that something must be wrong with them, that they are responsible for their own exclusion from this affluent society.[3]

Rejection of a victim analysis in favor of a clearly developed ideology of social and economic causation was not common, however. Most students in 1965 held ambivalent positions about the causes of inequities (Table 1). On the one hand, nearly all of them talked at some point in the interview about economic and social system problems; two-thirds discussed social, economic, and political determinants of racial inequality at least twice in the interview, and many more often. Generally, however, this did not represent a full-blown ideology of social

3. Bayard Rustin, "A Way Out of the Exploding Ghetto," *New York Times Magazine 13* (August, 1967), p. 16.

determinism; 92 percent also expressed elements of conventional individualism. In fact, few students were consistent on either side of the coin. Less than 10 percent repeatedly talked about system determinants without ever referring to victim deficiencies; likewise, only five percent persistently talked about the inadequacies of individuals while failing to mention any social or economic sources of inequity. It was in this area of their explanations of inequity that students were to change greatly as the ideas of Fanon and other revolutionary-collectivist writers gained a hearing later in the decade.

OPINIONS ABOUT SOCIAL CHANGE

Students generally were optimistic about change in 1965. The vast majority agreed a lot was happening in the South at the time we were interviewing, and that the future looked promising. Almost all the students who talked about differences between parents' and their own views about race described their parents as much more tolerant of gradualism and more skeptical about major social changes. "My father says he has seen these movements come and go; it is his feeling that I had better get my education since I'm going to face exactly the same knocks"; "My folks thought there was no way possible for change to occur. I guess they think education is the only way and then clearly just to teach or work in the post office. I don't agree; I think change can come about, although it will be up to us to make it happen"; "I don't blame my parents, seeing what they've seen, they're naturally suspicious of any real gains from all these demonstrations, and partly I think they're just worried I'll get hurt in all this, you know a typical mother's worry." These comments reflected the parents' interrelated concerns about their children's physical safety and fear that commitment to the movement might jeopardize their children's education and success; it was not simply that the parents were pessimistic about change. But it is safe to conclude that many students felt their parents were less optimistic then they.

Moreover, students reflected their optimism in other ways. When they were asked why they rejected the idea of a separate state, three-quarters expressed the conviction that current inequities could and would be altered; only a fifth showed even a slight resignation about change. Likewise, when students talked about their preferences and expectations for the racial compositions of their future work and neighborhood environments, almost all who preferred mixed settings felt they would indeed end up in a racially mixed situation. Less than a third of the group felt that the racial situation and current level of discrimination would continue so as to preclude the kind of integration they preferred.

Their optimism allowed them to advocate many different change strategies. Advocacy of collective pressure and Black power was to grow as students were increasingly to view the system as intransigent and their presumed successes as illusory. But in 1965 most students still believed that traditional reform methods would prove effective, even if protest were necessary to bring national attention to injustice and the plight of the southern Black. Half the students said the NAACP and legal strategies represented best what they felt were preferable approaches to change. The direct action style of CORE, SCLC, and SNCC were also approved; 40 percent mentioned one of these groups as reflecting their preferred strategy. Even the students who advocated direct action also approved of more traditional methods. Less than 10 percent of the students followed SNCC and rejected more conventional groups and tactics at the same time. Methods were simply not yet so polarized.

We also coded across questions in the interview for advocacy of individual and collective strategies. The modal response was to mention both, although self- and group-betterment projects predominated over collective action. Half the students talked about education as the key for change. At the very least they believed that preparation and training would be necessary to take advantage of the increased opportunities they thought would be available to their generation. At the extreme some students felt education and individual mobility were the only meaningful ways to bring about an aggregate change in the status of Black Americans. Eighty-five percent of the students mentioned self-advancement or group betterment projects at least once during the interview; half talked about individual mobility as a change strategy more than once. Howsoever, more than half the students also mentioned some form of collective action and the necessity of protest to force change, although only a fifth of the students brought up these collective approaches more than once (Table 1). We also see the predominance of conventional self-advancement because only 10 percent of the students advocated solely a collective approach while 30 percent advocated only individual mobility. The collective strategies they mentioned reflected the *era*: demonstrations, voter registration drives, marches to centers of political power, and picketing businesses that practiced discrimination in service or employment. Feelings about nonviolence were strong; 90 percent of the students advocated nonviolence as the technique for action; only a third of the students even felt there might be situations when civil rights' workers should be armed to protect themselves in self-defense and less than 10 percent of the students felt nonviolence was *not* a good idea when it came to the self-defense of civil rights' workers, urging instead that civil rights workers should always be armed and ready to protect themselves.

TRANSITION TO NATIONALISM

Turning Inward to Campus Politics

The targets of political action and the thinking of students changed remarkably in the last half of the decade. The shifts from community civil rights work to campus confrontations and from reformist to revolutionary or anarchist thinking were national in character. The increase in the political action of the nation's college students midway through the decade reflected primarily the increase in on-campus protests, sometimes about strictly campus issues, sometimes about the role of the college in abetting economic and social injustice in its host community, sometimes about national and international policies and events to which the college was not party. Students attending Black colleges likewise turned inward to campus protest, but they increasingly saw their concerns and activities in campus politics as aspects of Black Nationalism. Superficially like the shift in student political action nationwide, the growth of student unrest on Black campuses was attributed, by the leaders at least, to evidence of Nationalist thinking among the students. Demanding greater voice in campus governance represented to these students their commitment to the "self-determination of Black people." They wanted to "decolonize" Black colleges, to make them truly relevant for Black people. These students who came to feel that Blacks must control their own institutions understandably translated their broad concerns about political nationalism into a desire to determine educational policies of Black colleges. (See Appendix Table 8.1 for opinion shifts from 1964 to 1970 about traditional college governance.)

We saw all these shifts and eventual articulation of student power in nationalist terms in one college that we studied intensively from 1964 to 1968. In 1968 we reinterviewed seniors at this college who, as freshmen, had participated in large numbers in the famous Selma and Montgomery civil rights demonstrations. Sixty-two percent of the freshman class had joined in at least two demonstrations in the spring of 1965; a third had maintained a high level of activity from February to the close of the school year; 11 percent had affiliated with the campus action group that had provided the leadership and strategy direction for the on- and off-campus activities associated with the Montgomery march. Four years later only 17 percent of them, then seniors, were still active in such off-campus political action. Yet the campus was not dead; it was not even quiet. The issues that galvanized student action had shifted to campus affairs. The course of events here showed the tie between student concerns about college governance and Nationalist thinking in the campus unrest on Black campuses.

Student protest erupted in December, 1968. The first overt manifestation involved the desire of the students in one of the academic divisions to have a faculty member relieved of his teaching duties. The administration did not respond favorably to these demands. The second major incident was more political than academic, although it did involve academic freedom. Several students disrupted a lecture by representatives of the United States Department of State because of their concern about the Vietnam War. The next major issue grew out of this incident. Some students felt strongly when one of the student leaders of the incident was identified and threatened with disciplinary action.

Sensing the mood of the students, the president called a general campus meeting to discuss the problems that were disturbing them. He expressed the feeling that all problems could be resolved if lines of communication between students and the administration were kept open. The tension on campus remained high during the next week, however, partially because Stokely Carmichael was scheduled to speak. Actually no unusual incidents occurred when he spoke to an overflow audience. Students also continued to bring pressure on the administration about its policies for inviting speakers to campus. Some students felt that the administration was attempting to keep militant students of other colleges from meeting with local students. The administration had recently initiated a policy that required that they be notified at least 12 hours in advance of any meetings the students wanted to hold. Such meetings would require administrative approval; in other words, unofficial meetings were considered illegal, and students participating in such unofficial meetings would be subject to campus discipline. The students almost immediately challenged the new policy when a group of activist students from another campus called a meeting at the student union. Students were informed that this unofficial meeting could not be held. The meeting took place anyway; subsequently several students were placed on social and administrative probation. The next day approximately 200 students attempted to hold another unofficial meeting. They were informed by the dean of students that it could not be held on campus.

Student and faculty concern mounted during those days. Students met and proposed resolutions. They presented demands to the administration to: (1) make ROTC voluntary instead of compulsory; (2) give students representation on all committees involving student life; (3) provide amnesty for protest participants; (4) require that all teaching and nonteaching faculty publish in their field before being hired or by their first two years on campus; (5) revise policies on inviting speakers and authorizing student meetings; (6) clarify the role of the dean of students so that he could be a student advocate instead of an arm of the administration. While there were efforts to negotiate and respond to these demands, some were either not met or were referred to committees or to the board of trustees.

None of the initial incidents or the first set of demands cast the confrontation directly in Nationalist terms. Eventually, however, the students added a demand to turn the college into a Black university that would be truly responsive to the needs of Black people and would provide new curricular offerings in a wide array of Black studies. What had started as grievances of nonpolitical students about their strictly academic experiences had developed through response and counter-response into broader demands for student power on the campus, the demands increasingly cast by the leaders in the collectivist terms of Black Nationalism. Listen to the manifesto advocating a Black university:

> The Black University concept includes, among other things, a redirection of goals for the school as a whole and the instillment of a Black community concept within the Black students for generations to come. By this we mean a college that benefits and carries on a perpetual reciprocal relationship with the entire Black community . . . If the college cannot learn from and be designed to benefit from the Black community, then it does not need to exist; to hand America a carbon copy of itself is now archaic, insulting and irrelevant in terms of outlook and practicality to the Black community. We Black people need and will have educational institutions that speak from a Black experience and address themselves to Black collective needs. Individual considerations are now secondary to a collective ethos—this is the order of the day. Survival of the Black population is of primary concern; therefore, individual pursuits as a primary concern can only be looked upon in this light: "we all hang together, or we hang separately."[4]

As the intensity of the controversy increased and the issues proliferated, as many as three-quarters of the senior class participated in some capacity. Student opinion supported demands for participation in governance, although most students clearly did not support some of the strategies that were adopted during this period of unrest. Forty-

4. A manifesto presented by students to the administration of a Black college, 1968.

two percent of our sample of seniors felt that the college administration had too much authority; 76 percent felt students should have more power; 41 percent said the issue of student power was very important to them. Of course, far fewer were very active; only 10 percent considered themselves actively part of the leadership group; about 50 students were expelled or suspended; close to 100 others were placed on probation. Most of these students were readmitted by court order, although a few were later reexpelled after legally required due process had been afforded them. The year ended in an uneasy peace.

This campus was not alone in its distress. Two other campuses of the 10 that had participated in the first study in 1964 also experienced disruptions and protests over academic priorities and campus governance that year. In fact, more historically Black than white institutions experienced protests that year. Sixty percent of the Black colleges and universities but 43 percent of the white institutions that responded to a protest survey in May, 1968 reported some kind of protest.[5] Moreover, most of the Black colleges that experienced unrest reported that the protests, strikes, and confrontations had occurred between March and May, and especially just following the assassination of Martin Luther King in early April.

What had happened to explain why the center of student protest shifted from off-campus civil rights targets to campus issues concerning governance of student life and the school's authority structure? What had happened that also led these students to think in nationalistic terms by 1970? Very few Afro-American or Black student unions existed on either southern or northern campuses in 1964. By 1970 every school in our study had one. Demands for Black studies had been expressed everywhere. All the schools had traditionally taught courses in Negro History and the sociology of race relations. The new student demands for Black courses went far beyond that.

The social history of the sixties will be written by others. We do not presume to explain the subtleties of all these shifts, although we can point to the ways students were experiencing critical events of the second half of the decade: the escalation of the Vietnam War with its attendant threats to our national commitment to address problems of poverty and racial injustice; the urban revolts, beginning with Watts in the summer of 1965, which reflected, even in the words of the official Commission on Civil Disorders, responses to "white racism"; economic problems that found us adopting policies to fight inflation, including cutbacks to education that directly threatened the existence

5. Durward Long, "Black Protest," in Julian Foster and Durward Long, Editors, *Protest: Student Activism in America* (New York: William Morrow, 1970), p. 468, Table 1.

of Black colleges, while unemployment continued to rise; emergence of Black Power groups that seemed at first to speak only for the young and the less traditional but would lead to Black caucuses within our major political parties; the assassination of Malcolm X, Medgar Evers, Martin Luther King, and Robert Kennedy.

These events and their symbols became relevant to students as they faced local instances of the wider phenomena. Take the college where students had ridden the last wave of the southern student movement to the largely impotent demonstration in Montgomery and then had turned to campus protests by 1968. In 1966 several men students there had forcefully connected the war and the battle for justice at home by refusing induction. By the spring of 1968 the role of the ROTC on the campus had become one of the focal issues of student grievances. One of their fellow students had been murdered in 1966. A young man who had grown up in the local community and had dropped out of college to work full time in the movement, he had been shot down by the white owner of a local gas station while trying to use a white restroom. The accused, indicted for second degree murder by the grand jury, had admitted to the killing, but his claim of self-defense had been accepted by an all-white jury nearly a year after the murder. Although the students expected the verdict for acquittal as yet one more example of southern courtroom injustice, they were nonetheless angered, frustrated, and eventually embittered and cynical. Take the example of students at another of the 10 schools. During a civil rights protest in early 1968 three students had been shot and killed by policemen.

These killings and the untempered use of power against Blacks who challenged it were not new: lynchings, repression, and mockery of legal justice pervade our history. The direct action phase of the southern movement had produced its own tragedies, almost all of them deaths of Black people. Students who had been active from 1963 to 1965 had seen it all. Still, whereas the nation had cried out in anger earlier in the decade, the murder of these students in the late sixties went practically unnoticed; their insignificance tells the story. The demonstrations were over; they had led nowhere; they had simply subjected Black people to brutality without producing enough change. Students turned to other strategies and other targets as the course of events forced them. They also reanalyzed forces inhibiting change. By 1970 they were altogether more aware of systematic determinants of inequity; they were also more cynical. The second half of the decade was a period of the loss of innocence. When major economic and social change replaced public accommodations and voting rights as targets of change, students understandably became more aware of systemwide forces. Vis-á-vis the growing commitment of resources to the Vietnam War, they also became less optimistic about achieving the basic changes they increasingly realized were necessary for the freedom of Black Americans. Revolutionary-collectivist theories of change provided many students the framework for understanding the events of the sixties and for articulating their new perspectives. Although Nationalist thinking developed and spread as earlier analyses and change strategies failed to improve significantly the economic and social conditions most Black Americans faced, its responsive character soon shifted to an energizing force through which students came to accept group identification and collective concern as positive elements in their personal identities.

Ideological Shifts: Questionnaire Responses in 1964 and 1970

GROWTH OF COLLECTIVE CONSCIOUSNESS

We have already seen in the interviews conducted in the spring of 1965 that students were struggling then to discard victim perspectives and to revise their view of the group's history in terms of exploitation and oppression, thereby developing pride in the group's heritage of strength and endurability. Two sets of questionnaire items administered in both 1964 and 1970 showed that students were much more conscious of collective oppression and had thus taken a critical step toward Nationalism by 1970.

One set, comprising the Individual-System Blame index, directly questioned who is responsible for race inequities. Accepting the system blame alternative implied awareness of discrimination as the collective experience of Black Americans and at the same time expressed a positive group identity that comes from refusing to blame one's own group for the inequities it faces. Accepting the individual blame alternative showed adherence to the old victim perspective in which the individual Black is blamed for his own misfortunes. In 1964 half of the freshmen and a third of the seniors answered at least three of the four questions on this index by blaming Blacks instead of systematic discrimination. The picture was radically altered by 1970, when over half of both freshmen and seniors answered at least three of the four questions by blaming the system. Shifts on the individual items comprising the indices were striking. The proportion of students who shifted from individual to system blame was as much as 20 to 30 percent on the three questions in which majority opinion in 1964 had reflected a victim analysis (Table 2).

Shifts on the Control Ideology index likewise reflected growth in collective consciousness. (The index, developed from factor analyzing the Rotter Internal-External Control Scale, was previously described in Chapter 4.) Rejecting a rigid Protestant ethic explanation of success

TABLE 2. **Comparison of the Individual-System Blame Responses, 1964 and 1970**

Individual Items	1964[a]		1970[b]	
	Men	Women	Men	Women
1. a. The attempt to "fit in" and do what's proper hasn't paid off for Blacks. It doesn't matter how "proper" you are, you'll still meet serious discrimination if you are Black. (System Blame)	56%	52%	84%	86%
b. The problem for many Blacks is that they aren't really acceptable by American standards. Any Black who is educated and does what is considered proper will be accepted and get ahead. (Individual Blame)	44	48	16	14
	100%	100%	100%	100%
2. a. Many Blacks who don't do well in life do have good training but the opportunities just always go to whites. (System Blame)	24%	19%	53%	59%
b. Blacks may not have the same opportunities as whites but many Blacks haven't prepared themselves enough to make use of the opportunities that come their way. (Individual Blame)	76	81	47	41
	100%	100%	100%	100%
3. a. Many Blacks have only themselves to blame for not doing better in life. If they tried harder, they'd do better. (Individual Blame)	61%	67%	41%	44%
b. When two qualified people, one Black and one white, are considered for the same job, the Black won't get the job no matter how hard he tries. (System Blame)	39	33	59	56
	100%	100%	100%	100%

4. a. It's lack of skill and abilities that keeps many Blacks from getting a job.
   It's not just because they're Black. When a Black is trained to do something,
   he is able to get a job. (*Individual Blame*)

   b. Many qualified Blacks can't get a good job. White people with the same
   skills wouldn't have any trouble. (*System Blame*)

a. (*Individual Blame*)	33%	33%	20%	21%
b. (*System Blame*)	67	67	80	79
	100%	100%	100%	100%

Indexed based on these four items:

All four alternatives blaming other Blacks chosen.	14%	19%	6%	6%
Three out of four blaming Blacks.	28	24	14	12
Two blaming Blacks, two blaming discrimination.	29	29	22	26
Three out of four blaming discrimination.	21	20	29	28
All four alternatives blaming the system chosen.	8	8	29	28
	100%	100%	100%	100%

[a]These percents are based on the 2141 students (1141 men and 1000 women) attending the six colleges in 1964 that participated in both the 1964 and 1970 cross-sectional studies.

[b]These percents are based on the 1127 students (589 men and 538 women) attending the six colleges that participated in the cross-sectional study in 1970.

TABLE 3. Comparison of Control Ideology Responses, 1964 and 1970

Individual Items	1964[a]		1970[b]	
	Men	Women	Men	Women
Items showing sizable (more than 20%) shifts from 1964 to 1970:				
1. a. Becoming a success is a matter of hard work, luck has little or nothing to do with it. (*Internal*)	76%	79%	53%	54%
b. Getting a good job depends mainly on being in the right place at the right time. (*External*)	24	21	47	46
	100%	100%	100%	100%
2. a. Knowing the right people is important in deciding whether a person will get ahead. (*External*)	41%	51%	73%	75%
b. People will get ahead in life if they have the goods and do a good job; knowing the right people has nothing to do with it. (*Internal*)	59	49	27	25
	100%	100%	100%	100%
3. a. People who don't do well in life often work hard, but the breaks just don't come their way. (*External*)	34%	33%	69%	65%
b. Some people just don't use the breaks that come their way. If they don't do well, it's their own fault. (*Internal*)	66	67	31	35
	100%	100%	100%	100%
4. a. Leadership positions tend to go to capable people who deserve being chosen. (*Internal*)	73%	70%	42%	40%
b. It's hard to know why some people get leadership positions and others don't; ability doesn't seem to be the important factor. (*External*)	27	30	58	60
	100%	100%	100%	100%

Items showing moderate (10-20%) shifts from 1964 to 1970:

Item				
5. a. Without the right breaks one cannot be an effective leader. *(External)*	29%	23%	41%	40%
b. Capable people who fail to become leaders have not taken advantage of their opportunities. *(Internal)*	71% / 100%	77% / 100%	59% / 100%	60% / 100%
6. a. In the case of the well-prepared student, there is rarely if ever, such a thing as an unfair test. *(Internal)*	52%	46%	32%	33%
b. Many times exam questions tend to be so unrelated to course work that studying is really useless. *(External)*	48% / 100%	54% / 100%	68% / 100%	67% / 100%
7. a. Sometimes I can't understand how teachers arrive at the grades they give. *(External)*	32%	28%	48%	50%
b. There is a direct connection between how hard I study and the grades I get. *(Internal)*	68% / 100%	62% / 100%	52% / 100%	50% / 100%

Items showing reasonable stability (Less than 10% shift from 1964 to 1970:

Item				
8. a. No matter how hard you try, some people just don't like you. *(External)*	59%	58%	67%	67%
b. People who can't get others to like them don't understand how to get along with others. *(Internal)*	41% / 100%	42% / 100%	33% / 100%	33% / 100%
9. a. Who gets to be the boss often depends on who was lucky to be in the right place first. *(External)*	16%	16%	26%	20%
b. Who gets to be boss depends on who has the skill and ability, luck has little or nothing to do with it. *(Internal)*	84% / 100%	84% / 100%	74% / 100%	80% / 100%

TABLE 3 (Continued)

Individual Items	1964[a]		1970[b]	
	Men	Women	Men	Women
10. a. It is hard to know whether or not a person really likes you. (External)	48%	45%	52%	55%
b. How many friends you have depends upon how nice a person you are. (Internal)	52	55	48	45
	100%	100%	100%	100%
11. a. Without the right breaks, one cannot be an effective leader. (External)	16%	13%	24%	18%
b. Getting people to do the right thing depends upon ability; luck has little or nothing to do with it. (Internal)	84	87	76	82
	100%	100%	100%	100%
12. a. Most people don't realize the extent to which their lives are controlled by accidental happenings. (External)	60%	64%	64%	67%
b. There really is no such thing as "luck". (Internal)	40	36	36	33
	100%	100%	100%	100%
13. a. People are lonely because they don't try to be friendly. (Internal)	54%	50%	42%	39%
b. There's not much use in trying too hard to please people, if they like you, they like you. (External)	46	50	58	61
	100%	100%	100%	100%

Index based on above 13 items:
Mean scores
Range: 0-13, 0 = most internal, 13 = most external

	Men	Women	Men	Women
Total	$\chi=5.04$	$\chi=5.03$	$\chi=7.40$	$\chi=7.28$
Freshman	4.32	4.09	6.92	6.75
Seniors	5.43	5.75	7.94	7.89

[a]These percents are based on the 2141 students (1141 men and 1000 women) attending the six colleges in 1964 that participated in both the 1964 and 1970 cross-sectional studies.

[b]These percents are based on the 1127 students (589 men and 538 women) attending the six colleges that participated in the cross-sectional study in 1970.

implied the new consciousness by questioning the legitimacy of the dominant group's cultural norms, which, when internalized by subordinated groups, produces self-blame for their life situation. Students in 1970 much less consistently insisted that people get ahead because they work hard or in other ways possess the virtues of the Protestant ethic. In 1964 students typically chose many more internal than external explanations for success and failure. By 1970 they were considerably more balanced by seeing both internal and external forces operating in people's lives. This did not mean students had shifted to a rigid belief in fate. Instead, their increased externality represented awareness that internal virtues do not always pay off and that some outcomes in life are directed by forces individuals cannot control. We know this by examining which of the 13 questions on this index resulted in large external shifts from 1964 to 1970 (Table 3). The four that showed as much as a 20 percent shift away from a conventional work ethic stance did not refer to fate or chance but to other external determinants—knowing the right people, being in the right place at the right time, or just not knowing why some people succeed and others do not since ability does not seem to be the important factor. None of the questions in which "luck" or "fate" was explicitly used in the external explanation showed more than five percent shifts toward externality. The greater externality in 1970 reflected the students' criticisms of conventional individualism rather than the resignation to fate that is so often interpreted as the meaning of externality.

Students who discussed revolutionary-collectivist ideas in the latter half of the sixties contended that these shifts away from individualism to recognition of collective oppression conformed closely to Fanon's treatment of the critical shift from the colonial situation to decolonization. In the colonial situation, Fanon says, "Every effort is made to bring the colonized person to admit the inferiority of his culture which has been transformed into instinctive patterns of behavior, to recognize the unreality of his 'nation,' and in the last extreme, the confused and imperfect character of his own biological structure."[6] Fanon continues: "In decolonization, there is therefore the need of a complete calling in question of the colonial situation."[7] "Political education means opening their minds, awakening them, and allowing the birth of their intelligence; as Cesaire said, it is 'to invent souls . . .' Thus, the native discovers that his life, his breath, his beating heart are the same as those of the settler. He finds out that the settler's skin is not of any more value than a native's skin; and it must be said that

6. Frantz Fanon, *The Wretched of the Earth* (New York: Grove Press, 1963), p. 236.
7. *Ibid.,* p. 37. Copyright © 1963 by Presence Africaine.

TABLE 4. Comparison of Judgments of the Modifiability of Discrimination, 1964 and 1970

Individual Items	1964[a]		1970[b]	
	Men	Women	Men	Women
1. a. Racial discrimination is here to stay.	20%	18%	46%	42%
b. People may be prejudiced but it's possible for American society to completely rid itself of open discrimination.	80	82	54	58
	100%	100%	100%	100%
2. a. The so-called "white backlash" shows once again that whites are so opposed to Blacks getting their rights that it's practically impossible to end discrimination in America.	23%	26%	64%	65%
b. The so-called "white backlash" has been exaggerated. Certainly enough whites support the goals of the Black cause for Americans to see considerable progress in wiping out discrimination.	77	74	36	35
	100%	100%	100%	100%
3. a. The racial situation in America may be very complex, but with enough money and effort, it is possible to get rid of racial discrimination.	35%	38%	28%	24%
b. We'll never completely get rid of discrimination. It's part of human nature.	65	62	72	76
	100%	100%	100%	100%
Index based on above three items:				
All three alternatives that discrimination *can* be eliminated chosen.	29%	30%	11%	11%
Two out of three that discrimination *can.*	44	45	27	26
Two out of three that discrimination *cannot.*	19	21	31	32
All three alternatives that discrimination *cannot* be eliminated chosen.	8	4	31	31
	100%	100%	100%	100%

[a]These percents are based on the 2141 students (1141 men and 1000 women) attending the six colleges in 1964 that participated in both the 1964 and 1970 cross-sectional studies.

[b]These percents are based on the 1127 students (589 men and 538 women) attending the six colleges that participated in the cross-sectional study in 1970.

this discovery shakes the world in a very necessary manner. All the new revolutionary assurance of the native stems from it."[8]

Freeing oneself from the burden of responsibility for disadvantage was thus viewed as an essential predisposing attitude for taking the step to Black Nationalism. Most students had taken it by 1970. This reanalysis of history also meant they had to question their previously "unrelenting faith in the federal government and belief that changes in the laws would rapidly pave the ways for sweeping changes in the social structure."[9] They became altogether less optimistic about eliminating discrimination in American society. Indeed this shift from optimism to pessimism was even more marked than the shift to system blame (Table 4). The proportion of students who were optimistic about getting rid of open discrimination was down 25 percent. Opinion shifts about the meaning of the white backlash were even more evident. Forty percent fewer students in 1970 felt the white backlash had been exaggerated. It was only on a third question that most students in both 1964 and 1970 expressed pessimism about change.

DEVELOPMENT OF COLLECTIVE COMMITMENTS

Black Americans, like other minorities, historically have debated the wisdom of two modes of handling discrimination and promoting social change. Some, expressing a valued belief in the American experience that the good life follows as a reward to moral discipline, hard work, and ambition, have resolutely sought individual advancement both as their personal solution and as their strategy for aggregate change in the group's status as well. Others have insisted on the necessity of group action, since racial subordination violates two preconditions for individual mobility—access to favorable life opportunities, and evaluation of performance by nonracial, universal achievement standards. Still others have advocated both individual and collective strategies, the latter to reform institutions and alter discriminatory practices so that equal opportunity would allow for individual ascent. Individual and collective modes of social ascent are incorporated in two contrasting approaches to social change, an emphasis on individual achievement and the revolutionary-collectivist approach.

Achievement theory stresses the development of motivation to excel through family socialization, freedom from binding group obligations or ties, and a willingness to take advantage of opportunities

<hr>

8. *Ibid.,* p. 45.
9. Joyce Ladner, "What Black Power Means to Negroes in Mississippi," in August Meier, Editor, *The Transformation of Activism* (New York: Aldine Publishing Company, *Trans*-action Books, 1970), p. 137.

TABLE 5. Comparison of Individual Mobility-Collective Action Preferences, 1964 and 1970

Individual Items	1964[a]		1970[b]	
	Men	Women	Men	Women
1. a. The best way to overcome discrimination is through pressure and social action.	21%	13%	56%	51%
b. The best way to overcome discrimination is for each individual Black to be even better trained and more qualified than the most qualified white person.	79% 100%	87% 100%	44% 100%	49% 100%
2. a. Depending on biracial committees is just a dodge. Talking and understanding without constant protest and pressure will never solve the problems of discrimination.	42%	38%	72%	70%
b. Talking and understanding as opposed to protest and pressure is the best way to solve racial discrimination.	58% 100%	62% 100%	28% 100%	30% 100%
3. a. The best way to handle problems of discrimination is for each individual Black to make sure he gets the best training possible for what he wants to do.	72%	74%	46%	46%
b. Only if Blacks pull together in civil rights groups and activities can anything really be done about discrimination.	28% 100%	26% 100%	54% 100%	54% 100%
4. a. Organized action is one approach to handling discrimination, but there are probably very few situations that couldn't be handled better by Black leaders talking with white leaders.	50%	54%	32%	36%
b. Most discriminatory situations simply can't be handled without organized pressure and group action.	50% 100%	46% 100%	68% 100%	64% 100%

5. a. Discrimination affects all Blacks. The only way to handle it is for Blacks to organize together and demand rights for all.

   b. Discrimination may affect all Blacks but the best way to handle it is for each individual Black to act like any other American—to work hard, to get a good education, and mind his own business.

6. a. Blacks would be better off and the cause of civil rights advanced if there were fewer demonstrations.

   b. The only way Blacks will gain their civil rights is by constant protest and pressure.

5. a.	53%	47%	79%	80%
b.	47	53	21	20
	100%	100%	100%	100%
6. a.	16%	21%	14%	16%
b.	84	79	86	84
	100%	100%	100%	100%

Index based on above six items:

All six individual action alternatives chosen.	7%	7%	2%	1%
Five out of six individual.	12	18	6	6
Four out of six individual.	26	26	13	19
Three individual, three collective.	24	24	15	15
Four out of six collective.	18	16	22	20
Five out of six collective.	9	7	23	20
All six collective alternatives chosen.	4	2	19	19
	100%	100%	100%	100%

aThese percents are based on the 2141 students (1141 men and 1000 women) attending the six colleges in 1964 that participated in both the 1964 and 1970 cross-sectional studies.

bThese percents are based on the 1127 students (589 men and 538 women) attending the six colleges that participated in the cross-sectional study in 1970.

in areas away from home. Applied to majority-minority relations, this approach would view racial change as a consequence of the aggregated achievements of individual Negroes. Revolutionary-collectivist theory, on the other hand, sets forth the rationale for commitment to a collectivity, a belief that the deprived, apathetic masses can only achieve a better life through involvement in a collective, revolutionary struggle . . . While both theories view the disciplined effort of individuals as an essential determinant of change, revolutionary theory joins this quality with subordination of self to a collective cause and authority.[10]

A series of questions we gave both in 1964 and in 1970 asked students to choose between individual and collective modes. One alternative asserted that the individual mobility made possible through education and advanced training is the best way for individual Blacks to deal with the realities of discrimination; the other stressed that the nature of the race situation demands constant protest, pressure, and group action.

We have already seen from themes in the interviews conducted in the spring of 1965 that individual mobility took precedence over social action at that time, although students typically approved of both types of strategies. Preference for aggregate change through individual advancement also characterized their responses to these items that asked them to choose between individual and collective modes. In 1964 half of the students chose at least four of the six alternatives favoring individual mobility, and only about one-fifth chose four of the six collective strategies. In 1970 the situation was reversed. Sixty-two percent of the students then chose at least four of the six alternatives favoring group action. For example, 36 percent more of the students in 1970 agreed that "the best way to overcome discrimination is through pressure and social action"; 27 percent more said that "only if Blacks pull together in civil rights groups and activities can anything really be done about discrimination"; 31 percent more asserted that "discrimination affects all Blacks—the only way to handle it is for Blacks to organize together and demand rights for all." Even in 1964 most of the students preferred collective action on the other three questions; in 1970 collective choices were even more consensual, expressed then by 70 to 80 percent of the students (Table 5).

These shifts did not mean that students were indifferent to their own mobility and individual goals; they did indicate, however, a major departure from individualism to collectivism in their social change

10. Glen H. Elder, Jr., "Intergroup Attitudes and Social Ascent Among Negro Boys," *American Journal of Sociology* 76(4) (1971), p. 674.

theories. Many students argued that these shifts represented a second stage in the development of Nationalist thinking. First, individuals must become aware of collective oppression; then individualism can be replaced by collective commitments. Turner describes these sequential steps in becoming a Nationalist.

> Becoming a Black Nationalist involves the realization that persons of African descent are treated categorically by the dominant group. Subsequently, the firm conviction that Afro-Americans must become transmuted into a conscious and cohesive group develops. The rationale is that a group giving a unitary response can more effectively and honorably confront the constraining dominant group. Race, color, and resistance to the oppression of the dominant group and its imposed assumptions and definitions about the minority become the vehicle for realizing conversion from category to group. Loyalty to group cultural attributes and commitment to collective goals provide the adhesive for the group.[11]

By 1970 most students had taken these steps. They had shifted to the need for group action to alter the inequities they had come to believe were the collective experience of Black Americans. By these shifts they were predisposed to favor the political analysis of Black Nationalism.

BLACK NATIONALISM: STUDENT OPINIONS IN 1970

Black Nationalism represents a coherent ideology with both political and cultural elements. The ideology, however, contains many themes, not a single theme. In 1970 we asked students many questions about the political and cultural ideas implied by nationalist thought. Our factor analysis of their attitude responses supports work by Mathis[12] and Lessing[13] showing the multidimensionality of Black Nationalism. Four political factors resulted: advocacy of self-determination through separatism, community control of schools and other institutions, economic development or Black capitalism, and acceptance of the use of

---

11. James Turner, "Identity in Transition: A Theory of Black Militancy," in Roderick Aya and Norman Miller, Editors, *The New American Revolution* (New York: The Free Press, 1971), pp. 169-170.
12. Arthur Lee Mathis, "Social and Psychological Characteristics of the Black Liberation Movement: A Colonial Analogy," (Ph.D. Dissertation, University of Michigan, 1971).
13. Elise E. Lessing and Susan W. Zagorin, "Factor Structure and Concurrent Validity of a Black Power Ideology Scale," *Proceedings of the 78th Annual Convention of the American Psychological Association* 5, 1970, pp. 353-54 and Lessing and Zagorin, "Some Demographic, Value and Personality Correlates of Endorsement of Negro Militancy by Negro and White Youth," *Proceedings of the 77th Annual Convention of the American Psychological Association* 4 (1969), pp. 295-296.

TABLE 6. **Proportion of Men and Women Approving of Individual Items on the Black Nationalism Indices, and Average Scores of Men and Women on the Nationalism Summary Indices (1970)**[a]

	Percent Approving or Strongly Approving		
	Men	Women	Total Sample
POLITICAL NATIONALISM			
Self-Determination through separatism:			
Do you feel that Blacks should form their own political party?	44%	34%	40%
Do you approve of interracial marriage? (percent disapproving)	24%	39%	31%
My school should be an all-Black campus, a campus without whites as teachers or students.	20%	17%	18%
Do you feel that Blacks should have nothing to do with whites if they can help it?	15%	13%	14%
Do you think that Blacks should set up a separate Black nation in America?	14%	10%	12%
Total score (range 1–16)	$\chi=6.29$	$\chi=6.35$	
Community control			
Do you feel that Blacks should take more pride in Black history?	90%	91%	90%
Do you feel that stores in Black communities should be owned and run by Blacks?	81%	75%	79%
Do you agree that Black Americans should insist that schools in Black neighborhoods should have Black principals?	77%	71%	74%
Do you believe that schools with mostly Black children should have mostly Black teachers?	79%	61%	66%
Do you feel that Black parents should have the final word as to what is taught to their children in the public schools?	47%	44%	45%
Total score (range 1–16)	$\chi=11.13$	$\chi=11.03$	
Economic development:			
Do you think that educated Blacks who have good jobs should try to use their talents and leadership ability to help other Blacks?	97%	97%	97%
Do you feel that Blacks should try to get money for setting up businesses that will be run by Blacks in the Black community?	94%	94%	94%
Do you feel that Blacks should patronize Black businesses whenever possible?	93%	91%	92%
Total score (range 1–10)	$\chi=8.65$	$\chi=8.35$	

TABLE 6 (Continued)

	Percent Approving or Strongly Approving		
	Men	Women	Total Sample
Militancy: political use of violence:			
Some people say that events in Newark, Detroit, and Watts helped the Blacks. Others say it hurt. What do you think? (Percent saying helped some or a great deal.)	82%	74%	78%
Many different terms have been used to describe the events that took place in Newark, Detroit, Watts, and other places. (Percent saying that they should be called rebellion.)	52%	40%	46%
Do you approve of violence as a means of helping the Black cause?	56%	31%	44%
Civil rights workers should be armed, ready to protect themselves.	32%	16%	24%
Total score (range 1–13)	$\chi=9.00$	$\chi=7.88$	
	$F=51.5$ (.001)		

CULTURAL NATIONALISM

	Men	Women	Total Sample
Afro-American orientation			
Do you approve of Black women wearing Afro hair styles?	94%	95%	95%
Which name do you prefer being called? (Percent preferring either Afro-American or Black.)	87%	83%	85%
Which would you say was more important to you— being Black or being American or being both?			
(Percent saying both)	49%	56%	53%
(Percent saying Black)	35%	23%	29%
Total score (range 1–10)	$\chi=8.24$	$\chi=7.89$	
African identification			
Do you feel that Black children should study an African language?	72%	68%	70%
Do you think Blacks should identify themselves with Africa by wearing African-styled clothes?	35%	42%	38%
Total score (range 1–7)	$\chi=4.58$	$\chi=4.41$	

[a]This table is based on the 1127 students who participated in the six-college cross-sectional study in 1970.

violence as a political tool. Two cultural factors also emerged: assertion of an Afro-American identity and identification with African symbols.

Self-Determination Through Separatism

One of the most controversial issues among students in 1970 concerned the usefulness and feasibility of various modes of action and degrees of separation of Blacks in the United States. Nationalist thought advocates separatism as a route to self-determination: Black people must organize collectively through Black institutions that do not have white leadership, control, or membership. Separatism focuses upon the importance of self-reliance and the need to strengthen group consciousness and identity among Black people. It springs from the conviction that American society as presently structured cannot fully integrate or assimilate Afro-Americans. Racism is not an institutional anomaly but the essence of the system; Black people are exploited and subjugated as a group, not as individuals. Advocates of separatism believe that the prevailing values and institutional arrangements in American society are designed and maintained to sustain the subordinate position of Blacks. Thus, they reject American society, totally or partially, for being aggressively hostile to the interests and lives of Blacks. Contemporary separatists have urged Blacks to work toward building an autonomous nation-state. The Muslims, members of the Republic of New Africa and participants in the Black Power Conference of 1967 have all urged that the United States be partitioned into two separate nations, one for Blacks and one for other Americans. These separatists are convinced that Black people will never be allowed to live in peace and harmony as equal human beings in a white society.

As popularly used, separatism also denotes a process of group development, during which Blacks work on problems of group unity, solidarity, leadership, pride and political strength. In this sense separatism is seen as a necessary step toward attaining an equitable and effective share of the total power in American society. During this process of group development, Nationalists press for the development of, and maintenance of, autonomous Black cultural institutional values and for the strengthening of the group's racial identity. Group members are urged to reject these values and norms of the dominant culture that deny the authenticity of the African-American cultural heritage and function to colonize Blacks psychologically. This separatist mood has been reflected on college campuses across the nation in demands for all Black dormitories, Black organizations, lounges and buildings reserved for the use of Black students, and for autonomous Black Studies centers.

Separatist ideas were represented by one of the factors that emerged in factor analyzing a set of items that we first included in the 1970 study to measure the students' attitudes about Nationalism (Appendix Table 8.2). Students who supported separatism believed that "my school should be an all-Black campus, a campus without whites as teachers or students"; "Blacks should have nothing to do with whites if they can help it"; "Blacks should set up a separate Black nation in America"; "Blacks should form their own political party"; and "Blacks should not engage in interracial marriage."

Separatism was the most controversial of all the Nationalist themes for both men and women. The proportion who approved or strongly approved of these separatist items ranged from 12 to 40 percent, compared to rates of 92 to 97 percent for the most highly accepted nationalist theme, Black economic development (Table 6). The idea of a separate Black political party received the most support, although still only 40 percent of the students endorsed it. Geographical separatism was the least popular: only 12 percent of the students approved of Blacks setting up a separate Black nation; only 18 percent favored their school being all Black; only 14 percent felt that Blacks should have nothing to do with whites when possible. Interracial marriage was disapproved by 31 percent of the total sample. This was the only item on the separatism factor on which men and women expressed even somewhat different opinions. More women (30 percent) than men (24 percent) disapproved of interracial marriage. Men and women also viewed the meaning of interracial marriage somewhat differently. It was strictly a question of political strategy for men; it fell only on the separatism factor for men. For women, however, interracial marriage was also related to issues of racial pride and identity; its loadings were as high as on the separatism factor for two other factors, the Afro-American orientation and the African Identification factor. The issue of interracial marriage is much more personalized for Black women: Black women are threatened with the loss of marriage partners through interracial marriage.

What other attitudes and opinions correlated with self-determination through separatism? Did the advocates of separatism depart ideologically from other students in any other ways? To examine this, we correlated all six nationalism factors with the political beliefs already discussed as predispositions toward Nationalism: system blame, preference for collective action over individual mobility, and advocacy of student involvement in campus governance as a special instance of control of Black institutions.

Advocacy of self-determination through separatism articulated especially with those aspects of student power that concerned the philosophical and intellectual direction of the college (Appendix Table 8.3).

In fact, this was the only nationalism factor that related to the students' attitudes about curriculum and speaker issues. Students with strong feelings about self-determination also felt strongly that students should have the authority to determine whether or not outside speakers could speak on campus; they further felt that speakers should not require administrative clearance. They also advocated student authority in curricular decisions in the college. In contrast, the separatism factor was not unusually relevant for other aspects of student power. Thus, it was exactly those campus issues that had become politicized between 1968 and 1970—inclusion of Black studies in the curriculum, the opportunity of Nationalist speakers to address student groups, and the Blackness of the college's identity—that were uniquely connected with separatism.

Feelings about separatism also related particularly well to a special commitment to be part of Black life (Appendix Table 8.3). Students who were favorable toward separatism expressed strong preference for working in all Black settings, for living in Black neighborhoods, and for sending their children to all Black schools. (The taus between the separatism factor and the expressed preferences to be part of Black life ranged from .42 to .58 for both men and women; they were the highest correlations for any factor; others ranged between .13 and .33).

Students who strongly favored separatism also expressed strong doubts about the intentions or willingness of whites to make extensive social changes to benefit most Blacks. (Taus between the separatism factor and a measure of system distrust were .49 for men and .52 for women, again the highest obtained for any of the factors.) Separatists likewise blamed the social system, rather than Blacks themselves, for the group's low socioeconomic status in American society, although no more so than advocates of other aspects of Nationalism. They strongly approved of the Muslim organization and of the Panthers; they strongly disapproved of the policies and practices of the more traditional civil rights groups, the SCLC, Urban League, NAACP general organization, and the Legal Defense Fund of the NAACP (Appendix Table 8.3).

Community Control

The idea of community control as an aspect of Nationalism was represented by a second factor (Appendix Table 8.2). The community control concept requires that the resources and the publicly supported institutions in the Black community function to promote the interests and concerns of the people who live there. This idea should be basic to political processes in America. Generally, the local government, schools, recreational facilities, and other public institutions in American communities are controlled and administered by local people or at least by people who represent the attitudes, interests, and the values of the community residents. Sometimes policemen, teachers, school administrators, and local government officials are required to live within the community they serve. The Black Nationalist concept of community control demands that the constitutional right to self-government be extended to Black people and that Blacks act collectively in exercising this right. Thus, community control is a central aspect of the nationalist Black Power concept. Black Power ideology demands that Blacks participate fully in the decision-making processes affecting their lives; it also demands that Blacks retain and build their positive self-identity and their group consciousness.

The community control factor was primarily comprised of items about control of the public schools. In the urban areas of the North this has been among the salient issues in attempts to operationalize the concept of community control in the Black community. In the South's dual system of education Blacks traditionally have had greater influence on the direction of schools for Black children, although they, like northern Blacks, never had the control over resources that would have made them independent of the central administrations of the public schools. The schools are appropriate targets of political control in both regions of the country despite their different histories. Generally, Nationalists argue that the public school system is a key institution in the struggle for community control because it is responsible for transmitting to the younger generation the ideals, values, attitudes, and world view of the larger society. To build and retain a positive Black identity it is mandatory to determine what children learn about themselves. Schools must be controlled to insure that children acquire positive images of themselves as Black persons as well as a positive image of the group's place in contemporary society and in history.

Approval of community control was reasonably widespread, more so than advocacy of either separatism or militancy (Table 6). Seventy-four percent of the students in 1970 agreed that "Black Americans should insist that schools in Black neighborhoods have Black principals"; 66 percent said that "Schools with mostly Black students should have mostly Black teachers"; 45 percent felt that "Black parents should have the final word as to what is taught to their children in the public schools"; 90 percent felt that "Blacks should take more pride in Negro history." The only issue included in this factor that did not concern schools asserted that "Stores in the Black community should be owned and run by Blacks." Seventy-nine percent of the students agreed that they should.

The proportion of men and women who agreed with these items did not differ. However, the community control issue was very much linked to the issues of separatism for men, but not for women. The school-related items that made up the community control factor also carried high loadings on the separatism factor for men (Appendix Table 8.2). This suggests that community control as a separate nationalistic issue was more relevant to the political ideology of women. Men saw it more as just another instance of manning separate institutions.

Students who advocated community control were especially likely to attribute blame for the low socioeconomic condition of Blacks to systematic inequities in the social system rather than to a lack of skill, ability, motivation, or proper behavior by Black people. (The taus between our measure of system blame and community control, .45 for men and .44 for women, were higher than those with any other Nationalism factor; other taus ranged from .17 to .30). Advocates of community control were also unusually concerned about freedom for political participation of students. Students who urged community control were very much in favor of students themselves deciding whether or not to participate in civil rights activities held either off campus or on the campus itself (Appendix Table 8.3).

Black Economic Development

During the late sixties some Black Nationalists began arguing that the social problems experienced by Black people in America stemmed from a lack of economic development. Lack of capital, in turn, made the Black man politically powerless to effect social change and to secure equality in the United States. Floyd McKissick of CORE called for full-time commitment to Black business development with social commitments to Black communities.[14] He argued that equality depended upon Black control over Black industries, and he stressed economic independence through the rapid development of Black corporate structures. This idea of an all-Black capitalist economy is a bourgeoise nationalist notion that originated with Booker T. Washington around the turn of the century.[15] Washington advocated building an all-Black cooperative economy, arguing that:

> *Brains, property, and character for the Negro will settle the question of civil rights. The best course to pursue in regard to a civil rights bill in the South is to let it alone; let it alone and it will take care of itself. Good schools, teachers, and plenty of money to pay*

14. Floyd B. McKissick, "Black Business Development With Social Commitment to Black Communities," John H. Bracey, Jr., August Meier and Elliott Rudwick, Editors, *Black Nationalism in America* (Indianapolis and New York: Bobbs-Merrill, 1970), pp. 492-503.

15. Harold Cruse, *Rebellion or Revolution?* (New York: William Morrow, 1968), p. 157.

*them with will be more potent in settling the race question than
many civil rights bills and investigating committees . . .*[16]

Another of the factors from the 1970 analysis was made up of items
explicitly related to these ideas of self-help and economic development
(Appendix Table 8.2). The endorsement rates of these items showed
that the idea of Black economic development was the most popular
nationalistic concept among the students in our sample. Ninety-seven
percent felt that "Educated Blacks should try to use their talents and
leadership ability to help other Blacks"; 94 percent agreed that "Blacks
should try to get money for setting up businesses that will be run by
Blacks in the Black community"; 92 percent urged that "Blacks should
patronize Black businesses whenever possible." (Table 6.)

Commitment to Black economic development was especially associated with concern for programs and groups dealing with bread and
butter issues (Appendix Table 8.3). Students who strongly favored Black
economic development also felt very positive toward the SCLC,
sponsor of Operation Breadbasket, and toward the Urban League, an
organization traditionally involved with employment problems. Economic development was the only factor that was positively related to
attitudes about these two organizations. Indeed, students who favored
two other aspects of nationalism, separatism, and militancy were negative about these two groups. Although it could be argued that support
among advocates of economic development of the SCLC and the
Urban League simply represented their moderateness, the fact that
they also approved of the Muslims and the Panthers as heartily as
advocates of other aspects of nationalism showed that they were not
merely moderate. Instead, they seemed to approve of those groups and
strategies that addressed economic issues.

The pattern of these relationships between Black economic development, on the one hand, and between both separatism and militancy,
on the other, shows that Nationalism has several facets, some of them
reasonably independent. Advocating economic development seemed
to represent a distinct variety of Nationalist thought, not just another
theme within a highly cohesive ideology. A given student could
endorse separatism and militancy as well as Black economic development, but this pattern represented a differentiated ideology instead of
just a variation on a common theme.

Militancy

The Black Nationalist movement was accompanied during the 1960s
by an increase in militant activities. Malcolm X, Robert Williams, the
Panthers, and others asserted the constitutional right of Black people

16. *Ibid.,* Quoting Booker T. Washington in the Atlanta Exposition Speech, p. 159.

to defend themselves with arms if necessary. Large numbers of Black people were also engaged in direct confrontations with legal authorities during the urban rebellions from 1965 to 1968. A new militancy developed as more people began to question, even deny, the legitimacy of a political and legal system that historically has failed to represent the identity and needs of Black people. Indeed, some Nationalists have defined the situation of nonwhites as domestic colonization under a political, social, and cultural order intrinsically hostile to the interests of Blacks. Also, Blacks were provided new models by the successful decolonization movements among Black people on the African continent. Militant Black Nationalism asserts that some acts that are defined by the dominant group as violent may be necessary in the struggle for liberation.

The items on the militancy factor all speak to these issues of collective violence and armed self-defense (Appendix Table 8.2). While not as well supported as either community control or economic development, the idea of militancy was more accepted than separatism was (Table 6). Seventy-eight percent of the total sample believed that "events in Newark, Detroit, Watts, and other places helped Blacks"; 44 percent approved of "violence as a means of helping the Black cause"; 46 percent favored describing the events in Newark, Detroit, Watts, and other places as "rebellions" rather than "riots," "hoodlumism," or "civil disorders"; 24 percent felt that "civil rights workers should be armed, ready to protect themselves." The least militant act in a legal sense, the arming of civil rights workers for self-defense, was least approved by the students. Perhaps the idea was just too close to home since many had participated in civil rights activities or at least had friends and relatives who had been involved. The militant acts referred to in the other items primarily took place in urban areas outside the South.

This is the one factor on which men and women consistently disagreed. Women were less approving than men of the militant position on every item. Twice as many men (32 percent) as women (16 percent) felt that civil rights workers should be armed. Only 31 percent of the women, compared to 56 percent of the men, approved of violence as a means of helping the Black cause. Forty percent of the women, compared to 52 percent of the men, favored describing events that took place in Newark and other cities as rebellions. Eighty-two percent of the men but 74 percent of the women felt that events like those in Newark helped Black people.

Attitudes toward militancy stood out particularly in differentiating which students approved of protest and collective strategies of social change (Appendix Table 8.3). Students who approved of militancy also strongly favored handling problems of racial discrimination through tactics of organized group action and pressure rather than through strategies that stressed talking and understanding between Black and white leaders. (The taus, .45 for men and .44 for women, were the highest obtained for all factors with the measure of preferred strategies.) Students favoring militant actions also strongly favored collective actions that depended on group solidarity and social pressure rather than on actions stressing personal involvement and individual mobility. (These taus, .44 for men and .42 for women, were also higher than for any other factor.)

In most other ways the attitudinal correlates of militancy followed the same pattern as those connected with separatism. For example, approval of militancy was associated, although less strikingly than separatism was, with distrust of the sincerity or willingness of whites to correct social injustices affecting Black people. It was also positively related, although more weakly so than separatism was, to the students' commitments to live and participate in Black settings and institutions. In these ways separatism and militancy picked up the same feelings and opinions, understandably so since they were themselves more closely related than either was to any other nationalist theme. On the other hand, each carried distinct meanings as well. Militancy was especially relevant for the question about which strategies should be followed to effect social change. Separatism was especially important in distinguishing which students were concerned about college governance as an example of self-determination.

Cultural Nationalism

Cultural nationalism "contends that Black people—in the United States or throughout the world—have a culture, style of life, cosmology, approach to the problems of existence, and aesthetic values distinct from that of white Americans in particular and white Europeans or Westeners in general."[17] In its mildest form, cultural nationalism asserts that Afro-Americans have a distinct subculture within the many that make up pluralistic American society; more militant cultural nationalists assert the superiority of Afro-American culture to Western civilization. The movement for cultural nationalism or cultural autonomy is an attempt to establish and maintain a self-identity and a value system based on an awareness of and cultivation of the African-American heritage of Blacks. Cultural nationalists have attempted to reject the norms and values of American culture that classify Blacks as "culturally deprived," "a people without a culture or history," and "a people

17. Introduction, *Black Nationalism in America*, pp. XXVI-XXVII.

inherently incapable of intellectual achievement." Cultural nationalism thus redefines the Black self and its relationship to the dominant society. Manifestations of cultural nationalism include glorifications rather than rejection of Black color, hair, facial features ("Black is beautiful"); heightened interests in African and Afro-American history and culture; the wearing of African clothes, assuming African or Arabic names, speaking an African language, and positive identification with African origins and cultural heritage; the development of a body of social science literature written from an Afro-American perspective; the development of a distinct Afro-American literature, art, and music; the formation of media to transmit Afro-American culture—news-papers, journals, theaters, artistic workshops, and musical groups.

Two factors emerged that expressed these themes of cultural nation-alism (Appendix Table 8.2). The first, composed of items related to Black self-identity, represented an Afro-American orientation. Students in 1970 generally were supportive: 85 percent preferred being called either Afro-American or Black in contrast to Negro or Colored; 95 percent approved of Blacks wearing Afro-hair styles; when asked which was more important to them—being Black, being Black and American, being American, or neither—53 percent chose the dual identity of being Black and American and 29 percent preferred the exclusive identity of being Black (Table 6). The second factor referred explicitly to African identification—wearing of African clothes and studying African languages. Seventy percent of the students agreed that "Black children should study an African language"; 38 percent felt that "Blacks should identify themselves with Africa by wearing African-styled clothes."

Some political nationalists have asserted that strong feelings about cultural nationalism function to divert attention away from the more pressing political and economic problems faced by Afro-Americans; others have asserted that the cultural and political forms of Black Nationalism exist symbiotically and that both are necessary in a struggle for total decolonization. Were these two cultural factors separate from or subparts of political nationalism for the students we studied in 1970? The Afro-American orientation was part of their political nationalism: it correlated with advocacy of community control, economic develop-ment, separatism, and militancy; it related to the system attitudes and social change theories that predisposed students to nationalism in much the same fashion as these other dimensions of political nation-alism did (Appendix Table 8.3). In contrast, the African Identification Index was clearly independent of political meanings. Students who were strongly committed to the value of children studying an African language and of Blacks wearing African-styled clothes did not espouse political nationalism, system blame perspectives, or collective commitments more than those students with very little African Identification (Appendix Table 8.3). We will also see in Chapter 10 that African Identification likewise carried no collective action implications for students, while all of the political nationalism measures were significant, some more, some less, in distinguishing students who were active in either civil rights or student power issues from those who remained unengaged.

chapter 9

The Social Roots of Activism and Black Nationalism

In this chapter we explore the social roots of activist Black students over the changing decade of the sixties. We look at activism at three points in time: in 1964, at the end of the mass demonstration era; in 1968, when on-campus student administration confrontations had almost replaced conventional off-campus civil rights attacks; and again in 1970, when the newly emerging Black Nationalism and the psychological questions of Black consciousness provided the *raison d'etre* for student activists. First, we examine the participation rates of Black students, relative to other students, at these three points in time. We show that Black students were consistently more active than college students in the nation at large. Then, we turn to the social determinants of activism. The data we present address several questions. Did the social bases of participation change as the targets and issues changed? Did the leaders in the early days more often develop out of the experience of the southern working-class Black family?. Did casual participation in a single, isolated event more often characterize students from more affluent, elite families? Did the students who were still participating in civil rights activities in 1970 come from different backgrounds from their fellow students who expressed their commitments to Black Nationalism by turning to issues concerning campus governance and the development of a "relevant Black education?" Is Black Nationalism itself tied to social class experience?

THE POLITICAL ACTION OF STUDENTS AT BLACK COLLEGES

Participation Rates:
A National Perspective

During the first half of the sixties, when protest centered around civil rights issues, large numbers of the students who attended Black colleges

235

in the South participated in the southern student movement. Matthews and Prothro in *Negroes in the New Southern Politics* report that 24 percent of their sample of students attending 30 Black colleges had participated in some civil rights activity by the end of 1961.[1] A study of students attending four Black colleges in the Greensboro, North Carolina area provides even more striking figures for their involvement in the spring following the first sit-in in Greensboro in February, 1960. Virtually all the students had participated in some way; 24 percent were actively involved.[2] Three years later, the National Opinion Research Center surveying seniors who had entered Black colleges in 1960 found that 70 percent reported having participated in civil rights activities at some point during their college years; 32 percent claimed to have been active participants or leaders.[3] The participation rates of the seniors we studied in 1964 agree almost exactly with the NORC study. At a school near enough to Montgomery, Alabama for students to participate easily in the famous events of 1965, almost three-quarters of the student body took part in some way.

Blacks' participation in the Southern student movement, although varying according to time and place, rose generally over this period to include the vast majority of the student body on those campuses where a local movement provided easy opportunity. The lowest participation estimates still exceeded those for students in the nation at large during the same period. Baird reports from an American Council of Education survey administered to students in 31 institutions in the spring of 1964 and again in 1965 that less than three percent of the students were classified as activists, that is, those who had taken part in at least three of the five types of protests the survey listed; another 22 percent had participated in one or two types; 75 percent had not engaged in any at all.[4] The Harris and Gallup polls of 1965 show similar rates: only about a fifth of the students in their samples had participated in political activities.[5] It seems fair to conclude that, whereas only 20 to 30 percent of students in the nation at large had participated in some form of student protest or political action by 1965, the participation figure for students in Black colleges was closer to 70 percent.

1. Donald R. Matthews and James W. Prothro, *Negroes and the New Southern Politics* (New York: Harcourt, Brace and World, 1966), p. 412.
2. Ruth Searles and J. Allen Williams, Jr., "Negro College Students' Participation in Sit-Ins," *Social Forces 40* (March, 1962), pp. 215-220.
3. Anthony M. Orum and Amy W. Orum, "The Class and Status Bases of Negro Student Protest," *Social Science Quarterly 49* (December, 1968), pp. 521-533.
4. Leonard L. Baird, "Who Protests: A Study of Student Activists," in Julian Foster and Durward Long, Editors, *Protest: Student Activism in America* (New York: William Morrow, 1970), pp. 123-133.
5. Seymour M. Lipset "The Activist: A Profile," *The Public Interest 13* (Fall, 1968), p. 45.

Later in the decade—when protest focused as much or more on the Vietnam War, campus governance, and the relationship of the university to the wider society—the scope of student protest broadened to include many more of the nation's universities and colleges. For example, the number of campuses with New Left organizations and campuses experiencing student protest of the Vietnam War doubled between 1965 and 1968.[6] Though protest spread to more institutions, the proportion of the nation's college students who participated in political action stayed much the same.[7] The Harris and Gallup polls of 1967 and 1968 portrayed remarkable stability with the 1965 rate of participation: about 20 percent of their samples both at the midpoint and later in the decade said they had engaged in protest and political activities.[8] Some studies do show that participation rates varied according to the issue at stake. For instance, a study of freshmen entering 246 institutions in the fall of 1966 shows: (1) a range of zero to 31 percent of the students being involved in protest about racial discrimination, although half of the schools reported that no more than 2.1 percent of their students were involved; (2) a range of zero to 55 percent of the students involved in action against the Vietnam War, again with half of the schools estimating not more than 1.7 percent participation; and (3) a range of zero to 85 percent of the students involved in a protest of the administrative policies of the college, half of the institutions reporting only an 8.2 percent involvement.[9]

Comparable estimates have not been published for students attending Black colleges for the same period, although there were proportionately more Black than white institutions experiencing student protests in 1967 and 1968. According to Long, 60 percent of the 35 Black schools but only 43 percent of the 1217 white institutions that responded to a protest survey in May, 1968 reported some kind of protest during the academic year 1967-1968.[10] Data from the studies we conducted in the second half of the sixties are also pertinent. The longitudinal followup of seniors at one school in 1967-1968 shows

6. Richard E. Peterson, "The Scope of Organized Student Protest," in *Protest: Student Activism in America*, p. 78.
7. Another study, which depended on estimates of deans of students and was conducted in 1967-68, concluded that the average participation in the 849 institutions studied was somewhere between five and 10 percent. Moreover, this study asserts that participation had not increased since 1965, although more colleges around the country had experienced protest in 1968 than in 1965. *Ibid.*, pp. 59-80.
8. Lipset, "The Activist: A Profile," p. 45.
9. Alexander Astin, "Determinants of Student Activism," in *Protest: Student Activism in America*, Table 1, p. 94.
10. Durward Long, "Black Protest," in *Protest: Student Activism in America*, Table 1, p. 468.

that three-quarters of the senior class participated in at least one event in a three-month long protest about educational issues that eventually led to the closing of the school. Two years later, in 1970, the repeat cross-sectional study of students in six of the original 10 colleges we had studied in 1964 provided estimates of different kinds of protest action: 67 percent reported some activity during their college years aimed at changing administrative policies at their colleges, 75 percent reported some activity in civil rights protest (Table 1).

TABLE 1. **Proportion of Students Who Participated in Various Types of Collective Action in 1964, 1968, and 1970**

	Total Sample, Ten Colleges 1964[a]
Level of civil rights participation:	
Actively involved for at least a year plus jail experience	7%
Participated in several events	23
Participated in one event	16
Never participated	54
	100%

	Seniors, College H 1968[b]	Total Sample, Six Colleges 1970[c]
Current and past civil rights participation:		
Currently active	17%	10%
Previously active	77	65
Never active	6	25
	100%	100%
Current and past participation in student power activities:		
Currently active	75%	10%
Previously active	15	57
Never active	10	33
	100%	100%
Membership in Black student organization:		
Yes		7%
No	No data	93
		100%

[a]These percents are based on the 3639 students who participated in the cross-sectional study of 10 colleges in 1964.

[b]These percents are based on the 239 seniors at College H who participated in the longitudinal study from 1964 to 1968.

[c]These percents are based on the 1127 students who participated in the cross-sectional study of six colleges in 1970.

Comparing statistics from samples that vary widely always raises questions about the reliability of the estimates. Yet throughout the decade of the sixties the figures derived from our data and other studies on the participation of students from Black colleges are again and again so much larger than for students in the nation at large that we cannot escape the conclusion that Black college students were more active as a group. Indeed, the growth of student activism during the sixties cannot be understood without recognizing the role played by Black students, particularly at two significant moments. From 1960 to 1965 it was Black students attending colleges in the South, with support from northern students both Black and white, who led the assault on off-campus civil rights targets. Then in 1965, as white students began to attack the United States' growing commitment to the war in Vietnam, Black students on both Black and white college campuses raised other critical issues for the nation, and especially for higher education. Between 1967 and 1969 there were enough Black students at some white schools to make an important impact on re-shaping admission policies and on highlighting the problems inherent in the university's relation to its host community, especially when the university resided in a predominantly Black urban setting. At the same time, students in Black colleges were making major demands of their administrators and boards of trustees for changes in the substance and character of their own educational experiences.

Despite the numbers of Black students involved, social scientists have painted a picture of student activism that is almost totally white. Only 14 journal articles (or chapters) and three books on Black students or Black colleges are listed in two major bibliographies on student activism, one with 211[11] and the other with 188 entries.[12] In contrast, there has been an undue amount of discussion concerning a different kind of Black activism, the urban revolts of 1965 to 1968. At the very time that little attention was given to the Black aspect of the protest by the nation's educated young, over 50 articles were published on the urban protests. This has led to a further distortion of life in America which supposes that the outcry of educated young people comes from whites, while the anger of embittered urban dwellers comes from Blacks.

Why have Black student activists been neglected while "rioters" have been zealously studied? From a radical perspective, urban revolts

---

11. Kenneth Keniston and Michael Lerner, "Selected References on Student Protest," in Philip G. Altbach and Robert S. Laufer, Editor, *The New Pilgrims: Youth Protest in Transition* (New York: David McKay, 1972), pp. 313-326.

12. Julian Foster, "Student Protest: What is Known, What is Said," in *Protest: Student Activism in America*, pp. 48-58.

do deserve the greater attention since revolution is sparked from the protest of nonelites. Following a traditional Marxist position, Perkins and Higginson argue that students and other sectors of the petty bourgeoisie must be assigned the back seat in the present struggle for Black freedom since student movements, except on very rare occasions, have never been the detonators of social revolution. They view the urban disturbances as clearly more hopeful signs of an uprising of the "Black masses":

> Although the present form of struggle (nationalism) has been best articulated by the more radical wing of petty bourgeois intellectuals in the Black community, if one examines the pathways that this rhetoric has taken, one discovers a huge chasm of disparity between theory and practice, at least in terms of the petty bourgeoisie. The Black masses, on the other hand, have proven consistently that they are more radical than the most radical student or petty bourgeois leader. Theirs is a radicalism that grows out of the dimensions of colonial oppression and the radical indigence in which they are forced to live.[13]

We doubt that a revolutionary perspective explains the disproportionate concern of social scientists with urban revolts, for few social scientists speak from a Marxist position in commenting on the American scene. We wonder instead if the imbalance between research on urban revolts and on Black student activism does not stem from the implicit stance in social science and in the thinking of many Americans that looks at Blacks primarily as "a problem." Billingsley, in evaluating how Black families have been treated in American scholarship, notes that they either are ignored altogether or are considered only if they may be conceived of as a social problem.[14] Billingsley quotes the historian Benjamin Quarles in making this general point:

> When we pick up a social science book, we look in the index under "Negro," it will read, "see Slavery," "see Crime," see "Juvenile Delinquency," perhaps "see Commission on Civil Disorders;" perhaps see anything except the Negro. So when we try to get a perspective on the Negro, we get a distorted perspective.[15]

---

13. W. E. Perkins and J. E. Higginson, "Black Students: Reformists or Revolutionaries?" in Roderick Aya and Norman Miller, Editors, The New American Revolution (New York: The Free Press, 1971), pp. 199-200.

14. Andrew Billingsley, Black Families in White America (Englewood Cliffs, New Jersey: Prentice-Hall, 1968).

15. Ibid., p. 199, Quoting Benjamin Quarles, Jet Magazine 33(12) (December 28, 1967), p. 32.

There is also the less bigoted motivation of social scientists, who prefer to study what is close to established research sites. In that vein, Black students are not the only group ignored in studies of student activism. Most studies of student activism have been conducted on a few campuses by social scientists in residence who found data accessible and were better able to understand the historical and institutional context of the critical events.[16] The scholarly neglect of student activism on Black campuses may well represent the much wider phenomenon of neglecting events in the small schools and even in the larger ones that fall outside the circle of institutions that command the major resources for social science research. What we know about student activism comes mainly from the studies conducted by the social scientists at such elite institutions as the University of California at Berkeley, Columbia University, the University of Chicago, and Yale University. One major bibliography on student activism published in 1968 listed 12 books and 84 articles on Berkeley, one book and 16 articles on Columbia, and—with the exception of the less elite San Francisco State College about which there were two books and six articles—only one monograph and six articles dealing with events on various other campuses.[17] The national studies instigated primarily by the American Council on Education, from which we have reported participation rates, stand out as rare instances of transcending a provincial depiction of student politics.

Some would applaud the scholarly neglect of Black student activism as a protection of Black students because they suspect that repression of activists rather than institutional change is the major consequence of studies of activism. From this perspective the best research is no research. While we concur that Black people, Black institutions, and Black communities have been overstudied relative to the benefits they have derived from research, we also feel that ignoring Black student activism limits what we understand about student political action. We simply cannot grasp the full range of concerns of the young people, both Black and white, who have felt impelled to try to change some of our social institutions if we generalize from the information gained at a set of geographically restricted schools or from a limited sample of our nation's students.

16. A study of student unrest at several predominantly Black colleges was undertaken in 1968, supported by the Russell Sage Foundation, although the results have not yet been published.
17. Philip Altbach, *Student Politics and Higher Education in the United States: A Select Bibliography* (Cambridge, Massachusetts: Center for International Affairs, Harvard University, 1967).

The Social Backgrounds of Black
And White Activists

Consider what we may learn of the social backgrounds of activist college students if our knowledge depends too exclusively on studies of white activists. Flacks concludes that the following modal profile was repeatedly found in studies of white activists during the first half of the sixties: White students who were politically active were disproportionately the sons and daughters of highly educated, professional, high income parents; their mothers more often were employed; they grew up in atypical numbers in urban and suburban environments on the East and West coasts.[18] Flacks himself suggests that the students recruited to protest activity toward the end of the decade represented more heterogeneous backgrounds than this description implies.[19] But how distorted a picture of student activism was it even at the time it was drawn? Did the Black students who manned the southern movement during the first half of the sixties likewise come from elite backgrounds? The few studies that were conducted on participants in the southern student movement provided mixed results. The most systematic study, based on responses of 264 students attending 30 predominantly Black colleges, was made by Matthews and Prothro in 1962.[20] Their analyses, and Orbell's reanalysis of the same data,[21] show that participation in civil rights protest activities was greatest among students from higher income families who were attending high quality colleges in urban settings. According to Orbell, these variables interacted so that the highest rate of participation (67 percent) was found at high quality, urban schools among students from high income families, while the lowest rate (16 percent) of participation at lower quality, rural schools, attended by students from low income families.[22] (This difference was greater than would be expected if these social variables simply operated in an additive manner.) Another study of students in North Carolina, conducted in the spring of 1960—just after the first sit-ins—likewise concluded that comfortable socioeconomic status was more often a characteristic of the active students than of the

18. Richard Flacks, "Who Protests: The Social Bases of the Student Movement," in *Protest: Student Activism in America,* p. 137.
19. *Ibid.,* p. 138. *Also,* Milton Mankoff and Richard Flacks, "The Changing Social Base of the American Student Movement," in *The New Pilgrims: Youth Protest in Transition,* pp. 46-62.
20. Matthews and Prothro, *Negroes and the New Southern Politics.*
21. John M. Orbell, "Protest Participation Among Southern Negro College Students," *American Political Science Review 61* (June, 1967), pp. 446-456.
22. *Ibid.,* p. 451.

inactive ones.[23] Actually the data from this study do not support a socioeconomic effect on participation unless one compares only the 24 percent of the sample classified as having "high participation" and the 5 percent classified as showing "low participation." When the rest of the students falling between high and low participation groups are included, the data show no significant SES-participation relationships. Moreover, a third study of 3500 seniors graduating from Black colleges in 1964 reports that there were no family-income or parental-education correlates of the civil rights participation the students reported as having engaged in during their four years of college.[24] The authors of that study conclude that their failure to find social class determinants of participation, despite the few earlier studies that had, probably was the result of the difference in the level of participation in 1960 and 1961, when the movement was just getting off the ground, and the level during the next four years, when opportunities for involvement increased so greatly. They argue that the initial leadership for launching the movement came from elite Black students who nonetheless experienced a sense of deprivation relative to the wider society, but that as opportunities for participation broadened, then so would the social backgrounds of the participants broaden.

The impressions of observers who were closer to the leaders of the southern student movement question whether the active participants were more frequently from higher status families, even during the early years. Meier, a sociologist then teaching at a Black college, notes in reviewing the Matthews and Prothro study:

> My observations indicate that the low income students were the ones more likely to participate. In fact, many of the student protest leaders themselves characterized a type of student who was involved in the movement as belonging to the "striving working class." Perhaps upward mobility aspirations were more important than social class background in leading students to participate in the movement. There were variations, of course, and at some colleges the more elite students made up a substantial portion of the body of protestors . . . I suspect that the major reason for the discrepancy lies in the fact that Matthews and Prothro failed to distinguish between students who joined in demonstrations once or twice, and those who engaged in them over a sustained period. I believe that if they had measured this variable, they would have found a profile of the really dedicated protestors to be quite different from that of those whose involvement was of a more casual variety. And it is the former group,

23. Searles and Williams, "Negro College Students' Participation in Sit-Ins."
24. Orum and Orum, "The Class and Status Bases of Negro Student Protest."

after all, which was really the backbone of the student movement and the principal dynamic thrust within it. At any rate the question deserves careful further study.[25]

Zinn, also teaching at a Black college when he described the Student Nonviolent Coordinating Committee in *The New Abolitionists*, agrees that southern Black students who were committed full time to the movement were more likely to have grown up in families that were poor and of the working class than from elite southern Black families.

> *In late 1963 I checked the backgrounds of forty-one field workers for SNCC in Mississippi (roughly one-third of the total SNCC force in the Deep South). Thirty-five of them were Negro, and twenty-five of them came from the Deep South. Of the six white staff members, two were from the Deep South. The white youngsters and most of the Northern Negroes came from middle-class homes; their fathers were ministers or teachers or civil service workers. All of the Southern Negroes, and some of the Northern Negroes (twenty-one out of thirty-five) came from homes where their mothers were maids or domestics, the fathers factory workers, truck drivers, farmers, bricklayers, carpenters. Twenty-nine (about three-fourths) of the total SNCC Mississippi staff were between fifteen and twenty-two years old. There were twelve between twenty-two and twenty-nine and one person each in his thirties, forties, and fifties. Twenty-six, or about two-thirds, of the Mississippi SNCC staff were either college graduates or had some college education. Ten had finished high school or had some high school education . . . If one were to generalize roughly about the SNCC staff in the Deep South, one would say they were young, they are Negro, they come from the South, their families are poor and of the working class, but they have been to college. Northern middle-class whites and Negroes are a minority.*[26]

DEMOGRAPHIC CORRELATES OF ACTIVISM, 1964 TO 1970

We related degree of participation in civil rights activism, and later in student power protests and in Black student organizations, to six demographic variables: rural-urban location of the student's home, family income, family structure, the importance of religion in the family, and finally, level of education attained by the father and by the mother.

25. August Meier, "Black Power at the Ballot Box," in August Meier, Editor, *Black Experience: The Transformation of Activism* (New York: Aldine Publishing Company, *Trans-action Books*, 1970), pp. 127-128.
26. Howard Zinn, *SNCC: The New Abolitionists* (Boston: Beacon Press, 1964), pp. 9-10.

A few general conclusions about the demographic correlates of student activism should be noted before we present more specific results. First, in most respects the demographic correlates of activism remained reasonably stable over the decade of the sixties (Appendix Table 9.1). The aspects of students' precollege environments that distinguished who actively participated early in the civil rights movement also continued to differentiate activists from nonactivists later in the decade. Second, it was the rural-urban setting of the place where the student had grown up that proved consistently to be the strongest predictor of activism, especially of civil rights activism (Appendix Table 9.1). Third, of the three types of activism we examined—participation in civil rights, in student power activities, and in Black student organizations—civil rights participation was most closely tied to these demographic and family influences (Appendix Tables 9.1 and 9.2). For example, at a school closed by campus confrontations in 1968 the relationship of demographic characteristics of the seniors to their continued involvement in civil rights activities was far larger than their relationship to participation in the campus protest that embroiled the school for three months. In fact the students who took part in the campus protest did not differ from the nonparticipants in any way that had to do with demographic or family influences. In 1970 we again related the demographic variables to student involvement in both civil rights and student power activities. Again the demographic correlates were stronger with civil rights activism than with student power activism.

Let us turn, then, to civil rights participation for a closer examination of family and demographic influences where they operated most prominently. Data from the 10 colleges we studied in 1964, from our longitudinal follow-up in 1968 of seniors at one of those colleges, and from the six colleges studied in 1970 all show the specific significance of rural-urban background (Appendix Table 9.1). (The beta weights for rural-urban background range between .30 and .38 in these three studies, while the beta weights for the other demographic variables mostly fall below .20). Moreover, it was always the students from the farms and villages of less than 2500 population who participated least; students from cities of larger than 100,000 population consistently showed the highest rates of participation. In 1964, 31 percent of the farm and village students had taken part as opposed to 88 percent of those from metropolitan centers; in 1968 the figures were 47 percent as opposed to 94 percent; and in 1970, 16 percent as opposed to 93 percent. Rural-urban setting influenced students in two ways. Growing up on a farm or a village reduced the probability of participation. Attending a college in a rural setting did likewise. Growing up in the rural South *and* attending a college in a rural site virtually precluded participation. In 1964, when nearly half of the total sample had participated in at least one civil rights demonstration or activity, only 3 percent of those who had grown up in the rural South and were attending a rural college were participants (Chart A). Rural-urban influence persisted after controlling for the influence of other demographic and family variables.

It is customary in discussing rural-urban differences to attribute them to the greater conservatism and traditionalism of people of rural background. We will discuss such ideological issues later in this chapter.

CHART A.   Civil Rights Participation of Rural and Urban Students Attending Colleges Located in Rural and Urban Settings, 1964

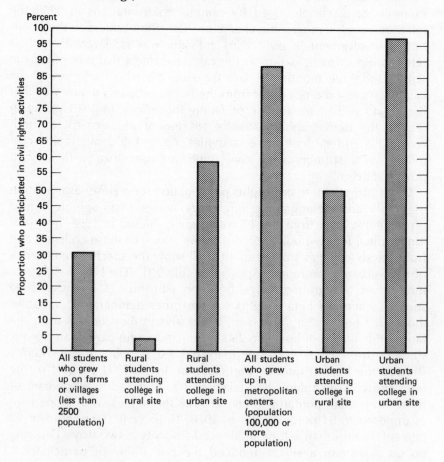

The interviews that we conducted both in 1964 and in 1968 suggested other, nonideological reasons that rural-urban background was relevant to Black student activism in the South, although it rarely stood out in studies about white student activism. Two reasons particularly were highlighted in the interview responses. Black students from farms and rural nonfarm homes repeatedly talked of their lack of opportunity for participation, since most southern campaigns occurred at least in small towns and usually in the larger towns. The southern movement, although not an urban phenomenon, was not a rural one either except insofar as those small towns and cities it made famous reflected the largely rural environment in which they were located. Rural students typically found their chance to participate only at college. If they went to colleges located in or near the more urban areas, they became much more involved than did the rural students who went to schools in rural areas. Fifty-eight percent of the farm and village students attending urban colleges, but only 3 percent attending rural colleges, reported having participated in 1964 (Chart A).

Rural students also cited as reasons for their nonparticipation their fears of reprisal against their families. In 1964 many of the families of rural students were still engaged in tenant farming. These students worried, quite realistically, lest their parents be thrown off their places or suffer from other economic hardships because their children had taken part in the civil rights movement. Most students, even the sons and daughters of professionals, mentioned fears of economic consequences to their families as prominent reasons for staying uninvolved or of being sources of anxiety once they had become involved. Few parents had job security or protection from the intense social and economic pressures in some communities. Farm families, however, faced the greatest threat. Physical brutality, burning of homes and churches, and shots in the night were all more prevalent in rural areas. Some rural students did participate despite risks to themselves and to their families, but clearly their risks were greater and their opportunities more limited.

This interpretation—that limited opportunity and fear of reprisals explain the lower activism of rural students—is supported by the fact that it was civil rights activism especially that pointed out the rural-urban effect. The intensive study of one college that experienced three months of serious campus protests in 1968 shows this most clearly. The seniors who were still active in civil rights activities on that campus at that time were drawn disproportionately from the ranks of urban students; the seniors who had never participated in civil rights activities were disproportionately from the rural South. In contrast, the seniors who were active in the student power protests on the same campus at the same time were indistinguishable from the nonactivists with respect to their precollege home environments: they were no more or less likely to have grown up in urban settings. Likewise, of the three forms of student political action we examined in 1970, the students' rural-urban background was important only in accounting for continued participation in civil rights action; it did not account for participation in either student power activities or for membership in Black student organizations. Campus-based as they are, neither of these latter activities carried the same economic and social pressures that threatened rural students who attacked race inequities in off-campus community campaigns.

In our analysis of the influence of socioeconomic status background variables (parental education and family income) we are particularly interested in how our data address the controversy about status correlates of participation that has appeared in the literature on the Black student movement. As we noted in the introductory discussion of this chapter, there are widely varying views about the socioeconomic characteristics of the Black student activists, particularly in the early years of the movement. Some authors[27] draw a picture that parallels the well-documented elitist background of the white student activists— they suggest that civil rights protest was greatest among Black students from higher income families and higher quality institutions. Others[28] claim that participants, particularly the leaders, came from less elite backgrounds. Meier[29] particularly has stressed the "striving working-class" background of the Black student leadership.

Our data indicate that parental education and family income were related to civil rights activism in ways that support Meier's personal observations of participants in the southern student movement during the first half of the decade. In 1964 the students who participated the most were from families in which the parents were either high school graduates or may have had a year or two of college and in which family incomes were only moderate (between $3600 and $6000 a year). The sons and daughters of college graduates or of people with professional degrees whose incomes were higher than $6000 resembled in their participation rates their fellow students whose parents were much less educated and at the bottom of the income scale. Both groups were less involved than what Meier calls the striving working class. This pattern prevailed in the data collected in the 10 colleges in 1964 and

27. Matthews and Protho, *Negroes and the New Southern Politics;* Searles and Searles, "Negro College Students' Participation in Sit-Ins"; and Orbell, "Protest Participation Among Southern Negro College Students."
28. Zinn, *The New Abolitionists;* Meier, "Black Power at the Ballot Box."
29. Meier, "Black Power at the Ballot Box."

again accounted for the continued involvement in civil rights activities of the seniors in one of the schools over the period from 1964 to 1968. It was only in 1970 that parental education and family income bore reasonably linear relationships to civil rights activism.

The 1964 data on civil rights participation were coded to check explicitly whether the controversy about the effects of social class on activism could be resolved, as suggested by Meier,[30] by differentiating leadership or sustained activity from more casual forms of participation. (Meier had suggested that the more casual participants were from elite backgrounds, while the leaders were more from working-class backgrounds.) We related the six demographic variables to two groups of participants—the 7 percent who had been actively involved for a sustained period of time *and* had been to jail at least once, and the 13 percent who had participated in just one isolated event. We found no evidence that the shorter term, more casual participants were typically from higher status families. In fact, none of the demographic variables successfully distinguished these two groups of participants. Apparently, parental education and family income worked primarily to distinguish participants from nonparticipants, and not to delineate the leaders from the more casual participants.

Overall, these data on parental education and family income do support the conclusion that there was some socioeconomic influence on participation. However, the influence was less striking than that of rural background. At the extreme we found no more than 15 to 20 percent differences in participation between the students from moderately well-educated families with moderate incomes who were the most active and the two less active groups—those from professional, higher income families and those from the least educated with the lowest incomes. The impression gained from studies of white student activism that family social class strongly influences participation, especially so in the early part of the sixties, is inappropriately generalized when activism includes the action of Black students as well. Family social status was less important in explaining which Black students participated in the first place. When it did operate, its effect was not the same as for white students. Instead of the most elite young people participating most actively, as most research indicates happened in the New Left white student movement at least up to about 1968, it was Black students from somewhat less affluent families who showed a slight edge in political involvement.

Family religion likewise turned out to be less important than previous work on white student activism has showed it to be. It was only

30. *Ibid.*

among the male seniors at the school where we conducted the longitudinal follow-up study in 1968 that religion related to activism at all and then only in civil rights action (Appendix Table 9.1). Senior men who came from the most and the least religious families were more active in civil rights protest than senior men from families where religion was only moderately important. Our failure to find a religious effect in these data departs from some national studies of activism. For instance, Astin found religion among the three best predictors for all three forms of activism he measured in 1966-1967.[31] The meaning of that religious effect, however, was not the same as the religiosity variable we have consistently used. In Astin's data it was primarily white students who considered themselves agnostic, in contrast to students who identified with some religious group, who were more active in all three types of activism—civil rights activities, protest against the Vietnam War, and student power confrontations. In contrast, we were interested in the importance of religion among the students who accepted a religious classification. Agnosticism could in no way carry the same meaning for Black college students that it does in a national sample of colleges since less than half of one percent of our sample of students from Black colleges considered themselves agnostic.

The final demographic variable we examined, family structure, also was unrelated to student activism (Appendix Tables 9.1 and 9.2). Whether a student grew up in a nuclear family with both a mother and father present in the home, in a family headed by the mother, or in another type of family structure never related to involvement in political action. Family structure was not important for any type of activism at any point in the sixties.

In general, then, the results of these social analyses of Black student activism point up the differences in the social roots of Black and white activism. Background factors—religion and social status—that were critical determinants of white activism were either irrelevant or operated very differently among Black student activists. And rural-urban background, the factor most related to the activism of the Black students we studied, is never mentioned as a critical determinant of student political action in the voluminous literature on activism of white students. To be sure, the white radical student is typically described as urban, although that description derives primarily from studies at elite institutions whose student bodies are predominantly urban anyway. The few available national studies of activism do not point to rural-urban background as a strong determinant. Astin did not find rural-urban background among the 10 student characteristics

---

31. Astin, in *Protest: Student Activism in America*, Table 2, p. 96.

that in 1966-1967 best predicted either civil rights action or involvement in protesting the Vietnam War among white college students, although growing up in a suburb of a large city was related to protest action against administrative policies (largely in loco parentis) of the college.[32] Braungart's sophisticated multivariate analyses of the demographic influences on white students' participation in political action did not even include a rural-urban variable.[33] This is one of the ways in which the characterization of student activism in the nation at large suffers from being restricted so predominantly to conclusions about white students. It has allowed us to overpsychologize the genesis of student protest since white students have not typically faced the same repression that southern, Black students—particularly those from rural areas—were forced to consider in the early sixties. Looking to family dynamics and to personality of individuals to explain who participates in political action may be more appropriate where the threat of reprisals impinges less severely. In contrast, opportunity factors hold much more promise in accounting for participation where control by repression prevails more widely. Whether police force is exercised more or less brutally in a specific social situation, thus determining the opportunity for participation, inevitably goes further than family interaction or psychodynamics to explain who, in a generally repressive environment, engages in action and who does not.

DEMOGRAPHIC CORRELATES OF IDEOLOGY, 1964 TO 1970

In the following chapter we will examine some of the ideological correlates of student activism, how action reflected students' attitudes toward the social system, their interpretations of the racial situation in America, their strategies for social change, their orientations toward student control and other college political issues, and their commitments to Black Nationalism. In the remainder of this chapter we will look at the demographic correlates of these ideologies. Since we will see in the following chapter that these ideological orientations were clearly related to action, the relationships between social background and ideology may help clarify the relationships between demographic factors and action that we have been discussing.

---

32. *Ibid.*
33. Richard G. Braungart, "Family Status, Socialization, and Student Politics," *American Journal of Sociology* 77(1) (July, 1971), pp. 108-130; Richard G. Braungart and Margaret M. Braungart, "Social and Political Correlates of Protest Attitudes and Behavior Among College Youth: A Case Study," unpublished paper, University of Maryland, 1971.

Demographic Correlates of System Attitudes, 1964-1970

We have noted that rural-urban differences were the major demo-graphic correlates of student civil rights activity in the period covered by our study. We will therefore look at the relationship between rural-urban background and six system attitudes we have explored in this study. These include: (a) two indicators of collective consciousness —*control ideology,* the measure of Protestant ethic beliefs in which students attributed the success and failure of other people to their internal virtues or to fate and other external forces, and, *individual-system blame,* in which students attributed the cause of race in-equities to system obstacles or to personal deficiencies of other Blacks; (b) one indicator of collective commitments—preferred change strate-gies, in which students stressed either *individual mobility or collective action;* (c) and three indicators of the students' attitudes toward the authority of college administrators—*control over student political action, in loco parentis control,* and *control over academic freedom issues.* (We will also be concerned with the demographic correlates of Black Nationalism ideology, but we will consider Black Nationalism separately in a later section of this chapter since we had no data on Black Nationalism in 1964.)

Generally we expected greater conventionality from young people who had grown up in the traditional ways of rural and small-town life. Rural youth enter college politically more conservative, more accepting of traditional patterns of authority, and expressing values and beliefs that, although previously normative, no longer command universal adherence.[34] Their ideological differences from more urban and sophisticated students should be particularly marked, therefore, during periods of social change because the rate of change should be more rapid in urban areas, especially among students whose family resources provide opportunities for travel and exposure to many and varied styles of life. Thus, we expected rural and urban students to differ most about those values and beliefs that showed the greatest population shifts between 1964 and 1970. We have already described in Chapter 8 the striking shifts in students' ideologies about what determines success and failure in American society, their increasing blame of the system for racial inequities, their preferences for collective over indi-

---

34. Claude S. Fischer, "A Research Note on Urbanism and Tolerance," *American Journal of Sociology* 76(5) (March, 1971), pp. 847-856; Hart Nelsen, Raytha L. Yokley, and Thomas W. Madron, "Rural-Urban Differences in Religiosity," *Rural Sociology* 36(3) (September, 1971), pp. 389-396; Hart Nelsen and Raytha Yokley, "Civil Rights Attitudes of Rural and Urban Presbyterians," *Rural Sociology* 35(2) (June, 1970), pp. 161-170.

vidual strategies of change, their heightened criticism of the traditional governance in their colleges. Unless television or other communication media had equalized rates of change throughout the society, we expected that the rural students would differ from their urban peers, particularly about these issues and especially in 1970. In 1970 it was always the rural and farm students who expressed the most individualistic, conventional views about success in our society; they also continued to accept traditional administrative authority at much the same level that was modal in 1964. In contrast, students from metropolitan centers stood out as the most system-blaming, most critical of conventional Protestant ethic explanations of success, most collective in their change preferences, and most disapproving of administrative control of student political action and a traditional parietal stance toward students (Appendix Tables 9.3 and 9.4).

Overall these results show that ecological influences cushion the impact of social change. In 1964 the rural-urban environments from which students entered college had very little influence on their views about the nature of society and legitimacy of established bases of power. Between 1964 and 1970 many conventional attitudes about what determines success in the culture at large and about the traditional causal analyses of race inequities in our society had come under attack. Many students had developed new ways of thinking about being Black in America and about the role of the college in determining policies that affected their lives. However, the shift was not evenly spread across students from all settings in the South. By 1970 the students from metropolitan centers stood out as the most critical of the social system as the source of race inequities, most rejecting of conventional individualistic explanations of success, most favorable about collective action as the best strategy for handling problems that all Blacks face, and most disapproving of administrative control of student political action and traditional protective policies regarding students' lives. Yet their peers from the rural South were still expressing beliefs that had been commonplace in 1964; they were both behind the times and most of their fellow students.

The other five demographic variables were only minimally related to ideology, just as they were only weakly related to action (Appendix Tables 9.3 and 9.4). In 1964 there were no significant relationships between the demographic variables and any of the six indices of system beliefs. Even in 1970, in contrast to the clear relationships between rural-urban background and ideology, relationships with the other demographic characteristics were minimal. The only consistent exception was family income, where several significant relationships appeared to indicate that the sons and daughters of

CHART B. Summary of Significant Demographic Relationships with Activism and Ideology.

	Significant Relationships	No Relationships
Rural-urban setting of place student lived while growing up	*Activism:* Civil Rights activism, men and women, 1964, 1968, 1970.	*Activism:* Student power activism, men and women, 1968, 1970.
	System attitudes: All six measures for men and women, 1970.	*System attitudes:* None in 1964 for either men or women.
	Black Nationalism: Militancy, men and women, 1970; African cultural identity, women, 1970.	*Black Nationalism:* None with self-determination, community control, economic development, men and women, 1970; African cultural identity, men, 1970.
Parental education	*Activism:* Curvilinear relationship with civil rights activism for men and women, 1964 and 1968—linear relationship for men and women, 1970; student power activism men and women, 1970; BSO membership men, 1970.	*Activism:* Student power activism, 1968; BSO membership, women, 1970.
		System attitudes: None in either 1964 or 1970 for either men or women.
		Black Nationalism: None in 1970 for either men or women.
Family income	*Activism:* Curvilinear relationship with civil rights activism for men and women, 1964 and 1968—linear relationship for men and women, 1970; student power for men, 1970.	*Activism:* Student power for men and women, 1968; student power for women, 1970; BSO membership for either men or women, 1970.

CHART B (Continued)

System attitudes: College governance of political action and general parietal policies for men and women, 1970.

System attitudes: None in 1964 for either men or women; none with control ideology, system blame, and preferred change strategies for men and women, 1970.

Black Nationalism: None in 1970 for either men or women.

Activism: None with activism for either men or women, 1964, 1968, 1970; none with student power activism, 1968, 1970, for either men or women.

System attitudes: None in either 1964 or 1970 for either men or women.

Black Nationalism: None for women, only the use of violence for men, 1970.

Family structure

Black Nationalism: Political use of violence, men, 1970.

Activism: Curvilinear relationship civil rights activism, men, 1968.

Activism: None with civil rights activism either men or women, 1964 or 1970 or for women, 1968; none with student power activism 1968, 1970.

System attitudes: None in either 1964 or 1970 for either men or women.

Black Nationalism: None in 1970 for either men or women.

Importance of religion to the family

higher income families adopted a more radical perspective. But even these relationships were restricted to issues of college governance: there were no significant income relationships with the broader system beliefs, namely, control ideology, system blame, or collective strategies for social change.

How do these ideological findings relate to the data on action discussed in the preceding section? Chart B summarizes all of the demographic correlates of activism and ideology. That we found no relationship between rural-urban background and system beliefs in 1964 supports our interpretation that the lower civil rights activity of rural students in 1964 sprang from less opportunity and greater fear of reprisals rather than from less ideological commitment. However, our data also suggest that the picture may have changed by 1970, when we found clear relationships between rural-urban background and ideology. By 1970 issues of opportunity and fear of reprisals may have become less relevant as inhibitors of the civil rights activity for rural students; a more critical issue may have become their greater geographical distance from the ideological radicalization that occurred in the second half of the decade.

Demographic Correlates of Black Nationalism, 1970

As a political ideology, Black Nationalism requires a process of reflection that translates the recognition of being Black in social terms into a caste and class consciousness.[35] Black Nationalism, like any political ideology, presumes an intellectual step that at once integrates and transforms feelings into ideas. It is a step that demands analytic sophistication, if not formal education, and protection from the worst daily preoccupations about survival. In most revolutionary models it is the role of elites to conceptualize the intellectually coherent base for these feelings and ideas. Thus, one might expect Black Nationalism to have been studied primarily among elites, the Black intellectuals responsible for giving it substance since Carmichael's first espousal of Black Power. In fact, Black Nationalism has been investigated primarily in national sample surveys, which never provide large numbers of intellectuals in any subgroup of the population, or in samples of riot participants and nonparticipants. It is difficult to tell from prior research, therefore, in what particular social situations nationalist ideas are most likely to flourish.

For two other reasons prior research is not very germane. First, most studies have been exclusively concerned with just one aspect of

35. James Turner, "Identity in Transition: A Theory of Black Militancy," in *The New American Revolution*, p. 169.

Nationalist ideology, the issue of using violence as a political strategy. Prior work primarily has set out to explain either riot participation or militancy attitudes, typically defined as feelings of sympathy toward riots or toward violence as a tool for change. Second, most studies have been conducted on adult samples where demographic variables pertain to the adult's own life situation rather than to the parents' social position. In our concerns with college students, the socialization implications of the student's family's social position are primary. Still, since these studies show reasonable convergence about the import of certain demographic variables, they can serve as a context for the data we have examined on the ideologies of college students.

These prior studies of militancy attitudes and participation in urban disturbances agree reasonably well regarding the impact of educational, regional, and rural-urban background, as well as the lack of impact of economic factors such as family income and relationship to the job world. Militants[36] and "rioters"[37] are generally described in these studies as better educated than less militant Blacks and those who did not participate in the riots. Very few studies fail to show an educational difference between the people who hold the most militant attitudes and those who are less militant.[38] Most studies also show that "rioters" and nonparticipants did not differ in their income levels. Studies of militancy attitudes indicate only a slight income effect: adults in only the lowest income group stand out as the least militant.[39] Likewise, militants and nonmilitants do not seem to differ in either their employment histories or job status.[40] Evidence about the influ-

36. T. M. Tomlinson, "Militancy, Violence, and Poverty: Ideology and Foundation for Action," in N. E. Cohen, Editor, The Los Angeles Riots: A Socio-Psychological Study (New York: Praeger, 1970); and Gary T. Marx, Protest and Prejudice: A Study of Belief in the Black Community (New York: Harper and Row, 1967).

37. Raymond J. Murphy and James M. Watson, "The Structure of Discontent," in The Los Angeles Riots; and Nathan Caplan and J. M. Paige, "A Study of Ghetto Rioters," Scientific American 219(2) (August, 1968), pp. 15-21.

38. An exception is a study by Campbell and Schuman in which militancy attitudes were not related to educational level. See Angus Campbell and Howard Schuman, Racial Attitudes in Fifteen American Cities, Supplement Studies for the National Advisory Commission on Civil Disorders (Washington, D.C.: Government Printing Office, 1968).

39. Murphy and Watson, "The Structure of Discontent"; Caplan and Paige, "A Study of Ghetto Rioters"; Charlotte Darrow and Paul Lowinger, "The Detroit Uprising: A Psychosocial Study" (paper presented at the American Academy of Psychoanalysis, New York, 1967); J. Shculman, "Ghetto Residence, Political Alienation and Riot Orientation," unpublished manuscript, Cornell University, 1967.

40. Robert M. Fogelson and Robert B. Hill, Who Riots? A Study of Participation in the 1967 Riots, Supplement Studies for the National Advisory Commission on Civil Disorders.

ences of labor force participation on "riot" participation is more equivocal largely because relationship to the job world has been measured in so many different ways in studies of "riot" participation. Most studies also show that the militant Blacks are atypically young and likely to be men;[41] they are more likely to be found in nonsouthern parts of the country and to have been born in, rather than migrated to, the North.[42] Several studies also conclude that the most militant come from big cities, whereas the least militant come from rural parts of the country.[43]

While few of these studies apply specifically to young people attending college, some commentators suggest that many of their findings might pertain to Black students on at least some college campuses as well. Noteworthy among these is Harry Edwards who relies heavily on precollege demographic and family influences in distinguishing among five types of Black students he interviewed, mostly at predominantly white colleges and universities, located mostly outside the Deep South.[44] Edwards suggests particularly that three of these five types of students—"militant students," "anomic activists," and "conforming Negro students"—reflect distinctive social backgrounds.

Other data, however, question the critical import of the student's social background. Even if Edwards' characterizations fit appropriately at the nonsouthern, predominantly white campus, at least in the last few years of the sixties when distinctions in ideology and political style took on heightened significance in what some critics called the "make-believe world of campus politics,"[45] they seemed not likely to apply so well at southern colleges in general or at predominantly Black colleges specifically. While very few studies speak directly to the historically Black colleges in the South and at the same time tap aspects of Nationalism other than just the issue of violence, the few there are agree that student opinions about Black Nationalism do *not* depend on the sex of the student or on socioeconomic background.[46] Men and

41. Marx, *Protest and Prejudice;* Nathan Caplan, "The New Ghetto Man: A Review of Recent Empirical Studies," *Journal of Social Issues* 26(1) (1970), pp. 59-73.
42. Murphy and Watson, "The Structure of Discontent"; Caplan and Paige, "A Study of Ghetto Rioters"; Fogelson and Hill, *Who Riots? A Study of Participation in the 1967 Riots;* D. O. Sears and J. B. McConahay, "Riot Participation," in *The Los Angeles Riots.*
43. Fogelson and Hill, *Who Riots? A Study of Participation in the 1967 Riots;* Caplan and Paige, "A Study of Ghetto Rioters."
44. Harry Edwards, *Black Students* (New York: The Free Press, 1970).
45. Perkins and Higginson, "Black Students: Reformists or Revolutionaries?" p. 222.
46. Elise E. Lessing and Susan W. Zagorin, "Factor Structure and Concurrent Validity of a Black Power Ideology Scale," *Proceedings of the 78th Annual Convention of the American Psychological Association* 5, 1970, pp. 353-354; Lessing and Zagorin,

women, and students from affluent, highly educated homes as well as from less comfortable socioeconomic backgrounds, share much the same attitudes that are generally supportive of Nationalism.

One of the previous studies, conducted by Mathis,[47] suggests that a most important demographic correlate of Black Nationalist ideology may be one not considered in our study—the North-South regional distinction. (It was not considered in our study because the student body was almost exclusively southern in origin.) Mathis's study included students attending three northern, predominantly white schools as well as students from two southern, predominantly Black institutions. The findings support the general view that northern Blacks are more committed to a Nationalist ideology. The urban, northern students were more nationalistic on all the dimensions Mathis included in that study: political nationalism, cultural nationalism, system distrust, and system blame. Rural and urban students from the South, however, rarely differed from each other; both were considerably less nationalistic than the northern urban students. The Mathis study also indicated a strong effect of religion: students who were not religious and did not attend church expressed much greater political nationalism than did those students who were religious and church attenders.

How do the results of the demographic analyses we conducted on the attitudes of students toward Black Nationalist ideology in 1970 compare with these earlier studies on militancy attitudes and the few studies specifically of Black students in college? The results were clear-cut. Precollege backgrounds influenced the stance of both the men and women toward Black Nationalism in just one significant way (Appendix Table 9.3). Again, as in our findings on activism and system ideology, the most significant determinant was rural-urban background. Men and women who grew up on farms or in villages in the rural South were much less approving than all other students of the use of violence as a political tool. (The beta weights attached to rural-urban background in predicting this one aspect of Nationalism were .34 for men and .35 for women.) In fact, only 3 percent of these rural students approved of violence sufficiently to put them above the median in the distribution of scores on this militancy index. Moreover, just these two

---

"Some Demographic, Value and Personality Correlates of Endorsement of Negro Militancy by Negro and White Youth," *Proceedings of the 77th Annual Convention of the American Psychological Association* 4, 1969, pp. 295-296; C. T. Willis and F. J. Goldberg, "Some Correlates of Militancy and Conservatism Among Black College Students in the North and South," *Psychiatry*, in press; Arthur Lee Mathis, "Social and Psychological Characteristics of the Black Liberation Movement: A Colonial Analogy," (Ph.D. Dissertation, University of Michigan, 1971).
47. Mathis, "Social and Psychological Characteristics."

groups of students from farms and villages stood out. The attitudes of students from all other settings were markedly homogeneous regarding the use of violence as a political strategy.

The other two effects of precollege background pertained either to men or to women but not both (Appendix Table 9.5). Rural-urban background further influenced the cultural identity of women. The women, but not the men, who grew up on farms or villages in the South were less identified than other women with cultural symbols such as African dress, African language, Afro-hair styles, the importance of being called Black instead of Negro, and the significance of thinking of themselves as Black rather than American. Family structure, however, related to the militancy attitudes of the men but not the women. Men who grew up in homes where the father had been absent during most of their elementary and high school years approved of the political use of violence more than other men.

Apart from the striking meaning of rural-urban background on the stance of both the men and women toward violence and these two effects that emerged either for men or for women, demographic and family background simply did not matter in explaining the Nationalist ideologies of these Black students. (Beta weights for other demographic and family variables in predicting most aspects of Nationalism generally fell between .01 and .15). Urban students, those from intact, affluent, educated, or less religious families, did not differ from rural students or those from father-absent, or low-income, less educated, or more religious families in their views about the self-determination meaning of Black Nationalism, the importance of politically controlling institutions in the Black community, or the advisability of developing an economic base for control.

These data on social status variables generally agree with the few studies that have been done on the political and cultural Nationalism of Black students in college. Ours and other studies together show that Black students identify with Black Nationalism without respect to their precollege social backgrounds. Family income and parental educational attainments seem not to influence the ideologies students hold. The effect of education noted in the studies of militancy attitudes and riot participation seems not to be a generational effect but rather an influence within a given age group that promotes thinking in nationalist perspectives. Young people generally are more supportive of Nationalism. The more educated among them are even more supportive. And among them the family's educational achievements are irrelevant.

We might note one significant way in which our findings differ from those of the Mathis study. We did not confirm Mathis's findings that a strong religious belief inhibited the development of Nationalism among the students. The fact that we found no relationship with religious beliefs may reflect the different measures of religion used in the two studies: Mathis measured the student's own religiosity, while we measured the student's perception of the importance of religion in his home. It is also possible that Mathis's findings are largely a reflection of the regional differences among his students, since northern students tend to be much less religious than those in the South.

Since the students attending the colleges we studied were so exclusively southern in origin, our results cannot speak to the highly significant meaning other research attributes to growing up in the urban North. Both the studies on militancy attitudes and "riot participation" among adults and Mathis's work on Nationalism among college students show a militancy-nationalistic edge to the northern experience. Our data understandably fail to substantiate this regional effect since only two schools we studied drew even as many as 10 percent of their students from states outside the Deep South. We were fortunate, however, in being able to combine the data we collected from students in the six southern colleges we studied in 1970 with the students Mathis studied in both northern and southern colleges in 1969. The two southern colleges he studied were among the six we studied a year later; we had used many of the questions Mathis previously used to tap Nationalism. First, we checked to see if his and our samples in these two colleges differed significantly on the questions both studies had in common. Since they did not, we combined responses from the two studies for those two colleges, thereafter comparing the data from the six southern schools with Mathis's data from the three northern schools. Generally, the results supported Mathis's conclusions that northern students were, on the average, more nationalistic than southern students. But the picture was somewhat complex. Although Nationalism was generally higher among northern students, the particular school the student attended mattered greatly also. Northern students attending *certain* northern schools were more nationalistic in their ideologies than southern students attending *certain* southern schools, but they looked very much like southern students attending *other* southern schools. These significant interactions between region of the country and specific college appeared for both men and women. In general, the level of Nationalism reflected by the students in the least nationalistic of the northern group of schools, a small community college located on the outskirts of a middle-sized city, conformed closely to the level expressed in the least nationalistic school in the southern set, a school of similar size serving predominantly rural students and located in a rural setting. The level of Nationalism of the two southern schools where the most nationalistic ideologies were held in 1970 resembled closely the level reflected by students attending a large, high status, residential university located in a small city in the North. It was only the third northern school, a large public commuter university located in a major metropolitan center, whose students were decidely more nationalistic than any student body in the six southern schools.

We point out these similarities between certain northern and southern campuses to highlight two things. First, data derived from small and special samples of either southern or northern colleges can result in exaggerated, if not erroneous, conclusions. Although we suspect that better, more representative samples would substantiate that Black students attending northern colleges are more nationalistic, on the average, than Black students attending southern, historically Black colleges, the data yet available are not conclusive on this issue. Second, comparing the aggregated attitudes of students from even a good sample of northern colleges with the aggregated attitudes of students from a good sample of southern, Black colleges can miss the important and interesting influences of particular social settings. Even if the average level of nationalism is higher among students attending northern schools, some northern and southern schools may share much the same ideological milieus. In fact, we suspect strongly that the attitudinal climates of most southern, Black colleges can be matched by the climates of the Black subgroups on many northern campuses. It is just that there are enough northern Black students attending community and four-year colleges in metropolitan centers of the North for which there are no attitudinal counterparts in the South to make the average level of nationalism higher among northern than among southern Black students.

chapter 10

Ideology
and Action

In the preceding two chapters we have examined trends in political action and ideology. At several points we suggested inherent connections between ideology and action: activists were motivated by ideological commitments that at once reflected a greater knowledge of politics and a stronger awareness of the social and economic determinants of inequities; the shift toward psychological questions of Black consciousness during the second half of the sixties was more than accidentally related to the simultaneous shift from community to campus targets of action; the rising concern for self-determination in discussions of Black Nationalism provided a special rationale for Black students to demand a piece of the action in determining college regulations and educational policies that affected their lives; the Black students' activism would come to reflect even more strongly a collectivist perspective as the ideas of Black Nationalism sharpened the polarity between individual advancement and collective welfare of the group.

In this chapter we will examine these connections, investigating the tie between ideology and action during the civil rights period and later in 1970 after Black Nationalism had dominated the political discussion of students. The data will be organized around the major issues of Black Nationalism that were delineated in Chapter 8: the action implications of (1) the twofold consciousness of the subordination of Black people and of a newly defined status and group pride; (2) the recognition of self as part of the collectivity and the commitment to collective action; and (3) the insistence on Black Power as reflected in advocating group self-determination, community control of major institutions located in the Black community, and economic development of the community. Then, we will turn to questions these results raise for the role of personal efficacy as a motivator of social action and the meaning of "powerlessness" as an aspect of alienation. Much

263

of the discussion of urban revolts and college student protest has been cast, erroneously we believe, as the expressive acts of the alienated. On the contrary, the social action of the students we have studied over the decade of the sixties reflects their awareness of social determination and their collective proclivities that combine into an activist ideology that is "external" but not "powerless."

NATIONALIST IDEOLOGY AND ACTION

Collective Consciousness of Racial Oppression

We have already seen how students in the early days of the movement were grappling simultaneously to discard victim perspectives and to revise their view of the group's history in terms of exploitation and oppression, thereby developing pride in the group's heritage of adaptive strength and endurability. How did this growing collective consciousness of racial oppression relate to taking action? We argued in Chapter 8 that the Individual-System Blame index directly tapped this aspect of Nationalist ideology by questioning who is responsible for race inequities. Accepting the system explanation implied both the awareness of discrimination and oppression and a positive group identity that comes from refusing to blame one's own group for the inequities it faces. This is the simultaneous process of becoming conscious of oppression and of developing group pride. Rejecting a rigid Protestant ethic viewpoint (as we interpreted external scores on the Control Ideology index to mean) likewise implied this consciousness because it questions the legitimacy of the dominant group's cultural norms which, when internalized by subordinated groups, produce self-blame for their life situation. If everyone is master of his fate, if success follows inevitably from hard work, then the status differential between my (minority) group and the majority group must reflect the personal deficiencies of my people. When traditional work ethic explanations of success are applied to minority status, it inevitably imputes a negative identity.

Students who had rejected traditional explanations for the status and life conditions of Black people should also have been more involved in trying to change the social forces they had come to view as the primary sources of inequities. What did the data show? In 1964 both indicators of collective consciousness significantly differentiated which students were actively involved in civil rights activities (Appendix Table 10.1). Students who blamed the system instead of other Blacks and who questioned the validity of a strict Protestant ethic ideology were significantly more involved in action at that time (Chart A). This tie between action and ideology that focused on social instead of individualistic interpretations of minority status characterized both the men and the women activists. Evidence from the college where freshmen were studied before and after taking part in the famous Selma and Montgomery campaigns in the spring of 1965 suggests, however, that this focus on social forces may have been the result of, rather than the source of, action in those days. System blame did not predict later action. Freshmen who subsequently became active in the local campus group that provided the leadership for the college's participation in these events entered college with views no different from those held by freshmen who later were only moderately involved or who took no part at all. By the end of the year, however, their explanations of race inequities and their stance toward the Protestant ethic as a cultural norm departed greatly from the less active freshmen (Appendix Table 10.2). Activism had changed the participants' ways of looking at the world; they looked much more than they had previously to social and economic determinants of racial inequality in our society.

By 1970, when collective consciousness of racial oppression had shifted to the point where system blame was the modal response, these indicators of collective consciousness still distinguished political

CHART A.   **Average Civil Rights Participation of Students above and below the Median on the Individual-System Blame, Internal-External Control Ideology, and Individual Mobility-Collective Action Strategy Measures**

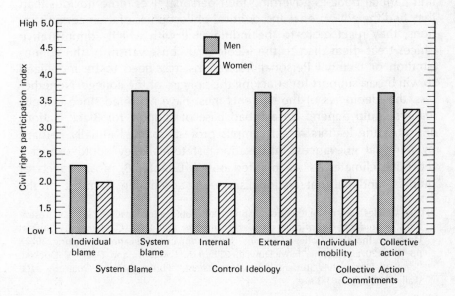

activists from nonparticipants (Appendix Table 10.3). Scores on the Control Ideology index distinguished active from inactive students in both civil rights and student power issues. Students who had rejected a rigid Protestant ethic interpretation of success were still more active in civil rights action and were also more involved in campus action for student power in governance. System blame also continued to differentiate activists, both men and women, from other students with respect to both civil rights and student power issues. Students who had rejected a victim blame perspective in favor of an external ideology were more involved in political action both on and off campus. These ideological differences between the active and the inactive students applied to all six colleges we studied in 1970, and they assumed striking proportions at the two colleges where student activism was particularly widespread (Table 1). Even at a time when collective consciousness of oppression had produced major shifts in students' analyses of their history and their relationships to white institutions, it was the activists who especially came to view that history in terms of oppression and to question the legitimacy of the work ethic.

We do not mean to imply that action was perfectly correlated with growth in collective consciousness. Some students who focused on the oppressor's role in inequities did not act, particularly at one college (discussed in the next chapter) where nationalist ideology was strong despite only moderate levels of activism. Likewise, some students participated in campus confrontations without strong ideological commitments. Many observers of student unrest agree that most students find parietal policies governing their personal lives more noxious than they find the educational and political philosophies of their administrations; they react more to the indifference with which administrative offices treat them than to the ideological conservatism of the administration or faculty.[1] Personal frustrations may need to be mobilized to win broad support for attacking the policies of the college. Nonetheless, the ideologies of the students must have mattered since campus leaders could depend on a broad base of support for Black Nationalism. As the leaders recast campus protest, sparked initially perhaps by personal grievances, into Nationalist terms, they could expect a receptive climate. As we pointed out in Chapter 8, most aspects of political and cultural Nationalism were acceptable to most of the

---

1. Two articles that made this point about the mobilization around personal frustrations of students, specifically on Black campuses are: Elton C. Harrison, "Student Unrest on the Black College Campus," *Journal of Negro Education 41* (Spring, 1972), pp. 113-120 and Sophia F. McDowell, Gilbert A. Lowe, Jr., and Doris A. Dockett, "Howard University's Student Protest Movement," *Public Opinion Quarterly 34*(3) (Fall, 1970), pp. 383-388.

Ideology and Action   **267**

students on most campuses. Numerous confrontations that began with attacks on curfews, food quality, inadequate scholarships for athletes, or some other nonideological issue developed into demands for "decolonizing Black institutions" by providing for the self-determination of Black students in influencing the rules, philosophies, and directions of "their" Black colleges.

Collective Commitments

Revolutionary-collectivist theory argues that collective consciousness of oppression inevitably leads to commitments to collective goals. While individuals may hold onto personal goals, and in this way fall short of true revolutionary vision, they come to view them as just personal choices that will not likely result in a meaningful aggregate change for the group. To change the life conditions of the group demands collective attacks. We argued in Chapter 8 that our measure of preferences for individual versus collective action strategies of handling discrimination directly taps this issue of collective commitments. Students chose between alternatives such as: "the best way to handle problems of discrimination is for each individual Black to make sure he gets the best training possible for what he wants to do" and "only if Blacks pull together in civil rights groups and activities can anything really be done about discrimination." Chapter 8 described the striking shift since 1964 in student opinion about these alternative approaches to social change. The shift represented a major step toward Nationalist thought.

Students whose ideologies reflected this determination to unite as a group should have taken a more active part in collective endeavors. This ideology measure was as close as any attitude indicator could be to actual behavior. In both 1964 and 1970 the more collectively oriented students clearly were the most active (Chart A). In 1970 these individual-collective preferences differentiated degree of activity in both the civil rights and student power arenas for both men and women; they even distinguished which men belonged to Black student organizations, even though membership in such groups only very rarely reflected ideology (Appendix Tables 10.4 and 10.5). To illustrate the size of these relationships in 1970, especially at the two most active campuses: 67 percent of the civil rights activists and 90 percent of the student power activists, compared to only 20 percent of the students who were not involved in civil rights and 10 percent of the nonparticipants in student power issues, chose at least five of the six collective alternatives on this index (Table 1). This does not mean that these collectivist-activist students were pursuing only collective goals. As we will see in the last section of the book, many of them managed

TABLE 1. System Blame Orientations and Collective Commitments of Students Who Were Currently Active, Previously Active and Never Active in Civil Rights and Student Power Activities on the Two Campuses Where Activism Was Especially Widespread, 1970.

	Civil Rights			Student Power		
	Currently Active	Previously Active	Never Active	Currently Active	Previously Active	Never Active
System-blame orientations Proportion who:						
Chose at least *three* of the four *system-blame* alternatives	75%	40%	5%	90%	38%	10%
Chose two system-blame and two individual-blame alternatives	25	38	50	10	34	55

	Col 1	Col 2	Col 3	Col 4	Col 5	Col 6
Chose at least three of the four *individual-blame* alternatives	— 100% (120)	22 100% (240)	45 100% (40)	— 100% (92)	28 100% (248)	35 100% (60)
Collective commitments Proportion who:						
Chose at least *five* of the six collective action strategies	67%	25%	20%	90%	35%	10%
Chose three of each or four of one and two of other	33	65	60	10	67	70
Chose at least *five* of the six *individual mobility* strategies	— 100% (120)	10 100% (240)	20 100% (40)	— 100% (120)	2 100% (240)	20 100% (40)

to maintain personal goals at the same time they committed themselves to collective action as the best method of social change. These data do show strikingly how a collectivist ideology was translated into action.

The "before-after" study of active and inactive freshmen at the one college where longitudinal data were collected also clarifies the dynamics of this relationship. Individual-collective preferences predicted subsequent action; heightened commitment to the collective approach also followed the experience of activism (Appendix Table 10.2). Students who subsequently participated actively in the local movement had entered college the previous fall, before the student body became activated, already predisposed to action through their preferences for collective strategies. They were significantly more collective in their orientations at time of entrance than the freshmen who never became involved in the movement. Nonetheless, action also had an effect. Controlling for these initial differences, the freshmen activists completed their freshman year with stronger collective commitments. Action reinforced the collectivist view that encouraged students to take action in the first place.

Political Nationalism

We have looked at the development of collective consciousness of oppression and the conversion from the sense of category to collectivity as the initial stages in the development of political nationalism. Chapter 8 described three indices that seemed to capture the students' ideas about political nationalism: (1) advocating political self-determination through separatism; (2) advocating community control, specifically control of the schools attended by Black children; and (3) advocating the development of Black businesses. These three indices all related significantly to activism in 1970, although the action relationships with the economic development index were clearly weaker than with the other two (Appendix Table 10.5). The separatism, self-determination index was especially relevant to action in student power for both men and women, while the community control index was unusually meaningful for civil rights action. These special connections make sense in light of other attitudinal correlates of these factors. We noted in Chapter 8 that the separatism measure bore a distinctive pattern of relationships with student attitudes about governance. Advocating self-determination through separatism was the only nationalism theme that correlated significantly with disapproval of administrative control over what speakers could be invited to campus and the curricular directions of the college. We argued that students with heightened sensitivities about the need for Blacks to control their own institutions understandably translated their broad concerns about self-determination into a desire to determine educational policies that would make "Black colleges really relevant for Black people." In addition, it was the concern about self-determination that really stood out among the student power activists. Similarly, the special tie between community control and civil rights action seemed to reflect the unique community base of each. Over the decade of the sixties and certainly by 1970 civil rights action had grown to depend on community development that would make a difference in Black people's control over their own lives and institutions. The model of activating change through a single-issue demonstration was increasingly replaced by a developmental model that depended on long-term commitment of local people.

A fourth index described in Chapter 8 as a dimension of political nationalism refers to types of action strategies that may need to be employed in the struggle for liberation. Students with high scores on this militancy index believed that defensive violence might be a political necessity. They were not advocating violence as either an ultimate value or a preferred strategy; they simply assumed that defensive violence might be necessary. We also pointed out in Chapter 8 that students with these attitudes about the political use of violence were particularly sympathetic, even more than those with high scores on other dimensions of political nationalism, to collective action as a mode of dealing with discrimination. Given the strong action theme in this attitude index, we expected it to correlate highly with actually taking action. It did, but only among the men (Appendix Table 10.5). Men who viewed violence as a possible political necessity were more active in collective endeavors, particularly in student power activities, but also in civil rights groups and in Black student organizations as well. Women's attitudes about the use of armed defense, however, were simply unrelated to whether they were involved in collective action. This is the one way in which the ideological correlates of action differed for men and women. We argued in Chapter 8 that the issue of violence carried different meanings for men and for women. On every item included in this index women were less positive than men about the use of violence. Furthermore, their attitudes did not relate to whether they were politically engaged. Repeatedly, therefore, we see that men and women did not share the same views about this particular issue of revolutionary thought.

Summary

Chart B summarizes the implications of all these ideology measures for political action for both men and women and in both 1964 and 1970. It shows that all aspects of political nationalism related positively to student activism among men. All but the question of violence as a political tool related to activism among women. The three measures that were repeated in both 1964 and 1970—system blame, work ethic or control ideology, and preference for individual versus collective

CHART B. **Summary of Significant Relationships between Ideology Measures and Student Activism**

Collective Consciousness Measures	Significant Relationships	No Relationships
External control Ideology	Civil rights activism, men and women, 1964, 1970 Student Power Activism, men and women, 1970	BSO membership, men and women, 1970
System blame	Civil rights activism, men and women, 1964, 1970 Student Power Activism, men and women, 1970	BSO membership, men and women, 1970
Collective Commitments		
Preference for collective action over individual mobility change strategies	Civil rights activism, men and women, 1964, 1970 Student Power Activism, men and women, 1970 BSO membership, men, 1970	BSO membership, women, 1970
Political Nationalism		
Self-determination through separatism	Civil rights activism, men and women, 1970 Student Power Activism, men and women, 1970 BSO membership, men and women, 1970	
Community control	Civil rights activism, men and women, 1970	Student power activism, and BSO membership, men and women, 1970
Black economic development	Civil rights activism, men and women, 1970	Student power activism, and BSO membership, men and women, 1970
Militancy: acceptance of the political use of violence	Civil rights activism, student power activism, and BSO membership, men, 1970	Civil rights activism, student power activism, and BSO membership, women, 1970

CHART B (Continued)

Collective Consciousness Measures	Significant Relationships	No Relationships
Cultural Nationalism		
Afro-American orientation		*Civil rights activism, student power activism*, and *BSO membership*, men and Women, 1970
African identification		*Civil rights activism, student power activism*, and *BSO membership*, men and women, 1970

strategies—showed consistently positive relationships at both points in time. Students who believed more in social than in individual determinism were more involved in efforts to change the racial inequities they felt were built into our social and economic system. In 1970, when the whole population showed a large shift away from conventional victim analyses to a critique of the social structure and to advocacy of collective rather than individual strategies of change, individual differences in these beliefs still correlated with level of involvement in action. Moreover, the action implications of these aspects of collective consciousness included taking action not only in race inequities but also in college educational and student life policies. Among men membership in the Black student organization also reflected stronger collective commitments.

Two other aspects of nationalist ideology carried special implications for both student power and civil rights action. Advocacy of separatism as a self-determination issue was especially prominent among those students who, in 1970, were very active in campus-based protest about educational policies and curricular reform. Although the self-determination index was significantly related to all three forms of student political action, its relationship to student power action was most pronounced. Similarly, the community control index operated particularly to distinguish actives from inactives in off-campus civil rights activities. A special concern with the community beyond the campus provided a thread connecting beliefs about Black control of community institutions and continued civil rights work in the community. Although we might have expected that the Black economic development measure would operate in much the same way as the community control index, it was altogether less important than the other ideology measures, nor did it connect to any extent with civil rights action.

Accepting action that implicated violence as a possible political strategy depended on the sex of the student. The men who believed that armed defense might be necessary in the struggle were more active in civil rights and student power, and more frequently belonged to Black student organizations. The issue of violence was quite irrelevant as to whether women became involved in action.

Finally, it was political nationalism rather than cultural nationalism that related to student activism. The two measures of cultural nationalism that were generated in the factor analyses of student attitudes in 1970, the measure of African Identification and the Afro-American Orientation, did not distinguish actives from inactives among either the men or the women, or in any arena of action. Of course, students varied less in their attitudes toward cultural symbols and their willingness to wear African dress, and Afro hair styles than they did in their opinions about the political aspects of nationalism. Their more homogenous stance toward cultural nationalism minimized the role it could play in explaining who acted and who did not. Moreover, even the most extreme differences in viewpoint about cultural nationalism failed to distinguish activists from nonactivists: the students in the top third on the cultural nationalism measures were no more active than those in the bottom third. We suspect that this reflects the varied motivations through which students come to express cultural identifications with an Afro-American style. There are many reasons to respond to Black pride and to distinctively African or Afro-American artifacts or lifestyle that have nothing to do with social change commitments. In contrast, the group of students who developed strong commitments to political nationalism necessarily had to think about social change and their role in it.

THE ROLE OF PERSONAL EFFICACY IN ACTIVISM

Some theories to explain collective movements, civil conflict, and revolution look to structural and economic forces;[2] others look to rates of socioeconomic change[3] or relative declines in the availability of eco-

2. Bruce M. Bassett, "Inequality and Instability: The Relation of Land Tenure to Politics," World Politics 16 (1964), pp. 442-454.
3. Ivo K. Feierabend, Rosalind L. Feierabend, and B. A. Nesvold, "Social Change and Political Violence: Cross-National Patterns," in H. D. Graham and Ted Robert Gurr, Editors, Violence in America: Historical and Comparative Perspectives (Washington, D.C.: National Commission on the Causes and Prevention of Violence, 1969), pp. 632-668.

nomic goods and political freedom;[4] still others look to political variables, such as the coerciveness of regimes and their legitimacy.[5] Many also depend on social-psychological arguments.[6] The sense of personal efficacy is one of the central concepts employed in these social-psychological theories to account for whether individuals will act or not. The feeling of efficacy is variously cast as the sense of civic competence,[7] a personal confidence,[8] a belief in internal control.[9] Each of these concepts refers to beliefs about the instrumentality of action. Individuals who view themselves as competent and who feel personally efficacious also believe that their action will matter. They feel they possess the means to accomplish their goals. This set of beliefs then motivates them to act.

The specific causal role attributed to feelings of efficacy varies somewhat in different social-psychological theories of collective movements. Some impute a direct causal role. More commonly, however, feelings of efficacy are not viewed as important independent motivators but gain significance only as they condition what individuals do with their perceptions of opportunity or with their feelings of discontent or frustration with their life condition. For example, the blocked opportunity theory advances the idea that militants and riot participants hold high aspirations and strong beliefs in their own competencies, but they recognize that discrimination blocks them from reaching their goals; conversely, nonmilitants do not react to blocked opportunity in the same way because they do not regard themselves

4. Ted Robert Gurr, "A Causal Model of Civil Strife: A Comparative Analysis Using New Indices," *American Political Science Review* 62 (1968b), pp. 1104-1124.

5. Ivo K. Feierabend and Rosalind L. Feierabend, "Aggressive Behaviors within Politics, 1948-1962: A Cross-National Study," *Journal of Conflict Resolution* 10 (1966), pp. 249-271; D. P. Bwy, "Political Instability in Latin America: A Preliminary Test of a Casual Model," *Latin America Research Review* 3 (1968); pp. 17-66; Ted Robert Gurr, "Urban Disorder: Perspectives from the Comparative Studies of Civil Strife," *American Behavioral Scientist* 11 (1968a), pp. 50-55; and Ted Robert Gurr, "A Causal Model of Civil Strife."

6. This categorization of theoretical perspectives on the issue of civil strife and revolution is taken from Ted Robert Gurr, "The Calculus of Civil Conflict," *Journal of Social Issues* 28(1) (1972), pp. 27-47.

7. Gabriel A. Almond and Sidney Verba, *The Civic Culture* (Princeton, New Jersey: Princeton University Press, 1963).

8. M. Brewster Smith, "A Map for the Analysis of Personality and Politics," *Journal of Social Issues* 24 (November, 1968a), pp. 15-27; M. Brewster Smith, "Competence and Socialization," in John A. Clausen, Editor, *Socialization and Society* (Boston: Little, Brown, 1968), pp. 271-320.

9. Julian B. Rotter, Melvin Seeman, and Shephard Liverant, "Internal Versus External Control of Reinforcements: A Major Variable in Behavior Theory," in N. F. Washburne, Editor, *Decisions, Values and Groups* (New York: Macmillan, 1962), pp. 473-516.

as so competent in the first place.[10] A recent variant of the blocked opportunity argument focuses on the discrepancy between feelings of personal efficacy and those of political efficacy as the precondition of action.[11] Other theorists argue that heightened feelings of discontent and frustration with one's status are the necessary precondition for action, although the form that the action will take depends on the individual's feelings of efficacy.[12]

Conclusions about empirical relationships between feelings of efficacy and action are made difficult by measurement problems raised by the commonly used Internal-External Control scale. As we will show in the next secton, it is frequently impossible to know whether results showing a connection between the Internal-External Control scale and action reflect personal feelings of efficacy or aspects of the scale that measure ideology and political beliefs. Still, Caplan concludes from studies of the urban disturbances in the late sixties that participants generally felt personally efficacious:

> *Findings from these studies show that Black militants feel keenly about their self-worth and their potential for acting competently, and are motivated to utilize their internal resources. They show a strong need for achievement. They make the most out of the external resources available to them to improve their social position, and they experience frustration when the opportunity to attain goals is blocked by forces outside their control. One conclusion that can be drawn from this accumulation of findings is that Black militants behave as one would predict if their sense of personal efficacy is higher than for comparable nonmilitants. . . . An additional source of evidence on higher personal efficacy among militants comes from responses to interview items that require the respondents to comment directly about their feelings of personal resourcefulness. Forward and Williams studied pre-riot and post-riot responses of Black senior high school students to the Rotter Internal-External Control Scale, which indicates confidence in one's ability, and found a strong relationship between pre-riot personal control scores and positive reaction to the riot on post-riot measures. . . . Similarly using a combination of items measuring attitudes toward oneself in relation to the environment, Gary Marx at Harvard concluded from*

---

10. Nathan Caplan and J. M. Paige, "A Study of Ghetto Rioters," *Scientific American* 219(2) (August, 1968), pp. 15-21.
11. Nathan Caplan, "A Causal Model of Black Militancy," (unpublished paper, 1972).
12. Thomas J. Crawford and Murray Naditch, "Relative Deprivation, Powerlessness, and Militancy: The Psychology of Social Protest," *Psychiatry* 33(2) (May, 1970), pp. 208-223; Leonard Berkowitz, "Frustrations, Comparisons and Other Emotion Arousal as Contributors to Unrest," *Journal of Social Issues* 28(1) (1972), pp. 77-91.

a study of 1,100 urban Blacks that the militant has a stronger sense of his own potential than those who are less willing to use violence in open confrontation in the pursuit of political objectives.[13]

Almost all these studies limit their concerns to riot participation, and sometimes not to action itself but only to militant attitudes. Most pertain to adults. How do feelings of efficacy operate in the activism of Black college students? We consistently included our measure of the sense of personal control in the analyses where we examined the relationship between ideology and action. We developed the measure of Personal Control, described in Chapter 4, from factor analyzing items from the Internal-External Control scale. The Personal Control factor included the five items that refer to the first person. Defined by the item with the highest loading, it measures the individual's feeling that "when I make plans, I am almost certain I can make them work." What do the results relating this measure to action show?

Only in 1964, and then primarily among women, did feelings of personal control (efficacy) correlate with involvement in political action (Appendix Tables 10.1 and 10.4). None of the analyses in 1970 showed the Personal Control measure significantly related to any type of action —civil rights, student power, or membership in Black student organizations. Instead it was the measures of nationalist ideology that differentiated activists from nonactivists in 1970. We consistently looked at each ideology measure in a multiple analysis of variance that used the Personal Control measure as the second possible predictor. The Personal Control measure showed neither a significant main effect nor did it even condition the meaning of ideology for action, with one exception (Appendix Table 10.6). That exception indicated that the heightened involvement in civil rights action of men with strong commitments to political self-determination occurred primarily among men who themselves felt personally efficacious. Otherwise, personal efficacy played no role in explaining student political action in 1970 either as an independent source of motivation or as a conditioner of the meaning of ideology for action.

In 1964 when feelings of efficacy did operate, at least somewhat for men and even more for women, the results showed that personal control and ideology independently facilitated action (Appendix Table 10.1). They combined additively so that the most active students were those who both felt efficacious about their own lives and held the attitudes that were later to be viewed as the precursors of nationalism, that is, blame of the system rather than personal deficiencies of Blacks themselves, critique of the cultural norm stressing individualistic ex-

13. Caplan, "A Causal Model of Black Militancy," p. 5.

planations of success for a more balanced view about the role of external and internal determinants, and a preference for collective action rather than individual mobility as the best strategy for handling racial discrimination.

Why should feelings of efficacy and control relate to action in 1964, albeit less importantly than ideology even then, but not in 1970? In 1964 individuals could still realistically believe that their actions would make an impact in changing social conditions. However recalcitrant Black activists in the South found local and state officials, they believed earlier in the sixties that the federal government, particularly the Justice Department, and the national press were behind their efforts to change voting rights and public accommodations discrimination. Enactment of the 1964 Civil Rights Act with provisions about voting rights and open accommodations reinforced that conviction. And, although some federal marshals looked away while civil rights workers were brutally beaten as they brought people to register, there were other instances when the Justice Department provided meaningful protection. A few Associated Press reporters likewise became famous because they could be depended on to get the news out. A SNCC worker recalled the time in 1963 that one of the Mississippi offices was bombed. Lying on the floor, anticipating the momentary entry of vigilantes, he managed to phone an AP reporter affiliated with the *New York Times,* who was known for his responsibility. He promised to get the information on the wire immediately and to alert the Justice Department. In this period when students had "an almost unrelenting faith in the Federal Government,"[14] they could legitimately believe that their own personal action mattered. An individual could get in touch with the right person in a reasonably responsive federal office or press room and it made a difference. The whole struggle was highly personalized. Although activists believed that the forces they were fighting were clearly of social and economic origin and that only collective action could change the life conditions of Black Americans as a group, they also felt that individuals could effectively daunt the forces of injustice if they tried.

After the Mississippi Summer Project in 1964 and the final burst of mass demonstrations in the spring of 1965, southern activists shifted their focus to problems such as unemployment and poverty, whose nature defied so obvious or personalized form of action. They increasingly doubted whether established power bases such as the northern

14. Joyce Ladner, "What Black Power Means to Negroes in Mississippi," in August Meier, Editor, *The Transformation of Activism* (New York: Aldine, *Trans*-action Books, 1970), 137.

liberal wing of the Democratic Party or the federal government or the liberal press would indeed continue to be the sources of support they had previously expected them to be. In describing the growth of the Black power thrust among activists in Mississippi, Ladner asserts that it was "an inevitable outgrowth of the disillusionment that Black people experienced in their intense efforts to become integrated into the mainstream of American society."[15] It was no longer viable to believe that the individual could alter the course of events—the problems were too complex. Intransigence was no longer romantically attributed to the South alone. The situation demanded collective attack. Thus, by 1970 the students had generally dropped the notion that the individual alone could make a difference; they came more and more to believe in the theme of nationalism, that only a group determined to act together could alter injustice. Is it surprising, then, that personal efficacy no longer related to action while nationalist ideology carried the major social psychological role in 1970?

The causal role Caplan attributes to personal efficacy underlines another possible reason why it may operate less critically than ideology among college students. If it is the discrepancy between feelings of competency and anticipation that they will be blocked, instead of efficacy per se, that motivates militancy among adults who have already tested the job market, we might not expect personal efficacy to count for much in explaining the political behavior of college students. They have not yet faced that discrepancy with the force felt by men and women already in the labor force. Of course, students are aware of this discrepancy. Their awareness is the basis of their nationalist ideology. Admittedly, they express concerns about their futures, but they can still believe that blocked opportunity will affect the collective condition of the group more than their own personal lives. When the discrepancy is less personal, ideology can provide the more critical basis of action.

In revolutionary thought ideology admittedly plays on feelings of frustration. Elites who attempt to activate "the masses" have to find the bases of their frustration. But the goal is to develop among workers, or the colonized, a sense of collective consciousness whereby they see that all people in their life condition indeed face the same forces. Personal frustration must be translated into collective consciousness and collective commitments. Thus, most analyses of Black Nationalism that follow the decolonization model delineated by Fanon underplay

15. *Ibid.*, p. 148.

personal factors in favor of the independent force of ideology itself.[16] Ideology rises out of and remains inherently tied to economic and social realities. But it is ideology, not personal frustration, that is seen as the yeast for action. Many social psychological theories of collective movements have perhaps relied too exclusively on notions of personal frustration.[17] Personal frustration may account for action among nonelites or in periods when group conflict has not emerged so pointedly. But they should not be treated as total depictions even of the social-psychological forces that promote civil conflict, revolution, or collective movements. There are certain times, conditions, and groups of people for whom ideology rather than personal frustration provides the social-psychological propulsion to act.

ALIENATION: THE CONTROVERSY OVER POWERLESSNESS

Because of the concepts and measures we have used, these data speak directly to a central controversy in the alienation literature over the meaning of powerlessness for action. Seeman argues that to be alienated means to be characterized by one (or several) of the following: (1) a sense of powerlessness, a low expectancy that one's behavior can control the occurrence of personal and social rewards; (2) a sense of meaninglessness, a sense of the incomprehensibility of social affairs, of events whose dynamics one does not understand and whose future course one cannot predict; (3) a sense of normlessness, a high expectancy that socially unapproved means are necessary to achieve given goals; (4) value isolation, the individual's rejection of commonly held values in the society; (5) self-estrangement, the individual sense of a discrepancy between his ideal and his actual self-image and failure to satisfy certain postulated human needs; (6) social isolation, the individual's low expectancy for inclusion and social acceptance expressed typically in feelings of loneliness or feelings of rejection or repudiation.[18] According to Seeman, the most solid evidence about the meaning of these types of alienation concerns the sense of powerlessness. Moreover, most of this evidence depends on data provided by Rotter's

16. Frantz Fanon, *The Wretched of the Earth* (New York: Grove Press, 1963); *Black Skins, White Masks* (New York: Grove Press, 1967); *A Dying Colonialism* (New York: Grove Press, 1965).

17. James A. Geschwender, "Social Structure and the Negro Revolt: An Examination of Some Hypotheses," *Social Forces* 43(2) (December, 1964), pp. 248-256; "Explorations in the Social Movements and Revolutions," *Social Forces* 47 (December, 1968), pp. 127-135.

18. Melvin Seeman, "Alienation and Engagement," in Angus Campbell and Philip E. Converse, Editors, *The Human Meaning of Social Change* (New York: Russell Sage Foundation, 1972), pp. 472-473.

Internal-External Control scale, which Seeman argues is in strict accord with his conceptual definition of powerlessness. For that reason, the data relating our Internal-External Control subscales to social action joins the controversy about the meaning of powerlessness.

Recent theorizing about powerlessness suggests that the critical difference between the powerless and the less alienated lies not so much in their propensity to act as in the form of their action. Seeman hypothesizes, for example, that "planned, instrumentally oriented action" is less likely to emanate from the powerless than from the less alienated; at the same time, the more "powerless are characterized by their readiness to participate in relatively unplanned and/or short-term protest activities."[19] Seeman argues that two things are implied in proposing this difference between expressive and instrumental action. First, the powerless outlook encourages a short-range view, the inability or unwillingness to plan, to defer gratification, or to coordinate steps toward a future state of affairs. Second, this short-range view is expressed in particular kinds of protest. It is a perspective that coincides with the temper of contemporary direct-action forms of protest. He concludes that one finds in these protests—in urban riots, student demonstrations, and local community conflicts—the evidence of a powerlessness factor.[20]

Crawford and Naditch[21] argue similarly in discussing how powerlessness conditions the meaning of relative deprivation for social change. For people to act to change social conditions, they must first experience the discontent that stems from a sense of relative deprivation. Feeling discontented, individuals may adopt one of two orientations that differ according to their levels of powerlessness. Discontent fatalism develops when individuals perceive a large gap between their desires and their accomplishments but feel powerless to do anything to reduce this gap. Discontent activism follows when individuals feel relatively deprived but expect they can perform some action that will help them obtain their goals. Crawford and Naditch make the same predictions as Seeman about the form action will take under these two orientations. Feeling discontented but personally powerful, the behavior of the discontented activist will be instrumental and planned. Feeling discontented and powerless, the behavior of the discontented fatalist will be expressive, although Crawford and Naditch suggest that the word "explosive" might be more appropriate. "A man with strong and salient goals but no perceived means for achieving his goals might

19. *Ibid.*, p. 482.
20. *Ibid.*, p. 483.
21. Crawford and Naditch, "Relative Deprivation, Powerlessness, and Militancy: The Psychology of Social Protest."

respond with despair or apathy, or he might respond with violent, destructive and 'unpredictable' outbursts, triggered by seemingly trivial incidents. The characteristic behavior pattern might alternate between these two modes of responding to frustration."[22] They then try to show, on the one hand, the way in which militancy attitudes and participation in urban protest fit the combination of discontent and powerlessness, and, on the other hand, the way in which the participation in nonviolent civil rights demonstrations (which they view as more "instrumental") fit the combination of discontent and a high sense of internal control. (Both violent and nonviolent confrontations are in turn distinguished from participation in instrumental but more traditional activities such as NAACP membership; traditional activities are then viewed as reflecting high internal control and content rather than discontent.)

Commentators on white student activism also join the debate.[23] Making exactly the same predictions, Silvern and Nakamura cast the controversy about expressive and instrumental action as follows:

> *Left-wing activists are sometimes described as quite the opposite of powerless; they are seen as participating in primarily instrumental activity, out of an optimistic assessment of their chances for success. . . .*[24] *But there are theoretical arguments that internality is not in fact associated with activism among left-wing white students and that instead these students experience a great deal of powerlessness. Block, et al. described left-wing activists as adopting an existential stance in the face of their perception of an uncertain, unresponsive world. They turn to the existential act of taking a stand and fighting for it as a way to create meaning in their lives. Although the authors do not draw it out, the implication of their description is that student activists act in defiance of pessimism rather than from an optimistic sense of power. Their action is primarily expressive, rather than instrumental goal seeking. The idea that activism can stem from an alienated sense of despair appears throughout the sociological literature of political extremism. This literature suggests that to the extent that powerlessness is the impetus, the resulting social-political action will be expressive, defiant, and often violent.*[25]

22. *Ibid.*, p. 214.
23. Louise E. Silvern and Charles Y. Nakamura, "Powerlessness, Social-Political Action, Social-Political Views: Their Interrelation Among College Students," *Journal of Social Issues* 27(4) (1971), pp. 138-139.
24. *Ibid.*, p. 139.
25. *Ibid.*, p. 140.

The data we just presented contradict these expectations in certain ways. Let us review briefly the pertinent results. First, we found in 1964 that internal scores on the measure of personal control but external scores on the control ideology measure were associated with participation in civil rights (Appendix Table 10.1). Since these measures of personal control and control ideology substantially come from the Rotter Internal-External Control scale, the 1964 results provide mixed support for the expected relationship between internality and action. One kind of powerlessness, the more personal aspect of not feeling able to control events in one's own life, *inhibits* taking action, particularly among women. But the other kind of powerlessness that derives from questioning the validity of the Protestant work ethic in accounting for success in our society *facilitates* involvement in social action. Given this pattern, the total Internal-External Control scale, representing a summary of these inhibiting and facilitating components, understandably bore no relationship at all to participation in civil rights activities for either men or women in 1964 (Appendix Table 10.7).

Did these two kinds of powerlessness relate to whether action was primarily expressive or instrumental? We further differentiated the civil rights participants to form two groups of students: (1) those who participated in only one demonstration, a group that ought to fit typical definitions of expressive, spontaneous action; and (2) those who sustained frequent involvement over at least a year and who were associated with some group that took responsibility for coordinating local activities, a group that ought to reflect planned, instrumental, and sustained action. Personal powerlessness as measured by the Personal Control measure did not distinguish between these two groups; both groups showed greater personal control than students who were not involved at all. In contrast, their control ideologies did successfully distinguish between them, but not as expected by the theoretical arguments in the literature on powerlessness. The sustained activists were more, not less, external on the Control Ideology scale. If rejecting the Protestant ethic in favor of more balanced views about the role of internal and external forces in determining success implies a sense of powerlessness (and we will argue that it reflects political ideology instead of powerlessness), then powerlessness was associated with sustained action. In contrast, the supposedly "less alienated" group who accepts more of the Protestant ethic were more likely to have participated in just the one, isolated event. The measure of Individual-System Blame that translates the question of internal or external attributions into the issue of race inequities followed the same pattern: blaming external forces such as discrimination or other social obstacles was more characteristic of the sustained activists; stressing the individual's responsibility for the status differentials of Blacks and whites was more characteristic of the expressive group.

The 1970 data further questioned the tie between powerlessness, as measured by the Internal-External Control scale, and expressive action. The questions about student power and civil rights activism each asked students to declare not only their current participation but also whether they had previously taken part but later dropped out of protest activities. This explicitly refers to the longevity difference between sustained action and the spontaneous outbursts presumably characteristic of expressive action. Externality on both the Control Ideology subscale and the Individual-System Blame measure was associated particularly with sustained action. There was a clear ordinal relationship between length of commitment and externality: the currently and previously active were more external than students who had never participated at all; students who had sustained their involvement over their college years were even more external than the protest dropouts. In 1970 the issue of personal powerlessness was simply irrelevant for student activism. The Personal Control subscale of the Internal-External Control scale was unrelated to both level and form of action.

Finally, much the same pattern characterized the results from the longitudinal study of freshmen in their senior year at the college we studied intensively. We looked at three groups of students: (1) the stable activists who had been active as freshmen and were still involved in civil rights as seniors; (2) the activist dropouts, who had been equally active as freshmen but were no longer involved as seniors; and (3) the stable inactives who had not participated either as freshmen or since their freshman year. Comparing the internal-external control scores of the sustained and dropout activists is especially pertinent for the instrumental-expressive predictions made in the powerlessness literature. The sustained activists were more external on both the Control Ideology scale and Individual-System Blame index (Appendix Table 10.8 A and B). In fact the dropouts looked almost exactly like the stable inactives with respect to their analyses of the determinants of success in American society and their explanations for race inequities. Both groups were significantly more internal on both measures than the stable activists, even though the three groups had entered college four years before with much the same perspectives on these issues. The students who maintained their involvement in social action over their college years developed a perspective that was external but not expressive or powerless. We see repeatedly, therefore, that the more external students were committed to social action in a sustained way. These results were too consistent, replicated as they were in the cross-section study in 1964, in the 1968 longitudinal investigation of students who were freshmen in 1964, and in the 1970 cross-section study that was repeated in six colleges, as well too general, since they referred not only to civil rights activities but also to campus governance, to be a chance phenomenon. Why should they depart so much from the arguments and the evidence advanced by others? We propose three reasons. One entails a critique of the data provided as evidence for expressive-instrumental action predictions; the second depends on showing a conservative ideological bias in the Internal-External Control scale; the third questions the personalization of the concept of powerlessness itself.

Differential predictions that tie efficacy to instrumental action and powerlessness to expressive action should be tested using indicators of both types of action. That happens rarely. Usually just the relationship between powerlessness and riot participation is cited as major evidence, although it speaks to only half of the prediction. For example, Ransford's study showing a significant correlation between powerlessness, measured by 12 of the Rotter Internal-External Control items, and militancy attitudes among Black residents in the Los Angeles area is frequently cited as supporting the tie between powerlessness and expressive action.[26] There is no question but that Ransford's data do show that Black Americans who adhered less rigidly to the Protestant ethic as the explanation for success in our society also more often approved of violence as a political tool and necessity. However, this association may reflect primarily the ideologically conservative bias in the Internal-External Control instrument that we turn to next; moreover, it says nothing about actual behavior or about the differential predictions as to the form of action that powerless and less alienated people will pursue. Ransford himself rejects the powerlessness-alienation theoretical perspective[27] that others have attributed to him.[28] In fact he now argues that external scores on the Internal-External items that he used primarily reflect awareness of system barriers instead of personal powerlessness and thus understandably correlate with approving of riot violence as an instrumental means of correcting racial injustice. Nonetheless, others continue to use his

26. Seeman, "Alienation and Engagement," pp. 483-484; Crawford and Naditch, "Relative Deprivation, Powerlessness and Militancy: The Psychology of Social Protest;" and John R. Forward and Jay R. Williams, "Internal-External Control and Black Militancy," *Journal of Social Issues 26* (Winter, 1970), pp. 75-91.

27. H. Edward Ransford, "Comment on Internal-External Control and Black Militancy," by John R. Forward and Jay R. Williams, *Journal of Social Issues,* (Winter, 1970), *Journal of Social Issues 27*(1) (1971), pp. 227-232.

28. John R. Forward and Jay R. Williams, "Rejoinder," *Journal of Social Issues 27*(1) (1971), pp. 233-236.

results as though they support at least the powerlessness-expressive action aspect of the theory.

Even where both expressive and instrumental action are purportedly examined, close examination too often reveals other problems that make valid conclusions difficult to draw. For example, Silvern and Nakamura set out to test the differential prediction by examining the pattern of internal and external correlates of five forms of action undertaken by UCLA undergraduates.[29] They contend that the connection between expressive action and powerlessness was demonstrated by the fact that only protest activities were associated with external scores on the Internal-External Control scale. They fail to tell us, however, whether the other four types of action that they view as more instrumental were related to internal scores. In fact, therefore, the differential prediction was not tested. The data reported by Crawford and Naditch to support the differential prediction about expressive and instrumental action[30] provide still another example of this problem. Crawford and Naditch do not use the same data base in testing the connection between powerlessness and expressive action as they use in testing the relationship between efficacy and planned action. They cite Ransford's data as demonstrating that powerlessness is associated with expressive action; they use data from a Civil Rights Commission survey to demonstrate that the more efficacious Black adults, as indicated by their more internal scores on the I-E scale, were more active in the three types of action that they defined as instrumental.

In trying to make sense of the evidence at hand, we also immediately run into wide inconsistencies in what indicates expressive and instrumental action. Involvement in protest action is sometimes used to indicate instrumental action, sometimes expressive action. Take the two studies just cited. Silvern and Nakamura treat protest activities as clearly expressive in nature. Crawford and Naditch, on the other hand, argue that participation in demonstrations and attendance at rallies both indicate instrumental action. Two other studies[31] showing a positive relationship between internality on the Internal-External Control scale and participation in civil rights protest are also cited to support the tie between efficacy and instrumental action.[32] Consider the

---

29. Silvern and Nakamura, "Powerlessness, Social-Political Action, Views."
30. Crawford and Naditch, "Relative Deprivation, Powerlessness and Militancy: The Psychology of Social Protest," pp. 208-223.
31. Pearl M. Gore and Julian B. Rotter, "A Personality Correlate of Social Action," *Journal of Personality 31* (March, 1963), pp. 58-64; and Bonnie R. Strickland, "The Prediction of Social Action from a Dimension of Internal-External Control," *Journal of Social Psychology 66* (August, 1965), pp. 353-358.
32. Seeman, "Alienation and Engagement," pp. 478 and 479.

discussion of riots and urban disturbances. Some people view participation as an instrumental means of correcting injustice.[33] Others
treat it as a prime example of expressive action.[34] No wonder the controversy generates heat.

We suspect that the writer's own political philosophy determines
what is defined as expressive and what instrumental. Generally the
more traditional forms of political activity are treated as instrumental.
For example, Silvern and Nakamura classify writing letters to Congress-
men, tutoring, volunteering for hospital work, and campaigning for
peace candidates as instrumental while they think of protest activities
as expressive.[35] We would naturally expect internal scores on the I-E
scale to correlate with such traditional types of instrumental action, at
least if we are right that there is a strong ideologically conservative
bias in the scale. We see this bias in the interpretation of some data
presented by Bullough in discussing alienation in the ghetto.[36] The
results showed: (1) that Black adults who had moved to the San Fer-
nando Valley from Los Angeles were more internal on the Internal-
External Control scale than equally middle-class Blacks who remained
in the urban area; (2) that residents of Los Angeles who lived a "more
integrated style of life" were likewise more internal than other ghetto
residents. These results are used to support the inference that it was
the "internals' relative sense of mastery that encourages them to take
action that leads to integrated housing."[37] To move or not to move
certainly shows an action decision. Whether it reflects feelings of
efficacy and powerlessness or the ideological controversy over integration and separatism is debatable. Black Americans who adopt a
conventional individualistic explanation of success might also be expected to subscribe to integration; we doubt that they are more efficacious than Blacks who reject integration.

We are not alone in questioning the ideological theme in the
Internal-External Control scale. Several writers have commented that

33. Ransford, "Comment on Forward and Williams; Forward and Williams, "Internal-
External Control," and "Rejoinder;" Caplan, "A Causal Model of Black Militancy;"
H. L. Nieberg, *Political Violence: The Behavioral Process* (New York: St. Martin's
Press, Inc., 1969); and St. C. Drake, "Urban Violence and American Social
Movements," in R. H. Connery, Editor, *Urban Riots: Violence and Social Change.
Proceedings of the Academy of Political Science 29* (1968), pp. 13-24.
34. Ransford, "Isolation, Powerlessness and Violence;" Crawford and Naditch, "Rela-
tive Deprivation, Powerlessness and Militancy: The Psychology of Social Protest;"
Seeman, "Alienation and Engagement."
35. Silvern and Nakamura, "Powerlessness, Social-Political Action, Views."
36. Bonnie L. Bullough, "Alienation in the Ghetto," *American Journal of Sociology 72*
(January, 1967), pp. 469-478.
37. Seeman, "Alienation and Engagement," p. 480.

many of the items scored as internal would be more congenial to a person holding a conservative than a liberal political ideology.[38] The internal response to several paired items state: "In the long run people get the respect in this world that they deserve;" "Becoming successful is a matter of hard work, luck has little or nothing to do with it;" "Most misfortunes are the result of lack of ability, ignorance, laziness, or all three." Thomas suggests: "Such emphasis on individualism and success through hard work sounds like statements from the National Association of Manufacturers or the United States Chamber of Commerce—the individual holding liberal social and political views, on the other hand, might well disagree with such statements because he feels strongly that slum conditions and racial prejudice deny many persons equal opportunity."[39] Data Thomas collected from a sample of 30 conservative and 29 liberal, white, upperclass parents and their college-age offspring indicate that there is a political aspect to the scale. Although the liberal parents were slightly more active politically, their scores were more external than those of the conservative parents. Furthermore, the left-wing students were more external than either the non-activists or right-wing activists. Silvern and Nakamura also demonstrate the externality is associated with left-wing views among white college students.

Finding this political bias, some writers question whether the Internal-External Control scale should be used to measure a person's expectancy of control of reinforcements. We continue to feel that the first person items that comprise our measure of personal control do indeed indicate what Rotter meant by the concept. As we have shown in Chapter 4, the Personal Control measure operates motivationally, as a generalized expectancy measure as it should. But the third person items that comprise our Control Ideology scale and account for most of the total Rotter score should be treated as measures of political posture rather than reflecting people's generalized expectancies about being able to control events in their own lives. Instead of externality on the Control Ideology scale reflecting a low personal expectancy and, in this sense, measuring powerlessness as defined by Seeman, it demands being aware of the role of sociological forces in accounting for success differentials in our society. To be external on many of the items pre-

---

38. Patricia Gurin, Gerald Gurin, Rosina C. Lao, and Muriel Beattie, "Internal-External Control in the Motivational Dynamics of Negro Youth," *Journal of Social Issues* 25(3) (1969); pp. 29-53; Silvern and Nakamura, "Powerlessness, Social-Political Action, Views;" and L. E. Thomas, "The Internal-External Scale, Ideological Bias, and Political Participation," *Journal of Personality* 38 (1970), pp. 273-286.
39. Thomas, "The Internal-External Scale, Ideological Bias, and Political Participation," p. 276.

sumes awareness of social causation in a complex society in which poverty and race inequities cannot legitimately be explained in individualistic terms.

Failure to recognize this ideological theme in this frequently used measure encourages the tendency to attribute powerlessness to any belief that focuses on the external forces, however reality-based they may be. Thus, "riot" participants have been described as better educated, more involved in organizations concerned with civil rights, more knowledgeable about politics, all of which generally indicate lack of alienation, but also more powerless since they attribute their employment troubles to external sources. Sixty-nine percent of the riot participants in the Kerner Commission Newark and Detroit data perceived discrimination as an obstacle to employment success and only 18 percent referred to lack of training; among the uninvolved, 41 percent chose the latter more internal explanation.[40] Why not the following description: better educated, more involved in organizations, more knowledgeable about politics, and more sophisticated about the causes of Blacks' unemployment?

Why does it matter if these biases on both sides of the powerlessness-action equation go unrecognized or unchallenged? If we insist on calling an external view, no matter how realistic or sophisticated, an indicator of powerlessness, we are ill-prepared to entertain the possibility that protest action, urban revolts, and other nontraditional forms of action are the instrumental acts of the more sophisticated and ideologically committed instead of the expressive outbursts of the more powerless elements of society. Nor can we understand when alienation, in the form of personal powerlessness, is truly increasing and when externality represents the growth of a sophisticated depiction of social causation. The students we studied over the decade of the sixties shifted toward a much more external view of the determinants of success in the culture at large and in the lives of Black Americans more specifically (Chapter 8, Tables 1 and 2). Others likewise report that college students have become more external on the Internal-External Control scale.[41] Often these shifts are interpreted as showing an increase in alienation among college youth when they found the decade of protest resulting in so few changes. Is it that, or is it a reflection of an ideological shift away from individualistic philosophies in favor of explanations stressing social and economic causation of suc-

---

40. Seeman, "Alienation and Engagement," p. 476.
41. Silvern and Nakamura, "Powerlessness, Social-Political Action, Views;" Julian B. Rotter, "External Control and Internal Control," *Psychology Today* 5(1) (June, 1971), pp. 37-42.

cess in our society? The fact that the students we studied in 1970 showed the same level of personal efficacy that we found in 1964 (Chapter 4, Table 1) but were much more external on the ideological aspects of the Internal-External Control scale suggests that the shift is in political ideology and not in personal powerlessness.

The ideological theme in the measure of powerlessness is not the only problem, however. The concept of powerlessness, even if it were to be measured independently of ideology, has been peculiarly personalized in much of the writing on powerlessness. Treatment of alienation in the mass society literature assumes that people are not alienated if they are connected to secondary groups and institutions that represent their interests and mediate between them and the state.[42] The sense of powerlessness, therefore, should not derive exclusively from whether people feel personally powerless but also whether they have identified with, or actually participated in, groups that they perceive as having power. No matter how personally impotent people may feel, they may not feel powerless if they believe that the groups with which they identify can influence social and political events. Measures of personal feelings of powerlessness, even if uncontaminated by ideology, may not predict whether the individual behaves as if powerless. We are not surprised, for example, that our measure of personal control no longer was associated with either amount or kind of student activism in 1970. It correlated with action only in 1964 when political institutions, the federal government especially, were rather directly accessible to the individual; it was a time when the individual could more validly expect an individual act to matter. At the present time it is more realistic for an individual to feel that individual acts cannot influence events very much. The nature of the problems we now face—war, ecological imbalance, racial oppression, and inflation—demand collective attacks. In fact we argue that this recognition of individual powerlessness may often be the precondition for action, although it will be collective rather than individual action. In instances of local problems personal efficacy probably does provide the source of motivation to act. The issue at the national and international level with respect to problems that defy easy solutions is whether individuals, recognizing their individual impotence, become committed to collective action and to groups with the potential power of changing what the individual alone cannot alter. The concept and the measure of powerlessness must include this possibility if they are to reflect the relationship of the individual to secondary institutions, a relationship that is presented as so critical to action in a mass society.

42. Seeman, "Alienation and Engagement," p. 476.

We agree that activists often take an existential step. They recognize the complexity of social events as well as the incredible odds against influencing their course, especially if individuals act alone. The action they take, however, goes far beyond the attempt to give meaning to their lives; they act out of the conviction that if anything can influence the course of events it must stem from a collective endeavor. In this sense many activists are not nihilists. Like the colonized facing the colonial power's military strength, the existential step is commitment to a revolutionary group, not individual revolt. The individual's commitment to the collectivity can provide the bridge between the sometimes overly personalized discussion of powerlessness in modern society and the sometimes depersonalized presentation of revolutionary thought.

chapter 11

Institutional Patterns of Ideology and Activism

The few available national studies of student activism agree that participation rates vary greatly in different kinds of institutions. Peterson examined how many of eight different kinds of colleges reported student protests in 1964 and again in 1968. Large public universities stood out, primarily because more of them had experienced protests around off-campus issues: in 1964-1965 more reported civil rights protests, and in 1968 disruptions over both civil rights and the Vietnam war.[1] Peterson also noted regional variation in off-campus protests; colleges in the South reported substantially less organized protest about both civil rights and the Vietnam war. Astin further comments that protests occurred more often in liberal arts colleges in the Northeast, least often in junior colleges.[2]

Certain kinds of Black colleges likewise have experienced more student activism. There is some evidence that participation in the southern movement early in the decade was greater among students in private than public colleges; colleges of high academic quality located in heavily urban counties with a comparatively small Black population also stood out for greater levels of student involvement.[3] Institutional variation in student activism at Black colleges continued into the latter part of the decade. Generally more Black institutions than white reported student disruptions in 1967-1968.[4] But Black colleges differed among themselves in the proportion of their student bodies who participated, the form protests took, and their subsequent responses to the

1. Richard E. Peterson, "The Scope of Organized Student Protest," in Julian Foster and Durward Long, Editors, *Protest: Student Activism in America* (New York: William Morrow, 1970), pp. 59-80.
2. Alexander Astin, "Determinants of Student Activism," *Ibid.*, pp. 89-101.
3. John M. Orbell, "Protest Participation Among Southern Negro College Students," *American Political Science Review 61* (June, 1967), pp. 446-456.
4. Durward Long, "Black Protest," in *Protest: Student Activism in America*, p. 467.

protests.[5] Prior research does not show, however, whether this variation in the late sixties represented systematic differences between public and private institutions or whether in other ways it reflected institutional type.

Overall, prior research has clearly demonstrated that colleges and universities differ greatly in level of student activism and that these differences are not random. Certain kinds of institutions are more protest-prone than others. Controversy does not focus on these facts but on the explanations for them. Do these variations reflect genuine differences in the environments and organizational characteristics of the different types of institutions, or do they primarily reflect the characteristics of the students who choose to attend one type of institution rather than another? Astin's data relating institutional type to student activism argue for the latter explanation. Although several of the correlations between environmental characteristics of the colleges and frequency of protest were quite high, virtually all those relationships disappeared when student input characteristics were controlled.[6]

In this chapter we describe student activism and ideological differences among the 10 institutions that participated in the 1964 cross-sectional study and the six institutions that participated again in 1970. Did they differ in both 1964 and 1970 regarding student power protest as well as civil rights activism? Was institutional variation greater regarding activism or ideology? Was Black Nationalism ascribed to by more students in certain colleges? Did these differences persist when we adjusted for the fact that certain colleges recruited more rural students, who were less active in civil rights protest? Did the campus climate condition whether students expressed their ideologies by becoming involved in action?

This chapter goes beyond differences between colleges, and examines the extent to which activism was associated with different experiences within the college. What aspects of the college experience were related to activism? Were activists somewhat marginal to traditional collegiate life or were they at least as much a part as other students? Was there any evidence in 1970 that student power and civil rights activists participated in different aspects of the college? Was there a distinctive subculture associated with activism on all campuses or only on campuses where activism itself was reasonably widespread? Finally, we examine whether the experience of being an activist served as one

5. Elton C. Harrison, "Student Unrest on the Black College Campus," *The Journal of Negro Education 41* (Spring, 1972), pp. 113-120; Long, "Black Protest," in *Protest: Student Activism in America*, pp. 459-481.
6. Astin, "Determinants of Student Activism," in *Protest: Student Activism in America*, pp. 89-101.

of the sources of college impact. Did activism produce personal changes in the participants?

INSTITUTIONAL DIFFERENCES, 1964 AND 1970

These colleges did differ greatly in student activism rates (Table 1). In 1964, 86 percent of the students at the most active college, compared to only 13 percent at the most inactive, and an overall average of 46 percent in the 10 institutions, had participated in civil rights. Furthermore, while 7 percent of the total sample had been actively involved for at least a year and had been jailed numerous times, this figure rose to 31 percent on one campus and fell to less than 1 percent at another. In 1970 the differences continued to be as striking (Table 2). Comparing the high and low colleges: 90 versus 42 percent of the students said they had been active in civil rights during their college years, 35 versus 4 percent of these students were still actively involved in 1970; 85 percent versus 42 percent had been active in student power issues, 27 percent versus 1 percent were still participating; 20 percent versus 2 percent reported belonging to a Black student organization. These differences were reduced when three student input characteristics— sex of the student, rural-urban background, and the father's education —were statistically controlled. As would be expected from the data reported in Chapter 9, it was particularly rural-urban background that served to diminish the size of these institutional differences. Nonetheless, the relationship between institution attended and participation in political action continued to be significant even after adjusting for institutional differences in these three student inputs (Appendix Table 11.1). Moreover, the size of these relationships remained reasonably constant from 1964 to 1970.

Ideology was a different matter. With or without controlling student input characteristics, most colleges looked reasonably similar as to their students' beliefs and race ideologies (Appendix Table 11.1). Only on two issues that we examined as part of ideology were there large institutional differences. First, in both 1964 and 1970, the institutions differed greatly in student reactions to campus regulations and governance. If we define the upper half of the total sample as the highly disapproving group, we can illustrate these institutional differences by comparing the proportion of students in the extreme colleges who fell in the high group (Table 3). Seventy-two percent at the most critical college, but only 25 percent at the least critical, expressed strong disapproval of the administration exercising control over student political action. The contrast in disapproval of traditional parietal policies and of the administration maintaining sole power to determine such

TABLE 1.   **Proportion of the Students Attending the 10 Colleges Studied in 1964-1965 Who Were Participating in Civil Rights Activities**

Civil Rights Participation	Institution										All Institutions
	A	B	C	D	E	F	G	H	I	J	
Actively involved for at least a year plus jail experience	*	7%	31%	19%	11%	2%	6%	1%	1%	7%	7%
Participated in several events	8%	20%	40%	33%	36%	11%	13%	19%	27%	28%	23%
Participated in one event	5%	21%	15%	26%	16%	25%	20%	10%	20%	16%	16%
Never participated	87%	52%	14%	22%	37%	62%	61%	70%	52%	49%	54%
	100%	100%	100%	100%	100%	100%	100%	100%	100%	100%	100%
	(400)	(400)	(400)	(400)	(317)	(400)	(381)	(400)	(343)	(198)	(3639)

TABLE 2. Proportion of Students Attending the Six Colleges Studied in 1970 with Civil Rights, Student Power, and Black Student Organization Participation

| | Institution | | | | | | All |
	A	B	C	H	I	J	Institutions
Civil rights participation:							
Currently active	4%	5%	35%	23%	10%	7%	10%
Previously active	38	57	55	67	70	83	65
Never active	58	38	10	10	20	10	25
	100%	100%	100%	100%	100%	100%	100%
Participation in student power activities:							
Currently active	1%	9%	27%	17%	11%	10%	10%
Previously active	41	59	58	49	74	46	57
Never active	58	32	15	34	15	44	33
	100%	100%	100%	100%	100%	100%	100%
Membership in Black Student Organizations:							
Now a member	2%	7%	3%	4%	20%	20%	7%
Not a member	98	93	97	96	80	80	93
	100%	100%	100%	100%	100%	100%	100%
	(200)	(197)	(233)	(200)	(161)	(136)	(1127)

TABLE 3.   **Range of Extreme Differences Between the High and Low Institutions[a] on Measures of Black Nationalism and Attitudes About Campus Governance in 1970**

	Institution with Highest Percent above the Median of Total Sample	Institution with Lowest Percent above the Median of Total Sample
Collective consciousness:		
System blame	66%	39%
External control ideology	61%	36%
Collective commitments:		
Preference for collective action over individual mobility change strategies	83%	28%
Political Black nationalism:		
ADVOCACY OF:		
Self-determination	61%	31%
Community control	60%	41%
Economic development	59%	54%
Political use of violence	67%	39%
Cultural Black nationalism:		
African identification	60%	35%
Afro-American orientation	59%	28%
Attitudes about campus governance:		
DISAPPROVAL OF:		
Control of student political action	72%	25%
Parietal policies	76%	21%
Administration exercising sole authority over academic freedom	67%	47%

[a]These percents are based on approximately 200 students in the high and 200 students in the low group. In most colleges that participated in 1970 we sampled 100 freshmen and 100 seniors, split evenly by sex.

policies was 76 percent at the most critical and only 21 percent at the least critical college. Thus, almost 50 percent more of the students at the most critical college than those on the campus where students were most accepting of traditional regulations and governance expressed what was high disapproval for the sample as a whole. Second, advocacy of collective action as the best means of dealing with race inequities varied from institution to institution: 53 percent of the students on the most collectively oriented campus, but only 13 percent on the least collectively oriented, chose at least five of the six collective strategies on the individual-collective strategies index. By comparing the proportion of students in the extreme colleges whose collective commitments fell above the median for the sample as a whole, we found 83 percent at the most collective, but only 28 percent at the least collective.

These two issues very closely reflected college differences in activism itself. Colleges differed not only in civil rights participation but also in student commitments to collective action to redress racism. Moreover, we showed in Chapter 10 that collective action preferences especially correlated with participation in civil rights. In the same vein, colleges differed greatly not only in participation rates in student power activities but also in student disapproval of traditional governance and campus regulations. And student power attitudes particularly correlated with student power activism. The consistency of these results supports the conclusion that there were reliable college differences in both activism and in the action-implicated aspects of ideology.

Otherwise, the colleges differed only slightly regarding their students' beliefs and race ideologies. Although most of the institutional comparisons resulted in statistical differences, their size was not impressive. (The beta coefficients for institutional differences in attitudes about campus governance were .24 and in collective commitments .26 while all other coefficients for college differences in nationalist ideology fell between .05 and .11—See Appendix Table 11.1.) The most extreme colleges showed genuinely different ideological climates, although the range between the high and low colleges was not nearly so great on other ideology measures as with attitudes about campus regulations, collective commitments, and participation in political action. Using the upper half of the total sample to define the "high group," the extreme colleges differed much less on all the other dimensions of ideology (Table 3). Instead of the 50 percent more who showed above median disapproval of traditional governance and the 55 percent more who preferred collective action change strategies, only 27 percent more at the high than at the low school expressed strong system blame; 25 percent more expressed above median rejection of the traditional work-ethic as an explanation of success; 31 percent more strongly advocated Afro-American identifications and self-determination through separatism; 25 percent more showed high commitment to African symbols; 28 percent more approved of violence as a possible political necessity; and only 19 percent and 5 percent more advocated community control and Black economic development, respectively.

CAMPUS PROFILES

Particular institutions stand out in these comparisons for a variety of reasons: for their students' consistently conventional or consistently nationalistic ideologies; for their consistently low or high levels of activism; for greater than average shift in student opinion since 1964; for a marked discrepancy between rank position on the ideology measures and on level of student activism. Brief sketches of four such campuses show unique environments despite the overall homogeneity in some aspects of student opinion. We had to depend on the 1970 questionnaire data for these profiles since we did not interview students or observe campus activities in 1970 as we had earlier in 1964.

The Nonpolitical Campus

This large, land-grant college serves almost exclusively in-state students, three-quarters of whom grew up on farms and in small towns. The campus itself stands isolated, 45 miles away from the nearest city of any size, seven miles from a small village. Few of its graduates have left the state to find jobs; typically, most have gone into teaching, many in rural schools in the state. The agricultural graduates, approximately 18 percent in 1964 and 10 percent even in 1970, generally have combined farming with either teaching or working as county agents. Given the dominance of rural influences, this college understandably showed the greatest conventionality in its students' attitudes. It was this college that consistently anchored the low end in all of the extreme college comparisons we just noted. In 1964 and 1970 its students expressed the least system blame, least rejection of conventional Protestant ethic beliefs, least commitment to collective action, and least rejection of traditional governance and student life regulations. Although student opinion about all these issues had shifted significantly here between 1964 and 1970, the college's position relative to others had not changed at all. Moreover, opinion shifts brought this college's average scores in 1970 only up to the level of the most unconventional school in 1964. For 1970 that meant an attitudinal climate very different from that on most of the other campuses. Civil rights activism also was consistently low; only 13 percent had participated in any civil rights activities in 1964; 42 percent had done so by 1970, but only 4 percent were still active. Participation in student power issues was also lower in 1970 here than elsewhere; only 42 percent of the students said they had ever been active, 1 percent still active. Finally, student opinion in 1970 showed the least approval of all six dimensions of Black Nationalism.

This description oversimplifies the situation, however. This campus errupted in 1966 because a small group of students led a boycott of classes to dramatize that they felt excellence in the academic arena was jeopardized by undue emphasis on and fiscal priority for the athletic program. While the boycott was not successful in closing classes, the campus was by no means the pastoral scene that might be expected to follow from our description of student opinion here. In fact, talking about average student opinion misses the fact that the distribution of opinion also looked different here than elsewhere. Although most students subscribed to individualistic theories of causation, preferred individual mobility strategies of change, and accepted the traditional authority of the college, a few—about 8 to 15 percent, depending on the issues at stake—held completely opposite views. Notably absent in 1964, and somewhat missing in 1970, were students who held moderate positions on these ideology measures. Moreover, the few "radical" students stood out on all ideology measures; the same students who advocated collective action were also the most unconventional on all other measures. The intercorrelations among these ideology measures for just the 10 percent who chose at least 5 out of 6 collective strategies were all above .8, although the ideological interrelationships for the total sample and for the rest of the students at this college fell closer to .4. Thus, a small group of students held a coherent ideology that departed greatly from modal opinion at this college.

With the seeds of discontent provided by this small group, the absence of a large moderate group meant that there were very few students prepared to hold the middle line. This was especially striking in 1964 regarding governance issues. Most students accorded legitimacy for decision making to the administration alone. Fewer students here than on any other campus advocated a decision-making model in which students and administrators shared responsibility for setting regulations, even about curfews. Without students who were committed to a consensual power model or those whose attitudes were moderate, this campus was set for a special kind of unrest once an issue had activiated the few who felt that students alone ought to exercise decision-making power. Repressive responses quicken in situations where conflict is polarized and the parties lack experience resolving it together. In fact, the 1966 campus unrest was handled by calling in the state police, an action that had not yet been taken by many administrators. Most students, understandably in light of the distribution of student opinion here, tolerated that administrative action. The dissident students were expelled; life returned to normal. We should not conclude, however, that the potential for unrest no longer existed since this skewed distribution of student opinion continued to characterize this institution's data in 1970, despite numerous changes in the college's regulations and stronger efforts to involve students in some aspects of governance.

The Ideological Campus

The same elite college described in Chapter 6 as maintaining, but not enhancing, the high motivations and aspirations its students brought to college, this institution attracts urban, sophisticated students who provide a strong ideological tone to the campus. Even after controlling for the ideological edge that results from selecting an atypically urban student body, its adjusted average scores on most of the ideology measures stood out in both 1964 and 1970. Its students led in blaming the system in both 1964 and 1970; they most strongly rejected a rigid Protestant ethic ideology in 1964 and held second rank in 1970; they were most critical of administrative control of academic freedom and of parietal rules in 1964 and they held second- and third-rank positions respectively in 1970. Furthermore, approval of militancy and Afro-American orientations were stronger here than elsewhere in 1970, although their other nationalism scores generally did not depart from those of other campuses. Its students also advocated collective strategies of change more than average, although admittedly not as whole-heartedly as students in two other institutions in 1964 and one other in 1970.

In contrast, this college did not rank among the top institutions in student activism despite its students' ideological commitments. Civil rights participation in 1964 was fourth among the 10 colleges; it shared with two others only moderate involvement in 1970. Participation in student power activities was second lowest among the six colleges, despite the second highest level of student advocacy of student power and rejection of traditional governance. Breadth of student participation in extracurricular affairs was generally low here, compared to other colleges and especially compared to those that even began to approximate the attitudinal stance of the students here.

There was only one exception to this discrepant picture of ideology and action. Its students did stand out in 1970 both for their advocacy of militancy and Afro-American orientations and for their membership in a Black student organization. Twenty percent of the students—here and at one other college, the activated one described below—belonged to a BSO in 1970, while less than 5 percent at most other colleges did. (Perhaps this is not such an exception since Black student organizations primarily provide an arena for ideological discussions instead of a base for action.)

Blackness was a dominant theme on this campus in 1970. Two questions that clearly distinguished it from other campuses referred to the importance of being Black. Ninety-five percent of the students at this college wanted to be referred to as Black, whereas closer to three-quarters of the students at four other colleges and only 40 percent of the nonpolitical college chose Black as preferred nomenclature. When students were asked how they thought of themselves—as American, as Black, as both Black and American, as neither—60 percent of the students here but as few as 20 percent at most other colleges and only 6 percent at the nonpolitical college chose the single identity of being Black. The modal response at most colleges (approximately 60 percent at four of the schools) was being both Black and American. In contrast, only a third of the students here accepted the double identity of being Black and American. With so much emphasis on identity issues, BSO membership may well have provided a forum for expression of these identity concerns rather than representing political action per se.

We do not mean to attribute widespread passivity to the students; they were not the least active student body either in 1964 or in 1970. Some students were very active throughout the decade of the sixties; many leaders of the southern student movement came from this college earlier in the decade. But the level of activism did not match the ideological climate. Fewer participated in action than their politically sophisticated stance might suggest would have been the case. This discrepancy stands in marked contrast to two other colleges; one that consistently showed high levels of student activism despite only moderate commitments to nationalism and one that became much more ideological and activist after 1964.

The Activist Campus

This large public university, located in an urban hub known for Black business and wealth, attracts in-state students who split almost evenly between rural and urban backgrounds. Many urban students commute; the residential students come disproportionately from rural areas and small cities in the state. Administrators viewed the commuter-residential mix as an important source of conflict and student protest on the campus. Campus rules and regulations, especially curfews and those concerning control of the students' personal lives, necessarily prevailed only for students living on campus. Commuters were responsible to their parents or relatives with whom they lived. They represented an envied group to the residential students, especially to the women whose lives were particularly affected by double standards in the parietal rules of the college. Although many rules were later reviewed and control lessened, the climate in 1964 was characterized by considerable student hostility toward the rules and even more toward the Dean of

Women, who was viewed as much too arbitrary and punitive. This was an environment in which the commuting students were free to come and go as they pleased while the lives of the residential students were carefully monitored. Its urban setting also provided attractive off-campus opportunities that invited the residential students, like students in generations past, to develop clever maneuvers to sneak out. Moreover, this particular urban center had a vital Black political movement that offered opportunities for participation in political action as well.

Is it any wonder that students here consistently stood out for their civil rights activism and their attack on traditional college governance? In 1964, 86 percent of the students reported having participated in some kind of civil rights activity. Thirty-one percent had been actively involved over a sustained period of time. In 1970, 90 percent of the students said they participated in civil rights during their college years; 35 percent were still active. These rates led all the other institutions. Student power participation tied for first with one other college; 85 percent at these two campuses reported having been engaged in some kind of student power activity. The rates at the other four colleges were much lower. Their feelings about student regulations and governance also put them in the lead. They tied for first in 1964 and second in 1970 in criticizing administrative control of student political action; they were second in both 1964 and 1970 in disapproving parietal policies; they tied for first in 1964 and were third in 1970 in criticizing policies that required administrative clearance of speakers, that provided for investigating the political involvements of faculty, and that raised other academic freedom issues. The students here also held unusually high commitment to collective action as a social change strategy in both 1964 and in 1970. Average scores on the individual-collective index put this college first in 1964, third in 1970. In contrast, neither their system attitudes, which we have viewed as precursors to nationalism, nor their scores on the nationalism dimensions were particularly noteworthy.

The campus stands out, therefore, for its consistently high level of activism and for the aspects of student opinion that seem to be central to action—the stance students took toward the college administration and traditional rules and regulations and the preferences they expressed for collective modes of dealing with race inequities. On the other ideological measures it was not nearly so politically sophisticated as the institution we previously described. Blackness was not nearly so important. But more students acted on what bothered them both within the college and the surrounding community.

The college's location in a politically active, socially exciting city and its rural-urban and residential-commuter mix in the student body go a long way in accounting for its heightened level of activism. The inequity of applying rules to some but not all students provided a basis of activation; moreover, the city's attractions for off-campus life provided an incentive that another campus with as many commuters lacked by being located in a smaller town where there was little to do anyway. The community civil rights movement likewise provided greater opportunities for political participation, especially since the leadership did not have to come exclusively from the college itself. When the right issue sparked student concern, the local leadership was organized to build upon this spark. Commuter status also enabled easier involvement of large numbers of the students.

The Activated Campus

Described in Chapter 6 as accentuating its students' initially high aspirations and motivation, this small isolated campus also showed the greatest shift in both ideology and activism between 1964 and 1970. All the other institutions remained close to their 1964 rank position, despite an absolute increase in their students' system awareness, collectivism, social determinism, and advocacy of student involvement in college decision making. The shifts here were marked enough that its 1970 average scores gave it a different position in the rank order of colleges. Its rank shifted from fifth to second place in system blame, fifth to first place in rejection of a rigid Protestant Ethic ideology, fourth to first in commitments to collective strategies, fourth to first place in concern about college control in the academic freedom area, fifth to first in criticism of traditional in loco parentis policies, and from fourth to first in disapproval of administrative control of student political action. Some shift also occurred in student activism. Although the students here continued to show only the moderate level of involvement in civil rights that had characterized them in 1964 as well, they had the highest rate of participation in student power and tied with one other school for BSO membership in 1970. This was the only college that stood out markedly on most dimensions of Black Nationalism in 1970. Over 70 percent of the students here scored above the median of the total sample on the self-determination, African identification, and community control indices. It was only with respect to militancy attitudes and feelings about Blackness as an identity issue that they did not lead in nationalism in 1970. Actually, the average scores probably underestimated nationalist attitudes here in 1970. Since student resistance to the study was stronger here than elsewhere, students who did participate were likely the most traditional. We know for sure that the most outspoken of the senior class refused to participate. Neither the overall refusal rate nor senior resistance at other colleges even began to approximate the problem here. This sample bias would have worried us had the data showed this college to be unusually conventional. Quite the contrary, however; despite the bias, it held the top rank of eight on the 11 ideology measures we have been discussing in these chapters on collective consciousnes and action.

What was it about this college that produced such a different student climate in 1970? Of course, in absolute terms student ideology on all the campuses in 1970 differed greatly from the climate in 1964. But what was it that resulted in a relatively greater shift here so that its position relative to other colleges had changed so much? This question particularly intrigued us since this was the college where the most sophisticated and affluent students in 1964 accused the faculty of holding hopelessly outmoded social attitudes and charged the school both with paternalism and irrelevance to Black needs. What had happened? Although we did not conduct intensive interviews in 1970, some plausible explanations were suggested by other aspects of the 1970 questionnaire data. For example, the freshman core program, once the souce of special criticism from its most outspoken students for its Western bias, had been greatly altered. All freshmen in 1970 were introduced to non-Western materials as an automatic part of the new core program. This was the only college where a non-Western and Black studies emphasis reached all students in 1970. Such courses were elective everywhere else; thus, many fewer students took them elsewhere and certainly not until after the freshman year. Students here also credited a particular social science professor, hired after 1964, for his role in curriculum change, his knowledge of Black literature and scholarship, and his own commitment to Black Nationalism. The very elements of the environment that some students criticized heatedly in 1964, its smallness, familialism, and faculty concern for student development, maximized the impact that such a professor could have. This college has also had a long history of educational innovation. It developed a general studies curriculum, a strong focus on community, and attracted an interracial staff with radical perspectives during the late forties and fifties when that was atypical of almost all southern colleges. Without fully appreciating the college's history, the 1964 student critics underestimated its potential for change when they justly criticized the most outdated aspects of the communal climate that had been radical itself 10 years before. Paternalistic as the faculty and administration could be, their strong commitment to student needs and to the development of each student also provided unusual openness to change when they were convinced that the needs of the students had changed.

The communal orientations of the college that historically provided for much more student involvement in decision making here than else-where also provided a base for working out student demands for an even greater role in determining their education. Moreover, once students pressed demands for curriculum revision and involvement in broader aspects of the college's functioning, their effectiveness was facilitated by the sheer smallness and isolation of the campus. Students could not remain untouched by the campus environment; it was all they had. While isolation militates against change promoted primarily from outside influences, it multiplies the impact a school can have if there are forces for change within the environment itself.

INSTITUTIONAL EFFECT

We cannot be sure that these pronounced differences in activism, student power attitudes, and collective commitments tell much about environmental effects since they may reflect the experience and the attitudinal differences that students brought with them to these differ-ent colleges. We reduced that possibility somewhat by statistically adjusting for the fact that certain colleges recruited more rural students, who participated less and especially in civil rights activities. College differences in activism and ideology at least did not reflect this partic-ular selectivity effect. But there may be other correlates of activism and ideology we did not control that varied across the colleges through the kinds of students they initially selected. Since the 1970 data were col-lected during the second academic term, comparisons of freshmen did not conclusively attest to such selectivity; but the fact that these col-lege differences were nearly as large among freshmen as among seniors at least suggests that certain colleges attracted students who entered with already greater activism experience and more ideo-logically committed. This was clearly the case in 1964 when question-naires were administered to freshmen at time of entrance rather than during the second term. Activism rates were significantly different among the freshmen entrants of the 10 colleges in 1964, although they were not so sizable as comparisons of seniors. Generally, therefore, we feel these differences must at least partially reflect selectivity factors. We cannot adjust for them as impressively as we could in exam-ining the impact of the colleges on their students' aspirations and motivations.

Two of the colleges did show clear evidence, however, of providing a climate that enhanced student participation. For example, the fresh-men who entered the college that became activated by the events in Selma and Montgomery had the second lowest participation rate as high school students. Only 10 percent of them had taken part in any civil rights activities before entering college. At the end of that year 62 percent of the freshman class had taken part in something. The fact that SNCC opened a field office in the town and promoted political organization of that county for the newly formed Black Panther Political Party provided strong support for the campus leadership group. Effective organization made buses available for the major demonstrations in Montgomery; open organizational meetings that gave direction to these events and to picketing local grocery stores likewise provided opportunity for widespread participation. It would be very hard to argue that this college simply selected students who were already political activists; the activities that developed that year created activists out of students who had not previously taken part. There was also the college that became activated between 1964 and 1970. Since most other colleges maintained their rank positions from 1964, the large shifts in ideology here indicate that something was happening to cause such a different ideological climate in 1970. Further substantiation is provided by the fact that this was the only college where the difference between freshmen and seniors in 1970 was strikingly greater than the difference between freshmen and seniors in 1964. Since we have taken the freshmen-senior difference as some indication of the impact of the college experience, this suggests something special about the experience of the 1970 seniors at this college.

Another way of approaching institutional effect depends on showing that the campus climate conditions whether ideological commitments actually turn into action. We noted in Chapter 10 that ideological correlates of action were particularly striking on the two campuses where activism was reasonably widespread. In contrast, ideology did not distinguish between activists and nonactivists nearly so well at the two where activism was much more rare. Where there were few opportunities for action or where the mood of the campus discouraged participation, nationalist students could do little to express their beliefs. They could talk about their beliefs, but actual participation in civil rights or student power was much less likely. Both the opportunities to participate and the campus ambience encouraged a stronger connection between ideology and action on the active campuses. The campus climate, defined by level of activism, served as a situational arousal of attitudes and beliefs. Where the situation made the attitudes salient, they were more likely to be acted upon. Where the situation minimized their significance, they were more likely to remain latent.

This effect of the level of campus activism showed especially with certain aspects of ideology (Appendix Tables 11.2 A and B). System blame related to all three forms of activism in 1970 much more highly at the two colleges where activism was more widespread (for men: the relationships between system blame and civil rights activism were .47 at the active, but only .12 at the inactive colleges; with student power activism .57 at the active, but only .16 at the inactive; with BSO membership .23 and .03, respectively; for women: with civil rights activism .30 at the active, but only .09 at the inactive; with student power .37 and .07, respectively; with BSO membership .19 and .01). Likewise, commitments to collective action differentiated whether students actually participated or not primarily at the two active campuses (for men: the relationships between preferences for collective action and civil rights activism were .33 at the active but only .11 at the inactive; with student power participation .48 and .16, respectively; with BSO membership .36 and .03; for women, differences in the size of the relationships were less striking: with civil rights activism .32 at the active and .18 at the inactive; with student power participation .36 and .10; and no relationship with BSO membership at either type). Concerns about self-determination also correlated with activism primarily where activism was more common (for men: the relationships between self-determination and civil rights activism was .39 at the active but .06 at the inactive colleges; with student power participation .62 and .09, respectively; with BSO membership .19 and .09; for women: with civil rights activism .32 at the active but only .11 at the inactive campuses; with student power, .49 and .14, respectively; with BSO membership .23 and .12). The other themes of nationalism related to activism in much the same fashion on both types of campuses. For example, militancy attitudes differentiated the male activists from other students regardless of campus activism level; they did not differentiate the women activists from nonactivists at either type. College effect is rarely thought about in these conditional (or mediating) terms in studies of institutional impact. Yet the capacity of an institution to encourage the individual to act on beliefs is a critical aspect of its effect. This should be particularly the case in higher education institutions since one of their primary functions, and products, is development of the student. Impact should not rest simply on whether a college changes the individual's beliefs and attitudes, but how it helps the student translate beliefs into meaningful commitments.

COLLEGE EXPERIENCES ASSOCIATED WITH ACTIVISM

We have seen that the colleges differed greatly in both 1964 and 1970 in student activism and in some aspects of ideology. These differences, great though they were, reflected average trends. Despite these differences between the institutions, the variation within each institution was also sizable. On even the most active campuses some students were committed activists, some completely uninvolved. In this section we explore some of the correlates of these within-college differences. We will look especially at the college experiences of activist and non-activist students. To a large extent we will show that both activists and nonactivists could be found within the same college because they experienced it very differently. In a sense they did not attend the "same" college. They participated in different extracurricular groups and identified with different campus subcultures.

The Intensive Study of Activism at College H in 1965 and 1968

The intensive four-year longitudinal study of one institution offers unusual data for exploring the experiences of activist students. It allows investigating whether activists showed the same pattern of experiences during the civil rights period as later when student power protests became more common. We interviewed students at the height of the college's involvement in one of the last mass demonstrations of the civil rights epoch in the spring of 1965 and again in the spring of 1968 during the last two months of campus unrest that focused on institutional policies. The longitudinal design also means we could trace the experiences of three groups of seniors in 1968: (1) stable activists, who had maintained active involvement in civil rights activities throughout their college years; (2) the activist dropouts, who had been active as freshmen but were no longer involved as seniors; and (3) the stable nonactivists, who had never taken part. Were the experiences that differentiated the activists from other students at the freshman level distinctive only of those activists who sustained their political participation or equally characteristic of those who later dropped out?

These data consistently demonstrated that the activists were integrated into the mainstream of campus life (Appendix Table 11.3). They were more active in extracurricular groups in 1965; they also were in 1968. Moreover, the students who had sustained their involvement in political action throughout their college years showed this pattern of campus leadership far more than the freshman activists who had later dropped away from political involvements. As freshmen the activists belonged to more groups and organizations on the campus: over half of them belonged to at least two groups while less than one-fourth of the nonactivists did. As seniors the stable activists stood out from both the dropouts and the stable nonactivists: 71 percent of the men and 77 percent of the women who had sustained their political activism belonged to at least two organizations, while among the dropouts the percent decreased to 42 percent of the men and 47 percent of the women and among the stable nonactivists 38 percent of both sexes.

Among the men it was also the stable activists who most often had held leadership positions in these campus groups: 76 percent of the men who were still activists as seniors had been an officer of some organization, 30 percent of them of at least two groups; only 40 percent of the dropouts and nonactivists had ever held office, and only 6 percent in two or more groups.

This heightened activity of the stable activists did not simply reflect participation in nontraditional or political groups; they had participated in traditional campus groups, too. As both freshmen and seniors the activists were as likely to have joined Greek organizations, and as seniors much more likely to have participated in campus government. A quarter of both the men and women who were still politically active as seniors also had served on the student government association, while only 6 percent of the other two groups had done so.

We asked the students about informal groupings as well. In 1965 we asked which, if any, of the following student types they felt similar to, which they would never want to be identified with, and which fit each of their three best friends on the campus.

Student Leaders. Students who think of themselves as leaders on the campus—students who are really influential around here.

Casual-type Students. Students with a relaxed attitude toward college.

The Student Union Crowd. Students who hang around the student union or spend a lot of time playing cards.

Students Interested in Political and Social Issues. Students who discuss political affairs—students interested in bringing political speakers to the campus—students concerned about Black issues in contemporary America.

The Intellectuals on Campus. Students who may or may not get good grades but who are really interested in talking about movies they have seen, books they are reading—students who like to analyze things, look for the meaning behind things.

The Really Serious Students. Students who are concerned about studying, keeping up with course work—students who care about achieving good grades.

Creative, Perhaps Somewhat Nonconformist Students. The literary types, writers or poets—musicians who spend a lot of time playing or listening to jazz or classical music—the dramatic types who are involved in acting or with the theater world.

In 1968 we asked these same questions and added a new group:

The Active Afro-American Students. Students who are very much involved in African heritage—students who may wear their hair and dress in a certain way—students who may be learning Swahili.

The results of these subcultural identifications show remarkable consistency (Appendix Table 11.3). As freshmen 67 percent of the activists but only 19 percent of the nonactivists had identified with the political types; also nearly a third of the activists but only 12 percent of the nonactivists felt they were similar to student leaders. While an equal number of both groups (about 20 percent) felt the student union crowd fit them, the casual type was four times more often accepted among the nonactivists as among the activists. Since the intellectual label likewise was accepted much more among the nonactivists, there seemed to be two types of nonactivists: intellectually identified nonparticipants, and casual students who hung around the student union. While sharing equally with the nonparticipants the student union identification, the activists were distinctively political and student leaders. This political cast went beyond their own self-descriptions. They much more often described their friends as political types: half of them said at least two of their three best friends were political types while none of the nonactivists said two of their friends were political and, indeed, only 17 percent said even one of their friends was. Even more impressive is the fact that 79 percent of the activists, but only 19 percent of the nonactivists, had among their three best friends at least one who participated in the SNCC-affiliated campus group that gave direction to the college's civil rights activities.

This pattern also continued to characterize the students who were still active as seniors, while the freshmen activists who later dropped their political involvements looked much more like the stable nonactivists as seniors. While all three groups identified equally often as student leaders (about 44 percent of each group), as the student union crowd (10 percent), as intellectuals (51 percent), as really serious students (41 percent), and as creative nonconformists (16 percent), over three times as many of the students who were still politically active as seniors identified with the political type. (Eighty-two percent of the stable activists but only 27 percent of the dropouts and 18 percent of the stable inactives accepted the political label.) Twice as many of the stable activists also described at least one of their three best friends as political. Many more of them also identified as Afro-American types: 28 percent of the stable activists but only 4 percent of the dropouts and none of the stable nonactivists viewed themselves as Afro-American types. A third of the stable activists also described at least one of their friends the same way, while less than 10 percent of the other two groups did. Moreover, just as the political identity continued to be distinctively activist, the casual type continued to be accepted by many more of the nonactivists at the senior level, just as it was at the freshman level. Fifty-six percent of the stable nonactivists and 39 percent of those who had dropped their activism but only 5 percent of the stable activists identified as the casual type at the senior level. Acceptance of being casual among the nonactivists also implied sub-cultural affiliations: a third of the two inactive groups said at least two of their three friends were also casual types while none of the stable activists viewed two friends as casual and only 15 percent even described one of their friends that way.

Repeatedly we learn that activists thought about themselves and their friends in distinctively political terms, while nonactivists considered themselves and their friends as distinctively casual. These groups shared many self-descriptions, but they parted company both at the freshman and senior levels in their identifications and associations as political and casual. Also, this demarcation held only for students who had sustained their freshman involvement in action. The dropouts were just as unlikely to identify as political and just as likely to view themselves as casual as were the students who had never participated in social action during their college years.

Although other studies have linked activism to certain academic experiences, especially to particular majors and academic units, notably to liberal arts and to social science and humanities majors within liberal arts, our results showed reasonably equal participation rates across the academic divisions of this one college. At both the freshman and senior level activists and nonactivists were equally spread across its eight major academic units. Activists and nonactivists were also equally involved in professional clubs and groups that honored academic excellence. This was true at both the freshman and senior levels. They did differ, however, in how much contact with faculty they reported (Appendix Table 11.3). As freshmen, two-thirds of the men and one-half of the women activists reported contact outside of the classroom with at least one faculty member. In sharp contrast, two-thirds of the nonactivists of both sexes reported no contact with faculty beyond the class room. In 1968 this heightened faculty contact among activists still prevailed, although only among men. Moreover, the men who had sustained their activism over their college years stood out: 83 percent of them but only 51 percent of the dropouts and stable nonactivists said there was a least one faculty member whom they had gotten to know outside of the classroom. More of the stable men activists (88 percent) than dropouts (68 percent) or stable non-activists (62 percent) also said they had gone to faculty members to talk about their futures and to get help with graduate school or job planning. Among those who had sought out faculty for this purpose, more activists (51 percent) also felt that the contact had proved very helpful; only 12 percent of the other two groups were that positive.

Finally, the most extreme measure of faculty contact, the percent who mentioned a faculty member among their three best friends at college, likewise distinguished activist men from other seniors. Eighteen percent of the men who were still active as seniors but only 4 percent of the dropouts and none of the stable nonactivists included a faculty person as a close friend.

The Black-oriented activities on a checklist of campus events also distinguished the male activists from other seniors. The list included many traditional, collegiate-social activities: the Paul Winter jazz group, the Gerry Butler Show, the homecoming parade, the homecoming dance, the student government association election, Greek night, the play *Waiting for Godot*. Participation in these was independent of activist involvements. But the men who were still politically active as seniors had more often than either the dropouts or stable nonactivists attended events with special implications for Black consciousness: 84 percent of the activists but 58 percent of the dropouts and 46 percent of the nonactivists had attended the Miriam Makeba concert; 32 percent of the activists but only 15 percent of the dropouts and 10 percent of the nonactivists had attended a symposium called the South African Speakout; 26 percent of the activists but none of the other two groups had gone to the film "Come Back Africa;" 52 percent of the activists but only 14 percent of the dropouts and 10 percent of the nonactivists had listened to a lecture by Ron Karenda.

To summarize: The college experiences reported by activist and nonactivist students both at the freshman and senior level showed that they equally often joined fraternities and sororities, participated in traditional collegiate social events, identified with the student union crowd, identified with really serious and creative nonconformist types of students, and at the senior level with intellectuals and student leaders; they also majored in much the same areas and participated equally in professional clubs and academic excellence groups on the campus. But the activists at the freshman level and those who had remained so through the four years of college had belonged to more campus groups; at the senior level they also had held more leadership positions and more often participated in student government; they expressed distinctively political identifications and much more often cast their friends as political types as well; as seniors they showed stronger Black commitments, reflected both in identifying more often as Afro-American types and in attending in larger numbers the prominent Black-oriented concerts, films, and lectures at the college. They reported more contact with faculty.

This is a picture of socially integrated students who just as often took part in the traditional aspects of college life but were even generally more active, particularly in political ways. These were not marginal students—not as freshmen, not as seniors. The factors that predisposed them to become activists in the first place, especially the fact that they more often came to college from urban backgrounds, may also have predisposed them to show this generally active, hooked-instance toward campus life. We do not argue cause and effect here. We do not know if activism encouraged broader involvements or vice versa. But the results do impressively attest that activism was embedded in a broader set of college experiences; that these experiences indicate that activists in no way stood apart from traditional college life as they expressed their heightened concerns about political and social issues.

The Cross-Sectional Study of Three Kinds of Activism in Six Colleges in 1970

The 1970 cross-sectional study lets us ask two further questions about the campus experiences of activist students. Did the picture that characterized the civil rights activists at the one college we studied intensively generalize to other colleges or only to campuses where activism itself was reasonably widespread, as it was at that one college? Did that same set of college experiences apply equally to civil rights participants, to student power activities, and to BSO members?

The answer to the first question is clear-cut. The campus involvements of civil rights activists were very different at the two active and two inactive colleges in 1970. *Among women the difference simply shows that it was only at the active colleges that civil rights activists participated in distinctive aspects of the campus* (Appendix Table 11.4B). At these two active colleges the women who were involved in civil rights in 1970 showed much the same set of experiences that were distinctive of activists at the college we just discussed: they saw themselves as political and as Afro-American types; they belonged to more campus organizations in which they more often held office; they especially participated more often in political and Afro-American groups. *Among men two different patterns of campus involvements emerged at the active and inactive colleges* (Appendix Table 11.4A). On the active campuses men who were active in civil rights in 1970, like the women activists on those campuses and like the activists we just described from our four-year longitudinal study of one college, were distinctively identified with political and Afro-American types, generally more active in campus organizations and in campus organizations and in campus leadership, more active in political and Afro-American organizations. In addition they more often participated in professional clubs and academic excellence groups; they also more often reported having taken Black studies courses. On the two inactive campuses men who were still involved in civil rights in 1970 did not show any of these distinctive experiences. Rather than thinking of themselves as political and Afro-American types, they identified as casual, creative nonconformists who were not serious students and who hung around the student union crowd. They were no more or no less active in campus organizations than other students on their campuses who did not participate in civil rights activities. Putting this together with what we learned about the implications of ideology on the active and inactive campuses, we see two very different profiles of activism, at least among the men students.

CHART A.   **Profile of the College Experiences of Men Civil Rights Activists on Active and Inactive Campuses**

Active Campuses	Inactive Campuses
Ideological correlates of activism:	*Ideological correlates of activism:*
1. System blame.	1. Commitment to community control.
2. Preference for collective strategies.	2. Approval of the political use of violence.
3. Concern with self-determination.	
4. Commitment to community control.	
5. Approval of the political use of violence.	
Subcultural identifications:	*Subcultural identifications:*
1. Political types.	1. Rejecting the label "really serious" student.
2. Afro-American types.	2. Creative, perhaps somewhat nonconformist.
	3. Casual types.
	4. Student union crowd.
Formal group memberships:	*Formal group memberships:*
1. Belonged to more organizations.	No relationships.
2. More leadership experience.	
3. Greater experience in student government and policy groups.	
4. Membership in Afro-American groups.	
5. Membership in professional, departmental clubs.	
6. Recognition by academic excellence clubs.	
Curricular experiences:	*Curricular experiences:*
1. Taken more Black studies courses.	No relationships.

These results suggest that when activism itself was more common-place, if not admired, the student leaders with political interests and ideological commitments participated most actively in civil rights action as well as in the formal government and academic clubs on the campus. When activism was "in," the "in" students took part. More-over, their political beliefs became salient to the question of partici-pation since there was ample opportunity to express what they be-lieved. In contrast, when campus activism involved many fewer stu-dents, more marginal students who thought of themselves as non-conformists and who indeed did not participate in unusual numbers in the traditional campus organizations atypically appeared in the activist subgroup. Since we will show in the next section that this nonconformist, casual image characterized only the civil rights activists but not the student power activists or BSO members on these inactive campuses, it was especially the kind of action that focused on off-campus issues and targets that attracted this type of male student who remained relatively marginal to traditional campus life. This makes a good deal of sense. When activism was not only rare but also oc-curred off campus, activism was the culture of students who were less integrated in traditional campus life and who thought of themselves as nonacademic and nonconformist types.

The second question that the 1970 data clarified was whether these experience patterns of the civil rights activists applied to other types of activism as well. The results of investigating the experience correlates of student power activists, civil rights participants, and BSO members were sharper among the men than among the women. The pattern for women was much the same for the men but the relationships were not as large (Appendix Table 11.4B). We describe here only the results for men.

For men the activism-campus experience correlates depended greatly on level of campus activism (Appendix Table 11.4A). On active campuses the three types of male activists shared much the same col-lege experiences—the ones we have already described as distinguish-ing civil rights activists from nonactivists on those campuses. At the inactive colleges, however, different patterns of experiences did charac-terize the three types of activists: the nonconformist image of the civil rights activist did not characterize either the student power activists or BSO members. Student power activists on these campuses were by no means marginal. They belonged to more organizations, had exercised greater campus leadership, and especially had participated in unusual numbers in government, policy, and political groups on the campus. They were hooked into traditional campus lives. The civil rights activists were not. Likewise, BSO members did not share the marginal stance of the civil rights activists but, rather than showing the generally greater involvement in campus groups of the student power activists, the BSO members differed from nonmembers only in associations that were clearly Afro-American in orientation. They identified more with the Afro-American campus subculture; they belonged to more Afro-American groups beyond the one that provided their classification as BSO members; they were more active in policy committees but not unusually active in other formal organizations on the campus. Moreover, it was only the BSO members who stood out for having been relatively more exposed to Black-oriented curriculums.

The picture that emerged of civil rights activists at the college we studied intensively did indeed generalize to other colleges but only to those where participation rates were reasonably high. Men and women civil rights activists on active campuses repeatedly turned out to be campus leaders who were generally active in campus organizations, particularly policy and political groups, and who participated in a political subculture on the campus. They had closer relationships with faculty. In 1970 they also had more often taken Black studies courses. A similar picture also characterized the male student power activists and BSO members on active campuses. At inactive colleges, however, three different experience patterns were associated for men with the three types of activism we studied in 1970. Civil rights activists on inactive campuses were nonconformists who remained relatively marginal to both the academic and "straight" collegiate-social aspects of college life. Student power activists were more socially integrated: they belonged to more campus groups and more often held leadership positions, particularly in student government and policy-setting groups. BSO members were unusually oriented to Blackness—to an Afro-American subculture, to Afro-American groups, and to Black studies.

A CASE STUDY: THE EFFECT OF ACTIVISM

We have just seen that civil rights activists, at least on reasonably involved campuses, participated in a subculture of politically identified students. Activists also stood out for their generally heightened activity and for their leadership in both political and traditional campus groups. They got to know faculty better. They participated at least as often in collegiate-social events and much more often in Black-oriented cultural and political events on the campus. Did their involvement in activism and the attendant college experiences change them in any way?

The data from the intensive longitudinal case study allow an unusual opportunity to study the effect of activism on students. The fact that the 1965 campus movement emerged between the time we administered questionnaires during freshman orientation and readministered them to freshmen at the end of the year provided a natural experiment on the effects of social action at this one college. It is rare that a collective movement just happens to occur in a setting where pertinent "before" measures had previously been collected; but without controlling for initial characteristics that might have predisposed certain people to take part, we do not know if later differences between activists and nonactivists say anything about the effect of action. In fact, almost all studies of student protest have depended on interviewing or testing activists only after their participation. Thus, our study offered an unusual social experiment. Moreover, the fact that we subsequently followed these freshmen activists through their college years offers even rarer data on persistence of change. Suppose the effect of action in the freshmen year were to encourage a nationalist perspective among the activists. Did that change in attitude persist through the four years of college, so that the freshman activists were still more nationalistic than other students as seniors? Or did the effect of activism in the freshman year depend on whether the students sustained their political involvements through the next four years? Does persistence depend on continued experience? Here the critical comparison is between freshman activists who were still active in civil rights as seniors and freshman activists who subsequently dropped out of political action.

The results from both the freshman and senior follow-up studies consistently showed that action affected ideology but had no effect on the students' personal goals or achievement motivation. First, the personal characteristics that were unaffected by action—action had no effect on the following characteristics either at the freshman or senior level:

Aspirations. Intention of going to graduate school, level of job aspiration, desire to get married, grades aspired for.

Expectancies. Certainty of going to graduate school, overall expectancy of achieving the desired job, expectancy of reaching the grade point average goal, certainty of getting married.

Assessment of competencies. Academic self-confidence, self-assessment of competence for desired job.

Achievement anxiety. Fear of failure, worries about future security.

The only motivational characteristic that was influenced by the experience of activism was the sense of personal control, and then more among men than among women. Freshmen men who had been active in the local campaign ended the year with a stronger sense of personal control, after adjusting for initial differences between them and the men who did not become involved in any civil rights activities that year. As seniors, both the men and the women activists expressed stronger efficacy. Moreover, it was only the freshmen who had sustained their involvement in action who stood out as seniors; the freshman activists who dropped out of action looked, as seniors, much like those who had never participated at all.

What about academic performance? Data from other studies on the performance records of activists offer only equivocal answers: some show that activists, especially radical left activists, perform better in college;[7] some show no differences.[8] To our knowledge no studies support the stereotyped expectation that activists perform worse than other students. Our results generally showed little difference in the grade point averages of activists and nonactivists. Since entrance scores were related to activism in the freshman year, it was important to control for verbal and quantitative scores. (The higher test-score students subsequently became more involved in political action: 47 percent of the students with above median scores but only 26 percent with below median scores were active in the freshman year). After adjusting for those differences, the activists and nonactivists showed very similar grade-point averages at the end of the freshman year. By the end of the senior year the relationship between participation and performance depended on the sex of the student. After adjusting for entrance test scores, the women who had sustained their freshman participation in civil rights ended the senior year with the highest grades; those who subsequently dropped away from political action had achieved almost exactly the same grades as the stable nonactivists. (On a 4-point system, the women stable activists showed 2.85, or close to a B average, while the dropouts and student nonactivists had 2.38 and 2.39, respectively.) In contrast, the cumulative grades of the three groups did not differ statistically among men. [The previously active men showed a slight edge (2.45) on the stable activists (2.31) and on the stable nonactivists (2.22).] Since only the women activists stood out and there were no differences at the freshman level for either sex, we feel safest concluding that the activists performed much like other students at this school.

7. Zelda F. Gamson, Jeffrey Goodman, and Gerald Gurin, "Radicals, Moderates and By-standers During a University Protest." Paper read at the August, 1967 Meetings of the American Sociological Association, San Francisco.
8. Jesse D. Geller and G. Howard, "Student Activism and the War in Vietnam," mimeographed (Yale University: Department of Psychology, N.D.); Richard G. Braungart and Margaret M. Braungart, "Social and Political Correlates of Protest Attitudes and Behavior Among College Youth: A Case Study," Unpublished Paper, University of Maryland, 1971.

At the very least, however, these results conclusively show that activists performed no worse than other students. Given the beliefs of some administrators, often fostered by a few notoriously antiacademic activists, these results showing similar performance records of activists and nonactivists themselves are very important.

Ideology was the area of personal change that was demonstrably tied to experience and activism. (See Chart B for a summary of all effects of action.) Activism during the freshman year produced ideological effects; the freshmen who had sustained their political commitment still stood out ideologically at the end of the senior year. Persistence of the effect depended on the continued action. The freshman activists who later became inactive shared, as seniors, almost the same ideological perspectives as the freshmen who had never participated in social action at all. Generally, the effect prevailed on all the measures we have discussed as precursors of nationalism.

We noted in Chapter 10 that the study of freshman change indicated that the correlation between taking action and holding the social system rather than individuals themselves responsible for race inequities primarily occurred as an effect of activism. The freshmen who subsequently took part in the local movement did not enter college with different analyses of racial inequities. At the end of the year their explanations of inequality differed greatly (Appendix Tables 10.3 and 11.5 A and B). Activists much more often talked about discrimination and systematic exclusion of Blacks from the opportunities and rewards of this society; nonactivists still held some of the older, victim explanations that put the burden of responsibility on Blacks themselves. Shifting from the victim to a system analysis when most Americans continued to believe in the American dream of unlimited mobility possibilities for the just and the deserving required an enormous shakeup in the thinking of many students. One student who was active in the movement that year put it this way:

> I learned a whole new history about myself in this thing. I do not mean that is the only reason the movement is important, but it sure does help. As a kid I really believed those lies—not just as a kid—I guess I really believed that stuff all the way through college, always trying to use the right tone of voice, dress the right way—man, I really let it put me in a straight jacket. That's why SNCC is so important; they go out there in those clay hills and really teach people about themselves, about how it really is.

Activism also affected the students' ideologies about the role of social and individual determinants of success in the culture at large. While the freshmen who became active and those who stayed uninvolved

CHART B.   Effects of Civil Rights Action Among Students at College H

Significant effects on:	No effects on:

	Individual Achievement
	    Aspirations: Desire to go to graduate school, level of job aspiration, grades aspired for.
	    Performance: Cumulative grade point average.

	Achievement Motivation *Expectancies:* Certainty of going to graduate school, overall expectancy of achieving desired job, expectancy of reaching grade point average goal, certainty of getting married.
Competency-based expectancies: Sense of personal control.	*Competency-based expectancies:* Academic self-confidence, self-assessment of competence for desired job.

Ideology
    System blame
    External control ideology
    Preference for collective action
    Specific strategies and groups approved
    Attitudes toward campus governance: Academic freedom policies among men.
	Attitudes toward campus governance: College control of student political action; parietal policies among men and women; academic freedom policies among women.

in civil rights entered college with much the same attitudes about the Protestant work ethic, the activists less often held to a rigid individualistic interpretation of success and failure after they had participated in the local movement (Appendix Tables 10.3 and 11.5 A and B). Although their average scores on the Control Ideology scale showed they still felt individual attributes were more important than external forces, this preference for individualism was less pronounced than among the nonactivist students.

Preference for collective action as a social change strategy likewise showed the impact of the activist experience (Appendix Tables 10.3, 11.5 A and B). First, students who advocated collective action as the best way to deal with the realities of discrimination were predisposed to action: freshmen who subsequently participated actively had entered college the previous fall, when the student body was not yet activated, already expressing stronger commitments to collective action. But activism also had an effect. Controlling for these initial differences, we found that the freshmen activists completed their freshman year still preferring, more than other freshman, a collective approach to the problems they also interpreted, more than others, as caused by social and economic forces.

Interviews we conducted with students at the height of the 1965 ferment brought out the impact the movement had on these aspects of ideology. When asked what kinds of things ought to be done, the students who were not engaged in the local movement were more likely to talk about self- or group-betterment strategies: "We should work to improve Black people—try and make a better impression, show them that they must always think that someone is looking at them as Blacks"; "Actually what has to be done is that the Black person has to do a little better than the next man; be a little more careful; strive a little harder; he's constantly up for inspection and has to prove that he's just as good as anyone else"; "My responsibility is being an American, not a Black person. If I can help a person who is white, blue, or green, I will if he accepts my help in a responding manner—that is, begins to help himself"; "The problem with a lot of Blacks is that they have not really tried to help themselves." The distancing of self from the group is also striking in these comments. In contrast, the activists were much more likely to analyze the social forces that act on Black people and to exhibit a sense of identification as part of the group. "It's the system itself that is one of the main things that keeps us from getting what is ours—you've got to work to attack the system, change it at the guts, not just hope it gets the talented tenth into the front desk jobs."

The meaning of the activist experience showed also in the way the students reacted to a question in the interview about the society they would like to live in and how they felt about American society in general. Most students chose the statement that said, "The present American system and the life it promises would be a full one if it provided for full integration of all races in the system—except for the racial issue I have no basic criticism of American society." A few, 20 of the 180 students interviewed, said they would not accept the American system even if there were integration. They preferred a statement that advocated "a radical change in the whole economic base of the American system, a revolution that goes much beyond race, challenging all the economic injustice of this society." Significantly, 16 of these 20 students were highly involved in the local move-ment. It was not just a matter of being pro- or anti-integration; it was that these activists were beginning to think about the way the social and economic system operates, especially about our system's capacity or lack of capacity to incorporate the underclass.

The specific strategies and civil rights groups they approved of dif-fered also from students who stayed on the sidelines. One consistent result showed that the students who did not participate at all entered college more undecided about what strategies and groups showed the most promise; more inactives entered with no opinions about all the groups and approaches we asked about. Their subsequent inactivity probably stemmed from their rather low interest in civil rights in general. They also knew less about important political figures when they entered college. Among men only 48 percent of the nonactivists but 72 percent of the students who later took part in the local campaign correctly identified at least half of the 10 people we asked about; among women the comparable figures were 25 percent of the non-activists but 62 percent of the activists.

The most committed of the activists also stood out in predictable ways not only from the nonactivists but also from students who attended all the local events but did not take part in the many strategy meetings of the campus leadership group. Those who became only moderately active entered college significantly more approving of groups known for conventional, reform methods—specifically the NAACP Legal Defense Fund, Biracial Councils, and the Urban League. In contrast, the core group of activists were initially more positive about more militant strategies and groups—rent strikes, economic boycotts, school boycotts, SNCC, and the formation of a Black political party. After controlling for these initial differences, the effect of action was to heighten the students' commitments to the groups and strategies that were predictive of how involved they became in the first place: the moderates still showed strongest approval of traditional groups; the activists ended the freshman year more supportive of militant strategies. Activism was also tied to an unusual positive shift in support of Black political parties. The ideology of the local leadership group rejected the notion of elite leadership, particularly where it meant Blacks acting as brokers to the "man downtown." Animosity was felt particularly for traditional leaders and groups who were believed to accommodate to whites. On the local scene, this took the form of criticizing those who advocated "going slow" in nominating Blacks for local office in an effort to convince the white community of their desire to "work with them." The issue of Black political power was becoming uppermost among the core of activist leaders on the campus. The ways that the activists' predispositions were heightened through their activist experience seemed to reflect the thinking of the local group: their negative shift away from the NAACP, of whom they were initially more critical anyway, reflected rejection of traditional leadership; their shift away from the biracial councils expressed their rejection of accommodation strategies; their increased support of a Black political party showed their advocacy of a mass movement of Black people who would wield power through coalitions rather than integration with white pressure groups. In contrast, the moderates' support for traditional groups was maintained; they also showed an unusual increase in support of both demonstrations and sit-ins. While it was true that local activities were largely these sorts of direct actions, the activists were highly critical of depending on this tried and "untrue" approach. In the strategy meetings that the moderates missed the activists argued long and heatedly about turning to less conventional approaches that would do more than open up lunch counters. Moderate action seemed to reinforce prior strategy preferences or bring the moderates to the point where the southern movement had previously been, particularly to heighten support for strategies the usefulness of which was already being questioned by committed activists during what would turn out to be the death knell of the demonstration period.

What about the persistence of these ideological effects of action? The effect of activism in increasing social determinism and system blame persisted only if students continued to take part in civil rights through their college years (Appendix Tables 11.5 A and B). As seniors the activist dropouts held almost identical views to the students who had never participated in civil rights. Both the dropouts and the stable nonactivists more often focused on individual deficiencies in explaining race inequities, although admittedly a little less so than at the end of their freshman year; they also still showed greater individualism in their general theories of success and failure. The students who were still active as seniors clearly stood out: they more often blamed systematic discrimination for the status differentials of Blacks and whites; they professed views that gave equal balance to internal and external determinants of success in the culture at large. Although they did not cast these beliefs in the language of decolonization, their reanalysis of the relationships between Blacks and whites showed their heightened Black consciousness even at a time that nationalist thinking was less commonplace.

Heightening of collective commitments through acting collectively persisted even for the freshmen who later dropped out of civil rights activities (Appendix Tables 11.5 A and B). As seniors they were still significantly more collective in their strategy preferences than the stable nonactivists. But it was the stable activists who were the most committed to collective action. They advocated collective action over individual mobility approaches more than both the other groups. Consistent with this, they departed from both groups on questions of Black Nationalism that we asked for the first time in their senior year. They more often approved of leaders who stood for nationalism; they favored separatism more than other students; they more often viewed armed defense as a right and a necessity; they advocated self-determination through Black political strength and community development.

We also asked seniors how they felt they had changed during their college years. Their subjective views supported the ideological changes that emerged from comparing their actual scores as freshmen and seniors. The stable activists felt they had developed greater interest in politics and world affairs, in African culture and heritage, in social issues and problems, in civil rights, and in issues concerning Blacks in America. Although a majority of even the stable nonactivists also said their interests in these issues had increased since coming to college, a significantly larger proportion of the students who were still politically active as seniors said they had experienced a marked increase in these matters. In contrast, the three groups of seniors expressed much the same level of change in nonideological characteristics. They fairly equally talked about greater clarity in their occupational plans and general direction to take in life, increase in ambition, and self-confidence, and greater enthusiasm about learning. They also as often said they had not changed much in their interests in art and music, their religious beliefs, their attitudes toward fraternities and sororities, or their feelings about getting married. Once again we see that activism affected students' ideological commitments while it had little impact on their personal goals òr their nonideological attitudes and feelings.

chapter 12

Collective Achievement: Summing Up

Students attending historically Black colleges during the sixties participated in large numbers in social change efforts. They triggered the decade of protest with the student sit-in movement. They led student participation in the civil rights movement in the South. Whereas only 20 to 30 percent of the students in the nation at large had participated in political action by 1965, the participation figure for students in Black colleges was closer to 70 percent. Later on the scope of student protest broadened to include many more of the nation's universities and colleges; even so more Black than white institutions experienced campus unrest during the academic year of 1967-1968 when student protest reached its highest peak. Also more Black than white students took part in the increasingly campus-based action of the second half of the decade. Three-quarters of the students in our sample reported in 1970 that they had participated in some form of political activity during their college years. By contrast, both the Harris and Gallup polls of 1967 and 1968 showed that the proportion of the nation's college students who had participated politically was still only about 20 percent.

While the rate of student action, and the participation gap between Black and white students, remained constant throughout the decade, the targets of protest changed greatly. Protest about racial issues had never assumed as great significance for white as for Black students. With growing commitment to the Vietnam War, the focus of concern for white students increasingly shifted to the war and to the university's role in it—through offering ROTC, allowing "military research," providing facilities for recruiters from companies with military contracts, and investing in companies whose policies were viewed as economically imperialistic. While university racial practices were attacked by some white students, most of the campus targets related either to grievances about governance or to the Vietnam War. Black students likewise turned inward to campus protest in the second half of the decade after they had become convinced that our domestic racial problems would not be daunted by demands for civil rights or by the strategies developed in the civil rights movement. Superficially like the shift in student political action nationwide, the growth of campus-based action among Black students was viewed more and more, by the leaders at least, as aspects of Black Nationalism. On white campuses Black students had important effects in reshaping admission policies and in developing curricula that would relate to the larger number of Blacks that were being admitted. At the same time students on Black campuses were making major demands of their administrators and boards of trustees for changes in the substance and character of their own educational experiences. Demanding greater voice in campus governance represented to these students on Black campuses their commitment to the self-determination of Black people. They wanted to "decolonize" Black colleges, to make them truly relevant for Black people. As they came to feel that Blacks must control their own institutions, they understandably translated their broad concerns about political nationalism into a desire to determine educational policies of Black colleges. By the end of the decade the action of Black students reflected the impressive shifts that had taken place in their political and racial ideologies.

Just as stability marked what happened to the students' aspirations and achievement motivation between 1964 and 1970, change marked what happened to their analyses of the race situation in America. By 1970 students were more aware of systematic determinants of racial inequities; they far less often blamed Black people themselves for their income, educational, and occupational status. The questions that probed for causes of inequity showed 20 to 30 percent shifts away from a victim analysis to blame of the social and economic system for systematic discrimination against Black people. Reanalyzing the history of Black people in America also meant they questioned their previously unrelenting faith in the federal government and their generally optimistic posture about change. They became much less optimistic about eliminating discrimination in American society. This shift from optimism to pessimism was even more marked than the shift to system blame. Struck by the complexity of the economic and social problems they increasingly viewed as responsible for racial inequities, they also changed what they advocated should be done about discrimination and racism. While ambivalent, most students in 1964 preferred individual mobility and group betterment strategies over collective action. With 30 to 40 percent shifts on questions that asked students to choose between individual and collective strategies, the vast majority favored collective action by 1970. These shifts did not mean that students were disinterested in their own mobility and individual goals; we have already seen that they were as motivated for personal achievement in 1970 as in 1964. The shifts in action preferences did indicate, however, a major departure from individualism to collectivism in their theories of social change.

Many students viewed these ideological shifts as the development of collective consciousness and collective commitments that set the stage for supporting Black Nationalism as a cultural and political ideology. Revolutionary-collectivist theory, especially as presented by Fanon, gained a hearing on Black campuses just as these changes in the students' thinking were occurring. The language of campus political debate reflected the impact of Fanon and exponents of Black Nationalism in the American scene. Growth in consciousness and collectivism was seen as a developmental progression. First, individuals had to become aware of collective oppression, thereby refusing to accept responsibility for the gross inequities between the oppressor and oppressed. Then, individualism could be replaced by collective commitments. The shifts from blame of individual Blacks to system blame implied this awareness of collective oppression and, at the same time, expressed a positive group identity that came from refusing to blame one's own group for the inequities it faces. Rejecting a rigid Protestant ethic explanation of success also implied the new consciousness by questioning the legitimacy of the dominant group's cultural norms, which, when internalized by subordinated groups, produces self-blame for their life situation. Seeing oppression as the collective experience of the group, the conversion from category to group, students then stressed the necessity of group rather than individual action. They had shifted to the need for group action to alter the inequities they had come to believe were the collective experience of Black Americans. By these shifts they were predisposed to favor the political analysis of Black Nationalism.

The students' political analyses of Black Nationalism were represented by four ideas, some approved more, some less, in 1970. Almost all students approved of the notion of developing Black corporate structures. Nearly as popular as Black economic development was the idea of community control, especially control of the schools attended by Black children. Far less consensually approved was the insistence in militant nationalist ideology that some acts which are defined by the dominant group as violent may be necessary to the struggle for liberation. Acceptance of the political use of violence, and in this sense approval of militancy, was the only aspect of nationalism about which men and women disagreed. Women disapproved of militancy even more than the men. Least approved by both men and women was the argument that self-determination must be achieved through separatism. These four political dimensions, interrelated but conceptually distinct, were all relevant for explaining which students took part in collective action in 1970. Commitment to the cultural symbols of an African identity proved to be clearly separate from acceptance of the political ideas of nationalism as well as irrelevant for participation in political action.

The tie between ideology and action remained intact even as the targets of action, form of action, and content of the ideology shifted over the decade of the sixties. In 1964 when system blame, questioning of the work ethic as determining success in the culture at large, and commitment to collective action were less commonplace, those students who had already developed collective consciousness and commitments were most active in civil rights activities. Their unusually strong preference for group action served as both a source and consequence of their action. Their focus on social forces in explaining racial inequities was mostly the result, rather than the source, of action. The longitudinal study of one college showed that freshmen who subsequently became active in the local civil rights group entered college more committed to collective action but with views about inequities no different from those held by freshmen who were later only moderately involved or who took no part at all. By the end of the freshman year their explanations of race inequities and their stance toward the Protestant Ethic as a cultural norm departed greatly from the less active freshmen. In 1970 when collective consciousness of racial oppression had shifted to the point where system blame was the modal response, the students who expressed the strongest social determinism and preference for group action over individual mobility as strategies of change were still most active politically, both in civil rights activities and in student power protest. Likewise in 1970 all the dimensions of political nationalism related positively to student activism among men. All aspects except approval of violence as a political tool related to activism among women. The ideological differences between the active and inactive students applied to all six colleges we studied in 1970, but they assumed striking proportions at the two where student activism was particularly widespread.

In contrast to these consistent ideological differences between activists and nonactivists, the sense of personal efficacy, sometimes suggested in social psychological discussion of collective movements as necessary to turn discontent into effective social action, distinguished activists from other students only in 1964. In 1970 the sense of personal control was simply irrelevant for action. This is one way in which the change in mood and in the targets of action conditioned the social-psychological correlates of activism. In 1964 the civil rights movement was personalized. The individual could realistically believe that personal action would matter in changing social conditions. However recalcitrant Black activists found local and state officials in the South, they believed that the federal government, especially the Justice Department, and the national press were behind their efforts to change voting rights and public accommodations discrimination. After the Mississippi Summer Project in 1964 and the final burst of mass demonstrations in the spring of 1965, southern activists shifted their focus to problems, such as unemployment and poverty, whose nature defied obvious or personalized forms of action. They doubted more and more whether previous bases of support could be depended upon. It was no longer viable to believe that the individual alone could alter the course of events. By 1970 the students believed in the theme of nationalism, that only a group determined to act together could alter injustice. The conditions that promoted the growth of nationalism also diminished the significance of individual action, and the individuals' sense of efficacy as a precursor of action.

Were these activists who focused so much on external forces as the critical determinants of success in life merely expressing a sense of powerlessness that can lead to expressive outbursts of anger? Did their ideology reflect powerlessness? Was their action expressive? We have argued that they were neither personally powerless nor was their action short-lived, spontaneous, and expressive. In fact, the students who sustained frequent involvement in civil rights for at least a year and were associated with a leadership group that took responsibility for coordinating local activities—in short those whose action was planned, instrumental, and sustained—were the most external on the system blame and control ideology indices in 1964. Likewise in 1970 it was the students who had sustained their activity over their college years who stood out as especially external. These sustained activists were at once more external in their ideologies and maintained about the same level of personal power or efficacy as students who had never participated or students whose commitment to social action had been short-lived. These data challenge much of the discussion of urban revolts and college student protest that is cast, erroneously we believe, as the expressive action of the alienated. The social action of the students we have studied reflects their awareness of social determination and their collective proclivities that combined into an activist ideology that was at once "external" but not "powerless."

The analyses we conducted of the social roots of activism highlighted the significance of opportunity for participation and relative freedom from reprisals in accounting for participation in civil rights. Activity in student power issues later in the decade depended very little on the social background of the students. But students who continued to be active in civil rights, even at the end of the decade, were more often from urban settings. Data from the cross-sectional study in 1964, from the longitudinal followup in 1968 of seniors at one of those colleges, and from the cross-sectional study in 1970 all showed the special significance of rural-urban background for civil rights activism. Rural-urban setting influenced students in two ways. Growing up on a farm or a village reduced participation. Attending a college in a rural setting also did. Growing up in the rural South and attending a college in a rural site virtually precluded participation. Rural students repeatedly talked of their lack of opportunity for participation since most southern campaigns occurred at least in small towns and generally in larger ones. Rural students found their chance to participate only at college. They also cited their fears of reprisal against their families. In 1964 many of their parents were still engaged in tenant farming. They worried, quite realistically, lest their parents be thrown off their places or suffer from other economic hardships because their children had taken part in the civil rights movement. Most students, even the sons and daughters of professionals, mentioned fears of economic consequences to their families as prominent reasons for staying uninvolved or as sources of anxiety once they had become involved. Farm families, however, faced the greatest threat. Physical brutality, burning of homes and churches, and shots in the night were all more prevalent in the rural South.

These results point up the differences in Black and white student activism. Background factors, especially religion and social status, that have proved to be critical determinants of white activism were either irrelevant or operated very differently for Black students. Religion consistently failed to distinguish activists from nonactivists. Social status, altogether less important than rural-urban background, showed a curvilinear rather than linear relationship to activism as it does among white students. It was the most elite white students who were the most active and radical, at least through the better part of the sixties. It was the Black students from families with only moderate incomes and educational attainments who were the most active. Even more striking is the fact that rural-urban background, the factor most related to the civil rights activism of the Black students we studied, is never mentioned as critical determinant of student political action in the voluminous literature on activism of white students. To be sure, the white radical student is typically described as urban, since most studies have been conducted at elite institutions whose students are predominantly urban anyway. The few national studies of activism have not pointed to rural-urban background as a strong determinant of action in either civil rights or in protests about the Vietnam War.

Analyses of institutional influences showed sizable college differences in activism rates. Many more students at certain colleges than at others had participated in civil rights activities both in 1964 and 1970; the same was true of involvement in student power activities in 1970. These college differences continued to be significant even after controlling for the entering students' rural-urban backgrounds that influenced who participated in civil rights activities.

Ideology was a different matter. Institutional differences were sizable only regarding their students' collective action commitments and their attitudes toward traditional college governance. Most other aspects of the system attitudes that predisposed students to nationalism and of nationalism itself were subscribed to at much the same level in most of the colleges. While meaningful differences between the two most extreme institutions could be noted for many dimensions of Black Nationalism, most of the colleges falling between the two extremes showed remarkably homogeneous climates. In general, most students at most colleges strongly supported cultural nationalism and also favored, although less universally, the basic aspects of political nationalism.

Moving within the college to examine the kinds of college experiences that were associated with political activism, we found consistently that activists were remarkably integrated into the mainstream of campus life. This was true of the civil rights activists we studied in the longitudinal study at one college and of both the civil rights activists and student power activists, at least on active campuses, in the study of six colleges in 1970. Activists saw themselves as distinctively political and Afro-American students; they belonged to more organizations in which they more often held office; they especially participated more often in student government and policy groups on the campus, although they just as often (more often in 1970) joined fraternities and sororities and took part in traditional collegiate-social life of the colleges as well. In addition to casting themselves as political, they more often described their best friends as political and Afro-American types, also. Moreover, just as the political identity was distinctively activist, the casual label was accepted by many more nonactivists. Acceptance of being a casual type who took a sort of relaxed attitude toward college also implied subcultural affiliations for the nonactivist since a third of them said at least two of their three best friends were also casual types. None of the activists who maintained their political involvements over their college years viewed two of their friends as casual types. Turning from extracurricular life to academic experiences, we found that activists performed at least as well as nonactivists. They also just as often belonged to professional and departmental clubs and groups that honored academic excellence; in fact, in 1970 there was some evidence that they belonged to such groups in somewhat greater numbers. They were spread rather uniformly across the academic departments and divisions of the colleges we studied; they were not unsually concentrated among the social sciences and the humanities, as some studies have indicated is true of white activists. The major way in which activists differed academically from other students was in their relationships with faculty. Activists repeatedly reported more outside contact with faculty members. This contact was not exclusively political. At the college we studied intensively for four years, more of the activists not only reported contact with more faculty members and more often listed a faculty person as one of their friends but also reported as seniors that they had gone to a faculty member to talk about their futures and to get help with graduate school or job planning.

Activism also turned out to be one of the ways in which the college experience influenced students. The longitudinal study of activists showed that they ended their senior year ideologically different from other students. They expressed much stronger collective consciousness of racial oppression and firmer collective commitments than either the students who had never participated in civil rights or those who had dropped out of political action after their freshman year. This was true even after adjusting for the differences in attitudes, which were minor in any case, that these three groups had brought with them to college. Persistence of commitment to action was clearly necessary for these effects. Students who had been politically active as freshmen but later dropped their activism left college with almost exactly the same ideologies as students who had never been active. Activism, however, had no effect on the students' personal aspirations, their expectancies of success, their assessments of their strengths or competencies, or their academic anxieties. When we asked seniors how they felt they had changed during their college years, their subjective views supported this picture that emerged from comparing their actual scores as freshmen and as seniors. More than other seniors they felt they had changed ideologically: they said they had developed greater interest in political and world affairs, in African culture and heritage, in social issues and problems, in civil rights, and in issues concerning Blacks in America. In contrast, they shared with other students the same sense of how much they had changed regarding their personal goals and nonpolitical attitudes and feelings.

We also explored the effect of the college by examining whether the campus climate conditioned the meaning of activism, its ties to certain college experiences, or its connection with ideology. The campus climate, defined by breadth of student activism, counted in two ways in understanding what activism meant. First, it was only where activism was reasonably widespread that ideology was strongly related to who participated. Most of the connections between collective consciousness, Black Nationalism, and activism were much stronger on the two campuses where 90 percent of the students had taken part in some political activity during their college years. We think of the institution's capacity to encourage students to act on their beliefs as a critical aspect of its effect. The medium through which this happened became clearer when we also found that the picture of the activist as an integrated, campus leader applied only on those campuses where civil rights activism was commonplace. By contrast, civil rights activists were marginal to traditional collegiate life at the two colleges where participation had been less universal, one where only 42 percent and another where 62 percent had ever taken part in civil rights activities and where only 4 and 5 percent were currently active. Instead of being unusually active in campus organizations and taking part in a political subculture that addressed typical problems on the campus as well as broader political questions, the civil rights activists on these two less active campuses thought of themselves as casual, creative nonconformists who were not serious students; they were involved in the community off the campus. Moreover, it was only the community control and militancy aspects of nationalism that they expressed more strongly than other students on their campuses.

We highlight these differences in civil rights activism on the active and less active campuses for two reasons. We do not want to overgeneralize the profile that applied to student power activists generally and to civil rights activists on active campuses. Most activists were successful, socially integrated, hooked-in students who took part not only in a political subculture but also broadly in campus life. But not all activists should be described that way. Furthermore, we think of the conditioning effect of campus climate as part of the college's impact on students. Nationalist students who attended a college where their beliefs could be expressed into action easily because political action was widespread, if not normative, experienced college very differently from students with much the same ideology who entered a college where political action was rare, if not deviant.

Finally, we highlight the fact that sex of the student mattered so little in these analyses of collective achievement. In contrast to the much higher level of aspiration that the men's educational and occupational goals represented, men and women shared very much the same commitments to action and political ideologies. Their level of activism was approximately the same. At most, only 10 percent more of the men than the women participated in collective action; even that differential occurred only in the 1968 follow-up of the students at College H. Comparisons of the participation of men and women in the 1964 and 1970 cross-sectional studies showed virtually the same rates. Their analyses of inequities, preferences for collective action, and attitudes toward Black Nationalism were likewise remarkably similar. The only way in which their approval of Nationalism differed was the fact that women disapproved more than men of using violence as a political tool. Whereas some writers have cast Black women as aggressively more active in change efforts, others have depicted Black women as less sophisticated politically, less militant, and likely to be pawns in the attempts of whites to co-opt Black leadership. We found neither characterization to be true. These Black men and women were together in their action and ideologies throughout the sixties.

part 3

Collective and Individual Achievement– Putting It All Together

chapter 13

Collective and Individual Achievement—Polarized, Independent, or Integrated?

We chose to organize this book around the individual achievement goals and the collective commitments of Black students because we believed these dual goals define a critical dilemma. How can Black students pursue personal predilections, strive to realize their own hopes, and simultaneously work to change the barriers and inequities built into the fabric of the Black experience in America? Obviously, the conflict between self-gain and group commitment can and often is encountered outside the Black and the minority experience. Many other students struggle with self-interest and social concern. Few of them, however, face the social pressures felt by minority students, and most of them can escape questions of obligations and commitments to a group. Black students, like students from other groups experiencing a rise in collective consciousness and nationalism, must cope with competing, powerful motives and pressures for selflessness rather than gain, for cooperation rather than competition, for collective rather than individual commitments. How do they put it all together? When can individual goals and collective commitments exist together and, even more positively, actually reinforce each other? When does polarization occur? What is it about the students' college experiences and personal strengths that promotes a life plan that allows the personal as well as the collective expression of achievement? What situations foster the integration of these goals? Some sudents see nothing contradictory in pursuing Black studies and computer sciences simultaneously. Their commitment to advanced education seems to be predicated on their consciousness of themselves as Blacks and their desire to be effective on behalf of others. They see it as George Jackson did when he wrote to his younger brother, Jonathan:

> *I hope you are involved in the academic program at your school, but knowing what I know about this country's schooling methods, they are not really directing you to any specialized line of study.*

339

They have not tried to ascertain what fits your character and disposition and to direct you accordingly. So you must do this yourself. Decide now what you would like to specialize in, one thing that you will drive at. Do you get it? Decide now. There are several things that we as a group, a revolutionary group, need badly: chemists, electronic engineers, surgeons, etc. Choose one and give it special attention at a certain time each day. Establish a certain time to give over to your specialty and let Robert know indirectly what you are doing. Then it only remains for you to get your A's on the little simple unnecessary subjects that the school requires. This is no real problem. It can be accomplished with just a little attention and study. But you must start now on your specialty, the thing that you plan to carry through this war of life. You must specialize in something. Just let it be something that will help the war effort.[1]

This chapter explores how students managed both their personal and their collective commitments. Thus far in the book we have treated each separately; we discussed the influences on individual achievement in Part 1, the influence on collective achievement in Part 2. We turn now to the relationship *between* these goals and to the forces that promoted their integration or their polarization. We are not free of values and biases. We hope that students can maintain and express both individual and collective commitments. Our preference for the resolution that combines these two sets of commitments rests on the belief, fantasy in the eyes of some, that critical social changes can be forced without the exclusively collective stance that revolutions must exact.

TWO FORMS OF SOCIAL CHANGE: INDIVIDUAL MOBILITY AND COLLECTIVE ACTION

Historically most civil rights groups have operated on the assumption that change in the status and life conditions of Black Americans would occur primarily through the aggregated achievements of individuals. Problems of unequal opportunity and prejudiced evalution of performance admittedly were attacked through group action, legal battles, and political pressure. Still, most people believed that if discrimination were adequately controlled and opportunity truly equalized, the mobility of the individual would provide the mechanism for aggregate change in the status of Black Americans. Group effort would play a role, but the primary responsibility would fall to individuals to prepare

1. George Jackson, *Soledad Brother: The Prison Letters of George Jackson* (New York: Bantam Books, 1970), pp. 145-146. Copyright 1970 by World Entertainer's, Ltd. Published by Coward, and McCann and Geoghegan, Inc. and Bantam Books, Inc.

themselves to take advantage of new opportunities. If enough individuals achieved individual success, the status of the group eventually would improve, especially as the next generation benefited educationally from their parents' mobility.

In this traditional view of change must the personal gain of the individual conflict with commitment to the group? If the ascent of the group depends on the achievements of individuals, must the individual view self-gain as conflicting with concern about others? Personal advancement theoretically advances the group. The individual's accomplishment presumably by example assures the same possibilities for others. With the first cracks in housing, school, or job discrimination many Blacks felt it was their obligation to pioneer so that previously closed doors would open even wider. While moving up and out brought wealth and prestige to the individual, it was not simply a rationalization to argue that personal mobility was gained for the sake of the group, that it broke down barriers for others. Increased status also provided a basis for greater personal influence that in turn could be used for the political advantage of the group.

Many people have used their own mobility and increased personal power to benefit others. But conflicts have also existed. Pursuing personal goals, becoming a model for others, using the personal influence that accrues to an improved status to advance the group can hold real and genuine conflicts. Lorraine Hansberry wrote of her own conflict between personal comfort and group commitment as she faced her own death:

> Do I remain a revolutionary? Intellectually—without a doubt. But am I prepared to give my body to the struggle or even my comforts? This is what I puzzle about.
>
> Am now sitting thinking about many things. All the narrowness and selfishness of this last year of my life seems to crowd in on me. I've just finished reading an article on Harlem in the current Look and hardly feel that my existence is justified, let alone the "style" of life I lead . . .
>
> And then again a month later:
> Have the feeling I should throw myself back into the movement. Become a human being again.
>
> But that very impulse is immediately flushed with a thousand vacillations and forbidding images. I see myself lying in a pool of perspiration in a dark tenement room recalling groton and the trees and longing for death . . .
>
> Comfort has come to be its own corruption. I think of lying without a painkiller in pain. In all the young years no such image ever

occurred to me. I rather looked forward to going to jail once. Now I can hardly imagine surviving it at all. Comfort. Apparently I have sold my soul for it.

I think when I get my health back I shall go into the South to find out what kind of revolutionary I am . . .[2]

Frazier's classic analysis of the marginal man also attests to the pressures brought on the successful individual to lose commitment to, if not contact with, less advantaged Blacks.[3] Although reliable data on the extensiveness of the separation of the middle class from the Black masses never existed, Frazier's indictment rang true to many people. The central theme of the southern movement in the early sixties called for the dedivorcement of the privileged from the masses. In a meeting in 1961 between celebrated Black artists and the then Attorney General, Robert Kennedy, Lorraine Hansberry spoke about the shift in thinking that was taking place then:

. . . the qualitative change in the struggle for Negro freedom is that we are not, any of us, remotely interested in the all-insulting concept of the 'exceptional Negro.'

We are not remotely interested in any tea at the White House.

What we are interested in is making perfectly clear that between the Negro intelligentsia, the Negro middle class, and the Negro this-and-that—we are one people. And that as far as we are concerned, we are represented by the Negroes in the streets of Birmingham! . . .[4]

The struggle to reidentify that grew out of the direct-action period in the sixties shows that many people did believe that individual mobility previously had cut into the cohesiveness of the Black community and had threatened cooperative action.

Revolutionary-collectivist theory minces no words about this. Individual achievement, concern with self, or any other aspect of individualism cannot coexist with collective commitments. Fanon lays it out sharply in *The Wretched of the Earth:*[5]

Individualism is the first to disappear. The native intellectual has learned from his masters that the individual ought to express himself fully. The colonialist bourgeoisie has hammered into the native's mind the idea of a society of individuals where each person shuts himself up in his own subjectivity and whose only wealth is indivi-

2. Lorraine Hansberry, *To Be Young, Gifted and Black,* Adapted by Robert Nemiroff (Englewood Cliffs, New Jersey: Prentice-Hall, 1969), pp. 249-250. Copyright © 1969 by Robert Nemiroff and Robert Nemiroff as the Executor of the Estate of Lorraine Hansberry.

3. Franklin Frazier, *Black Bourgeoisie* (Glencoe, Illinois: The Free Press, 1957).

4. Hansberry, *To Be Young, Gifted and Black,* p. 220.

5. Frantz Fanon, *The Wretched of the Earth* (New York: Grove Press, 1963), p. 47. Copyright © 1963 by Presence Africaine.

dual thought. Now the native who has the opportunity to return to the people during a struggle for freedom will discover the falseness of the theory. The very forms of organization of the struggle will suggest to him a different vocabulary. Brother, Sister, Friend—these words outlawed by the colonialist bourgeoisie because for them my brother is my purse, my friend is part of my scheme for getting on. The native intellectual takes part, in a sort of auto-da-fé, in the destruction of all his idols: Egoism, recrimination that springs from pride, and the childish stupidity of those who always want to have the last word. Such a colonized intellectual, dusted over the colonial culture, will in the same way discover the substance of village assemblies, the cohesion of people's committees, and the extraordinary fruitfulness of local meetings and groupments. Hence-forward, the interests, of one will be the interests, of all, for in concrete fact everyone will be discovered by the troops, everyone will be mas-sacred—or everyone will be saved. The motto "lookout for yourself," the atheist's method of salvation, is in this context forbidden.

Just as Fanon addressed the intellectuals of Algeria, Black Nation-alists here challenged Black college students whose privileged posi-tions marked them for special sensitivity to the conflict of self-interest and group commitment. Carmichael pulled no punches when he spoke to students at one of the colleges we were studying:[6]

One of the things that you are going to have to do is realize that Black people, especially in the colleges, can no longer afford the luxury of being an individual. We must see ourselves as a people. We can no longer accept that which white society calls success because to be successful, for Black people, in this country is to be anti-Black. I will explain that a little bit for you. They tell us all the time about Ralph Bunche. And they are going to tell others about you. You have got to be careful because you are used against Black people in the ghettos. See, everytime they rebel, they yell and scream, someone will pull you forward and say, "She went to col-lege, you can do it too." You stand there and say, "Yeah, anybody can go to college." Can't anybody go to college—college is for the elite and you better learn to understand THAT. This country is not inclusive; it is exclusive . . . Where is your political analysis? How do you serve Black people whom you are supposed to be serving? Do you see yourselves as part of Black people striving towards libera-tion or are you isolated as white people would have you be, different from the winos in the ghetto, different from the dirty, filthy people in the rural South? Are you different from your mothers who scrub

6. Stokely Carmichael, taped speech at School H.

floors to send you here? And the minute you walk out you leave her where she was. Can't you go back? . . . You are Black, brothers and sisters, and you better come on home. The Black people of this country need your skills. They do not need you telling them how much money you make every year. They are not impressed . . . You are Black, brothers and sisters, and you better come on home. You had better come on home.

To go to college motivated by typical collegiate impulses—by the desire for self-expression, for personal advancement, for material gain—showed that you held white values. To be Black meant a return to peoplehood and a loss of individualism. Pressures for polarization were building up as Nationalist thinking sharpened the issues for students in the late sixties.

The experiences of students who had tried to bridge the two worlds of school and community action often bore out these Nationalist warnings. You had to choose. Having daily touch with the suffering of mass poverty, experiencing directly the atrocious brutality that had provided the social control of Black people in the South over the years, understanding that the abstract principles of democratic theory simply never prevailed in the rural South—these experiences widened the rift between their individual purposes in attending college and their concerns for Black people, inhibiting an easy shift back and forth from community to campus. Students and their parents correctly feared that involvement would threaten staying in school. The last four months in the life of a young SNCC worker who entered one of the colleges in the fall of 1964 show us the pain, vacillation, and ambivalence that characterized many of the committed activists. Sammy Younge first dropped out of school during his freshman year to work full time in the movement. He returned to school in September, 1965. His friends described his turmoil that fall:

September 1965
Gwen Patton: He came into the office and told me, "Gwen I'm going to school. That's the purpose of me being here." I couldn't believe it. It was a parody of what people always said. Then he went into my office and got a piece of paper. He pecked it out on the typewriter—his resignation from TIAL.[7]

Eldridge Burns: For the first couple of weeks, we used to go to the library and study for about five minutes and then get up and go someplace else. Just a big fake. One day I said, "Well, man, I think I'll go back out in the country. I think I'll go up to Brownsville." So we rode up there and he talked to all the people he had organ-

7. James Forman, *Sammy Younge, Jr.* (New York: Grove Press, 1968), p. 174. Copyright © 1968 by Grove Press.

ized up there. He came back and said, "Aw, man, I ain't going to mess with that stuff." So we left it alone. He'd jump in his car and go to Atlanta, Montgomery, Columbus or Birmingham, or any place.

Then one day he withdrew from school. He said, "Yeah, man, don't tell my mama, but I withdrew from school." I said, "What did you do that for?" He said, "Oh, man, I'm tired. I haven't been studying. I can't make it."[8]

Then, feeling there was no other way to deal with the conflict between self and commitment, he tried again to sever his ties with the movement:

November, 1965

Stokely Carmichael: He was high that night, and we had a talk. He said he was putting down civil rights. He wanted to get into the bag, and he was going to be out for himself; that was what he was going to do. So I told him, "It's still cool, you know. Makes me no never mind." He said he thought a lot of SNCC people were putting him down because he was going back into the bag, but that didn't make any difference to him because cats put him down when he went SNCC. I told him that I thought there would be some people who would do that, but as far as I was concerned, we could still drink wine any time.[9]

But that didn't last either.

December 30, 1965

Stokely Carmichael: On December 30, we were putting up tents to house the people who had been evicted. Sammy came over to help. He just drove up one day. He had on his dungarees, overalls, jacket, everything. I said to him, "What's happening, baby?" He said, "I can't kick it man. I got to work with it. It's in me." We talked a little, but there was so much to do that we didn't talk too long. He just said that he had tried to kick it, but couldn't."[10]

Four days later Sammy Younge was killed.

What wonder that we expected the students we studied over the decade of the sixties to reflect strain between individual and collective goals. Although we knew that students still in college would not show the intensity of conflict felt by those who already had dropped out, we thought that personal and group commitments would be polarized even as the general rule. At the very least we expect to find an inverse relationship between activism and commitment to individual achievement. What did the data show?

---

8. *Ibid.*, p. 178.
9. *Ibid.*, pp. 181-182.
10. *Ibid.*, p. 183.

Individual and Collective Commitments: Independent or Related?

These two sets of commitments—to individual achievement goals and to activism and social change—were repeatedly unrelated. Both in 1964 and again in 1970 it was a picture of independence, not polarization. That students were activists said nothing about their educational or occupational goals or their performance in college. That students aspired for demanding professions said nothing about whether they had taken part in political action during their college years.

Let us be more specific. We pointed out in Chapter 11 that grade performance in college, as one indicator of individual achievement, was not related to activism. The independence of collective and individual commitments went far beyond that. We checked whether activists and nonactivists aspired to different educational and occupational goals. We examined the individual goals of activists and nonactivists in 1964 and in 1970. We explored whether the type of activism in 1970 mattered as to the ease with which students handled personal and collective commitments. With only two exceptions the results repeatedly showed that high aspirations and performance just as often characterized the activist as the nonactivist student—no more, no less. Individual and collective commitments generally were not polarized, nor were they complementary to each other. Whether students engaged in one said nothing about their commitments or actions in the other.

Chart A shows the general independence of personal and collective commitments.

One of the two exceptions to the general rule of independence supported a complementary relationship between these two types of goals. Men activists in both civil rights and student power issues in 1970 were more likely than nonactivists to aspire to graduate or professional school. Independence held even then, however, among the women. The second exception supported polarization, at least to some extent. The men who were only moderately involved in civil rights in 1964 aspired to jobs that were the most nontraditional for Blacks and reflected the strongest ability demands. In contrast, the most involved activist men intended to enter jobs that were similar to those of the nonactivists and clearly reflected lower levels of aspiration than those of the moderately involved. This suggests that holding on to high achievement, personal goals may have been somewhat easier if activism was not too involving and all consuming. On the whole, however, these data showed that conflict and polarization were not broadly experienced, at least by students who stayed in college.

Chart A

1964 Civil Rights Activism	1970 Civil Rights Activism	1970 Student Power Activism
Unrelated to the following individual achievement indicators:	*Unrelated* to the following individual achievement indicators:	*Unrelated* to the following individual achievement indicators:
Graduate school aspirations	Graduate school aspirations of women	Graduate school aspirations of women
Certainty of graduate school enrollment	All dimensions of job aspirations	All dimensions of job aspirations
Performance on achievement tasks	Self-reports of college grades	Self-reports of college grades
College grades		
Prestige of job aspirations		
Ability and nontraditionality of women's aspirations		
Related to the following:	*Related* to the following:	*Related* to the following:
Ability and nontraditionality of men's job aspirations	Graduate school aspirations of men	Graduate school aspirations of men

We grew to feel that dropout was the critical criterion of conflict. When individual and collective commitments produced too much strain, the student left college, at least temporarily. The strain probably never reached intense levels among those who could tolerate staying in school. In the stable college population, commitment to individual achievement did not have to imply anything about commitment to collective action, or vice versa. We were able to explore whether dropout did carry special significance as an indicator of polarization in the longitudinal study of one school where dropout and activism data were collected over a four-year period. Large numbers of freshmen in 1964 had participated in demonstrations during their freshman year. That we followed this class through their four years of college provided an unusual opportunity to chart the dropouts among the strongly committed and nonactivists alike. Activists, disproportionately, dropped out at the end of their freshman year. Among men, 50 percent of the most actively involved, but only 25 percent of the non-activists, dropped out before their sophomore year; among women, the dropout figures were 50 percent of the activists and 30 percent of the nonactivists. The relationship between activism and dropout was especially pronounced among freshmen who entered college with above-median test scores. (The tau between dropout and activism was .44 among the high-scoring men and .40 among the high-scoring women, but only .17 and .23 among men and women, respectively, in the group with below-median test scores.) This was clear evidence of the polarization of individual achievement (defined by staying in college) and collective commitments. Dropout data after the sophomore year continued to support the polarization thesis. Again, dropout was greatest among students who had been actively involved in civil rights as freshmen. After the end of the sophomore year the altogether smaller dropout rate evened out between activists and nonactivists so that by senior year the percent of the freshmen activists and nonactivists who were still attending college did not differ.

Some of these activists who felt the contradictions too keenly to stay in school probably attended other colleges later on. At least temporarily, however, collective and individual achievements were polarized for many of them. One activist from this freshman class explained to James Forman why she could no longer stay in school as she got increasingly committed to political work during her sophomore year.

I quit school in February to work with SNCC in Lowndes County. I always knew that I would drop out of school because, at this point, it was useless and irrelevant to me. There I was, a biology major, sitting in a classroom learning about the green stuff that grows on trees while there are people out here who like to hang people from trees. So, this little green stuff that grows on trees had no relevance in life at all. I couldn't see the classroom situation unless I could apply it to my everyday life. And I couldn't do that.

My first year in school, I had been a typical (   ) student. I was in the dormitory and ate my meals in the cafeteria. I didn't have to leave campus for a thing. It's all provided for you right there. But I could see there is so much in life I was missing. You pass a shack coming into Macon County on your way to school, but that's sort of irrelevant to you because you're coming to the campus where you're going to be in a nice warm dormitory. If somebody's outside in the cold it's not your problem. And then the answers people will give you in terms of what you're moving toward. You're moving toward the fact that some day you'll be able to afford a nice house and a nice big car, and I just couldn't see that being everything. So I started looking for the answers myself. Like what am I living for? Like what meaning does my life have?

Then, during the summer of 65 I worked a nine-to-five job in New York, for cancer research. I had all these great promises of how, when I finished school, I could move right into this top position, and how the institution would pay half my expenses if I would go to Cornell and work on my Master's. It was really a great life. But while I was up there working this nine-to-five job, I was reading everyday about Jimmy Rogers and Ruby Sales down in Lowndes County. All the while, I felt out of place, because I should have been in Lowndes County. I should have been in Alabama. When Jonathan Daniels got killed I felt I should have been here.

The first semester back here at (   ), I worked with Jimmy in Macon County to ease my conscience about not being here over the summer. Most of the kids in school are working toward the day when they get their degrees, and then the first thing they talk about doing is leaving the South for good. In school, you learn to exclude people—and these people are just like your parents and your grandparents. They live in shacks and they're "nasty." People go to school and they get in these nice little middle-class positions and then they can't talk to their grandparents or their parents because they're ashamed of them. You go to New York and you forget the South is here. But I plan to live in the South.

To me, this is just a big classroom right here in Alabama. I'm still reading a lot: I can read things now and see what answers the particular author has for the problems. There are some changes I can bring about myself, by being out in Lowndes County. If I do nothing *but get more students involved, that will be something. In a class-room, you hera all about the great theory of democracy and you swear that it's working. Out here, you know it isn't. This is where it really is.*[11]

Separate Sources of Motivation for Individual and Collective Commitments

Political experience clearly pushed some students to choose between college and the world of action. A few vacillated, choosing to be "in the bag," then choosing to be "out county where it was happening." However, the decision to stay in school, once made, resolved these stresses for most students. Students who tolerated staying in college during these years of ferment handled their individual goals and feelings of responsibility to the group without intense conflict. There was apparently nothing in the general experience of the stable college population that pushed for polarization of collective and personal commitments. Activism and traditional achievement were simply independent of each other among students who elected to stay in school.

The motivations that prompted these two separate commitments likewise were independent of each other. What facilitated one goal had nothing to do with the source of motivation for the other. Collective commitments related to one unique set of attitudes, personal career commitments to another unique set. In short, commitments to individual achievement goals were correlated with traditional indicators of achievement motivation *but not with racial ideology;* commitments to collective action were correlated with racial ideology *but not with traditional achievement* motivation.

We have noted aspects of these separate sources of motivation first in Chapter 4, where we discussed the association of individual achievement motivation to individual aspirations and performance, then in Chapter 10, where we examined the relationship of ideology to activism. However, we have not described heretofore the consistent lack of relationship between racial ideology and personal achievement goals nor the independence of achievement motivation and collective action. *The system attitudes, collective commitments, and Nationalist ideology that distinguished activists from nonactivists in both 1964 and 1970 were almost always unrelated to how well students performed in college, whether they aspired for graduate school, or what kinds of jobs they intended to enter after completing their training. Conversely, the personal expectancies, feelings of competency, and achievement*

11. *Ibid.*, pp. 214-216.

motives that related to achieving better grades and striving for high aspirations practically never distinguished activists from nonactivists.

Chart B summarizes and highlights these separate sources of motivation. It is broken into quadrants. The frequent checks in the upper left quadrant show the general tie of individual achievement motivation to traditional individual achievement; the absence of checks in the upper right quadrant demonstrates the lack of relationship between individual achievement motivation and collective action. Conversely, the frequent checks in the lower right quadrant illustrate the special connection between system attitudes and nationalist ideology to collective action; the absence of checks in the lower left quadrant testifies to the irrelevance of race ideology to individual goals and behavior.

Again and again we see independence and separation. Two separate sources of motivation related to individual and collective choices that were themselves independent. This implies that students managed to combine collective and individual commitments when they managed to develop both sources of motivation. But how did students do that? What made it possible for them to integrate their Nationalist ideology and achievement concerns into strong commitment to both personal goals and collective commitments? What encouraged some students to follow just the activist path, renouncing—or perhaps not developing—strong personal aspirations? When were students predominantly motivated to "look out for Joe," to pursue their own high achievement goals with no involvement in collective action at all? What accounted for letting it all pass by—proceeding through college without strong commitments to either individual achievement or to collective endeavors to effect social change? The next chapter addresses itself to these questions.

CHART B. **Summary of Relationships of Achievement Motivation and Ideology Measures to Individual and Collective Achievement, 1964 and 1970**[a]

	Individual Achievement														Collective Achievement			
	Educational and Occupational Aspirations								Performance: (1964 Data Only)						Civil Rights Activism		Student Power Participation (1970 Data Only)	
	Planning to Go to Graduate School		Prestige of Occupational Choice		Ability Demands of Occupational Choice		Nontraditionality of Occupational Choice		Percentile Rank GPA		Correct Performance Anagrams		Number Errors Anagrams					
	Men	Women	Men	Women	Men	Women	Men	Women	Men	Women	Men	Women	Men	Women	Men	Women	Men	Women
ACHIEVEMENT MOTIVATION																		
Competency judgments Personal efficacy	√	√	√√	√√	√√	√√	0	0	√	√	√	0	0	√	√0	0	0	0
Academic self-confidence	√	√	√√	√√	√√	√√	√√	√√	√	√	√	√	√	√	00	00	0	0
Job ability confidence	√	√	√√	√√	√√	√√	√0	√0	0	0	√	0	√	0	00	00	0	0
Achievement motives (1964 data only)															No motives measures in 1970			
Achievement orientation	0		√	√	√	√	0	0	0	√	0	√	0	0	0	0		
Fear of failure	√	0	√	√	√	√	√	0	0	√	√	0	0	0	0	0		

IDEOLOGY MEASURES																	
Control ideology	00*	00	0*0	00	0*0	00	0*0	00	0*	0*	0	0*	0	✓✓	✓0	✓✓	0
System blame	00	00	0*0	00	00	00	✓✓	00	0*	0*	0	0*	0	✓✓	✓✓	✓✓	✓
Preference for Collective action	00	00	00	00	00	00	0✓	00	0	0	0	0	0	✓✓	✓✓	✓✓	✓
Black Nationalism (1970 data only)																	
Self-determination	0	0	0	0	0	0	0	0						✓	✓	✓	✓
Community control	0	0	0	0	0	0	0	0						✓	✓	0	0
Militancy	0	0	0	0	0	0	0	0						✓	0	✓	0
Black economic development	0	0	0	0	0	0	0	0						✓	✓	0	✓
Afro-American orientation	0	0	0	0	0	0	0	0						✓	✓	✓	✓
African orientation	0	0	0	0	0	0	0	0						0	0	0	0

No Nationalism measures in 1964.

*No relationship for this total sample although there was for particular subgroup, such as men with low personal control.

ªThe 1964 results are in the first column, the 1970 results in the second.

chapter 14

Collective and Individual Achievement– Putting It All Together

We have seen in the previous chapter that the general experience of the stable college population did not polarize collective and individual achievement, at least during the period we studied. Activism as collective achievement was simply independent of individualistic achievement goals among students who elected to stay in college. Also independent were the motivations that correlated with these two sets of commitments. Collective commitments related to collectivist ideology; personal and career commitments related to individualistic achievement motivation. This fact of independence of the two sets of goals and two sources of motivation meant that students theroretically could "put it all together." But how many did? Who were they? What aspects of the college experience fostered the integration and mutual reinforcement of collective and individual achievement?

FOUR RESOLUTIONS: INDIVIDUALISTIC ACHIEVERS, COMMITTED ACHIEVERS, ACTIVISTS, AND THE UNENGAGED

Four groups of seniors represented four different patterns of responding to individual and collective achievement. We used three criteria to distinguish these four groups. Two criteria defined unusually high individual aspirations: (1) the intention to pursue the Ph.D. or professional degrees at the graduate level, (2) aspirations for jobs whose ability demands or nontraditionality fell in the top quartile for this student population. Seniors who met either or both of these criteria were classified as high in traditional achievement orientation; seniors who failed to meet either showed lower stress on achievement in their future goals. This residual group obviously represented a wide range of individual goals since it included all but the top aspirants. The third criterion defined commitment to collective action. Seniors who had been involved in civil rights or student power activities throughout their college years were considered the committed group; seniors who had never been involved in either were classified as uncommitted.

Two of the four groups held in common the intention of pursuing major professions, medicine, law, architecture, or engineering, or working toward the Ph.D. in graduate school; they differed in whether they had been committed over their college years to collective achievement as well. *The Individualistic Achievers'* strong personal goals existed at the expense of collective commitments. They reported as seniors that they had never participated in any form of social action. The equally high personal goals of the *Committed Achievers* coexisted with strong, stable commitments to collective action. The *Activists,* like the Committed Achievers, had been politically involved throughout college but approached graduation with lower personal goals. They either considered the B.A. a terminal degree or talked about advanced education as a more remote goal. If they expected to go eventually to graduate or professional school, they talked about training for lower status professions such as education, social work, the ancillary medical careers, or other jobs that fell below the top quartile in their ability demands and nontraditionality. Even as a remote goal graduate school was thought of as a master's degree. Students in this group had not necessarily rejected personal goals, as the activist committed to revolution would have done, but they had not integrated their collective commitments with the same high level of personal aspiration that characterized the Committed Achievers. The fourth group, the *Unengaged,* had neither been active in collective endeavors nor did they end college with personal goals that reflected unusual individual achievement.

The four groups excluded the seniors who said they had previously participated in civil rights or student power activities but were no longer active as seniors.

We used two sources of data for examining these four resolutions and types of commitments. One set of analyses was based on responses of the seniors from the six colleges who participated in the cross-sectional study in 1970; the second set was based on the responses of seniors at the college where the longitudinal study was conducted between 1965 and 1968. Chart A shows the number of seniors who were Individualistic Achievers, Committed Achievers, Activists, and the Unengaged in these two sets of data.

The breakdown of the four groups among just the students who were included for these analyses from the longitudinal study of College H in 1968 was as following: *Individualistic Achievers,* 30 percent men and 27 percent women; *Committed Achievers,* 28 percent men and 29 percent women; *Activists,* 19 percent men and 20 percent women; and the *Unengaged,* 23 percent men and 24 percent women. In the 1970 six college study the groups were distributed as following: *Individualistic Achievers,* 23 percent men and 35 percent women; *Committed Achievers,* 26 percent men and 12 percent women; *Activists,* 17 percent men and 16 percent women; and the *Unengaged,* 34 percent men and 37 percent women.

CHART A.   **Breakdown of the Four Groups in Two Data Sets**

	Seniors in the Six College Cross-Sectional Study, 1970		Longitudinal Followup of Seniors at College H, 1968	
	Men	**Women**	**Men**	**Women**
Individualistic Achievers	40	46	22	28
Committed Achievers	45	16	21	30
Activists	30	20	15	21
Unengaged	59	48	18	25
Group left out of these analyses	71	96	27	32
	245	226	103	136

Postcollege Plans of the Four Groups

The future educational and occupational goals of these four groups of students differed by definition, but the differences extended beyond the criteria by which the four groups were originally selected. Let us look first at the Committed and Individualistic Achievers who shared top career aspirations and expected to complete the Ph.D. or professional degrees. Despite a commonality of goals, their postcollege plans differed greatly in several ways. Almost all of the Committed Achievers (95 percent) expected to enter professional schools rather than academic graduate programs. In contrast, the Individualistic Achievers preponderantly (67 percent) talked about Ph.D. programs. The Committed Achievers almost exclusively looked to law and medicine while the Individualistic Achievers chose among a much broader range of careers: 33 of the 61 Committed Achievers intended to be lawyers; only 8 of the 86 Individualistic Achievers aspired to the law. None of the Committed Achievers mentioned engineering or business; almost none talked about scientific research. The choices of the Individualistic Achievers had much greater diversity. In the areas of biology and chemistry: of the 32 Individualistic Achievers who talked about these fields only 14 expected to become doctors or pharmacists; 18 aspired for scientific research careers in biology, biochemistry, chemistry, and pharmacology. In contrast, the Committed Achievers who held these scientific interests aimed almost exclusively to practice their professions. Again and again we found that the Committed Achievers held more professional and practical goals. In addition, nearly half of the Committed Achievers voluntarily talked about using their future jobs as avenues for helping Black people and for contributing to community development. Given that only 11 percent of the total sample in 1970 specifically talked about responsibility to the Black community when they described their future careers, the high level of collective concern among the Committed Achievers was all the more striking. None of the Individualistic Achievers mentioned commitments to the Black community when they described what they expected to do.

The Committed Achievers were strongly motivated to express social commitments through their occupational roles, whereas the job choices of the Individualistic Achievers were not motivated by Black consciousness in such explicit ways. The Committed students, however, had somehow come to an unduly restrictive notion of the jobs that would integrate their personal and collective motivations. Table 1 shows this. Surely law and medicine, while very appropriate, are not the only ways to effect change through one's professional life.

Social commitment likewise distinguished the choices of the Activists and Unengaged, although both groups were at a lower level of aspiration than that held by the Committed and Individualistic Achievers. By definition, the seniors in these two groups did not plan to enter professional training for the major professions or to pursue the Ph.D. At a lower level, however, we again found that the politically involved seniors chose careers they thought would make them useful to the Black community. They disproportionately chose jobs that required preparation in social science—social work, guidance and counseling, public administration, urban planning, and the like. Half of the Activists but only 6 percent of the Unengaged mentioned social science as the area they would study if they managed to work for a master's degree someday. Rather than showing a press toward social science, the Unengaged chose among a wide range of fields: 40 percent in education, 30 percent in business, 9 percent in agriculture, 10 percent in science, 6 percent in social science, and 5 percent in the arts. Their descriptions of their future jobs likewise showed the same differences in Black consciousness that distinguished the Committed from the Individualistic Achievers. A quarter of the Activists but practically none of the Unengaged voluntarily mentioned that they wanted to use their careers to help Black people.

TABLE 1.   **Career Aspirations of Committed and Individualistic Achievers in 1970**

Committed Achievers	Individualistic Achievers
33 Lawyers	8 Lawyers
17 Doctors	10 Doctors
3 Pharmacists	4 Pharmacists
3 Public Health	14 Engineers
Nursing administrators	10 Biologists
4 Researchers in natural science	8 Mathematicians
1 Writer	2 Physicists
⎯	2 Chemists
61	2 Biochemists
	4 Pharmacological researchers
	1 College professor:
	Romance language
	1 College professor: English
	1 Artist
	2 Sociologists
	9 Psychologists
	2 Economists
	4 Business administrators
	1 Educational administrator
	⎯
	86
58 Professional degrees	20 Professional degrees
1 Ph.D.	62 Ph.D.'s
2 Master's degrees	4 Master's degrees

Precollege Backgrounds

Given the only small relationships between demography and traditional indicators of achievement (Chapter 5) and with activism (Chapter 9), we did not expect sharp distinctions in the precollege histories of these four groups of students. Nor did we find them. They came to college from much the same backgrounds. In fact, only the Unengaged stood out at all; they more often grew up on farms or villages (41 percent versus less than 12 percent of the other groups); their fathers had attained less education (48 percent of their fathers but less than 20 percent of the fathers of the other groups had only grammar school educations). Otherwise, even the Unengaged looked much like the other groups. All four groups shared similar family incomes and family structures; religion carried much the same significance to their families.

Performance Histories

We did not collect records of college grades in 1970, although we asked the students to tell us their grade averages. The self-reported grades of the four groups did not differ. Likewise, the longitudinal study at the one college where we had also collected entrance test scores and actual grade records failed to show performance differences among the four groups. Since the Committed Achievers and Activists less often chose occupations that reflected interest in science, we checked to see whether they might have performed less well in science and math courses. They took fewer courses in those fields, but their average grades were not lower.

With such similar performance histories, the differences in the aspirations and future commitments of these four groups clearly had to reflect something other than performance, at least as it is measured by standard tests and college grades. What was it, then, about their motivations and ideologies that promoted such different commitments?

Motivations of the Four Groups: Achievement Motivation and Social Ideology

We expected that the achievement motivation of the two groups with high aspirations would differ from the two groups who expressed lower educational and job goals. It did, in the ways discussed in Chapter 4 and just summarized in Chapter 13 as one independent source of motivation. The Individualistic Achievers and Committed Achievers expressed stronger personal efficacy, less anxiety about tests, stronger convictions about their own academic competence and ability to succeed in their future occupational roles (Appendix Table 14.1). For example, in the 1970 data 68 percent of the Committed Achievers and 52 percent of the Individualistic Achievers, as compared to about a fourth of the other two groups, felt that their academic potential would put them in the top quarter of their classes; between 35 and 40 percent of the Committed and Individualistic Achievers but only 10 percent of the other two groups were completely sure of their abilities to perform well in jobs that they had chosen, although the Individualistic and Committed Achievers had chosen jobs that were considered more difficult and demanding in the first place; over half of the Committed and Individualistic Achievers but less than 30 percent of the other groups answered all or all but one of the five personal control questions affirming that they felt they could control what happened in their own lives; the test anxiety scores of the Committed and Individualistic Achievers were both significantly lower than those of the other two groups. These differences held equally well in the 1968 longitudinal study as in the 1970 cross-sectional study.

We also expected stronger ideological commitments from both the Committed Achievers and the Activists than from either of the non-activist groups. As the results discussed in Chapter 10 and just summarized in Chapter 13 as the other independent source of motivation suggest, it was the activism that these two groups shared that distinguished them ideologically from the Individualistic Achievers and the Unengaged (Appendix Table 14.2). For example, 93 percent of the Committed Achievers and 81 percent of the Activists, as compared to 29 percent of the Individualistic Achievers and 23 percent of the Unengaged, chose at least three of the four system blame alternatives on the individual-system blame index; 74 percent of the Committed Achievers, 71 percent of the Activists, but only 22 and 27 percent of the Individualistic Achievers and Unengaged chose five out of six alternatives favoring collective action on the individual-collective strategy measure; both activist groups more often rejected traditional work-ethic explanations of success and instead attributed success in the culture at large to both internal virtues and social determinants; they were consistently more nationalistic on all the dimensions of political nationalism—self-determination, Black economic development, community control, and political use of violence. Finally, the Committed Achievers and Activists stood out as especially critical of traditional governance in all aspects of student life on their campuses.

Despite these predictable differences in which either the aspiration or activism criterion carried the major explanatory burden, certain comparisons among these four groups of seniors provided unexpected information. It was especially the longitudinal study of shifts from the freshman to senior year that extended what we have presented already about aspiration and activism. The longitudinal analyses revealed distinctive motivational dynamics behind the different resolutions of individual and collective commitments.

Let us look first at the Committed Achievers. This group of politically active, high aspirant students completed their senior year with heightened feelings of competence and potential for effectiveness (Appendix Table 14.1). In fact they were the only group who assessed their personal competencies more favorably at the senior level than at the freshman level. The increase showed up in how they judged their potential for academic success, their ability to get and perform well on the jobs they had chosen, and their overall sense of personal control. The positive effect of the four years in college that was reflected by the increase in senior over freshman scores countermands the regression effects that typically would be expected, since the Committed Achievers entered college as reasonably confident freshmen. Adjusting for freshman scores, the Committed Achievers finished the senior year the most self-assured group, even when they were compared with the Individualistic Achievers who shared equally ambitious goals (Appendix Table 14.1). Something happened during their college years that encouraged these politically active students to feel generally more efficacious and surer of themselves academically and occupationally. Since they had performed at much the same level as other students, the positive experiences had to go beyond sheer academic success. After looking at the motivations of the other groups, we will turn to the college experiences that may have fostered the Committed Achievers' feelings of confidence.

The Committed Achievers also looked at the role of discrimination differently from the Individualistic Achievers, even somewhat differently from the Activists. They were unusually sensitive to discrimination. They shared with other Activists greater awareness of systemic problems, which they considered to be more often the source of race differentials in status in our society; together with the Activists they also criticized conventional explanations of success in favor of more balanced views that stressed both personal and social determination (Appendix Table 14.2). But the Committed Achievers, even more than the Activists, emphasized the *collective* impact of social inequities (Appendix Table 14.3). Ninety percent of the Committed Achievers, but only about half of the other groups including the Activists, insisted that discrimination affects everyone and cannot be avoided by special privilege or status; 78 percent of the Committed Achievers, contrasted to between a third and a half of the other groups, stressed that discrimination specifically limits job success at all levels of the occupational structure. This strong identification with the collectivity had not daunted the expression of the Committed Achievers' own personal goals. They held onto highly prestigious and demanding career goals at the same time that they stressed the collective impact of discrimination and racism. These Committed Achievers especially countered the previously more common individualism that had sometimes produced marginality from the group. They were more, not less, conscious of discrimination as the shared experience of the group; they set demanding personal objectives without denying the impact of social inequities. Their heightened concern about these issues stood out even from the Activists. Their stance could not have been more different from the older, more conventional beliefs of the Individualistic Achievers who repeatedly stressed the irrelevance of race.

The Individualistic Achievers' conventionality and acceptance of the social order as reasonably just were their distinctive features. They professed unusually individualistic and optimistic beliefs, even compared to the Unengaged with whom they shared less commitment to nationalism and political activities. For example, only eight percent of the Individualistic Achievers, contrasted to a third of the Unengaged and about half of the Committed Achievers and Activists, rejected conventional work ethic explanations of success on at least eight of the thirteen questions on the control ideology scale. The longitudinal analyses of freshman-senior shifts further explained why the Individualistic Achievers, as seniors, looked so different from other students (Appendix Table 14.4). They had entered college thinking much like other freshmen. All the other groups, even the Unengaged, left college much less individualistic and conventional than when they entered. Only the Individualistic Achievers maintained the position they had held as freshmen: as seniors they still favored individualistic interpretations of success and failure, while most other seniors stressed as many external as internal reasons why people manage to succeed in our society. Applied to the Black experience, their individualism produced unusual insistence that race was truly an irrelevant factor both in the success of Blacks generally and in their own success specifically. They believed that individual talents and strengths would reap their own rewards irrespective of external barriers and inequities. In 1970 nearly 80 percent of the Individualistic Achievers but no more than half of even the Unengaged and only a fifth of the Committed Achievers argued that discrimination would not exist in the types of jobs they had chosen (Appendix Table 14.3). Of course, the jobs that the Individualistic Achievers expected to enter were unusually centered in scientific and academic fields where one might argue that discrimination would not operate as obviously as in other fields, at least for the "talented tenth." Actually, discrimination has intruded every bit as much into those fields. Morever, 37 percent of the Individualistic Achievers, but no more than 15 percent of the other groups, said race was generally irrelevant in the life chances of Black people as a group. Even more striking, 54 percent of the Individualistic Achievers, but no more than a quarter of the others, said that race would be generally irrelevant in their own lives. Consonant with these beliefs, Individualistic Achievers were also unusually sanguine about social change and progress. Sixty percent of them, but only between 25 to 33 percent of the other groups, chose at least two out of three alternatives on the discrimination modifiability index that stressed that discrimination can be controlled or at least greatly reduced. They did not attribute as much responsibility to racial discrimination in the life situation of Black Americans in the first place and held atypically that it was more modifiable anyway. Although more commonly held in 1964, these beliefs put this group out of step with the modal stance of students in 1970. Where we could use longitudinal data we saw that the Individualistic Achievers departed from others as seniors because they had not shifted toward the greater social awareness, cynicism, and collectivism that typified the population in general. They had held on to conventional views in a period when rethinking of racial issues was the norm. Their stability extended beyond their social ideologies even to aspects of their achievement motivation. Whereas the Committed Achievers had become more self-confident, the Individualistic Achievers appraised themselves as seniors much as they had as freshmen.

The Activists presented yet another motivational issue, especially compared to the Committed Achievers with whom they shared so much politically. The longitudinal analyses showed that the Activists approached graduation with lower achievement goals than the Committed Achievers because their aspirations had decreased greatly during their college years (Appendix Table 14.1). They had entered as freshmen just as certain as the Committed Achievers of going on to graduate or professional schools and with equally strong commitments to advanced degrees. As freshmen their job choices had indicated aspiration, on all three dimensions of aspiration, as high as the choices of both the Individualistic and Committed Achievers. However, their job aspiration scores were the only ones that were considerably lower at the senior than at the freshman level. In the face of the more common pattern of maintaining earlier aspirations, the adjusted aspiration scores of the senior Activists understandably departed from those of the equally politically committed students. The Activists had lowered their personal aims while the Committed Achievers had not. What explained this difference? We suggest that it lay in their college experiences.

Most of these dynamics were revealed in the interviews we conducted in 1968 with seniors we had studied since their freshman year. Six of these interviews are presented at the end of this chapter. They show the increased confidence and strong collective identifications of two Committed Achievers—a young man who had been politically active throughout college and as a senior planned to enter law school to become a criminal lawyer, and a young woman who planned to study for the Ph.D. in sociology and regional planning; the steadfast ideological and psychic stance of two Individualistic Achievers—a young man who expected to enter graduate school to become a research chemist, a young woman headed for a career in engineering; the decreased aspirations of two Activists—a young man who entered college with his sight on a career as a research scientist but planned at graduation to teach science in high school, a young woman who was not even sure as a senior that she could work in a poverty program as a youth worker, or for that matter get a Civil Service job, but might have to settle instead for teaching social science in high school.

College Experiences: Clues to the Resolutions

We drew a picture in Chapter 11 of the politically committed student, at least on active campuses, as socially integrated, broadly active in campus organizations, in closer touch with the faculty, and just generally engaged in college life. Examining the college experiences of these four types of seniors, we found, however, that it was *only* the Committed Achievers, *not the other Activists,* who could be characterized that way (Appendix Table 14.5). The Committed Achievers, and only they, stood out in both 1968 and 1970 for:

contact with more faculty outside the classroom,

greater use of faculty in planning for the future,

finding these faculty contacts more helpful,

belonging to more campus groups,

holding more leadership positions on the campus,

participating especially in more governance committees and Afro-American groups,

identifying more often as student leaders and less often as casual types,

participating more often in at least some Black-oriented events, especially those concerned with the politics of Africa and political nationalism at home.

The Committed Achievers and Activists did experience some aspects of college life similarly. They both identified more often than other seniors as political types and Afro-American students; together they more often participated in political events on the campus; they more frequently had taken Black studies courses. Nonetheless, the differences in their experiences, despite their common ideological proclivities and overlap in political activities, seemed to have mattered in important ways. Here were two groups who had entered college with similar personal goals; they had expressed similar views about the world. Yet, they left college four years later with very different personal goals, one group having lowered their sights, the other having maintained strong commitments to individual achievement as they found paths they believed would make their personal goals of benefit to others. The Committed Achievers may have been deluding themselves; they may have been rationalizing to protect strong personal ambitions. The truly committed revolutionary would argue they were. The choices they were making, primarily for law and medicine, and the ways they talked about using their professional skills rang true to us. In fact, they seemed so genuine and serious that we feared they had unduly restricted their aims to only the most obvious avenues of service. The Activists wanted to serve, too, but they had lowered their aims to goals that no longer required prolonged advanced training and would not provide so obvious a challenge to their talents or gratification of status and power motivations. We suggest that they were not as motivated by these personal ambitions.

Why had these two groups of activists increasingly diverged despite showing equivalent performance histories? We do not offer final answers to such a complicated issue, but some clues do flow from their college experiences. College had not been the same broad success experience for the Activists as for the Committed Achievers. The Activists had not been especially active in campus affairs other than their political affiliations. They had not experienced the confirmation of success that comes from being a leader on the campus. They had not developed close ties with the faculty despite having performed as well as the Committed Achievers academically (Appendix Table 14.5). Faculty have sometimes been viewed as exclusively fostering militancy and radicalism among activists. Our results suggest that such a stereotype of faculty influence misses the critical difference that the faculty made in the college experience of these two groups of activists. When the faculty was most influential, it was because of their career guidance and their personal interest in the student's future. The Committed Achievers had had closer ties with faculty altogether; that resulted in career effects that the other group of Activists had missed. Of course, we do not know how the Committed Achievers developed these ties. It is hard to argue clear-cut effects from these data, and it is far too simple to urge the faculty to "do something" about the other Activists. Most students, not just Activists, probably would benefit from closer ties with the faculty. The Activists needed something—faculty models, successful leadership, social experiences—to help them put it all together, as the Committed Achievers had done. There was nothing about their activism per se that distinguished them from the Committed Achievers. They were not more marginal; they were not alienated—just less successful. They were not ideologically different, not more militant, not more rigid. This group of Activists seemed to have lowered their personal goals not because they felt high achievement was inconsistent with commitment but because they did not know how to integrate their personal and collective commitments. They lacked experiences the Committed Achievers had had.

The contrast in the college experiences of the Committed and Individualistic Achievers focused on much the same issues, the role of the faculty and meaning of social success on the campus (Appendix Table 14.5). Despite similar grades and equally high aspirations, the Individualistic and Committed Achievers had experienced college differently. The Individualistic Achievers had not had the same general success. They had not been leaders on the campus. They had not been especially active, even in conventional collegiate activities. Their peculiar reduction in confidence, despite reasonable performance, might not have occurred had their worth been rewarded in nonacademic ways. Nor did they show a distinctive subcultural pattern. Their confidence might not have eroded even without nonacademic successes and leadership had they atypically identified as scholars or as intellectuals, or had they participated in a "main-chance" subculture. But they did not cast their friends as any particular types of students. Their own identifications were not distinctive. Overall they seemed less integrated into campus life. They dated less; they more often named someone off campus among their three best friends; they less often mentioned cross-sexed relationships among their closest friends on campus. We would not make much of friendship data if they did not support a picture of the Individualistic Achievers as loners who found college less successful generally. They were less touched by the experience of going to college. When we asked seniors how they felt they had changed, this group reported less change across the board. By their own admission they ended college much the same as they had entered it. Was there also something special that promoted ideological insulation? When they had participated more than other students, it was always in conventional events, like attending Greek Nite or going to hear popular artists who came to the campus. What they did in atypical numbers reinforced their conventionality rather than shaking them up. These students needed to be challenged—psychically, ideologically. Standing still had not stood them well. The example of the Committed Achievers shows that a more critical, somewhat cynical social perspective will not dampen personal commitments even when expressed in political activity. Engaging these Individualistic Achievers in debate, challenging their conventional outlooks, and encouraging them to think about broader and specifically political questions might have helped, rather than threatened, the personal goals that motivated them so exclusively.

PROFILES: INDIVIDUALISTIC ACHIEVERS, COMMITTED ACHIEVERS, AND ACTIVISTS

Committed Achiever (Female)

R planned to work for a year with the Urban League prior to entering graduate school to study for a Ph.D. in sociology and regional planning. Eventually she intended to take a professional, nonacademic position in community development. She anticipated that her Ph.D. training would provide the technical research skills she would need in a planning job. As a freshman she had planned to become a social worker and to study for a master's degree. Her career interests had continued to be in the same field, but meantime she had learned about the opportunities for greater influence and challenge that would be opened by attaining a doctoral degree. She was very clear that this was not to take her away from an activist role. "I don't really know whether training in sociology will put me where I want to go. One of the reasons I want a year out is to find a place where I can get the planning and policy skills that might not be available in academic sociology. But I know I want a Ph.D. because I want to get into a situation where I have some real power and influence over development issues."

Absolutely sure of her ability to handle the work she was planning for her future, she also viewed herself as academically competent. She thought her performance would be better than 90 percent of the class, set A as the highest grade she could get, and felt completely certain she could achieve that. She thought her verbal and oral skills were in the top 5 percent of her class although she considered herself in the bottom half in mathematical and scientific skills. Her test anxiety scores put her in the middle third of the sample, indicating more anxiety than was typical of the Committed Achieving group. When she talked about her doubts about realizing her aspirations, she focused exclusively on financial concerns. She was already helping to support a younger sister who was just beginning college and believed that a year of working and looking around for the right graduate school would help the family out greatly. She added: "I just hope I don't get trapped into finding it hard to go back to making less money and contributing a lot less to my family when the year is over." Since she added that she was completely certain of going to graduate school in another year, the risks she described were probably not too important.

In some ways her college experiences were not typical of the Committed Achievers since she defined herself as fairly uninterested in campus affairs. She had not been active in campus government although she had worked on the campus paper, been active in both a dance and a theater group, as well as been active in the political activities. She also had participated in all of the Black-oriented lectures, concerts, and other special events that took place during her senior year and identified as a political and Afro-American type of student. Although she did not see herself as a student leader, she did go beyond political identifications, accepting the description of the "creative, somewhat nonconformist students" as appropriate for her. She seemed to combine political and artistic interests and activities in ways that were not typical for either the Committed Achievers or Activists.

She stressed "strong identification with my race" when she talked about how she had changed since she came to college. "Before I came to school I identified with whites more than I do now. I mean white values at least. Here I became more aware and proud of the fact that I was part of a Black group. I'm not sure I would have said those things about myself as a freshman but I think I've really changed." She also felt she had learned to "think for myself without being influenced by my family. College has made me realize what my purpose in life is and being willing to go after it in ways my folks think is pretty unrealistic. I'm sure they still believe I'm just going into social work like other people they know." When asked if there were any of these changes she was not too happy about, she added "I guess I'd say I've become prejudiced and suspicious of white people. I mean I question their intents very often and sometimes I wonder if I haven't gotten too cynical about the whole thing. Maybe that happens when you come to see things in a different light from what you always believed."

With a history of four years of consistent involvement in civil rights activities and political organization, she was not very interested as a senior in student power issues. She agreed that the college exercised too much authority over students and felt that students ought to have much more power than they did. She just was not personally committed to student power activities. In fact she had not gotten involved in the campus unrest that had turned the campus upside down in her senior year. As she put it, "I've been too busy doing things out in the community to care very much about what goes on on campus."

Arguing that being Black hurts the life chances of Black people in this country, she stressed that discrimination occurs in every section of the country. "Too many students think that discrimination is less vicious in the North. Having lived in California for part of my life, I know things are bad everywhere. It makes it twice as hard for Black people to obtain their goals as white people." She believed that the field she was going into would make race somewhat less of a factor in her own situation, but she stressed that discrimination would probably operate even for her. "The idea that all these new programs are looking for Blacks is only partially true, at least at the level I want. First of all there aren't very many jobs where there's real policy authority. And there's still a lot of prejudice of wanting whites in those jobs with Blacks carrying our program implementation. My eyes aren't closed about that." Like other Committed Achievers and Activists, she consistently blamed the system for race inequities and favored collective over individual strategies of change.

She said she particularly admired W. E. B. Dubois, Malcolm X, Sojourner Truth, Frederick Douglass, and John F. Kennedy; her favorite authors, Lorraine Hansberry, Richard Wright, Albert Camus, James Baldwin, and Nikki Giovanni. Favoring nationalism over integration, she explained nationalism as the idea that Blacks should "have control of economic enterprises and political control in areas where they live." She added, "It also has a cultural aspect—it means an awareness and subsequent pride in yourself and therefore the ability to bring about significant political and social changes."

R named the Dean of Students at the college as having had the greatest influence on her by providing opportunities for her to actually work in community development while she was in school. "We had lots of long talks and he opened my eyes to the things I could do if I was willing to make the big commitment to the Ph.D. I wouldn't have known about things like regional planning and public administration or research evaluation if it hadn't been for him. I guess you could say he took me seriously and that really meant a lot." She mentioned further having been close to two other faculty members, both women, both examples of "doing your own thing."

Her aunt had "made me realize the need to identify and work with my people. She's been involved in the NAACP and political activities all her life, and on top of being a mother and holding a top job in welfare administration. She didn't have any daughters and has always been close to me. She's my father's sister and just a very different kind of woman from my mother. I mean I feel close to my mother too but it was different with my aunt. She made me realize that being just a good mother wasn't the salvation of Black people. Maybe I'm not expressing it very well but I guess I learned through seeing what she's done with her life that you can be strong and effective without being domineering." When we asked how the aunt's example made her realize the need to identify and work with Black people, she added, "Well, it's sort of like my mother's way is just a personal and private solution. I don't think that having just a personal commitment to yourself and the family is enough anymore. I want to do something that makes a difference for the Black community in general."

She was sure that she wanted to marry some day and thought it would probably happen while she was in graduate school. She expected to continue working after marriage to pursue her career interests. When asked what she would do about working if she had children, she gave a response rare for women in this student population. "I expect to work because I think you can be a better mother if you have things you care about yourself. Sitting at home and playing middle-class mommy isn't going to help Black children deal with the world they face. My kids have got to learn that you have to get out there and be involved if anything is going to change. I can be an example for that and still be a good mother in the usual sense of that."

Repeatedly, we saw a pattern of influences that encouraged two aspects of unconventionality in this young woman. Some influential people stood for individualistic, but nonetheless unconventional, insistence on doing what you want to do, even as a woman. Others stood for collective comitments. She was merging these two into personal aspirations that set her apart from most women students and at the same time represented her strong ideological commitments.

R was born in Montgomery, Alabama, but had lived in California during her high school years.

Individualistic Achiever (Female)

S had entered college planning to go into electrical engineering and as a senior she still intended to pursue a career in engineering. She expected to go ahead to graduate school immediately following college but she was not at all certain of entering a Ph.D. program. As she talked about her future educational and job plans, she expressed a great deal of concern about both her ability and sex-role conflict. She said she had "some doubt about my ability but it's probably adequate to do this kind of work," a response that put her in the least self-confident quarter of her class. Admittedly her choice was demanding and, therefore, that she questioned her talent could be expected from the choice she was making. She also lacked academic confidence, however. She thought her academic performance would be better than only 50 percent of her class, again putting her in the bottom quarter of the confidence scale. She felt that B− was the highest grade she could get and felt there was some possibility she couldn't achieve even that. She felt she was in the top 10 percent of her class as to mechanical, scientific, and mathematical skills, but in the bottom half in English and reading skills and in the bottom quarter in oral skills. Actually she had been performing at sightly above a B average throughout her college career despite having been enrolled mostly in engineering courses. Somehow she seemed less confident of her talent than her performance should have led her to feel. In addition, she also expressed many doubts about the fit between engineering and getting married. She felt there was some possibility she wouldn't actually end up as an engineer because "I have plans of getting married and am not completely sure that this is a field for a married woman whose husband will not be in the same or a similar field." She expected to get married after finishing a year of graduate school. Although she said she wanted to continue to work after marriage to pursue her career interests, she admitted being very uncertain about whether she would work while her children were small. When asked about her major reasons for not wanting to work after having children, she said, "I think I ought to give my children the love and attention they need. The guy I plan to marry feels very strongly that a mother's care cannot be substituted for by babysitters or anybody else. I agree with him but I would like to work so that I can provide my children all the necessities as well as luxuries that I feel are important to them. Probably what I'll do is work just part-time while they're little." Having put herself through college and feeling keenly the negative consequences of having to work too much, she was especially concerned about making sure her own children would have it easier in life. In fact the major way she felt she had changed since coming to college was, "facing up to my own responsibilities, that I would have to work and take care of myself entirely." She continued, however, "I'm not happy about having to do that. I don't see it as a positive change at all. It isn't what I expected would happen when I came to college. I really thought my parents could help me more than it turned out. So I've had to adjust to a way of living that I don't think has contributed anything except making me too busy to do as well as I should have. Everything has been an uphill fight for me and sometimes I'd just like to get married and be taken care of for the rest of my life. But I know you can't depend on that. I'm going to make sure that I can earn a good living in my own right, no matter what happens."

This young woman was highly motivated but at the same time ambivalent not only about her career goals but about the reasons behind her choice. Her assessment of how she had changed since coming to college fits with all this. She felt she had undergone a marked increase in ambition and now held somewhat clearer occupational plans and a much clearer view of the general direction she wanted to take in life. But she felt much less self-confidence and somewhat less excitement and enthusiasm about learning than when she entered college. Her achievement goals seemed predominantly based on necessity and on fears of economic insecurity rather than on intrinsic challenge and gratification. Her test anxiety understandably was very high, in the top 10 percent of her class. Yet, despite the general lack of self-confidence and anxiety about achievement, she had a very strong sense of general efficacy in life. She answered all the personal control questions, indicating that she would be able to control what happened in her life. Repeatedly, therefore, we see a pattern of unusual aspiration, especially for a woman, as well as a strong sense of both her capacity to take care of herself and insistence that she would be prepared to do so if necessary. At the same time she seemed to long for a situation where some of her dependency could be met and comforted.

When we asked her what were the important influences since coming to college, she stressed, "My experiences are what have changed me and made me feel so strongly about what I'm going to do in life. I always wanted to be an engineer but I have new reasons for wanting to do it." She added that her advisor in engineering had also been very helpful to her. "Everytime I had a problem he would always help me, whether it was personal or about college life. He gave me an incentive to stay in school and keep at the engineering and he seemed to understand why I wasn't sure I could do it. He knew perfectly well that it was strange for me as a woman to be in engineering but he never seemed to think it peculiar himself. I guess that mattered a lot, too." When asked if there was anyone outside of college whom she felt had had an effect on her, she adamantly answered no. "I wish there had been somebody who'd been influential. I've always done it on my own."

No one else in college other than the advisor in engineering had been very helpful to her. She had never tried to use the placement office or the residence hall advisors, faculty members, or any of the student personnel services on the campus. When asked if she had found the faculty helpful in planning about what to do after college, she said she had tried once or twice but found it very unhelpful. She had taken no part in any extracurricular groups or activities at college. It was not just that she was politically inactive; she was generally inactive. She viewed herself as a casual type and an ordinary, average type of student. These same characteristics fit all three of the friends whom she talked about, all of whom were women majoring in sciences. When she was asked if there was a student whom she particularly admired or respected, she answered: "There's no one around here who's very admirable. The students who get picked out as the leaders around here are really out for themselves. But I guess everybody is, to some extent. If you don't look out for yourself, nobody else will." In this account of her college experience we see the same theme of almost exaggerated autonomy, of not being hooked in to any particular subgroups or areas of college life, and of some distrust of student leaders who stood out as success examples. She shared with the male Individualistic Achiever an aloofness from the college scene, although her distance seemed to be based more on conflict about being alone than on wanting to be autonomous.

Predictably, her ideological stance was conventional. Despite her unusual job aspirations, she held reasonably conventional views about the woman's role in motherhood. The issue of student power was not too important: "The things that have been done around here have been really ridiculous. Nothing has ever happened after any of the marches or demonstrations that the students have initiated." She also felt that students had quite a bit of power at this school already and added that, "It's about the right amount." She answered five of the six individual-collective questions favoring individual mobility as the way to handle discrimination. She also favored individualistic interpretations of race inequities; she answered three of the four individual system blame measures by asserting that Black people have mostly not taken advantage of the opportunities that came their way. Favoring integration over nationalism, she also looked to the Southern Christian Leadership Conference as the best civil rights group and picked out Martin Luther King, Whitney Young, and James Meredith as the best leaders.

She particularly admired Booker T. Washington, George Washington Carver, John F. Kennedy, and Edward Brooke. Her favorite authors were James Baldwin, Ralph Ellison, and Ayn Rand. Like the male Individualistic Achiever, she consistently insisted that race was irrelevant to what generally happens both for other Blacks and herself. She felt that "Race rarely enters into a teacher's decisions about grades; it is how good a student is that counts"; "Getting into predominantly white colleges depends solely on individual merit"; "Getting promoted on the job depends only on ability, creativity, and hard work"; "Ability in past performance is the only criterion for who gets admitted to graduate and professional school"; "If I'm not successful in achieving my goals in life, it will be because I didn't work hard enough or use enough initiative." When asked whether being Black has something to do with the life chances of Black people, she said it is "irrelevant depending on their qualifications. I don't think being Black ever hurts. I think if you are prepared and can meet competition, you can get the job." She viewed most things in individual terms, just as she analyzed the forces that operated in her own life. She did not view herself or her situation as connected with a more commonly shared Black experience. Her doubts and uncertainties seemd to center in the stance of aloneness; she was a loner all the way.

S grew up in Riveria Beach, Florida.

Activist (Female)

T entered college expecting to major in general science and to teach science at the high school level or to work as a lab technician in a research laboratory. She had switched to a major in social studies and listed three possible job directions she might take—work in a poverty program with disadvantaged youth, teach social studies at the high school level, or take the civil service examination and work somewhere with the government. She really wanted to work with the poverty program, but she wasn't sure she could find a job there with just a BA degree. When she did not mention going to graduate school among the things she might do in the few years following graduation, we asked how she felt about that as something to do some time in the future. 'Maybe I might want to go someday but I'm not sure I'd be accepted, and I really want to rest from the whole academic thing. I just don't know if I'll ever really want to go back." She ended by saying there was "a pretty strong possibility" she would not go. Since her real job aspirations were unclear, we could not interpret her job confidence assessments. She said she was pretty sure she had the ability to do the kind of work she had chosen, a not very optimistic assessment for this population. Since she had already indicated that she feared she was not qualified for a poverty program job and did not have the background for graduate school, she seemed to be admitting to doubt even about her ability for teaching or taking a civil service job that she, herself, viewed as less demanding. Saying that she could perform better only than 50 percent of the class, she also set C+ as the highest grade she could get. Yet she had entered as a freshman with entrance scores in the top quarter of her class and with a confidence that seemed to match. As a freshman she had thought that she could do better than 75 percent of the class and set B+ as the grade she felt matched her potential and that she was trying to achieve. By the time she was a senior her grade aspirations had dropped to around C; C was indeed the average she had achieved. She thought of herself as in only the upper half of her class in all of the skill areas we asked about—mathematical, scientific, English, oral, and manual-mechanical. She was not particularly anxious about tests; her test anxiety scores were in the bottom third of this sample.

When asked how she had changed in school, she referred to a decrease in aspiration. She said, "The things I used to think were important I just don't see that way now. I feel now that if an A is gotten and nothing is gotten from the class, it is to no avail. I'm just not very concerned about making good grades or being the success I used to think I wanted. My whole outlook has broadened. The things my parents taught me were very narrow. They thought the most important thing was 'getting on,' especially making a mark that other people admired. I don't want to do that at all anymore. I just want to find a way to help kids who haven't had the opportunities I've had." Her level of aspiration and the bases of her goals had both shifted. She developed a genuine service orientation away from the science stance she brought with her from high school.

Other students were able to combine a service orientation with achievement at a higher level than she admitted having. She herself saw the shift as carrying a double meaning: a drop in ambition, and an increase in the commitment to others. When she evaluated the ways she had changed on the dimensions we gave, she talked about having much less ambition than when she entered college, somewhat less self-confidence, somewhat less clarity about the direction she wanted to take in life, but marked increase in interest in politics and world affairs, in African culture and heritage, in social issues and social problems, and in civil rights.

When we asked about who had an effect on her since coming to college, she talked about three students, two of whom had also been active in the local movement. "I've come to evaluate what I want out of life very differently because of all the talks we've had. In some way or other we were all sort of looking out for ourselves when we got to school. I don't mean we didn't care about other people but mostly we just never thought about what our responsibilities were. Getting active in the movement and seeing people in real poverty really opened my eyes. I've come to feel you can't think about what's best for you and ever make the choices that help other people. If you think about personal advancement, there'll always come a time when you rationalize taking a better job that makes you leave the people you've been working with. It just always happens." The same theme emerged when she talked about the faculty member she viewed as having been most influential for her at school. "I admire him because he seems to understand and is concerned about students. He makes me feel that when I'm out of school, I will be concerned and not just out there because of the pay. I think a teacher should really put himself into it and that's what his actions have taught me."

Her ideological commitments were characteristic of Activists. She insisted that being Black hurts the life chances of Blacks in America because "racism is everywhere. No matter how much education or experience you have, the color of your skin is the determining factor in whether you get a job. These are just facts that more Black people should face up to." She felt that the kinds of choices she was making might make being Black a job asset. But she added, "It all depends on who's in power. If I'm being interviewed by a white person, even for a poverty program, the same old prejudice will enter in. I'd like to work for a community-controlled program, not because I think Blacks will always be fair. It's just that I think it is bound to be a fairer situation both for me and for the kids in the program." She favored Nationalism over integration, viewed the events in Newark and Detroit the preceding summer as a revolt rather than a riot, looked to the leadership of Stokely Carmichael, Adam Clayton Powell, Rap Brown, and Martin Luther King as positive forces. She felt that the college exercised too much authority over students and that students should have much more power than they held, especially in disciplinary actions and in curriculum. She added that the issue of student power was very important to her; she had been among the active group in the campus confrontations during her senior year. She had also been consistently involved in civil rights activities and in political organization work during her college years. She preferred collective strategies of handling discrimination and believed that discrimination and other system obstacles accounted for race inequities in this society. She particularly admired Frederick Douglass, Harriet Beecher Stowe, W. E. B. DuBois, Franklin Roosevelt, and Malcolm X. Her favorite authors were James Baldwin, Richard Wright, John Donne, and Langston Hughes.

In addition to political activities she had been active in the Association of Women Students, although she had never been an officer in that organization. She had not affiliated with a sorority and said that she "would not want to do so." She thought of herself as a political and Afro-American type, and she accepted the last phrase in the description of intellectuals on campus—"students who talk a lot about the meaning of life, students who like to analyze things and look for meaning behind events."

Her closest friends were also politically oriented. The student she most admired on the campus had been class president and she viewed him as a student leader.

She did not present the same picture of marginality that the male Activist did, although she certainly had not had the leadership experience that the female Committed Achiever had had. The most important aspect of the college for her had been what the movement and her friends in the movement had provided, that is, to question the success motif, a stance that probably was of less concern for students who exercised real leadership on the campus.

T grew up in a small town of South Carolina.

Committed Achiever (Male)

D came to college intending to go into chemical research and switched fields because of receiving an undeservedly low grade in his sophomore year. "I might not have switched just because of that but at the same time I was getting more and more interested in economics and political science while taking part in the political organizing of Lowndes County. The more I worked out in the community the more I felt law was the way I could be most effective politically." He now intended to go into law school after completing his ROTC obligation. "If I could do anything I wanted next year, I would spend the year studying in Africa and then come back to law school. But I am absolutely certain I will go into law after the army. My experiences have made me much more aware of the pervasive implications of racism in this country and I want to do something about it. Being Black hurts Black people's life chances because the very roots of this country are racist." He felt that his own life chances would be hurt too, "because there is no such thing as individual exceptions; we're all Black together and somehow the general conditions here affect everyone to some degree. It used to be that Blacks could consider themselves just as individuals—but no more. You can't delude yourself anymore."

D believed that going to a Black college had prepared him for his life work in a way that an integrated school could not have. "I absolutely need knowledge and experience as a Black. I want to work with and for Black people. People who go off to integrated schools lose a lot by just having to defend themselves and their integrity in that environment. I have been able to deepen my understanding in a more open way."

The person at school who had had the greatest influence on D was an African instructor. "He is from Biafra but his knowledge is much broader than that. He has forced many of us to go beyond the obvious, almost doctrinaire, point of view that says we are Afro-Americans; he's made us want to dig in and really find out about peoples in Africa. Also he forces students to think, to be creative and to assert themselves. He has shown me that I am significant, that I count because I can do these things."

In answer to structured probes about how he had changed since coming to college he said, "I have become much more clear about my occupational plans, have had a marked increase in ambition, in interests in politics and world affairs, in African culture and heritage, in social issues and social problems, and greater clarity about the direction I want my life to take. I don't think I have changed in my interest in civil rights and issues concerning Blacks in America because I was always interested. I'd say I am a much better student. But there are ways I haven't changed at all: I feel as I always did about religion, about getting married, about fraternities and sororities, about art and music. I wasn't ever very excited about those things; I'm still not."

D had been active politically all through college. He took part in the local affiliate of SNCC as a freshman, continued to work in Lowndes County the next year, and was active in the campus protests in his senior year. In addition, he was active in student government, in a jazz club with special concerns about African music, in the political science club, and the campus newspaper. He participated in every Black-oriented event that occurred during his senior year: he had attended the film, Come Black Africa, the symposium, "Speak Out on South Africa," the Miriam Makeba concert, the lecture by Ron Karenda, as well as the student meetings that focused on the campus unrest of that year. Consistent with his general participation in campus life, he also attended most of the more typical collegiate social activities, all of the outside music groups that came to campus, and voted in the campus elections. But he did not participate in any Homecoming events or in the Greek Nite activities. He felt that the college exercised too much authority over students but added that the worst part of it was the "generally cold atmosphere that makes students feel the administration doesn't care." Thinking that students should have "much more power than they have," he stressed especially that they should have more to say about course requirements and about the selection of instructors and the Board of Trustees. These issues were not typical student power concerns; most students stressed student life regulations rather than curriculum and high-level authority.

He most admired Nat Turner, Denmark Vessey, Toussaint L'Overture, Frederick Douglass, and Malcolm X. The authors he liked best were Harold Cruse, Eldridge Cleaver, W. E. B. DuBois, James Baldwin, and Richard Wright. He viewed the events that had taken place the previous summer in Newark and Detroit as a "rebellion," felt that they had helped the Black cause, and favored Nationalism over integration. He talked of Nationalism in political terms: "Black people in control of their own political, economic, and social institutions." Black leaders he considered "good" included Muhammed Ali, Rap Brown, Stokely Carmichael, Martin Luther King, Floyd McKissick, and James Meredith. At the opposite pole, he considered Edward Brooke, Roy Wilkins, and Whitney Young "harmful to us." He answered all the system-blame questions by blaming discrimination rather than inadequacies of Blacks themselves; he also answered all of the individual-collective questions favoring collective strategies of social change.

He felt more self-confident as a senior and pointed to a faculty member's influence as critical. He said he was "absolutely sure" about his ability to become a lawyer; he felt he could do better than 90 percent of the class academically; he believed that "A" was the highest grade he could make and was "pretty certain" he could get at least that, although he more often aimed for something between B+ and A−. He viewed himself in the upper 5 percent of his class in reading or English and oral skills but only in the upper half in mathematical or scientific skills. These judgments reflect the switch he had made from science to law. His test anxiety scores were in the bottom half of the sample. He answered all but one of the personal control questions expressing strong convictions about his capacity to control what happened in his own life.

Unconventionally for Committed Achievers, he liked the idea of his wife having her own career. "She should have interests of her own that motivate her and it would also mean a better material life for the whole family."

D grew up in Savannah, Georgia.

Individualistic Achiever (Male)

B was quite certain that he would go to graduate school in chemistry, although his draft status might make it impossible the next year. He had known he wanted to be a chemist in high school and his college years had reinforced his determination. He did not believe that being Black would be a handicap to his career. "Being Black is irrelevant to what happens in life because it is the initiative of the person that counts. If he wants to do anything, and has the initiative, he can do it. Being Black will be irrelevant for me personally; I'm just as good as another person. If I want to do something I will do it. I will not let my race interfere with anything I want to do. I got a lot of this from my mother who is the person I would say has had the greatest effect on me. She instilled in me since I was very little that I could do anything I wanted and that I should make decisions on my own." His years in college had had very little influence: "When I think about how I have changed in college, I would say I've just gotten more sure of the things I felt before coming here. I'm very much the same person, only more convinced, more solid that way." Consistent with his sense of initiative, he also expressed very high personal control: he answered all five questions indicating he can control what happens in his life.

He had joined only the YMCA and the chemistry club in college. He had not attended any of the Black-oriented events in college but he did go to the Homecoming parade and dance, Greek Nite, and the Paul Winter Jazz Ensemble. As yet another indicator of his conventionality, he felt that the students should have about the same amount of power as they then held and, in fact, said that there were no areas of campus life in which students should exercise the major influence. Moreover, he would not approve of his wife coupling marriage and a career because "a woman might put her career ahead of marriage."

Despite his determination and his sense of autonomy, he thought of himself as being able to do better than only 50 percent of the class (a response that put him in the bottom quartile of confidence for this student population); he also listed B− as the highest grade he could get and was only "pretty," not completely, certain of being able to attain that—and this despite being in the upper two stanines on both verbal and quantitative scores. His academic anxiety also put him in the top third of this student population.

He named Presidents Roosevelt, Kennedy, and Lincoln, as well as Booker T. Washington and George Washington Carver, as historical figures he particularly admired, and Steinbeck as the author he most admired. He urged stepping up the bombing and invading the North as United States policy in Vietnam, strongly agreed that "a former member of the Communist Party who refuses to reveal the names of Party members he had known should not be allowed to teach in a college or university" and that "it is proper for the government to refuse a passport to a Socialist"; he felt that things in Newark and Detroit the summer before his senior year hurt the Black cause, adding that "Black Power means the same as white supremacy." His preferred civil rights organization was the NAACP. Muhammed Ali, Martin Luther King, Thurgood Marshall, Carl Stokes, Roy Wilkins, and Adam Clayton Powell were all considered as showing "good leadership," while Rap Brown and Stokely Carmichael were both judged as providing "bad leadership." He preferred to be called "Negro." He answered all four system-blame questions by blaming the deficiencies of Blacks rather than discrimination; he answered all three questions about modifiability by seeing discrimination as modifiable. The one thing that does not fit neatly in his strong preference for collective action: he answered five of the six questions favoring collective action rather than individual mobility.

He further showed the same pattern of optimism and feeling of the irrelevance of race in the following responses: He agreed that "The average Black can have an influence in political decisions," "Today when Blacks make plans, they are almost certain they can make them work," "Race rarely enters into a teacher's decisions about grades; it is how good a student is that counts," "A Black has a much better chance of getting ahead today than ten years ago because of social change," "Black students find it easier to get into white colleges today than ten years ago because white colleges are actively recruiting Blacks," "Getting to be an executive in a major company depends on ability and training alone; race has little or nothing to do with it," "Ability and past performance are the only criteria of who gets admitted to graduate or professional school"; "If I am not successful in achieving my goals in life, it will be because I didn't work hard enough or use enough initiative." He answered 11 of the 13 Protestant ethic questions indicating a strong belief in the role of internal virtues in determining success in life.

Over and over this young man's beliefs, experiences, and goals showed an overriding individualism that he expressed simultaneously in enormous personal initiative and in traditional judgments of the role of race in the social order.

B grew up in Eldridge, Alabama.

Activist (Male)

C had entered college intending to become a mathematician or research physical scientist. As a senior he intended to teach physical science at the high school level. When asked why he changed his career goal, he said: "I didn't really change my interests; I just can't hack the math at the level it would take to use it as the primary part of a job. It got to seem like a career in research would be years and years of preparation and then wouldn't put me in touch with people. I got more people-oriented." Actually he would like to become a counselor in a college if "I could do anything I really would like." Settling for teaching high school represented a compromise both with his freshman aspirations and even his ideal goal as a senior. Part of his doubts about accomplishing what he would like ideally centered on his ROTC obligations. "I will have to serve four years in the Air Force as a result of AFROTC. I just think that will mean that I won't go to graduate school because I'll want to settle down when I get out. I couldn't get into college guidance work without graduate training. I am just being realistic."

C was "absolutely sure" about his ability to teach high school, but that after all was less challenging even in his own mind than his other two goals. He became less confident of his academic strengths during college. As a senior he felt he could "do better than 50 percent of the class"; as a freshman he had felt the potential to "do better than 90 percent of the class." In talking about the "highest grade he could get," he settled on a solid B; he also felt that was what he had been aiming for in college and what he had accomplished. As a senior he did not judge himself as in even the upper quarter of his class in any skill area. As a freshman he had considered himself in the top 5 percent in English skills and the top 10 percent in both mathematical and scientific skills. All of this points to reduced aspiration and confidence, some of which may have been realistic. Yet his entrance scores and actual grades had matched the levels of both the Committed and Individualistic Achievers just described. It was reduction beyond the necessary.

Like the Committed Achiever, C consistently focused on negative implications of discrimination. "Being Black hurts the life chances of most Black Americans"; "Being Black will hurt my life chances just because there is an element of racism and prejudice everywhere; anyone who doubts that is just kidding himself." He particularly admired Denmark Vessey, Toussaint L'Overture, John Brown, Nat Turner, Stokely Carmichael, John F. Kennedy, and Horace Greely; his favorite authors were W. E. B. DuBois, E. Franklin Frazier, Ann Petry, Malcolm X, and Truman Capote. Favoring Nationalism instead of integration, he felt that Nationalism meant that "Black people get the power of the vote, money, and education to raise themselves from second-class citizenship." He did not differentiate among leaders, however, in the way the Committed Achiever did. All Black leaders were evaluated as "good," even those representing more moderate ideologies and strategies.

In talking about one or two of the biggest areas of change since coming to college, C said "I have developed more race awareness. Before I came here I was like most typical Blacks. My values were white-oriented; I was ashamed to be Black. Now my values are its great to be Black." His responses to structured questions about change confirmed this. He agreed he showed a "marked increase in interest in politics and world affairs, in African culture and heritage, in social issues and social problems, in civil rights, in issues concerning Blacks in America." He felt "much more clear about my occupational plans" but felt "somewhat less ambition" and "somewhat less enthusiasm about learning," and "much less self-confidence than when I entered college." When asked if anyone at college had influenced him or had been really important in the ways he had changed, he simply answered no. The greatest influence on him during the previous four years had come from Malcolm X. "His writings and speeches simply changed my outlook on being Black in America. I believed all kinds of delusions until his writings and my experience in the movement opened my eyes." He also denied that he especially admired any student at college.

Consistent with his insistence that no one had influenced him, he also denied having gotten to know any teachers outside of the classroom. When asked about opportunity to get to know faculty, however, he said he was "fairly satisfied." He identified with "students interested in political and social issues," "the Afro-American students," and "the ordinary, average type students" but selected the political label as most appropriate to him. None of his three best friends were politically involved despite his own long history of political involvement. Two of them were "really serious students," the third an "ordinary, average type student." While he belonged to a fraternity, he said as a senior that he had not taken part in any other group or activities at college. His political activity—he had taken part in every single political event of note during his four years of college—was not prompted by a friendship group nor connected with other campus activities. He felt especially keenly about the school exercising authority over what students did off campus, arguing that students should have "much more power" than they did. When the areas of power were further probed, he listed also that students should have a greater role in choosing speakers and that students should decide under what circumstances another student should be dismissed. Finally, C had not attended the Ron Karenda lecture or either of the programs on Africa, although he had participated in the student power meetings in his senior year and had attended the Miriam Makeba concert. Consistent with his Greek affiliation, he had also taken part in Greek Nite. All in all, college had not involved him terribly much. He added that "my own reading and working in voter registration and out in Lowndes County were my real education."

C grew up in Montgomery, Alabama.

chapter 15

Highlights and Implications

INDIVIDUAL AND COLLECTIVE ACHIEVEMENT

We have organized the results of the several studies we conducted between 1964 and 1970 around one central question: How did students attending Black colleges integrate their collective commitments as Blacks with their goals for individual achievement and personal fulfillment? The first part of the book examined the students' future educational and occupational commitments as the individual achievement dimensions of personal identity. The second explored their collective action experiences as indicative of collective achievement and the collective medium for forming personal identity. The third focused on students who did manage to integrate these individual and collective aspects of identity—the Committed Achievers who had been involved throughout their college years in collective efforts to change the conditions of life for Black people and who finished college planning to pursue professional training for personally challenging occupations through which they could also continue to serve the Black community. What have we learned that challenges traditional thinking about achievement?

Since individualism underlies so much conceptualization in social science, it is difficult even to think about involvement in collective action as a form of achievement. It is hard to conceive of achievement as pride in seeing one's group gain power or pleasure in having contributed to an improved standard of living for other group members. Yet many people intuitively understand psychologists when they talk of the individual's anticipated pleasure of meeting a personal standard of excellence as the need for achievement. Perhaps we might as easily imagine the anticipated pleasure of helping the group achieve its goals as related to achievement if we lived in a society, a Chinese collective or an Israeli kibbutzim, that stresses collectivist goals. The students who were caught up in the early days of the southern student movement knew what such pleasure was. But for the most part Americans simply do not conceive of group products and accomplishments as relevant to achievement because the cultural stress on individualism has been so well internalized.

Why, then, insist on viewing these collective change efforts as collective achievement, as we have done in this book? Why not reserve the concept of achievement for the individual student's efforts for personal advancement and fulfillment? Why not characterize the student's collective action experience simply as "student activism?" Why insist on setting the student's involvement in social action within the context of achievement? First, the motivation of the students who were committed to collective goals carried all the usual connotations of achievement motivation. Their collective commitments and group identifications prompted hard and persistent effort as well as the setting of group goals that were both difficult and realistic. They showed pleasure with the *process* of trying to create change as well as with the *product* of change as defined by a specific target or campaign goal. Second, reserving the term achievement only for the accomplishments of the individual misses important elements of achievement motivation for the personal identities of minority students. Group identification and collective commitments play an important role in identity formation. We foster the minority student's ambivalence about achievement if an exclusive press for individualistic mobility cements the fear that individual accomplishments must come at the expense of, or at least from the indifference to, other members of the group. No wonder some students experienced guilt over personal success and even occasionally defined their presence in college as evidence that they had irrevocably turned their backs on home and the group.

Our results showed that collective achievement and consciousness of self as part of a collectivity did not destroy individual achievement motivation. Traditional academic achievement and individual goals were not necessarily in conflict with strong commitments to the group and collective action. Some students managed to do both. Some held onto high levels of personal aspiration for educational and occupational achievement and gained pleasure from meeting personal standards of excellence while they also worked persistently throughout their college years to improve the conditions of life for others. So why do many people fear that collective commitments will jeopardize individual achievement? Partly the fear is legitimated by the stress in collectivist-revolutionary thought itself on the irreconcilability of personal goals and collective commitments. Partly the fear is reinforced by any one example of a student whose commitments to civil rights, to protest of the war, or to institutional change in higher education overrode academic and traditional achievement commitments. We suspect, however, that revolutionary writing and case examples of the revolutionary dropouts are only minimally important in accounting for the prevailing uneasiness, especially among educators, about the implication of collective commitments for individual achievement. We believe that the individualism implicit in traditional thinking about achievement motivation goes further in explaining why many are wary of group consciousness, group action, and ideologies that stress collective responsibility. Achievement theory typically presents familial and group loyalties as inhibitors of individual achievement because they may reduce the individual's willingness to leave the group or home when opportunities for individual advancement appear. Competition, rather than cooperation, with others and thus with other group members is generally stressed as fostering individual achievement motivation. If readiness to leave the group and to engage in competition with other members is deemed necessary for individual achievement, should we wonder that collective commitments are considered antithetical to personal achievement? Fortunately, we believe that these precursors of individual achievement have been grossly exaggerated. Geographical mobility, and thus the willingness to break family and group ties, is necessary for individual advancement in only certain occupations and at only certain periods in the process of industrialization. Very little evidence has been marshaled to show the necessity of competition with other individuals for the development of achievement motivation. Indeed, we often forget that the original conceptual definition of achievement motivation emphasized competition with one's *own* standard of excellence rather than competition with others. The necessity of individual competition also flies in the face of solid evidence that Russian schoolchildren do achieve and develop individual achievement motivation from cooperative, rather than competitive, experiences within the peer group. Competition plays a role, but it is competition between groups, not between individuals. Our own data have shown that one of the college environments that most promoted the students' personal educational and occupational goals, as well as their personal expectancies of success, stressed communal and familial themes, especially the idea that success need not depend on the failure of others. This college more than any other minimized individual competition as a motive for personal achievement; yet it was singularly effective in enhancing its students' commitments to individual achievement.

Individual and collective commitments can coexist and neither has to threaten the other. Both are also necessary for personal identity, especially so for students from minority groups who, in periods of nationalism, press group members to fight oppression and to commit themselves to the collective welfare. What have we learned about the Committed Achievers that enabled them to integrate these two levels of identity and two types of achievement?

The Significance of the College Experience

The analyses and profiles reported in Chapter 14 highlight the significance of the college experience. The social backgrounds of the Committed Achievers were not atypical. Their personal strengths and ideologies as freshmen were not atypical. They differed from the Activists who had shared their political experiences, but only as seniors, not as freshmen. They differed from the Individualistic Achievers who matched their unusually high levels of individual aspiration, but only as seniors, not as freshmen. Where we could unravel the dynamics of change from the longitudinal study of one college, we learned that the Committed Achievers departed from other students as seniors because they had managed to maintain, even increase, the personal aspirations and individual achievement motivation with which they had entered college while they used the activism experience to develop much stronger collective consciousness and group commitments. The Committed Achievers were the only group who assessed their personal competencies more favorably at the senior than at the freshman year. The increase in confidence characterized how they judged their potential for academic success, their abilities to get jobs and perform well on them, and their overall sense of personal control. Something happened during their college years to make these politically active students feel generally more efficacious and surer of themselves occupationally and academically. They were also unusually sensitive to the social world. They showed that strong identification with the collectivity need not daunt expression of personal goals. They held on to highly prestigious and demanding career goals at the same time they stressed the collective impact of discrimination and racism. They talked more than any other group about social restrictions and conditions of oppression. They emphasized systemic problems as the source of race inequities. They criticized conventional explanations of success in favor of more balanced views that stressed social as well as individual determination. They nearly unanimously agreed that discrimination affects all Black people and cannot be avoided by special privilege or status. They argued that discrimination operates at all levels of the occupational structure and thus must be seen as a collective phenomenon. These students—who possessed more than the average consciousness of discrimination—stood in sharp contrast to the view that awareness of restriction necessarily produces hopelessness.

A broadly successful college experience seemed to foster the mutual development and reinforcement of individual and collective achievement among the Committed Achievers. The study of the effects of activism demonstrated that taking part in collective action fostered the preferences for collective change strategies that had predisposed students to get involved in the first place. Participation also promoted new ways of thinking about inequities and prepared students to respond positively to the press for collectivism in the writings by Black Nationalists later in the decade. Most students shifted from individualistic to collectivist theories of change, but it was particularly the stable activists who most reflected the new consciousness and collectivist ideology. Taking part in collective action was a clear source of ideological impact. Additionally, when activism was embedded in a broader set of leadership and success experiences on the campus, individual achievement goals did not suffer. The Activists lowered their personal aims; the Committed Achievers did not. The difference seemed to lie in their campus experiences beyond the political activities they shared in common. The Committed Achievers, but not the Activists, stood out for having had contact with more faculty outside the classroom, turning to faculty specifically for help in planning their future careers, finding these faculty contacts more helpful, belonging to more campus groups, holding more leadership positions on the campus, having had more experience in campus governance committees and groups concerned with educational policies, and having taken advantage of more campus events with a distinctively Black political perspective. Activism alone did not promote the integration of collective and individual achievement. Activism in a particular context did. The critical context was provided by certain aspects of the college environment—faculty-student contact and diverse extracurricular offerings broadly available to students—that also facilitated individual aspirations. In addition, the campus culture had to support the importance of political action. On the campuses where participation was very rare, the activist student was marginal to other aspects of campus life and the activist experience was not a prime source of ideological development.

The contrast of the Committed Achievers with both the Activists and Individualistic Achievers points to the significance of the combination of these college experiences—activism itself, meaningful contact with the faculty, broad leadership success, and subcultural supports—as conditioning when collective and individual achievement were mutually reinforcing. For example, the Activists had lowered their personal goals, but not because they felt high achievement was inconsistent with collective commitments. Nothing in the experience of activism per se produced polarization, at least during the period we studied, which included two periods when activism and radicalization were especially pronounced. The Activists were not more marginal; they were not alienated—just less successful. They were not ideologically different, not more militant, not more rigid. Had they entered college with less promise for traditional achievement, or with much lower aspirations, or with more rigid collectivist views, some might argue that their activism expressed different motivations from the activism of the Committed Achievers; some might feel that the college experience should not be expected to alter the differences. This was simply not the case where we could use the longitudinal data over the four years of college to unravel the dynamics of activism and achievement goals. The Activists ended their senior year with lower goals because they did not seem to know how to integrate their personal and collective commitments. What they lacked—and the Committed Achievers had—were faculty models, success in leadership, subcultural supports, and social experiences that proved to them it was possible to combine their freshman goals with their increasing activism and collectivist thought. We also saw that the Committed Achievers differed ideologically and personally from the Individualistic Achievers whose high achievement goals they shared, but they differed only as seniors, not as freshmen. The Individualistic Achievers had entered college thinking much like other freshmen. But as seniors, they held different ideological views because they did not move with the other students toward greater social awareness, cynicism, and collectivism. They held onto conventional views in a period when rethinking racial issues was the norm. Moreover, their stability extended beyond their social ideologies even to aspects of their achievement motivation. Whereas the Committed Achievers had become more self-confident, the Individualistic Achievers appraised themselves as seniors much as they had as freshmen. Even in their own subjective views they reported less change during the college years. The contrast in the college experiences of the Committed and Individualistic Achievers centered on many of the same issues that separated the Committed Achievers and Activists—the role of the faculty, and the meaning of social success on the campus. The Individualistic Achievers had not had the same general success; they had not been especially active, even in conventional collegiate activities. They had not developed subcultural identifications. Overall, they seemed less integrated into campus life, less touched by the experience of going to college. What they did in atypical numbers reinforced their conventionality rather than shaking them up. They needed what colleges ideally can do best: they needed to be challenged, personally and ideologically.

We will not prescribe how colleges might do this. We have seen that faculty contact mattered greatly, and not simply to foster radicalization and activism but to help the Committed Achievers think through and actualize their future goals. But how fruitful is it to appeal to faculty to help more students and to extend themselves outside the classroom when they already teach more courses and spend more hours in the classroom than seems tolerable? While their strictly curricular work loads conform to the other small colleges with equally low resources, their teaching commitments do not allow much time for counseling and getting to know students. Certainly not all faculty extend themselves even where resources are greater and work loads are lighter. At least the appeal to faculty would not then come as a hollow cry. Indeed, we have been repeatedly struck with the enormous commitment to students by large numbers of the faculties, despite pressures that militated against it. The very fact that their influence proved so critical attests to their commitment. Increases in institutional resources that allow more faculty to be hired and work loads to be lightened would help. Every college administrator has known that for a long time. The difficult problem is mustering the resources. As the financial base for higher education has become increasingly insecure, it has also become popular in some circles to suggest that inventiveness and flair thrive best when they must. We do not agree. Although resources are no substitute for educational inventiveness, neither can much happen without them. Some experiments made possible through increased support to small and developing colleges during the sixties did prove useless; many others, especially in special freshman programs for the "new students," in work-study arrangements, in faculty counseling, both excited and helped many students. We need not excuse the dim financial picture by seeing it as cause for hope.

The Significance of a Differentiated Conception of Internal and External Control

The fact that the Committed Achievers simultaneously expressed a strong sense of personal control and showed such sensitivity to external causes of racial inequities raises implications about the meaning of internal and external control. Literally hundreds of studies have examined the determinants and consequences of internal and external control. Since performance on standard tests has generally correlated positively with internal scores on the I-E scales, and especially so for minority students, many people suggest that everything possible should be done to increase the minority person's sense of internal control. Numerous interventions—such as personal counseling, behavior modification programs, and participation in decision making—have been used to increase the sense of control. Indeed, some theoretical models of minority achievement make internality the central issue.

While we agree that a personal sense of control can contribute to many positive outcomes, our results suggest that the meaning of internal and external control is far too complicated to advocate simply increasing internality as a global personality disposition. We have shown that only some types of internal control carried positive motivational implications, even when used to explain indicators of conventional individual achievement. To review briefly: a personal sense of control, where success in one's own life was attributed to one's own effort or ability, generally promoted positive motivation. Students with a strong sense of personal control more often aspired to advanced education and to challenging and difficult careers; they performed better on traditional achievement tasks and received higher grades in college. By contrast, external control scores were associated with several of these achievement indicators when externality pertained to the role of social and economic forces in determining race inequities. Men who were especially aware of racial discrimination and blamed it for status differentials between Blacks and whites also more often aspired to jobs heretofore closed to Blacks. These externally oriented, system-blaming students were unusually attuned to the social and economic realities that produce both constraints and opportunities. This reality interpretation of the meaning of system blame was buttressed by the fact that men who chose occupations that realistically challenged their talents particularly stood out for their system-blame ideology. Blaming the system was also associated with more effective performance, at least among students who felt personally efficacious themselves. These results clearly showed that an external orientation promoted rather than inhibited healthy motivation when it depended on assessing systematic social forces that do realistically structure the achievements of minorities. We also saw repeatedly that this kind of external orientation was associated with collective achievement throughout the period we studied. Stress on economic and social determination, an ideology that was at once external but not powerless, was positively related to civil rights participation in 1964, 1968, and 1970 and to participation in campus-based change efforts in both 1968 and 1970.

Over and over these results point to the significance of a combination of internal and external control beliefs. Students who managed to feel personally efficacious but recognized the critical role of systematic external forces in determining what happens in the lives of Black Americans also showed they could integrate collective and individual achievement. The pattern found most frequently among the Committed Achievers was one of internal scores on the measure of personal control but external scores on the system blame and control ideology indices. The Individualistic Achievers believed just as firmly in their own sense of personal control but they were not as sensitive to social and economic forces. The Activists believed just as firmly in an ideology that held social and economic forces responsible for race inequities, but they were not as sure of their own sense of personal control. Surely, then, we would not want to convince students that internal control is always better. Instead we must be guided by a much more differentiated conception of internal control. We do want to help students develop greater control over their personal lives. We should try many approaches—counseling, providing personal success experiences, involving students in decisions that do affect their lives—to encourage a sense of personal efficacy. But the targets of control should be clearly personal: you can control how you behave toward your friends, whether you learn anything new today, how you use your time, whether you choose to work; maybe you can even control some of the things that happen in your classroom, although instructor's biases and behaviors are not completely controllable by students' efforts and behaviors. By contrast, we should not convince students that they can individually control what happens more broadly in their schools and colleges since many external forces control finances, programs, personnel, and so forth. We would be sorely remiss if we tried to convince students that they can control even more distant people, institutions, and events. Unemployment, subemployment, low pay scales, the location of factories beyond the central city, and inadequate transportation facilities probably go further than anything about workers' lack of internal control or other personal characteristics in explaining why incomes are so low in most American cities. We surely want to help students understand the complicated dynamics behind poverty and race inequality in our society. We would do them a grave disservice if we simply tried to make them generally more internal. They need to understand the complex set of forces that do influence the problems we are up against. Only some can be affected by personal action; more by their collective action; and some only by social and economic readjustments that they can influence only very minimally. Overall, students will behave more effectively if they recognize that there are limits to internal control and personal action while they are motivated to influence the external forces that may be subject to the political power of the group. The Committed Achievers seemed to have done exactly that.

FACTS AND FANCIES

We have presented data that either counter common expectations or provide new information about Black students. Although we already have stressed these results at several points in the book, we also want to highlight them here.

The Insignificance of Family Background

The students' social backgrounds influenced individual achievement far less than some, although by no means all, previous research suggests. None of the family and social background measures significantly influenced the grades students earned, their performance on standard achievements tests and on tests typically used in achievement motivation research, or their scores on measures of achievement motives and values. It was only the students' educational and occupational aspirations and expectancies of success that correlated significantly with precollege background. Moreover, the link between aspirations and home background existed only among freshmen; by the senior year the effect had disappeared. Furthermore, the dynamic of the precollege influence supported the importance of current environmental resources and opportunities more than the impact of early family socialization. We have argued this because (a) social background influenced expectancies (which at the psychological level reflect the objective possibilities and constraints of the environment) more than it influenced motives and values that presumably arise out of early family socialization and (b) the influential aspects of the precollege background that pertained especially to expectancies of success were family income and rural-urban residency, each of which indicates that objective differences in opportunities between the poor and the more well-off, the urban and the rural students. Finally, the results of the social background analyses of collective achievement likewise supported the insignificance of family status or socialization. Instead, it was the opportunity to participate, as reflected in rural-urban residency, that was the most important influence on collective achievement, especially on participation in civil rights activities. Growing up in a rural part of the South and attending a rural college virtually precluded participation in civil rights.

The Absolute Irrelevance of Father Absence

The common belief that father absence negatively influences the achievement of Black students likewise received no support. Family structure characteristics were consistently included in the analyses of both individual and collective achievement. Whether the student grew up in a nuclear, two-parent family or in one of two father-absent families (a mother-headed family or an extended family) simply had no bearing on: *individual achievement*—college grades, college entrance test scores, performance on achievement tasks, job aspirations of men students, expectancies of achieving career goals, graduate or professional school goals and expectancies, commitments to education, self-confidence about ability, achievement motives and values, work-ethic values; *collective achievement*—system-blame ideology, preferences for collective action, political nationalism, civil rights participation, involvement in student power activities, or Black student organization membership. Its only effect was the positive relationship of growing up in a mother-headed family on the women students' aspirations for demanding careers that were viewed as unconventional for women.

We can only conclude that family characteristics, especially father absence and the family's socialization effects, have been exaggerated far beyond their actual impact on either the individual or collective achievements of Black students, certainly at the college level but probably at the high school level as well. We are by no means the first to question the prevailing acceptance of home factors as critically determining the achievement outcomes of minority students. Although much research does support the point that students' socioeconomic characteristics account for a large part of the variance in performance on achievement tests, very little research has actually isolated how much of the impact follows from social inheritance and how much from current inequities and discrimination by class and by race. Results from appropriate block-recursive designs in which it is possible to tease out the relative importance of family influences at different points in the life cycle are just now gaining a hearing. The important work of the Duncans, which tries to explain achievement outcomes later in the life cycle, especially race differentials in wages, points to the greater significance of various sources of current discrimination than to even the combined direct and indirect effects of family characteristics. Much more work of that nature needs to be done. The controversy about the import of the home versus schooling or the significance of family socialization versus present discrimination is not solved. Our data should be viewed as part of a continuing research endeavor on a critical problem in American society. In that context these data add evidence that questions the role of family status and socialization and supports the role of environmental opportunities and college socialization.

The Myth of Female Dominance

Instead of enjoying favored status relative to Black men, Black women face the inequities of both race and sex discrimination. The college-educated Black woman shows the effects not only in actual employment patterns but in her job and educational aspirations as well. She is not, as the widely held stereotype suggests, more ambitious than the Black man. The goals of the women reflected lower levels on almost every measure of educational and occupational aspiration. Although their desire to go to graduate school nearly matched the aspirations of the men, many fewer women intended to pursue professional degrees and many more expected to terminate graduate work at the master's level. The occupations women chose indicated considerably lower aspiration: they accorded less prestige, demanded less ability, and fell more often in the female sector of the labor market. Moreover, this pattern of sex differences in aspiration closely resembles data from national studies of college students. Three times as many men as women, both in the college population at large and the Black colleges we studied, plan to pursue doctoral or professional degrees. Figures on graduate degrees awarded show that the male edge for doctorates earned is nine to one in the nation at large, eight to two among Blacks. The size of the male edge in aspiration for traditionally masculine fields—law, medicine, physical sciences, and engineering—and the female edge for traditionally feminine fields —social work and teaching at the elementary and secondary levels—is approximately the same among Black and white graduating seniors. The fact that the colleges we studied influenced the future goals of the men more than the women again parallels national data. The accentuation of sex differences during the college years in orientations about career and marriage, in preferences of academic majors and occupational fields, and in number of years of desired education is one of the most reliable facts about change in college. We do not conclude that Black and white women, or Black and white men (even among the college population) experience life the same way or hold the same attitudes about themselves and their worlds. We do argue that the demands of sex role and patterns of sex discrimination in the society at large critically determine role-appropriate educational and occupational choices, be the women Black or white. Black women, compared to Black men and contrary to myth, will go on entering doctoral and professional training at a much lower rate, will end up in predominantly female jobs located disproportionately at the lower end of each category of job status, and will earn lower wages unless the sex-role constraints on Black women are faced for what they are. Again, we are not the first to point to the lack of empirical support for the presumed employment and economic edge of Black women over Black men. Our data add to other statistics showing the opposite picture. We want to stress, however, that these restrictions on Black women's aspirations are changeable. Colleges where faculty and students interacted frequently and where the student culture pressed intellectual values did positively influence the aspirations of women students, and specifically for careers that counter common sex-role stereotypes about feminine jobs. Colleges can challenge and encourage their women students to disregard the effect of these sex constraints on their future goals, although they will hardly do so if educators accept the common misconceptions about Black women in higher education and the labor market. Finally, we emphasize that the sex of the student was of little importance in the analyses of collective achievement. Whereas some writers have cast Black women as more aggressive and active in efforts at change, others have depicted Black women as less sophisticated politically, less militant, and likely to be pawns in the attempts of whites to coopt Black leadership. We found neither characterization to be true. These Black men and women were together in their action and ideologies throughout the sixties.

Black Activism: An Expression of Ideology, Not Powerlessness

A disproportionate concern with the urban revolts and complementary neglect of the political action of Black college students has distorted the picture of Black activism and left the impression that student activism was a white phenomenon. We pointed out in Chapter 9 that only 14 articles and three books on Black students or historically Black colleges are referenced in two major bibliographies on student activism, one with 211 and the other 188 entries. This neglect occurred even though we have shown that Black college students were always more active politically during the decade of the sixties. Although we have had to depend on estimates from inadequate data bases and often noncomparable samples, the contrast between the participation of Black and white students is so striking that we feel safe in drawing the conclusion we have. Whereas only 20 to 30 percent of the students in the nation at large had participated in political action by 1965, the participation figure for students in Black colleges was closer to 70 percent. Later on the scope of student protest broadened to include many more of the nation's universities and colleges; even so, a larger proportion of Black than of white institutions experienced campus unrest during the academic year 1967-1968 when student protest reached its highest peak. Also more Black than white students took part in the increasingly campus-based action of the second half of the decade. Three-quarters of the students in our sample reported in 1970 that they had participated in some form of political activity during their college years. By contrast, both the Harris and Gallup polls of 1967 and 1968 showed that the proportion of the nation's college students who had participated politically was still only about 20 percent.

This neglect of the significance of the action of Black college students has distorted the social and psychological meaning of both student activism and Black activism. We have already stressed that the social roots of activism among Black and white college students differed greatly. By having left the impression that student activism was a white phenomenon, social science has also drawn a portrait of the college activist as expressing the liberal values of "elite" families. This characterization became inaccurate even for white activists as their base of action broadened to include more colleges and universities at the end of the decade. It was inaccurate for politically engaged students from Black colleges throughout the decade. The critical social determinant of participation for Black students from southern Black colleges was whether they had the opportunity to participate, especially whether they had grown up in the rural South and were attending colleges located in rural areas where opportunities were restricted and reprisals more threatening. Had more attention been given to the action of Black college students, the popular literature on student activism might not have stressed family dynamics and personality of individuals nearly so much. Looking to family values, socialization practices, and personality to explain who participated in political action may be appropriate where the threat of reprisals impinges less severely. They were *not* the critical determinants of which Black students were active on Black colleges we studied, not in 1964, 1968, or 1970. Student activism is simply not well understood if information about it depends so exclusively on white students who were active at white colleges and universities. Likewise, Black activism has been misunderstood by overemphasizing the urban revolts and underemphasizing the action of college-educated Black youth. "Riot" participation and militancy attitudes have been cast, erroneously we believe, as reflecting the alienation, especially the sense of powerlessness, of the urban Black population. Because we used many of the same measures that have provided the interpretation of urban participants as external and "powerless," we have been able to show that Black student activists reflected the same set of beliefs about internal and external control. They, too, stressed that external forces largely account for social inequities in our society. We have contended, however, that this external ideology represents a sophisticated political stance in which social rather than individual determination is stressed. Furthermore, we presented data that directly contradicts the interpretation that the externality of "riot" participants represents the translation of powerlessness into "spontaneous, expressive" action rather than "sustained, planned" action. The students who had sustained their political action longest and who were active in the leadership that gave direction to civil rights activities, like the "riot" participants, held the most external ideologies. These students were the sustained, instrumental activists, but they scored most external on our measures of both control ideology and system blame. Their action reflected their awareness of social determination and their collective proclivities that combined into an activist ideology that was at once external but not "powerless." Inadequate attention to the action of Black college students made it possible to miss the common ideological commitments of Blacks on college campuses and of those involved in the urban revolts. Black activism, regardless of where it has occurred, has reflected the impact of a collectivist ideology that simultaneously puts the responsibility for inequities in the social and economic order and advocates the necessity of a collective, rather than an individual, response. If we insist on calling an external view, no matter how realistic or sophisticated, an indicator of powerlessness, we are ill-prepared to entertain the possibility that nontraditional forms of political action, whether they occur on college campuses or in our urban centers, are the instrumental acts of the more sophisticated and ideologically committed instead of the expressive outbursts of the more powerless elements of society.

Heterogeneity of the 10 Colleges

We have repeatedly stressed the heterogeneity of these 10 historically Black colleges. The differences among them were statistically significant and the range represented by them was striking on almost every characteristic we examined. To recapitulate briefly: They varied in academic status as judged by the Southern Association of Schools and Colleges. Some were privately, some publicly sponsored. Some had exercised considerable constraint over student and faculty participation in political action, some none at all. Sex ratios varied from one college where women represented 68 percent of the student body to another in which they were only 32 percent. Emphasis on liberal arts ranged from one college where 93 percent of the students were enrolled in liberal arts to another where only 29 percent were. The largest college enrolled 4088 students in 1964, the smallest only 498. They attracted students from different social backgrounds. One attracted a student body that was predominantly from college-educated and professional families while the college at the other extreme enrolled less than a fifth of its students from such backgrounds. While all the colleges served almost exclusively southern students, they varied from one where 59 percent were out-of-state residents to one where only 4 percent grew up in other states. Campus life characteristics also varied considerably. Amount of faculty student interaction ranged from one college where 90 percent reported nonclass contact with at least one faculty member to a college where only 40 percent did. Extracurricular activities outside the traditional collegiate social arena were much more numerous at certain of the colleges: on one campus 58 percent had taken part in such activities, while on another only a third of the students had. Civil rights participation ranged in 1964 from one college with 86 percent to another with only 13 percent of the students having participated, and, in 1970 from one with 85 percent to another with just 45 percent who had been active at some point during college. Academic values received greater stress by students at some colleges than at others. Disapproval of traditional college governance was stronger on some campuses and, although students at all the colleges were much more critical of parietal policies in 1970 than in 1964, the range of opinion among the colleges was considerable even in 1970. Finally, the colleges showed significant variation on almost all aspects of student achievement motivation and future aspirations. Even after adjusting for college differences in sex ratios and demographic characteristics of their students, the colleges still differed in the average level of their students' occupational and educational aspirations, college grades, academic self-confidence, sense of personal efficacy, and personal expectancies of being able to realize their goals. In only a few ways could these 10 colleges be described as serving homogeneous student bodies: it was only on the average level of the students' achievement motives and approval of Black Nationalism that the 10 colleges did not differ significantly.

Documentation of these institutional variations should reduce the tendency to view all historically Black colleges as homogeneous institutions. While people who know Black colleges are fully aware of both their common and unique patterns of historical development as well as their current heterogeneity, the wider public often is not. Even this small group of 10 colleges represented striking variability. Furthermore, while it is possible to show that Black colleges serve students who, on the average, come from somewhat different backgrounds and somewhat different viewpoints from those of Black students attending predominantly white colleges and those of white students in the nation at large, many of these southern Black colleges attract students who are remarkably like students attending other kinds of institutions. These data on the variation within the historically Black colleges add to other recent work on Black colleges that stresses their variability and the commonality between them and other colleges, especially between them and predominantly white colleges of the same size in the same states. This emphasis on heterogeneity in no way undercuts the strength of unity among the historically Black colleges. Black colleges can speak in one voice about policies and developments that affect them all while they also address issues they face in common with other types of institutions.

Beyond highlighting the heterogeneity of these 10 colleges, the data we have presented also show the importance of disaggregating the study of college impact. The analyses presented in Chapter 6 showed that positive motivational consequences generally resulted from frequent faculty-student interaction and from a student culture that provided diverse extracurricular activities and stressed academic values. Even so, the case examples of two colleges—one that accentuated its students' already initially high aspirations and expectancies and another that enhanced their level of aspiration beyond what would have been expected—indicate that these generally significant institutional characteristics assumed somewhat different meaning on the two campuses. The influence of the faculty, while important on both campuses, was especially critical in the heightened expectancy environment of the accentuation college where the faculty believed that absolutely every student could achieve and insisted that they would. The influence of diverse options for activity while important on both campuses, assumed unusual significance in the open, lively, exciting environment of the college that showed redirection effects. Civil rights activities, work-study opportunities, political and intellectual debates, and the college's special history as an intellectual and cultural center in the state exposed students to new opportunities far beyond what more conventional colleges could offer.

In a similar way, the college environment conditioned the motivational dynamics of traditional achievement outcomes. The material presented in Chapter 4 showed that expectancies of success were generally more important than either positive or negative achievement measures in accounting for the level of aspiration that the students' occupational and educational aspirations represented. We also pointed out, however, that certain college environments heightened the significance of motives and values. This was clearly true at one college where fear of failure and desire of security turned out to be the best predictors (in this instance, negative) of the men's job aspirations. In this particular environment the motivational strengths needed to hold onto higher levels of occupational achievement depended on an unusual commitment to achievement values and on limiting one's fears about security and anxiety about possible failure. While expectancies also influenced the men's aspirations somewhat, they mattered less in this particular setting than at colleges where social pressures for settling for comfortable opportunities in the local labor market and for the social status accorded by family position in the local Black community were less pronounced; expectancies were clearly less important than were the strengths to resist these kinds of social pressures at this college. We highlighted this unique pattern not to belittle the decision to live and work in this community or the reasons underlying the decision. Rather, the results underline the point that the dynamics of motivation depend heavily on environmental pressures and supports. While it was true that expectancies and feelings of competency generally assumed greater significance than most measures we had of achievement values and motives, that was not always the case.

The college environment also conditioned the dynamics behind collective achievement. We saw this occur in two ways. First, the climate of the campus, defined by whether activism was commonplace or not, influenced whether collectivist ideology actually was expressed in action. It was only where activism was reasonably widespread that ideology was strongly related to who participated. Most of the connections between collective consciousness, collective commitments, Black Nationalism, and activism were much stronger on the two campuses where the vast majority of the students had taken part in some political activity during their college years. We think of the institution's capacity to encourage students to act on their beliefs as a critical aspect of its effect. Second, the medium through which this happened became clearer when we also found that the picture of the activist as an integrated, campus leader applied only on those campuses where civil rights activism was commonplace. Indeed, the civil rights activists were marginal to traditional collegiate life at the two colleges where participation had been less universal. Instead of being unusually active in campus organizations and taking part in a political subculture that addressed typical problems on the campus as well as broader political questions, the civil rights activists on these two less active campuses thought of themselves as casual, creative nonconformists who were not serious students. They were involved instead in the community off the campus.

These examples all attest to the importance of looking not only for general effects but also for the unique effects that may stem from particular college environments. Some people argue that science is advanced only by general propositions and by empirical generalizations that hold in all conditions. That may be true. Nonetheless, we believe that the nature of the social world and the state of social science both demand appreciation of conditioning analyses. Most social and psychological relationships do not hold in all conditions. Instead we need to examine the conditions where a given relationship—for example, between expectancies and individual achievement or between ideology and collective achievement—applies and where it does not. The issues we have examined are far too complex to expect simple effects or to generalize too broadly. We personally feel that more is learned when the conditioning effect of the unique college environment can be specified, even when it is possible to demonstrate more general effects as well. Here are the facts. Not only did the 10 colleges represent heterogeneous environments, but certain of them also influenced students very differently from others. Black colleges cannot be viewed as a homogeneous group of institutions.

Support of Black Students and the Historically Black Colleges

The data we have presented in this book have documented the extraordinary commitment of Black students and their families to education. Black students are motivated: they persist in college despite grave financial obstacles; they hold high career aspirations; they want graduate and professional education every bit as much as white students; they work more frequently and more hours and end college with greater indebtedness as proof of their educational commitments. They also have to consider issues of group responsibility more than most other college students. Many of them evince unusual strength in pulling it all together. Their families often sacrifice more because so many more Black students come from very low income families than is true of the nation's college population. Facing their hardships, Black students have achieved an unusual feat by graduating from college in the numbers they do. The strength of their motivation is simply not the problem. The problem is finding the financial resources with which they can get the education that will allow them to achieve occupational parity with whites. We do not pretend that education is enough. The discrimination that reduces the income and occupational benefit to education for Black people must be wiped out. But education is necessary. The slight increase in Black enrollment in higher education that showed up nationally in 1965 was not sustained by 1973. Moreover, even stabilizing those gains would not suffice. Enormous expansion must occur. At the graduate and professional level admission of Black students would have to be multiplied by 15 even to reach the proportion of Blacks in the population at large.

The income distribution of Black people in the United States necessitates that any meaningful admission expansion has to draw most of the additional Black students from families with only moderate or low incomes. The data we have presented comparing the students from poverty backgrounds with those from more comfortable economic situations augur well for recruiting these additional low income Black students. The students who grew up in poverty attending these Black colleges were hardly distinguishable in motivation or performance from their financially more comfortable peers. Yet, despite their apparent motivational readiness for college, they had not experienced equal educational opportunities, if only because of financial inequities. Their parents obviously had not been able to provide them with as much financial support. Unfortunately, this differential in source of support had not been compensated by enough scholarship aid; the proportion of the lowest income group who reported receiving scholarship assistance was almost exactly the same as that of the highest income group. Black colleges have simply not had the resources to make scholarships a major aspect of financial support to students. Instead, students from poverty backgrounds were markedly distinguished by more frequent dependence on loans. Three times as many of them reported having all of their college costs covered by some kind of loan. Moreover, virtually all the students from the lowest income group, as compared to 40 percent of the most comfortable group, not only worked but, on the average, worked twice as many hours. Having to work as many hours as they did and ending college with so much indebtedness clearly put these low income students at a disadvantage in financing graduate or professional education.

Because these financial problems are real and because expansion of Black enrollment in higher education necessarily means recruiting students from low income backgrounds, Bowles and DeCosta conclude that achievement of universal higher education opens the only foreseeable opportunity to recruit and enroll the additional Black students who are needed to begin to close the professional gap between Black and white.[1] They advocate making the concept of universal higher education realistic by means of a national student finance program that would provide an education salary of at least $3000 to any student who wishes it. Many other proposals have been advanced.[2] Those least likely to be effective in promoting educational opportunity for students from very poor families are the educational opportunity bank and tax credit proposals. Those most likely to go to the heart of the problem are plans providing straight grants in aid to students based on

1. Frank Bowles and Frank A. DeCosta, *Between Two Worlds: A Profile of Negro Higher Education* (New York: McGraw-Hill, 1971).
2. John P. Mallan, "Current Proposals for Federal Aid to Higher Education," in M. D. Orwig, Editor, *Financing Higher Education: Alternatives for the Federal Government* (Iowa City, Iowa: American College Testing Program, 1971), pp. 303-330; and William H. Sewell, "Inequality of Opportunity for Higher Education," *American Sociological Review 36* (October, 1971), pp. 793-809.

need[3] and the ones providing capital facilities to provide space for these students and a cost-of-education supplement to institutions.[4] Clearly the larger aspects of the task can be undertaken only by the federal government. Despite passage of the recent higher education bills, there is no reason at the moment to feel reassured that the necessary commitment will in fact be made.

With sufficient financial assistance, the expansion of admission to students not now attending college would not only maintain current enrollment rates but provide for growth as well. This need not mean a loss in the student attributes important for high quality education even if the students were increasingly from homes with fewer economic resources. It is to this point that our data are most relevant. In fact, with sufficient financial support for the students and for the colleges, greatly expanding the admission of low income students would present the historically Black colleges, as well as other types of institutions, with the opportunity to have an additional educational impact, assuming that impact is thought of as student development and change and not a guaranteed output by the selection of the lowest risk students available. The most elite American institutions of higher education show little evidence of impact beyond their power to attract students whose precollege experiences virtually guarantee high levels of postcollege achievement.[5] Colleges could provide opportunities and develop the talents of low-income students who have the academic strengths characteristic of the students from poverty backgrounds who were already attending the Black colleges we studied. They were basically motivated, and their aspirations were low enough and flexible enough to be changed; they did not present personality deficits so often assumed to result from cultural restriction and deprivation. If colleges were to recruit more such students, they will need the kind of help colleges are uniquely prepared to provide. They need experiences that reinforce their self-confidence; they need information, exposure, and models who represent the viability of realizing high educational and occupational achievement. We do not mean that admitting more such low income, rural youth will produce a level of urbaneness and

3. Sewell, "Inequality of Opportunity"; Stephen J. Wright, "The Financing of Equal Opportunity in Higher Education: The Problems and the Urgency," in *Financing Equality of Educational Opportunity in Higher Education* (New York: College Entrance Examination Board, 1970), pp. 1-5; and Bowles and DeCosta, *Between Two Worlds.*
4. Wright, "The Financing of Equal Opportunity in Higher Education: The Problems and the Urgency"; and Bowles and DeCosta, *Between Two Worlds.*
5. Alexander W. Astin and Robert J. Panos, *The Education and Vocational Development of College Students* (Washington: American Council on Education, 1969).

social sophistication that many of the highest status students have traditionally brought to the most elite Black colleges. But we wish to stress,
from the data we have presented, the strong probability that they will
bring academic commitments and motivational strengths that should
make their potential for change and development the kind of challenge that higher education should symbolize.

We do not mean to minimize the applicability of these data for
predominantly white schools as well. However, we expect that the
historically Black colleges will continue to appeal to many Black
students; we also suspect that rural, low income students from the
South will be better served by the historically Black colleges. The
campus ambience is more familiar and less hostile to their needs and
concerns. Administrators and teachers in predominantly white schools
know so little of Black life that they find it hard not to confuse student
styles with student ability, motivation, or educability. Black faculty can,
although admittedly do not always, use their own experiences to make
these critical distinctions. The distinctions must be made if increased
enrollment is not largely compensated for by increased attrition. We
think Black colleges will want to promote the education and mobility
of such students. Black colleges have always served as a mobility route
for Black youth. As other institutions begin to serve similar functions
for some Black students, Black colleges can continue to do what they
have always done and done very well.

This book represents eight years of work in which we have seen
many shifts in mood on the campuses of these colleges. At no time has
pessimism been more pronounced than now. We hope that talking
about students will dramatize the costs of cutting support. We cannot
fool ourselves that Black students do not want to go to college and to
graduate and professional schools; that they do not share the professional aspirations of all college students; and that financial resources
are not necessary to turn their motivation into educational gains for the
Black community. Their motivation and educational commitments are
not problematic; financial support is. In more optimistic times Lorraine
Hansberry spoke to young Black writers, saying that "though it be a
thrilling and marvelous thing to be merely young and gifted in such
times, it is doubly so, doubly dynamic—to be young, gifted, and
black."[6] The pride and confirmation of personal authenticity that these
students spoke about as they described their struggle for personal and
group identity attested to the special privilege of being young, gifted,
and Black. It remains for the nation to make possible the full realiza-
tion of the gift of being Black.

6. Lorraine Hansberry, *To Be Young Gifted and Black,* Adapted by Robert Nemiroff
   (Englewood Cliffs, New Jersey: Prentice-Hall, 1969), pp. 256-257.

bibliography

Almond, Gabriel A., and Sidney Verba, *The Civic Culture* (Princeton: New Jersey, Princeton University Press, 1963).

Altbach, Philip, *Student Politics and Higher Education in the United States: A Select Bibliography* (Cambridge, Massachusetts: Center for International Affairs, Harvard University, 1967).

American Council on Education Research Reports, "National Norms for Entering College Freshmen, Fall, 1970," 5(6), p. 22.

Angrist, S. S., "The Study of Sex Roles," *Journal of Social Issues 25*(1) (1969), pp. 215-232.

Astin, Alexander W., "Determinants of Student Activism," in Julian Foster and Durward Long, Editors, *Protest: Student Activism in America.* (New York: William Morrow, 1970), pp. 89-101.

Astin, Alexander W., "Racial Considerations in Admissions," in David C. Nichols and Olive Mills, Editors, *The Campus and the Racial Crisis* (Washington: American Council on Education, 1970), pp. 113-141.

Astin, Alexander W., and Robert J. Panos, *The Educational and Vocational Development of College Students* (Washington: American Council on Education, 1969).

Astin, Helen, *The Woman Doctorate* (Hartford, Connecticut: The Russell Sage Foundation, 1969).

Atkinson, John W., *An Introduction to Motivation* (Princeton, New Jersey: Van Nostrand, 1964).

Atkinson, John W., and N. T. Feather, *Theory of Achievement Motivation* (New York: John Wiley and Sons, 1966).

Atkinson, J. W., and P. O'Connor, *Effects of Ability Grouping in Schools Related to Individual Differences in Achievement-Related Motivation,* Report to the U. S. Office of Education, 1963.

Atkinson, John W., and Joel O. Raynor, *Motivation and Achievement* (Washington, D.C.: V. W. Winston, in press).

407

Bachman, J. G., *The Impact of Family Background and Intelligence on Tenth Grade Boys,* Youth in Transition, Volume II (Ann Arbor, Michigan: Institute for Social Research, 1970).

Back, K. W., and I. H. Simpson, "The Dilemma of the Negro Professional," *Journal of Social Issues XX* (1964), pp. 60-70.

Baird, Leonard L., "Who Protests: A Study of Student Activists," in Julian Foster and Durward Long, Editors, *Protest: Student Activism in America* (New York: William Morrow, 1970), pp. 123-133.

Bassett, Bruce M., "Inequality and Instability: The Relation of Land Tenure to Politics," *World Politics 16* (1964), pp. 442-454.

Battle, Esther S., and J. B. Rotter, "Children's Feelings of Personal Control as Related to Social Class and Ethnic Group," *Journal of Personality 31* (1963), pp. 482-490.

Bayer, Alan E., "The New Student in Black Colleges," *School Review 81* (May, 1973), pp. 415-426.

Bayer, A. E., and R. F. Boruch, "The Black Student in American Colleges," *ACE Research Reports, 4*(2) (1969).

Bayer, Alan E., and Robert F. Boruch, "Black and White Freshmen Entering Four-Year Colleges," *Educational Record 50* (1969), pp. 371-386.

Becker, Gary S., *Human Capital* (New York: Columbia University Press, 1946).

Bell, R. L., "Lower Class Negro Mothers and Their Children," *Social Forces XLIII* (1965), pp. 493-501.

Bennett, W. S., and N. P. Gist, "Class, Family, and Student Aspirations," *Social Forces 53* (1964), pp. 167-173.

Berkowitz, Leonard, "Frustrations, Comparisons and Other Emotion Arousal as Contributors to Unrest," *Journal of Social Issues 28*(1) (1972), pp. 77-91.

Billingsley, Andrew, *Black Families in White America* (Englewood Cliffs, New Jersey: Prentice-Hall, 1968).

Billingsley, Andrew, "Black Families and White Social Science," *Journal of Social Issues, 26* (March, 1970), pp. 127-142.

Black, K. W., and I. H. Simpson, "The Dilemma of the Negro Professional," *Journal of Social Issues XX* (1964), pp. 60-70.

Blake, Elias, Jr., "Future Leadership Roles for Predominantly Black Colleges and Universities in American Higher Education," *Daedalus, 100* (Summer, 1971), pp. 745-771.

Bond, Horace Mann, *Black American Scholars: A Study of Their Beginnings* (Detroit, Michigan: Balamp Publishing, 1972).

Bond, Horace Mann, *The Education of the Negro in the American Social Order* (New York: Octagon Books, 1970).

Bond, Horace Mann, "The Negro Scholar and Professional in America," in John P. Davis, Editor, *The American Negro Reference Book* (Englewood Cliffs, New Jersey: Prentice-Hall, 1966), pp. 535-568.

Bowles, Frank, and Frank A. DeCosta, *Between Two Worlds: A Profile of Negro Higher Education* (New York: McGraw-Hill, 1971).

Bowman, Mary Jean, "Economics of Education," in Orwig, Editor, *Financing Higher Educational Alternatives for the Federal Government* (Iowa City: American College Testing Program, 1971), pp. 37-70.

Bracey, John H., Jr., August Meier, and Elliott Rudwick, Editors, Introduction, *Black Nationalism in America* (Indianapolis and New York: Bobbs-Merrill, 1970), pp. XXVI-XXVII.

Braungart, Richard G., "Family Status, Socialization, and Student Politics," *American Journal of Sociology 77*(1) (July, 1971), pp. 108-130.

Braungart, Richard G., and Margaret M. Braungart, "Social and Political Correlates of Protest Attitudes and Behavior Among College Youth: A Case Study," (Unpublished Paper, University of Maryland, 1971).

Brookover, W., A. Peterson, and S. Thomas, *Self-Concept of Ability and School Achievement: Final Report of Cooperative Research Project 845* (East Lansing, Michigan: Michigan State University, 1967).

Bryant, James A., *A Survey of Black American Doctorates* (New York: The Ford Foundation, n.d.).

Bullough, Bonnie L., "Alienation in the Ghetto," *American Journal of Sociology 72* (January, 1967), pp. 469-478.

Bwy, D. P., "Political Instability in Latin America: A Preliminary Test of a Causal Model," *Latin America Research Review 3* (1968), pp. 17-66.

Campbell, Angus and Howard Schuman, *Racial Attitudes in Fifteen American Cities,* Supplement Studies for the National Advisory Commission on Civil Disorders (Washington, D.C.: Government Printing Office, 1968).

Caplan, Nathan, "A Causal Model of Black Militancy," (Unpublished Paper, 1972).

Caplan, Nathan, "The New Ghetto Man: A Review of Recent Empirical Studies," *Journal of Social Issues 26*(1) (1970), pp. 59-73.

Caplan, Nathan, and J. M. Paige, "A Study of Ghetto Rioters," *Scientific American 219*(2) (August, 1968), pp. 15-21.

Carmichael, Stokeley, taped speech at The College H.

Carnegie Commission on Higher Education, *From Isolation to Mainstream: Problems of the Colleges Founded for Negroes* (New York: McGraw-Hill, 1971).

The Carnegie Commission on Higher Education, *Less Time, More Options: Education Beyond the High School* (New York: McGraw-Hill, 1971).

The Chronicle of Higher Education (May 30, 1972), p. 2.

Clift, Virgil A., "Educating the American Negro," in John P. David, Editor, *The American Negro Reference Book* (Englewood Cliffs, New Jersey: Prentice-Hall, 1966), pp. 347-377.

Coleman, J. S. et al., *Equality of Educational Opportunity* (Washington, D. C.: U. S. Government Printing Office, 1966).

Crawford, Thomas J., and Murray Naditch, "Relative Deprivation, Powerlessness, and Militancy: The Psychology of Social Protest," *Psychiatry 33*(2) (May, 1970), pp. 208-223.

Cross, K. Patricia, *Beyond the Open Door* (San Francisco: Jossey-Bass, 1971).

Crowley, J., T. Levitin, and R. Quinn, "The Seven Deadly Half-Truths About Women," *Psychology Today* (March, 1973), pp. 94-96.

Cruse, Harold, *Rebellion or Revolution?* (New York: William Morrow, 1968).

Darrow, Charlotte, and Paul Lowinger, "The Detroit Uprising: A Psychosocial Study," (Paper presented at the American Academy of Psychoanalysis, New York, 1967).

Davis, J. A., *Great Aspirations* (Chicago: Aldine, 1964).

Drake, St. Clair, "The Black University in the American Social Order," *Daedalus 100*(3) (Summer, 1971), pp. 833-897.

Drake, St. Clair, "Urban Violence and American Social Movements," in R. H. Connery, Editor, *Urban Riots: Violence and Social Change. Proceedings of the Academy of Political Science 29* (1968), pp. 13-24.

Duncan, Otis Dudley, "Discrimination Against Negroes," *Annals of the American Academy of Political and Social Science 371* (May, 1967), pp. 85-103.

Duncan, Otis Dudley, "Inheritance of Poverty or Inheritance of Race?" in Daniel P. Moynihan, Editor, *On Understanding Poverty* (New York: Basic Books, 1968), pp. 85-110.

Edwards, Harry, *Black Students* (New York: The Free Press, 1970).

Elder, Glen H., Jr., "Intergroup Attitudes and Social Ascent Among Negro Boys," *American Journal of Sociology 76*(4) (1971), pp. 673-697.

Epps, E. G., *Family and Achievement: A Study of the Relation of Family Background to Achievement Orientation and Performance Among Urban Negro High School Students* (Ann Arbor, Michigan: Institute for Social Research, 1969).

Epps, Edgar G., and Glenn R. Howze, *Survey of Black Social Scientists* (Tuskegee, Alabama: Tuskegee Institute, 1971).

Erikson, Erik H., "Identity and the Life Cycle," *Psychological Issues,* Monograph 1 (New York: International Universities Press, 1959).

Fanon, Frantz, *Black Skin, White Masks* (New York: Grove Press, 1967).

Fanon, Frantz, *A Dying Colonialism* (New York: Grove Press, 1965).

Fanon, Frantz, *The Wretched of the Earth* (New York: Grove Press, 1963).

Feierabend, Ivo K., and Rosalind L. Feierabend, "Aggressive Behaviors within Politics, 1948-1962: A Cross-National Study," *Journal of Conflict Resolution 10* (1966), pp. 249-71.

Feierabend, Ivo K., Rosalind L. Feierabend, and B. A. Nesvold, "Social Change and Political Violence: Cross National Patterns," in H. D. Graham and Ted Robert Gurr, Editors, *Violence in America: Historical and Comparative*

Perspectives (Washington, D.C.: National Commission on the Causes and Prevention of Violence, 1969), pp. 632-668.

Feldman, K., and Theodore M. Newcomb, *The Impact of College on Students* (San Francisco: Jossey-Bass, 1969).

Fichter, Joseph H., *Neglected Talents: Background and Prospects of Negro College Graduates* (Chicago: National Opinion Research Center, 1966), Report No. 112.

Fischer, Claude S., "A Research Note on Urbanism and Tolerance," *American Journal of Sociology* 76(5) (March, 1971), pp. 847-856.

Flacks, Richard, "Who Protests: The Social Bases of the Student Movement," in Julian Foster and Durward Long, Editors, *Protest: Student Activism in America* (New York: William Morrow, 1970), pp. 134-157.

Fogelson, Robert M. and Robert B. Hill, *Who Riots? A Study of Participation in the 1967 Riots,* Supplement Studies for the National Advisory Commission on Civil Disorders. (Washington, D.C.: Government Printing Office, 1968).

Folger, John K., Helen S. Astin, and Alan E. Bayer, Editors, *Human Resources and Higher Education: Staff Report of the Commission on Human Resources and Advanced Education* (New York: Russell Sage Foundation, 1970).

Forman, James, *Sammy Younge, Jr.* (New York: Grove Press, 1968).

Forward, John R., and Jay R. Williams, "Internal-External Control and Black Militancy," *Journal of Social Issues* 26 (Winter, 1970), pp. 75-91.

Forward, John R., and Jay R. Williams, "Rejoinder," *Journal of Social Issues* 27(1) (1971), pp. 233-236.

Foster, Julian, "Student Protest: What is Known, What is Said," in Julian Foster and Durward Long, Editors, *Protest: Student Activism in America* (New York: William Morrow, 1970), pp. 48-58.

Franklin, John Hope, *From Slavery to Freedom* (New York: Vintage Books, 1969).

Frazier, Franklin, *Black Bourgeoisie* (Glencoe, Illinois: The Free Press, 1957).

Gamson, Zelda F., Jeffrey Goodman, and Gerald Gurin, "Radicals, Moderates and By-standers During a University Protest." Paper read at the August, 1967 Meetings of the American Sociological Association, San Francisco.

Geller, Jesse E., and G. Howard, "Student Activism and the War in Vietnam," mimeographed (Yale University: Department of Psychology, n.d.).

Geschwender, James, "Explorations in the Social Movements and Revolutions," *Social Forces* 47 (December, 1968), pp. 127-135.

Geschwender, James A., "Social Structure and the Negro Revolt: An Examination of Some Hypotheses," *Social Forces* 43(2) (December, 1964), pp. 248-256.

Gore, Pearl M., and Julian B. Rotter, "A Personality Correlate of Social Action," *Journal of Personality* 31 (March, 1963), pp. 58-64.

412   Bibliography

Gropper, G. L., and R. Fitzpatrick, *Who Goes to Graduate School?* (Pittsburgh: American Institute for Research, 1959).

Gurin, Gerald, *Inner-City Negro Youth in a Job Training Project: A Study of Factors Related to Attrition and Job Success* (Ann Arbor: Institute for Social Research, University of Michigan, 1968).

Gurin, Gerald, *A National Attitude Study of Trainees in MDTA Institutional Programs* (Ann Arbor: Institute for Social Research, University of Michigan, 1970).

Gurin, Gerald, Study at the Institute for Social Research, The University of Michigan, Ann Arbor, Michigan.

Gurin, Patricia, Gerald Gurin, Rosina C. Lao, and Muriel Beattie, "Internal-External Control in the Motivational Dynamics of Negro Youth," *Journal of Social Issues 25*(3) (1969), pp. 29-53.

Gurin, Patricia, and Daniel Kutz, *Motivation and Aspiration in the Negro College* (Ann Arbor, Michigan: Institute for Social Research, 1966).

Gurr, Ted Robert, "The Calculus of Civil Conflict," *Journal of Social Issues 28*(1) (1972), pp. 27-47.

Gurr, Ted Robert, "A Causal Model of Civil Strife: A Comparative Analysis Using New Indices," *American Political Science Review 62* (1968b), pp. 1104-1124.

Gurr, Ted Robert, "Urban Disorder: Perspectives from the Comparative Studies of Civil Strife," *American Behavioral Scientist 11* (1968a), pp. 50-55.

Hall, Eleanor R., *Motivation and Achievement in Negro and White Students* (Final Report, U. S. Department of Health, Education and Welfare, 1971).

Hansberry, Lorraine, *To Be Young, Gifted and Black,* Adapted by Robert Nemiroff (Englewood Cliffs, New Jersey: Prentice-Hall, 1969).

Harrison, Elton C., "Student Unrest on the Black College Campus," *The Journal of Negro Education 41* (Spring, 1972), pp. 113-120.

Harwood, Edwin, and Claire C. Hodge, "Jobs and the Negro Family: A Reappraisal," *The Public Interest 23* (Spring, 1971), pp. 125-131.

Havemann, Ernest, and Patricia Salter West, *They Went to College* (New York: Harcourt, Brace, 1952).

Herzog, Elizabeth, *About the Poor: Some Facts and Fictions* (Washington, D.C.: U. S. Department of Health, Education and Welfare, 1967).

Herzog, Elizabeth, "Social Stereotypes and Social Research," *Journal of Social Issues 26* (March, 1970), pp. 109-125.

Hill, Robert, *Strengths of Black Families* (New York: Emerson Hall, 1971).

Holland, J. L., "Exploration of a Theory of Vocational Choice and Achievement. A Four-Year Prediction Study," *Psychological Reports 12* (1963), pp. 547-594.

Horner, Matina, "Toward an Understanding of Achievement-Related Conflicts in Women," *Journal of Social Issues 28*(2) (1972), pp. 157-175.

Innes, J. T., P. B. Jacobson, and R. J. Pellegrin, *The Economic Returns to Higher Education: A Survey of Findings* (Eugene: The Center for Advanced Study of Educational Administration, University of Oregon, 1965).

Jackson, George, *Soledad Brother: The Prison Letters of George Jackson* (New York: Bantam Books, 1970).

Jackson, Jacquelyne J., "But Where Are the Men?" *The Black Scholar* (December, 1971), pp. 30-41.

Jaffe, A. J., Walter Adams, and Sandra G. Meyers, *Negro Higher Education in the 1960's* (New York: Frederick A. Praeger, 1968).

Jones, Lewis Wade, "Vantage Points for Viewing the Negro College," (Unpublished Paper, Tuskegee Institute, Alabama, 1968).

Jones, Mack H., "The Responsibility of the Black College to the Black Community: Then and Now," *Daedalus 100*(3) (Summer, 1971). pp. 745-771.

Jorgensen, Carl Christian, *The Socialization and Meaning of Sense of Internal Versus External Control Among Black High School Students* (The University of Michigan: Unpublished Ph.D. Dissertation, 1971).

Kahl, J. A., "Educational and Occupational Aspirations of 'Common Man' Boys," *Harvard Education Review XXIII* (1953), pp. 186-203.

Karabel, J., and A. W. Astin, "Social Class, Academic Ability and College 'Quality'," (Unpublished Manuscript).

Keniston, Kenneth, and Michael Lerner, "Selected References on Student Protest," in Philip G. Altbach and Robert S. Laufer, Editors, *The New Pilgrims: Youth Protest in Transition* (New York: David McKay, 1972), pp. 313-326.

Ladner, Joyce A., *Tomorrow's Tomorrow: The Black Woman* (Garden City, New York: Doubleday, Anchor Books, 1972).

Ladner, Joyce, "What Black Power Means to Negroes in Mississippi," in August Meier, Editor, *The Transformation of Activism* (New York: Aldine Publishing Company, Trans-action Books, 1970), pp. 131-154.

Lefcourt, H. M., and G. W. Ladwig, "The American Negro: A Problem in Expectancies," *Journal of Personality and Social Psychology 1* (1965), pp. 377-380.

Lerner, Gerda, *Black Women in White America: A Documentary History* (New York: Pantheon Books, 1972).

Lessing, Elise E. and Susan W. Zagorin, "Factor Structure and Concurrent Validity of a Black Power Ideology Scale," *Proceedings of the 78th Annual Convention of the American Psychological Association 5*, 1970, pp. 353-354.

Lessing, Elise E., and Susan W. Zagorin, "Some Demographic, Value and Personality Correlates of Endorsement of Negro Militancy by Negro and White Youth," *Proceedings of the 77th Annual Convention of the American Psychological Association 4*, 1969, pp. 295-296.

Lewis, Hylan, "Race, Class, and Culture in the Sociopolitics of Social Welfare," *Race, Research, and Reason: Social Work Perspectives* (New York, New York: National Association of Social Workers, 1969).

Lewis, Oscar, *The Children of Sanchez* (New York: Random House, 1961).

Lewis, Oscar, "The Culture of Poverty," in Daniel P. Moynihan, Editor, *On Understanding Poverty* (New York: Basic Books, Inc., 1968), pp. 187-200.

Lewis, Oscar, *La Vida* (New York: Random House, 1966).

Liebow, Elliott, *Tally's Corner* (Boston: Little, Brown, 1967).

Lipset, Seymour M., "The Activist: A Profile," *The Public Interest 13* (Fall, 1968), pp. 39-51.

Long, Durward, "Black Protest," in Julian Foster and Durward Long, Editors, *Protest: Student Activism in America* (New York: William Morrow, 1970), pp. 459-482.

Mahone, C. H., "Fear of Failure and Unrealistic Vocational Aspirations," *Journal of Abnormal and Social Psychology* 60 (1960), pp. 253-261.

Mallan, John P., "Current Proposals for Federal Aid to Higher Education," in M. D. Orwig, Editor, *Financing Higher Education: Alternatives for the Federal Government* (Iowa City, Iowa: American College Testing Program, 1971), pp. 303-330.

Mandler, G., and S. B. Sarason, "A Study of Anxiety and Learning," *Journal of Abnormal and Social Psychology* 47 (1952), pp. 166-173.

Manifesto presented by students to the administration of a Black college, 1968.

Mankoff, Milton, and Richard Flacks, "The Changing Social Base of the American Student Movement," in Philip G. Altbach and Robert S. Laufer, Editors, *The New Pilgrims: Youth Protest in Transition* (New York: David McKay, 1972), pp. 46-62.

Marx, Gary T., *Protest and Prejudice: A Study of Belief in the Black Community* (New York: Harper and Row, 1967).

Mathews, Donald R., and James W. Prothro, *Negroes and the New Southern Politics* (New York: Harcourt, Brace and World, 1966).

Mathis, Arthur Lee, "Social and Psychological Characteristics of the Black Liberation Movement: A Colonial Analogy," (Ph.D. Dissertation, University of Michigan, 1971).

Meier, August, "Black Power at the Ballot Box," in August Meier, Editor, *Black Experience: The Transformation of Activism* (New York: Aldine Publishing Company, Trans-action Books, 1970), pp. 121-129.

Merton, R. K., *Social Theory and Social Structure* (New York: Free Press, 1964).

Miller, Jerry Lee Lamasnez, "Occupational Choice: The Construction and Testing of a Paradigm of Occupational Choice for the College Graduate," (Doctoral Dissertation, Florida State University, 1959).

Miller, Walter, "The Elimination of the American Lower Class as a National Policy: A Critique of the Ideology of the Poverty Movement of the 1960's" in Daniel Moynihan, Editor, *On Understanding Poverty* (New York: Basic Books, 1968), pp. 260-315.

Miller, Walter, "Lower Class Culture as a Generating Milieu of Gang Delinquency," *Journal of Social Issues 14* (1958), pp. 5-19.

Mirels, H. L., "Dimensions of Internal Versus External Control," *Journal of Consulting and Clinical Psychology 34* (1970), pp. 226-228.

Mischel, W., and E. Staub, "Effects of Expectancy of Working and Waiting for Larger Rewards," *Journal of Personality and Social Psychology 3* (1965), pp. 625-633.

Mitchell, David C., *Urban Community College Students' Beliefs in Internal-External Control,* (Case Western Reserve University: Unpublished Ph.D. Dissertation, 1970).

Mommsen, K. G., "Professionalism and the Racial Context of Career Patterns Among Black American Doctorates: A Note on the 'Brain Drain' Hypothesis," (Unpublished article, 1972).

Morgan, J. N., and M. H. David, "Education and Income," *Quarterly Journal of Economics* (August, 1963), pp. 423-437.

Morgan, James, and M. H. David, "Race, Economic Attitudes and Behavior," *Proceedings The Social Statistics Section, American Statistical Association,* 1962.

Morris, J. L., "The Relation Between Perceived Probability of Success in Chosen Occupations and Achievement-Related Motivation," (University of California, Berkeley: Ph.D. Thesis, 1964).

Moynihan, Daniel P., *The Negro Family: The Case for National Action* (Washington, D.C.: U. S. Department of Labor, Office of Planning and Research, 1965).

Murphy, Raymond J., and James M. Watson, "The Structure of Discontent," in N. E. Cohen, Editor, *The Los Angeles Riots: A Socio-Psychological Study* (New York: Praeger, 1970), pp. 140-157.

McClelland, David C., *The Achieving Society* (Princeton, New Jersey: Van Nostrand, 1961).

McDowell, Sophia F., Gilbert A. Lowe, Jr., and Doris A. Dockett, "Howard University's Student Protest Movement," *Public Opinion Quarterly 34*(3) (Fall, 1970), pp. 383-388.

McKissick, Floyd B., "Black Business Development With Social Commitment to Black Communities," in John H. Bracey, Jr., August Meier, and Elliot Rudwick, Editors, *Black Nationalism in America* (Indianapolis and New York: Bobbs-Merrill, 1970), pp. 492-503.

Nash, J., "The Father in Contemporary Culture and Current Psychological Literature," *Child Development 36* (1965), pp. 261-297.

Nelsen, Hart, and Raytha Yokley, "Civil Rights Attitudes of Rural and Urban Presbyterians," *Rural Sociology 35*(2) (June, 1970), pp. 161-170.

Nelsen, Hart, Raytha L. Yokley, and Thomas W. Madron, "Rural-Urban Differences in Religiosity," *Rural Sociology 36*(3) (September, 1971), pp. 389-396.

Nichols, R. C., and A. W. Astin, *Progress of the Merit Scholars: An Eight-Year Follow-Up,* NMSC Research Reports 1 (Evanston, Illinois: National Merit Scholarship Corporation, 1965).

Nieberg, H. L., *Political Violence: The Behavioral Process* (New York: St. . Martin's Press, 1969).

Orbell, John M., "Protest Participation Among Southern Negro College Students," *American Political Science Review 61* (June, 1967), pp. 446-456.

Ornati, Oscar, "Poverty in America," in L. A. Ferman, J. L. Kornbluh, A. Haber, Editors, *Poverty in America* (Ann Arbor, Michigan: The University of Michigan Press, 1965), pp. 24-39.

Orum, Anthony M., and Amy W. Orum, "The Class and Status Bases of Negro Student Protest," *Social Science Quarterly* 49 (December, 1968), pp. 521-533.

Perkins, W. E., and J. E. Higginson, "Black Students: Reformists or Revolutionaries?" in Roderick Aya and Norma Miller, Editors, *The New American Revolution* (New York: The Free Press, 1971), pp. 195-222.

Peterson, Richard E., "The Scope of Organized Student Protest," in Julian Foster and Durward Long, Editors, *Protest: Student Activism in America* (New York: William Morrow, 1970), pp. 59-80.

Population Characteristics, Negro Population: March, 1965, Series P-20, No. 145, U. S. Department of Commerce, Bureau of the Census, December, 1965.

Population Characteristics, Negro Population: March, 1965, Series P-20, No. 155, U. S. Department of Commerce, Bureau of the Census, September, 1966.

Quinn, Robert P., Joyce M. Tabor, and Laura K. Gordon, *The Decision to Discriminate: A Study of Executive Selection* (Ann Arbor: Survey Research Center, Institute for Social Research, The University of Michigan, 1968).

Ransford, H. Edward, "Comment on 'Internal-External Control and Black Militancy'" by John R. Forward and Jay R. Williams, *Journal of Social Issues* Winter, 1970), *Journal of Social Issues 27*(1) (1971), pp. 227-232.

Ransford, H. Edward, "Isolation, Powerlessness and Violence: A Study of Attitudes and Participation in the Watts Riot," *American Journal of Sociology 73* (March, 1968), pp. 581-591.

Reiss, Albert J., *Occupations and Social Status* (Glencoe, Illinois: The Free Press, 1961).

Rosen, B. C., "Race, Ethnicity, and Achievement," *American Sociological Review XXIV* (1959), pp. 47-60.

Rotter, Julian B., "External Control and Internal Control," *Psychology Today 5*(1) (June, 1971), pp. 37-42.

Rotter, Julian B., "Generalized Expectancies for Internal Versus External Control of Reinforcement," *Psychological Monographs 80*(1) whole No. 609, 1966, pp. 1-28.

Rotter, Julian B., Melvin Seeman, and Shepard Liverant, "Internal Versus External Control of Reinforcements: A Major Variable in Behavior Theory," in N. F. Washburne, Editor, *Decisions, Values and Groups* (New York: MacMillan, 1962), pp. 473-516.

Rustin, Bayard, "A Way Out of the Exploding Ghetto," *New York Times Magazine* 13 (August, 1967), pp. 16, 54, 59-65.

Schulman, J., "Ghetto Residence, Political Alienation and Riot Orientation," (Unpublished Manuscript, Cornell University, 1967).

Shultz, Theodore W., *The Economic Value of Education* (New York: Columbia University Press, 1963).

Searles, Ruth, and J. Allen Williams, Jr., "Negro College Students' Participation in Sit-Ins," *Social Forces 40* (March, 1962), pp. 215-220.

Sears, D. O., and J. B. McConahay, "The Politics of Discontent," in N. E. Cohen, Editor, *The Los Angeles Riots:* A Socio-Psychological Study (New York: Praeger, 1970), pp. 258-287.

Seeman, Melvin, "Alienation and Engagement," in Angus Campbell and Philip E. Converse, Editors, *The Human Meaning of Social Change* (New York: Russell Sage Foundation, 1972), pp. 467-527.

Sewell, William H., "Inequality of Opportunity for Higher Education," *American Sociological Review* 36 (October, 1971), pp. 793-809.

Sewell, W. H., and V. P. Shah, "Parents' Education and Children's Educational Aspirations and Achievements," *American Sociological Review* 33 (1968), pp. 191-209.

Sewell, W. H., and V. P. Shah, "Socioeconomic Status, Intelligence, and the Attainment of Higher Education," *Sociology of Education 40* (1967), pp. 1-23.

Sewell, W. H., A. O. Haller, and M. A. Straus, "Social Status and Educational and Occupational Aspiration," *American Sociological Review XXII* (1957), pp. 67-73.

Sharp, Laure M., *Education and Employment* (Baltimore: Johns Hopkins University Press, 1970).

Shaw, Ralph L., and Norman P. Uhl, "Control of Reinforcement and Academic Achievement," *The Journal of Educational Research 64*(5) (1971), pp. 226-228.

Siegel, P. M., "On the Cost of Being a Negro," *Sociological Inquiry XXXV* (April, 1965), pp. 41-57.

Silvern, Louise E., and Charles Y. Nakamura, "Powerlessness, Social-Political Action, Social-Political Views: Their Interrelation Among College Students," *Journal of Social Issues 27*(4) (1971), pp. 137-157.

Smith, M. Brewster, "Competence and Socialization," in John A. Clausen, Editor, *Socialization and Society* (Boston: Little, Brown, 1968), pp. 271-320.

418   Bibliography

Smith, M. Brewster, "A Map for the Analysis of Personality and Politics," *Journal of Social Issues 24* (November, 1968a), pp. 15-27.

Spaeth, Joe L., "The Allocation of College Graduates to Graduate and Professional Schools," *Sociology of Education 41* (Fall, 1968), pp. 342-349.

Spranger, E., *Types of Men.* Translated from the fifth German edition of *Lebensformen by P. J. Pigors* (Halle: Max Niemeyer Verlof, 1928. American Agent: Stechert-Hafner, New York).

Sprey, J., "Sex Differences in Occupational Choice Patterns Among Negro Adolescents," *Social Problems X* (1962), pp. 11-22.

Stanfiel, James D., "Education and Income of Parents at Predominantly Black Colleges," *Journal of Negro Education XLI*(2) (Spring, 1972), pp. 170-176.

Staples, Robert, *The Black Family* (Belmont, California: Wadsworth, 1971).

Strickland, Bonnie R., "The Prediction of Social Action from a Dimension of Internal-External Control," *Journal of Social Psychology 66* (August, 1965), pp. 353-358.

Tangri, Sandra Schwartz, "Determinants of Occupational Role Innovation Among College Women," *Journal of Social Issues 28*(2) (1972), pp. 177-199.

Tangri, S. S., "Role Innovation in Occupational Choice Among College Women," (Unpublished Doctoral Dissertation, The University of Michigan, 1969).

Thomas, L. E., "The Internal-External Scale, Ideological Bias, and Political Participation," *Journal of Personality 38* (1970), pp. 273-286.

Tomlinson, T. M., "Ideological Foundations for Negative Action: Militant and Non-Militant Views," in N. E. Cohen, Editor, *The Los Angeles Riots: A Socio-Psychological Study* (New York: Praeger, 1970), pp. 326-379.

Turner, James, "Identity in Transition: A Theory of Black Militancy," in Roderick Aya and Norman Miller, Editors, *The New American Revolution* (New York: The Free Press, 1971), pp. 166-194.

Turner, Ralph, *The Social Context of Ambition* (San Francisco: Chandler, 1964).

United States Bureau of the Census, Series P-20, No. 155, March, 1965.

United States Bureau of the Census, Series P-20, No. 145, March, 1965.

United States Bureau of the Census, Series P-23, No. 38, July, 1971.

United States Bureau of the Census, Series P-20, No. 234, March, 1972.

"Voting Rights," *Civil Rights Digest 4*(4) (December, 1971), p. 32.

Wallace, W. L., *Student Culture: Social Structure and Continuity in a Liberal Arts College* (Chicago: Aldine, 1966).

Weiner, Bernard, Irene Frieze, Andy Kukla, Linda Reed, Stanley Rest, and Robert M. Rosenbaum, "Perceiving the Causes of Success and Failure" in Edward E. Jones *et al.*, Editor, *Attribution: Perceiving the Causes of Behavior* (Morristown, New Jersey: General Learning Corporation, 1973), pp. 95-120.

Weisbrod, B. A., and P. Karpoff, "Monetary Returns to College Education, Student Ability, and College Quality," *Review of Economics and Statistics* (November, 1968), pp. 491-497.

Weston, Peter J., and Martha T. Mednick, "Race, Social Class and the Motive to Avoid Success in Women," *Journal of Cross-Cultural Psychology 1*(3) (September, 1970), pp. 284-291.

Willis, C. T., and F. J. Goldberg, "Some Correlates of Militancy and Conservatism Among Black College Students in the North and South," *Psychiatry,* in press.

Wilson, Alan B., "Residential Segregation of Social Classes and Aspirations of High School Boys," *American Sociological Review 24* (1959), pp. 836-845.

Wittes, S., *School Power Structure and Belief in Internal-External Control: A Study of Secondary Schools in Conflict* (The University of Michigan: Unpublished Ph.D. Dissertation, 1969).

Wright, Stephen, J., "The Financing of Equal Opportunity in Higher Education: The Problems and the Urgency," in *Financing Equality of Educational Opportunity in Higher Education* (New York: College Entrance Examination Board, 1970), pp. 1-5.

Wolfe, Dael, *The Uses of Talent* (Princeton, New Jersey: Princeton University Press, 1971).

Zinn, Howard, *SNCC: The New Abolitionists* (Boston: Beacon Press, 1964), p. 16.

Zytkoskee, Adrian, Bonnie R. Strickland, and James Watson, "Delay of Gratification and Internal Versus External Control Among Adolescents of Low Socioeconomic Status," *Developmental Psychology 4*(1) (1971), pp. 93-98.

Appendix

chapter 3

TABLE 3.1. Occupational Aspirations of Men and Women, 1964 and 1970:
Job Titles of the Most Probable Future Occupation

Job Titles	1964[a]		1970[b]	
	Men	Women	Men	Women
Medicine				
Dental or medical technician	.7%	1.8%	.2%	.4%
Dentist	1.1	—	1.3	—
Doctor, private practice	9.2	1.4	5.1	.6
Doctor: staff surgeon at large hospital; other hospital staff position	—	—	.7	—
Psychiatrist	—	—	.2	—
Registered nurse	—	7.3	—	5.6
Nursing administrator	—	—	—	.4
Pharmacist	1.3	—	1.8	1.0
Physical or occupational therapist	1.5	2.0	.4	1.4
Veterinarian	.7	—	.7	—
Business and sales				
Accountant	3.9	.8	6.2	2.2
Actuary	—	—	—	.2
Bank teller	—	—	—	.2
Bookkeeper	.4	.4	.7	.8
Investment broker	—	—	.2	.2
Business executive, administrator	3.7	.2	4.5	.6
Manager: office manager of large concern	1.2	.6	3.5	.6
Sales manager	.4	.2	.4	.2
Cashier	—	—	.2	—
Clerk	—	—	.2	.6
Marketing, advertising executive	—	—	.7	.2
Marketing, advertising assistant	—	—	—	.4
Personnel, public relations	1.1	.2	2.9	.8
Sales representative for firm	—	—	.8	—
Retail sales	—	—	—	.2
Secretary	—	6.1	—	4.2
Public advisors; social science; social welfare, government				
Administrator in social welfare agency	—	—	1.1	.2
Civil rights organizational work	—	—	.7	1.6
Counselor, psychological or guidance	1.3	3.6	3.5	4.2

TABLE 3.1. **Occupational Aspirations of Men and Women, 1964 and 1970:**
(Cont'd) **Job Titles of the Most Probable Future Occupation**

Job Titles	1964[a]		1970[b]	
	Men	Women	Men	Women
Child developmentalist	—	—	—	.2
Economist	—	—	.2	.2
Foreign service or diplomatic corps	.9	—	.5	—
Forest ranger, conservationist	—	—	.5	—
Interpreter, translator	.2	.8	.2	.4
Minister	.9	—	.5	—
Officer, armed services	2.6	.2	.9	—
Public official: local level	.2	—	.2	—
Public official: national level	.2	—	.2	—
Social scientist	—	—	1.1	.6
Social worker	4.5	11.7	5.3	17.7
Working with youth groups	—	.2	.3	—
The arts and fashion				
Artist: painter or sculptor, etc.	—	—	.2	—
Composer	.2	—	.2	—
Conductor, symphony orchestra	—	—	.2	—
Conductor, jazz or dance group	.2	—	.2	—
Designer: fashion	—	1.4	.2	1.0
Illustrator	.6	—	.9	.2
Interior decorator	—	.2	.2	—
Musician, general	.9	.2	.2	.2
Musician: instrumentalist or vocalist in jazz or popular music-group	—	—	.2	—
Musician: instrumentalist or vocalist in symphony	.9	.4	—	.2
Writer: novelist, playwright, poet	—	—	.2	—
Basic and applied science and mathematics				
Architect, designer	1.1	—	.4	—
Draftsman	.9	—	1.1	—
Engineer	6.8	.2	4.4	—
Consulting engineer in industry	—	—	1.1	—
Computer programmer	.6	.6	4.4	2.4
Computer operator	.4	.4	.4	.6
Mathematician	2.6	1.0	.2	.2
Scientist, industrial scientist, natural scientist	1.8	.2	4.5	2.4
Science: laboratory assistant	2.6	2.0	—	1.0
Statistician	.4	.2	.4	—
Technician: aeronautical, automotive, other	.2	—	2.0	.4

| | 1964[a] | | 1970[b] | |
Job Titles	Men	Women	Men	Women
Agriculture, home economics				
County agricultural agent	.6	—	1.1	.2
Dietician	.4	2.8	—	1.0
Farm manager, owner	.6	—	.4	—
Home economics demonstrator	—	—	—	.4
Home economist	—	2.2	—	.2
Sports				
Coach, college athletic team	.2	—	.2	—
Coach, high school athletic team	1.1	—	.9	—
Professional player	.4	—	.7	—
Education				
High school teacher of:				
Agriculture	.9	—	.7	.4
Art	—	—	.5	—
Music	1.7	.8	.5	1.8
Commercial subjects	.4	2.4	.5	2.0
English	.7	3.0	.4	6.4
Industrial arts, home economics	.6	.2	.7	.9
Mathematics	2.0	2.4	.4	1.0
Physical education	1.8	1.4	2.9	2.8
Science	.6	.4	1.1	.8
Social studies	1.5	.6	2.0	1.8
Special education	.4	1.2	—	2.4
Elementary education, or type not specified	11.5	28.9	3.3	17.7
College Teaching, higher education				
Art	—	.2	—	—
Literature	—	.2	.2	—
Mathematics	.2	—	.4	.2
Music	.6	.2	.2	—
Science	4.1	.8	.2	.2
College professor, not specified	4.1	2.2	1.1	1.2
Library work				
Librarian	—	2.6	—	1.4
Mass communication; entertainment				
Copy writer	—	—	.2	—
Newspaper editor	—	—	.2	—

TABLE 3.1.   Occupational Aspirations of Men and Women, 1964 and 1970:
(Cont'd)   Job Titles of the Most Probable Future Occupation

| | 1964[a] | | 1970[b] | |
Job Titles	Men	Women	Men	Women
Newspaper reporter	.4	—	.2	.6
Photographer	—	—	.2	—
Professional model	—	—	—	.2
Actor	—	—	.2	.2
Law				
Lawyer	6.5	1.2	7.1	.6
Lawyer, civil rights	.2	—	2.9	.2
Skilled workers not classified elsewhere				
Electrician	1.3	—	—	—
Foreman, construction work	—	—	.4	—
Machinist	.2	—	—	—
Mechanic	.4	—	.2	—
Radio-TV repair	.2	—	—	—
Electronic technician	—	—	.2	—
Service workers				
Airline stewardess	—	—	—	.2
Beautician	—	.2	—	.2
Policeman (policewoman)	—	—	.4	.2
Other	.2	1.8	1.9	.3
	100%	100%	100%	100%

[a]These percents are based on the 1964 data from 535 seniors, 285 men and 250 women, attending the six colleges that participated in the cross-sectional studies in both 1964 and 1970.
[b]These percents are based on 536 seniors, 280 men and 256 women, who participated in the 1970 cross-sectional study of six Black colleges.

TABLE 3.2.   Educational Aspirations of Men and Women, 1964 and 1970:
Field of Intended Graduate or Professional School Study

| | 1964[a] | | 1970[b] | |
	Men	Women	Men	Women
Major Professions	24%	8%	30%	7%
Medicine	8	3	4	1
Dentistry	1	—	1	—
Law	7	1	14	2
Veterinary medicine	1	—	1	—
Journalism	*	—	—	—

TABLE 3.2. **Educational Aspirations of Men and Women, 1964 and 1970:**
(Cont'd) **Field of Intended Graduate or Professional School Study**

	1964[a]		1970[b]	
	Men	Women	Men	Women
Engineering	5	*	5	*
Architecture	1	—	*	—
Social work	1	4	4	4
Other major professions; professional school; NA whether major or minor	—	—	—	—
Minor Professions	2%	6%	1%	9%
Dental hygiene	*	—	—	—
Medical technology	*	*	—	—
Nursing and public health	—	4	—	6
Pharmacy	*	—	1	1
Physical and vocational therapy	1	1	*	1
Speech therapy	—	*	—	*
Other minor professions	—	*	—	*
Minor professions, NA what kind	—	—	—	*
Humanities (philosophy, religion, language and literature)	4%	8%	1%	7%
Philosophy	*	*	*	*
Religion and ministry	*	—	*	—
English language and literature	2	5	*	5
Romance and Germanic language and literature	*	*	*	*
Other languages and literature (Far Eastern, African, etc.)	—	*	—	*
Creative writing	—	—	—	—
Humanities general area	—	—	—	*
Literature; NA what kind	—	*	—	—
Language, NA what kind	*	1	—	*
Fine Arts	5%	3%	1%	2%
Art studies	—	—	*	—
Applied art	*	*	*	*
Commercial art	*	—	*	*
Musical studies	—	*	*	*
Applied music	3	2	*	*
Dance	—	—	*	*
Drama	*	—	—	*
Speech, radio, TV	—	*	—	—
Other fine arts	—	—	—	—
Fine arts, NA what kind	—	—	—	—

	1964[a]		1970[b]	
	Men	Women	Men	Women
Social Sciences, History and Special Area Studies	*14%*	*13%*	*20%*	*20%*
Anthropology	—	*	—	—
Economics	1	1	1	1
Political science	3	—	6	*
Psychology	3	3	6	6
Sociology	3	4	5	10
History	3	2	1	1
Near Eastern and other special area studies	—	—	—	—
Other social sciences	*	*	*	—
Social science, NA what kind	*	2	1	2
Basic Sciences and Mathematics	*21%*	*9%*	*11%*	*7%*
Astronomy	—	—	—	—
Chemistry	5	*	1	1
Geology, minerology, petrography, volcanology, oceanography, etc.	*	—	1	*
Physics	1	*	*	*
Biology	5	3	4	3
Physiology	*	—	*	*
Math	8	4	4	3
Other basic sciences	—	*	*	—
Basic science, NA what kind	1	1	*	*
Education and Library Science	*8%*	*21%*	*5%*	*22%*
Elementary education	*	3	—	4
Secondary education	*	*	*	*
Special education	—	1	*	5
Physical education	2	3	3	3
Guidance and personnel work	*	1	*	5
Public health education or health education	*	1	*	*
Library science	—	3	—	2
Other education	*	1	*	1
Education, NA what kind	4	8	1	2
Agriculture and Home Economics	*4%*	*5%*	*2%*	*3%*
Agricultural education	*	—	*	—
Agricultural administration or economics	*	—	*	*

428

TABLE 3.2. **Educational Aspirations of Men and Women, 1964 and 1970:**
(Cont'd) **Field of Intended Graduate or Professional School Study**

	1964[a]		1970[b]	
	Men	Women	Men	Women
Agricultural science	2	—	1	—
Agriculture, NA what kind	1	—	*	—
Home economics education	—	*	1	—
Child development and nursery school education	—	*	—	*
Foods and nutrition	*	2	—	1
Home economics	—	1	*	*
General home economics	*	2	—	*
Business (Commerce)	*5%*	*7%*	*20%*	*11%*
Business education	*	2	*	2
Specific professional-type business areas	1	1	5	2
General business administration	3	*	6	2
Bookkeeping	—	*	—	*
Secretarial or clerical skills	*	*	—	*
Business machines	—	*	*	—
Business, NA what kind	—	4	9	5
Technical	*2%*	*1%*	*1%*	*0*
Technical or vocational or industrial education	*	—	*	—
Construction (or civil) technology	*	—	—	—
Electrical technology	*	—	—	—
Mechanical technology	*	—	—	—
Technical skills training, NA kind	*	1	*	—
Not Intending to Go to Graduate or Professional School	*11%*	*19%*	*8%*	*12%*
	100%	100%	100%	100%

[a]These percents are based on the 1964 data from 535 seniors, 285 men and 250 women, attending the six colleges that participated in the cross-sectional studies in both 1964 and 1970.

[b]These percents are based on 536 seniors, 280 men and 256 women, who participated in the 1970 cross-sectional study of six Black colleges.

TABLE 3.3. **Interrelationships among Several Dimensions of Level of Aspiration Reflected by the Occupational Choices of Men and Women in 1964**[a]

	1	2	3	4	5
1. *Desirability* of the choice to like-sexed peers	1.00				
2. *Prestige* the choice is judged to have	+.89 (+.31)	1.00			
3. *Ability demands* the choice is judged to have	+.64 (−.31)	+.69 (+.51)	1.00		
4. *Social difficulty* the choice is judged to have for Blacks	+.58 (−.12)	+.52 (+.43)	+.67 (+.79)	1.00	
5. *Nontraditionality* of the choice (percent Black in the chosen occupation by 1960)	+.61 (−.16)	+.54 (+.13)	+.57 (+.18)	+.68 (+.36)	1.00

[a]This analysis is based on the 3639 students, 1880 men and 1759 women, who participated in the 1964 cross-sectional study of 10 Black colleges. The correlations for women are in parentheses.

chapter 4

TABLE 4.1A. Performance and Aspiration Implications of a Sense of Personal Control and Control Ideology for Men. (Multiple Analyses of Variance Using Personal Control and Control Ideology[a] to Explain Occupational and Educational Aspirations of Men in 1964 and in 1970 and to Explain Performance Measures in 1964)

Performance and Aspirations	1964[b]				1970[c]			
	High Personal Control		Low Personal Control		High Personal Control		Low Personal Control	
	Internal Control Ideology	External Control Ideology	Internal Control Ideology	External Control Ideology	Internal Control Ideology	External Control Ideology	Internal Control Ideology	External Control Ideology
Average Scores On:								
Occupational aspirations:								
Prestige of the choice (Range 1–5, 5 = high)	3.10	3.11	2.47	2.83	3.04	3.10	2.72	2.73
	F, interaction PC and CI = 6.72 (.01)				*F*, interaction PC and CI = (NS)			
	F, effect of PC = 27.14 (.001)				*F*, effect of PC = 5.63 (.025)			
	F, effect of CI = (NS)				*F*, effect of CI = (NS)			
Ability demands of the choice (Range 1–7, 7 = high)	3.89	3.98	3.20	3.55	3.80	3.74	3.16	3.42
	F, interaction PC and CI = 3.86 (.05)				*F*, interaction PC and CI = 3.92 (.05)			
	F, effect of PC = 28.24 (.001)				*F*, effect of PC = 9.97 (.01)			
	F, effect of CI = (NS)				*F*, effect of CI = (NS)			
Nontraditionality of the choice (average percent Black in the occupation)	2.99	3.03	4.23	3.33	2.76	2.52	4.73	3.73
	F, interaction of PC and CI = 5.36 (.025)				*F*, interaction PC and CI = 4.01 (.05)			
	F, effect of PC = 3.82 (.05)				*F*, effect of PC = 9.34 (.01)			
	F, effect of CI = (NS)				*F*, effect of CI = (NS)			

Educational aspirations:

Intention of going to graduate or professional school (Range 1–5, 5 = high)

2.76	2.75	2.29	2.32	2.86	2.90	2.08	2.45

F, interaction PC and CI = .47 (NS) F, interaction of PC and CI = 3.42 (almost .05)
F, effect of PC = 3.98 (.05) F, effect of PC = 11.88 (.001)
F, effect of CI = (NS) F, effect of CI = (NS)

Performance Measures:

Correct performance on 6th trial of anagrams (Range 0–13)

6.96	8.00	4.71	7.37	No data in 1970

F, interaction PC and CI = 2.92 (almost .05)
F, effect of PC = 7.62 (.01)
F, effect of CI = 5.32 (.025)

Total number of errors on six anagrams trials (Range 0–78)

5.44	4.25	9.31	4.61	No data in 1970

F, Interaction of PC and CI = 2.89 (almost .05)
F, effect of PC = (NS)
F, effect of CI = 4.02 (.05)

Percentile position within college on cumulative grades (Range 00–90)

63.7	65.0	39.6	51.2	No data in 1970

F, interaction of PC and CI = 4.01 (.05)
F, effect of PC = 3.72 (almost .05)
F, effect of CI = (NS)

[a]High and low status on these variables represents a median split.

[b]These analyses in 1964 were done controlling for entrance test scores and father's education (used as covariates). The occupational aspiration analyses are based on 1580 men remaining after deleting 300 men who said the issue of future occupational choice was very unimportant to them. The performance analyses are based on 1680 men for whom we collected performance data.

[c]Since we did not collect any performance data, either college grades or entrance scores, in 1970, these analyses are uncontrolled for test scores position. The analyses did include a control for father's education. They are based on 539 men remaining after deleting the 52 men who said occupation was unimportant to them.

TABLE 4.1B. Performance and Aspiration Implications of a Sense of Personal Control and Control Ideology for Women. (Multiple Analyses of Variance Using Personal Control and Control Ideology[a] to Explain Occupational and Educational Aspirations of Women in 1964 and in 1970 and to Explain Performance Measures in 1964)

| | 1964[b] | | | | 1970[c] | | | |
| | High Personal Control | | Low Personal Control | | High Personal Control | | Low Personal Control | |
Performance and Aspirations	Internal Control Ideology	External Control Ideology	Internal Control Ideology	External Control Ideology	Internal Control Ideology	External Control Ideology	Internal Control Ideology	External Control Ideology
Average Scores On:								
Occupational aspirations								
Prestige of the choice (Range 1–5, 5 = high)	2.82	2.82	2.62	2.68	2.77	2.81	2.45	2.46
F, interaction of PC and CI = (NS) F, effect of PC = 9.50 (.005) F, effect of CI = (NS)					F, interaction of PC and CI = (NS) F, effect of PC = 8.87 (.05) F, effect of CI = (NS)			
Ability demands of the choice (Range 1–7, 7 = high)	2.97	3.01	2.54	2.59	3.08	3.05	2.70	2.71
F, interaction of PC and CI = (NS) F, effect of PC = 4.21 (.05) F, effect of CI = (NS)					F, interaction of PC and CI = (NS) F, effect of PC = 3.68 (almost .05) F, effect of CI = (NS)			
Nontraditionality of the choice (Average percent Black in the occupation)	4.98	5.42	5.02	5.18	6.46	5.45	6.73	6.22
F, interaction of PC and CI = (NS) F, effect of PC = (NS) F, effect of CI = (NS)					F, interaction of PC and CI = (NS) F, effect of PC = (NS) F, effect of CI = (NS)			

434

Educational aspirations:											
Intention of going to graduate or professional school (Range 1–5, 5 = high)	1.73	3.00	2.28	2.10	F, interaction of PC and CI = 3.28 (almost .05) F, effect of PC = (NS) F, effect of CI = (NS)	2.53	2.60	2.01	2.30	F, interaction of PC and CI = 3.44 (almost .05) F, effect of PC = 3.65 (almost .05) F, effect of CI = (NS)
Performance measures:											
Correct performance	6.40	7.67	3.51	6.15	F, interaction of PC and CI = 4.03 (.05) F, effect of PC = (NS) F, effect of CI = (NS)			No data in 1970		
Total number of errors on six anagrams trials (Range 0–13)	3.09	1.33	6.62	4.05	F, interaction of PC and CI = 3.84 (.05) F, effect of PC = 5.94 (.025) F, effect of CI = (NS)			No data in 1970		
Percentile position within college on cumulative grades (Range 00–90)	66.7	74.0	38.3	52.5	F, interaction of PC and CI = (NS) F, effect of PC = 3.89 (.05) F, effect of CI = (NS)			No data in 1970		

[a] High and low status on these variables represents a median split.

[b] These analyses in 1964 were done controlling for entrance test scores and father's education (used as covariates). The occupational aspiration analyses are based on 1349 women remaining after deleting 410 women who said the issue of future occupational choice was very unimportant to them. The performance analyses are based on 1559 women for whom we collected performance data.

[c] Since we did not collect any performance data, either college grades or entrance scores, in 1970, these analyses are uncontrolled for test scores position. The analyses did include a control for father's education. They are based on 438 women remaining after deleting the 98 women who said occupation was unimportant to them.

TABLE 4.2A. **Level of Significance of the Relationships between Two Competency Measures (Sense of Personal Control and Academic Self-Confidence)[a] and the Aspirations and Performance of Men. (Summary of Multiple Analyses of Variance Using Personal Control and Academic Self-Confidence to Explain Occupational and Educational Aspirations in 1964 and 1970 and to Explain Performance in 1964)**

Performance and Aspirations	1964[b]			1970[c]		
	Interaction of Personal Control and Academic Self-Confidence	Main Effect of Personal Control	Main Effect of Academic Self-Confidence	Interaction of Personal Control and Academic Self-Confidence	Main Effect of Personal Control	Main Effect of Academic Self-Confidence
Occupational aspirations:						
Prestige of the choice (Range 1–5, 5 = high)	F(NS)	F(.001)	F(.001)	F(NS)	F(.025)	F(.01)
Ability demands of the choice (Range 1–7, 7 = high)	F(NS)	F(.001)	F(.001)	F(NS)	F(.001)	F(.001)
Nontraditionality of the choice (Average percent Black in the occupation)	F(NS)	F(.05)	F(.001)	F(NS)	F(.001)	F(NS)

Educational aspirations:

Intention of going to graduate or professional school (Range 1–5, 5 = high)	F(NS)	F(.05)	F(.001)	F(NS)	F(.001)	F(.001)

Performance measures:

Correct performance on 6th trial of anagrams (Range 0–13)	F(NS)	F(.01)	F(.01)	No data in 1970	
Total number of errors on six anagrams trials (Range 0–78)	F(NS)	F(NS)	F(.01)	No data in 1970	
Percentile position within college on cumulative grades (Range 00–90)	F(NS)	F(.05)	F(.01)	No data in 1970	

[a]High and low status on these variables represent a median split.

[b]These analyses in 1964 were done controlling for entrance test scores and father's education (used as a covariate). The occupational aspiration analyses are based on 1580 men remaining after deleting 300 men who said the issue of future occupational choice was very unimportant to them. The performance analyses are based on 1680 men for whom we collected performance data.

[c]Since we did not collect any performance data, on either college grades or entrance scores, in 1970, these analyses are uncontrolled for test score position. The analyses did include a control for father's education. They are based on 977 students, 539 men remaining after deleting the 52 men who said occupation was unimportant to them.

TABLE 4.2B. Level of Significance of the Relationships between Two Competency Measures (Sense of Personal Control and Academic Self-Confidence)[a] and the Aspirations and Performance of Women. (Summary of Multiple Analyses of Variance Using Personal Control and Academic Self-Confidence to Explain Occupational and Educational Aspirations in 1964 and 1970 and to Explain Performance in 1964)

Performance and Aspirations	1964[b]			1970[c]		
	Interaction of Personal Control and Academic Self-Confidence	Main Effect of Personal Control	Main Effect of Academic Self-Confidence	Interaction of Personal Control and Academic Self-Confidence	Main Effect of Personal Control	Main Effect of Academic Self-Confidence
Occupational aspirations:						
Prestige of the choice (Range 1–5, 5 = high)	$F(NS)$	$F(.005)$	$F(.001)$	$F(NS)$	$F(.05)$	$F(.05)$
Ability demands of the choice (Range 1–7, 7 = high)	$F(NS)$	$F(.05)$	$F(.01)$	$F(NS)$	$F(.05)$	$F(.05)$
Nontraditionality of the choice (Average percent Black in the occupation)	$F(NS)$	$F(NS)$	$F(.05)$	$F(NS)$	$F(NS)$	$F(.05)$

Educational aspirations:					
Intention of going to graduate or professional school (Range 1–5, 5 = high)	F(NS)	F(NS)	F(.05)	F(NS)	F(.05)
Performance measures:					
Correct performance on sixth trial of anagrams (Range 0–13)	F(NS)	F(NS)	F(.05)	No data in 1970	
Total number of errors on six anagrams trials (Range 0–78)	F(NS)	F(.025)	F(.001)	No data in 1970	
Percentile position within college on cumulative grades (Range 00–90)	F(NS)	F(.05)	F(.01)	No data in 1970	

[a] High and low status on these variables represent a median split.

[b] These analyses in 1964 were done controlling for entrance test scores and father's education (used as a covariate). The occupational aspiration analyses are based on 1349 women remaining after deleting 410 women who said the issue of future occupational choice was very unimportant to them. The performance analyses are based on 1559 women for whom we collected performance data.

[c] Since we did not collect any performance data, on either college grades or entrance scores, in 1970, these analyses are uncontrolled for test score position. The analyses did include a control for father's education. They are based on 438 women remaining after deleting the 98 women who said occupation was unimportant to them.

439

TABLE 4.3. **Motivational Characteristics of Three Groups of Men Who Entered College with above Median Test Scores, Those Whose Occupational Aspirations Indicated Underaspiration, Realism and Overaspiration, 1964**[a]

Motivational Characteristics	Occupational Aspiration Groups		
	Under Aspirants	Realistic Aspirants	Over Aspirants
Realism of grade aspirations:			
Underaspirant: expected lower grades than their current GPA	48%	20%	14%
Realistic aspirant: grade level expected close to current GPA	19%	48%	23%
Overaspirant: expected higher grades than their current GPA	33%	32%	63%
	100%	100%	100%
		$\chi^2(.02)$	
Competency assessments:			
Average Sense of personal control (Range 1–6, 6 = high)	2.97	3.95	3.00
		$F(.005)$	
Average academic self-confidence (Range 1–5, 5 = high)	2.21	3.89	3.25
		$F(.001)$	
Job self-confidence (Range 1–4, 4 = high)	1.82	2.57	2.15
		$F(.001)$	
Achievement-related motives:			
Average fear of failure (Range 0–98, high represents high anxiety)	57.0	53.2	52.1
		$F(.001)$	
Average security orientation (Range 0–3, 3 = high concern with security)	1.20	1.29	1.35
		$F(NS)$	

TABLE 4.3.   **Motivational Characteristics of Three Groups of Men Who**
(Cont'd)   **Entered College with above Median Test Scores, Those Whose Occupational Aspirations Indicated Underaspiration, Realism and Overaspiration, 1964**[a]

Motivational Characteristics	Occupational Aspiration Groups		
	Under Aspirants	Realistic Aspirants	Over Aspirants
Average success orientation (Range 0–2, 2 = high desire for success)	.55	.63 F(NS)	.54
Average achievement orientation (Range 0–3, 3 = high concern with achievement)	1.10	1.06 F(NS)	1.37
Average control ideology (Range 0–13, 0 = most internal, 13 = most external)	4.15	5.72 F(.01)	4.87
Average system blame (Range 0–4, 4 = high)	2.05	2.40 F(.001)	1.72

[a]The realism score, corresponding to the goal discrepancy score traditionally used in experimental studies of level of aspiration, is the discrepancy between the ability required for the student's occupational choice (the percent judged by peers to have the ability for it) and the percentile of the class that is represented by his cumulative grade point average. Any student who aspired to an occupation whose ability requirements were no more than 10 percent higher or 10 percent lower than his own performance was defined as making a realistic choice. When the discrepancy was more than 10 percent, he was classified as an overaspirant; when it was more than a minus 10, he was classified as an underaspirant. The men used in this analysis attended four colleges where raw scores on the SAT were available; there were 297 men above the median SAT score for these four colleges. After deleting those with missing data on other variables, a total of 207 were available, distributed as following: *underaspirants*, 38; *realistic aspirants*, 74; and *overaspirants*, 95.

TABLE 4.4A. **Level of Significance of the Relationships between Positive Achievement Motives (and Negative Achievement Motives) and the Aspirations and Performance of Men, 1964[a]. (Summary of Multiple Analyses of Variance Using Two Positive Motives, Achievement Orientation and Success Orientation[b], and Two Negative Motives, Fear of Failure and Desire for Security[b], to Explain Aspirations and Performance)**

Performance and Aspirations	Positive Motives			Negative Motives		
	Interaction of Achievement and Success Orientations	Main Effect of Achievement Orientation	Main Effect of Success Orientation	Interaction of Fear of Failure and Desire for Security	Main Effect of Fear of Failure	Main Effect of Desire for Security
Occupational aspirations:						
Prestige of the choice (Range 1–5, 5 = high)	F(NS)	F(.001)	F(NS)	F(NS)	F(.001)	F(.001)
Ability demands of the choice (Range 1–7, 7 = high)	F(NS)	F(.001)	F(NS)	F(NS)	F(.001)	F(.001)
Nontraditionality of the choice (Average percent Black in the occupation)	F(NS)	F(NS)	F(.05)	F(NS)	F(.001)	F(NS)

Educational aspirations:						
Intention of going to graduate or professional school (Range 1–5, 5 = high)	F(NS)	F(NS)	F(NS)	F(NS)	F(.001)	F(.05)
Performance measures:						
Correct performance on sixth trial of anagrams (Range 0–13)	F(NS)	F(NS)	F(NS)	F(NS)	F(.001)	F(NS)
Total number of errors on six anagrams trials (Range 00–78)	F(NS)	F(NS)	F(NS)	F(NS)	F(.001)	F(NS)
Percentile position within college on cumulative grades (Range 00–90)	F(NS)	F(NS)	F(NS)	F(NS)	F(.001)	F(NS)

[a] These analyses in 1964 were done controlling for entrance test scores and father's education (used as covariates). The occupational aspiration analyses are based on 1580 men remaining after deleting 300 men who said the issue of future occupational choice was very unimportant to them. The performance analyses are based on 1680 men for whom we collected performance data.

[b] High and low status on these variables represents a median split.

TABLE 4.4B. **Level of Significance of the Relationships between Positive Achievement Motives (and Negative Achievement Motives) and the Aspirations and Performance of Women, 1964[a]. (Summary of Multiple Analyses of Variance Using Two Positive Motives, Achievement Orientation and Success Orientation[b], and Two Negative Motives, Fear of Failure and Desire for Security[b], to Explain Aspirations and Performance)**

Performance and Aspirations	Positive Motives			Negative Motives		
	Interaction of Achievement and Success Orientations	Main Effect of Achievement Orientation	Main Effect of Success Orientation	Interaction of Fear of Failure and Desire for Security	Main Effect of Fear of Failure	Main Effect of Desire for Security
Occupational aspirations:						
Prestige of the choice (Range 1–5, 5 = high)	F(.05)	F(.05)	F(NS)	F(NS)	F(.05)	F(NS)
Ability demands of the choice (Range 1–7, 7 = high)	F(NS)	F(.05)	F(NS)	F(NS)	F(.05)	F(NS)
Nontraditionality of the choice (Average percent Black in the occupation)	F(NS)	F(NS)	F(NS)	F(NS)	F(NS)	F(NS)

Educational aspirations:					
Intention of going to graduate or professional school (Range 1–5, 5 = high)	F(NS)	F(.05)	F(NS)	F(NS)	F(NS)
Performance measures:					
Correct performance on sixth trial of anagrams (Range 0–13)	F(NS)	F(NS)	F(NS)	F(NS)	F(NS)
Total number of errors on six anagrams trials (Range 00–78)	F(NS)	F(NS)	F(NS)	F(NS)	F(NS)
Percentile position within college on cumulative grades (Range 00–90)	F(NS)	F(.001)	F(NS)	F(NS)	F(NS)

[a]These analyses in 1964 were done controlling for entrance test scores and father's education (used as covariates). The occupational aspiration analyses are based on 1349 women remaining after deleting 410 women who said the issue of future occupational choice was very unimportant to them. The performance analyses are based on 1559 women for whom we collected performance data.

[b]High and low status on these variables represents a median split.

TABLE 4.5. Motivational Characteristics at Time of Entrance of Men and Women Who Dropped Out of College H after the Freshman Year, Compared to Men and Women Who Were Still in Residence Four Years Later, Controlling for Entrance Test Scores[a]

Motivational Characteristics	Men				Women			
	Below Median Entrance Scores		Above Median Entrance Scores		Below Median Entrance Scores		Above Median Entrance Scores	
	Dropouts	Stayers	Dropouts	Stayers	Dropouts	Stayers	Dropouts	Stayers
Competency expectancy assessments:								
Average sense of personal control (Range 1–6, 6 = high)	2.91	2.22	2.54	3.24	2.89	2.91	2.63	2.48
	F, effect of test scores (NS) *F*, effect of dropouts (NS) *F*, effect of interaction of test scores and dropout (.05)				*F*, effect of test scores (NS) *F*, effect of dropouts (NS) *F*, effect of interaction (NS)			
Academic self-confidence (range 1–5, 5 = high)	3.16	2.25	2.40	3.59	2.99	3.02	2.87	3.01
	F, effect of test scores (NS) *F*, effect of dropouts (NS) *F*, effect of interaction of test scores and dropout (.01)				*F*, effect of test scores (NS) *F*, effect of dropouts (NS) *F*, effect of interaction (NS)			

Achievement-related motives:

Fear of failure (Total score collapsed into thirds; range 1–3, 3 = high)	1.74 2.61 2.40 1.15	F, effect of test scores (.05) F, effect of dropouts (NS) F, effect of interaction of test scores and dropout (.01)	2.41 2.43 2.12 2.10	F, effect of test scores (.05) F, effect of dropouts (NS) F, effect of interaction of test scores and dropout (NS)		
Security orientation (Range 0–3, 3 = high)	1.24 1.27 1.31 1.26	F, effect of test scores (NS) F, effect of dropouts (NS) F, effect of interaction of test scores and dropout (NS)	1.28 1.20 1.36 1.28	F, effect of test scores (NS) F, effect of dropouts (NS) F, effect of interaction of test scores and dropout (NS)		
Success orientation (Range 0–2, 2 = high)	.52 .59 .61 .57	F, effect of test scores (NS) F, effect of dropouts (NS) F, effect of interaction of test scores and dropout (NS)	.50 .60 .54 .55	F, effect of test scores (NS) F, effect of dropouts (NS) F, effect of interaction of test scores and dropout (NS)		
Achievement orientation (Range 0–3, 3 = high)	1.12 1.23 1.28 1.25	F, effect of test scores (NS) F, effect of dropouts (NS) F, effect of interaction of test scores and dropout (NS)	1.20 1.24 1.29 1.32	F, effect of test scores (NS) F, effect of dropouts (NS) F, effect of interaction of test scores and dropout (NS)		

[a]This analysis was done only at College H. It was carried out on the 100 freshman men and 100 freshman women who were randomly sampled from all entering freshmen in 1964 to be the freshman analysis sample for College H. Four years later these 200 students broke down as following: 49 women with below median entrance scores, 25 of whom had dropped out and 26 of whom were still in residence; 51 women with above median entrance scores, 14 of whom had dropped out and 37 of whom were still in residence; 48 men with below median entrance scores, 25 of whom had dropped out and 23 of whom were still in residence; 52 men with above median entrance scores, 13 of whom had dropped out and 39 of whom were still in residence.

447

TABLE 4.6. **Relative Importance of Expectancies and Motives in Explaining the Occupational Aspirations of Men at College G, Compared to Men in All 10 Colleges, 1964**

	Beta Weights in Predicting					
	Prestige of the Occupational Choice		Ability Demands of the Occupational Choice		Nontraditionality of the Occupational Choice	
	Men at All Ten Colleges	Men at College G	Men at All Ten Colleges	Men at College G	Men at All Ten Colleges	Men at College G
Competency-expectancy assessments:						
Sense of personal control	.28	.06	.25	.05	.10	.11
Academic self-confidence	.35	.10	.40	.07	.35	.11
Achievement motives:						
Fear of failure	.19	.34	.16	.31	.12	.36
Desire for security	.12	.34	.14	.40	.05	.24
Achievement orientation	.12	.24	.17	.09	.02	.24
Success orientation	.01	.10	.03	.09	.01	.14

TABLE 4.7A. **Performance and Aspiration Implications of a System Blame Ideology for Men. (Multiple Analyses of Variance Using Personal Control and System Blame[a] to Explain Occupational and Educational Aspirations of Men in 1964 and in 1970, and to Explain Performance Measures in 1964)**

Performance and Aspirations Average Scores On:	1964[b]				1970[c]			
	High Personal Control		Low Personal Control		High Personal Control		Low Personal Control	
	Blame of Individuals	System Blame	Blame of Individuals	System Blame	Blame of Individuals	System Blame	Blame of Individuals	System Blame
Occupational aspirations:								
Prestige of the choice (Range 1–5, 5 = high)	3.10	3.13	2.68	2.62	3.05	3.06	2.70	2.74
	F, interaction of PC and SB = (NS)				*F*, interaction of PC and SB = (NS)			
	F, effect of PC = 13.36				*F*, effect of PC = 5.10 (.025)			
	F, effect of SB = (NS)				*F*, effect of SB = (NS)			
Ability demands of the choice (Range 1–7, 7 = high)	3.81	3.92	3.42	3.43	3.86	3.77	3.26	3.47
	F, interaction of PC and SB = (NS)				*F*, interaction of PC and SB = (NS)			
	F, effect of PC = 14.02				*F*, effect of PC = 10.27			
	F, effect of SB = (NS)				*F*, effect of SB = (NS)			

[a]High and low status on these variables represents a median split.

[b]These analyses in 1964 were done controlling for entrance test scores and father's education (used as covariates). The occupational aspiration analyses are based on 1580 men remaining after deleting 300 men who said the issue of future occupational choice was very unimportant to them. The performance analyses are based on 1680 men for whom we collected performance data.

[c]Since we did not collect any performance data, neither college grades nor entrance scores, in 1970, these analyses are uncontrolled for test scores position. The analyses did include a control for father's education. They are based on 539 men remaining after deleting the 52 men who said occupation was unimportant to them.

449

TABLE 4.7A. Performance and Aspiration Implications of a System Blame Ideology for Men. (Multiple Analyses of Variance Using Personal Control and System Blame[a] to Explain Occupational and Educational Aspirations of Men in 1964 and in 1970, and to Explain Performance Measures in 1964)
(Cont'd)

Performance and Aspirations Average Scores On:	1964[b]				1970[c]			
	High Personal Control		Low Personal Control		High Personal Control		Low Personal Control	
	Blame of Individuals	System Blame	Blame of Individuals	System Blame	Blame of Individuals	System Blame	Blame of Individuals	System Blame
Nontraditionality of the choice (Average percent Black in the occupation)	3.16	2.85	4.13	3.01	2.96	2.41	5.09	3.58
	F, interaction of PC and CI = (NS) F, effect of PC = 3.09 (almost .05) F, effect of SB = 7.92 (.005)				F, interaction of PC and SB = (NS) F, effect of PC = 4.35 (.05) F, effect of SB = 6.70 (.01)			
Educational aspirations:								
Intention of going to graduate or professional school (Range 1–5, 5 = high)	2.66	3.00	2.36	2.29	2.81	2.94	2.39	2.30
	F, interaction of PC and SB = (NS) F, effect of PC = 4.22 (.05) F, effect of SB = (NS)				F, interaction of PC and SB = (NS) F, effect of PC = 8.94 (.01) F, effect of SB = (NS)			

Performance measures:

Correct performance on sixth trial of anagrams (Range 0–13)	6.89	8.00	6.20	4.07	No data in 1970
	F, interaction of PC and SB = 5.51			
	F, effect of PC = 5.22			
	F, effect of SB = (NS)			
Total number of errors on six anagrams trials (Range 0–78)	6.58	1.87	5.52	10.85	No data in 1970
	F, interaction of PC and SB = 8.86			
	F, effect of PC = (NS)			
	F, effect of SB = (NS)			
Percentile position within college on cumulative grades (Range 00–99)	60.6	72.5	59.6	35.7	No data in 1970
	F, interaction of PC and SB = (NS)			
	F, effect of PC = 3.84 (.05)			
	F, effect of SB = (NS)			

[a]High and low status on these variables represents a median split.

[b]These analyses in 1964 were done controlling for entrance test scores and father's education (used as covariates). The occupational aspiration analyses are based on 1580 men remaining after deleting 300 men who said the issue of future occupational choice was very unimportant to them. The performance analyses are based on 1680 men for whom we collected performance data.

[c]Since we did not collect any performance data, neither college grades nor entrance scores, in 1970, these analyses are uncontrolled for test scores position. The analyses did include a control for father's education. They are based on 539 men remaining after deleting the 52 men who said occupation was unimportant to them.

TABLE 4.7B. Performance and Aspiration Implications of a System Blame Ideology for Women. (Multiple Analyses of Variance Using Personal Control and System Blame[a] to Explain Occupational and Educational Aspirations of Women in 1964 and in 1970, and to Explain Performance Measures in 1964)

Performance and Aspirations Average Scores On:	1964[b]				1970[c]			
	High Personal Control		Low Personal Control		High Personal Control		Low Personal Control	
	Blame of Individuals	System Blame	Blame of Individuals	System Blame	Blame of Individuals	System Blame	Blame of Individuals	System Blame
Occupational aspirations:								
Prestige of the choice (Range 1–5, 5 = high)	2.79	2.82	2.60	2.67	2.75	2.79	2.43	2.47
	F, interaction of PC and SB = (NS) F, effect of PC = 9.05 (.005) F, effect of SB = (NS)				F, interaction of PC and SB = (NS) F, effect of PC = 3.92 (.05) F, effect of SB = (NS)			
Ability demands of the choice (Range 1–7, 7 = high)	2.92	3.04	2.51	2.55	3.06	3.01	2.77	2.73
	F, interaction of PC and SB = (NS) F, effect of PC = 3.99 (.05) F, effect of SB = (NS)				F, interaction of PC and SB = (NS) F, effect of PC = 3.71 (almost .05) F, effect of SB = (NS)			
Nontraditionality of the choice (Average percent Black in the occupation)	5.01	5.46	5.22	5.08	6.48	5.59	6.43	6.37
	F, interaction of PC and SB = (NS) F, effect of PC = (NS) F, effect of SB = (NS)				F, interaction of PC and SB = (NS) F, effect of PC = (NS) F, effect of SB = (NS)			

Educational aspirations:							
Intention of going to graduate or professional school (Range 1–5, 5 = high)	2.33	2.41	2.17	2.10	2.23	2.94	2.19	2.06

Educational aspirations:

Intention of going to graduate or professional school (Range 1–5, 5 = high)

2.33 2.41 2.17 2.10   2.23 2.94 2.19 2.06

F, interaction of PC and SB = (NS)   *F*, interaction of PC and SB = 3.06 (almost .05)
F, effect of PC = (NS)   *F*, effect of PC = 3.81 (.05)
F, effect of SB = (NS)   *F*, effect of SB = (NS)

Performance measures:

Correct performance on sixth trial of anagrams (Range 0–13)

6.46 7.66 6.30 6.58   No data in 1970

F, interaction of PC and SB = (NS)
F, effect of PC = (NS)
F, effect of SB = (NS)

Total number of errors on six anagrams trials (Range 0–78)

2.46 2.66 3.33 7.36   No data in 1970

F, interaction of PC and SB = 3.02 (almost .05)
F, effect of PC = 4.56 (.05)
F, effect of SB = (NS)

Percentile position within college on cumulative grades (Range 00–90)

61.2 75.4 50.2 38.7   No data in 1970

F, interaction of PC and SB = (NS)
F, effect of PC = 3.93 (.05)
F, effect of SB = (NS)

[a]High and low status on these variables represents a median split.

[b]These analyses in 1964 were done controlling for entrance test scores and father's education (used as covariates). The occupational aspiration analyses are based on 1349 women remaining after deleting 410 women who said the issue of future occupational choice was very unimportant to them. The performance analyses are based on 1559 women for whom we collected performance data.

[c]Since we did not collect any performance data, neither college grades nor entrance scores, in 1970, these analyses are uncontrolled for test scores position. The analyses did include a control for father's education. They are based on 438 women, remaining after deleting the 98 women who said occupation was unimportant to them.

chapter 5

TABLE 5.1.   **Relationships between Family Background and Demographic Variables and Performance Measures for Men and Women, 1964**[a]

Family Background and Demographic Variables	Percentile Score[b] Within the College on Cumulative Grade Point Averages		Percentile Score[c] Within the College On Entrance Scores		Number Anagrams Correctly Answered	
	Eta	Beta	Eta	Beta	Eta	Beta
A. Men:						
Rural-urban setting of place student lived most of life	.06	.06	.10	.10	.02	.02
Family income	.03	.01	.05	.03	.01	.01
Family structure	.06	.06	.03	.02	.01	.01
Father's education	.08	.07	.11	.09	.03	.02
Mother's education	.06	.05	.08	.05	.03	.03
B. Women:						
Rural-urban setting of place student lived most of life	.10	.08	.17	.18	.05	.04
Family income	.10	.08	.09	.10	.03	.03
Family structure	.01	.01	.03	.03	.01	.01
Father's education	.09	.08	.07	.08	.03	.03
Mother's education	.09	.06	.05	.05	.02	.01

[a]This analysis includes 3639 students in 1964.

[b]We controlled for the college the student was attending by assigning each student a percentile score within his or her college. This was necessary since the same entrance tests were not given in all 10 schools; likewise, the grade point average distribution differed greatly between some colleges.

[c]These multivariate analyses were carried out with the Multiple Classification Analysis Program. The eta is the correlation ratio which, when squared, indicates the proportion of the variance explainable by a predictor operating alone (i.e., without adjustment for correlation with other predictors as in this example the correlation of rural urban setting with cumulative grades without controlling for a family income, family structure, mother's education, father's education). The beta coefficients provide a measure of the relationship of each predictor to the dependent variable, after adjusting for the effects of all other predictors. They are analogous to the standardized regression coefficient. This table and most other tables on demographic relationships show that these multiple controls made very little difference; the etas and betas were very similar in most instances.

TABLE 5.2. Relationships[a] between Family Background and Demographic Variables and Three Dimensions of the Occupational Aspirations of Freshmen Men and Women, 1964 and 1970[b]

Family Background and Demographic Variables	1964 Prestige of Choice		Ability Demands of Choice		Nontraditionality of Choice		1970 Prestige of Choice		Ability Demands of Choice		Nontraditionality of Choice	
	Eta	Beta	Eta	Beta	Eta	Beta	Eta	Beta	Eta	Beta	Eta	Beta
A. Men:												
Rural-urban setting of place student lived most of life	.12	.12	.13	.13	.11	.12	.25	.17	.14	.13	.15	.20
Family income	.16	.11	.14	.15	.22	.24	.22	.18	.11	.11	.29	.23
Family structure	.03	.02	.07	.04	.02	.01	.03	.04	.07	.04	.07	.07
Father's education	.21	.11	.16	.08	.16	.11	.28	.31	.17	.24	.28	.33
Mother's education	.26	.24	.21	.19	.18	.13	.20	.25	.13	.17	.19	.17
B. Women:												
Rural-urban setting of place student lived most of life	.24	.23	.19	.16	.11	.11	.19	.14	.16	.16	.18	.19
Family income	.14	.13	.19	.15	.12	.20	.09	.13	.15	.27	.21	.26
Family structure	.07	.08	.03	.03	.05	.08	.02	.03	.06	.02	.04	.03
Father's education	.17	.17	.15	.13	.13	.21	.17	.17	.21	.26	.28	.29
Mother's education	.07	.10	.16	.13	.13	.16	.17	.17	.17	.13	.17	.20

[a]The italic betas are statistically significant beyond the .001 level.

[b]This analysis includes 940 freshmen in 1964 and 591 freshmen in 1970.

TABLE 5.3. **Relationship between Family Background and Demographic Variables and Measures of Achievement Motives for All Men and Women in 1964[a]**

Family Background and Demographic Variables	Negative Motives				Positive Motives					
	Fear of Failure[b]		Security Orientation		Achievement Orientation[c]		Success Orientation[c]		Preference for Intermediate Risks[d]	
	Eta	Beta	Eta	Beta	Eta	Beta	Eta	Beta	Eta	Beta
A. Men:										
Rural-urban setting of place student lived most of life	.07	.08	.05	.05	.08	.08	.10	.10	.04	.04
Family income	.04	.04	.01	.01	.06	.07	.05	.03	.01	.01
Family structure	.02	.02	.04	.04	.03	.03	.01	.01	.03	.03
Father's education	.05	.08	.03	.03	.03	.04	.06	.05	.03	.03
Mother's education	.08	.08	.06	.06	.02	.02	.06	.05	.05	.05
B. Women:										
Rural-urban setting of place student lived most of life	.09	.09	.06	.05	.02	.01	.07	.08	No	
Family income	.03	.04	.08	.07	.08	.07	.05	.06	Data	
Family structure	.02	.02	.02	.02	.03	.02	.02	.02	for	
Father's education	.04	.05	.02	.12	.11	.11	.09	.12	Women	
Mother's education	.09	.10	.03	.07	.08	.08	.04	.07		

[a]This analysis includes 3639 students in 1964.

[b]The measure of fear of failure is the Mandler-Sarason Test Anxiety Scale. (G. Mandler and S. B. Sarason, "A Study of Anxiety and Learning," *Journal of Abnormal and Social Psychology*, 16, 1952, pp. 115-118.)

[c]The measures of security orientation, achievement orientation, and success orientation were derived content-analyzing responses to unstructured questions about how the students would like their future lives to work out and what they admired about influential people in their lives.

[d]The measure of preference of intermediate risks was developed by Atkinson and O'Connor (J. W. Atkinson and P. O'Connor, *Effects of Ability Grouping in Schools Related to Individual Differences in Achievement-Related Motivation.* Report to the U.S. Office of Education, 1963).

TABLE 5.4. **Relationship between Family Background and Demographic Variables and Measures of Work Ethic Values and General Life Values in 1964**[a]

Family Background and Demographic Variables	Work-Ethic Values[b]		Top Ranked General Value[c]	
	Eta	Beta	Eta	Beta
A. Men:				
Rural-urban setting of place student lived most of life	.11	.10	.05	.06
Family income	.06	.05	.04	.04
Family structure	.05	.05	.04	.05
Father's education	.07	.07	.07	.08
Mother's education	.06	.05	.06	.04
B. Women:				
Rural-urban setting of place student lived most of life	.07	.06	.06	.06
Family income	.06	.07	.07	.07
Family structure	.02	.01	.05	.05
Father's education	.01	.01	.03	.04
Mother's education	.05	.04	.06	.09

[a]This analysis includes 3639 students in 1964.

[b]The measure of work-ethic values was derived from factor analyzing the Internal-External Control Scale developed by Julian B. Rotter, "Generalized Expectancies for Internal versus External Control of Reinforcement," *Psychological Monographs: General and Applied*, 80, 1966, pp. 1-28.

[c]The measure of theoretical pragmatic, social, political, religious, and aesthetic values was developed by E. Spranger, *Types of Men*. Translated from the fifth German ed. of *Lebensformen* by P. J. Pigors (Halle: Max Niemeyer Verlof, 1928. American Agent: Stechert-Hafner, New York).

TABLE 5.5. **Relationship between Family Background and Demographic Variables and Measures of Student Values for All Men and Women in 1964**[a]

Family Background and Demographic Variables	Value Attributed to Nine Possible Goals for College																	
	Preparation for Marriage		Career and Skill Development		Receiving Academic Recognition		Intellectual Exploration		Establishing Permanent Friendships		Proof of Academic Ability		Identity: Finding Niche for Oneself		Commitment to Lifelong Values		Professional Development	
	Eta	Beta	Eta	Beta	Eta	Beta	Eta	Beta	Eta	Beta	Eta	Beta	Eta	Beta	Eta	Beta	Eta	Beta
A. Men:																		
Rural-urban setting of place student lived most of life	.06	.05	.07	.08	.04	.05	.06	.04	.07	.06	.06	.06	.08	.08	.09	.08	.10	.09
Family income	.03	.01	.09	.08	.02	.02	.07	.07	.07	.07	.07	.07	.03	.02	.05	.05	.05	.04
Family structure	.01	.01	.03	.03	.01	.01	.03	.03	.02	.02	.06	.06	.02	.01	.02	.01	.05	.05
Father's education	.10	.08	.08	.07	.11	.07	.10	.09	.06	.06	.05	.05	.03	.03	.09	.10	.04	.03
Mother's education	.08	.07	.07	.05	.13	.11	.06	.06	.05	.04	.06	.09	.06	.06	.06	.08	.02	.03
B. Women:																		
Rural-urban setting of place student lived most of life	.09	.09	.06	.05	.08	.08	.11	.10	.06	.07	.11	.11	.08	.07	.13	.12	.08	.08
Family income	.07	.07	.04	.04	.08	.11	.05	.05	.04	.03	.08	.09	.02	.03	.06	.04	.02	.02
Family structure	.04	.05	.05	.05	.04	.04	.04	.01	.01	.01	.03	.04	.02	.03	.02	.02	.01	.02
Father's education	.04	.04	.04	.03	.06	.06	.08	.06	.05	.05	.05	.05	.05	.06	.09	.09	.04	.04
Mother's education	.07	.08	.04	.04	.06	.06	.06	.04	.05	.06	.09	.09	.09	.11	.07	.07	.07	.07

[a]This analysis includes 3639 students in 1964.

459

TABLE 5.6. Relationship between Family Background and Demographic Variables and the Value Attached to Education, Contrasted to the Expectancy of Achieving Higher Education, Men and Women, 1964 and 1970

	1964								1970							
	Value of Education Importance of:[a]				Expectancies of Achieving Educational Goals Certainty of:				Value of Education Importance of:[a]				Expectancies of Achieving Educational Goals Certainty of:			
	A College Degree		Going to Graduate or Professional School		Completing College[b]		Continuing Beyond the Baccalaureate Degree[c]		A College Degree		Going to Graduate or Professional School		Completing College[b]		Continuing Beyond the Baccalaureate Degree[c]	
Family Background and Demographic Variables	Eta	Beta	Eta	Beta	Eta	Beta	Eta	Beta	Eta	Beta	Eta	Beta	Eta	Beta	Eta	Beta
A. Men:																
Rural-urban setting of place student lived most of life	.08	.08	.10	.08	.22	.19	.20	.21	.07	.06	.09	.08	.31	.32	.25	.22
Family income	.05	.04	.04	.03	.29	.26	.38	.36	.03	.04	.05	.03	.40	.39	.39	.39
Family structure	.03	.04	.01	.01	.01	.01	.01	.02	.01	.01	.02	.01	.03	.04	.01	.01
Father's education	.08	.06	.09	.07	.10	.10	.03	.04	.08	.06	.09	.07	.10	.10	.04	.03
Mother's education	.06	.04	.07	.06	.06	.05	.12	.13	.04	.03	.05	.04	.06	.07	.01	.02
B. Women:																
Rural-urban setting of place student lived most of life	.05	.06	.13	.13	.24	.22	.31	.31	.03	.04	.10	.09	.30	.29	.30	.30
Family income	.01	.01	.06	.04	.32	.30	.32	.33	.09	.07	.05	.04	.33	.33	.41	.40
Family structure	.04	.03	.02	.05	.03	.01	.04	.06	.01	.01	.03	.02	.04	.01	.03	.02
Father's education	.04	.06	.06	.06	.10	.10	.11	.09	.05	.06	.08	.07	.11	.10	.12	.11
Mother's education	.06	.08	.10	.08	.06	.05	.12	.08	.03	.03	.06	.05	.08	.09	.09	.08

[a] This analysis includes 3639 students in 1964 and 1127 students in 1970.

[b] This analysis includes 940 freshmen students in 1964 and 591 freshmen in 1970. Demographic variables were not significantly related to certainty of finishing college among seniors.

[c] This analysis includes 897 seniors in 1964 and 536 seniors in 1970. Demographic variables were not significantly related to expectancy of going on to graduate or professional school among freshmen.

TABLE 6.1. **Multiple Classification Analysis of the Relationship between College Attended and Student Aspiration and Motivation, Controlling Three Student Input Characteristics (Sex, Rural-Urban Background, and Father's Education), 1964 and 1970**

| | Eta and Beta Coefficients for College Attended | | | |
| | 1964[a] | | 1970[b] | |
	Eta	Beta	Eta	Beta
ASPIRATIONS				
Dimensions of occupational aspiration:				
Prestige of the choice	.30	.24	.35	.26
Ability demands of the choice	.28	.21	.32	.19
Nontraditionality of the choice	.18	.08	.28	.15
Educational aspirations:				
Intention of going to graduate or professional school	.18	.10	.27	.22
PERFORMANCE				
Grade point average	.52	.52	No data	
Anagrams performance	.23	.24	No data	
Total number errors on Anagrams task	.25	.25	No data	
ACHIEVEMENT-RELATED MOTIVATION				
Motives and values:				
Achievement orientation	.09	.08	No data	
Success orientation	.05	.06	No data	
Security concerns	.18	.17	No data	
Test anxiety	.05	.06	No data	
Control ideology: work ethic values	.10	.10	.10	.08
Expectancies and competency assessments:				
Sense of personal control	.15	.15	.19	.16
Academic self-confidence	.22	.19	.24	.21
Level of expectancy of achieving occupational goal	.11	.09	.17	.18

[a]Where the same measures were repeated in 1964 and 1970, the analyses of 1964 data include the 2141 students attending the six colleges that participated at both points in time. Where measures were administered only in 1964 (performance and motive measures) the analyses of 1964 data include the 3639 students attending the 10 colleges that participated in 1964.

[b]These analyses are based on the 1127 students attending the six colleges that participated in both the 1964 and 1970 cross-sectional studies.

TABLE 6.2. Institutional Differences in the Occupational Aspirations of Men and Women Students at Time of College Entrance and at the End of the Freshman Year, 1964[a]

	Average Levels of Aspiration on Three Dimensions of Occupational Aspiration								
	Prestige of the Choice (Range 1–5, 5 = High)			Ability Demands of the Choice (Range 1–7, 7 = High)			Nontraditionality of the Choice (Average Percent Black in Occupation)		
College	Initial Scores	Post Scores	Post Scores Adjusted For Initial Differences	Initial Scores	Post Scores	Post Scores Adjusted For Initial Differences	Initial Scores	Post Scores	Post Scores Adjusted For Initial Differences
				A. Men					
College A	2.87	2.69	2.71	3.41	3.21	3.33	3.14	3.93	3.82
College C	2.97	2.82	2.82	3.57	3.49	3.54	2.76	3.66	3.75
College D	2.92	2.85	2.88	3.62	3.63	3.67	3.08	3.26	3.17
College E	3.02	2.99	2.97	3.59	3.96	4.13	3.00	2.62	2.58
College F	2.88	2.79	2.82	3.40	3.16	3.28	4.37	5.40	4.95
College G	3.01	2.84	2.87	3.81	3.77	3.72	2.64	2.77	2.92
College H	2.98	2.99	2.98	3.94	3.88	3.78	2.17	3.75	4.15
College I	3.08	3.14	3.10	4.03	4.19	4.12	2.27	1.84	2.04
College J	3.09	3.01	2.96	4.08	4.05	3.82	2.44	2.40	2.65
	$F=2.68$ (.01)	$F=5.82$ (.001)	$F=4.13$ (.001)	$F=3.51$ (.001)	$F=8.65$ (.001)	$F=5.93$ (.001)	$F=3.56$ (.001)	$F=7.40$ (.001)	$F=5.52$ (.001)

				B. Women					
College A	2.71	2.72	2.74	2.65	2.69	2.73	5.31	5.29	5.27
College C	2.74	2.76	2.74	2.99	2.99	3.08	5.17	5.27	5.35
College D	2.67	2.70	2.75	2.78	3.01	3.27	5.21	5.40	5.54
College E	2.86	2.79	2.78	3.12	3.19	3.22	4.95	5.14	5.64
College F	2.71	2.70	2.73	2.77	2.71	2.72	5.45	5.51	5.64
College G	2.82	2.80	2.79	3.03	3.05	3.14	4.92	4.94	4.91
College H	2.77	2.76	2.77	3.13	3.10	3.08	5.53	5.43	5.47
College I	2.83	2.81	2.82	3.18	3.24	3.30	5.31	5.61	5.78
	F=9.73	F=5.71	F=1.44	F=2.96	F=6.45	F=4.22	F=.30	F=.83	F=.83
	(.001)	(.001)	(NS)	(.01)	(.001)	(.001)	(NS)	(NS)	(NS)

[a]This covariance analysis of "institutional effect" is based only on 1964 data since we collected data on freshmen at the beginning and end of the freshman year only in 1964. Only nine colleges are included in the analysis since the data on the freshman sample at the end of year were very incomplete at the tenth institution (College B). 440 men and 400 women were included.

463

TABLE 6.3. Significance Level of Institutional Differences in the Educational Aspirations and Achievement-Motivation of Men and Women Students at Time of College Entrance and at the End of the Freshman Year, 1964[a]

	Freshman Men			Freshman Women		
	Initial Scores At College Entrance	Post Scores At End of the Freshman Year	Post Scores, Adjusted for Initial Differences	Initial Scores At College Entrance	Post Scores At End of the Freshman Year	Post Scores, Adjusted for Initial Differences
Educational aspirations:						
Intention of going to graduate school	F(NS)	F=3.29 (.001)	F=3.26 (.001)	F(NS)	F=2.68 (.01)	F=2.09 (.05)
Motives and values:						
Achievement orientation	F(NS)	F(NS)	F(NS)	F(NS)	F(NS)	F(NS)
Security concerns	F=1.98 (.05)	F=1.99 (.05)	F(NS)	F=2.04 (.05)	F(NS)	F(NS)
Test anxiety	F(NS)	F(NS)	F(NS)	F(NS)	F(NS)	F(NS)
Control ideology: Protestant ethic values	F=2.13 (.05)	F=3.06 (.01)	F=2.71 (.01)	F=2.49 (.05)	F=1.78 (NS)	F=2.09 (.05)
Expectancies and competency assessments:						
Sense of personal control	F=2.27 (.05)	F=5.96 (.001)	F=3.92 (.001)	F=2.32 (.05)	F(NS)	F(NS)
Academic self-confidence	F=2.02 (.05)	F=3.32 (.001)	F=2.63 (.01)	F=2.24 (NS)	F(NS)	F(NS)

[a]This covariance analysis of "institutional effect" is based only on 1964 data since we collected data on freshman at the beginning and end of the freshman year only in 1964. Only nine colleges are included in the analysis since the data on the freshman sample at the end of year were very incomplete at the 10th institution (College B). 440 men and 400 women were included.

TABLE 6.4. **Institutional Differences in Students' Grade Point Averages and in Performance on an Anagrams Task Administered in 1964**

Presentation of Colleges In Order of Rank Position On Cumulative Grades:	Cumulative Grade Point Averages[a]	Average[b] Number Anagrams Done Correctly On Sixth Trial (Range 0–13)	Cumulative Grades, Adjusted for SAT Entrance Scores In Five Colleges That Administered Them
I	2.49	9.55	2.65
H	2.22	No data	2.10
B	2.18	8.13	—
J	2.14	8.84	2.24
D	2.10	8.55	—
G	1.89	6.89	1.82
C	1.54	7.17	—
A	1.38	6.57	—
E	1.31	7.79	1.11
F	No data	7.63	—
	$F = 18.9$ (.001)	$F = 17.4$ (.001)	$F = 11.4$ (.001)

[a]This analysis was based on 3239 students attending the nine colleges in 1964 from whom we collected student grade reports. These grade averages are adjusted for the effect of three student input characteristics: sex, rural-urban background, and father's education.

[b]This analysis likewise was based on 3239 students attending the nine colleges where we administered the anagrams task. Again the performance averages are adjusted for the effect of the same three student characteristics.

[c]This analysis was based on 1639 students attending the five colleges that administered the SAT in 1964.

TABLE 6.5A. Significance Level of Differences, at Time of College Entrance and at End of Freshman Year 1964-1965, in the Aspirations of Freshman Women in Colleges That Varied in Institutional Features Presented to the Students[a]

			Institutional Features			
Aspirations	Public-Private Sponsorship	Liberal Arts Emphasis	Academic Status	Social Status of the Student Body	Cosmopolitanism of the Student Body	Sex Ratio: Percent Women in the College
EDUCATIONAL ASPIRATIONS *Intention of pursuing the Ph.D. or professional degree:*						
Initial scores	F(NS)	F(NS)	F(NS)	F(NS)	F(NS)	F(NS)
Post scores	F(NS)	F(NS)	F(NS)	F(NS)	F(NS)	F(NS)
Post scores adjusted for initial differences	F(NS)	F(NS)	F(NS)	F(NS)	F(NS)	F(NS)
OCCUPATIONAL ASPIRATIONS *Prestige of the choice:*						
Initial scores	$F = 38.1(.001)$	$F = 17.1(.001)$	$F = 48.3(.001)$	$F = 25.3(.001)$	$F = 15.4(.001)$	F(NS)
Post scores	$F = 17.5(.001)$	$F = 9.31(.001)$	$F = 32.3(.001)$	$F = 17.6(.001)$	$F = 9.03(.001)$	F(NS)
Post scores adjusted for initial differences	F(NS)	F(NS)	$F = 4.71(.05)$	F(NS)	F(NS)	F(NS)

Ability demands of the choice:					
Initial scores	$F= 9.16(.01)$	$F= 5.84(.001)$	$F=16.8(.001)$	$F= 9.3(.001)$	$F= 5.57(.01)$
Post scores	$F(NS)$	$F= 4.79(.01)$	$F=23.2(.001)$	$F=12.4(.001)$	$F= 4.04(.05)$
Post scores adjusted for initial differences	$F(NS)$	$F(NS)$	$F=11.15(.001)$	$F(NS)$	$F(NS)$
Nontraditionality of the choice:					
Initial scores	$F(NS)$	$F(NS)$	$F(NS)$	$F(NS)$	$F(NS)$
Post scores	$F(NS)$	$F(NS)$	$F(NS)$	$F(NS)$	$F(NS)$
Post scores adjusted for initial differences	$F(NS)$	$F(NS)$	$F(NS)$	$F(NS)$	$F(NS)$

[a]These analyses are based on the 450 freshman women in 1964. The colleges were grouped in the following way: two groups for academic status and public-private sponsorship; three groups for social status of student body, for cosmopolitanism, and for sex ratio; four groups for liberal arts emphasis.

TABLE 6.5B. **Significance Level of Differences, at Time of College Entrance and at End of Freshman Year 1964-1965, in the Aspirations of Freshman Men in Colleges That Varied in Institutional Features Presented to the Students**[a]

	Institutional Features					
Aspirations	Public-Private Sponsorship	Liberal Arts Emphasis	Academic Status	Social Status of the Student Body	Cosmopolitanism of the Student Body	Sex Ratio: Percent Women in the College
EDUCATIONAL ASPIRATIONS *Intention of pursuing the Ph.D. or professional degree:*						
Initial scores	F(NS)	F(NS)	F(NS)	F(NS)	F(NS)	F(NS)
Post scores	F(NS)	F=4.6(.01)	F=18.6(.001)	F=10.2(.001)	F=5.4(.001)	F(NS)
Post scores adjusted for initial differences	F(NS)	F=3.2(.05)	F=15.7(.001)	F=8.1(.001)	F=4.4(.01)	F(NS)
OCCUPATIONAL ASPIRATIONS *Prestige of the choice:*						
Initial scores	F=5.5(.05)	F=4.5(.01)	F=14.9(.001)	F=8.6(.001)	F=4.9(.01)	F(NS)
Post scores	F=15.2(.001)	F=10.6(.001)	F=22.4(.001)	F=15.1(.001)	F=9.5(.001)	F(NS)
Post scores adjusted for initial differences	F=9.8(.01)	F=6.9(.001)	F=10.1(.001)	F=7.6(.001)	F=5.6(.001)	F(NS)

468

Ability demands of the choice:						
Initial scores	$F=7.6(.01)$	$F=6.6(.001)$	$F=20.1(.001)$	$F=10.9(.001)$	$F=8.0(.001)$	$F(NS)$
Post scores	$F=10.9(.001)$	$F=12.2(.001)$	$F=36.4(.001)$	$F=20.5(.001)$	$F=12.3(.001)$	$F(NS)$
Post scores adjusted for initial differences	$F=4.3(.05)$	$F=6.2(.001)$	$F=17.4(.001)$	$F=9.9(.001)$	$F=5.4(.001)$	$F(NS)$
Nontraditionality of the choice:						
Initial scores	$F(NS)$	$F=3.6(.05)$	$F=15.4(.001)$	$F=7.8(.001)$	$F=4.7(.001)$	$F(NS)$
Post scores	$F(NS)$	$F=9.8(.001)$	$F=19.7(.001)$	$F=9.3(.001)$	$F(NS)$	
Post scores adjusted for initial differences	$F(NS)$	$F=9.2(.001)$	$F=7.8(.01)$	$F=12.2(.001)$	$F=6.2(.001)$	$F(NS)$

[a]These analyses are based on the 490 freshman men in 1964. The colleges were grouped in the following way: two groups for academic status and public-private sponsorship; three groups for social status of student body, for cosmopolitanism, and for sex ratio; four groups for liberal arts emphasis.

TABLE 6.6A. Significance Level of Differences, at Time of College Entrance and at the End of Freshman Year 1964-1965, in the Aspirations of Freshman Women in Colleges That Varied in Student Culture Characteristics[a]

Aspirations		Student Culture Characteristics				
	Academic Press	Diversity of Extracurricular Activities	Amount Faculty Student Interaction	Rejection of Traditional Governance	Breadth of Extracurricular Participation	Participation Rates in Student Elections
EDUCATIONAL ASPIRATIONS						
Intention of pursuing the Ph.D. or professional degree:						
Initial scores	F(NS)	F(NS)	F(NS)	F(NS)	F(NS)	F(NS)
Post scores	$F = 3.82(.05)$	F(NS)	$F = 3.89(.05)$	F(NS)	F(NS)	F(NS)
Post scores adjusted for initial differences	$F = 3.08(.05)$	F(NS)	$F = 3.06(.05)$	F(NS)	F(NS)	F(NS)
OCCUPATIONAL ASPIRATIONS						
Prestige of the choice:						
Initial scores	$F = 17.5(.001)$	$F = 17.8(.001)$	$F = 25.7(.001)$	$F = 6.0(.01)$	F(NS)	F(NS)
Post scores	$F = 11.6(.001)$	$F = 10.4(.001)$	$F = 16.4(.001)$	F(NS)	F(NS)	F(NS)
Post scores adjusted for initial differences	F(NS)	F(NS)	F(NS)	F(NS)	F(NS)	F(NS)

Ability demands of the choice:						
Initial scores	$F= 5.7(.001)$	$F= 6.8(.001)$	$F= 8.5(.001)$	$F(NS)$	$F(NS)$	$F(NS)$
Post scores	$F=11.6(.001)$	$F=10.4(.001)$	$F=11.8(.001)$	$F= 4.7(.01)$	$F(NS)$	$F(NS)$
Post scores adjusted for initial differences	$F= 8.7(.001)$	$F= 3.4(.05)$	$F= 5.7(.01)$	$F= 3.9(.01)$	$F(NS)$	$F(NS)$
Nontraditionality of the choice:						
Initial scores	$F(NS)$	$F(NS)$	$F(NS)$	$F(NS)$	$F(NS)$	$F(NS)$
Post scores	$F(NS)$	$F(NS)$	$F(NS)$	$F(NS)$	$F(NS)$	$F(NS)$
Post scores adjusted for initial differences	$F(NS)$	$F(NS)$	$F(NS)$	$F(NS)$	$F(NS)$	$F(NS)$

[a]These analyses are based on the 450 freshman women in 1964. The colleges were grouped in the following way: three groups for diversity of extracurricular activities, amount of faculty-student interaction, breadth of student extracurricular participation, participation rates in student elections; four groups for academic press and rejection of traditional governance.

TABLE 6.6B. Significance Level of Differences, at Time of College Entrance and at the End of Freshman Year 1964-1965, in the Aspirations of Freshman Men in Colleges That Varied in Student Culture Characteristics[a]

Aspirations	Student Culture Characteristics					
	Academic Press	Diversity of Extracurricular Activities	Amount Faculty Student Interaction	Rejection of Traditional Governance	Breadth of Extracurricular Participation	Participation Rates in Student Elections
EDUCATIONAL ASPIRATIONS						
Intention of pursuing the Ph.D. or professional degree:						
Initial scores	F(NS)	F(NS)	F(NS)	F(NS)	F(NS)	F(NS)
Post scores	$F=7.5(.001)$	$F=6.8(.001)$	$F=9.8(.001)$	$F=3.9(.01)$	F(NS)	F(NS)
Post scores adjusted for initial differences	$F=7.3(.001)$	$F=4.2(.001)$	$F=7.9(.001)$	$F=3.9(.01)$	F(NS)	F(NS)
OCCUPATIONAL ASPIRATIONS						
Prestige of the Choice:						
Initial scores	$F=5.4(.001)$	$F=4.8(.01)$	$F=8.2(.001)$	$F=2.7(.05)$	F(NS)	F(NS)
Post scores	$F=11.9(.001)$	$F=8.7(.001)$	$F=12.5(.001)$	$F=5.4(.001)$	F(NS)	F(NS)
Post scores adjusted for initial differences	$F=7.3(.001)$	$F=5.4(.001)$	$F=5.6(.01)$	$F=4.0(.01)$	F(NS)	F(NS)

Ability demands of the choice:						
Initial scores	$F= 8.4(.001)$	$F= 7.9(.001)$	$F=10.2(.001)$	$F= 2.7(.05)$	$F(NS)$	$F(NS)$
Post scores	$F=19.1(.001)$	$F=13.4(.001)$	$F=18.9(.001)$	$F= 9.1(.001)$	$F(NS)$	$F(NS)$
Post scores adjusted for initial differences	$F=11.0(.001)$	$F= 8.7(.001)$	$F= 4.2(.001)$	$F= 6.5(.001)$	$F(NS)$	$F(NS)$
Nontraditionality of the choice:						
Initial scores	$F= 6.4(.001)$	$F= 3.8(.05)$	$F=13.8(.001)$	$F(NS)$	$F(NS)$	$F(NS)$
Post scores	$F=11.5(.001)$	$F= 9.1(.001)$	$F=11.8(.001)$	$F= 5.9(.001)$	$F(NS)$	$F(NS)$
Post scores adjusted for initial differences	$F= 6.2(.01)$	$F= 7.0(.001)$	$F= 7.1(.001)$	$F= 4.5(.001)$	$F(NS)$	$F(NS)$

[a]These analyses are based on the 490 freshman men in 1964. The colleges were grouped in the following way: three groups for diversity of extracurricular activities, amount of faculty-student interaction, breadth of student extracurricular participation, participation rates in student elections; four groups for academic press and rejection of traditional governance.

TABLE 6.7A. **Significance Level of Differences, at Time of College Entrance and at End of Freshman Year 1964-1965, in the Achievement Motivation of Freshman Women in Colleges That Varied in Institutional Features Presented to the Students**

			Institutional Features			
Achievement Motivation	Public-Private Sponsorship	Liberal Arts Emphasis	Academic Status	Social Status of the Student Body	Cosmopolitanism of the Student Body	Sex Ratio: Percent Women in the College
MOTIVES						
Achievement orientation:						
Initial scores	F(NS)	F(NS)	F(NS)	F(NS)	F(NS)	F(NS)
Post scores	F(NS)	F(NS)	F(NS)	F(NS)	F(NS)	F(NS)
Post scores adjusted for initial differences	F(NS)	F(NS)	F(NS)	F(NS)	F(NS)	F(NS)
Fear of failure:						
Initial scores	F(NS)	F(NS)	F(NS)	F(NS)	F(NS)	F(NS)
Post scores	F(NS)	F(NS)	F(NS)	F(NS)	F(NS)	F(NS)
Post scores adjusted for initial differences	F(NS)	F(NS)	F(NS)	F(NS)	F(NS)	F(NS)

VALUES							
Control ideology:							
Initial scores	F(NS)	F(NS)	F(NS)	F(NS)	F(NS)	F(NS)	F(NS)
Post scores	F(NS)	F(NS)	F(NS)	F(NS)	F(NS)	F(NS)	F(NS)
Post scores adjusted for initial differences	F(NS)	F(NS)	F(NS)	F(NS)	F(NS)	F(NS)	F(NS)
COMPETENCY-BASED EXPECTANCIES							
Sense of personal control:							
Initial scores	$F=3.96(.05)$	$F=2.69(.05)$	$F=6.44(.05)$	$F=3.3(.05)$	$F=2.71$(almost .05)	F(NS)	F(NS)
Post scores	F(NS)	$F=3.04(.05)$	F(NS)	$F=3.2(.05)$	$F=3.78(.05)$	F(NS)	F(NS)
Post scores adjusted for initial differences	F(NS)	F(NS)	F(NS)	F(NS)	F(NS)	F(NS)	F(NS)
Academic self-confidence:							
Initial scores	F(NS)	F(NS)	F(NS)	F(NS)	F(NS)	F(NS)	F(NS)
Post scores	F(NS)	F(NS)	F(NS)	F(NS)	F(NS)	F(NS)	F(NS)
Post scores adjusted for initial differences	F(NS)	F(NS)	F(NS)	F(NS)	F(NS)	F(NS)	F(NS)

[a]These analyses are based on the 450 freshman women in 1964. The colleges were grouped in the following way: two groups for academic status and public-private sponsorship; three groups for social status of student body, for cosmopolitanism, and for sex ratio; four groups for liberal arts emphasis.

TABLE 6.7B. **Significance Level of Differences, at Time of College Entrance and at End of Freshman Year 1964-1965, in the Achievement Motivation of Freshman Men in Colleges That Varied in Institutional Features Presented to the Students**[a]

	Institutional Features					
Achievement Motivation	Public-Private Sponsorship	Liberal Arts Emphasis	Academic Status	Social Status of the Student Body	Cosmopolitanism of the Student Body	Sex Ratio: Percent Women in the College
MOTIVES						
Achievement orientation:						
Initial scores	F(NS)	F(NS)	F(NS)	F(NS)	F(NS)	F(NS)
Post scores	F(NS)	F(NS)	F(NS)	F(NS)	F(NS)	F(NS)
Post scores adjusted for initial differences	F(NS)	F(NS)	F(NS)	F(NS)	F(NS)	F(NS)
Fear of failure:						
Initial scores	F(NS)	F(NS)	F(NS)	F(NS)	F(NS)	F(NS)
Post scores	F(NS)	F(NS)	F(NS)	F(NS)	F(NS)	F(NS)
Post scores adjusted initial differences	F(NS)	F(NS)	F(NS)	F(NS)	F(NS)	F(NS)

VALUES						
Control ideology:						
Initial scores	$F=5.3(.05)$	$F(NS)$	$F=9.9(.01)$	$F=5.1(.01)$	$F(NS)$	$F(NS)$
Post scores	$F(NS)$	$F=3.9(.01)$	$F=8.9(.01)$	$F=6.9(.01)$	$F=6.1(.001)$	$F(NS)$
Post scores adjusted for initial differences	$F(NS)$	$F=2.6(.05)$	$F(NS)$	$F=3.8(.05)$	$F=5.6(.001)$	$F(NS)$
COMPETENCY-BASED EXPECTANCIES						
Sense of personal control:						
Initial scores	$F(NS)$	$F=5.3(.01)$	$F=7.8(.01)$	$F=4.3(.05)$	$F=6.1(.001)$	$F(NS)$
Post scores	$F(NS)$	$F(NS)$	$F=4.1(.05)$	$F(NS)$	$F(NS)$	$F(NS)$
Post scores adjusted for initial differences	$F(NS)$	$F(NS)$	$F(NS)$	$F(NS)$	$F(NS)$	$F(NS)$
Academic self-confidence:						
Initial scores	$F(NS)$	$F(NS)$	$F(NS)$	$F(NS)$	$F=4.2(.01)$	$F(NS)$
Post scores	$F(NS)$	$F=3.2(.05)$	$F(NS)$	$F(NS)$	$F(NS)$	$F=7.65(.01)$
Post scores adjusted for initial differences	$F(NS)$	$F=3.9(.01)$	$F(NS)$	$F(NS)$	$F(NS)$	$F=5.82(.05)$

[a]These analyses are based on the 490 freshman men in 1964. The colleges were grouped in the following way: two groups for academic status and public-private sponsorship; three groups for social status of student body, for cosmopolitanism, and for sex ratio; four groups for liberal arts emphasis.

TABLE 6.8A. Significance Level of Differences, at Time of College Entrance and at End of Freshman Year 1964-1965, in the Achievement Motivation of Freshman Women in Colleges That Varied in Student Culture Characteristics[a]

Achievement Motivation	Student Culture Characteristics					
	Academic Press	Diversity of Extracurricular Activities	Amount Faculty Student Interaction	Rejection of Traditional Governance	Breadth of Extracurricular Participation	Participation Rates in Student Elections
MOTIVES						
Achievement orientation:						
Initial scores	F(NS)	F(NS)	F(NS)	F(NS)	F(NS)	F(NS)
Post scores	F(NS)	F(NS)	F(NS)	F(NS)	F(NS)	F(NS)
Post scores adjusted for initial differences	F(NS)	F(NS)	F(NS)	F(NS)	F(NS)	F(NS)
FEAR OF FAILURE						
Initial scores	F(NS)	F(NS)	F(NS)	F(NS)	F(NS)	F(NS)
Post scores	F(NS)	F(NS)	F(NS)	F(NS)	F(NS)	F(NS)
Post scores adjusted for initial differences	F(NS)	F(NS)	F(NS)	F(NS)	F(NS)	F(NS)

VALUES						
Control ideology:						
Initial scores	F(NS)	F(NS)	F(NS)	F=3.9(.01)	F(NS)	F(NS)
Post scores	F(NS)	F(NS)	F(NS)	F(NS)	F(NS)	F(NS)
Post scores adjusted for initial differences	F(NS)	F(NS)	F(NS)	F(NS)	F(NS)	F(NS)
COMPETENCY-BASED EXPECTANCIES						
Sense of personal control:						
Initial scores	F(NS)	F=3.8(.01)	F(NS)	F(NS)	F(NS)	F(NS)
Post scores	F(NS)	F=7.2(.001)	F=6.20(.01)	F=2.8(.05)	F(NS)	F(NS)
Post scores adjusted for initial differences	F(NS)	F=3.9(.01)	F=3.4(.05)	F=2.9(.05)	F(NS)	F(NS)
Academic self-confidence:						
Initial scores	F(NS)	F(NS)	F(NS)	F(NS)	F(NS)	F(NS)
Post scores	F(NS)	F(NS)	F(NS)	F(NS)	F(NS)	F(NS)
Post scores adjusted for initial differences	F(NS)	F(NS)	F(NS)	F(NS)	F(NS)	F(NS)

aThese analyses are based on the 450 freshman women in 1964. The colleges were grouped in the following way: three groups for diversity of extracurricular activities, amount of faculty-student interaction, breadth of student extracurricular participation, participation rates in student elections; four groups for academic press and rejection of traditional governance.

TABLE 6.8B. Significance Level of Differences, at Time of College Entrance and at End of Freshman Year 1964-1965, in the Achievement Motivation of Freshman Men in Colleges That Varied in Student Culture Characteristics[a]

Achievement Motivation	Student Culture Characteristics					
	Academic Press	Diversity of Extracurricular Activities	Amount Faculty Student Interaction	Rejection of Traditional Governance	Breadth of Extracurricular Participation	Participation Rates in Student Elections
MOTIVES						
Achievement orientation:						
Initial scores	F(NS)	F(NS)	F(NS)	F(NS)	F(NS)	F(NS)
Post scores	F(NS)	F(NS)	F(NS)	F(NS)	F(NS)	F(NS)
Post scores adjusted for initial differences	F(NS)	F(NS)	F(NS)	F(NS)	F(NS)	F(NS)
Fear of failure:						
Initial scores	F(NS)	F(NS)	F(NS)	F(NS)	F(NS)	F(NS)
Post scores	F(NS)	F(NS)	F(NS)	F(NS)	F(NS)	F(NS)
Post scores adjusted for initial differences	F(NS)	F(NS)	F(NS)	F(NS)	F(NS)	F(NS)

VALUES						
Control ideology:						
Initial scores	$F = 3.3(.05)$	$F(NS)$	$F = 5.9(.01)$	$F = 3.2(.05)$	$F(NS)$	$F(NS)$
Post scores	$F = 3.6(.05)$	$F = 5.8(.001)$	$F = 7.4(.001)$	$F = 3.8(.01)$	$F(NS)$	$F(NS)$
Post scores adjusted for initial differences	$F(NS)$	$F = 5.1(.001)$	$F = 3.2(.05)$	$F(NS)$	$F(NS)$	$F(NS)$
COMPETENCY-BASED EXPECTANCIES						
Sense of personal control:						
Initial scores	$F = 3.00(.05)$	$F = 3.1(.05)$	$F = 2.9(.05)$	$F = 3.7(.05)$	$F(NS)$	$F(NS)$
Post scores	$F(NS)$	$F = 8.2(.001)$	$F = 6.1(.01)$	$F(NS)$	$F = 7.1(.001)$	$F = 6.72(.01)$
Post scores adjusted for initial differences	$F(NS)$	$F = 3.4(.05)$	$F = 3.2(.05)$	$F(NS)$	$F = 4.2(.01)$	$F = 4.4(.05)$
Academic self-confidence:						
Initial scores	$F(NS)$	$F(NS)$	$F(NS)$	$F(NS)$	$F(NS)$	$F(NS)$
Post scores	$F = 3.6(.05)$	$F(NS)$	$F(NS)$	$F(NS)$	$F(NS)$	$F(NS)$
Post scores adjusted for initial differences	$F = 3.5(.05)$	$F(NS)$	$F(NS)$	$F(NS)$	$F(NS)$	$F(NS)$

[a]These analyses are based on the 490 freshman men in 1964. The colleges were grouped in the following way: three groups for diversity of extracurricular activities, amount of faculty-student interaction, breadth of student extracurricular participation, participation rates in student elections; four groups for academic press and rejection of traditional governance.

TABLE 8.1. **Proportion of Men and Women Disapproving Traditional Student Regulations and Traditional Governance, 1964 and 1970**

	Percent Disapproving or Strongly Disapproving					
	1964[a]			1970[b]		
	Men	Women	Total	Men	Women	Total
Attitude toward authority in the area of student political action:						
Students should not be allowed to conduct any civil rights demonstrations *on* campus while enrolled at the college.	66%	61%	63%	89%	86%	87%
Students should not be allowed to participate in any civil rights activities or demonstrations *off* campus in the community while enrolled at the college.	79%	71%	75%	90%	86%	88%
Who should: decide whether students should conduct any civil rights activities or demonstrations on campus.						
(Percent saying: Students	24%	19%	21%	46%	28%	37%
College and Students	51%	54%	52%	47%	62%	55%
College)	25%	27%	27%	7%	10%	8%
	100%	100%	100%	100%	100%	100%
Mean on Total score: range 1–9	5.78	5.48	5.64	7.23	6.59	6.92
		$F=6.88(.01)$			$F=44.1(.001)$	
Attitude toward authority in the parietal policies:						
Women students must have "hours"—be in their dormitories not later than certain specified hours at night.	17%	13%	15%	62%	58%	60%
Students should not be allowed to leave campus without a written permission from parents each time they wish to do so.	73%	51%	62%	94%	89%	91%
Who should: decide what students should be allowed to do when spending time off-campus.						

TABLE 8.1.
(Cont'd) **Proportion of Men and Women Disapproving Traditional Student Regulations and Traditional Governance, 1964 and 1970**

| | Percent Disapproving or Strongly Disapproving | | | | | |
| | 1964[a] | | | 1970[b] | | |
	Men	Women	Total	Men	Women	Total
(Percent saying: Students	50%	40%	46%	88%	82%	85%
College and Students	34%	41%	37%	9%	15%	12%
College)	16%	19%	17%	3%	3%	3%
	100%	100%	100%	100%	100%	100%
Who should: discipline students, short of dismissal from school						
(Percent saying: Students	12%	7%	9%	14%	5%	10%
College and Students	56%	56%	56%	69%	72%	70%
College)	32%	37%	35%	17%	23%	20%
	100%	100%	100%	100%	100%	100%
Who should: determine what time girls should be in at night						
(Percent saying: Students	7%	10%	8%	32%	31%	32%
College and Students	49%	56%	52%	56%	57%	56%
College)	44%	34%	40%	12%	12%	12%
100%	100%	100%	100%	100%	100%	100%
Mean on Total score: range 1–13	6.69	5.99	6.35	9.40	8.72	9.07
		$F=25.4(.001)$			$F=30.09(.001)$	
Attitude toward authority about academic freedom issues:						
Student organizations shall not invite any speaker to the college without clearing first with the administrative office of the college.	20%	13%	17%	40%	25%	32%
Who should: determine what speakers a student organization can invite to speak on campus.						
(Percent saying: Students	28%	28%	28%	53%	41%	47%
College and Students	58%	56%	57%	44%	56%	50%
College)	14%	16%	15%	3%	3%	3%
	100%	100%	100%	100%	100%	100%
Mean on Total score: range 1–7	4.20	4.04	4.12	4.95	4.54	4.75
		$F=6.63(.05)$			$F=35.2(.001)$	

[a]These percents are based on the 2141 students (1141 men and 1000 women) attending the six colleges in 1964 that participated in both the 1965 and 1970 cross-sectional studies.

[b]These percents are based on the 1127 students (589 men and 538 women) attending the six colleges that participated in the cross-sectional study in 1970.

TABLE 8.2. Factor Analysis of Black Nationalism Items (1970)[a]

	Varimax Rotation Factors											
	Self-Determination Through Separatism		Community Control		Economic Development		Militancy: Political Use of Violence		Afro-American Orientation		African Identification[b]	
	Men	Women	Men	Women	Men	Women	Men	Women	Men	Women	Men	Women
1. My school should be an all-Black campus, a campus without whites as teachers or students.	.69	.54	.03	.11	.06	.05	.09	.09	.04	.26		.00
2. Do you feel that Blacks should have nothing to do with whites if they can help it?	.56	.65	.09	.18	.04	.04	.08	.10	.02	.00	.02	.33
3. Do you approve of interracial marriage?	.66	.33	.01	.12	.07	.06	.08	.00	.12	.31		.07
4. Do you feel that Blacks should set up a separate Black nation in America?	.28	.56	.07	.14	.17	.00	.03	.06	.13	.10		.19
5. Do you think that Blacks should form their own political party?	.42	.53	.20	.23	.06	.02	.05	.00	.09	.05		
6. Do you feel that stores in the Black communities should be owned and run by Blacks?	.00	.07	.61	.69	.02	.00	.11	.07	.04	.04		.12
7. Do you agree that Black Americans should insist that schools in Black neighborhoods should have Black principals?	.43	.22	.48	.61	.07	.22	.28	.22	.11	.11		.13
8. Do you feel that Black parents should have the final word as to what is taught to their children in the public schools?	.43	.23	.32	.58	.10	.06	.12	.00	.08	.11		.16

Item	1	2	3	4	5	6	7	8	9	10	11
9. Do you feel that Blacks should take more pride in Negro history?	.06	.23	.63	.46	.02	.02	.06	.21	.17	.08	.21
10. Do you believe that schools with mostly Black children should have mostly Black teachers?	.64	.34	.58	.52	.12	.29	.15	.09	.22	.03	.21
11. Do you feel that Blacks should try to get money for setting up businesses that will run by Blacks in the Black community?	.03	.09	.08	.17	.76	.78	.01	.03	.15	.00	.17
12. Do you think that educated Blacks who have good jobs should try to use their talents and leadership ability to help other Blacks?	.08	.10	.05	.04	.71	.78	.00	.05	.02	.11	.10
13. Do you feel that Blacks should patronize Black businesses whenever possible?	.05	.10	.04	.01	.52	.48	.18	.30	.09	.05	.08
14. Some people say that events in Newark, Detroit, and Watts helped the Blacks. Others say it hurt. What do you think?	.03	.06	.18	.01	.00	.12	.67	.60	.04	.05	.09
15. Do you approve of violence as a means of helping the Black cause?	.14	.14	.06	.06	.03	.14	.68	.41	.14	.08	.20
16. Civil rights workers should always be armed, ready to protect themselves.	.18	.26	.03	.17	.10	.06	.61	.21	.04	.21	.20
17. Many different terms have been used to describe the events that took place in Newark, Detroit, Watts, and other places. Which of the following (hoodlumism, riot, civil disorder, rebellion) do you think best describes what happened?	.04	.14	.14	.07	.03	.04	.51	.09	.22	.02	.08
18. Which name do you prefer being called (colored, Negro, Afro-American, Black)?	.23	.02	.00	.00	.10	.06	.20	.11	.48	.58	.10

TABLE 8.2. (Cont'd) Factor Analysis of Black Nationalism Items (1970)[a]

	Varimax Rotation Factors											
	Self-Determination Through Separatism		Community Control		Economic Development		Militancy: Political Use of Violence		Afro-American Orientation		African Identification	
	Men	Women	Men	Women	Men	Women	Men	Women	Men	Women	Men[b]	Women
19. Which would you say was more important to you—being Black or being American or both?	.13	.26	.05	.09	.15	.04	.10	.41	.33	.20		.08
20. Do you approve of Black women wearing Afro-hair styles?	.01	.00	.03	.09	.17	.10	.01	.22	.72	.60		.28
21. Do you think Blacks should identify themselves with Africa by wearing African-styled clothes?	.08	.07	.16	.13	.01	.07	.06	.17	.66	.14		.62
22. Do you feel that Black children should study an African language?	.06	.14	.75	.33	.12	.17	.01	.13	.16	.02		.50
23. Do you believe that Blacks have more to be proud of than any other ethnic group in America?	.07	.01	.22	.17	.29	.19	.06	.57	.16	.12		.10

[a]This analysis is based on 1127 students in 1970.
[b]No such factor for men.

TABLE 8.3. Attitudinal Correlates of Nationalism Factors, 1970[a] (Tau Measures of Association)

	Self-Determination		Political Use of Violence		Community Control		Black Economic Development		Afro-American Orientation		African Identification	
	Men	Women	Men	Women	Men	Women	Men	Women	Men	Women	Men	Women
System attitudes:												
System blame	.25	.28	.28	.30	.45	.44	.27	.21	.17	.26	NS	NS
System distrust	.49	.52	.41	.36	.33	.34	.22	.29	.35	.35	.18	NS
Strategies:												
Preference for protest over negotiation	.18	.20	.45	.44	.34	.35	.31	.26	.29	.26	NS	NS
Preference for collective action over individual mobility	.35	.27	.44	.42	.29	.25	.19	.28	.19	.26	NS	NS
Specific action groups:												
SCLC	-.34	-.24	-.37	-.27	NS	NS	.28	.23	NS	NS	NS	NS
NAACP (general)	-.31	-.25	-.34	-.29	NS	NS	NS	NS	NS	NS	NS	NS
NAACP Legal Defense	-.34	-.28	NS	NS	NS	NS	NS	NS	NS	NS	NS	NS
Urban League	-.32	-.26	NS	NS	NS	NS	.37	.39	NS	NS	NS	NS
Biracial councils	NS	NS	NS	NS	NS	NS	NS	NS	NS	NS	NS	NS
CORE	NS	NS	NS	NS	NS	NS	NS	NS	NS	NS	NS	NS
SNCC	NS	NS	NS	NS	NS	NS	NS	NS	NS	NS	NS	NS
Nation of Islam	.25	.34	.27	.34	.20	.21	NS	.25	.20	.32	.17	.22
Black Panthers	.32	.39	.44	.49	.35	.28	.28	.26	.33	.21	.21	.27

487

TABLE 8.3. (Cont'd) Attitudinal Correlates of Nationalism Factors, 1970[a] (Tau Measures of Association)

	Self-Determination		Political Use of Violence		Community Control		Black Economic Development		Afro-American Orientation		African Identification	
	Men	Women	Men	Women	Men	Women	Men	Women	Men	Women	Men	Women
Student power attitudes:												
Decisions about civil rights activities on campus	NS	NS	.23	.19	.16	.19	NS	NS	.21	.29	NS	NS
Decisions about civil rights activities off campus	NS	NS	.25	.36	.27	.32	.26	.33	.21	.31	NS	NS
Decisions about what speakers can come to campus	.28	.29	NS	NS	NS	NS	NS	NS	NS	NS	NS	NS
Disapprove administrative clearance of speakers	.35	.25	NS	NS	NS	NS	NS	NS	NS	NS	NS	NS
Decisions about curriculum	.21	.17	NS	NS	NS	NS	NS	NS	NS	NS	NS	NS
Race cosmos:												
Prefer Black work setting	.42	.54	.24	.29	.29	.27	.19	.14	.22	.19	NS	.17
Prefer Black neighborhood	.42	.58	.28	.22	.27	.28	.13	NS	.13	.24	NS	.17
Prefer Black schools	.48	.49	.17	NS	.24	.33	NS	NS	.23	NS	NS	NS

[a]This analysis was based on 1127 students.

chapter 9

TABLE 9.1. Relationship between Family and Demographic Variables and Civil-Rights Activism for Men and Women, 1964, 1968, 1970

| | Civil Rights Activism | | | | | |
| Demographic and Family Variables | 1964 Ten College Cross-Sectional Study[a] | | Longitudinal Followup at One College of Freshmen of 1964 as Seniors in 1968[b] | | 1970 Six College Cross-Sectional Study[c] | |
	Eta	Beta	Eta	Beta	Eta	Beta
A. Men:						
Rural-urban setting of place student lived most of life	.31	.31	.41	.36	.31	.30
Family income	.16	.13	.17	.24	.19	.22
Family structure	.05	.04	.09	.03	.05	.04
Father's education	.11	.11	.25	.24	.17	.17
Mother's education	.16	.14	.23	.22	.21	.21
Importance of religion in the family	.06	.05	.36	.38	.06	.05
B. Women:						
Rural-urban setting of place student lived most of life	.30	.30	.37	.38	.31	.27
Family income	.09	.11	.34	.22	.18	.14
Family structure	.03	.03	.09	.10	.07	.08
Father's education	.13	.18	.23	.23	.21	.10
Mother's education	.23	.24	.24	.22	.23	.13
Importance of religion in the family	.15	.13	.16	.18	.04	.03

[a]This analysis includes 3639 students in 1964. Level of participation was measured on a six-point scale ranging from no participation to continuing commitment that included jail experience.

[b]This analysis includes 239 students who had been studied as freshmen in 1964 and again as seniors in 1968 at one participating college. Civil rights activism was measured for stability of involvement, ranging from those who had never been active to those who reported continual participation over the four years of college.

[c]This analysis includes 1127 students. Civil rights activism was measured for stability of involvement, ranging from those who reported never having been active to those who said they had been active more than two years.

TABLE 9.2. **Relationship between Family and Demographic Variables and Two Types of Activism in 1968 and 1970 for Men and Women**

Demographic and Family Variables	Student Power Activism				Membership in Black Student Organizations	
	Longitudinal Followup at One College of Freshmen of 1964[a] as Seniors in 1968[a]		1970 Six College Cross-Sectional Study[b]		1970 Six College Cross-Sectional Study[b]	
	Eta	Beta	Eta	Beta	Eta	Beta
A. Men:						
Rural–urban setting of place student lived most of life	.13	.10	.10	.11	.12	.13
Family income	.06	.06	.19	.22	.09	.09
Family structure	.02	.01	.04	.02	.11	.11
Father's education	.10	.11	.16	.17	.20	.19
Mother's education	.09	.10	.11	.12	.14	.11
Importance of religion in the family	.04	.03	.03	.04	.03	.08

TABLE 9.2. Relationship between Family and Demographic Variables and Two Types of Activism in 1968 and 1970 for Men and Women (Cont'd)

Demographic and Family Variables	Student Power Activism				Membership in Black Student Organizations	
	Longitudinal Followup at One College of Freshmen of 1964[a] as Seniors in 1968[a]		1970 Six College Cross-Sectional Study[b]		1970 Six College Cross-Sectional Study[b]	
	Eta	Beta	Eta	Beta	Eta	Beta
B. Women:						
Rural-urban setting of place student lived most of life	.10	.11	.11	.11	.13	.13
Family income	.09	.09	.08	.08	.07	.10
Family structure	.01	.01	.06	.09	.03	.03
Father's education	.11	.10	.12	.15	.10	.14
Mother's education	.07	.06	.07	.07	.11	.14
Importance of religion in the family	.03	.02	.01	.02	.03	.02

[a]This analysis includes 239 students who had been studied as freshmen in 1964 and again as seniors in 1968 at one participating college. Student power activism referred to participation in campus protest activities in 1968 and included three groups of students, those who had been active and had been suspended from school, those who had taken part but had not been suspended, and those who had not participated at all.
[b]This analysis includes 1127 students. Student power activism likewise measured stability of participation. Membership in a Black student organization was a simple dichotomous measure of membership versus no membership.

TABLE 9.3. **Relationship between Family and Demographic Background Variables and Collective Consciousness and Collective Commitments of Men and Women, 1964 and 1970**

Demographic and Family Variables	1964[a]						1970[b]					
	Collective Consciousness				Collective Commitments		Collective Consciousness				Collective Commitments	
	Control Ideology		Individual System Blame		Preference for Individual Collective Change Strategies		Control Ideology		Individual System Blame		Preference for Individual Collective Change Strategies	
	Eta	Beta	Eta	Beta	Eta	Beta	Eta	Beta	Eta	Beta	Eta	Beta
A. Men:												
Rural-urban setting of place where student lived most of life	.11	.10	.09	.09	.10	.11	.31	.31	.23	.24	.35	.30
Family income	.06	.06	.03	.03	.03	.04	.14	.11	.10	.07	.16	.11
Family structure	.05	.05	.04	.04	.02	.02	.07	.07	.04	.08	.05	.06
Father's education	.08	.08	.04	.05	.07	.07	.16	.14	.15	.18	.19	.19
Mother's education	.06	.06	.08	.09	.02	.07	.11	.15	.07	.10	.13	.10
Importance of religion in the family	.03	.02	.03	.02	.09	.10	.08	.08	.04	.03	.04	.06

493

TABLE 9.3. **Relationship between Family and Demographic Background Variables and Collective Consciousness and Collective Commitments of Men and Women, 1964 and 1970** (Cont'd)

Demographic and Family Variables	1964[a]						1970[b]					
	Collective Consciousness				Collective Commitments		Collective Consciousness				Collective Commitments	
	Control Ideology		Individual System Blame		Preference for Individual Collective Change Strategies		Control Ideology		Individual System Blame		Preference for Individual Collective Change Strategies	
	Eta	Beta	Eta	Beta	Eta	Beta	Eta	Beta	Eta	Beta	Eta	Beta
B. Women												
Rural-urban setting of place where student lived most of life	.07	.07	.03	.04	.09	.10	.20	.20	.23	.22	.24	.22
Family income	.06	.07	.07	.06	.03	.04	.10	.10	.09	.03	.15	.07
Family structure	.02	.01	.01	.03	.02	.02	.09	.06	.01	.03	.01	.03
Father's education	.07	.07	.05	.04	.07	.08	.12	.12	.22	.18	.16	.18
Mother's education	.05	.04	.08	.08	.05	.06	.12	.15	.14	.14	.18	.18
Importance of religion in the family	.03	.03	.02	.02	.04	.03	.07	.06	.04	.03	.04	.03

[a]This analysis includes 2141 students attending the six colleges in 1964 that participated in the cross-sectional studies in both 1964 and 1970.
[b]This analysis includes 1127 students who participated in the cross-sectional study of six colleges in 1970.

TABLE 9.4. **Relationships between Family and Demographic Background Variables and Student Attitudes toward Administrative Authority in the College, Men and Women, 1964 and 1970**

	Attitudes toward Administrative Control over:											
	1964[a]						1970[b]					
Demographic and Family Variables	Student Political Action		Parietal Policies		Academic Freedom Issues		Student Political Action		Parietal Policies		Academic Freedom Issues	
	Eta	Beta	Eta	Beta	Eta	Beta	Eta	Beta	Eta	Beta	Eta	Beta
A. Men:												
Rural-urban setting of place where student lived most of life	.08	.09	.07	.07	.09	.08	.32	.32	.29	.22	.09	.14
Family income	.05	.04	.04	.03	.06	.06	.27	.24	.37	.30	.10	.10
Family structure	.01	.01	.02	.02	.05	.05	.07	.07	.11	.10	.10	.10
Father's education	.07	.07	.06	.06	.07	.07	.14	.18	.12	.12	.17	.18
Mother's education	.05	.04	.05	.05	.06	.06	.12	.17	.11	.13	.09	.05
Importance of religion in the family	.01	.02	.03	.02	.03	.02	.10	.09	.08	.04	.03	.04
B. Women:												
Rural-urban setting of place where student lived most of life	.06	.06	.02	.01	.11	.10	.22	.26	.29	.22	.13	.12
Family income	.07	.06	.08	.07	.07	.06	.22	.24	.24	.20	.06	.07
Family structure	.03	.02	.03	.01	.01	.01	.06	.04	.24	.23	.02	.02
Father's education	.08	.07	.07	.06	.08	.07	.18	.18	.16	.06	.15	.17
Mother's education	.04	.03	.08	.08	.06	.06	.17	.16	.17	.07	.13	.09
Importance of religion in the family	.01	.01	.03	.01	.03	.02	.03	.02	.03	.01	.04	.06

[a]This analysis includes 2141 students attending the six colleges in 1964 that participated in the cross-sectional studies in both 1964 and 1970.
[b]This analysis includes 1127 students who participated in the cross-sectional study of six colleges in 1970.

TABLE 9.5. Relationship between Family and Demographic Variables and Five Dimensions of Black Nationalist Ideology of Men and Women, 1970[a]

Demographic and Family Variables	Self-Determination and Separatism		Community Control		Economic Development		Political Use of Violence		Cultural Identity	
	Eta	Beta	Eta	Beta	Eta	Beta	Eta	Beta	Eta	Beta
A. Men:										
Rural-urban setting of place where student lived most of life	.15	.13	.09	.07	.04	.03	.37	.34	.09	.09
Family income	.14	.15	.18	.14	.11	.11	.08	.16	.12	.14
Family structure	.07	.04	.08	.08	.10	.10	.18	.23	.04	.05
Father's education	.14	.09	.10	.09	.04	.05	.09	.09	.09	.06
Mother's education	.12	.08	.13	.09	.07	.08	.14	.15	.14	.10
Importance of religion in the family	.05	.06	.15	.12	.07	.08	.08	.07	.07	.05
B. Women:										
Rural-urban setting of place where student lived most of life	.09	.09	.12	.13	.03	.06	.34	.35	.25	.28
Family income	.05	.05	.12	.10	.08	.07	.04	.05	.04	.06
Family structure	.05	.04	.08	.06	.08	.07	.07	.07	.07	.03
Father's education	.17	.12	.08	.05	.11	.14	.11	.09	.07	.07
Mother's education	.17	.16	.12	.10	.12	.13	.14	.15	.13	.10
Importance of religion in the family	.04	.03	.02	.01	.05	.04	.03	.03	.05	.03

[a]This analysis includes 1127 students who participated in the cross-sectional study of six colleges in 1970.

TABLE 10.1. **Average Level of Participation in Civil Rights Activities of Students in 1964[a] Who Expressed High and Low[b] Personal Control, Individual Versus System Blame,[c] and an Internal Versus External Control Ideology[d]**

Collective Consciousness Measures	Men		Women	
Control Ideology	Personal Control		Personal Control	
	Hi	Low	Hi	Low
Internal	2.41	2.14	2.17	1.70
External	3.80	3.54	3.54	3.17
	$F, PC = 4.82(.05)$		$F, PC = 11.60(.001)$	
	$F, SB = 16.85(.001)$		$F, SB = 16.82(.001)$	
	$F, PC \times SB = (NS)$		$F, PC \times SB = (NS)$	
Individual-System Blame	Personal Control		Personal Control	
	Hi	Low	Hi	Low
Blame individuals	2.38	2.20	2.28	1.58
Blame the system	3.88	3.49	3.60	3.07
	$F, PC = 3.92(.05)$		$F, PC = 28.03(.001)$	
	$F, SB = 16.43(.001)$		$F, SB = 18.81(.001)$	
	$F, PC \times SB = (NS)$		$F, PC \times SB = (NS)$	

[a]Level of participation in civil rights was measured in 1964 on a five-point scale ranging from no participation, coded 1, to continuing action including jail experience, coded 5. The 1964 analysis includes 3010 students, the 3639 minus those who had missing data on any of the variables included in this analysis.

[b]High and low personal control was determined by a median split on a six-point index.

[c]Individual versus system blame was determined by a median split on a five-point index.

[d]Internal versus external control ideology was determined by a median split on a 14-point index.

TABLE 10.2. Collective Consciousness and Commitments of Civil Rights Activists and Nonactivists before and after Participation in Events at College H. Longitudinal Study of Freshmen,[a] Beginning to End of Academic Year 1964–1965

	Men				Women			
	Mean Scores Fall 1964		Adjusted[b] Mean Scores Spring 1965		Mean Scores Fall 1964		Adjusted[b] Mean Scores Spring 1965	
Collective Consciousness	Nonactivists	Activists	Nonactivists	Activists	Nonactivists	Activists	Nonactivists	Activists
System blame (Range 0–4)	1.08	1.74	1.59	2.86	1.18	1.61	1.61	2.93
	F = NS		F = 9.01 (.025)		F = NS		F = 8.99 (.025)	
External control ideology (Range 0–13)	3.42	3.77	3.51	5.23	3.23	3.42	3.68	5.13
	F = NS		F = 10.01 (.025)		F = NS		F = 9.84 (.025)	
Collective Commitments								
Preference for collective action over individual mobility (Range 0–6)	2.19	2.81	2.19	3.75	2.19	2.98	2.38	3.87
	F = 3.91 (almost .05)		F = 7.10 (.01)		F = 4.24 (.05)		F = 6.99 (.01)	

[a] This analysis includes 117 freshman women, 61 inactives and 56 activists, and 94 freshman men, 42 inactives and 52 activists, who answered our questionnaires at time of entrance to college in the fall of 1964 and again at the end of their freshman year in the spring of 1965 after nearly half of their class had participated in civil rights events in nearby communities.

[b] The end of the freshman year mean scores are adjusted through covariance procedures for any initial differences between the groups at the time they entered college the previous fall.

TABLE 10.3. **Average Level of Participation in Civil Rights Activities of Students in 1970[a] Who Expressed High and Low[b] Personal Control, Individual versus System Blame,[c] and an Internal versus External Control Ideology[d]**

Collective Consciousness Measures	Men		Women	
Control-Ideology	Personal Control		Personal Control	
	Hi	Low	Hi	Low
Internal	1.44	1.59	1.52	1.31
External	2.02	1.99	1.83	1.69
	F, PC = NS F, SB = 9.92(.005) F, PC × CI = NS		F, PC = NS F, SB = 5.85(.025) F, PC × CI = NS	
Individual-System Blame	Personal Control		Personal Control	
	Hi	Low	Hi	Low
Blame individuals	1.36	1.42	1.45	1.40
Blame the system	2.14	1.84	1.94	1.72
	F, PC = NS F, SB = 11.05(.001) F, PC × SB = NS		F, PC = NS F, SB = 10.98(.001) F, PC × SB = NS	

[a]Participation in civil rights was measured in 1970 on a three point scale, ranging from those who had never participated, coded 1, to those who had been active for more than two years, coded 3. The 1970 analysis includes 1024 students, the 1127 minus those who had missing data on any of the variables included in this analysis.

[b]High and low personal control was determined by a median split on a six-point index.

[c]Individual versus system blame was determined by a median split on a five-point index.

[d]Internal versus external control ideology was determined by a median split on a 14-point index.

TABLE 10.4. Average Level of Participation in Civil Rights Activities of Students in 1964[a] and in 1970[b] Who Expressed High and Low Personal Control[c] and Advocated Individual Mobility Strategies and Collective Action Strategies[d] to Handle Race Inequities

	1964				1970			
	Men		Women		Men		Women	
	Personal Control		Personal Control		Personal Control		Personal Control	
	Hi	Low	Hi	Low	Hi	Low	Hi	Low
Individual mobility	2.52	2.24	2.17	1.85	1.57	1.42	1.35	1.55
Collective action	3.91	3.42	3.48	3.19	2.18	1.79	1.71	1.82
	F, PC = 3.98(.05)		F, PC = 11.88(.005)		F, PC = NS		F, PC = NS	
	F, IC = 11.24(.001)		F, IC = 9.19(.005)		F, IC = 11.39(.001)		F, IC = 14.81(.001)	
	F, PC × IC = NS		F, PC × IC = NS		F, PC × IC = NS		F, PC × IC = NS	

[a]Level of participation in civil rights was measured in 1964 on a five-point scale ranging from no participation, coded 1, to continuing action, including jail experience, coded 5. The 1964 analysis includes 3139 students, the 3569 minus those who had missing data on any of the three variables included in this analysis.

[b]Participation in civil rights was measured in 1970 on a three-point scale, ranging from those who had never participated, coded 1, to those who had been active for more than two years, coded 3. The 1970 analysis includes 1075 students, the 1127 minus those who had missing data on any of the three variables included in this analysis.

[c]High and low personal control was determined by a median split on a six-point index.

[d]Individual versus collective strategy was determined by a median split on a seven-point index.

TABLE 10.5. Tau[a] Measures of Association between Dimensions of Nationalism and Three Forms of Action in 1970 for Students in All Six Colleges[b] and for Students at the Two Most Active Campuses[c]

| | Civil Rights Participation | | | | Student Power Activism | | | | Membership in Black Student Organizations | | | |
| | All Colleges | | Two Most Active Colleges | | All Colleges | | Two Most Active Colleges | | All Colleges | | Two Most Active Colleges | |
	Men	Women	Men	Women	Men	Women	Men	Women	Men	Women	Men	Women
Collective consciousness of racial oppression:												
External control ideology	.21	.20	.32	.29	.20	.22	.30	.34	.09	.07	.18	.14
System blame	.27	.20	.47	.30	.37	.28	.57	.39	.13	.14	.28	.19
Collective commitments:												
Preference for collective action over individual mobility change strategies	.28	.24	.33	.32	.33	.26	.48	.36	.27	.03	.36	.03

TABLE 10.5. Tau[a] Measures of Association between Dimensions of Nationalism and Three Forms of Action in 1970 for Students in All Six Colleges[b] and for Students at the Two Most Active Campuses[c] (Cont'd)

	Civil Rights Participation				Student Power Activism				Membership in Black Student Organizations			
	All Colleges		Two Most Active Colleges		All Colleges		Two Most Active Colleges		All Colleges		Two Most Active Colleges	
	Men	Women	Men	Women	Men	Women	Men	Women	Men	Women	Men	Women
Black power:												
Advocacy of: Political Self-determination	.23	.25	.39	.32	.41	.41	.62	.49	.15	.17	.19	.23
Community control	.31	.32	.36	.42	.13	.16	.13	.16	.05	.07	.05	.07
Economic development	.18	.35	.18	.45	.07	.16	.07	.19	.01	.09	.01	.19
Action strategies:												
Approval of political use of violence	.28	.10	.35	.15	.43	.16	.45	.24	.27	.01	.29	.04

[a]Tau represents the degree of association between two ordinal variables; it varies between 0 and 1.0, the closer to 1.0 the more closely related the two variables are. With the size N in these analyses, any tau measure greater than .15 indicates a statistically significant relationship between the two variables.
[b]This analysis includes 1127 students.
[c]This analysis includes 397 students at the two campuses where activism was most widespread.

502

Multiple Analyses of Variance[d] of Personal Efficacy and Several Dimensions of Nationalist Ideology	Civil Rights Participation[a]		Student Power Activism[b]		Membership in Black Student Organizations[c]	
	Men	Women	Men	Women	Men	Women
Personal control	NS	NS	NS	NS	NS	NS
External control ideology	.005	.025	.01	.01	NS	NS
Interaction of PC,CI	NS	NS	NS	NS	NS	NS
Personal control	NS	NS	NS	NS	NS	NS
System blame	.001	.001	.001	.001	NS	NS
Interaction of PC,SB	NS	NS	NS	NS	NS	NS
Personal control	NS	NS	NS	NS	NS	NS
Collective action commitments	.001	.001	.001	.025	.05	NS
Interaction of PC,CA	NS	NS	NS	NS	NS	NS
Personal control	NS	NS	NS	NS	NS	NS
Advocacy of self-determination	.025	.025	.001	.001	NS	NS
Interaction of PC,SD	.05	NS	NS	NS	NS	NS
Personal control	NS	NS	NS	NS	NS	NS
Advocacy of community control	.001	.001	.05	.025	NS	NS
Interaction of PC,CC	NS	NS	NS	NS	NS	NS
Personal control	NS	NS	NS	NS	NS	NS
Advocacy of economic development	.05	.001	NS	.05	NS	NS
Interaction of PC,ED	NS	NS	NS	NS	NS	NS
Personal control	NS	NS	NS	NS	NS	NS
Approval of political use of violence	.005	NS	.001	NS	.05	NS
Interaction of PC,PUV	NS	NS	NS	NS	NS	NS

[a]Civil rights participation was measured in 1970 on a three-point scale, ranging from those who had never participated, coded 1, to those who had been active for more than two years, coded 3. These analyses were based on the 1127 students who participated in the 1970 cross-sectional study minus those who had missing data on either the action variables or the measure of personal control or the measures of ideology. The actual numbers vary somewhat analysis to analysis, although the total N never drops below 1024.

[b]Student power activism was measured by differentiating three groups of students, those who had never taken part in a student power confrontation at their schools, coded 1, to those who had been active for more than two years, coded 3.

[c]Membership in Black student organizations was measured by simply asking students to state whether they were currently members of such campus groups or not.

[d]This table shows the probability levels associated with the F statistics provided in analysis of variance. Any F statistic that shows that the difference in means could have occurred by chance more than five out of 100 instances; that is, a probability level that does not reach at least .05 is considered not significant (NS).

TABLE 10.7. **Average Level of Participation in Civil Rights Activities of Men and Women with Internal and External Scores[a] on the Personal Control, Control Ideology, and Total Rotter Internal-External Scales, 1964[a]**

	Average Civil Rights Participation[b]	
	Men	Women
Personal control:		
Internal	3.10	2.95
External	2.84	2.43
	$F = 4.82$ (.05)	$F = 11.60$ (.001)
Control ideology:		
Internal	2.27	1.93
External	3.66	3.35
	$F = 16.85$ (.001)	$F = 16.82$ (.001)
Total Rotter scale:		
Internal	2.66	2.52
Moderate	2.89	2.48
External	2.77	2.61
	$F = 2.34$ (NS)	$F = 1.66$ (NS)

[a]Internal and external scores represented a median split on the sense of personal control and control ideology scales; internal, moderate and external groups on the total I-E scale represented approximately a third of the sample in each.

[b]Level of participation in civil rights was measured in 1964 on a five-point scale ranging from no participation coded 1, to continuing action including jail experience, coded 5.

TABLE 10.8A. Collective Consciousness of Stable Activists, Activist Dropouts and Stable Nonactivists for Men at College H.[a] Longitudinal Study of the Class of '68 from Time of Entrance to College, Fall 1964 to End of the Senior Year, Spring 1968

Collective Consciousness	Mean Scores as Freshmen Fall 1964			Adjusted Mean Scores[b] as Seniors Spring 1968		
	Inactives	Activist Dropouts	Stable Activists	Inactives	Activist Dropouts	Stable Activists
System blame (Range 0–4)	1.06	1.59 F = NS	1.86	1.47	1.86 F = 15.89 (.001)	3.19
External control ideology (Range 0–13)	3.00	3.41 F = NS	4.16	5.72	5.41 F = 7.03 (.001)	8.57

[a]This analysis includes 101 senior men, 28 stable inactives, 33 activist dropouts and 40 stable activists.

[b]The senior year means are adjusted through covariance procedures for any initial differences between the three groups at the time they entered College H. Since the three groups did not differ significantly at time of entrance, these adjustments make only minor departures from the senior year raw scores.

TABLE 10.8B. Collective Consciousness of Stable Activists, Activist Dropouts and Stable Nonactivists for Women at College H.[a] Longitudinal Study of the Class of '68 from Time of Entrance to College, Fall 1964 to End of the Senior Year, Spring 1968

Collective Consciousness	Mean Scores as Freshmen Fall 1964			Adjusted Mean Scores[b] as Seniors Spring 1968		
	Inactives	Activist Dropouts	Stable Activists	Inactives	Activist Dropouts	Stable Activists
System blame (Range 0–4)	1.12	1.47 F = NS	1.75	1.02	1.43 F = 20.97 (.001)	3.04
External control ideology (Range 0–13)	3.00	3.14 F = NS	3.67	5.35	5.63 F = 7.44 (.001)	8.37

[a]This analysis includes 131 senior women, 41 stable inactives, 50 activist dropouts, and 40 stable activists.

[b]The senior year means are adjusted through covariance procedures for any initial difference between the three groups at the time they entered College H. Since the three groups did not differ significantly at time of entrance, these adjustments make only minor departures from the senior year raw scores.

TABLE 11.1. Multiple Classification Analyses[a] of the Relationship of Institution, Controlling Sex, Rural-Urban Background and Father's Education as Student Input Characteristics, to Level of Student Activism and Political-Nationalism Attitudes

	1964[b]	1970[c]
Student activism:		
Civil rights participation	.45	.32
Participation in student power activities	No data	.37
Membership in Black student organizations	No data	.19
Mention of belonging to some other kind of political group on the campus	No data	.22
Collective consciousness:		
System blame	.12	.16
External control ideology	.10	.08
Collective commitments:		
Preference for collective over individual mobility change strategies	.18	.26
Political Dimensions of Black nationalism, 1970 only:		
Advocacy of self-determination	No data	.12
Advocacy of community control	No data	.12
Advocacy of economic development	No data	.05
Acceptance of political use of violence	No data	.12

TABLE 11.1. Multiple Classification Analyses[a] of the Relationship of Institution, Controlling Sex, Rural-Urban Background and Father's Education as Student Input Characteristics, to Level of Student Activism and Political-Nationalism Attitudes
(Cont'd)

	1964[b]	1970[c]
Cultural dimensions of Black nationalism, 1970 only:		
African identification	No data	.11
Afro-American orientation	No data	.12
Attitudes about campus governance in:		
Control of student political action	.25	.23
Parietal policies	.27	.24
Academic freedom issues	.15	.08
Attitudes toward specific civil rights groups and strategies:		
Southern Christian Leadership Conference	.13	.10
Student Non-Violent Coordinating Committee	.13	.14
NAACP — Legal Defense Fund	.11	.09
NAACP — General Activities	.18	.08
Biracial councils	.09	.14
Congress of Racial Equality	.10	.12
Urban League	.11	.20
Nation of Islam	.06	.16
Black Panthers	No data	.18

GENERAL POLITICAL OPINIONS

Attitudes toward Communism:

	[b]	[c]
The United States should not have any economic or diplomatic relations with the Castro government in Cuba.	.17	.21
Communist China should be admitted to the United Nations.	.14	.12

Civil liberties attitudes:

A former member of the Communist Party who refuses to reveal the names of Party members he had known should not be allowed to teach in a college or university.	.18	.17
Legislative committees should not investigate the political beliefs of university faculty members.	.12	.09
It is proper for the government to refuse a passport to a Socialist.	.20	.16

Domestic social welfare attitudes:

The way they are run now, labor unions do this country more harm than good.	.08	.04
Social security should be extended to cover medical care for older people.	.09	No data
Any mother who gives birth to an illegitimate child while already on ADC should have her public assistance cut off.	.07	.13

[a] The coefficients in the body of the table are the beta coefficients provided by Multiple Classification Analysis and described in footnotes of Chapter 5. They can be used here to assess the relative importance of college attended for activism and ideology: the larger the coefficient, the more closely associated the particular aspect of activism or ideology is to college attended.

[b] This analysis is based on the 2141 students attending the six colleges in 1964 that participated in both the 1964 and 1970 cross-sectional studies.

[c] This analysis is based on the 1127 students attending the six colleges that participated in the cross-sectional study in 1970.

TABLE 11.2A. **Conditioner Effects of Level of Campus Activism for Men on the Relationship between Ideology and Action, 1970[a]. (Comparison of the Tau Measures of Association between Three Types of Activism and Ideology at the Most Active and the Least Active Campuses)**

	Civil Rights Activism		Student Power Activism		Membership in Black Student Organizations	
	Active Campuses	Inactive Campuses	Active Campuses	Inactive Campuses	Active Campuses	Inactive Campuses
Collective consciousness:						
System blame	.47	.12	.57	.16	.23	.03
External control ideology	.32	.05	.30	.04	.18	.01
Collective commitments:						
Preference for Collective action over individual mobility strategies	.33	.11	.48	.16	.36	.03
Political Black nationalism:						
Self-determination	.39	.06	.62	.09	.19	.09
Community control	.36	.23	.13	.20	.05	.09
Economic development	.18	.20	.07	.09	.09	.03
Political use of violence	.35	.24	.45	.32	.29	.05

[a]The civil rights relationships are based on 400 men attending the two colleges with the most students with a history of civil rights involvement (average of 90 percent), and 400 men attending the two colleges with the fewest involved (average of 52 percent participation). The student power relationships are based on 343 men attending the two colleges with the most students with a history of participation in student power activities (average of 85 percent), and the 398 men attending the two least active campuses (47 percent participation). The BSO relationships are based on 341 men attending the two colleges with the most students (20 percent) belonging to BSO and the 200 men attending the one college with the fewest BSO members (2 percent).

TABLE 11.2B. **Conditioner Effects of Level of Campus Activism for Women on the Relationship Between Ideology and Action, 1970[a]. (Comparison of the Tau Measures of Association between Three Types of Activism and Ideology at the Most Active and the Least Active Campuses)**

	Civil Rights Activism		Student Power Activism		Membership in Black Student Organizations	
	Active Campuses	Inactive Campuses	Active Campuses	Inactive Campuses	Active Campuses	Inactive Campuses
Collective consciousness:						
System blame	.30	.09	.39	.07	.19	.01
External control ideology	.29	.03	.34	.04	.14	.02
Collective commitments:						
Preference for collective action over individual mobility strategies	.32	.18	.36	.10	.03	.01
Political Black nationalism:						
Self-determination	.32	.11	.49	.14	.23	.12
Community control	.42	.14	.16	.17	.07	.08
Economic development	.45	.12	.19	.15	.19	.02
Political use of violence	.15	.03	.24	.12	.04	.03

[a]The civil rights relationships are based on 400 women attending the two colleges with the most students with a history of civil rights involvement (average of 90 percent), and 400 women attending the two colleges with the fewest involved (average of 52 percent participation). The student power relationships are based on 400 women attending the two colleges with the most students with a history of participation in student power activities (average of 85 percent), and the 200 women attending the two least active campuses (47 percent participation). The BSO relationships are based on 200 women attending the two colleges with the most students (20 percent) belonging to BSO and the 200 women attending the one college with the fewest BSO members (2 percent).

TABLE 11.3. Comparison[a] of the College Experiences of Activist and Nonactivist Students in the Class of 1968 at College H, First as Freshmen in 1964 and Then as Seniors in 1968

| | Freshman Year 1964[b] | | | | Senior Year 1968[c] | | | | | |
| | Men | | Women | | Men | | | Women | | |
	Inactives	Activists	Inactives	Activists	Stable Inactives	Activist Dropouts	Stable Activists	Stable Inactives	Activist Dropouts	Stable Activists
Extracurricular Groups										
Percent who belonged to at least two groups other than political Greek organizations.	21% χ^2(.001)	55%	18% χ^2(.001)	49%	38%	42% χ^2(.001)	71%	38%	47% χ^2(.001)	77%
Percent who had been an officer of at least one organization other than political.	* χ^2(NS)	4%	1% χ^2(NS)	5%	40%	40% χ^2(.01)	76%	41%	47% χ^2(NS)	53%
Percent who belonged to Greek organizations.	6% χ^2(NS)	8%	4% χ^2(NS)	5%	33%	39% χ^2(NS)	40%	22%	16% χ^2(NS)	18%
Percent who belonged to some kind of student government group—campus wide, dormitory, et cetera.	No data		No data		6%	9% χ^2(.05)	29%	4%	7% χ^2(.05)	25%
Percent who belonged to departmental clubs.	No data		No data		42%	39% χ^2(NS)	41%	22%	36% χ^2(NS)	46%

Subcultural Identification

Percent Identifying as:

Subculture							
Student Leaders	12% 32% χ²(.05)	10% 34% χ²(.05)	44%	44% χ²(NS)	47%	41%	39% χ²(NS)	34%
Student Union Crowd	18% 21% χ²(NS)	21% 19% χ²(NS)	17%	8% χ²(NS)	9%	4%	7% χ²(NS)	8%
Intellectuals	63% 30% χ²(.05)	70% 28% χ²(.05)	50%	49% χ²(NS)	50%	50%	56% χ²(NS)	54%
Creative Nonconformists	4% 7% χ²(NS)	3% 6% χ²(NS)	27%	21% χ²(NS)	18%	17%	10% χ²(NS)	23%
Political Type	18% 62% χ²(.001)	21% 73% χ²(.001)	17%	30% χ²(.001)	81%	22%	26% χ²(.001)	84%
Afro-American Type	No data	No data	0%	4% χ²(.01)	28%	0%	3% χ²(.01)	27%
Casual Types	44% 11% χ²(.001)	41% 5% χ²(.001)	59%	38% χ²(.01)	7%	54%	40% χ²(.01)	4%

TABLE 11.3. **Comparison[a] of the College Experiences of Activist and Nonactivist Students in the Class of 1968 at College H, First as Freshmen in 1964 and Then as Seniors in 1968** (Cont'd)

| | Freshman Year 1964[b] | | | | Senior Year 1968[c] | | | | | |
| | Men | | Women | | Men | | | Women | | |
	Inactives	Activists	Inactives	Activists	Stable Inactives	Activist Dropouts	Stable Activists	Stable Inactives	Activist Dropouts	Stable Activists
Contact with Faculty										
Percent who said they had gotten to know at *least* one faculty member well.	32%	67% $\chi^2(.05)$	31%	51% $\chi^2(.05)$	49%	56% $\chi^2(.05)$	83%	49%	52% $\chi^2(NS)$	62%
Percent who said they had talked to faculty members about post-college plans.	No data		No data		62%	68% $\chi^2(.05)$	88%	58%	59% $\chi^2(NS)$	62%
Percent who mentioned a faculty member among three best friends.	No data		No data		0%	4% $\chi^2(.05)$	18%	0%	1% $\chi^2(NS)$	2%

[a]Differences in college experiences were tested by Chi-Square statistics. The table shows the probability level attached to the Chi-Square values for each comparison. Where the Chi-Square could have occurred more than five out of 100 instances by chance, we have simply indicated that the percents are not significantly (NS) different.

[b]This analysis includes 117 freshman women (61 Inactives and 56 Activists) and 94 men (42 Inactives and 52 Activists) at College H.

[c]This analysis includes 131 senior women (41 Stable Inactives, 50 Civil Rights Dropouts and 40 Stable Activists) and 101 senior men (28 Stable Inactives, 33 Civil Rights Dropouts and 40 Stable Activists) at College H.

TABLE 11.4A. Conditioner Effects of the Level of Campus Activism on the Relationship[a] between Three Types of Activism and Other College Experiences for Men, 1970[b]

	Civil Rights Activism		Student Power Activism		Membership in Black Student Organizations	
	Active Campuses	Inactive Campuses	Active Campuses	Inactive Campuses	Active Campuses	Inactive Campuses
Other College Experiences:						
Subcultural identification						
Student leaders	.31		.32	.06		
Political types	.01	.03	.22	.01	.22	.03
Really serious students	.01	-.27				
Creative nonconformists	.01	.20				
Casual types		.26	-.26	-.04	-.26	.01
Student union crowd	.02	.28				
Afro-American type	.28	.03			.25	.27
Ordinary, average students			-.22	.10	-.29	.01

TABLE 11.4A. Conditioner Effects of the Level of Campus Activism on the Relationship[a] between Three Types of Activism and Other College Experiences for Men, 1970[b] (Cont'd)

	Civil Rights Activism		Student Power Activism		Membership in Black Student Organizations	
	Active Campuses	Inactive Campuses	Active Campuses	Inactive Campuses	Active Campuses	Inactive Campuses
Extracurricular groups:						
Membership in fraternities-Sororities	.31	.03	.41	.25	.31	.32
Number of groups other than Greek or political to which belong	.25	.02	.31	.31	.34	.04
Number of offices held	.31	.03	.44	.30	.30	.22
Number of Government or policy groups	.25	.02	.31	.31	.34	.15
Number of professional clubs	.29	.02	.22	.04		
Number of Afro-American groups	.29	.01	.23	.02		
Curricular Experiences:						
Taken *any* Black studies courses	.26	.08	.37	.16	.43	.31
Number of Black studies courses	.25	.07	.41	.15	.42	.30

[a]The coefficients in the body of the table are the contingency coefficients based on Chi-square statistics. To simplify reading the table and to highlight the comparisons between active and inactive campuses, we have not included the coefficients that did not represent statistical significance on *either type of campus*.

[b]The civil rights relationships are based on 400 men attending the two colleges with the most students with a history of civil rights involvement (average of 90 percent), and 400 men attending the two colleges with the fewest involved (average of 52 percent participation). The student power relationships are based on 343 men attending the two colleges with most students with a history of participation in student power activities (average of 85 percent), and the 398 men attending the two least active campuses (47 percent participation). The BSO relationships are based on 341 men attending the two colleges with the most students (20 percent) belonging to BSO and the 200 men attending the one college with the fewest BSO members (2 percent).

TABLE 11.4B. Conditioner Effects of the Level of Campus Activism on the Relationship[a] between Three Types of Activism and Other College Experiences for Women, 1970[b]

	Civil Rights Activism		Student Power Activism		Membership in Black Student Organizations	
	Active Campuses	Inactive Campuses	Active Campuses	Inactive Campuses	Active Campuses	Inactive Campuses
Other College Experiences:						
Subcultural identification						
Student leaders						
Political types	.25	.06				
Really serious students						
Creative nonconformists						
Casual types						
Student union crowd						
Afro-American type	.28	.07				
Ordinary, average students						

TABLE 11.4B. Conditioner Effects of the Level of Campus Activism on the Relationship[a] between Three Types of Activism and Other College Experiences for Women, 1970[b] (Cont'd)

	Civil Rights Activism		Student Power Activism		Membership in Black Student Organizations	
	Active Campuses	Inactive Campuses	Active Campuses	Inactive Campuses	Active Campuses	Inactive Campuses
Extracurricular groups:						
Membership in fraternities-sororities	.21	.24	.37	.28		
Number of groups other than Greek or political to which belong	.24	.21	.21	.04	.21	.21
Number of offices held	.21	.20	.24	.03		
Number of government or policy groups	.24	.04	.21	.10	.21	.22
Number of professional clubs						
Number of Afro-American groups						
Curricular Experiences:						
Taken *any* Black studies courses	.31	.02			.32	.06
Number of Black studies courses	.31	.02			.32	.01

[a]The coefficients in the body of the table are the contingency coefficients based on Chi-square statistics. To simplify reading the table and to highlight the comparisons between active and inactive campuses, we have not included the coefficients that did not represent statistical significance on *either type of campus.*

[b]The civil rights relationships are based on 400 women attending the two colleges with a history of civil rights involvement (average of 90 percent), and 400 women attending the two colleges with the fewest involved (average of 52 percent participation). The student power relationships are based on 400 women attending the two colleges with the most students with a history of participation in student power activities (average of 85 percent), and the 200 women attending the two least active campuses (47 percent participation). The BSO relationships are based on 200 women attending the two colleges with the most students (20 percent) belonging to BSO and the 200 women attending the one college with the fewest BSO members (2 percent).

TABLE 11.5A. Collective Consciousness, Collective Commitments and Student Power Attitudes of Senior[a] Men at College H Who Had Never Participated in Civil Rights (Inactives), Those Previously Active (Dropouts), and Those Who Had Maintained Their Activity All Four Years in College (Stable Activists)

	Mean Scores as Freshmen At Time of Entrance Fall 1964			Adjusted[b] Mean Scores as Seniors at the End of the Senior Year Spring 1968		
	Inactives	Activist Dropouts	Stable Activists	Inactives	Activist Dropouts	Stable Activists
Collective consciousness:						
System blame (Range 0–4)	1.06	1.59 F = NS	1.86	1.47	1.86 F = 15.89(.001)	3.19
External control ideology (Range 0–13)	3.00	3.41 F = NS	4.16	5.72	5.41 F = 7.03(.001)	8.57
Collective commitments:						
Preference for collective action over individual mobility (Range 0–6)	2.18	2.18 F = 4.69(.01)	3.14	3.02	3.18 F = 5.89(.025)	4.82

TABLE 11.5A. (Cont'd) Collective Consciousness, Collective Commitments and Student Power Attitudes of Senior[a] Men at College H Who Had Never Participated in Civil Rights (Inactives), Those Previously Active (Dropouts), and Those Who Had Maintained Their Activity All Four Years in College (Stable Activists)

	Mean Scores as Freshmen At Time of Entrance Fall 1964			Adjusted[b] Mean Scores as Seniors at the End of the Senior Year Spring 1968		
	Inactives	Activist Dropouts	Stable Activists	Inactives	Activist Dropouts	Stable Activists
Student power attitudes:						
Control of student political action (Range 1–9, Hi = disapproval of restrictions)	4.69	5.43 F = NS	5.67	6.23	6.92 F = NS	7.43
Parietal policies (Range 1–13, Hi = disapproval of restrictions)	7.92	7.92 F = NS	9.71	9.77	9.77 F = NS	10.04
Academic freedom policies (Range 1–6, Hi = disapproval of restrictions)	4.00	4.21 F = NS	4.17	4.15	4.29 F = 3.19(.05)	4.87

[a]This analysis includes 131 senior women, 41 stable inactives, 50 civil rights dropouts, and 40 stable activists, and 101 senior men, 28 stable inactives, 33 civil rights dropouts, and 40 stable activists at College H.

[b]The senior year means are adjusted through covariance procedures for any initial differences between the three groups at the time they entered College H.

TABLE 11.5B. Collective Consciousness, Collective Commitments and Student Power Attitudes of Senior[a] Women at College H Who Had Never Participated in Civil Rights (Inactives), Those Previously Active (Dropouts) and Those Who Had Maintained Their Activity All Four Years in College (Stable Activists)

	Mean Scores As Freshmen at Time of Entrance Fall 1964			Adjusted[b] Mean Scores as Seniors at the End of the Senior Year Spring 1968		
	Inactives	Activist Dropouts	Stable Activists	Inactives	Activist Dropouts	Stable Inactives
Collective consciousness:						
System blame (Range 0–4)	1.12	1.47 $F = $ NS	1.75	1.02	1.43 $F = 20.97(.001)$	3.04
External control ideology (Range 0–13)	3.00	3.14 $F = $ NS	3.67	5.35	5.63 $F = 7.44(.001)$	8.37
Collective commitments:						
Preference for collective action over individual mobility (Range 0–6)	2.10	2.59 $F = 2.99(\text{almost }.05)$	3.00	2.71	3.28 $F = 4.89(.01)$	4.81

TABLE 11.5B. Collective Consciousness, Collective Commitments and Student Power Attitudes of Senior[a] Women at College H Who Had Never Participated in Civil Rights (Inactives), Those Previously Active (Dropouts) and Those Who Had Maintained Their Activity All Four Years in College (Stable Activists) (Cont'd)

	Mean Scores As Freshmen at Time of Entrance Fall 1964			Adjusted[b] Mean Scores as Seniors at the End of the Senior Year Spring 1968		
	Inactives	Activist Dropouts	Stable Activists	Inactives	Activist Dropouts	Stable Inactives
Student power atttidues:						
Control of student political action (Range 1–9, Hi = disapproval of restrictions)	4.93	5.00 F = NS	5.44	5.93	6.13 F = NS	6.69
Parietal policies (Range 1–13, Hi = disapproval of restrictions)	6.69	7.05 F = NS	6.93	9.75	9.64 F = NS	10.20
Academic freedom policies (Range 1–6, Hi = disapproval of restrictions)	3.93	3.87 F = NS	4.00	3.80	3.83 F = NS	4.19

[a]This analysis includes 131 senior women, 41 stable inactives, 50 civil rights dropouts, and 40 stable activists, and 101 senior men, 28 stable inactives, 33 civil rights dropouts, and 40 stable activists at College H.

[b]The senior year means are adjusted through covariance procedures for any initial differences between the three groups at the time they entered College H.

chapter 14

TABLE 14.1. Covariance Analysis of Competency-Assessments and Level of Job Aspiration of Individualistic Achievers, Committed Achievers, Activists, and the Unengaged[a] — Longitudinal Study of the Class of 1968 at College H

	Means Scores Beginning Freshman Year				Mean Scores End of Senior Year				Mean Senior Scores Adjusted for Entrance Differences			
	IA (50)	CA (51)	A (36)	U (43)	IA (50)	CA (51)	A (36)	U (43)	IA (50)	CA (51)	A (36)	U (43)
Self-assessment of competency for chosen job	2.07	2.13	2.00	2.00	2.07	2.50	1.86	1.43	2.06	2.48	1.87	1.44
(Range 1–4, 4 = most certain of own competence)		$F = .08$(NS)				$F = 4.98$(.01)				$F = 4.96$(.01)		
Academic self-confidence	3.43	3.25	2.76	2.56	2.87	3.44	2.13	2.56	2.71	3.61	1.81	2.49
(Range 1–5, 5 = most confidence)		$F = 2.06$(NS)				$F = 2.93$(.05)				$F = 5.46$(.001)		

Sense of personal control	3.00	3.13	2.69	2.22	3.27	3.73	2.16	1.99	2.99	3.65	2.29	2.02
(Range 1–6, 6 = high)		$F = 1.84$(NS)				$F = 3.98$(.01)				$F = 3.84$(.01)		
Prestige of job aspirations	2.89	3.11	2.94	2.77	2.94	3.12	2.08	2.54	2.94	3.12	2.02	2.45
(Range 1–5, 5 = high)		$F = 1.99$(NS)				$F = 11.04$(.001)				$F = 9.90$(.001)		
Ability demands of job aspirations	3.46	3.92	3.46	2.94	3.63	4.08	2.77	2.81	3.93	3.65	2.69	2.87
(Range 1–7, 7 = high)		$F = 1.40$(NS)				$F = 15.98$(.001)				$F = 13.73$(.001)		
Nontraditionality of job aspirations	3.62	2.58	3.63	5.35	2.91	2.02	4.21	4.72	2.91	2.07	4.73	4.44
(Average percent Black in the job by 1960)		$F = 3.13$(.05)				$F = 3.53$(.05)				$F = 2.25$(NS)		

[a]Since the separate analyses of men and women produced similar results, this analysis combines them to increase the total number in each group.

TABLE 14.2. Comparison of Nationalist Ideology of Individualistic Achievers, Committed Achievers, Activists and the Unengaged, 1970[a]

	Individualistic Achievers (86)	Committed Achievers (61)	Activists (50)	The Unengaged (107)
Collective consciousness of racial oppression				
External control ideology (Range 0–13)	4.61	7.58	8.50	6.01
		$F = 4.38(.005)$		
System blame (Range 0–4)	2.27	3.54	3.25	2.44
		$F = 7.28(.001)$		
Collective commitments				
Preference for collective action over individual mobility change strategies (Range 0–6)	3.06	4.77	4.36	3.15
		$F = 14.09(.001)$		
Political nationalism				
Advocacy of:				
Political self-determination (Range 1–16, 16 = high)	5.41	7.23	7.15	5.82
		$F = 3.79(.01)$		
Community control (Range 1–16, 16 = high)	10.02	11.78	11.30	10.26
		$F = 4.29(.005)$		
Economic development (Range 1–10, 10 = high)	7.63	9.21	8.90	7.37
		$F = 4.05(.01)$		
Approval of political use of violence (Range 1–13, 13 = high)	8.00	10.01	9.33	7.52
		$F = 8.59(.001)$		

[a]Since the separate analyses of men and women produced similar results, this analysis combines them to increase the total number in each group.

TABLE 14.3. Comparison of the Race Cosmos of the Individualistic Achievers, Committed Achievers, Activists and the Unengaged 1970[a]

	Individualistic Achievers (86)	Committed Achievers (61)	Activists (50)	The Unengaged (107)
Do you feel that being Black has something to do with what happens in life for most Blacks in this country?				
Hurts life chances	46%	90%	50%	47%
Irrelevant	37%	4%	16%	14%
Helps life chances	17%	6%	34%	39%
	100%	100%	100%	100%
		Overall χ^2 = 62.46 (.001)		
What about you personally – do you think that being Black will:				
Hurt your life chances	24%	47%	46%	29%
Be irrelevant	54%	21%	23%	29%
Help your life chances	22%	32%	31%	42%
	100%	100%	100%	100%
		Overall χ^2 = 29.04 (.001)		

TABLE 14.3. Comparison of the Race Cosmos of the Individualistic Achievers, Committed Achievers, Activists and the Unengaged 1970[a] *(Cont'd)*

	Individualistic Achievers (86)	Committed Achievers (61)	Activists (50)	The Unengaged (107)
How much do you think discrimination operates in the job you have chosen?				
Percent saying:				
Discrimination matters at least somewhat	23%	78%	52%	49%
Discrimination does not matter at all	77%	22%	48%	51%
	100%	100%	100%	100%
		Overall $\chi^2 = 44.58(.001)$		
What type of job setting would you prefer?				
Percent saying:				
Mostly Black	18%	69%	52%	30%
Not mostly Black	82%	31%	48%	70%
	100%	100%	100%	100%
		Overall $\chi^2 = 47.81(.001)$		

In what type of neighborhood would you prefer to live?

Percent saying:					
Mostly Black	57%		5%		47%		23%
Not mostly Black	43%		95%		53%		77%
	100%		100%		100%		100%

Overall $\chi^2 = 53.57$ (.001)

What kind of school would you want your children to attend?

Percent saying:					
Mostly Black	39%		56%		78%		59%
Not mostly Black	61%		44%		22%		41%
	100%		100%		100%		100%

Overall $\chi^2 = 19.39$

[a]Since the separate analyses of men and women produced similar results, this analysis combines them to increase the total number in each group.

TABLE 14.4. Covariance Analysis of Collective Consciousness and Collective Commitments of Individualistic Achievers, Committed Achievers, Activists, and the Unengaged[a] — Longitudinal Study of the Class of 1968 at College H

	Mean Scores Beginning Freshman Year				Mean Scores End of Senior Year				Mean Senior Scores Adjusted for Entrance Differences			
	IA (50)	CA (51)	A (36)	U (43)	IA (50)	CA (51)	A (36)	U (43)	IA (50)	CA (51)	A (36)	U (43)
Collective consciousness:												
System blame	1.22	1.86	1.83	1.06	1.37	2.93	3.29	1.56	1.43	2.94	3.20	1.62
(Range 0–4)		$F = 1.38$(NS)				$F = 12.59$(.001)				$F = 10.62$(.001)		
External control ideology	3.75	4.00	4.07	3.15	5.10	7.80	8.36	6.01	4.99	7.80	8.36	5.89
(Range 0–13)		$F = 1.59$(NS)				$F = 3.10$(.025)				$F = 2.64$(.05)		
Collective commitments												
Preference for collective action over individual mobility	2.37	3.21	3.01	2.00	3.00	4.36	4.29	3.01	3.06	4.84	4.42	2.88
(Range 0–6)		$F = 3.16$(.025)				$F = 3.92$(.01)				$F = 2.82$(.05)		

[a]Since the separate analyses of men and women produced similar results, this analysis combines them to increase the total number in each group.

TABLE 14.5. The College Experiences of the Committed Achievers, Individualistic Achievers, Activists and the Unengaged, 1968 and 1970

	Longitudinal Followup of Seniors at College H in 1968				Cross-Sectional Study in 1970 Seniors in Six Colleges in 1970			
	Committed Achievers	Individualistic Achievers	Activists	Unengaged	Committed Achievers	Individualistic Achievers	Activists	Unengaged
Relationships with faculty								
Percent who have gotten to know several faculty members outside of class.	39%	14%	0%	0%	38%	10%	11%	9%
		Partition of χ^2: CA v IA NS CA v A .01 CA v U .01				Partition of χ^2: CA v IA .05 CA v A .05 CA v U .05		
Use of faculty for future planning:								
Percent used faculty and found helpful.	67%	25%	12%	0%	No data	No data	No data	No data
Percent used faculty but not helpful.	16%	12%	38%	10%	No data	No data	No data	No data
Percent never used faculty.	17%	63%	50%	90%	No data	No data	No data	No data
	100%	100%	100%	100%	No data	No data	No data	No data
		Overall $\chi^2 > .001$						

TABLE 14.5. The College Experiences of the Committed Achievers, Individualistic Achievers, Activists and the Unengaged, 1968 and 1970 (Cont'd)

	Longitudinal Followup of Seniors at College H in 1968				Cross-Sectional Study in 1970 Seniors in Six Colleges in 1970			
	Committed Achievers	Individualistic Achievers	Activists	Unengaged	Committed Achievers	Individualistic Achievers	Activists	Unengaged
Extracurricular group experiences:								
Percent fraternity-sorority membership	24%	37%	20%	30%	35%	25%	32%	20%
		Overall χ² NS				Overall χ² NS		
Percent belong to at least two groups other than Greek organizations.	81%	39%	60%	40%	60%	18%	25%	20%
		Partition χ²: CA v IA .05	CA v A NS	CA v U .05		Partition χ²: CA v IA .05	CA v A .05	CA v U .05
Percent officer in at least two.	81%	20%	18%	12%	30%	7%	4%	0%
		Partition χ²: CA v IA .01	CA v A .01	CA v U .01		Partition χ²: CA v IA .05	CA v A NS	CA v U .05

Percent active in at least one government and policy group	32%	10%	5%	1%	60%	18%	35%	11%
		Partition χ²:	CA v IA NS			Partition χ²:	CA v IA .05	
			CA v A .05				CA v A .05	
			CA v U .05				CA v U .05	
Percent active in Afro-American groups	No data	No data	No data	No data	32%	0%	15%	0%
						Partition χ²:	CA v IA .05	
							CA v A NS	
							CA v U .05	
Percent active in at least one professional club	36%	42%	31%	21%	38%	55%	34%	30%
		Overall χ² NS				Overall χ² NS		
Percent active in at least one service organization	No data	No data	No data	No data	3%	8%	10%	14%
						Overall χ² NS		

TABLE 14.5. The College Experiences of the Committed Achievers, Individualistic Achievers, Activists and the Unengaged, 1968 and 1970 (Cont'd)

	Longitudinal Followup of Seniors at College H in 1968				Cross-Sectional Study in 1970 Seniors in Six Colleges in 1970			
	Committed Achievers	Individualistic Achievers	Activists	Unengaged	Committed Achievers	Individualistic Achievers	Activists	Unengaged
Percent active in at least one academic excellence organization	No data	No data	No data	No data	12%	13%	11%	0%
Percent identifying with: student leaders	60%	25%	25%	11%	44%	16%	17%	11%
		Partition χ²: CA v IA .05 CA v A .05 CA v U .05				Partition χ²: CA v IA .05 CA v A .05 CA v U .05		
Casual type	5%	42%	55%	50%	13%	53%	65%	68%
		Overall χ² .05 No partitioned χ² significant				Partition χ²: CA v all others .05		
Student union crowd	12%	12%	6%	20%	11%	12%	16%	11%
		Overall χ² NS				Overall χ² NS		
Politically involved	88%	15%	68%	10%	71%	18%	60%	14%
		Partition χ²: Both CA & A v IA .05 CA v U .05				Partition χ²: CA v IA .05 CA v U .05 A v TA.05 U v U .05		

Intellectuals	43%	37%	56%	60%	51%	43%	47%	37%
		Overall χ² NA				Overall χ² NS		
Scholars	38%	38%	25%	50%	38%	58%	40%	53%
		Overall χ² NS				Overall χ² NS		
Creative nonconformists	31%	38%	6%	10%	29%	27%	27%	10%
		Overall χ² NS				Overall χ² NS		
Afro-American	25%	1%	30%	0%	39%	10%	47%	9%
		Partition χ²: both CA & A v IA .05 both CA & A v U .05				Partition χ²: both CA & A v IA .05 both CA & A v U .05		
Atheletes	8%	12%	7%	5%	9%	10%	11%	12%
		Overall χ² NS				Overall χ² NS		
Ordinary, average students	50%	50%	50%	50%	No data	No data	No data	No data
		Overall χ² NS						
Black studies: Percent taking at least one Black studies course	No data	No data	No data	No data	40%	7%	27%	8%
						Partition χ²: CA v IA .05 CA v D .05		

TABLE 14.5. The College Experiences of the Committed Achievers, Individualistic Achievers, Activists and the Unengaged, *(Cont'd)* 1968 and 1970

	Longitudinal Followup of Seniors at College H in 1968				Cross-Sectional Study in 1970 Seniors in Six Colleges in 1970			
	Committed Achievers	Individualistic Achievers	Activists	Unengaged	Committed Achievers	Individualistic Achievers	Activists	Unengaged
Awards–honors:								
Percent on Dean's List at least two semesters	13%	10%	7%	27%	No data	No data	No data	No data
		Overall χ² NS						
Participation in campus events:								
Black-oriented events:								
South Africa Speak Out	33%	5%	16%	2%	No data	No data	No data	No data
	Partition χ²: CA v IA & U .05				No data	No data	No data	No data
Come Back Africa	20%	6%	17%	4%	No data	No data	No data	No data
	Overall χ² NS				No data	No data	No data	No data
Ron Karenda	60%	18%	17%	16%	No data	No data	No data	No data
	Partition χ²: CA v all others .05				No data	No data	No data	No data
Miriam Makeba	80%	60%	81%	47%	No data	No data	No data	No data
	Overall χ² NS				No data	No data	No data	No data

Political events:									
Boycott meeting	79%	41%	62%	39%	No data	No data	No data	No data	No data
Draft forum	41%	6%	20%	7%	No data	No data	No data	No data	No data
		Partition χ²: CA v IA & U .05							
	Partition χ²: CA v IA & U .05								
Collegiate events:									
Homecoming parade	61%	98%	70%	62%	No data	No data	No data	No data	No data
		Overall χ² NS							
Homecoming dance	43%	68%	31%	45%	No data	No data	No data	No data	No data
		Overall χ² NS							
Greek Nite	34%	70%	30%	58%	No data	No data	No data	No data	No data
		Partition χ²: IA v CA & A .05							
Vote SGA elections	89%	92%	93%	89%	No data	No data	No data	No data	No data
		Overall χ² NS							
Jerry Butler Show	24%	68%	43%	33%	No data	No data	No data	No data	No data
		Partition χ²: IA v CA & U .05							
Paul Winter Jazz	40%	71%	29%	22%	No data	No data	No data	No data	No data
		Partition χ²: IA v all others .05							

index